D1348200

L. S. R. BYRNE AND E. L. CHURCHILL

A Comprehensive French Grammar

Third edition completely revised by
GLANVILLE PRICE
Professor of French
at the University College of Wales,
Aberystwyth

Basil Blackwell

© The Provost and Fellows of Eton College and Glanville Price 1986

First published 1950
Reprinted 1952
Second edition 1956
Reprinted 1957, 1964, 1967, 1970, 1974, 1978
Reprinted and first published in paperback 1980
Reprinted 1982
Third edition 1986

Reprinted with corrections 1987

Reprinted 1988

Reprinted 1989

Basil Blackwell Ltd
108 Cowley Road, Oxford OX4 1JF, UK

Basil Blackwell, Inc.
3 Cambridge Center
Cambridge, Massachusetts 02142, USA

British Library Cataloguing in Publication Data
Byrne, L.S.R.
  A comprehensive French grammar.—New ed.
  1. French language—Grammar—1950-
  I. Title   II. Churchill, E.L.   III. Price,
  Glanville
  448.2'421   PC2112

  ISBN 0–631–13013–6
  ISBN 0–631–14595–8 Pbk

Library of Congress Cataloging in Publication Data
Byrne, L.S.R. (Lionel Stanley Rice), 1863-1948.
  A comprehensive French grammar.
  Includes index.
  1. French language—Grammar—1950-
  I. Churchill, E.L. (Ernest Lee)   II. Price,
  Glanville.   III. Title.
  PC2111.B95   1986   448.2'421   85—15683
  ISBN 0–631–13013–6
  ISBN 0–631–14595–8

Typeset by Photo-Graphics, Honiton, Devon, England.
Printed in Great Britain by Billing & Sons Ltd, Worcester

Contents

Preface   *pages* xi–xiii
Technical terms and abbreviations   xiv–xvi

Introduction

Alphabet   *paragraphs* 1
Phonetic transcriptions   2
The two varieties of 'H' in French   3
Capitals   4
Punctuation   5
Division into syllables   6–7
Hyphens   8
Accents and symbols   9–11
Elision   12

The Noun Phrase

Introduction   13
The functions of the noun phrase   14–22
Determiners   23
Articles
    Introduction   24
    Definite article   25–33
    Indefinite article   34–39
    Partitive article   40–46
Gender
    Introduction   47
    Gender according to meaning
        Gender and sex   48–49

Other categories   50–51
The gender of place-names   52
Gender shown by ending
     Introduction   53
     Masculine endings   54
     Feminine endings   55
     Problematic endings   56
The gender of compound nouns   57–63
Words that are identical in form but different in gender   64
Some anomalies of gender   65–73
Gender of adjectives used as nouns   74
The feminine of nouns and adjectives
     Introduction   75–76
     Spoken French   77–81
     Written French   82–96
The plural of nouns
     Spoken French   97–100
     Written French   101–108
     Compound nouns   109–116
     Miscellaneous   117–121
The plural of adjectives   122–126
Agreement of adjectives   127–138
The position of adjectives   139–154
The comparison of adjectives and adverbs   155–174
Adjectives used as nouns   175–177
Numerals   178–187
Fractions   188–192
Pronouns and pronominal determiners
     Personal pronouns
        Introduction   193–197
        Conjunctive personal pronouns   198–214
        Disjunctive personal pronouns   215–220
        Adverb replacing preposition + pronoun   221
     Possessive determiners and pronouns
        Introduction   222
        Possessive determiners   223–230
        Possessive pronouns   231–233
     Demonstrative determiners and pronouns
        Introduction   234
        Demonstrative determiners   235–237
        Demonstrative pronouns   238

The neuter demonstrative pronouns   239–244
The simple demonstrative pronouns   245–247
C'est and *il est*   248–261
Relative pronouns   262–277
Interrogative determiners and pronouns
    Introduction   278
    Interrogative determiners   279
    Interrogative pronouns   280–290
Indefinite adjectives, adverbs, determiners
    and pronouns   291–319
Quantifiers   320–337

Verbs

Introduction   338
A The conjugations   339
B Names of moods and tenses   340–341
C The persons of the verb   342–343
D Defective verbs   344
E The morphology (forms) of the verb
    The endings   345
    The stems   346
    The verbs *avoir* and *être*   347
    A note on the subjunctive   348
    Avoir   349
    Être   350
    First conjugation – verbs in *-er*   351–358
    Second conjugation – verbs in *-ir*   359–366
    Third conjugation – verbs in *-re*   367–374
    Verbs in *-oir*   375
    Irregular verbs   376–378
F Reflexive verbs   379–381
G The passive   382–385
H Negative and interrogative conjugations   386–389
I Person and number
    Introduction   390
    A Composite subject   391–392
    B Collective subject   393–396
J Tenses
    Introduction   397–403
    The 'historic present'   404

The imperfect, the preterite and the perfect   405–410
The pluperfect and the past anterior   411–412
Tenses with *depuis (que), il y a, (voici, voilà)* . . . *que*   413
The future, *aller faire*, etc.   414
The conditional   415–417
Tenses in conditional sentences with *si* 'if'   418–422
Tenses in indirect questions after *si* 'if, whether'   423–424
K The infinitive   425–438
L The present participle   439–447
M The past participle
  Introduction   448–449
  Compound tenses with *avoir*   450
  Compound tenses with *être*   451–452
  Verbs compounded with *avoir* or *être*   453–456
  The absolute use of the past participle   457–458
  The agreement of the past participle   459–470
  Past participles used as nouns   471
N The moods   472
O The subjunctive
  Introduction   473–475
  Fixed expressions   476
  Constructions allowing a minimum of variation 477
  Constructions allowing a greater degree of variation   478
  The subjunctive introduced by *que* (introduction)   479
  The subjunctive in independent clauses   480
  The subjunctive in dependent *que*-clauses   481–485
  The subjunctive after conjunctions formed on the basis
    of *que*   486–491
  The subjunctive in relative clauses   492–495
  The tenses of the subjunctive   496–506
P 'May, might, must, ought, should, would'   507–513
Q The imperative   514–517
R The complement of verbs   518–538
S Idioms with *avoir*, *être*, *faire*   539–541

The Structure of the Sentence

Negation
  Introduction   542
  A Negation with a verb
    Introduction   543

Ne and another element | 544–556
Negation without *ne* | 557–558
Ne alone | 559–567
De, *du*, etc., *un(e)* and the direct object of negative
    verbs | 568–570
B The negative conjunction *ni* 'neither, nor' | 571
C Negation of an element other than a verb | 572–580
Interrogative sentences (questions)
Introduction | 581–582
A Direct questions – total interrogation | 583–587
B Direct questions – partial interrogation | 588–593
C Indirect questions | 593–595
Inversion | 596–601

Adverbs, Prepositions and Conjunctions

Adverbs
Introduction | 602
A Adverbs of manner | 603–613
B Adverbs of time | 614–623
C Adverbs of place | 624–625
D Adverbs of quantity | 626
E Adverbs of affirmation or doubt | 627–628
F Adverbs of negation | 629
G Interrogative adverbs | 630–633
The comparison of adverbs | 634
The position of adverbs | 635–643
Prepositions
Introduction | 644
Simple prepositions | 645–646
Compound prepositions | 647–648
Government of verbs by prepositions | 649
Repetition of prepositions | 650–651
The meaning and use of individual prepositions | 652–685
Prepositions used with adjectives | 686–690
Conjunctions
Introduction | 691
Conjunctions not requiring the subjunctive | 692–696
Conjunctions requiring the subjunctive | 697–698
Que as a subordinating conjunction | 699–705

Appendices

I   The expression of age, time, price, dimensions, speed
     Age   706
     Time   707–716
     Price   717
     Dimensions   718
     Speed and fuel consumption   719
II   Glossary of words easily confused   720
III Proverbs   721

Index   *page* 543

Preface

This new edition of 'Byrne and Churchill' has been not only extensively revised but in parts completely rewritten. In particular, the sections on 'Gender' (47–74), 'The demonstratives' (234–261), 'The subjunctive' (473–506) and 'Negation' (542–580) are almost entirely new. Many other sections have been radically revised and, indeed, there is barely a paragraph that has not been in some way modified, even if only in respect of minor details.

A far-reaching structural change as compared with the first and second editions lies in the abandonment of the division into two parts, each with a number of appendices. The original authors in their Preface justified this organization on the grounds that the type of French grammar they wanted did not exist:

> They had looked in vain for a complete compendium with a first part providing a plain statement of the more essential rules of the language backed by numerous examples, and a second part, complementary to the first, with fuller explanations of the more difficult sections, already partially dealt with, and some additional matter for more advanced students. So they were driven to produce what they wanted.

Understandable and valid though this policy is, the disadvantages outweighed the advantages. Reviewers and users of the book have commented on the inconvenience of having to search through two widely separated sections for information on a given topic. Sometimes, indeed, given that particular points are taken up further in the appendices, the relevant material is distributed among three or more sections. The publishers and I had no hesitation in deciding that, as far as possible, material on a given topic should be brought

together within the same section. There is all the more justification
for this in that, in the thirty-five years since the book was first
published, language-teaching methods have changed, more informal approaches are used in the early stages, and so a book such as
this is likely to be used mainly for reference purposes, by those
who are already familiar with the basic essentials of French
grammar.

Finally, in the interests of saving space and thereby keeping
down the cost of the volume, the word-lists that featured in the
original without serving to illustrate any particular point of grammar have been omitted.

Users of the original 'Byrne and Churchill' may then well fail, at
first sight, to recognize it in its new guise. Certainly it has been
drastically changed but in fact this new edition contains far more of
the original material than may at first be apparent, though it has
often been redistributed.

No grammar can answer all the questions that an advanced
learner of a language is likely to ask. Such a student will also need
to consult grammars written for native speakers (though these too
will leave some problems unsolved). The most widely used is
probably M. Grevisse, *Le bon usage*, 11th edition, Gembloux and
Paris, 1980. But dictionaries too must be consulted. The two best
and most widely used dictionaries of French and English are:

1 J. E. Mansion, *Harrap's New Standard French and English
Dictionary*, revised and edited by D. M. Ledésert and R. P. L.
Ledésert: Volumes One and Two, *French–English*, 1972;
Volumes Three and Four, *English–French*, 1980.
2 The *Collins–Robert French–English English–French Dictionary*,
London and Glasgow, Collins, 1978.

By far the best one-volume French–French dictionary is Paul
Robert's *Dictionnaire alphabétique et analogique de la langue
française* (usually known as *Le Petit Robert* to distinguish it from
Le Robert in seven volumes), Paris, Société du Nouveau Littré,
1967.

I am profoundly grateful to my colleague, Mrs Claude Young,
and to my wife, who have each read the complete text from the
points of view respectively of a native speaker of French and a
native speaker of English, but both with long experience of
teaching French to advanced English-speaking learners. Their
observations and suggestions have been shrewd, varied and quite

invaluable. They have each saved me from a number of errors and, of course, they are not in any way responsible for those that remain.

Mrs D. O. Evans has typed much of the text and to her too I am greatly indebted.

It is anticipated that this edition, like its predecessors, will go through a number of reprints and so I should be grateful to anyone who might take the time and trouble to draw my attention to anything that needs correcting.

G.P.

Technical terms and abbreviations

It is assumed that most users of this grammar will be familiar with the basic traditional terminology for the parts of speech (noun, adjective, verb, etc.) and a few other concepts such as 'clause', 'subject', 'gender', 'tense', 'active', 'passive', etc.

Among the terms (some of which, though now in general use, are not traditional) defined in particular sections of the book are the following (the list is not complete):

accusative (case)	17
complement of a preposition	20
complement of the subject	16
complement of the verb 'to be'	250, 518
complement of verbs	519
compound tense	340, 449
conjugation	339
conjunctive pronoun	193
dative (case)	18
defective verb	344
determiner	23
direct object	17
disjunctive pronoun	193
double-compound tenses	412
equative	156, 157
finite verb	341
genitive (case)	19
gerund	442
impersonal verb	343

indirect object	18, 21
intransitive verb	17
inversion	596
linking verb	518
mood	472
mute *h*	3
nominative (case)	15
noun phrase	13
partial interrogation	581
persons of the verb	342
quantifier	320
referent	250
simple tense	340
total interrogation	581
transitive verb	17

The following abbreviations have been used.

adj.	adjective
adv.	adverb
art.	article
compl.	complement
condit.	conditional
conjug.	conjugation
constr.	construction
def.	definite
demonst.	demonstrative
disjunct.	disjunctive
Eng.	English
fem.	feminine
Fr.	French
fut.	future
imper.	imperative
imperf.	imperfect
indef.	indefinite
indic.	indicative
infin.	infinitive
masc.	masculine
obj.	object
part.	participle
past ant.	past anterior
perf.	perfect

pers.	person
pluperf.	pluperfect
plur.	plural
poss.	possessive
pres.	present
pret.	preterite
pron.	pronoun
q. ch.	*quelque chose*
q. un	*quelqu'un*
ref.	reference
refl.	reflexive
rel.	relative
sing.	singular
subjunct.	subjunctive
transl.	translated

Introduction

Alphabet

1   The alphabet is the same as in English:

A	B	C	D	E	F	G	H
[a]	[be]	[se]	[de]	[ə]	[ɛf]	[ʒe]	[aʃ]
I	J	K	L	M	N	O	P
[i]	[ʒi]	[ka]	[ɛl]	[ɛm]	[ɛn]	[o]	[pe]
Q	R	S	T	U	V	W	X
[ky]	[ɛːr]	[ɛs]	[te]	[y]	[ve]	*	[iks]
Y	Z						
*	[zɛd]						

* The letters *w* and *y* are known as *double v* and *i grec* ('Greek i').
For the values of the phonetic symbols used above to transcribe
the names of the other letters, see section 2. (Note that *w*, which
occurs only in words borrowed from other languages, is pronounced [v] in *le wagon* '(railway-)carriage' and in a few other,
relatively uncommon, words but [w] in other borrowings from
English, e.g. *le week-end, le whisky, le whist.*)

The names of all the letters are now usually considered to be
masculine, e.g. *un a bref* 'a short *a*', *«Londres» s'écrit avec un s*
'*Londres* is written with an *s*', *Le d de «pied» ne se prononce pas*
'The *d* in *pied* is not pronounced'.

Phonetic transcriptions

2   To indicate pronunciation, we use symbols of the International Phonetic Alphabet, as follows:

Vowels

    [i]   as in *lit*
    [e]   as in **été**, *j'***ai**
    [ɛ]   as in *b***ê***te,* **fai***tes*
    [a]   as in *date*
    [ɑ]   as in *p***a***s, p***â***te*
    [ɔ]   as in *b***o***tte*
    [o]   as in *d***o***s,* **beau**
    [u]   as in *t***ou***t*
    [y]   as in *t***u**
    [ø]   as in *f***eu**
    [œ]   as in *p***eur**
    [ə]   as in *j***e***, premier*
    [ɛ̃]   as in *v***in***,* **m***ain*
    [œ̃]   as in **un**
    [ɔ̃]   as in *b***on**
    [ɑ̃]   as in *bl***anc***, d***ent*

Semi-vowels

    [j]   as in **y***eux,* **pi***ed*
    [ɥ]   as in *h***ui***le*
    [w]   as in **ou***i*

Consonants

    [t]   as in *t***out**
    [d]   as in *d***ent**
    [p]   as in *p***omme**
    [b]   as in *b***eau**
    [k]   as in *c***amp***,* **qui***,* **k***ilo*
    [g]   as in *g***outte**
    [f]   as in *f***ou**
    [v]   as in *v***ie**
    [s]   as in *s***ou***,* **f***ace*
    [z]   as in **z***éro, mai***s***on*
    [ʃ]   as in **ch***apeau*

[ʒ]   as in j*e, rou*g*e*
[l]   as in l*une*
[r]   as in r*ouge*
[m]   as in m*adame*
[n]   as in n*ez*
[ɲ]   as in si*gne*
[ŋ]   as in parki*ng*

A colon, [ː], after a vowel indicates that the vowel is long, e.g.:
[myːr] *mur*, [pɑːt] *pâte*, [pœːr] *peur*, [mɔ̃ːd] *monde*.

The two varieties of 'H' in French

3 The French *h* is never pronounced. However, some words
beginning with *h* (which is always followed by a vowel) function as
if they began with a vowel, while others function as if they began
with a consonant. These two varieties of *h* are known respectively
as 'mute *h*' and 'aspirate *h*' (in French, *h muet* and *h aspiré*).

(i) Mute *h*. Words (most of them of Latin or Greek origin)
beginning with mute *h* function as if it were not there, i.e. as if they
began with a vowel. (Indeed, in many such words it used *not* to be
there but has been introduced under the influence of Latin
spelling, e.g. medieval French *erbe* 'grass', *abiter* 'to dwell', *ier*
'yesterday', which have since had an *h* added to them, i.e. *herbe,
habiter, hier*, because it was realized that they came from Latin
herba, habitare, heri.) Like other words beginning with a vowel,
these words give rise to the processes of elision (see 12) (e.g.
l'herbe, j'habite) and liaison (see 7,c) (e.g. *les hommes* [lez ɔm]
'the men'), they take the masculine demonstrative *cet* not *ce* (e.g.
cet homme this man – see 235) and the feminine possessives *mon,
ton, son* not *ma, ta, sa* (e.g. *mon habitude*, my custom – see 223).

(ii) Aspirate *h*. On the other hand, a number of words beginning
with *h* function as if they began with a consonant. (In fact, though
the *h* is now silent, it *was* pronounced until perhaps the sixteenth
century, and in fact still remains in some provinces.) These are
mainly words borrowed from languages other than Latin or Greek
and, in particular, words borrowed in the early medieval period
from the Germanic speech of the Franks, or, much more recently,

from English. Such words do *not* give rise to elision (e.g. *le hêtre* 'beech-tree', *la hache* 'axe', *je hais* 'I hate', *je le hais* 'I hate him') or liaison (*les hibous* [le ibu] 'the owls'), and they take the masculine demonstrative *ce* (e.g. *ce hachoir* 'this chopper') and the feminine possessives *ma, ta, sa* (e.g. *ma honte* 'my shame').

Capitals

4 Capitals are called in French *majuscules*, small letters *minuscules*. Capital letters are used in French as in English:

(i) at the beginning of a sentence

(ii) with names.

Contrary to the English practice the following are spelt with small letters unless they stand first in a sentence:

(i) The names of the days of the week and the months (see **707**), e.g. *lundi* 'Monday', *janvier* 'January'.

(ii) Adjectives derived from or corresponding to proper names, e.g. *braver les tempêtes atlantiques* 'to face the Atlantic gales', *un printemps parisien* 'a Parisian spring', *l'ère napoléonienne* 'the Napoleonic era'.

This includes adjectives of nationality and also applies when they are used as nouns denoting a language, e.g.:

le gouvernement français	the French government
la langue italienne	the Italian language
Il comprend l'anglais	He understands English
Le russe est une langue difficile	Russian is a difficult language

but, when used as nouns with reference to people, they take a capital, e.g.:

C'est un Canadien	He's a Canadian
Les Allemands sont partis	The Germans have left

(iii) Titles, e.g. *le colonel Blanc, le docteur Dupont, le duc de Bourgogne* 'the Duke of Burgundy', *le président Coty* 'President Coty', *le professeur Mornet* 'Professor Mornet', *la reine Élisabeth* 'Queen Elizabeth', *saint Paul*. Note too *monsieur, madame, mademoiselle Dupont*, without capitals except (a) when addressing someone, e.g. in a letter (*Mon cher Monsieur Dupont*), (b) when abbreviated to *M., Mme, Mlle*.

Punctuation

5 Most French and English punctuation marks are the same:

.	*point*	full stop
,	*virgule*	comma
;	*point-virgule*	semi-colon
:	*deux points*	colon
?	*point d'interrogation*	question mark
!	*point d'exclamation*	exclamation mark
–	*tiret*	dash
-	*trait d'union*	hyphen
. . .	*points de suspension*	dots
( )	*parenthèses*	round brackets
[ ]	*crochets*	square brackets

The principal difference between the two languages relates to the use of quotation marks. There are two aspects to this:

(i) Quotations or other items that in English would be enclosed in inverted commas are usually placed between *guillemets*, i.e. « . . . », in French, e.g. *Il a répondu: «C'est impossible!»* 'He answered: "It's impossible!"', *Comment dit-on «magnétophone» en allemand*? 'What's the German for "tape-recorder"?'

(ii) Dialogue may be enclosed in *guillemets* or not. If not, then the beginning of the dialogue is indicated by a dash. In either case, each change of speaker is indicated by a dash and *not* by *guillemets* which, when used, mark only the beginning and end of the complete exchange. Note, too, that there is no formal indication (i.e. neither a dash nor *guillemets*) that phrases such as *dit-il* 'he said', *répondis-je* 'I answered', do not form part of the quotation. These points are all illustrated by the following passage from Alexandre Dumas:

Joseph entra là-dessus.
«Monsieur, me dit-il de l'air d'un homme enchanté de lui, les malles sont faites.

– *Entièrement?*
– *Oui, monsieur.*
– *Eh bien, défaites-les: je ne pars pas.»*

Thereupon Joseph came in.
'Sir,' he said with the air of a man who is feeling very pleased
with himself, 'the trunks are packed.'
'Entirely?'
'Yes, sir.'
'Well, unpack them: I'm not leaving.'

Division into syllables

6   (i) The following rules apply to the *written* language:

(a) A single consonant between vowels goes with the following
syllable, e.g. *au-to-mo-bi-le, ra-pi-di-té*; note that, for this purpose, the groups *ch* [ʃ], *ph* [f], *th* [t], *gn* [ɲ], which each represent
one sound, count as single consonants and are never split, e.g.
ma-chi-nal, té-lé-pho-ner, ma-thé-ma-ti-que, dé-si-gner.

(b) Except for the groups mentioned under a and c, two consonants occurring together are divided, the first going with the
preceding syllable, the second with the following, e.g. *ar-gent,
por-ter, ap-par-te-ment, al-ti-tu-de, oc-cu-per*.

(c) Pairs of consonants, the second of which is *l* or *r* (except the
group *-rl-*) are *not* divided and go with the following syllable, e.g.
ci-tron, li-brai-rie, ou-vrir, pu-bli-ci-té, re-plet, rè-gle-ment.

(d) Where three or more consonants come together, the first two
usually go with the preceding syllable, except that the groups
referred to in a and c above are not of course divided, e.g.
*obs-ti-né, pers-pec-ti-ve, promp-ti-tu-de, sculp-teur, ron-fle-ment,
ins-truc-tion, con-trai-re*.

(e) Occasionally, the rules set out in c and d are not observed, a
division according to etymology being preferred, e.g. *hé-mi-sphè-
re* (cf. *sphère*), *con-stant, in-stant* (both from a prefix and the root
of the Latin verb *stare*, to stand).

(f) Adjacent vowels that fall into separate syllables in pronunciation are also theoretically in separate syllables in the written
language, but see (ii), c, below.

(ii) When words are divided at the end of a line, the division is indicated as in English by a hyphen. Note that:

(a) The division should always coincide with a division between syllables, e.g. *cha-ritable* or *chari-table*, not *char-itable*.

(b) A syllable consisting only of one or more consonants and *-e* should never be carried over on its own, so, *pu-blique*, *impossible*, not *publi-que*, *impossi-ble*.

(c) Adjacent vowels should never be divided even when theoretically they fall into separate syllables, so *che-vrier* not *chevri-er*; this means that, since both *po-ète, thé-âtre* and (in accordance with b above) *poè-te, théâ-tre* are unacceptable, words such as these should not be divided.

7 In the spoken language, similar rules apply. In particular:

(a) A single consonant between vowels goes with the following syllable, e.g. [de-zi-ɲe] *désigner*, [de-za-kɔːr] *désaccord*, [vi-laːʒ] *village*.

(b) Pairs of consonants, other than those ending in [l] or [r], are split, e.g. [a-plo-dis-mã] *applaudissement*, [par-ti] *parti*, [py-blik] *publique*, [skyl-tœːr] *sculpteur*, (but [par-le] *parler*, cf. 6,i,c, above).

(c) A final consonant that is normally silent is pronounced in certain circumstances before a word beginning with a vowel, and then counts as part of the following syllable, e.g. [le-za-ni-mo] *les animaux*, [œ̃-le-ʒɛ-rɛ̃-si-dã] *un léger incident*, [œ̃-na-mi] *un ami*. This running on of a final consonant is known as *liaison*.

Hyphens

8 Hyphens are inserted

(a) between the elements of which compound nouns, adjectives or adverbs are formed, e.g.:

   par-dessous, underneath
   un passe-partout, a master key
   semi-circulaire, semicircular

(b) in a large number of proper names, e.g.:

Aix-en-Provence
Boulogne-sur-mer
les États-Unis
la Grande-Bretagne
Marie-Antoinette
le pape Jean-Paul

(c) in compound numbers, both cardinal and ordinal, except before and after *et, cent* (or *centième*), *mille* (or *millième*), e.g. *dix-sept* '17', *vingt-deux* '22', *trente-quatre* '34', *quatre-vingts* '80', *quarante-sixième* '46th', but *vingt et un* '21', *trois cent cinquante* '350', *mille cinq cents* '1500', *trente et unième* '31st', *cent deuxième* '102nd'. (See also **178** and **180**.)

(d) with personal pronouns (including *y* and *en*), *ce* and *on* following the verb; if there are two such personal pronouns they are also linked to one another by a hyphen except when the first is an elided form (i.e. *m', t'* or *l'* for *me, te, le* or *la*), e.g.:

Regardez-la! 'Look at her!', Donnez-le-moi 'Give it to me', Allez-vous-en! 'Go away!', Réfléchissez-y! 'Think about it!', Voulez-vous? 'Will you?', Puis-je vous aider? 'May I help you?' Oui, dit-il, ' "Yes", he said', Est-ce vrai? 'Is it true?', Que peut-on dire? 'What can one say?', Donne-m'en trois 'Give me three of them', Va-t'en! 'Go away!'.

If one of the pronouns *il, elle* or *on* follows a verb ending in a vowel, a -*t*- preceded and followed by hyphens is inserted, e.g. *Où va-t-il?* 'Where is he going?', *Peut-être viendra-t-il demain* 'Perhaps he will come tomorrow', *Oui, ajoute-t-elle* ' "Yes"' she adds', *Chante-t-elle?* 'Does she sing?' *A-t-on le temps d'y aller?* 'Has one time to go there?'.

(e) with *ci* and *là* used before about half a dozen adverbs apiece to form compound adverbs, e.g.:

ci-dessus, above (i.e. earlier in the same book or document)
ci-après, ci-dessous, below (in a book, etc.)
là-bas, over there
là-dedans, inside, therein
là-haut, over there

with *ci* in *ci-inclus* 'enclosed', *ci-joint* 'attached', and, on tombstones, *ci-gît, ci-gisent* 'here lies, here lie'
with the demonstrative pronouns *celui-ci, celles-là*, etc. (see **238**) and with *ci* and *là* following nouns preceded by a demonstra-

tive determiner (see 237), e.g. *ce livre-ci* 'this book', *cette maison-là* 'that house', *ces jours-ci* 'these days'

with the compound adverbs *de-ci de-là, par-ci par-là* 'here and there', *jusque-là* 'until then'

(f) with *même* 'self' emphasizing a disjunctive pronoun, e.g. *lui-même* 'himself', *elles-mêmes* 'themselves'

(g) as in English, when a word is divided between two lines (see also 6,ii).

Accents and symbols

9 There are three accents:

(i) The **acute** (*aigu*) may be used only over an *e*, and this *e* must be the last letter of a syllable, except when followed by an *e* mute at the end of a word, e.g. *ré-pé-tée*.

(ii) The **grave** (*grave*) may be used over an *e* (*i*) when the following syllable is mute (except for *-ée*), e.g. *mère* 'mother', *sèche* 'dry' (fem.), *je mènerai* 'I shall lead', and (*ii*) sometimes before a final *-s*, e.g. *très* 'very', *succès* 'success'.

The grave is used over an *a* in the following words: *à* 'at, to'; *çà* (now only in *çà et là* 'here and there'); *deçà* (now only in *en deçà de* 'on this side of', and, in literary usage, *deçà, delà* 'here and there'); *delà* (mainly in *au delà (de)* 'beyond'); *holà* (an interjection); *là* 'there'; *voilà* 'there is, there are'. Note that there is no accent on *cela* 'that' or its reduced form, *ça*.

The grave is used over *u* in the one word *où* 'where'.

(iii) The **circumflex** (*circonflexe*) may be used over *a, e, i, o* or *u*. (In some words it denotes the omission of an *s* that was there in earlier spelling, e.g. *bête, maître, pâte, hôte, île*, for medieval French *beste, maistre, paste, (h)oste, isle* – these words passed into English where the *s* remains in *beast, master, paste, host*, and, in spelling only, *isle*.)

Accents over capital vowels other than E are sometimes omitted; in particular, the grave accent is often omitted over a capital A representing the preposition *à*.

The cedilla

10 The **cedilla** is placed under a *c* before *a, o* or *u* to indicate that the *c* is pronounced [s], not [k], e.g. *je commençais, nous plaçons, reçu*, from the verbs *commencer, placer, recevoir*. Note that *c* is *always* pronounced [s] before *e* or *i* and so *never* takes a cedilla before either of these two vowels.

Diaeresis

11 The **diaeresis** (known in French as *le tréma*) consists of two dots placed over a vowel. In French, it occurs:

(a) over the second of two vowels, to show that it belongs to a separate syllable, e.g. present (*je*) *hais* 'I hate', pronounced as one syllable, [ɛ], but preterite (*je*) *haïs* 'I hated', pronounced as two syllables, [ai], *Paul* [pɔl] but *Saül* [sayl]

(b) over the *-e* of the feminine form of adjectives in *-gu* (see **92**), to indicate the pronunciation [gy], e.g. *aigu*, fem. *aiguë*. (Otherwise, the *-gue* would be pronounced [g] as in *vague, fatigue*, etc.

(c) in a few proper names, e.g. *Saint-Saëns* [sɛ̃sɑ̃ːs], *madame de Staël* [stal].

Elision

12 Elision in French occurs when the final vowel of a word is dropped before another word beginning with a vowel (this term includes words beginning with mute *h* – see **3**). The fact that a vowel has been elided is indicated by an apostrophe. Note that, with the exception of the words *la* (see a and b below) and *si* (see f below), the only vowel that can be elided in French is *e*.

Elision occurs in the following circumstances (for exceptions, see the end of this section):

(a) The *e* of the pronouns *je, me, te, se, le, ce* and the *a* of *la* are elided before a verb beginning with a vowel or mute *h* and, provided the pronouns precede the verb, before the pronouns *y* and *en*, e.g. *J'ai* 'I have', *Il m'avait vu* 'He had seen me', *Je t'offre ce livre* 'I am offering you this book', *Il s'est levé* 'He stood up',

Elle l'adore 'She adores him', *Je l'aime* 'I love her', *J'y habite* 'I live there', *Je l'y ai vue* 'I have seen her there', *Je t'en donnerai* 'I'll give you some'. (Note that the forms *-m'en* and *-t'en* can occur *after* a verb in the imperative, e.g. *Donnez-m'en* 'Give me some', *Va-t'en* 'Go away'.) These words are not elided in writing in other circumstances, e.g. *Puis-je en prendre?* 'May I take some?', *Dois-je y aller?* 'Am I to go there?', *Donnez-le à Henri* 'Give it to Henry'.

(b) The vowel of the definite articles *le* and *la* is elided before a noun or adjective beginning with a vowel or mute *h*, e.g. *le grand homme* 'the great man' but *l'homme* 'the man', *l'autre homme* 'the other man', *la petite île* 'the small island' but *l'île* 'the island'.

(c) The *e* of *de, ne, que* and *jusque* 'up to, until' is elided before a vowel or mute *h*, e.g. *Il est parti d'Amiens* 'He has set off from Amiens', *N'ouvrez pas la porte!* 'Don't open the door!', *Je crois qu'elle viendra* 'I think she'll come', *Il chante mieux qu'Henri* 'He sings better than Henry', *jusqu'alors* 'up till then', *jusqu'en 1984* 'up to 1984', *jusqu'où?* 'how far?'

(d) The *e* of the conjunctions *lorsque* 'when', *puisque* 'since', *quoique* 'although', is elided before the pronouns *il, elle, ils, elles, on*, and the indefinite articles *un* and *une*, e.g. *lorsqu'un enfant naît* 'when a child is born', *puisqu'on ne peut pas partir* 'since one cannot leave', *quoiqu'elle soit malade* 'although she is ill', but *quoique Alfred soit malade* 'although Alfred is ill', *lorsque arrivera le beau temps* 'when the fine weather arrives', etc.

(e) The *e* of *presque* 'almost' and *quelque* 'some' is elided *only* in the words *la presqu'île* 'peninsula', *quelqu'un* 'someone', and the infrequently used *quelqu'un de . . .*, *quelqu'une de . . .* 'one or other of . . .', e.g. *quelqu'une de mes publications* 'one or other of my publications', but *presque impossible* 'almost impossible', *presque à la fin* 'almost at the end', *avec quelque impatience* 'with some impatience'.

(f) The *i* of *si* 'if' is elided *only* before the pronouns *il, ils*, e.g. *s'il peut, s'ils peuvent* 'if he (they) can', but *si elle peut* 'if she can', *si Ibsen vivait toujours* 'if Ibsen were still living'.

Note that there is no elision before *oui* 'yes' (e.g. *Ce oui m'a surpris* 'That yes surprised me'), or before the numerals *huit* 'eight', *onze* 'eleven', and their ordinals, e.g. *le huit janvier* 'the eighth of January', *le onze de France* 'the French eleven (= team)', *la onzième fois* 'the eleventh time'. Note too the lack of elision before *un* and *une* meaning 'number one', e.g. *la porte du un* 'the door of (room) number one', *la une* 'page one, the front page (of a newspaper)'.

There is usually no elision (though it is possible) before the names of letters, e.g. *le a, le i, en forme de S* (də ɛs] 'S-shaped'. There is sometimes no elision before words in quotation marks, e.g. *«aveine» est l'ancienne forme de «avoine»* 'aveine is the old form of *avoine* ("oats")'.

The Noun Phrase

Introduction

13 A noun phrase always includes either

(a) a **noun** (e.g. *book, truth, elephants*), which may be accompanied by a determiner (see **23**) and/or an adjective or adjectives, and/or an adjectival phrase (e.g. 'a *coffee* cup', 'une tasse *à café*') or adjectival clause (e.g. 'the man *who came to dinner*'), or

(b) a **pronoun** (e.g. *I, him, these, mine, someone, nothing, themselves, who*?), some of which may (like nouns, but much less frequently) be accompanied by adjectival expressions, or

(c) a **noun clause**, i.e. a clause fulfilling similar functions to a noun (e.g. 'I believe *what he says*' = more or less 'I believe *his statement*', '*that he is angry* distresses me' = more or less '*his anger* (or *the fact of his anger*) distresses me').

For the functions of the noun phrase, see **14–22**.

The functions of the noun phrase

14 The functions of a noun phrase in a sentence, as far as English and French (but not necessarily other languages) are concerned, can be classified as follows (**15–22**). The noun phrase may be:

15 (i) The **subject**, e.g.:

The boy is reading a book
My friends work well
When **his brother** was killed
Where are **the books**?
These will never please him
If **she** speaks French
It is raining
Have **you** finished?

which in French would be:

Le garçon lit un livre
Mes amis travaillent bien
Quand son frère fut tué
Où sont les livres?
Ceux-ci ne lui plairont jamais
Si elle parle français
Il pleut
Avez-vous fini?

(In Latin, the subject was expressed by a form known as the *nominative* case, and the term is retained in some grammars with reference to English or French.)

16 (ii) The **complement of the subject**, after the verb 'to be' or another linking verb (see **518**), e.g.:

He is **a doctor**	*Il est **médecin***
It's **me**!	*C'est **moi**!*
He became **a soldier**	*Il est devenu **soldat***

17 (iii) The **direct object**, e.g.:

The boy is reading **a book**	*Le garçon lit **un livre***
Do you know **them**?	***Les** connaissez-vous?*

(In Latin, the direct object was expressed by the *accusative* case. Since both English and French have a distinct form of the personal pronouns (though not of nouns) to indicate the direct object – 'I see **him**, je **le** vois, he sees **me**, il **me** voit' – the use of the term 'accusative case' as occurs in many grammars of English or French is defensible.)

Note that verbs that have a direct object are known as **transitive** verbs while those that do **not** have a direct object are known as **intransitive** verbs.

18   (iv) The **indirect object**, e.g.:

I am sending **my brother** a book (= 'to my brother')
He will give **you** it (= 'to you')

or, in French:

J'envoie un livre à mon frère
Il vous le donnera

Note that, except with personal pronouns, the indirect object in French always requires the preposition *à* 'to' (or occasionally *pour* 'for') (see **21**).
(In Latin, the indirect object was expressed by the *dative* case. Since, in the case of the third person pronouns, French has distinct forms for the direct object (**le, la, les** 'him, her, them') and the indirect object (**lui**, '[to] him', '[to] her', **leur** '[to] them') (see **198**), the use of the term 'dative case' is defensible with reference to French).

19   (v) The **genitive**, e.g.:

the lady's book (= 'the book of the lady')
my brother's children (= 'the children of my brother')

Note that in French, there is no genitive – the construction with *de* 'of' must be used (see **22**) – so the equivalents of the above phrases are:

le livre de la dame
les enfants de mon frère

(Latin also had a *genitive* case. Our reason for retaining this term is that English nouns do have a special genitive form, viz. a form ending in 'apostrophe *s*' (**boy's**) or in an apostrophe alone (**boys'**) (see **22**).)

20   (vi) The **complement of a preposition**, e.g.

with **his friends**	*avec **ses amis***
under **the table**	*sous **la table***
without **me**	*sans **moi***

The indirect object

21   English in certain circumstances expresses the indirect object (i.e. the person or – occasionally – thing to whom or for whom something is given, sent, lent, shown, told, bought, etc.) merely by using the appropriate noun or pronoun without any preposition, e.g.:

(a) He gave John a present = He gave a present to John

(b) How many letters have you sent your brother = to your brother?

(c) He won't lend anyone his video-recorder = He won't lend his video-recorder to anyone

(d) You'll have to show someone your passport = You'll have to show your passport to someone

(e) He has bought his wife a car = He has bought a car for his wife.

This is not possible in French – the indirect object is always (except for personal pronouns, see **198**) indicated by the preposition *à* 'to' (or, with some verbs, *pour* 'for'). So the equivalents of the above sentences are:

(a) *Il donna un cadeau à Jean*

(b) *Combien de lettres avez-vous envoyées à votre frère?*

(c) *Il ne veut prêter son magnétoscope à personne*

(d) *Il vous faudra montrer votre passeport à quelqu'un*

(e) *Il a acheté une voiture pour sa femme*

The possessive relationship

22   English often expresses a possessive relationship between two nouns by means of the 'genitive case' (see **19**), i.e. by a form of the noun ending in 'apostrophe *s*' (*the boy's book* = 'the book of the boy', *the children's toys, Thomas's business*) or, in the case of some nouns (mainly plurals but also some personal names) ending in *-s*, by the apostrophe alone (*the boys' books* = 'the books of the boys', *Euripides' plays* = 'the plays of Euripides'). French has no such construction and expresses the possessive relationship by means of the preposition *de* 'of', e.g.:

le père de Jean	John's father = 'the father of John'
la maison de mon ami	my friend's house = 'the house of my friend'
le livre du garçon	the boy's book
les jouets des enfants	the children's toys
le sommet de la colline	the top of the hill

(For *du = de + le* and *des = de + les*, see **25**,b.)
Similarly when the possessor is a pronoun:

la maison de quelqu'un que je connais
the house of someone I know

Je n'aime pas cette robe, je préfère la couleur de la mienne
I don't like this dress, I prefer the colour of mine

Moi, je préfère la couleur de celle-ci (de celles-ci)
I prefer the colour of this one (of these)

Note that English phrases in which a pronoun relating to the object possessed is omitted must be rendered in French by the construction *celui de* . . ., *ceux de*, etc. 'the one(s) of' (see **245**), e.g.:

Ce jardin est plus grand que celui de Jean
This garden is bigger than John's

nos enfants et ceux de mon frère
our children and my brother's

Determiners

23 French has a variety of forms that serve to introduce the noun, and which, in most cases, also indicate the gender and number of the noun. These are known as determiners. They are:
(i) the definite, indefinite and partitive articles (**26–46**), e.g. *le livre* 'the book', *une belle maison* 'a beautiful house', *du pain* '(some) bread', *les enfants* 'the children', *des enfants* '(some) children'

(ii) the so-called 'possessive adjectives' (222–230), e.g. *mon chapeau* 'my hat', *leurs crayons* 'their pencils'

(iii) the so-called 'demonstrative adjectives' (234–237), e.g. *cette maison* 'this/that house', *ces disques* 'these/those records'

(iv) the relative determiner, *lequel* (as in *laquelle somme*) (270)

(v) the interrogative determiner, *quel?* 'which?' (279)

(vi) the negative determiners, *aucun* (546) and *nul* (547)

(vii) various indefinites and quantifiers, viz. *certains* (294), *chaque* (295), *différents* and *divers* (297), *maint* (324,viii), *plusieurs* (331), *quelque(s)* (306), and *tout* (317)

(viii) the cardinal numerals (178).

Articles

Introduction

24 There are three articles in French:

A: Definite
B: Indefinite
C: Partitive

The forms of the partitive article are identical with the construction '*de* + definite article' (see 25,b,c). In none of the articles is there a distinction between masculine and feminine in the plural. The basic forms are:

	masc. sing.	fem. sing.	plur.
Definite article	*le*	*la*	*les*
Indefinite article	*un*	*une*	*des*
Partitive article	*du*	*de la*	*des*

Notes
(a) for *l'* and *de l'*, see 27 and 31
(b) views differ as to whether (i) the indefinite article has no

plural, or (ii) the partitive article has no plural, or (iii) the plural form *des* is both an indefinite and a partitive; in practice, it makes no difference which view we adopt; purely for convenience, we shall deal with it under the heading of the partitive.

Definite article

25 The definite article is:

masc. sing.	fem. sing.	plur.
le	*la*	*les*

le livre, les livres	the book, the books
la porte, les portes	the door, the doors

Before a vowel or 'mute *h*' (see **3**), *le* and *la* become *l'*, e.g.:

l'arbre (m.), *l'homme* (m.)	the tree, the man
l'autre maison (f.), *l'heure* (f.)	the other house, the hour

Note that before an aspirate *h* the definite article has the same form as before a consonant, e.g.:

le hibou, owl	*la honte*, shame

Note too that:

(a) the preposition *à* combines with the articles *le* and *les* to give *au* and *aux* respectively, e.g.:

au père, au hasard	to the father, at random
aux professeurs, aux enfants	to the teachers, to the children

(b) the preposition *de* combines with the articles *le* and *les* to give *du* and *des* respectively, e.g.:

le prix du billet	the price of the ticket
Il vient du port	He's coming from the harbour
la fin des vacances	the end of the holidays

(c) *à* and *de* do not combine with *la* and *l'*, e.g.:

à la maison, à l'enfant	at the house, to the child

| *au sommet de la colline* | at the top of the hill |
| *à la fin de l'hiver* | at the end of (the) winter |

Position of the definite article

26   The definite article stands before the noun, and, if the noun is preceded by an adjective, before that adjective, e.g. *le tournant dangereux* 'the dangerous bend', *la petite maison* 'the little house'.

The article comes after *tout* 'all, whole' (see **317**) and sometimes after *feu* 'late', e.g.:

tout le comité	the whole committee
toute la journée	all day
tous les enfants	all the children
feu la reine (or *la feue reine*)	the late queen

'The' in English

27   The definite article must be used in French whenever the word 'the' occurs in English, or is implied by *s* with an apostrophe (as in 'my son's book' = 'the book of my son' *le livre de mon fils*, see **22**).
Exceptions:

(a) There is generally no article before a noun in apposition, but the article may be inserted for the sake of emphasis, or to distinguish between people or places of the same name, e.g.:

Amiens, chef-lieu du département de la Somme
Amiens, the capital of the Department of the Somme

Monaco, la ville non pas la principauté
Monaco, the town not the principality

(b) With *être, devenir* and verbs of making, calling and thinking, such as *faire, nommer, croire*, the article is omitted in French more commonly than in English when the noun that follows (whether complement or object) denotes a class or category to which any living being can be assigned, such as a bishop, colonel, doctor, man-eater, thief, etc.

In both languages the insertion or omission of the article in such cases is a matter of taste, e.g.:

Il est devenu (sera élu, était appelé, se croyait) chef (or *le chef*)
du parti

He became (will be elected, was called, thought himself)
leader (*or* the leader) of the party

(c) The article is always omitted with the numeral in a line of kings
of the same name, etc., e.g.:

Henri premier, Henri deux	Henry the First, Henry the Second

Observe that in a rapid enumeration of a number of nouns not
linked by a conjunction such as *et* 'and', *ou* 'or', there is no article
in either language, e.g.:

Hommes, femmes, enfants, tous s'y sont rendus
Men, women and children have all gone there

Article required in French where English has none

28 The definite article is required in French, though not in
English:

(a) before abstract nouns used in a general sense, e.g.:

L'union fait la force	Unity means strength
Aimez-vous la musique?	Do you like music?
La beauté n'est pas tout	Beauty isn't everything

(b) before names of substances used in a general sense, e.g.:

Le fer est plus dur que le bois	Iron is harder than wood
J'aime mieux le vin que la bière	I prefer wine to beer

(c) before plural nouns denoting a class, e.g.:

Les insectes ont six pattes	Insects have six legs
Les magnétoscopes coûtent cher	Video-recorders are expensive

(d) in brief commands to those of inferior age or rank, e.g.:

Tais-toi, l'enfant là-bas!	Be quiet, you boy over there!
Avancez, les soldats!	Forward, men!

(e) with names of languages, e.g.:

Il apprend l'anglais	He is learning English
Comprenez-vous le russe?	Do you understand Russian?
Le danois ressemble beaucoup au suédois	Danish is very like Swedish

But the article is not usually used with the verb *parler*, e.g. *Parlez-vous français?* 'Do you speak French?', *Il parle très bien anglais* 'He speaks English very well' (though the article also occurs, e.g. *Il parle l'allemand sans accent* 'He speaks German without an accent'), and never after *en*, e.g. *en français* 'in French', *en japonais* 'in Japanese'

(f) with words meaning 'last' or 'next' in expressions of time, e.g.:

le mois (l'an) dernier ⎫ *le mois (l'an) passé* ⎬	last month (year)
la semaine prochaine	next week

(g) when the definite article is not repeated in English before nouns referring to different entities, e.g.:

> *J'ai mis le beurre et le fromage dans le frigo*
> I've put the butter and cheese in the fridge

> *Les Belges et les Hollandais s'opposent à cette proposition*
> The Belgians and Dutch are opposed to the proposal

Title, rank, profession, saints' days

29 The definite article must be used in French before a noun denoting title, rank or profession, or before an adjective, when such noun or adjective precedes a proper name, e.g.:

> *Le colonel Gervais (le comte Richard, le docteur Guérin, la vieille Mme Moraud) lisait le journal*
> Colonel Gervais (Count Richard, Dr Guérin, old Madame Moraud) was reading the paper

In talking of saints' days the definite article is used in the feminine, *fête de* being understood, e.g.:

la Saint-Jean	St John's day, Midsummer day
la Toussaint	All Saints' day

Similarly, *à la Noël* (or *à Noël*) 'at Christmas'.

Geographical names

30 (i) As a rule, the definite article is used with names of continents, countries, regions and rivers, e.g.:

(a) (masculine) *le Brésil* 'Brazil', *le Portugal, l'Anjou, le Périgord, le Transvaal, le Valais, le Yorkshire, le Danube, le Nil* 'Nile', *le Rhône*

(b) (feminine) *l'Afrique* 'Africa', *l'Europe, l'Égypte, la France, la Grande-Bretagne* 'Great Britain', *l'Andalousie* 'Andalusia', *la Bavière* 'Bavaria', *la Bohême* 'Bohemia', *la Moldavie* 'Moldavia', *la Normandie* 'Normandy', *la Sibérie* 'Siberia', *la Toscane* 'Tuscany', *la Seine, la Tamise* 'Thames'

But it is not used:

(a) after the preposition *en* – see **656**

(b) with *Israël* (which was originally a personal name, that of the patriarch Jacob)

(c) with the names of the following islands (see **31**) that are also countries: *Chypre* 'Cyprus', *Cuba, Malte* 'Malta' (all feminine).

(ii) There is some fluctuation in the use of the definite article with names of countries and regions after the preposition *de* 'of, from', but in general the following indications apply:

(a) with masculine singular names, the article is used, e.g.:

Il revient du Portugal	He's coming back from Portugal
la reine du Danemark	the Queen of Denmark
l'histoire du Japon	the history of Japan
l'ambassade du Brésil	the Brazilian Embassy
les vins du Languedoc	Languedoc wines

(b) with feminine singular names, the article is not used when *de* means 'from' e.g.:

Il revient de Grande-Bretagne	He's coming back from Britain
Il arrive d'Espagne	He's arriving from Spain.

and after certain nouns such as *roi* 'king', *reine* 'queen', *ambassade* 'embassy', *histoire* 'history', *vin* 'wine', e.g.:

le roi d'Angleterre	the King of England
l'histoire de France	the history of France
les vins d'Italie	Italian wines
l'ambassade de Nouvelle-Zélande	the New Zealand Embassy

But, on the other hand, note for example *l'histoire littéraire de la France* 'the literary history of France', *la géographie de la France* 'the geography of France', *le président de l'Italie* 'the President of Italy', *le nord de la France* 'the north of France', *la politique agricole de la Grande-Bretagne* 'Britain's agricultural policy'. The distinction seems to be that expressions like *le roi de . . .*, *les vins de. . .*, etc., in most cases go back to a period when the article was not normally used with names of countries ('France' was just *France*, not *la France*), while those that involve the use of the article are usually of more recent coinage.

(c) with plural names, masculine or feminine, the article is used (as it is in English) e.g.:

l'ambassade des États-Unis	the United States Embassy
l'histoire des Pays-Bas	the history of the Netherlands
Il arrive des Philippines	He's arriving from the Philippines

31 As a rule the definite article is not used with the names of towns and islands, e.g. *Londres* 'London', *New-York, Paris, Aurigny* 'Alderney', *Bornéo, Corfou* 'Corfu', *Guernesey* 'Guernsey', *Java, Jersey, Madère* 'Madeira', *Majorque* 'Majorca', *Sercq* 'Sark', *Taïwan*.

The principal exceptions to this rule are:

(a) certain towns in France, e.g. *Le Bourget, Le Havre, Le Mans, La Rochelle*

(b) certain foreign towns, e.g. *Le Caire* 'Cairo', *L'Écluse* 'Sluys', *La Havane* 'Havana', *La Haye* 'the Hague', *La Mecque* 'Mecca', *La Nouvelle-Orléans* 'New Orleans'

(c) certain islands, some of which are also countries, e.g. *la Barbade* 'Barbados', *la Grande-Bretagne* 'Great Britain', *la Grenade* 'Grenada', *l'Irlande* 'Ireland', *l'Islande* 'Iceland', *la Jamaïque* 'Jamaica', *la Nouvelle-Zélande* 'New Zealand', *la Trinité* 'Trinidad', and some of which are not, e.g.: *la Corse* 'Corsica', *la Crète, la Guadaloupe, la Martinique, la Réunion, la Sardaigne* 'Sardinia', *la Sicile* 'Sicily'.

32 Problems sometimes arise in connection with the preposition *de*. It is not always possible to distinguish clearly between the use of *de* + the definite article and of *de* alone. Some tendencies can be suggested, but the great difficulty is that in a good many cases either form is possible. Sometimes there is a slight difference in meaning, sometimes there is none. Note for example:

le vent du nord, the north wind   *le vent d'est*, the east wind
le vent du sud, the south wind   *le vent d'ouest*, the west wind

and expressions such as *à portée de la main* 'within reach' but *à portée de vue* 'within sight', where the article seems to be inserted or omitted quite arbitrarily. These differences of idiom can only be learnt by observation.

Two tendencies in particular can be noted:

First, that the more completely the qualifying words are regarded as a mere adjective, the more likely it is that *de* alone will be used, e.g.:

le bateau de commerce, but   the trading vessel
le Ministère du Commerce   the Ministry of Trade

because the trading vessel is actually engaged in trade; its owners are traders. The Ministry of Trade is not trading; its officials are not traders, they are the authority that regulates the trade conducted by others.

Secondly, that when the first noun is preceded by the definite article, the definite article is more usual before the second noun; when the first noun is preceded by the indefinite or partitive article, *de* alone seems to be preferred before the second noun, e.g.:

the horrors of war   is   *les horreurs de la guerre*
a misfortune of war   is   *un malheur de guerre,*
but
misfortunes of war   may be   *des* or *les malheurs de
                                  guerre*

For *de* or *de* + article before names of countries etc., see **30**,ii.

33 For the use of the definite article where English uses the indefinite article, see **36**. For its use where English uses the possessive, see **228–230**.

Indefinite article

34   The forms of the indefinite article in the singular are:

masc.   fem.
un   *une*

These are used very much as in English; that is to say, 'a' or 'an' should usually be translated by the French indefinite article (but see **35** to **39** for exceptions).

On the form *des* as the plural of the indefinite article, see **24**, note b, and **40**.

35   Exceptions to the above rule regarding the use of the singular of the indefinite article fall under five headings:

(i)   Where French has nothing to represent 'a', or 'an', namely:

(a)   In apposition, e.g. *Son père, boucher de son état, est mort en 1950* 'His father, a butcher by trade, died in 1950'

(b)   After *être* 'to be', *devenir* 'to become', *paraître* 'to appear', *sembler* 'to seem', and verbs such as *faire* 'to make', *nommer* 'to appoint', *élire* 'to elect', *croire* 'to believe' | when the noun that follows, whether complement or object, denotes nationality, profession, rank, family status or some other long-term situation in life,

e.g. *Le père était avocat. Son fils est devenu général pendant la guerre. Plus tard, il a été élu sénateur, mais il n'a jamais été nommé ministre* 'The father was a barrister. His son became a general during the war. Later, he was elected a senator, but he was never appointed a minister'

Elle est Française	She is a Frenchwoman
Je suis citoyen américain	I am an American citizen
Il est grand-père	He is a grandfather

But the article is inserted if the noun is qualified, e.g. *Son père était un avocat distingué* 'His father was a distinguished barrister'.

(c)   After *quel* (m.), *quelle* (f.) 'what a . . .!', e.g. *Quel homme intelligent!* 'What an intelligent man!', *Quelle famille!* 'What a family!'.

(d)   When the direct object of a verb in the negative is introduced by *pas de* (or, but much less usually, *point de*) (see **568**), e.g.:

Je n'ai pas de crayon	I haven't got a pencil
Il n'a pas acheté de voiture	He didn't buy a car

(e) When the subject of the verb is preceded by *jamais* 'never', e.g. *Jamais enfant n'a été plus charmant* 'Never has a child been more charming'.

(f) In a number of miscellaneous expressions, e.g.:

nombre de	a number of
C'est chose facile	That's an easy thing (easily done)
C'est mauvais signe	That's a bad sign
porter plainte contre	to lodge a complaint against
à grande/faible allure	at a great/slow speed
en lieu sûr	in a safe place

36 (ii) Where French has the definite article to represent 'a' or 'an', namely:

(a) With nouns of measure, weight or quantity to denote the value of anything, e.g. *vingt francs le mètre* 'twenty francs a metre', *six francs le kilo/la douzaine* 'six francs a kilo/dozen'. Note *rouler à 50 km à l'heure* 'to travel at 50km an hour'

(b) With nouns denoting parts of the body, or mental or bodily faculties, e.g. *Elle avait la mémoire fidèle* 'She had a retentive memory', *Il a le nez pointu* 'He has a pointed nose'. Likewise in the plural, *Il avait les lèvres gonflées* 'He had swollen lips (his lips were swollen)'.

If, however, the noun is qualified by an adjective or a relative clause expressing a judgement or reaction rather than an objective description, then the indefinite article is generally used, e.g. *Il avait une tête gigantesque et un grand nez pointu* 'He had a gigantic head and a big pointed nose', *Il avait une vive intelligence, et un corps qui lui avait valu le nom de Colosse* 'He had a lively intelligence, and a body which had won for him the name of Colossus'.

37 (iii) Where French has *par* to represent 'a' or 'an'. This occurs mostly with nouns denoting a period of time, e.g. *trois fois par semaine* 'three times a week'. Cf. *dix francs par personne* 'ten francs a head (per person)'.

38 (iv) In French, as in English, a noun is often used with a preposition to take the place of an adverb. As a rule the use of the article in such phrases is the same as in English. But with *avec*, if the noun is qualified by an adjective, the French has the indefinite article where English sometimes has none, e.g.:

par hasard	by chance, accidentally
par un hasard malheureux	by an unlucky chance
Il se bat avec courage	He fights with courage, bravely
Il se bat avec un grand courage	He fights with great courage, very bravely

39   (v) Where two or more nouns occur in a series, the article must always be repeated in French with each noun, though in English it is often omitted with all but the first, e.g.:

Un père et un fils étaient assis devant le feu
A father and son were sitting in front of the fire

Vous trouverez sur la table une plume, un crayon et une feuille de papier
You will find a pen, pencil and sheet of paper on the table.

Partitive article

40   The forms of the partitive article are:

masc. sing.	fem. sing.	plural
du, de l'	*de la, de l'*	*des*

The form *de l'* is used instead of *du* or *de la* before a vowel or a mute *h* (cf. **25**, notes b and c), e.g. *du pain* 'bread', *de la viande* 'meat', but *de l'or* (m.) 'gold', *de l'eau* (f.) 'water'.

The form *des* can also be considered as the plural of the indefinite article (see **24**, note b).

41   English has no partitive article and no plural of the indefinite article, and nouns taking either of these forms in French often stand alone in English. Frequently, however, they are represented by 'some' or 'any', e.g.:

Voulez-vous du vin?   Do you want (some/any) wine?

Il y a du pain sur la table	There's (some) bread on the table
Il a acheté des biscuits	He bought (some) biscuits

42 The distinction between these and the definite article (which can also be used when English has no article, see **28**, especially **a**, **b** and **c**) is that the definite article indicates that the noun is being used in a general sense whereas the partitive article refers to only a part of the whole (and, likewise, the plural indefinite article indicates 'some' as opposed to 'all' members of a class), e.g.:

J'aime le café	I like coffee (in general)
J'aimerais du café	I'd like (some) coffee
Je bois du café	I'm drinking coffee
Les moutons ont quatre pattes	Sheep have four legs
Il y a des moutons dans le champ	There are (some) sheep in the field

Cf. the following, in which either the definite or the partitive article is possible, with a slight but real difference in meaning, since 'books' may mean 'books (in general)' (generic) or 'some books' (partitive):

Par les longues soirées d'hiver c'est avec $\left\{ \begin{array}{l} les \\ des \end{array} \right\}$ *livres qu'on*

s'amuse le mieux
In the long winter evenings it is from books that one gets most enjoyment

43 After (*ne . . .*) *pas* or *point* 'not', *guère* 'scarcely, hardly', *jamais* 'never', *plus* 'no longer, no more', the partitive article is normally replaced by *de* alone (see **568** – but see also **569–570**), e.g.:

Je ne veux pas de fromage	I don't want (any) cheese
Je n'ai pas acheté de pain	I haven't bought any bread
Ils n'ont guère d'argent	They have hardly any money
Vous ne buvez jamais de bière?	Don't you ever drink beer?
Nous ne mangeons plus d'œufs	We don't eat eggs any more.

Ne . . . que 'only', being restrictive rather than negative in sense, does not follow this rule, e.g.:

Il n'achète que du vin	He only buys wine
Nous n'avons que des cerises	We only have cherries

44 The plural partitive (or indefinite) article *des* is replaced by *de* when an adjective precedes the noun, e.g.:

> *Il nous a dit d'affreux mensonges*
> He told us (some) dreadful lies

> *Vous avez de belles fleurs dans votre jardin*
> You have (some) beautiful flowers in your garden

This does not apply when adjective and noun are virtually combined, expressing one idea, e.g. *des jeunes gens* 'youths, young men', *des petits pains* 'rolls', *des petits pois* 'peas'. The rule is often ignored elsewhere, especially in speech, e.g. *des vieilles chansons* 'old songs', *des petits yeux* 'small eyes'. A similar rule used to apply in the singular (*de bon vin* 'good wine', *de belle musique* 'beautiful music'), but nowadays it has virtually ceased to apply, in writing as well as in speech, e.g. *du bon vin, de la belle musique*.

45 The partitive article is omitted after *de*, in the following circumstances in particular:

(a) after expressions of quantity such as:

> *assez*, enough
> *autant*, as much, as many
> *beaucoup*, much, many, a lot of
> *combien*? how much? how many?
> *moins*, less
> *peu*, little, few
> *un peu*, a little
> *plus*, more
> *tant*, as much, so much as, so many
> *trop*, too much, too many

e.g. *assez de pain* 'enough bread', *J'ai autant de problèmes que vous* 'I have as many problems as you (have)', *beaucoup de difficulté* 'much (a lot of) difficulty', *beaucoup de gens* 'many (a lot of) people', *combien de fois*? 'how many times?', *peu de difficulté* 'little difficulty', *un peu de difficulté* 'a little (= some) difficulty', *trop de temps*, 'too much time'.

Similarly after nouns expressing quantity, e.g.:

une bouteille de vin	a bottle of wine
un kilo de viande	a kilo of meat
l'absence de témoins	the absence of witnesses
son manque d'intelligence	his lack of intelligence
un certain nombre de	a certain number of
personnes	people
une tranche de jambon	a slice of ham

(b) when *de* means 'with' or 'by' after one of the verbs listed in 524 (which see for further examples), e.g.:

Couvre-toi de gloire, Tartarin!
Cover yourself with glory, Tartarin!

Nous étions entourés d'ennemis
We were surrounded by enemies

Il me comble d'amitié	He overwhelms me with friendship
couronné de succès	crowned with success
couvert de boue	covered with mud
rempli de sable	filled with sand

(c) after certain adjectives, e.g.:

Le verre est plein d'eau
The glass is full of water

La place était vide de passants
The square was empty of passers-by

dépourvu d'intelligence
devoid of intelligence

But note that if *de* is followed by a definite article, then it combines with it in the normal way (see 25, b), e.g.:

Son verre était rempli (plein) de vin
His glass was filled with (full of) wine

Son verre était rempli (plein) du vin qu'il aimait le mieux
His glass was filled with (full of) the wine he liked best

46 The partitive article can however be used after prepositions other than *de*, e.g.:

Vous pouvez raconter ça à des imbéciles
You can tell that to fools

Avec du courage tout est possible
With courage anything is possible

Il se trouvait entouré par des voleurs
He found himself surrounded by robbers

Je l'ai fait pour des raisons valables
I did it for valid reasons

Note too (in accordance with **44**) *Je l'ai fait pour de très bonnes raisons* 'I did it for very good reasons'.

But no article is used when a noun is combined with a preposition to form an adjectival or adverbial expression, or when an abstract noun, or a noun denoting material, is governed by the preposition *en*, e.g.:

On répand des bruits sans fin
Endless rumours are being circulated

Gardez les portes avec soin
Guard the gates carefully

Pourquoi tous ces blocs en béton?
Why all these concrete blocks?

Ils sont pour l'écluse qui est en réparation
They are for the lock which is under repair

Gender

Introduction

47   Although the two grammatical genders of French are referred to by the terms 'masculine' and 'feminine', in the case of most (though not all) words these terms are utterly meaningless and, were it not for the fact that they are so well established, we might do better to abandon them altogether and use some such terms as 'gender A' and 'gender B'. It is impossible to give simple – or, indeed, complicated – rules that will enable the learner to determine the gender of each and every noun he comes across. However, it is possible to draw up certain categories of words that are likely to be of one gender rather than the other. In particular:

(1) Words standing for male or female human beings are likely to

be masculine or feminine respectively – but not necessarily so (see **48**). (For animals, see **49**.)

(2) Words falling into certain other categories depending on their meaning are likely to be of one gender rather than the other even though, in this case, sex is not a relevant factor (see **50–52**).

(3) Words with certain endings are likely to be of one gender rather than the other (see **53–55**); in most cases, not only sex (as in 1 above) but meaning in general (as in 2 above) is irrelevant.

(4) Special rules apply to compound nouns (see **57–63**).

Gender according to meaning

Gender and sex

48 (i) Humans

(a) Generally speaking, nouns referring to male humans are masculine and nouns referring to female humans are feminine, e.g.:

masc.	fem.
un avocat, barrister	*la cantatrice*, (opera) singer
le boucher, butcher	*la couturière*, seamstress
un étudiant, (male) student	*une étudiante*, (female) student
le musicien, musician	*une ouvreuse*, usherette
le père, father	*la princesse*, princess
le prêtre, priest	*la reine*, queen
le romancier, novelist	*la tante*, aunt
le voyageur, traveller	*la veuve*, widow

(b) Some nouns however are masculine even when they refer to females, in particular:

un architecte
un auteur, author(ess)
le brise-fer ⎫
le brise-tout ⎬ destructive child
le contralto
le docteur, doctor
un écrivain, writer
le médecin, doctor

    le ministre, (government) minister
    le peintre, painter
    le professeur, teacher, professor
    le sculpteur, sculptor, sculptress
    le témoin, witness

Many of these may be preceded by *femme* when it is wished to specify that the individual concerned is a woman, e.g. *une femme auteur, une femme médecin, une femme sculpteur. La doctoresse* also exists as the feminine of *docteur. Soprano* is usually masculine but occasionally feminine.

   Un ange 'angel', even when referring to a woman or a girl (or a heavenly being in female form), is always masculine.

(c) Some nouns are always feminine, even when they refer to males (and some of them refer only to males), e.g.:

    la brute
    la connaissance, acquaintance
    la dupe
    la personne, person
    la recrue, recruit
    la sentinelle, sentry
    la vedette, film star, etc.
    la victime, victim
    la vigie, look-out man (at sea)

(d) Some nouns take either gender, depending on the sex of the person concerned, e.g.:

    un or *une aide*, assistant
    le or *la camarade*, friend
    le or *la collègue*, colleague
    le or *la concierge*, caretaker
    un or *une élève*, pupil
    un or *une enfant*, child
    un or *une hypocrite*
    un or *une locataire*, tenant
    un or *une patriote*, patriot
    un or *une pupille*, ward
    un or *une propriétaire*, owner
    un or *une secrétaire*, secretary

and all words ending in *-iste* referring to humans:

    un or *une socialiste*   *un* or *une touriste*

49 (ii). **Animals**

The relation between gender and sex is far less close in the case of animals than it is in the case of humans. Note the following categories:

(a) Many nouns referring to animals have only a masculine form, used for both males and females, e.g.:

> *le blaireau*, badger
> *le chacal*, jackal
> *un écureuil*, squirrel
> *un éléphant*
> *le gorille*, gorilla
> *le hérisson*, hedgehog
> *un hippopotame*, hippopotamus
> *le jaguar*
> *le léopard*
> *le rat*
> *le renne*, reindeer
> *le rhinocéros*

If it is necessary to specify that the animal is female, one can say *un léopard femelle* 'leopardess', *un éléphant femelle*, etc.

Many nouns referring to the young of animals are of this type, e.g.:

> *l'éléphanteau*, elephant calf   *un ourson*, bear-cub
> *le levraut*, leveret   *le poulain*, foal
> *le lionceau*, lion-cub   *le renardeau*, fox-cub
> *le louveteau*, wolf-cub   *le veau*, calf

(b) Many nouns that are normally used in the masculine as generic terms, i.e. with reference both to males and females, do however have a feminine equivalent for use when one wishes to specify that a particular animal is female. In some cases, the two words are related, e.g.:

> *un agneau, une agnelle*, lamb
> *un âne, une ânesse*, donkey
> *le chameau, la chamelle*, camel
> *le chien, la chienne*, dog, bitch
> *le lapin, la lapine*, rabbit, doe
> *le lion, la lionne*, lion(ess)

le loup, la louve, wolf
un ours, une ourse, bear
le renard, la renarde, fox, vixen
le tigre, la tigresse, tiger, tigress

In other cases, quite different words are used, e.g.:

le cerf, la biche, stag (*or* deer), doe
le lièvre, la hase, hare, doe
le singe, la guenon, monkey

(c) With reference to some animals, there is a generic word (which in every case is masculine) referring to individuals of either sex, but also special words for specifying male and female respectively:

le chat, cat	*le matou*, tomcat	*la chatte*, female cat
le cheval, horse	*un étalon*, stallion	*la jument*, mare
le mouton, sheep	*le bélier*, ram	*la brebis*, ewe
le porc, le cochon, pig	*le verrat*, boar	*la truie*, sow

Note that, corresponding to *le taureau* 'bull', *la vache* 'cow', there is no generic term in the singular, though the collective noun *le bétail*, and the plural *les bestiaux*, both meaning 'cattle', exist.

(d) For certain animals, the generic (and only) word is feminine, e.g.:

la baleine, whale	*la loutre*, otter
la belette, weasel	*la panthère*, panther
la girafe, giraffe	*la souris*, mouse
la grenouille, frog	*la taupe*, mole
une hyène, hyena	*la tortue*, tortoise

Note that *la chèvre* 'goat' is used as a generic but that there is also a specifically 'male' word, *le bouc* 'he-goat'.

La bête 'animal' is always feminine, even with reference to male animals.

Gender according to meaning – other categories

50 (i) Masculine.
Most nouns falling into the following categories are masculine:

(a) Names of trees and shrubs

(b) Names of common fruits and vegetables not ending in -*e* (no exceptions)

(c) Names of metals and minerals

(d) Names of languages (no exceptions)

(e) Names of colours

(f) Names of weights and measures of the metric system, cardinal numbers, fractions, letters of the alphabet

(g) Names of days of the week, months, seasons, points of the compass.

Examples:

(a) Names of trees and shrubs, e.g.:

le chêne, oak
un érable, maple
le hêtre, beech
le laurier, laurel

le platane, plane-tree
le pommier, apple-tree
le sapin, fir
le troène, privet

The principal exceptions are;

une aubépine, hawthorn
la bruyère, heather

la ronce, bramble
la vigne, vine

(b) Names of common fruits and vegetables *not* ending in -*e* (for those ending in -*e*, see **51**), e.g.:

un abricot, apricot
le brugnon, nectarine
le citron, lemon
le melon

un artichaut, artichoke
le céleri, celery
le chou, cabbage
le haricot, bean

(c) Most names of metals and minerals (including precious stones), e.g.:

le cuivre, copper
le fer, iron

le sel, salt
le silicium, silicon

le plomb, lead	*le souffre*, sulphur
l'anthracite	*le diamant*, diamond
le carbone, carbon	*le rubis*, ruby
le charbon, coal	*le saphir*, sapphire

Exceptions:

la chaux, chalk	*une émeraude*, emerald
la pierre, stone	*la perle*, pearl
la roche, rock	

and some technical names of minerals in *-ite* (e.g. *la malachite*, see 56).

(d) Names of languages are all masculine, e.g.:

le français, French	*le russe*, Russian
le grec, Greek	*le swahili*

(e) Most names of colours, e.g.:

le bleu, blue   *le jaune*, yellow   *le rouge*, red

Exceptions: *l'écarlate* 'scarlet' and *l'ocre* 'ochre' are feminine.

(f) Names of weights and measures of the metric system, cardinal numbers, most fractions, and the letters of the alphabet, e.g.:

le gramme	*un tiers*, one third
le kilogramme	*un quart*, a quarter
le litre	*un dixième*, a tenth
le mètre	*un e*
un sept, a seven	*un m*

Exception: *la moitié*, half. Note that numerals in *-aine* indicating approximate quantities are feminine, e.g. *une dizaine* 'about ten', *une trentaine* 'about thirty', *une centaine* 'about a hundred'.

(g) The names of days of the week, months, seasons, and points of the compass, e.g.:

lundi dernier, last Monday
janvier prochain, next January
au printemps, in spring
en plein été, in the middle of summer
un automne agréable, a pleasant autumn
cet hiver, this winter

le nord, north
le sud, south
l'est, east
l'ouest, west

51 (ii) **Feminine**
The names of most common fruits and vegetables ending in *-e* (for others, see 50,i, b) are feminine, e.g.:

la banane, banana	*la betterave*, beetroot
la fraise, strawberry	*la carotte*, carrot
la pomme, apple	*la fève*, broad bean

Exceptions: *le pamplemousse* 'grapefruit', *le concombre* 'cucumber'.

52 (iii) **The gender of place names**
(a) There are no clear rules for determining the gender of names of towns. In many cases there is a good deal of hesitation and fluctuation but there is a marked tendency to treat them as masculine, e.g. *Paris est plus grand que Lyon* 'Paris is bigger than Lyon', *Venise est beau* 'Venice is beautiful', *le grand Londres* 'Greater London', *Grenoble est devenu un centre industriel* 'Grenoble has become an industrial centre', *le musée du vieux Marseille* 'the Museum of Old Marseilles'. However, names in *-e* and *-es* and occasionally others can also be treated as feminine, e.g. *Londres fut sévèrement bombardée en 1940* 'London was heavily bombed in 1940', *Bruxelles fut libérée en 1944* 'Brussels was liberated in 1944', *Nice fut fondée en 350 av. J.-C.* 'Nice was founded in 350 BC', *Marseille contemporaine* 'present-day Marseilles'.

(b) As a general rule, names of countries, of French provinces and regions, and of French rivers, are feminine if they end *-e*, masculine if they do not:

Countries, e.g.:

le Canada	*la Chine*, China
le Danemark, Denmark	*la Finlande*, Finland
le Japon, Japan	*la Norvège*, Norway
le Maroc, Morocco	*la Roumanie*, Romania
le Nigeria	*la Suisse*, Switzerland
le Portugal	*la Syrie*, Syria

Exceptions: *le Cambodge* 'Cambodia', *le Mexique* 'Mexico', *le Mozambique, le Zaïre*, and, with the *-e* pronounced, *le Zimbabwe*.
French provinces and regions, e.g.:

le Languedoc	*l'Aquitaine*
le Limousin	*la Bourgogne*, Burgundy
le Poitou	*la Champagne*
le Roussillon	*la Provence*

Exceptions: *le Maine, la Franche-Comté*
French rivers:

le Doubs	*la Durance*
le Lot	*la Loire*
le Rhin, Rhine	*la Maine*
le Tarn	*la Seine*

Exceptions: *le Rhône, la Lys*. Note that the rule does not apply to foreign rivers, many of which are masculine even though they end in *-e*, e.g. *le Danube, le Gange* 'Ganges', *le Tage* 'Tagus', *le Tibre* 'Tiber', *le Tigre* 'Tigris'.

(c) The gender of the names of French *départements* is as follows:

Names based on river-names take the gender of the corresponding river or, where there are two, of the first, e.g. *le Doubs, le Haut-Rhin, la Somme, la Loire-Atlantique, le Loir-et-Cher, le Lot-et-Garonne, la Meurthe-et-Moselle*.

Plural names (based on the names of mountains or other geographical features) happen in most cases to be feminine, e.g. *les Alpes Maritimes, les Ardennes, les Bouches-du-Rhône, les Côtes-du-Nord, les Deux-Sèvres, les Landes, les Pyrénées-Orientales, les Vosges, les Yvelines*. One, *les Hauts-de-Seine*, is masculine. In practice, however, the need to indicate gender with these names rarely arises.

Others are masculine if the name (or, in the case of compounds, the first element) does *not* end in *-e*, feminine if it does:

le Calvados	*la Corse du Sud*
le Cantal	*la Haute-Corse*
le Jura	*la Haute-Savoie*
le Morbihan	*la Lozère*
le Nord	*la Manche*
le Pas-de-Calais	*la Savoie*

le Puy-de-Dôme
le Val-de-Marne
le Val-d'Oise

Exception: *le Vaucluse*.

Gender shown by ending

53 We shall discuss successively endings that always or usually indicate that the noun is (i) masculine or (ii) feminine, and (iii) a few problematic endings.

54 (i) **Masculine endings**

-age

A few monosyllables:

le gage, pledge, guarantee
le mage, Magus (*les rois Mages*, the Three Wise Man)
le page, page-boy
le sage, wise man
le stage, short course, training period

and several hundred polysyllables (many of them corresponding to English words in *-ing*), e.g.:

l'atterrissage, landing (of a plane)
le barrage, dam
le bavardage, chatter(ing)
le chômage, unemployment
le cirage, waxing, polishing
le courage
l'étage, floor, storey
le fromage, cheese
le garage
le gaspillage, waste, wasting
le mariage, marriage, wedding
le message
le nettoyage, cleaning
l'orage, (thunder)storm
le paysage, scenery
le potage, soup

le pourcentage, percentage
le village
le visage, face
le voyage, journey

Exceptions: five monosyllables:

la cage
la nage, swimming (in certain expressions only)
la page
la plage, beach
la rage, fury, rabies

and four polysyllables (three of them names of plants):

l'image   *la solidage*, golden rod
la passerage, pepperwort   *la saxifrage*, saxifrage

-ai, -oi

Most nouns in *-ai, -oi* are masculine, e.g.:

le balai, broom   *le beffroi*, belfry
le délai, time limit *l'emploi*, use, job
l'essai, attempt   *l'envoi*, sending
le geai, jay   *le roi*, king
le quai, quay, platform   *le tournoi*, tournament

Exceptions: *la foi* 'faith', *la loi* 'law', *la paroi* '(inside) wall'.

-ail, -eil (including **-ueil**), **-euil**

All masculine, e.g.:

l'ail, garlic
le chandail, sweater
le corail, coral
le détail
l'émail, enamel
l'épouvantail, scarecrow
l'éventail, fan
le portail, portal
le travail, work
le vitrail, stained-glass window
l'appareil, apparatus
le conseil, piece of advice
l'orteil, toe

le réveil, waking up
le soleil, sun
le sommeil, sleep
l'accueil, welcome
le cercueil, coffin
l'écueil, reef
l'orgueil, pride
le recueil, collection (of poems, etc.)
le deuil, mourning
l'écureuil, squirrel
le seuil, threshold

-at

All masculine, e.g.:

le championnat, championship
le chocolat, chocolate
le climat, climate
le combat, fight
le consulat, consulate
le contrat, contract
le débat, debate
l'état, state
le forçat, convict
le nougat
le résultat, result
le secrétariat
le sénat, senate
le syndicat, trade-union

-c, -d, etc.

All words ending in *-c* or *-d*, and the relatively few words ending in *-b*, *-g*, *-k*, *-p*, *-q* or *-z*, are masculine, whether or not the consonant is pronounced, e.g.:

(a) **-c**:

l'aqueduc, aquaduct
le bec, beak
l'estomac, stomach
le franc
le jonc, reed
le lac, lake
le sac, bag
le porc, pig

(b) **-d**:

le bord, edge
l'étendard, flag, standard
le fond, bottom
le gland, acorn
le pied, foot
le regard, glance, look
le retard, delay
le standard, (telephone) switchboard

(c) others:

le club	*le steak*
le plomb, lead	*le coup*, blow
l'étang, pond	*le loup*, wolf
le hareng, herring	*le coq*, cock
le poing, fist	*le gaz*, gas
le bifteck, steak	*le nez*, nose
le snack, snack-bar	*le riz*, rice

-é

Nearly all words ending in *-é* except those in *-té, tié* (see below, 55) are masculine, e.g.:

le blé, wheat	*le délégué*, delegate
le café, café, coffee	*le fossé*, ditch
le carré, square	*le gué*, ford
le clergé, clergy	*le marché*, market
le cuirassé, battleship	*le pavé*, paving-stone
le dé, dice, thimble	*le péché*, sin
le défilé, procession	*le pré*, meadow
le degré, degree, step	*le thé*, tea

Exceptions: *l'acné* 'acne', *la clé* 'key', *la psyché* 'psyche'.

-eau

Four monosyllables

le beau, that which is beautiful
le sceau, seal
le seau, bucket
le veau, calf, veal

and some two hundred polysyllables, e.g.:

l'anneau, ring	*le gâteau*, cake
le bateau, boat	*le marteau*, hammer
le bouleau, birch-tree	*le morceau*, piece
le cadeau, present	*le niveau*, level
le cerveau, brain	*le râteau*, rake
le chapeau, hat	*le réseau*, network
le château, castle	*le rideau*, curtain
le couteau, knife	*le tableau*, picture
le drapeau, flag	*le tombeau*, tomb

Exceptions: Only two: *l'eau* 'water', *la peau* 'skin'.

-ède, -ège, -ème

> *l'intermède*, interlude
> *le quadrupède*, quadruped
> *le remède*, remedy
> *le collège*, type of secondary school
> *le cortège*, procession
> *le liège*, cork
> *le manège*, merry-go-round
> *le piège*, trap
> *le sacrilège*
> *le siège*, seat, siege
> *le sortilège*, magic spell
> *le chrysanthème*, chrysanthemum
> *le diadème*, diadem
> *l'emblème*, emblem
> *le poème*, poem
> *le problème*, problem
> *le système*, system
> *le thème*, theme, etc.

and the names of fractions, *un dixième* 'a tenth', *un vingtième* 'a twentieth', *un centième* 'a hundredth', etc.

Exceptions: The only common exception is *la crème* 'cream' (but note the use of *un crème*, short for *un café crème* 'coffee with cream or milk'). A few rare or technical terms include *la pinède* 'pine-forest', *l'allège* 'lighter (boat)', *la drège* 'drag-net', *la trirème* 'trireme'.

-er (for **-ier** see below):

(a) (*-r* pronounced). Nearly all masculine, e.g.:

> *le cancer*
> *l'enfer*, hell
> *le fer*, iron
> *l'hiver*, winter
> *le laser*
> *le leader*
> *le reporter*
> *le revolver*
> *le starter*, choke (of a car)
> *le speaker*, (radio, TV) announcer

Only two exceptions: *la cuiller* 'spoon', *la mer* 'sea'.

(b) (*-r* not pronounced). All masculine, e.g.:

le boucher, butcher	*le foyer*, hearth
le boulanger, baker	*le laisser-passer*, pass, permit
le clocher, church tower	*le loyer*, rent
le déjeuner, lunch	*l'oranger*, orange-tree
le dîner, dinner	*le plancher*, floor

-ès

All masculine, e.g.:

(a) (Final *-s* pronounced)

l'aloès, aloe	*le palmarès*, list of winners
le cacatoès, cockatoo	*le xérès*, sherry

(b) (Final *-s* not pronounced)

l'abscès, abscess	*le grès*, sandstone
l'accès, access	*le procès*, trial
le congrès, congress	*le progrès*, progress
le cyprès, cypress	*le succès*, success

-et

Some three hundred words, all masculine, e.g.:

le ballet	*le perroquet*, parrot
le banquet	*le poulet*, chicken
le béret	*le projet*, project
le billet, ticket	*le regret*
le bonnet	*le robinet*, tap
le buffet	*le roitelet*, wren
le carnet, notebook	*le secret*
le filet, net	*le sommet*, summit
le fouet, whip	*le sujet*, subject
le jouet, toy	*le ticket*

-i (pronounced [i], i.e. excluding -ai, -oi)

Most nouns in *-i* are masculine, e.g.:

l'abri, shelter	*le merci*, thanks
l'appui, support	*le pari*, bet
le colibri, humming bird	*le parti*, (political) party
le cri, shout	*le pli*, fold

le défi, challenge
l'ennui, boredom
l'épi, ear (of corn)

le raccourci, short cut
le ski, ski, skiing
le souci, care, worry

and the days of the week, *le lundi, le mardi,* etc.

Exceptions: *la fourmi,* ant, *la merci,* mercy.

Note that *un après-midi* and *une après-midi* 'afternoon' are both used.

-ier

A couple of hundred words, many of them referring to (a) male humans, or (b) trees, and all masculine:

(a) Male humans, e.g.:

le banquier, banker
le chevalier, knight
le conférencier, lecturer
l'épicier, grocer
le guerrier, warrior

l'héritier, heir
l'hôtelier, hotel-keeper
l'officier, officer
le romancier, novelist
le sorcier, sorcerer

(b) Trees, e.g.:

le dattier, date-palm
le figuier, fig-tree
le laurier, laurel
le marronier, chestnut tree
le noisetier, hazel-tree

le palmier, palm-tree
le peuplier, poplar
le poirier, pear-tree
le pommier, apple-tree
le rosier, rose-bush

(c) Others, e.g.:

l'acier, steel
le cahier, note-book
le casier, pigeonhole
le cendrier, ashtray
le chantier, building site
le clavier, keyboard
le collier, necklace
le dossier, file, dossier
le gosier, throat
le grenier, attic

le guêpier, wasps' nest
le métier, job, profession
le palier, landing
le panier, basket
le papier, paper
le pétrolier, (oil) tanker
le quartier, district (of a town)
le saladier, salad-bowl
le sentier, path
le tablier, apron

-ing

A few words borrowed from English (or, in the case of *schilling*, from German), are all masculine, e.g.:

le brushing, blow-dry
le building, office-block, etc.
le camping, camp-site
le jogging, jogging, track-suit
le meeting, rally, (political) meeting
le parking, car-park
le schilling, (Austrian) schilling
le shopping

-isme

Some four hundred words, all masculine, e.g.:

le catéchisme
le christianisme, Christianity
le cubisme
l'idiotisme, idiom
le prisme, prism

le rhumatisme, rheumatism
le romantisme, Romanticism
le socialisme
le tourisme
l'urbanisme, town-planning

-ment

With one exception, the scores of words in *-ment* are all masculine, e.g.:

l'abonnement, subscription
l'avertissement, warning
le bâtiment, building
le ciment, cement
le commencement, beginning
le désarmement, disarmament

le gouvernement, government
le logement, lodging
le moment
le monument
le mouvement, movement
le recensement, census

Exception: *la jument* 'mare'.

-oir

Over a hundred words, all masculine, e.g.:

le couloir, corridor
le désespoir, despair
le dortoir, dormitory
l'espoir, hope
le miroir, mirror

le mouchoir, handkerchief
le rasoir, razor
le soir, evening
le tiroir, drawer
le trottoir, pavement

-ou

All masculine, e.g.:

le bijou, jewel
le caillou, pebble

le genou, knee
le hibou, owl

le chou, cabbage

le clou, nail

le cou, neck

le coucou, cuckoo

le pou, louse˙

le trou, hole

le verrou, bolt

le voyou, lout

55   (ii) **Feminine endings**

-ace

Words in *-ace* are all feminine, e.g.:

l'audace, daring

la glace, ice, mirror

la menace, threat

la place, (public) square

la race, breed, race

la surface

la trace

-ade

Some two hundred words (many of them uncommon), the great majority of them feminine, e.g.:

l'ambassade, embassy

la bourgade, large village

la cascade

la façade

l'œillade, wink

l'orangeade

la promenade, walk

la saccade, jerk

la salade, salad

la tornade, tornado

Exceptions:

le or *la camarade*, friend

le or *la garde-malade*, home nurse

le or *la malade*, sick person

le or *la nomade*, nomad

le grade, rank

le jade

le stade, stadium

-aie

All nouns in *-aie* are feminine:

(a) Collective nouns for trees, etc.:

la châtaigneraie, chestnut grove

l'oliveraie, olive grove

la palmeraie, palm grove

la peupleraie, poplar grove

    la ronceraie, bramble patch
    la roseraie, rose garden

(b) Others, e.g.:

la baie, bay, berry	*la plaie*, wound
la haie, hedge	*la raie*, furrow, stripe
la monnaie, currency, change	*la taie*, pillow-case

-aine, -eine, -oine

Most nouns with these endings are feminine, e.g.:

l'aubaine, windfall	*la semaine*, week
la fontaine, fountain	*la peine*, trouble, difficulty
la gaine, sheath	*la reine*, queen
la graine, grain	*la veine*, vein
la haine, hatred	*l'avoine*, oats
la laine, wool	*la macédoine (de légumes)*,
la migraine	mixed vegetables
la plaine, plain	*la pivoine*, peony
la porcelaine	

Also *la douzaine* 'dozen', *la quinzaine* 'about fifteen, a fortnight', *la vingtaine* 'score', *la centaine* 'about a hundred', and similar forms derived from other numerals.

Exceptions:

le capitaine, captain	*le moine*, monk
l'antimoine, antimony	*le patrimoine*, heritage
le chanoine, canon	

-aison

All feminine, e.g.:

la comparaison, comparison	*la maison*, house
la conjugaison, conjugation	*la raison*, reason
la crevaison, puncture	*la saison*, season
la liaison	*la terminaison*, ending (of
la livraison, delivery	a word)

-ance, -anse, -ence, -ense

With only two exceptions, these words are feminine, e.g.:

l'ambulance	*la panse*, paunch
la confiance, confidence	*la transe*, trance

la correspondance, correspondence
la croyance, belief
la distance
l'espérance, hope
la lance
la naissance, birth
la puissance, power
la souffrance, suffering
l'anse, handle (of cup, etc.)
la danse, dance

l'agence, agency
la conscience
la différence
l'essence, petrol
l'influence
la patience
la présence
la violence
la défense, defence
la dépense, expenditure

Exceptions: *le silence, le suspense.*

-èche, -èque, -èse, -ève

The great majority of these are feminine, e.g.:

la brèche, breach
la crèche, crib, creche
la flèche, arrow
la mèche, wick
la bibliothèque, library
la discothèque, disco, record library

la pastèque, water-melon
la genèse, genesis
l'hypothèse, hypothesis
la synthèse, synthesis
la thèse, thesis
la fève, broad bean
la grève, strike
la sève, sap

Exceptions: *le* or *la métèque* (derogatory term for a foreigner), *le diocèse, un* or *une élève* 'pupil'.

-ée

Most nouns in *-ée* (but with a substantial number of exceptions, mostly technical or otherwise uncommon words) are feminine, e.g.:

l'araignée, spider
la buée, condensation, steam
la cactée, cactus
la cuillerée, spoonful
la dictée, dictation
la durée, duration
l'épée, sword
l'épopée, epic
la fée, fairy

la fusée, rocket
la journée, day
la marée, tide
la mosquée, mosque
la pensée, thought
la poignée, fistful, handful
la rosée, dew
la traversée, crossing
la vallée, valley

Exceptions include:

un or *une athée*, atheist
l'apogée, peak, climax, apogee
le camée, cameo
le colisée, coliseum
le lycée, (French) secondary school
le mausolée, mausoleum
le musée, museum
le pygmée, pygmy
le scarabée, scarab (beetle)
le trophée, trophy

-euse

All feminine:

(a) Female humans, e.g.:

la blanchisseuse, laundress
la maquilleuse, make-up girl
la menteuse, liar
l'ouvreuse, usherette
la religieuse, nun
la vendeuse, saleswoman

(b) Mechanical objects, e.g.:

l'agrafeuse, stapler
la cireuse, floor polisher
la mitrailleuse, machine-gun
la moissonneuse, harvester
la perceuse, drill
la tondeuse (de gazon), lawn-mower
la tricoteuse, knitting-machine
la tronçonneuse, chain-saw

(c) Others, e.g.:

la berceuse, lullaby
la nébuleuse, nebula
la vareuse, kind of tunic
la veilleuse, night-light

-ie (including **-uie**, but excluding **-aie** and **-oie**)

Several hundred words (including about four hundred in *-erie*), of which all except a handful are feminine, e.g.:

la biologie, biology
la boucherie, butcher's shop
la bougie, candle
la chimie, chemistry
la colonie, colony
la compagnie, company
la copie, copy
la démocratie, democracy
la folie, madness
la galerie, gallery
la géographie, geography
la jalousie, jealousy
la librairie, bookshop
la magie, magic
la maladie, illness
la partie, part
la pharmacie, pharmacy
la pie, magpie
la plaisanterie, joke
la pluie, rain

la prairie, meadow	*la symphonie*, symphony
la scie, saw	*la tragédie*, tragedy
la série, series	*la truie*, sow
la suie, soot	*la vie*, life

Exceptions:

l'amphibie, amphibian	*l'incendie*, fire
le coolie	*le Messie*, Messiah
le génie, genius; engineering corps	*le parapluie*, umbrella
	le sosie, double, look-alike

-ière

Well over a hundred words, nearly all feminine, e.g.:

la bannière, banner	*la lumière*, light
la barrière, barrier	*la manière*, manner, way
la bière, beer	*la matière*, matter
la cafetière, coffee-pot	*la paupière*, eye-lid
la chaumière, cottage	*la poussière*, dust
la croisière, cruise	*la prière*, prayer
la fermière, farmer's wife	*la rivière*, river
la frontière, frontier	*la théière*, tea-pot

Exceptions: *le cimetière* 'cemetery', *le derrière* 'backside, rear'.

-ine

Over a hundred words, nearly all feminine, e.g.:

la colline, hill	*la poitrine*, chest
la cuisine, kitchen	*la racine*, root
la farine, flour	*la routine*
la guillotine	*la ruine*, ruin
la machine	*la saccharine*
la marine, navy	*la sardine*
la médecine	*la scarlatine*, scarlet fever
la narine, nostril	*la turbine*
la pénicilline	*la vitrine*, shop window, showcase.
la piscine, swimming-pool	
la platine, tape-deck, etc.	

Only two exceptions: *le magazine, le platine* 'platinum'.

-ise

About fifty words, nearly all of them feminine, e.g.:

la bêtise, folly	*une église*, church
la brise, breeze	*la franchise*, frankness
la cerise, cherry	*la marchandise*, goods
la chemise, shirt	*la surprise*
la crise, crisis	*la valise*, suit-case

Exceptions: *le cytise* 'laburnum', *le pare-brise* 'windscreen'.

-sion, -tion

With one exception, the many nouns in *-sion, -tion* are all feminine, e.g.:

la confusion	*l'action*
la décision	*la civilisation*
l'émission, broadcast	*la condition*
l'occasion, opportunity	*la destination*
la possession	*la fiction*
la pression, pressure	*la nation*
la provision	*la position*
la télévision	*la question*
la tension	*la situation*
la vision, eye-sight	*la traduction*, translation

Exception: *le bastion*.

-lle, -sse, -tte, -ffe, -nne, -ppe

Many hundreds of words ending in a double consonant + *-e* are feminine. This does not apply to words in *-mme* and *-rre* (see vi below), but, otherwise, there are relatively few exceptions, all of which, apart from a few highly technical or very rare words, are listed below.

(a) **-lle** (pronounced [l]), e.g.:

la balle, ball	*la poubelle*, dustbin
la malle, trunk	*la selle*, saddle
la salle, room, hall	*la semelle*, sole (of shoe)
la chapelle, chapel	*la vaisselle*, dishes, crockery
la dentelle, lace	*la voyelle*, vowel

l'échelle, ladder	*la ville*, town
la ficelle, string	*la bulle*, bubble

Note that even *la sentinelle* 'sentry', referring to a male human, is feminine.

Exceptions:

l'intervalle, interval	*le violoncelle*, cello
le libelle, lampoon	*le mille*, thousand
le polichinelle, Punch, buffoon	*le vaudeville*
le or *la rebelle*, rebel	*le tulle*
le vermicelle, vermicelli	

(b) **-ille** (pronounced [j] – see 2), e.g.:

la bataille, battle	*l'aiguille*, needle
la ferraille, scrap iron	*l'anguille*, eel
la muraille, (high) wall	*la bille*, marble
la paille, straw	*la cheville*, ankle
la taille, waist, size	*la famille*, family
la volaille, poultry	*la faucille*, sickle
la bouteille, bottle	*la fille*, daughter
l'oreille, ear	*la pupille*, pupil (of eye)
la veille, eve, day before	*la grenouille*, frog
la feuille, leaf	*la patrouille*, patrol

Exceptions:

le chèvrefeuille, honeysuckle	*le gorille*, gorilla
le portefeuille, wallet	*le* or *la pupille*, ward

(c) **-sse**

All nouns in *-esse* are feminine; many of them denote either female beings, e.g.:

la déesse, goddess	*la princesse*, princess
la maîtresse, mistress	*la tigresse*, tigress

or qualities, e.g.:

la faiblesse, weakness	*la tendresse*, tenderness
la jeunesse, youth	*la tristesse*, sadness
la paresse, laziness	*la vieillesse*, old age
la politesse, politeness	*la vitesse*, speed

Other feminine nouns in *-sse* include:

la chasse, hunting	*la forteresse*, fortress
la classe, class	*la messe*, (religious) mass
la potasse, potassium	*la presse*, press
la tasse, cup	*la cuisse*, thigh
la terrasse, terrace	*la saucisse*, sausage
la baisse, lowering	*la brosse*, brush
la caisse, cash-desk	*la fosse*, pit
la graisse, grease, fat	*l'angoisse*, anxiety
la hausse, rise (in prices, etc.)	*la paroisse*, parish
la caresse, caress	*la mousse*, moss, mousse

Exceptions:

le or *la gosse*, kid
le or *la Russe*, Russian
le carrosse, (horse-drawn) coach
le colosse, colossus, giant
le molosse (rare), huge dog
le mousse, cabin-boy
le narcisse, narcissus
le pamplemousse, grapefruit
le petit-suisse, kind of cream cheese
le Suisse, Swiss

(d) -tte

A large group of nouns in *-ette*, the vast majority of them feminine, e.g.:

l'allumette, match	*la fourchette*, fork
la camionnette, van	*l'omelette*
la chaussette, sock	*la recette*, recipe
la cigarette	*la serviette*, towel, brief-case
la côtelette, chop, cutlet	*la silhouette*
la dette, debt	*la trompette*, trumpet

Exceptions: *le squelette* 'skeleton, *le trompette* 'trumpeter'.

Note that *la vedette* '(film-)star', etc., is feminine even when it refers to a man.

Other nouns in *-tte*, **all** feminine, include:

la datte, date (fruit)	*la botte*, boot, bunch
la patte, paw	*la carotte*, carrot

la grotte, cave, grotto
la goutte, drop

la hutte, hut
la lutte, struggle

(e) -ffe, -nne, -ppe

Most of these words are feminine, e.g.:

l'étoffe, cloth, material
la gaffe, blunder
la greffe, graft, transplant
la griffe, claw
la touffe, tuft
le truffe, truffle
l'antenne, aerial
la colonne, column
la couronne, crown
la panne, (mechanical) breakdown
la personne, person
la tonne, ton, tonne
l'enveloppe, envelope
la grappe, bunch (of grapes)
la grippe, flu
la nappe, tablecloth
la trappe, trap-door

Exception: *le renne* 'reindeer'.

-té, -tié

Several hundred nouns in *-té* and **all** nouns in *-tié* (there are only four) are feminine, e.g.:

la bonté, goodness
la cécité, blindness
la cité, city
la cruauté, cruelty
la difficulté, difficulty
la fierté, pride
la lâcheté, cowardice
la majorité, majority

la qualité, quality
la quantité, quantity
la santé, health
la vérité, truth
l'amitié, friendship
l'inimitié, enmity
la moitié, half
la pitié, pity

Exceptions:

l'aparté, (theatrical) aside
l'arrêté, order, decree
le comité, committee

le *comté*, county
le *côté*, side
le *décolleté*, low neckline
le *doigté*, fingering, tact
l'*été*, summer
le *pâté*, pie, pâté; block of houses; etc.
le *traité*, treaty, treatise

-tude

All feminine, e.g.:

l'*attitude*
la *certitude*, certainty
l'*étude*, study
l'*habitude*, habit

l'*inquiétude*, anxiety
la *multitude*
la *servitude*
la *solitude*

-ure

Over three hundred words, nearly all of them feminine, e.g.:

la *ceinture*, belt
la *confiture*, jam
la *couverture*, blanket
la *créature*
la *dictature*, dictatorship
la *doublure*, lining
la *fermeture*, closing
la *figure*, face
la *fourrure*, fur
une *injure*, insult

la *lecture*, reading
la *nature*
la *nourriture*, food
la *peinture*, painting, paint
la *reliure*, binding (of a book)
la *serrure*, lock
la *signature*
la *température*
la *torture*
la *voiture*, car, carriage

Exceptions:

(i) Chemical substances, e.g.:

le *bromure*, bromide
le *carbure*, carbide
le *chlorure*, chloride
le *fluorure*, fluoride

l'*hydrocarbure*, hydrocarbon
le *mercure*, mercury
le *phosphure*, phosphide
le *sulfure*, sulfide

(ii) Others:

l'*augure*, soothsayer
le *murmure*, murmur
le *parjure*, perjury

56 (iii) Problematic endings

-a

Those who know Latin, Italian or Spanish, in which languages nouns in -a are usually feminine, may well think the same is true of French. This is not so – many, though by no means all, French nouns in -a are masculine.

(a) Masculine nouns in -a include:

l'agenda, diary	*le sofa*
l'opéra	*le tapioca*
le panda	*le tibia*
le panorama	*le visa*
le rutabaga, swede	

and a number of names of flowers, e.g. *le bégonia, le dahlia, le gardénia, le pétunia.*

(b) Feminine nouns in -a include:

la malaria	*la toundra*, tundra
la marina	*la vendetta*
la paranoïa	*la véranda*
la razzia, raid, foray	*la villa*
la tombola, lottery	*la vodka*

and a number of names of dances, including *la mazurka, la polka, la rumba, la samba.*

-ène

(a) Masculine nouns in -ène are mainly technical terms of chemistry, e.g.:

l'acétylène	*le méthylène*
l'hydrogène	*le molybdène*, molybdenum
le kérosène	*l'oxygène*

but also include:

un or *une aborigène*	*le troène*, privet

(b) Feminine nouns in -ène include:

l'arène, arena	*l'hygiène*
l'ébène, ebony	*la patène*, paten
la gangrène, gangrene	*la scène*, scene, stage
l'hyène, hyena	*la sirène*, siren; mermaid

-ère

Nouns in -*ère* referring to humans are male or female according to the sex of the individual concerned. Apart from that, no very helpful rules can be given for determining the gender of nouns in -*ère*.

(a) Masculine nouns include:

Referring to males:

> *le compère*, accomplice
> *le confrère*, colleague, confrere
> *le frère*, brother
> *le père*, father
> *le trouvère*, trouvère (medieval bard)

Others:

> *le caractère*, character
> *le conifère*, conifer
> *le cratère*, crater
> *le critère*, criterion
> *le débarcadère*, landing stage
> *l'hélicoptère*, helicopter
>
> *l'hémisphère*
> *le ministère*, ministry
> *le monastère*, monastery
> *le mystère*, mystery
> *le réverbère*, street lamp
> *l'ulcère*, ulcer

(b) Feminine nouns include:

Referring to females:

> *la bergère*, shepherdess
> *la boulangère*, baker's wife
> *la conseillère*, adviser
>
> *l'étrangère*, foreigner
> *la ménagère*, housewife
> *la mère*, mother

Others:

> *l'artère*, artery
> *l'atmosphère*
> *la bruyère*, heather
> *la cuillère*, spoon
> *l'ère*, era
>
> *la misère*, dire poverty
> *la panthère*, panther
> *la sphère*
> *la stratosphère*
> *la vipère*, viper

-ète

(a) Masculine nouns include:

> *le diabète*, diabetes   *le prophète*, prophet

(b) Feminine nouns include:

l'arbalète, crossbow	*la diète*, diet (assembly)
la cacahuète, peanut	*l'épithète*, epithet
la comète, comet	*la planète*, planet .

(c) Nouns that can be of either gender, in accordance with the sex of the individual referred to, include:

un or *une ascète*, ascetic
un or *une athlète*
un or *une esthète*, aesthete
· *un* or *une interprète*, interpreter

-eur

Words in *-eur* fall into four groups:

(a) Nouns referring to male humans are masculine, e.g.:

le cambrioleur, burglar	*le pêcheur*, fisherman
le facteur, postman	*le sculpteur*, sculptor
le lecteur, reader	*le voleur*, thief
le menteur, liar	*le voyageur*, traveller

Note that *le professeur* 'teacher, professor', is masculine, even with reference to a woman.

(b) Nouns referring to physical (in many cases mechanical) objects are masculine, e.g.:

l'accélérateur, accelerator	*le moteur*, engine
l'aspirateur, vacuum-cleaner	*l'ordinateur*, computer
le carburateur, carburettor	*le radiateur*, radiator
le condenseur, condenser	*le récepteur*, receiver
le croiseur, cruiser	*le téléviseur*, TV set
le démarreur, starter (of car)	*le tracteur*, tractor
l'échangeur, interchange (on motorway)	*le vapeur*, steamship

(c) Abstract nouns, referring to qualities, feelings, colours, etc., are in most cases feminine, e.g.:

la blancheur, whiteness	*la faveur*, favour
la couleur, colour	*la fraîcheur*, coolness
la douceur, sweetness, softness	*la fureur*, fury
la douleur, pain, grief	*la grandeur*, size

la hauteur, height   *la profondeur*, depth
l'humeur, mood   *la rougeur*, redness
la largeur, width   *la stupeur*, daze
la pâleur, paleness   *la terreur*, terror
la peur, fear   *la valeur*, value

Exceptions:

le bonheur, happiness   *le labeur*, toil
le déshonneur, dishonour   *le malheur*, misfortune
l'honneur, honour

(d) Miscellaneous, e.g.:

masc.   fem.

le chœur, choir   *la fleur*, flower
le cœur, heart   *la liqueur*
le dénominateur, denominator   *la lueur*, glow
l'équateur, equator   *la sueur*, sweat
l'extérieur, outside   *la vapeur*, steam
le secteur, sector

-ite

(a) Words referring to humans are masculine or feminine according to the sex of the person referred to, e.g.:

le Jésuite, Jesuit
la Carmélite, Carmelite nun
un or *une antisémite*
un or *une Israélite*
le or *la Maronite*, Maronite (Christian)
le or *la Moscovite*, Muscovite
le or *la Sunnite*, Sunni Muslim

(b) Names of salts of acids are masculine:

l'arsénite   *le nitrite*
l'hypochlorite   *le phosphite*
l'hyposulfite   *le sulfite*

(c) Some names of minerals in fairly common use are masculine:

l'anthracite   *le graphite*
le granite (also *le granit*)   *le lignite*

but more technical names of minerals in *-ite* are feminine, e.g.:

la bauxite	*la magnésite*
la calcite	*la marcassite*
la ferrite	*la mélanite*
la lazalite	*la néphrite*
la malachite	*la wolframite*

(d) Medical terms in *-ite* (corresponding to English *-itis*) referring to various types of inflammation are feminine, e.g.:

l'appendicite	*la gastrite*
l'amygdalite, tonsilitis	*la laryngite*
l'arthrite	*la méningite*
la bronchite	*la phlébite*
la conjonctivite	*la poliomyélite*

(e) Other masculine nouns include:

le mérite. merit	*le satellite*
le parasite	*le termite*
le plébiscite	

(f) Other feminine nouns include:

la dynamite	*l'orbite*, orbit, eye-socket
la faillite, bankruptcy	*la réussite*, success
la guérite, sentry-box	*la stalactite*
la marguerite, ox-eye daisy	*la stalagmite*
la marmite, cooking-pot	*la site*
la mite, clothes moth	*la visite*

-mme, -rre

Note that there are more masculine than feminine words in *-mme* and *-rre*, e.g.:

(a) Masculine

le dilemme 'dilemma'	*le somme* 'nap'
l'homme 'man'	

Also masculine are *le gramme* 'gram', other metric units of measurement in *-gramme* (*le centigramme, le kilogramme*, etc.), and *le cryptogramme, le diagramme, le monogramme, le parallélogramme, le programme*, and *le télégramme* (for two feminine words in *-gramme*, see below).

le beurre, butter
le cimeterre, scimitar
le leurre, snare, delusion
le lierre, ivy
le paratonnerre, lightning conductor
le parterre, flowerbed, stalls (theatre)
le tintamarre, din, racket
le tonnerre, thunder
le verre, glass

(b) Feminine

une anagramme, anagram
une épigramme, epigram
la femme, woman
la flamme, flame
la gamme, scale, gamut
la gemme, gem
la gomme, rubber (eraser)

la pomme, apple
la somme, sum, amount
la barre, bar
la guerre, war
la pierre, stone
la serre, greenhouse
la terre, earth

-o

A majority of the small group of words in *-o* are masculine, but there are some important exceptions.

(a) Masculine words include:

le bistro(t), pub, café
le cargo, cargo-boat
le casino
le duo, duet
le credo, creed
l'écho
le kilo, kilo(gram)

le numéro, number, numeral
le piano
le trio
le porto, port (drink)
le studio, studio, flatlet
le verso, back (of page)
le zéro

(b) Feminine nouns include:

une auto, car
la dactylo, typist, typing
la dynamo

la photo
la polio
la radio, radio, X-ray photo

-oire

(a) Masculine nouns include:

l'auditoire, audience
l'ivoire, ivory

le laboratoire, laboratory
le mémoire, memoir

l'observatoire, observatory	le réfectoire, refectory
le pourboire, tip	le répertoire .
le promontoire, headland	le territoire, territory

(b) Feminine nouns include:

l'armoire, cupboard	l'histoire, history, story
la balançoire, swing	la mâchoire, jaw
la baignoire, bath-tub	la nageoire, fin
la bouilloire, kettle	la mémoire, memory
la foire, fair	la poire, pear
la gloire, glory	la victoire, victory

-te (other than **-ète, -ite** and **-tte**, see above)

(a) Nouns referring to humans are masculine or feminine according to the sex of the individual concerned, e.g.:

un or une adulte
un or une artiste
un or une astronaute
le or la démocrate
le or la dentiste
le or la diplomate
un or une enthousiaste, enthusiast
un or une hôte, guest
le or la linguiste
le or la patriote

Note le comte 'count, earl' (feminine la comtesse), le despote, un hôte 'host, landlord' (feminine une hôtesse), le pilote, le pirate.

(b) Names of chemicals and minerals in -ate, -lte, -ste are masculine, e.g.:

le carbonate	le sulfate, suphate
le chlorate	l'asphalte
le nitrate	le basalte
le phosphate	l'asbeste, asbestos
le silicate	le schiste, schist

(c) Most other nouns in -te (but with some important exceptions) are feminine, e.g.:

l'arête, fish-bone	la boîte, box
la bête, animal	la carte, map, card

la chute, fall	*la perte*, loss
la côte, coast	*la peste*, plague
la crainte, fear	*la piste*, track, runway
la cravate, tie	*la plainte*, complaint, groan
la crête, crest	*la porte*, door
la croûte, crust	*la poste*, postal service
la date	*la récolte*, crop
la découverte, discovery	*la route*, road
la dispute	*la sieste*, siesta
l'émeute, riot	*la sonate*, sonata
la faute, mistake	*la sorte*, sort
la fente, crack	*la tarte*, tart
la flûte, flute	*la tempête*, storm
la honte, shame	*la tente*, tent
la minute	*la tomate*, tomato
la note, note, bill	*la vente*, sale
la pâte, dough	*la veste*, jacket
la pente, slope	*la voûte*, vault

Exceptions include:

l'acte, act	*le faîte*, top, summit
l'antidote	*l'insecte*, insect
l'arbuste, small shrub	*le jute*
le buste, bust	*le parachute*
le compte, count, account	*le poste*, job, etc.
le conte, tale	*le reste*, remainder, rest
le contexte, context	*le texte*, text
le contraste, contrast	*le tumulte*, tumult
le doute, doubt	*le vote*

The gender of compound nouns

57 In what follows, only nouns formed of two or more words joined by hyphens are counted as compound nouns. Nouns that were originally compounds but are now written as one word without hyphens (e.g. *le chèvrefeuille*, honeysuckle) are treated as simple nouns and so are covered by the rules given above.

Compound nouns can be divided, for our present purposes, into six classes:

58 (i) **Nouns composed of a noun and a following or preceding adjective**

The gender of the compound is normally that of the simple noun, e.g.:

le bas-relief, low relief, bas relief
le cerf-volant, kite, stag-beetle

la basse-cour, farmyard
la belle-fille, daughter-in-law

Exceptions:

le Peau-Rouge, Redskin
le terre-neuve, Newfoundland dog (short for *le chien de Terre-Neuve*)

and some birds' names, including *le rouge-gorge* 'robin', *le rouge-queue* 'redstart'.

59 (ii) **Nouns having the construction noun + noun**

The gender is that of the principal noun, which is normally the first noun, e.g.:

le bateau-école, training-ship (i.e. a ship, *bateau*, serving as a school)
le camion-citerne, tanker (-lorry)
le chou-fleur, cauliflower (i.e. a 'flowering' cabbage)
un homme-grenouille, frogman
le mot-clé, keyword
un oiseau-mouche, humming-bird
le timbre-poste, (postage-) stamp
le wagon-lit, sleeping-car
une année-lumière, light-year
la porte-fenêtre, french window (i.e. a door, *porte*, serving also as a window)
la voiture-restaurant, dining-car (i.e. a coach, *voiture*, serving as a restaurant)

60 (iii) **Nouns having the construction noun + preposition + noun**

The gender is usually that of the first noun, e.g.:

masc.

un arc-en-ciel, rainbow
le chef-d'œuvre, masterpiece
le mont-de-piété, pawnshop
le pot-de-vin, bribe

fem.

la langue-de-chat, type of biscuit
la main-d'œuvre, work-force
la patte-d'oie, crow's foot (wrinkle)
la tête-de-loup, ceiling brush

Exceptions: *le face-à-main* 'lorgnette', *le tête-à-queue* 'spin, slew round (in horse-riding)', *le tête-à-tête*.

61 (iv) **Nouns having the construction adverb or prefix + noun**
The gender is that of the simple noun, e.g.:

masc.

l'arrière-plan, background
l'ex-roi, ex-king
le demi-tarif, half-fare
le mini-budget
le non-paiement, non-payment
le vice-président

fem.

l'arrière-pensée, mental reservation
l'ex-femme, ex-wife
la demi-bouteille, half-bottle
la mini-jupe, miniskirt
la non-agression
la vice-présidence, vice-presidency

62 (v) **Nouns having the construction preposition + noun**
These are usually masculine, e.g.:

l'après-guerre, post-war period (even though *la guerre*, war, is feminine)
l'en-tête, heading (e.g. headed writing-paper)
le sans-gêne, lack of consideration for others
le sous-main, desk blotter

Exceptions: words referring to a female person, e.g.:

une sans-abri, homeless woman
une sans-cœur, heartless woman

Many apparent exceptions are accounted for by the fact that the first element is not a preposition but an adverb (so they are, in fact, type iv nouns), e.g. *l'avant-scène* 'proscenium, apron-stage' is feminine because the word is to be analysed not as something that is in front of the stage (*scène*), but as that part of the stage, *scène*, which is in front, *avant*, and so it takes the feminine gender of *scène*; *la contre-attaque* 'counter-attack' is not something that is against (*contre*) an attack, but an attack that goes counter to a previous one; *la sous-alimentation* 'malnutrition, under-feeding' is obviously not something that is beneath (*sous*) nutrition (*alimentation*), but nutrition that is of an inferior level.
Likewise:

une avant-garde, vanguard
la sous-commission, sub-committee
la sous-location, sub-letting
la sous-préfecture, sub-prefecture

63 (vi) Words having the construction verb + noun
These are nearly all masculine, e.g.:

le casse-noisettes, nutcracker
le coupe-papier, paper-knife
le cure-dent, toothpick
un essuie-main, hand-towel
le fume-cigarette, cigarette-holder
le gratte-ciel, skyscraper
l'ouvre-boîte, tin-opener
le pare-brise, windscreen
le porte-avions, aircraft carrier
le porte-monnaie, purse
le taille-crayon, pencil sharpener
le tire-bouchon, corkscrew

Exceptions: *le* or *la garde-barrière* 'level-crossing keeper', *le* or *la garde-malade* 'home nurse', according to the sex of the individual, *la garde-robe* 'wardrobe'.

A few uncommon names of fruit and flowers in *passe-* or *perce-* are feminine, e.g. *la passe-crassane* (variety of winter pear), *la passe-pierre* or *perce-pierre* 'samphire', *la passe-rose* 'hollyhock', *la perce-feuille* 'hare's ear', *la perce-muraille* 'wall pellitory'.

Note that *le brise-fer, le casse-tout* 'a child who breaks everything', are masculine even with reference to girls.

Words that are identical in form but different in gender

64   As we have seen (in particular in 48,i,d), words such as *élève* 'pupil', *secrétaire* 'secretary', and many others can be of either gender depending on the sex of the person concerned. Quite apart from these, French has a number of pairs or sets of words whose members are identical in spelling and pronunciation but different in gender and meaning. They include:

(a) **Words ending in a consonant**

	masc.	fem.
faux	forgery	scythe
mort	dead man	death
souris	(archaic, poetical) smile	mouse
tour	turn, walk, lathe, trick, etc.	tower
vapeur	steamship	steam, vapour

(b) **Words ending in mute *e***

	masc.	fem.
aide	male assistant	help; female assistant
aigle	eagle	female eagle; eagle standard
cartouche	scroll	cartridge
couple	couple (e.g. man and wife); pair (e.g. of dancers)	(archaic) *une couple de. . .* a couple of. . .
crêpe	crepe	pancake
critique	critic	criticism, review

enseigne	sub-lieutenant, ensign (officer)	(shop-)sign, ensign (flag)
faune	faun	fauna
finale	finale	last letter or syllable of a word
foudre	tun	thunderbolt, lightning
garde	keeper, guardsman	guard (duty), guardianship
gîte	shelter, lair, (mineral) deposit	list (of ship) (*donner de la gîte* 'to list')
greffe	record office (of law court, etc.)	graft(ing), (heart) transplant, etc.
guide	(male)guide; guidebook, etc.	(female) guide; *les guides* 'reins'
hollande	Dutch cheese	holland (linen); Dutch porcelain
laque	lacquer ware	shellac, lacquer, hairspray
livre	book	pound
manche	handle (e.g. of a broom)	sleeve; *la Manche* 'English Channel'
manille	manilla cigar	shackle; card-game
manœuvre	labourer	manoeuvre
martyre	martyrdom (a male martyr is *un martyr*)	female martyr
matricule	reference number	membership list
mauve	mauve	mallow (plant)
mémoire	memorandum	memory
mode	method, way; (grammatical) mood	fashion
mousse	cabin-boy	moss, froth, lather, mousse, etc.
nielle	niello (enamel inlay)	blight
office	office (= duties), bureau, agency; religious service	servants' kitchen

ombre	grayling	shade, shadow
page	page(-boy)	page (of book)
paillasse	clown	straw mattress
palme	handsbreadth	palm leaf, (symbolic) palm
parallèle	resemblance; line of latitude	parallel line
pendule	pendulum	clock
période	climax	period
physique	the physical, that which is physical	physics
pique	spades (cards)	pike (weapon); cutting remark
platine	platinum	platen (printing or typing)
pneumatique	tyre (now abbreviated to *pneu*)	pneumatics
poêle	stove; pall	frying-pan
poste	position, job; (police) station, etc; (radio, TV) set; (telephone) extension; etc.	post (= postal service)
pourpre	crimson (colour)	the purple (sign of royalty or cardinalate)
réglisse	liquorice (product)	liquorice plant
rose	pink (colour)	rose
scolastique	scholastic (theologian)	scholasticism
sixième	sixth (fraction); sixth floor, etc.	lowest form in a *lycée*
solde	balance (of account); sale	(soldier's) pay
somme	sleep, nap	sum, amount
statuaire	sculptor (who makes statues)	statuary

tonique	tonic (medical)	keynote, tonic (in music)
trompette	trumpeter	trumpet
vague	vagueness	wave
vase	vase	silt
voile	veil	sail

(c) **Words ending in another vowel**

	masc.	fem.
merci	thank-you (e.g. *un grand merci*)	mercy
radio	radiogram; wireless (radio) operator	radio; X-ray (photograph)

Some anomalies of gender

65 *Amour* 'love' is normally masculine, but in the plural, in the sense of 'love affairs', it is sometimes (but not necessarily) feminine.

66 *Chose* 'thing' is feminine (*une bonne chose* 'a good thing'), but *quelque chose* 'something' is masculine *un petit quelque chose* 'a little something', *quelque chose s'est produit qui m'a beaucoup étonné* 'something happened which surprised me very much' in which the masculine agreement of *produit* (see **461**) shows that *quelque chose* is masculine. (Note too the construction *quelque chose d'intéressant* 'something interesting' – see **667**.)

67 *Délice* 'delight' is masculine in the singular but feminine in the plural.

68 *Gens* 'people'. Adjectives and participles qualifying *gens* are always masculine except when an adjective with a distinctive form in the feminine comes immediately before the word *gens*. In this case this adjective itself becomes feminine; and so do any other adjectives which precede it, such as *quel, tout*, etc.
  Observe, however, that *tout* (see **317**), being separated from the noun by the article, is masculine, unless another feminine adjec-

tive with a distinctive feminine form comes between the article and
gens, e.g.:

des gens ennuyeux	boring people, bores
de vieilles gens	old people
Quelles bonnes gens!	What good people!; *but*
Quels braves gens!	What nice people! (because *brave* has no distinctive feminine form)
tous les gens	all people, *or* all the people
toutes les vieilles gens	all (the) old people

Note however that *jeunes gens* often means specifically 'young
men', so *de nombreux jeunes gens* 'many young men', etc.

These rules produce the odd result that, in theory at any rate, *gens*
may have to be simultaneously qualified by both masculine and
feminine adjectives, e.g.:

> *Toutes les vieilles gens ne sont pas ennuyeux*
> All old people are not bores

– but, in practice, such sentences should be avoided.

69 *Œuvre* 'work' is usually feminine (*une œuvre littéraire* 'a
literary work', *une œuvre de longue haleine* 'a long-term piece of
work') and is always feminine in the plural (*de bonnes œuvres*
'good works', *les dernières œuvres de Balzac* 'Balzac's last works').
It may however be masculine when referring to the complete work
of a writer, composer or other artist (*l'œuvre entier* or *l'œuvre
entière de Balzac* 'the complete works of Balzac').

70 *Orge* 'barley' is feminine (*cette orge est mûre* 'this barley is
ripe') except in the terms *orge mondé* 'husked barley' and *orge
perlé* 'pearl barley'.

71 *Orgue* 'organ' is masculine (*un orgue électrique* 'an electric
organ', *deux orgues excellents* 'two excellent organs'), but note the
use of a feminine plural (e.g. *les grandes orgues* 'the great organ')
with reference to a singular instrument, especially a church organ.

72 *Pâque(s)*. The Jewish festival of Passover is feminine, *la
Pâque* (*célébrer la Pâque* 'to celebrate Passover').

The Christian festival of Easter, *Pâques* (no article), is feminine plural in a few expressions such as *bonnes Pâques!* or *joyeuses Pâques!* 'Happy Easter', *souhaiter de bonnes* (or *joyeuses*) *Pâques à quelqu'un* 'to wish someone a happy Easter', *faire de bonnes Pâques* 'to take communion at Easter' (also *Pâques fleuries* 'Palm Sunday'), but elsewhere is usually treated as masculine singular, e.g. *quand Pâques sera arrivé* 'when Easter arrives', *à Pâques prochain* 'next Easter'.

73 *Personne.* As an ordinary noun, meaning 'person', *personne* is feminine, e.g. *Il y a de la place pour une personne* 'There is room for one person', but in negative constructions where it means 'nobody' (see **551**) it is masculine, e.g. *Personne n'est venu* 'Nobody has come'.

Gender of adjectives used as nouns

74 Whatever their ending, adjectives used as nouns are masculine when the noun denotes something which has the characteristic expressed by the adjective, e.g.:

> *un solide*, a solid, i.e. something of which the chief characteristic is its solidity
>
> *je ferai mon possible*, I will do my utmost, i.e. what is possible to me, or something of which the chief characteristic is its possibility.

Adjectives which denote persons, when used as nouns, take their gender from the sex of the person, e.g.:

> *un aveugle* 'a blind man'   *une aveugle* 'a blind woman'

Many adjectives used as nouns (see **176**) take their gender from some noun implied, but not expressed, e.g.: *un transatlantique* 'a liner', masculine because of the gender of *le paquebot* 'liner'; *le complet* 'suit' because of the gender of *le costume* 'suit'; *la pénultième* 'the last syllable but one', feminine because of the gender of *la syllabe*; *la capitale* 'capital (city)' because of the gender of *la ville* 'city'; *la majuscule* 'capital (letter)' because of the gender of *la lettre* 'letter'.

The feminine of nouns and adjectives

Introduction

75 The question of what words are used for corresponding male and female beings (e.g. *le père* 'father', *la mère* 'mother'; *le roi* 'king', *la reine* 'queen'; *le taureau* 'bull', *la vache* 'cow'; *le jars* 'gander', *l'oie* 'goose') is a matter of lexicon not of grammar and so will not be dealt with here. The student should refer to a dictionary.

76 However, in certain cases corresponding masculine and feminine nouns were originally adjectives. In other cases, the feminine is derived from the masculine by change of suffix. These types can be considered as being on the fringes of grammar and so will be dealt with here.

Spoken French

77 In this section we shall deal only with adjectives.
There is no constant relationship between the masculine and feminine forms of adjectives in the spoken language. The main types of relationship are the following (for the phonetic symbols, see 2):

78 The feminine is identical with the masculine, e.g.:

[ʃɛːr] *cher–chère*, dear   [naval] *naval–navale*
[dirɛkt] *direct–directe*   [ruːʒ] *rouge*, red
[fɛrm] *ferme*, firm   [vrɛ] *vrai–vraie*, true

79 The feminine is formed from the masculine by the addition of a consonant, e.g.:

[blɑ̃] *blanc* – [blɑ̃ːʃ] *blanche*, white
[fo] *faux* – [foːs] *fausse*, false
[ʒɑ̃ti] *gentil* – [ʒɑ̃tij] *gentille*, nice
[grɑ̃] *grand* – [grɑ̃ːd] *grande*, big

[o] *haut* – [o:t] *haute*, high
[œrø] *heureux* – [œrø:z] *heureuse*, happy
[lɔ̃] *long* – [lɔ̃:g] *longue*
[su] *soûl* – [sul] *soûle*, drunk
[vɛ:r] *vert* – [vɛrt] *verte*, green

80 The feminine is formed from the masculine by changing the final consonant, e.g.:

[sɛk] *sec* – [sɛʃ] *sèche*, dry
[vif] *vif* – [vi:v] *vive*, living, etc.

81 The feminine is formed from the masculine by changing the vowel and adding a consonant, e.g.:

[bo] *beau* – [bɛl] *belle*, beautiful
[fu] *fou* – [fɔl] *folle*, mad
[leʒe] *léger* – [leʒɛ:r] *légère*, light, slight
[so] *sot* – [sɔt] *sotte*, foolish
[vjø] *vieux* – [vjɛj] *vieille*, old
[bɔ̃] *bon* – [bɔn] *bonne*, good
[brœ̃] *brun* – [bryn] *brune*, brown
[fɛ̃] *fin* – [fin] *fine*, fine, delicate
[peizɑ̃] *paysan* – [peizan] *paysanne*, peasant
[sɛ̃] *sain* – [sɛn] *saine*, healthy

Written French

82 The vast majority of adjectives form their feminine by adding *-e* to the masculine, e.g.:

masc.	fem.
bleu, blue	*bleue*
clair, clear	*claire*
différent, different	*différente*
grand, big	*grande*
gris, grey	*grise*
musulman, Moslem	*musulmane*
royal, royal	*royale*
vrai, true	*vraie*

Nouns falling into this category include many deriving from adjectives of nationality, e.g.:

un Américain, American	*une Américaine*
un Espagnol, Spaniard	*une Espagnole*
le Français, Frenchman	*la Française*

83 If the masculine already ends in *-e* the masculine and the feminine are the same, e.g.:

faible, weak	*faible*
rouge, red	*rouge*
le Russe, Russian	*la Russe*

84 In adjectives and nouns with the following endings, some further change, besides the addition of *-e*, takes place in the feminine:

-c becomes

(1) *-che* in

blanc, white	*blanche*
franc, frank, candid	*franche*
sec, dry	*sèche*

(2) *-que* in

ammoniac	*ammoniaque*
caduc, deciduous, etc.	*caduque*
franc, Frankish	*franque*
le Franc, Frank	*Franque*
public, public	*publique*
turc, Turkish	*turque*
le Turc, Turk	*la Turque*

(3) *-cque* in

grec, *le Grec*, Greek	*grecque*, *la Grecque*

-f becomes *-ve*, e.g.:

bref, brief	*brève*
neuf, new	*neuve*
le veuf, widower	*la veuve*, widow
vif, lively	*vive*

-g becomes *-gue* in

long, long	*longue*
oblong, oblong	*oblongue*

85   Adjectives and nouns in *-l* are regular except that: *-el* becomes *-elle*, e.g.:

mortel, mortal, deadly	*mortelle*

-eil becomes *-eille*, e.g.:

pareil, like	*pareille*

Note too

gentil, nice	*gentille*
nul, no, none	*nulle*

86   Five adjectives have a second masculine form in *-l* when they stand before a noun beginning with a vowel or mute *h*, and it is from this second form that the feminine is derived:

beau, *bel*, fine	*belle*
fou, *fol*, mad	*folle*
mou, *mol*, soft	*molle*
nouveau, *nouvel*, new	*nouvelle*
vieux, *vieil*, old	*vieille*

The use of the second masculine forms is illustrated in such contexts as *un bel homme* 'a handsome man' (cf. *un beau monsieur* 'a handsome gentleman'), *un fol espoir* 'an insane hope' (cf. *il est fou* 'he's mad'), *un mol oreiller* 'a soft pillow' (cf. *cet oreiller est mou* 'this pillow is soft'), *un nouvel élève* 'a new pupil' (cf. *un nouveau professeur* 'a new teacher'), *un vieil ami* 'an old friend' (cf. *un vieux film* 'an old film').

The following nouns in *-eau* form their feminine in the same way as *beau* and *nouveau*:

le chameau, camel	*la chamelle*
(le) jumeau, twin	*(la) jumelle*
le Tourangeau, native of Tours or of Touraine	*la Tourangelle*

87 Words in *-n* are regular except that:

-en becomes *-enne*, e.g.:

ancien, former	*ancienne*
européen, European	*européenne*
italien, Italian	*italienne*

-on becomes *-onne*, e.g.:

le baron	*la baronne*, baroness
bon, good	*bonne*
breton, Breton	*bretonne*
le lion	*la lionne*, lioness

and *-an* becomes *-anne* in:

(*le*) *paysan*, peasant	(*la*) *paysanne*
rouan, roan	*rouanne*

(but *afghan, musulman* 'Muslim', *persan* 'Persian', *le sultan*, etc., are regular – *afghane, la sultane*, etc.)

Notice also:

bénin, kindly, benign	*bénigne*
malin, cunning, malign	*maligne*

88 Words in *-r*, other than those in *-er* (see below) and *-eur* (see **89**) are regular, e.g.:

dur, hard	*dure*
noir, black	*noire*

The ending *-er* becomes *-ère*, e.g.:

le boulanger, baker	*la boulangère*, female baker, baker's wife
cher, dear	*chère*
un écolier, schoolboy	*une écolière*, schoolgirl
(*un*) *étranger*, foreign(er)	(*une*) *étrangère*
premier, first	*première*

89 Words in *-eur* are of various kinds:

(a) Comparatives, including all adjectives in *-érieur* (which derive from Latin comparatives), are regular:

majeur, major	*majeure*
mineur, minor	*mineure*

meilleur, better	*meilleure*
supérieur, superior	*supérieure*
ultérieur, later	*ultérieure*

(also *antérieur, extérieur, inférieur, intérieur, postérieur*).

(b) A number of adjectives and nouns in *-eur* form their feminine in *-euse*, e.g.:

le chanteur, singer	*la chanteuse*
le danseur, dancer	*la danseuse*
(le) flatteur, flattering, flatterer	*(la) flatteuse*
(le) menteur, lying, liar	*(la) menteuse*
pleureur, weepy	*pleureuse*
trompeur, deceitful, deceptive	*trompeuse*
(le) voleur, thieving, thief	*(la) voleuse*
le vendeur, shop assistant	*la vendeuse*

Note that these all have the same stem as that of the corresponding verb (*danseur* like *danser*, *menteur* like *mentir*, etc.).

(c) Three forms in *-eur* that correspond to verbs have however a feminine in *-eresse*:

(un) enchanteur, enchanter, enchanting	*(une) enchanteresse*
(le) pécheur, sinner, sinful	*(la) pécheresse*
(le) vengeur, avenging, avenger	*(la) vengeresse*

Two legal terms also fall into this category:

le défendeur, defendant	*la défenderesse*
le demandeur, plaintiff	*la demanderesse*

(Note that 'defender' is *le défenseur*, which has no feminine, and that *le demandeur* in the more general sense of 'someone who asks' has the feminine *la demandeuse*.)

Five others that also share a stem with a corresponding verb form their feminine in *-trice* (cf. d below):

(un) émetteur, transmitting (station etc), transmitter	*émettrice*
un exécuteur, executor	*une exécutrice*
un inspecteur, inspector	*une inspectrice*
un inventeur, inventor	*une inventrice*
(le) persécuteur, persecuting, persecutor	*(la) persécutrice*

(d) A large number of nouns and a few adjectives in *-teur* whose stem is *not* also that of a corresponding verb (e.g. *protecteur* 'protective, protector' but *protéger* 'to protect', *collaborateur* but *collaborer*) form their feminine in *-trice*, e.g.:

(un) accusateur, accusing, accuser	*(une) accusatrice*
un acteur, actor	*une actrice*, actress
(le) consolateur, comforting, comforter	*(la) consolatrice*
(le) destructeur, destructive, destroyer	*(la) destructrice*
un instituteur, schoolmaster	*une institutrice*, school-mistress
le lecteur, reader	*la lectrice*
le traducteur, translator	*la traductrice*

(e) Note the following: *l'ambassadeur* 'ambassador', *l'empereur* 'emperor', have the feminine forms *l'ambassadrice* 'ambassador's wife' (a woman ambassador is either *l'ambassadeur* or *l'ambassadrice*), *l'impératrice* 'empress'. *Le docteur* (but only in the sense of a medical doctor) sometimes has the feminine *la doctoresse*, but *la femme docteur* or just *le docteur* (cf. *ma femme est docteur* 'my wife is a doctor') are more usual.

(f) Some nouns in *-eur* have no feminine, including *l'amateur*, *l'auteur* 'author', *le défenseur* 'defender', *l'imprimeur* 'printer', *l'orateur* 'speaker, orator', *le possesseur* 'owner', *le professeur* 'teacher, professor', *le sculpteur* 'sculptor', *le vainqueur* 'winner, victor'.

90 Forms in *-s* are regular (e.g. *gris, grise* 'grey'), except for:

bas, low	*basse*
épais, thick	*épaisse*
exprès, formal, express	*expresse*
gras, fat	*grasse*
gros, big	*grosse*
las, tired	*lasse*
frais, fresh	*fraîche*
tiers, a third (part)	*tierce*

91 Forms in *-t* are regular (e.g. *plat, plate* 'flat'), except that:

(a) Nine adjectives in *-et* make their feminine in *-ète*, viz:

complet, complete	*complète*
incomplet, incomplete	*incomplète*
concret, concrete	*concrète*
désuet, antiquated, obsolete	*désuète*
discret, discreet	*discrète*
indiscret, indiscreet	*indiscrète*
inquiet, uneasy	*inquiète*
replet, stout, podgy	*replète*
secret, secret	*secrète*

The rest make their feminine in *-ette*, e.g. *muet* 'dumb', *muette*.

(b) A few adjectives in *-ot* make their feminine in *-otte*, in particular:

boulot, tubby	*boulotte*
maigriot, skinny	*maigriotte*
pâlot, palish	*pâlotte*
sot, foolish	*sotte*
vieillot, antiquated, quaint	*vieillotte*

92 Forms in *-u* are regular except that *-gu* becomes *-guë*, e.g.:

aigu, sharp	*aiguë*
ambigu, ambiguous	*ambiguë*
exigu, exiguous, scanty	*exiguë*

(otherwise the *-ue* would not be pronounced – e.g. *aigue*, with no *ë*, would be pronounced [ɛg] not [egy].)

Observe that *hébreu* 'Hebrew' has no feminine form. The adjective *hébraïque* is used instead, e.g. *l'Université hébraïque de Jérusalem* 'the Hebrew University of Jerusalem'.

93 As a rule *-x* becomes *-se*, e.g.:

heureux, happy	*heureuse*
jaloux, jealous	*jalouse*

But note:

doux, sweet, soft	*douce*
faux, false	*fausse*
roux, reddish-brown	*rousse*
vieux, old	*vieille*

94 A few adjectives fall under none of the rules given above:

andalou, Andalusian	*andalouse*
favori, favourite	*favorite*

Also *coi*, feminine *coite*, now used only in the expressions *se tenir coi(te)* 'to remain silent', *en rester coi(te)* 'to be rendered speechless'.

95 A certain number of adjectives (in addition to those having *-e* in the masculine, see **83**) have no special feminine form (and no special plural form, see **125**). They are:

(i) some words that were originally nouns but are now used as adjectives of colour, e.g. *une chaussure marron* 'a brown shoe', *une robe lilas* 'a lilac dress', *une jupe saumon* 'a salmon-pink skirt'; also *chamois* 'fawn, buff', *indigo*.

(ii) a very few other adjectives, mainly of foreign origin, e.g.:

une femme chic	a smartly dressed woman
une toile kaki	a khaki cloth
une pendule rococo	a rococo clock
une langue standard	a standard language
une livre sterling	a pound sterling

96 A few adjectives are used with nouns of one gender only. In the examples below, words marked with an asterisk occur (in normal usage, at least) only in the expressions given.

masc. only

un nez aquilin*, a hooked nose
benêt, simple-minded
un vent coulis*, a draught
un piano discord, an out-of-tune piano
un esprit dispos, an alert mind
le feu grégeois*, Greek fire
pantois, flabbergasted
un hareng saur*, a smoked herring

fem. only

bouche bée*, open-mouthed
une année bissextile*, a leap-year
une porte cochère*, a carriage entrance

de l'ignorance crasse, crass ignorance
la pierre philosophale*, the philosopher's stone
une œuvre pie*, a pious or charitable work

The plural of nouns

Spoken French

97 In spoken French, most nouns are invariable in the plural –
that is, there is no *audible* distinction between singular and plural,
e.g.:

> *le lit*, bed, plur. *les lits*, both pronounced [li]
> *la ville*, town, plur. *les villes*, both pronounced [vil]

The principal exceptions are:

(i) Most nouns ending in *-al* (see **105**), e.g. *le cheval* [ʃəval]
'horse', plural *les chevaux* [ʃəvo]

(ii) Some nouns in *-ail* (see **106**), e.g. *le travail* [travaj] 'work',
plural *les travaux* [travo]

(iii) *l'aïeul* [ajœl] 'grandfather', plural *les aïeux* [ajø] 'ancestors'; *le
ciel* [sjɛl], 'sky', plural *les cieux* [sjø]; *l'œil* [œj] 'eye', plural *les yeux*
[jø] (see **108**)

(iv) *monsieur* [məsjø], *madame* [madam], *mademoiselle* (madmwazɛl],
plurals *messieurs* [mesjø], *mesdames* [medam], *mesdemoiselles*
[medmwazɛl], *un bonhomme* [bɔnɔm] 'chap, bloke'; plural *des
bonshommes* [bõzɔm] *gentilhomme* [ʒãtijɔm] 'gentleman, squire',
etc., plural *des gentilshommes* [ʒãtizɔm] (see **109**)

(v) *l'os* [ɔs] 'bone', plural *les os* [o], *le bœuf* [bœf] 'ox', and *l'œuf*
[œf] 'egg', plurals *les bœufs* [bø], *les œufs* [ø].

98 In fact, the main indication as to whether a noun is singular or
plural is provided not by the form of the noun itself but by its
determiner (article, demonstrative, possessive, etc., see **23**), e.g.:

le chat [lə ʃa], the cat	*les chats* [le ʃa], the cats
la femme [la fam], the woman	*les femmes* [le fam], the women

l'enfant [lɑ̃fɑ̃], the child	*les enfants* [lezɑ̃fɑ̃], the children
un pied [œ̃ pje], a foot	*des pieds* [de pje], feet
une boîte [yn bwat], a box	*des boîtes* [de bwat], boxes
mon fils [mɔ̃ fis], my son	*mes fils* [me fis], my sons
sa main [sa mɛ̃], his/her hand	*ses mains* [se mɛ̃], his/her hands
votre jardin [vɔtrə ʒardɛ̃], your garden	*vos jardins* [vo ʒardɛ̃], your gardens
ce livre [sə li:vr], this book	*ces livres* [se li:vr], these books
cette pomme [sɛt pɔm], this apple	*ces pommes* [se pɔm], these apples

But sometimes the system breaks down – there is, for example, no audible distinction between *leur chapeau* 'their hat' and its plural *leurs chapeaux*, both pronounced [lœr ʃapo], or between *quelle porte?* 'which door?' and *quelles portes?* 'which doors?', both pronounced [kɛl pɔrt].

99 Sometimes the distinction between singular and plural is made clear in pronunciation by the presence of a liaison [z] in the plural, e.g. *leur enfant* [lœr ɑ̃fɑ̃] 'their child', *quel arbre?* [kɛl arbr] 'which tree?', plural *leurs enfants* [lœrz ɑ̃fɑ̃], *quels arbres?* [kɛlz arbr]. (Liaison can of course also occur even when the determiner itself indicates whether the noun is singular or plural, e.g. *mon cher ami* [mɔ̃ ʃɛr ami] 'my dear friend', plural *mes chers amis* [me ʃɛrz ami].)

100 Occasionally, when all else fails, the form of the verb may be the only way in which one can tell whether the subject of the sentence is singular or plural, e.g. *leur frère va* [va] *partir demain* 'their brother is going to leave tomorrow', plural *leurs frères vont* [vɔ̃] *partir demain*. But sometimes all possible devices fail. There is, for example, no way at all of distinguishing in pronunciation between *Quel livre voulez-vous acheter?* 'What book do you want to buy?' and the plural *Quels livres voulez-vouz acheter?* 'What books do you want to buy?' If it is essential to make the distinction, then the sentence must be phrased differently, e.g.:

Quel est le livre }
Quels sont les livres } *que vous voulez acheter?*

Written French

101   In the written language, the plural is regularly formed by adding -*s* to the singular, e.g.:

le livre, book	*les livres*
la femme, woman	*les femmes*

102   Nouns that end in -*s, -x* or -*z* in the singular remain unchanged, e.g.:

le mois, month	*les mois*
la voix, voice	*les voix*
le nez, nose	*les nez*

103   Nouns ending in -*au, -eau* or -*eu* add -*x* instead of -*s* to the singular, e.g.:

le noyau, stone (of fruit), nucleus	*les noyaux*
le tuyau, tube, pipe	*les tuyaux*
le chapeau, hat	*les chapeaux*
le seau, bucket	*les seaux*
le jeu, game	*les jeux*
le neveu, nephew	*les neveux*
le vœu, wish, vow	*les vœux*

Exceptions: *le landau* 'pram, landau', *les landaus*; *le bleu* 'blue, bruise', *l'émeu* 'emu', *le pneu* 'tyre', *les bleus* (which also means 'overalls'), *les émeus, les pneus*.

104   The following seven nouns in -*ou* also add -*x* to the singular:

le bijou, jewel	*le hibou*, owl
le caillou, pebble	*le joujou*, toy
le chou, cabbage	*le pou*, louse
le genou, knee	

– plurals *les bijoux, les cailloux, les choux*, etc.

Other nouns in -*ou* add -*s*, e.g. *le clou* 'nail', *le matou* 'tom-cat', *les clous, les matous*.

105 Most nouns ending in *-al* form their plural in *-aux*, e.g.:

le cheval, horse	*les chevaux*
le général, general	*les généraux*
le journal, newspaper	*les journaux*

Exceptions: *un aval* 'backing, guarantee', *le bal* 'dance', *le cal* 'callus', *le carnaval* 'carnival', *le chacal* 'jackal', *le choral* 'chorale', *le festival* 'festival', *le narval* 'narwhal', *le récital* 'recital', *le régal* 'treat', form their plural in *-s*, e.g. *des avals*, *les bals*, *les chacals*, *les récitals*, etc. *Le val* 'dale' has the plural *vals*, but note the expression *par monts et par vaux* 'over hill and dale'. *L'idéal* 'ideal' has both *idéals* (the more usual form) and *idéaux*.

106 About half the nouns ending in *-ail* form their plural in *-aux*. Of these by far the commonest is *le travail* 'work', plural *les travaux*.
Others include:

le bail, lease	*les baux*
le corail, coral	*les coraux*
l'émail, enamel	*les émaux*
le soupirail, basement window	*les soupiraux*
le vantail, leaf of door	*les vantaux*
le vitrail, stained-glass window	*les vitraux*

107 Nouns in *-ail* forming their plural in *-ails* include:

le chandail, (thick) sweater	*les chandails*
le détail, detail	*les détails*
l'épouvantail, scarecrow	*les épouvantails*
l'éventail, fan	*les éventails*
le gouvernail, helm	*les gouvernails*
le portail, portal	*les portails*
le rail, rail	*les rails*

L'ail 'garlic' has both *les ails* and *les aulx*, the latter being somewhat archaic. *Le bétail* 'cattle, livestock' is a collective word and has no plural.

108 The following words have two plurals which differ in sense:

aïeul, grandfather   *aïeuls*, grandfathers   *aïeux*, ancestors

ciel, sky	*ciels*, skies in paintings, canopies of beds, climates	*cieux*, skies, heavens
œil, eye	*œils*, in compound nouns with *de*; e.g. *œils-de bœuf*, round or oval windows, *œils-de-perdrix*, corns (on the feet)	*yeux*, eyes

Compound nouns

109 As in the section on gender (57–63), only nouns formed of two or more words joined by hyphens are here counted as compound nouns.

Nouns that were originally compounds but are now fused, i.e. written as one word without hyphens, present little difficulty as far as their plural goes – they are treated like any other noun, e.g.:

une entrecôte, (rib) steak	*des entrecôtes*
le passeport, passport	*les passeports*
le pourboire, tip	*les pourboires*

Note however the following exceptions (for their pronunciation, see 97(iv)):

(le) monsieur, gentleman, Mr	*(les) messieurs*
madame, mademoiselle, Mrs, Miss	*mesdames, mesdemoiselles*
le bonhomme, chap, bloke	*les bonshommes*
le gentilhomme, gentleman, squire, etc.	*les gentilshommes*

Locutions like *la pomme de terre* 'potato', in which the various elements are neither fused nor joined by hyphens, present even less difficulty: the first noun, and the first noun only, is made plural, *les pommes de terre*, cf.:

le coup d'œil, glance	*les coups d'œil*
l'hôtel de ville, town hall	*les hôtels de ville*
le ver à soie, silk-worm	*les vers à soie*
le verre à vin, wine-glass	*les verres à vin*

110 Compound nouns are constantly coming and going, in the sense that new ones are being created and others, that still figure in many grammars, have largely or entirely gone out of use. What is more, in many cases opinions differ as to the recommended plural. In these circumstances, the following indications do not aim to be exhaustive but only to cover most cases that the student is likely to come across. They must be supplemented by reference to a good dictionary.

The following classes are the same as those adopted with reference to gender (sections **58–63**).

111 (i) **Nouns composed of a noun and a preceding or following adjective**

Both elements become plural:

la basse-cour, farmyard	*les basses-cours*
la belle-mère, mother-in-law	*les belles-mères*
le grand-père, grandfather	*les grands-pères*
le haut-relief, high relief	*les hauts-reliefs*
le rouge-gorge, robin	*les rouges-gorges*
le cerf-volant, kite, stag-beetle	*les cerfs-volants*
le coffre-fort, safe	*les coffres-forts*

Note the following:

(a) Feminine nouns in *grand-* (which represents an early form of the feminine adjective – it is **not** a shortened form of *grande*): generally speaking, *grand* remains invariable – *la grand-mère* 'grandmother', *la grand-route* 'main road', plural *les grand-mères, les grand-routes* – but *grands-mères, grands-routes*, etc., are also acceptable.

(b) in *le haut-parleur* 'loudspeaker', *le nouveau-né* 'newly born child', *le sauf-conduit* 'safe conduct', the first element is not an adjective but an adverb (*haut* = 'aloud', *nouveau* = 'newly', *sauf* = 'safely') and so does not change: *les haut-parleurs, les sauf-conduits, les nouveau-nés*. (But, inconsistently, *le premier-né* 'firstborn', *le dernier-né* 'lastborn', *le nouveau-marié* 'newly-wed', and *le nouveau-venu* 'newcomer' have the plurals *les premiers-nés, les derniers-nés, les nouveaux-mariés, les nouveaux-venus*.)

112 (ii) Nouns composed of noun + noun

In most cases, both nouns become plural, e.g.:

le bateau-phare, light-ship	*les bateaux-phares*
le camion-citerne, tanker (lorry)	*les camions-citernes*
le chef-lieu, county town	*les chefs-lieux*
l'homme-grenouille, frogman	*les hommes-grenouilles*
l'oiseau-mouche, humming-bird	*les oiseaux-mouches*
le wagon-lit, sleeper	*les wagons-lits*

Exceptions include:

l'année-lumière, light-year	*les années-lumière*
le soutien-gorge, bra	*les soutiens-gorge*
le timbre-poste (for *timbre de poste*), postage-stamp	*les timbres-poste*

113 (iii) Nouns having the construction noun + preposition + noun

In most cases the first noun (only) becomes plural, e.g.:

l'arc-en-ciel, rainbow	*les arcs-en-ciel*
le chef-d'œuvre, masterpiece	*les chefs-d'œuvre*
le face-à-main, lorgnette	*les faces-à-main*
la langue-de-chat (type of biscuit)	*les langues-de-chat*

Some nouns, however, remain invariable, e.g.:

le pied-à-terre	*les pied-à-terre*
le pot-au-feu, stew	*les pot-au-feu*
le tête-à-tête	*les tête-à-tête*

114 (iv) Nouns having the construction adverb or prefix + noun

The second element, i.e. the noun, becomes plural, e.g.:

l'arrière-pensée, mental reservation	*les arrière-pensées*
l'avant-projet, pilot study	*les avant-projets*
la demi-heure, half-hour	*les demi-heures*
l'ex-roi, ex-king	*les ex-rois*
le haut-parleur, loudspeaker	*les haut-parleurs*

la mini-jupe, mini-skirt   *les mini-jupes*
le sous-titre, subtitle   *les sous-titres*
le vice-président   *les vice-présidents*

115   (v) Nouns having the construction preposition + noun

Here, there is considerable fluctuation. Some, including *le, la sans-cœur* 'heartless person', *le sous-main* 'desk blotter', are invariable, *les sans-cœur, les sous-main*. *L'à-côté* 'side issue', *l'en-tête* 'heading', usually have the plurals *les à-côtés, les en-têtes*, while *l'après-midi* 'afternoon' has either *les après-midi* or *les après-midis*.

116   (vi) Words having the construction verb + noun

To say that chaos reigns would be an unfair comment on the rules for the formation of the plural of nouns of this type. But that there are numerous uncertainties and inconsistencies is indisputable. We shall however try and give as much reliable guidance as possible, based on two general principles, and advise readers, in cases not covered here, to consult a good dictionary (while warning them that, if they consult *two* dictionaries, they may well find two different answers).

The first general principle is that the first element, being a verb, never varies. The apparent exception found in the case of a few compounds in *garde-*, all of them referring to people, is accounted for by the fact that *garde-*, though originally it *was* a verb, is here treated as a noun – e.g. *le garde-chasse* 'game-keeper', *les gardes-chasse* (*chasse* remains invariable – cf. c below), *le/la garde-malade* 'home-nurse', *les gardes-malade(s)* (*malade* may or may not take the plural -*s*, cf. a and b below).

The second principle, by no means always observed in practice as we shall see, is that the second element takes an -*s* when, and only when, it stands for a noun that can itself be plural in the particular sense in question. On this basis, the nouns in question fall into three groups:

(a) Those that have an -*s* even in the singular, e.g. *le compte-tours* 'rev counter', i.e. an instrument serving to count revolutions, *compter les tours* (in the plural) or *le brise-lames* 'breakwater', a construction serving to break the force of the waves, *briser les lames*. Such words are, of course, invariable in the plural – *les compte-tours, les brise-lames*. Other examples are:

le chauffe-plats, dish-warmer
le coupe-tomates, tomato-slicer
le gobe-mouches, flycatcher (bird)
le pare-balles, bullet-shield
le pare-chocs, bumper (of a car)
le porte-avions, aircraft-carrier
le porte-cigarettes, cigarette-case
le porte-clefs, key-ring
le presse-papiers, paper-weight
le protège-dents, gum-shield

(b) Those that add a plural marker to the noun; the justification for this is presumably that, to take an obvious example, *un tire-bouchon* 'a corkscrew', can only be used for drawing one cork at a time, whereas several corkscrews can draw several corks, hence the plural *des tire-bouchons*. Cf.:

un accroche-cœur, kiss-curl	*des accroche-cœurs*
le bouche-trou, stop-gap, stand-in	*les bouche-trous*
le couvre-lit, bedspread	*les couvre-lits*
le cure-pipe, pipecleaner	*les cure-pipes*
un ouvre-boîte, tin-opener	*des ouvre-boîtes*
le pèse-lettre, letter-scales	*les pèse-lettres*
le perce-oreille, earwig	*les perce-oreilles*
le vide-pomme, apple-corer	*les vide-pommes*

At least one category b noun, *le cure-dent* 'tooth-pick', which can be defined as something one uses *pour se curer les dents* (in the plural), and one which hesitates between categories a and b, viz. *le porte-cartes* or *le porte-carte* 'card-holder, map-case', i.e. something for containing cards or maps (in the plural), might have been expected to fall clearly into category a. Others that hesitate, e.g. *le coupe-cigare* or *le coupe-cigares* 'cigar cutter', *le taille-crayon* or *le taille-crayons* 'pencil sharpener', are very similar to *ouvre-boîte, vide-pomme*, and so ought to fall clearly into category b.

The inconsistencies in fact relate mainly to those nouns that do, or ought to but do not, fall into this category. They are well illustrated by the absurdity of the fact that *le coupe-tomates* 'tomato slicer' falls into category a, *le vide-pomme* 'apple-corer' into category b, and *le presse-citron* 'lemon-squeezer' into category c.

(c) Where the sense of the second element clearly remains singular (i.e. where we have to do with mass-nouns), the compound as a whole is invariable in the plural – e.g. several ice-breakers break ice (in the singular), so *le brise-glace, les brise-glace*, several waterheaters heat water (in the singular), so *le chauffe-eau, les chauffe-eau.* Cf.:

un abat-jour, lamp-shade	*des abat-jour*
un aide-mémoire, memor-andum	*des aide-mémoire*
le coupe-feu, fire-break	*les coupe-feu*
le garde-boue, mudguard	*les garde-boue*
le garde-manger, larder, pantry	*les garde-manger*
le gratte-ciel, skyscraper	*les gratte-ciel*
le pare-brise, windscreen	*les pare-brise*
le porte-bonheur, lucky charm	*les porte-bonheur*
le porte-monnaie, purse	*les porte-monnaie*
le rabat-joie, killjoy, spoilsport	*les rabat-joie*

Unfortunately, and inexplicably, a few nouns whose second element is not a mass-noun, i.e. it *could* have taken the plural marker, follow the same pattern as category c instead of falling, as might have been expected, into b, e.g.: *le fume-cigarette* 'cigarette-holder', *les fume-cigarette, le porte-plume* 'pen-holder', *les porte-plume, le presse-citron* 'lemon-squeezer', *les presse-citron.* Others fluctuate between the two forms, e.g. in *attrape-nigaud* 'con(fidence) trick', *des attrape-nigaud* or *attrape-nigauds, le porte-couteau* 'knife-rest', *les porte-couteau* or *porte-couteaux.* Likewise *les essuie-main(s)* 'hand-towels', *les essuie-glace(s)* 'windscreen-wipers', *les grippe-sou(s)* 'skinflints', *les porte-drapeau(x)* 'standard-bearers', *les porte-savon(s)* 'soap-dishes'.

Miscellaneous

117 The letters of the alphabet, phrases used as nouns, numerals and various other parts of speech such as adverbs or prepositions when used as nouns, do not vary in the plural, e.g.:

'Cannes' s'écrit avec deux n
'Cannes' is spelt with two *n*'s.

mettre les points sur les i
to dot the *i*'s

Ce ne sont que des on-dit
It's only hearsay

des meurt-de-faim
paupers

des va-et-vient
comings and goings

les oui et les non
the ayes (yeses) and the noes

des laissez-passer
passes, permits

écrire deux quatre
to write two fours

les ci-devant
pre-Revolutionary aristocrats

Vos pourquoi sont hors de saison
Your questions (whys) are out of place

118   (i) Generally speaking, words of foreign origin, even when they keep their original form, are treated as French words and form their plural in -*s*, e.g. (from Latin) *les albums, les ultimatums, les référendums, les sanatoriums, les tumulus*; (from English) *les best-sellers, les meetings, les snack-bars, les week-ends*; (from Italian) *les adagios, les concertos, les solos, les pizzas*; (from Spanish) *les matadors*.

(ii) Latin phrases used as nouns (cf. 117) and a few Latin words (many though not all of them to do with the Church) are invariable, e.g. *des ex-voto, des Te Deum, des confiteor* 'general confessions', *des credo* 'creeds', *des post-scriptum* 'postscripts'. *Le maximum* and *le minimum* have the Latin plurals *les maxima, minima*, in addition to the more usual *les maximums, minimums*.

(iii) English words in -*man* (including such false anglicisms as *le rugbyman* 'rugby player') normally form their plural in -*men*, e.g. *les gentlemen, les rugbymen*, but *le barman* has both *les barmen* and *les barmans*, and (obsolete) *le wattman* 'tram-driver' has only *les wattmans*.

English words in -*y* have either -*ies* or *ys* (depending perhaps on how well the writer knows English), e.g. *les dandies* or *dandys, les ladies* or *ladys, les whiskies* or *whiskys*.

Le match, le sandwich have *les matches,* or *matchs, les sandwichs* or *sandwiches*, but *le flash* has only *les flashes*.

(iv) Among words of Italian origin, *le dilettante* and *le, la soprano* have *les dilettanti, les soprani* beside the more usual *les dilettantes, les sopranos*.

119   Personal names.

Considerable uncertainty remains as to when personal names take a plural. The following indications cover most cases that occur with any frequency:

(i) Names of dynasties and certain eminent families, etc., usually take a plural form, e.g. *les Ptolémées, les Césars, les Bourbons, les Tudors* (but note *les Romanov, les Habsbourg*).

(ii) Otherwise, a name referring to a number of people of the same name is usually invariable, e.g. *les deux Corneille* (i.e. Pierre and Thomas Corneille), *le 'Journal' des Goncourt* (i.e. of the Goncourt brothers), *les Dupont* (i.e. the members of the Dupont family), *les Borgia* (the Borgias).

(iii) Proper names taken as representing a *type* of person are usually plural, e.g. *Combien de Mozarts naissent chaque jour en des îles sauvages!* (J. Rostand) (i.e. potential Mozarts), *les Cicérons de notre époque* (the Ciceros, i.e. orators, of our time), *il n'y a pas beaucoup de Pasteurs* (i.e. people like Pasteur); but some writers leave such names invariable, e.g. *les Boileau de l'avenir* (A. Hermant), *il y a peut-être eu des Shakespeare dans la lune* (Duhamel).

(iv) Names referring to makes of car, aeroplane, etc., are usually invariable, e.g. *des Ford et des Chevrolet, plusieurs Concorde, deux Leica* (cameras).

(v) Usage varies considerably in respect of proper names denoting the works (e.g. editions of literary texts, paintings) of the individual concerned. These sometimes take a plural form and are sometimes invariable, *des Rembrandts* or *des Rembrandt* 'Rembrandts' (i.e. paintings by Rembrandt), *trois Picassos* or *Picasso, il possède plusieurs Racines* or *Racine* (i.e. editions of Racine).

The conclusion seems to be that, except in cases such as those included under (i) above, it is never wrong to leave a proper name invariable even if, in some circumstances, it is more usual to add an -*s* in the plural.

120   Though this is not strictly a grammatical point, it is worth pointing out that some words in the plural have a different meaning or an additional meaning to that which they have in the singular. In particular:

l'affaire, matter	*les affaires*, affairs, business
le ciseau, chisel	*les ciseaux*, chisels, scissors
le gage, pledge	*les gages*, pledges, wages
la lettre, letter	*les lettres*, letters, arts (subjects), literature
la lunette, telescope, etc.	*les lunettes*, telescopes, etc., spectacles
l'ouïe, (sense of) hearing	*les ouïes*, gills
la vacance, vacancy (i.e. time during which a post is vacant)	*les vacances*, vacation, holiday(s)

121   Finally, note that some words are singular in French but correspond to a plural in English, in particular various words denoting items consisting of two symmetrical parts such as *une lorgnette* 'opera-glasses', *un soufflet* '(a pair of) bellows', and a number of words for items of leg-wear that may or may not be preceded by 'a pair of' in English, e.g. *un caleçon* '(a pair of) (men's) (under) pants', *un collant* 'tights', *une culotte* '(women's) pants', *un maillot (de bain)* 'swimming trunks', *un pantalon* 'trousers', *un short* 'shorts', *un slip* 'panties'.

The plural of adjectives

122   Most adjectives follow the same rules as nouns for the formation of their plural.

As all feminine adjectives (apart from a few invariables, see **95**) end in -*e*, they form their plural by adding -*s* to the singular, e.g.:

la grande maison, the big house   *les grandes maisons*
une fleur blanche, a white   *des fleurs blanches*
  flower

Apart from the exceptions dealt with below (123–126), masculine adjectives form their plural in *-s*, e.g.:

le grand chien, the big dog   *les grands chiens*
un livre difficile, a difficult book   *des livres difficiles*

123   Adjectives in *-eau*, like nouns in *-eau* (see 103), form their plural in *-x*, viz. *beau* 'fine, beautiful', *nouveau* 'new', *tourangeau* (the adjective corresponding to *Tours* and *Touraine*), plural *beaux, nouveaux, tourangeaux*.

Hébreu 'Hebrew' has the plural *hébreux*, but *bleu* 'blue' has *bleus*.

124   Most adjectives in *-al*, like nouns in *-al* (see 105), form their plural in *-aux*, e.g. *égal* 'equal', plural *égaux*, *social*, plural *sociaux*, *normal*, plural *normaux*, *spécial*, plural *spéciaux*. But *banal*, *bancal* (said of someone who has a twisted leg or legs and therefore limps), *fatal*, *final*, *natal* and *naval* take *-s*, e.g. *des incidents banals, des enfants bancals, des chantiers navals* 'naval dockyards', *fatals, finals, natals*. *Idéal* usually has *idéaux*, though *idéals* also occurs. Much uncertainty surrounds the plural of some adjectives in *-al*, e.g. *estival* '(to do with) summer', *frugal, glacial, pascal* '(to do with) Easter', and in consequence there is a tendency to avoid using them in the masculine plural.

125   Masculine adjectives (like nouns, see 102) ending in *-s* or *-x* (there are no adjectives ending in *-z*) do not change in the plural, e.g. *un gros livre* 'a big book', *trois gros livres* 'three big books', *il est heureux* 'he is happy', *ils sont heureux* 'they are happy'.

126   Adjectives that are invariable for gender (see 95) are also invariable for number, i.e. they have no special plural form:

(i) Words that were originally nouns but are now used as adjectives of colour: *des gants marron* 'brown gloves', *des rubans cerise* 'cherry-coloured ribbons', *des rideaux orange* 'orange curtains', *crème* 'cream', *olive* 'olive(-green)', *paille* 'straw-coloured', *puce*, etc. But note that the adjectives *écarlate* 'scarlet', *mauve, pourpre* 'crimson', *rose* 'pink', that were also originally nouns, are now treated as ordinary adjectives and so agree in number, e.g. *des rubans écarlates et mauves* 'scarlet and mauve ribbons', *des nuages roses* 'pink clouds'.

(ii) Miscellaneous, e.g. *des vêtements chic* 'smart clothes', *des uniformes kaki* 'khaki uniforms', *des églises rococo* 'rococo churches', *cinq livres sterling* 'five pounds sterling'.

Agreement of adjectives (including participles used as adjectives)

127 (i) Adjectives agree in gender and number with the noun they qualify, e.g.:

un homme intelligent, a clever man

une femme intelligente, a clever woman

des hommes intelligents, clever men

des femmes intelligentes, clever women

(ii) If an adjective qualifies two nouns, the adjective is plural, e.g. *un père et un fils intelligents* 'a clever father and son'.

(iii) If the two nouns are of different genders, the adjective is masculine plural, e.g. *Cet homme et sa femme sont très intelligents* 'This man and his wife are very clever'.

However, though it is certainly possible to have constructions such as *le charme et la politesse français* 'French charm and politeness', *des souliers et des chaussettes gris* 'grey shoes and socks', the fact that a feminine noun (*politesse, chaussettes*) is immediately followed by a masculine adjective means that the construction is much better avoided – which can easily be done by putting the feminine noun first, *la politesse et le charme français*, *des chaussettes et des souliers gris*. Admittedly, the expressions in question are now theoretically ambiguous (they *could* mean 'politeness and French charm', 'socks and grey shoes'), but in practice it will usually be clear from the context that the adjective refers to both nouns.

128 Where the adjective refers to two nouns linked by *ou* 'or', the adjective is usually plural if the idea is 'either [of the nouns mentioned] – it does not much matter which', e.g. *Je cherche un livre ou un journal allemands* 'I'm looking for a German book or [a German] newspaper', *Il mange chaque jour une pomme ou une poire mûres* 'He eats a ripe apple or pear every day'.

129 Note that an adjective qualifying two nouns is singular when the nouns are joined by *ainsi que, aussi bien que, autant que, comme, de même que* ('as, as well as, as much as, in the same way as, like', etc.), *plus que* (more than), and the like; e.g. *Sa main, ainsi que (aussi bien que, pas moins que) son pied, a été échaudée* 'His hand, as well as his foot, was scalded'.

The reason is that the basic structure of the sentence is *sa main a été échaudée* (note that the verb is singular) and the sentence as a whole could be translated as 'his hand was scalded, and so was his foot'. This is therefore not in fact an exception to the general rule. (See also **396**.)

130 In certain contexts, the agreement of the adjective is illogical and inconsistent. In particular:

(i) Logically, we would expect an adjective used with the expression *avoir l'air* to agree with *air*, i.e. one would expect to find not only *Il a l'air heureux* 'He looks happy' (literally 'He has a happy air'), but also *Elle a l'air heureux*. In practice, however, *avoir l'air* is often treated as the equivalent of *sembler, paraître*, etc., and the adjective usually (though not always) agrees with the subject, e.g. *Elle a l'air heureuse* 'She looks happy', *Ils ont l'air tristes* 'They look sad', etc.

(ii) *On* 'one' (see **302**) is normally masculine singular (in conformity with its origin – it comes from the Latin *homo* 'man'). However, there is a growing tendency in familiar speech to use it as the equivalent of any personal pronoun, i.e. to mean 'I, we, you, he, she or they' (especially 'we'). In such cases, adjectives relating to it agree according to the sense, i.e. they may be feminine and/or plural (even though the verb is always singular), e.g. *On est malades?* 'Are you [plural] ill?', *On a été contentes de les voir* 'We [feminine] were glad to see them'.

(ii) For the agreement of adjectives with *gens* 'people' (e.g. *Certaines* [feminine] *gens ne sont jamais heureux* [masculine] 'Some people are never happy'), see **68**.

131 *Demi* 'half', when it stands before its noun, is joined to that noun by a hyphen, and is invariable; when after its noun, it takes the gender of that noun, e.g.:

une demi-heure	half an hour
une heure et demie	an hour and a half; half past one
trois mois et demi	three and a half months
deux heures et demie	two hours and a half; half past two.

Note that *mi-* 'half' and *semi-* occur only as prefixes and are invariable, e.g. *à mi-côte* 'half-way up (or down) the slope', *à mi-distance* 'half-way, midway', *des pierres semi-précieuses* 'semi-precious stones', *la semi-voyelle* 'semi-vowel'.

132 *Nu* 'naked' used before a noun without any article is invariable, and is joined to the noun by a hyphen. After the noun it agrees in the usual way, e.g.:

travailler nu-tête, la tête nue	to work bare-headed
marcher nu-pieds, (les) pieds nus	to walk barefoot
nu-jambes, (les) jambes nues	barelegged

133 *Possible*, after a superlative, is invariable:

les plus grands malheurs possible
the greatest possible misfortunes

les robes les plus élégantes possible
the smartest dresses possible

J'ai fait le moins d'erreurs possible
I made the fewest possible mistakes (= as few mistakes as possible)

The reason is that *possible* is taken as agreeing with an unexpressed impersonal pronoun subject *il* (e.g. the first example above is the equivalent of something like *les plus grands malheurs qu'il est possible d'imaginer* 'the greatest misfortunes that it is possible to imagine').

Elsewhere, it agrees quite normally with its noun, e.g. *tous les malheurs possibles* 'all possible misfortunes'.

134 When placed before a noun, certain past participles and in particular *attendu, compris* (especially in the expression *y compris* 'including', *non compris* 'not including'), *excepté, passé,* and *vu* are treated as prepositions and so remain invariable; some of them can also follow the noun, in which case they agree with it in gender and number:

> *attendu* (or *vu*) *ces circonstances*
> considering (in view of) these circumstances
>
> *tous mes parents, y compris ma tante* (or *ma tante (y) comprise*)
> all my relations including my aunt
>
> *Personne n'est venu, excepté sa mère* (or *sa mère exceptée*)
> Nobody came except his mother
>
> *Passé dix heures, je ne travaille plus*
> After ten o'clock, I don't work any more
>
> *Passé ces maisons, on est en pleine campagne*
> Beyond these houses you are right in the country.

The expression *étant donné* 'given, in view of', is also usually invariable when it precedes, but may agree, e.g. *étant donné* or *étant données les difficultés* 'given the difficulties'.

The expression *ci-joint, ci-inclus* 'enclosed (herewith)', agree when they follow the noun immediately (*la lettre ci-jointe* 'the enclosed letter'), but elsewhere may either agree or (more usually) remain invariable, e.g.:

> *Vous trouverez ci-joint* (or *ci-jointe*) *une copie de ma lettre du 10 juin*
> You will find enclosed a copy of my letter of 10 June
>
> *Je me permets de vous envoyer ci-joint(es) les lettres dont je vous ai parlé*
> I take the liberty of enclosing the letters I told you about
>
> *Ci-joint(s) les documents que vous avez demandés*
> Herewith the documents you asked for.

135 Note the following special cases:

Plein 'full' is invariable when it precedes both the noun and its article in such expressions as *avoir de l'argent plein les poches* 'to have plenty of money' (literally 'to have one's pockets full of money'), *J'ai de l'encre plein les mains* 'I've got ink all over my hands', *en avoir plein la bouche de (quelque chose)* 'to be always on about (something)' (literally 'to have one's mouth full of it').

The adjective *feu*, late, deceased, is variable when placed between the article (or possessive determiner) and the noun, invariable when placed before them, e.g.:

la feue reine ⎱
feu la reine ⎰ the late queen

ma feue mère ⎱
feu ma mère ⎰ my late mother

Note however that *feu* is now not much used – use, for example, *ma pauvre mère, le regretté Charles Dupont.*

136 Compound adjectives

(i) When two adjectives, or an adjective and a participle, are used as one compound adjective, both halves agree with the noun qualified, e.g.:

des oranges aigres-douces
bitter-sweet oranges

une jeune fille sourde-muette
a deaf-and-dumb girl

(ii) But if the first half of the compound is adverbial, naturally only the second half agrees, e.g.:

des hommes haut-placés   highly placed men

(iii) *Tout-puissant* 'almighty, all-powerful, omnipotent', agrees as follows:

masc.	fem.
sing. *tout-puissant*	*toute-puissante*
plur. *tout-puissants*	*toutes-puissantes*

(iv) *Soi-disant* 'so-called' does not agree, e.g. *ces soi-disant professeurs* 'these so-called teachers', *une soi-disant preuve* 'a so-called proof'. (The reason is that it is treated as though it were still a present participle, 'calling oneself' – cf. the non-agreement of the participle in *Voyant cela, elle est partie* 'seeing that, she left'.)

137 Adjectives of colour that are themselves modified by another adjective (or a noun used as an adjective) do not agree in either gender or number, e.g. *une robe vert foncé* 'a dark-green dress', *une écharpe bleu vif* 'a bright-blue scarf', *la mer gris perle*

'the pearl-grey sea', *des chaussures vert pomme* 'apple-green shoes', *des yeux bleu clair* 'pale blue eyes', *des cheveux brun foncé* 'dark brown hair', *des uniformes bleu marine* 'navy-blue uniforms', *gris ardoise* 'slate grey', *jaune citron* 'lemon yellow', *rouge sang* 'blood-red', etc.

138 For adjectives that are invariable for gender and number (*une robe marron, des vêtements chic*, etc.), see **95** and **126**.

The position of adjectives

139 Adjectives in French tend to follow the noun (e.g. *un livre difficile* 'a difficult book'). However, some adjectives must and others may precede the noun (e.g. *un petit garçon* 'a little boy'), and there is indeed an increasing tendency on the part of journalists and others to put in front of the noun adjectives that would more usually be found after it (e.g. *une importante décision* for *une décision importante* 'an important decision') (see **148**). A safe principle to follow is that the adjective should be placed after the noun unless there is some reason for doing otherwise. The main rules and tendencies relating to contexts in which the adjective must or may come before the noun are set out in sections **140–150**.

140 The following adjectives nearly always precede the noun:

beau, beautiful, fine	*mauvais*, bad
bon, good	*meilleur*, better, best
bref, brief	*moindre*, less, least
grand, big, great	*petit*, little, small
gros, big	*sot*, foolish
haut, high	*vaste*, immense
jeune, young	*vieux*, old
joli, pretty	*vilain*, ugly, nasty

This remains true even when these adjectives are preceded by one or other of the short adverbs *assez* 'rather, quite', *aussi* 'as', *bien* 'very', *fort* 'very', *moins* 'less', *plus* 'more', *si* 'so', *très* 'very', e.g. *un assez bon rapport* 'quite a good report', *une plus jolie robe* 'a prettier dress', *un très grand plaisir* 'a very great pleasure'. (For adjectives qualified by a longer adverb or other expression, see **147,d.**)

Note however:

(i) *d'un ton bref* 'curtly', *une voyelle brève* 'a short vowel'; (ii) *la marée haute* 'high tide', *à voix haute* (or *à haute voix*) 'aloud'; (iii) *un sourire mauvais* 'a nasty smile' (and also with various other nouns – consult a good dictionary).

141 *Court* 'short' and *long* 'long' tend to precede the noun (e.g. *un court intervalle* 'a short interval', *une courte lettre* 'a short letter', *un long voyage* 'a long journey', *une longue liste* 'a long list') except when (as frequently happens) there is a contrast or an implied contrast, i.e. 'short as opposed to long' or *vice versa*, e.g. *une robe courte, une robe longue* 'a short/long dress', *des cheveux courts/longs* 'short/long hair', *une voyelle courte/longue* 'a short/ long vowel'.

142 *Dernier* 'last' (see also **184**) and *prochain* 'next' meaning 'last or next as from now' follow words designating specific moments or periods of time such as *semaine* 'week', *mois* 'month', *an, année* 'year', *siècle* 'century', names of the days of the week or of the seasons, and (in the case of *dernier* only) *nuit* 'night', e.g. *la semaine dernière* 'last week', *le mois prochain* 'next month', *l'an dernier/prochain, l'année dernière/prochaine* 'last/next year', *le siècle dernier* 'last century', *lundi prochain* 'next Monday', *l'été dernier* 'last summer', *la nuit dernière* 'last night'. Otherwise they precede the noun, e.g. *la dernière/prochaine fois* 'last time, next time', *la dernière semaine des vacances* 'the last week of the holidays', *la prochaine réunion* 'the next meeting', *le dernier mardi de juin* 'the last Tuesday in June', *le prochain village* 'the next village'.

143 *Nouveau* 'new' follows the noun when it means 'newly created' or 'having just appeared for the first time', e.g. *du vin nouveau* 'new wine', *des pommes (de terre) nouvelles* 'new potatoes', *un mot nouveau* 'a new (i.e. newly coined) word', *une mode nouvelle* 'a new fashion'; otherwise – and most frequently – it precedes the noun, e.g. *le nouveau gouvernement* 'the new government', *j'ai acheté une nouvelle voiture* 'I've bought a new (i.e. different) car'.

144   *Faux* 'false' usually precedes the noun, e.g. *un faux problème* 'a false problem', *une fausse alerte* 'a false alarm', *une fausse fenêtre* 'a false window', *un faux prophète* 'a false prophet', *de faux papiers* 'false papers', but follows it in certain expressions such as *des diamants faux* 'false diamonds', *des perles fausses* 'false pearls', *un raisonnement faux* 'false reasoning', *des idées fausses* 'false ideas'.

145   *Seul* before the noun means 'single, sole, (one and) only', e.g. *c'est mon seul ami* 'he is my only friend', *la seule langue qu'il comprenne* 'the only language he understands'. After the noun it means 'alone, on one's own', e.g. *une femme seule* 'a woman on her own'. Note too the use of the adjective *seul* in contexts where English uses 'only' as an adverb, e.g. *Seuls les parents peuvent comprendre* 'Only parents can understand', *Seule compte la décision de l'arbitre* 'Only the referee's decision (the referee's decision alone) counts'.

146   Some other adjectives have one meaning when they precede the noun and a very different one when they follow the noun. These include:

	meaning before the noun	*meaning after the noun*
ancien	former, ex-	old, antique, ancient
brave	nice, good, decent	brave
certain	certain, some	certain, undoubted, sure
cher	dear, beloved	dear, costly
chic	first-rate, nice	fashionable, smart
différent	(pl. only) various, several	(sing. and pl.) different
digne	deserving, worthy	dignified
divers	(pl. only) various, several	(sing. and pl.) diverse, opposed
fameux	real, out and out (only before)	celebrated, famous, notorious (both before and after)
franc	(pejorative) utter, downright, sheer	1. free (both before and after); 2. frank, outspoken (after only)
méchant	poor, second-rate	spiteful, malicious
même (see 300)	the same (preceded by definite article)	self, very
pauvre	poor (pitiable, or bad of its kind)	poor, needy
plaisant	ridiculous, silly	pleasant, amusing
propre	own	clean, proper, right
sale	nasty, dirty (figurative)	dirty (literal)

simple	mere, nothing but	simple, single
triste	poor of its kind, sad	sad
véritable ⎫	real, genuine	true
vrai ⎭		

Examples:

un ancien cinéma
a former cinema

la ville ancienne
the old city

Après un certain temps il partit
After some time he departed

On n'a trouvé aucun témoin certain
No reliable witness was forthcoming

C'est un fait certain
It is an undoubted fact

un chic type
a nice fellow

un type chic
a smart fellow

Différentes personnes me l'ont dit
Various people have told me so

Je suis d'avis différent
I am of a different opinion

une franche canaille
a sheer scoundrel

des paroles franches
frank words

les plus méchantes raisons du monde
the poorest arguments imaginable

une épigramme méchante
a spiteful epigram

C'est toujours la même chose
It is always the same thing

Mes pensées mêmes me font horreur
My very thoughts horrify me

le même soir
the same evening

ce soir même
this very evening

pauvre jeune homme!
poor young man!

le roman d'un jeune homme pauvre
the tale of a penniless young man

mes propres mains
my own hands

mes mains propres
my clean hands

le mot propre
1. the exact word; 2. the right expression

un sale tour a dirty trick	*des mains sales* dirty hands
une simple formalité a mere formality	*une explication simple* a simple explanation
	un billet simple a single ticket

147   The following normally go after the noun:

(a) Adjectives denoting nationality or derived from proper names, or relating to political, philosophical, religious, artistic movements, etc., e.g.:

la langue française
the French language

une actrice américaine
an American actress

les provinces danubiennes
the Danubian provinces

la politique gaulliste
Gaullist policy (i.e. that of General de Gaulle)

un personnage cornélien
one of Corneille's characters

les théories marxistes
Marxist theories

la religion chrétienne
the Christian religion

la peinture surréaliste
surrealist painting

(b) Adjectives denoting colour, shape or physical qualities (other than those, many of which relate to size, listed in **140**), e.g.:

une robe blanche	a white dress
une fenêtre ronde	a round window
un toit plat	a flat roof
une rue étroite	a narrow street
un oreiller mou	a soft pillow
une voix aiguë	a shrill voice
de l'or pur	pure gold
un goût amer	a bitter taste

Some of these however may occur in front of the noun, particularly when they are used figuratively, e.g. *le noir désespoir* 'black despair', *une étroite obligation* 'a strict obligation', *une molle résistance* 'feeble resistance', *la pure vérité* 'the plain truth'. But they by no means invariably precede the noun even when used figuratively (e.g. *l'humour noir* 'sick humour', *une amitié étroite* 'a close friendship').

(c) Present and past participles used as adjectives, e.g.:

un livre amusant	an amusing book
un verre cassé	a broken glass

Exceptions:

maudit 'accursed' and *prétendu* 'alleged' regularly stand before the noun qualified, e.g.:

cette maudite guerre	this accursed war
mon prétendu ami	my alleged friend

dû 'due' only stands first in the expression

en bonne et due forme	in due form

mort 'dead' only in a few compound nouns such as *du mort-bois* 'brushwood, useless wood (briars, brambles, etc.)', *la morte-saison* 'the slack season', *la morte-eau* 'neap-tide'.

sacré generally changes its sense with its position, e.g.:

cet endroit sacré	this holy place
ce sacré endroit	this damn place

soi-disant 'so-called' always stands before its noun and is invariable (see **136,iv**), e.g. *la soi-disant actrice* 'the so-called actress'.

(d) Adjectives qualified by an adverb in *-ment* or followed by any words depending on them, e.g.:

une décision indubitablement juste
an undeniably just verdict

un mendiant vieux comme Mathusalem
a beggar as old as Methuselah

Note however that the position of adjectives that would normally precede the noun is unaffected by the presence of a short adverb such as *si, plus, très*, etc. (see **140**).

148 In general, polysyllabic adjectives tend to follow rather than precede the noun. However, there seems to be an increasing tendency for such adjectives to be placed before the noun when they express a value judgement or, even more so, a subjective or emotional reaction. Such adjectives include *adorable, affreux* 'dreadful', *délicieux* 'delightful', *effrayant* 'frightful', *effroyable* 'appalling', *énorme* 'enormous', *épouvantable* 'terrible', *excellent, extraordinaire* 'extraordinary', *important, inoubliable* 'unforgettable', *magnifique* 'magnificent', *superbe, terrible*, and many others, e.g. *un adorable petit village* 'a delightful little village', *une épouvantable catastrophe* 'a terrible catastrophe', *un magnifique coucher de soleil* 'a magnificent sunset'.

149 It is perfectly possible for a noun to take adjectives both before and after it, as in *une belle robe bleue* 'a beautiful blue dress', *un jeune homme habile* 'a capable young man'.

150 A noun may be preceded and/or followed by two or more adjectives; except in the type of construction dealt with in **151** below, two adjectives preceding or following the noun are linked by *et* 'and' (or by *ou* 'or' if two following adjectives are presented as alternatives), e.g.:

une belle et vieille cathédrale
a beautiful old cathedral

un étudiant intelligent et travailleur
an intelligent, hard-working student

des journaux anglais ou français
English or French newspapers

Where more than two adjectives are associated in a similar way with the same noun, the last two are linked by *et* or *ou*, e.g. *des étudiants intelligents, travailleurs et agréables* 'intelligent, hard-working, pleasant students'.

151 In the examples given in **150**, each adjective modifies the noun so to speak independently and equally. Sometimes, however, one adjective modifies not just the noun but the group adjective + noun or noun + adjective, in which case there is no linking *et*, e.g. in *un gentil petit garçon* 'a nice little boy' the adjective *gentil* modifies the whole phrase *petit garçon*, and in *la* *poésie française contemporaine* 'contemporary French poetry' (in which the reference is not to poetry which happens to be both French and contemporary but to French poetry of the present time) *contemporaine* modifies the whole of the phrase *la poésie française*.

152 An adjective qualifying two or more nouns is put in the plural after the last noun, and, if either noun is masculine, the adjective is masculine (see also **127**), e.g.:

un printemps et un été secs
a dry spring and summer

un fils et une fille intelligents
a clever son and daughter

though, in practice, it is better to avoid having a feminine noun immediately followed by a masculine adjective as in this last example. If the adjective is placed before the nouns, it must be repeated with each noun, e.g.:

un beau printemps et un bel été
a fine spring and summer

153 Two or more adjectives, each in the singular, can modify the same plural noun when each refers to one instance of the plurality expressed by the noun, e.g. *les dix-neuvième et vingtième siècles* 'the nineteenth and twentieth centuries', *les religions chrétienne, musulmane et juive* 'the Christian, Moslem and Jewish religions', *les gouvernements espagnol et italien* 'the Spanish and Italian governments'.

154 Besides the fact that in English adjectives generally precede the noun qualified, but in French frequently come after it, the following differences between the two languages in the position of the adjective should be noted:

(a) With 'how' (*combien*, *comme* and exclamatory *que*), or 'so' (*tant*) in English the adjective is placed directly after 'how' or 'so', but in French after the verb, e.g.:

Comme il est (Qu'il est) facile de se tromper!
How easy it is to make mistakes!

Je n'avais pas compris combien il était difficile d'apprendre à fond le français
I never realized how hard it was to learn French thoroughly

Tant ils se montrèrent cruels qu'on finit par se soulever contre eux
So cruel did they show themselves that in the end there was a general rising against them.

(b) The adjective (or adverb) also follows the verb in French where English has two comparatives with 'the' before one or both of them (see 172), e.g.:

Plus il y réfléchissait, plus il en devenait triste
The more he thought it over, the gloomier (more gloomy) he became

The irregular comparatives, *meilleur, mieux*, etc. (see 161) cannot be used in this way, e.g.:

Plus nous approchons du sommet, plus nous nous sentons bien
The nearer the top we get, the better we feel

(c) In English, adjectives precede the word 'enough' but in French they follow the word *assez* 'enough' (see also 322), e.g.:

Il est assez intelligent pour comprendre
He is intelligent enough to understand

The comparison of adjectives and adverbs

155   As adjectives and adverbs have the same degrees of comparison and as the constructions involved are the same in each case we shall discuss them together.

156   There are four degrees of comparison, but one, the comparison of equality or inequality, sometimes known as the equative, has no special forms in either English or French (see 157). They are:

(i) the positive – e.g. (in English) *good, hard, difficult, easily*
(ii) the equative – e.g. (*not*) *as good as*, (*not*) *as easily as*

(iii) the comparative, which can be subdivided into:
    (a) the comparative of superiority, e.g. *better, harder, more difficult, more easily*
    (b) the comparative of inferiority, e.g. *less good, less easily*
(iv) the superlative – e.g. *the best, the hardest, the most difficult, (the) most easily.*

The comparative of equality or inequality (the equative)

157 In affirmative sentences the comparative of equality (English 'as . . . as . . .') is expressed by *aussi . . . que . . .*, e.g.:

Il est aussi grand que vous
He is as big as you (are)

Elle est aussi intelligente que belle
She is as intelligent as she is beautiful

Il comprend aussi facilement que vous
He understands as easily as you (do)

Ils sont aussi charmants que vous le dites
They are as charming as you say

In negative sentences, *aussi* is usually replaced by *si*, e.g.:

Il n'est pas si grand que vous
He is not as big as you (are)

Ils ne sont pas si charmants que vous le dites
They are not as charming as you say

though *aussi* is possible (*Il n'est pas aussi grand que vous*).
  On constructions of the type *Il est aussi grand que vous* 'He is as big as you (are)', *Vous travaillez aussi énergiquement que nous* 'You work as energetically as we (do)', i.e. where English has the option of using after a comparative a verb that repeats or stands for that of the previous clause, see **173**.

158 As in English, the second half of the comparison may be omitted, e.g.:

Je n'ai jamais vu un si (or *aussi*) *beau spectacle*
I never saw so fine a sight

159   *Tellement*, not *si*, must be used for 'so much' before *plus* or *moins*, e.g.:

> *Il n'est pas tellement plus grand que vous*
> He is not so much (all that much) taller than you

The comparative and superlative of superiority or inferiority

160   In French this comparative is formed by placing *plus* 'more' or *moins* 'less' before the adjective or adverb, the superlative by adding a definite article to the comparative, e.g.:

positive	comparative	superlative
stupide	*plus stupide*	*le plus stupide*
	moins stupide	*le moins stupide*
stupid	more stupid, stupider	(the) most stupid, stupidest
	less stupid	(the) least stupid
étrangement	*plus étrangement*	*le plus étrangement*
	moins étrangement	*le moins étrangement*
strangely	more strangely	(the) most strangely
	less strangely	(the) least strangely

Note the following constructions:

> *la plus jolie fleur*
> the prettiest flower

> *la question la plus difficile*
> the most difficult question

> *son élève le plus (moins) intelligent*
> his most (least) intelligent pupil

With an adjective preceding its noun, a possessive adjective may take the place of the definite article in the superlative, e.g.:

> *C'est mon plus grand ami*
> He is my greatest friend

161   In comparisons with *moins* there are no exceptions to the above rule; in those with *plus*, three adjectives and the corresponding adverbs are sometimes irregular, viz.:

positive	comparative	superlative
bon, good	*meilleur*, better	*le meilleur*, best
mauvais, bad	*pire*, worse	*le pire*, worst

petit, little, small	*moindre*, less, lesser	*le moindre*, least, smallest
bien, well	*mieux*, better	*le mieux*, best
mal, badly	*pis*, worse	*le pis*, worst
peu, little	*moins*, less	*le moins*, least

The adjectives agree in gender and number with their noun as follows:

masc. sing.	fem. sing.	masc. plur.	fem. plur.
(le) meilleur	*(la) meilleure*	*(les) meilleurs*	*(les) meilleures*
(le) pire	*(la) pire*	*(les) pires*	
(le) moindre	*(la) moindre*	*(les) moindres*	

The adverbs are of course invariable.

Note that some, but not all, of these forms are subject to certain restrictions and that, for some of them, 'regular' comparatives and superlatives such as *(le) plus mauvais* occur – see **163–164**.

162 The comparative and superlative of *bon* and *bien* are always *(le) meilleur* and *(le) mieux* respectively, e.g.:

Ce pain est meilleur que l'autre
This bread is better than the other

Leurs meilleurs amis
Their best friends

Il chante mieux que vous
He sings better than you (do)

C'est le matin que je travaille le mieux
It's in the morning that I work (the) best

The rule applies even to expressions such as *bon marché* 'cheap' (*meilleur marché* 'cheaper', *le meilleur marché* 'cheapest') and *de bonne heure* 'early' (*de meilleure heure* 'earlier' – though a more usual rendering for 'earlier' is *plus tôt*). Note that *plus ou moins bon* is only an apparent exception since it means 'more or less good', not 'better or worse'.

163 The comparative and superlative of *mauvais* are either *(le) pire* or *(le) plus mauvais*. The two are often interchangeable, but insofar as there is any distinction it is (a) that *(le) pire* occurs more widely in literary than in spoken usage, and (b) that *(le) pire* in any case tends to be restricted to contexts in which it refers to abstract nouns, e.g.:

> *Votre attitude est pire que la sienne*
> Your attitude is worse than his

> *le pire danger*
> the worst danger

but:

> *Ce vin est plus mauvais que l'autre*
> This wine is worse than the other

> *le plus mauvais restaurant de la ville*
> the worst restaurant in town

(Note however that French often says *moins bon* 'less good' where English says 'worse', e.g. *Cette route est moins bonne que l'autre* 'This road is worse than (*or* not as good as) the other'.)

The adverb (*le*) *pis* 'worse, worst' is even less used than *pire* and, for practical purposes, it can be assumed that the normal comparative and superlative of *mal* 'badly' are *plus mal* and *le plus mal*. *Pis* can never be used as an alternative to *plus mal* in, for example, a context such as *Il chante plus mal que vous* 'He sings worse than you'. Apart from the one expression *tant pis (pour vous, pour lui,* etc.) 'so much the worse (for you, for him, etc.)', it is rarely heard in conversational usage and even in literary usage it is confined to a few expressions like *aller de mal en pis* 'to go from bad to worse', *qui pis est* 'what is worse', *rien de pis* 'nothing worse', *le pis* 'the worst thing', *mettre les choses au pis* 'to put things at their worst, to assume the worst', and even in some of these it can be replaced by *pire*, e.g. *ce qui est pire* 'what is worse', *rien de pire, le pire, mettre les choses au pire*. (Note too the use of *moins bien* 'less well' as a frequent alternative to *plus mal*.)

164 As the comparative and superlative of *petit*, the form (*le*) *plus petit* must always be used when reference is to physical size, e.g.:

> *Il est plus petit que je ne croyais*
> He is smaller than I thought

> *le plus petit verre*
> the smallest glass

The form *moindre* occasionally occurs as the equivalent of 'less', e.g. *des choses de moindre impòrtance* 'things of less importance', but is more common as a superlative, particularly as the equivalent of English 'least, slightest', e.g.:

son moindre défaut	his slightest failing
les moindres détails	the smallest details
sans la moindre difficulté	without the slightest difficulty
Je n'ai pas la moindre idée	I haven't the slightest idea
la loi du moindre effort	the law of least effort

On the other hand, the comparative and superlative of the adverb *peu* are invariably *moins* and *le moins* 'less, (the) least', e.g.:

moins difficile
less difficult

J'ai moins de temps que vous
I have less time than you

C'est lui que j'aime le moins
He is the one I like (the) least

Note that, where English uses 'the least' with a noun, meaning 'the least amount of', French uses *le moins de* (with the optional addition, as in English, of the adjective *possible*), e.g.:

De cette façon vous le ferez avec le moins de difficulté (possible)
In this way you will do it with the least (possible) difficulty

Do not confuse this with constructions involving a negative or *sans* 'without', e.g.:

De cette façon vous n'aurez pas la moindre difficulté	In this way you will not have the least difficulty
De cette façon vous le ferez sans la moindre difficulté	In this way you will do it without the least difficulty

in which the meaning is not 'the least amount of difficulty' but 'the smallest difficulty'.

165 The adverb *beaucoup* 'much, many, a lot' has as its comparative and superlative *plus* and *le plus*, e.g.:

J'ai plus de temps que vous
I have more time than you (have)

C'est le soir que je travaille le plus
It's in the evening that I work most

166   'Than' (unless followed by a numeral, see **167**) is translated by *que*. In an affirmative sentence *ne* is often put before the verb (see **563**) and *le* may have to be added (see **213,vi**), e.g.:

Il est plus fort que son frère
He is stronger than his brother
Il en sait plus qu'il n'avoue
He knows more than he admits

Il a agi avec plus d'imprudence que je ne (le) croyais
He acted more rashly than I thought

167   Except in the type of sentence referred to in **168** below, 'than' followed by a numeral (including fractions) is translated by *de* instead of *que*, e.g.:

J'en ai plus de trente
I have more than thirty of them

Cela coûte plus de dix mille francs
That costs more than ten thousand francs

Il en a mangé plus de la moitié
He has eaten more than half of it

Plus des trois cinquièmes de l'équipage ont péri
More than three-fifths of the crew perished

Il a vécu moins de dix ans
He lived less than ten years

168   In the type of sentence discussed in **167**, 'more than' means 'in excess of' and 'less than' means 'a quantity less than'. There is however a totally different construction in which 'than' is followed by a numeral and in which it is translated not by *de* but, as in most other contexts, by *que*. In the construction in question, 'than' introduces a new clause in which the numeral, or phrase introduced by a numeral, serves as the subject of a verb either expressed or understood – e.g. 'This man is worth more than three others' = 'This man is worth more than three others are worth', so, in French, we have *Cet homme vaut plus que trois autres (ne valent)*.

169 Whereas, in English, two or three adjectives or adverbs can be made comparative or superlative by the addition of 'more', 'most', etc., to the first of the series, in French *plus, le plus*, etc., must be repeated before each adjective or adverb, e.g.:

He is more energetic and ambitious than I
Il est plus énergique et plus ambitieux que moi

170 There is another superlative which, though sometimes confused with the absolute superlative – see below – is really a superlative of superiority or inferiority. In this a person or thing is compared with the same person or thing in different circumstances, e.g.:

Une mère est le plus contente lorsqu'elle est avec ses enfants
A mother is happiest when she is with her children (i.e. 'at her happiest', not 'the happiest mother')

In this class of superlative the *le* is invariable, as *le plus, le moins*, are mere adverbs qualifying the adjective which follows.

171 After comparatives and superlatives the amount by which one thing differs from another is expressed by *de*, e.g.:

Il est de trois centimètres plus grand que son frère
He is three centimetres taller than his brother

Il est de beaucoup le plus intelligent de cette famille
He is (by) far the cleverest of this family

After a superlative the English preposition 'in' must also be translated by *de*, e.g.:

C'est l'élève le plus paresseux de la classe
He is the idlest boy in the class

le meilleur restaurant de Paris
the best restaurant in Paris

172 *Plus* and *moins* are used without any article before them, where English has two comparatives with 'the' before one or both of them, e.g.:

Plus il attendait, plus la nuit devenait noire
The longer he waited, the darker grew the night; *or*
The night grew darker the longer he waited

In such sentences *et* may be inserted between the two clauses:

Plus il attendait, et plus la nuit devenait noire

173   After a comparative of equality (see the end of section **157**), superiority or inferiority, French normally does not use a second verb that merely repeats or stands for (like 'did' in the third example below) the verb of the previous clause, e.g.:

Il est plus grand que moi
He is taller than I (am)

J'ai plus de temps que vous
I have more time than you (have)

Il a chanté mieux que son frère
He sang better than his brother (did)

Absolute superlative

174   Besides the ordinary superlative (which expresses the best, worst, highest, etc., of a group of persons or things) there is also what is called the absolute superlative, denoting an extremely high level of the quality described by the adjective, e.g.:

Le soir elle devenait des plus violentes
In the evening she became most violent (i.e. reached a very high level of violence)

une situation des plus difficiles
a most difficult situation

un enfant des plus exaspérants
a most exasperating child

The use of the plural will be understood if it is appreciated that *un enfant des plus exaspérants*, for example, means something like 'a child from among the most exasperating ones of his kind'.

In the absolute superlative ambiguity is caused by the English use of 'most', e.g. 'She became most violent in the evening' may mean

(i) 'more violent than at other times of day', i.e. *C'est le soir qu'elle devenait le plus violente*, a superlative of superiority or inferiority (see **170**),

(ii) 'exceedingly violent', an absolute superlative, i.e. *Le soir elle devenait des plus violentes* or, more commonly, *extrêmement violente*, or *violente au plus haut degré*.

Adjectives used as nouns

175   (i) Many adjectives of colour and some others are used as nouns with a variety of meanings for which a dictionary must be consulted, e.g.:

le beau	the beautiful, that which is beautiful
le blanc	the white (of an egg, of the eye)
un bleu	a bruise
le noir	darkness

176   (ii) Some adjectival nouns originate in expressions of the type noun + adjective; as a result of ellipsis of the noun, the adjective has taken on the function of a noun carrying the meaning of the whole expression, e.g.:

du bleu	for *du fromage bleu,* 'blue cheese'
un noir	for *un café noir,* 'a black coffee'
du rouge	for *du vin rouge,* 'red wine'
un complet	for *un costume complet,* 'a suit'
la capitale	for *la ville capitale,* 'capital (city)'
la majuscule	for *la lettre majuscule,* 'capital (letter)'

177   (iii) Adjectives can be used as nouns with reference to humans more freely in French than in English. Note in particular that, whereas in English a nominalized adjective with reference to humans is normally plural (e.g. 'the poor' = 'poor people', 'the blind' = 'blind people'), the fact that French has distinct masculine singular, feminine singular, and plural articles and other determiners (see **23**) means that one can have, e.g., *un pauvre* 'a poor man', *une pauvre* 'a poor woman', *des pauvres* 'poor people', *le muet* 'the dumb man', *la muette* 'the dumb woman', *cet aveugle* 'this blind man', *cette aveugle* 'this blind woman', *les aveugles* 'blind people', and, in cases where there are distinct forms for the masculine and feminine adjectives, a distinction in the plural between, for example, *les sourds* 'the deaf men' or 'the deaf (in general)' and *les sourdes* 'the deaf women'.

Numerals

178 Numerals are of two kinds:

1 cardinal, giving the number of items in question.

2 ordinal, giving the place of each item in numerical order.

	Cardinal		Ordinal
0	*zéro*		
1	*un* (m.), *une* (f.)	1st	*premier* (m.), *première* (f.)
2	*deux*	2nd	*deuxième, second* (m.), *seconde* (f.)
3	*trois*	3rd	*troisième*
4	*quatre*	4th	*quatrième*
5	*cinq*	5th	*cinquième*
6	*six*	6th	*sixième*
7	*sept*	7th	*septième*
8	*huit*	8th	*huitième*
9	*neuf*	9th	*neuvième*
10	*dix*	10th	*dixième*
11	*onze*	11th	*onzième*
12	*douze*	12th	*douzième*
13	*treize*	13th	*treizième*
14	*quatorze*	14th	*quatorzième*
15	*quinze*	15th	*quinzième*
16	*seize*	16th	*seizième*
17	*dix-sept*	17th	*dix-septième*
18	*dix-huit*	18th	*dix-huitième*
19	*dix-neuf*	19th	*dix-neuvième*
20	*vingt*	20th	*vingtième*
21	*vingt et un* (or *une*)	21st	*vingt et unième* (not *premier*)
22 etc.	*vingt-deux*, etc.	22nd etc.	*vingt-deuxième*, etc.
30	*trente*	30th	*trentième*
31	*trente et un* (or *une*)	31st	*trente et unième* (not *premier*)
32 etc.	*trente-deux*, etc.	32nd etc.	*trente-deuxième*, etc.
40	*quarante*	40th	*quarantième*
41	*quarante et un* (or *une*)	41st	*quarante et unième* (not *premier*)
42 etc.	*quarante-deux*, etc.	42nd etc.	*quarante-deuxième*, etc.

50	cinquante	50th	cinquantième
51	cinquante et un (or une)	51st	cinquante et unième (not premier)
52 etc.	cinquante-deux, etc.	52nd etc.	cinquante-deuxième, etc.
60	soixante	60th	soixantième
61	soixante et un (or une)	61st	soixante et unième (not premier)
62 etc.	soixante-deux, etc.	62nd etc.	soixante-deuxième, etc.
70	soixante-dix	70th	soixante-dixième
71	soixante et onze	71st	soixante et onzième
72 etc.	soixante-douze, etc.	72nd etc.	soixante-douzième, etc.
80	quatre-vingts	80th	quatre-vingtième
81	quatre-vingt-un (or une)	81st	quatre-vingt-unième (not premier)
82 etc.	quatre-vingt-deux, etc.	82nd etc.	quatre-vingt-deuxième, etc.
90	quatre-vingt-dix	90th	quatre-vingt-dixième
91	quatre-vingt-onze	91st	quatre-vingt-onzième
92 etc.	quatre-vingt-douze, etc.	92nd etc.	quatre-vingt-douzième, etc.
100	cent	100th	centième
101	cent un (or une)	101st	cent unième (not premier)
102 etc.	cent deux, etc.	102nd etc.	cent deuxième, etc.
200 etc.	deux cents, etc.	200th etc.	deux centième, etc.
257	deux cent cinquante-sept	257th	deux cent cinquante-septième
1000	mille	1000th	millième
1001	mille un (or une)	1001st	mille unième (not premier)
1500	mille cinq cents or quinze cents	1500th	mille cinq centième or quinze centième
10,000 etc.	dix mille, etc.	10,000th etc.	dix millième, etc.

179 Notes on pronunciation (for phonetic symbols, see 2):

(a) *Cinq* is pronounced [sɛ̃ːk] when final (e.g. *j'en ai cinq* 'I have five of them') and [sɛ̃k] in liaison (e.g. *cinq enfants* 'five children') but [sɛ̃] before a consonant (see note c) (e.g. *cinq jours* 'five days' though there is an increasing tendency in conversational speech to pronounce [sɛ̃k] even there).

(b) *Six* and *dix* are pronounced [sis] and [dis] when final (e.g. *j'en ai six* 'I have six of them'), [siz] and [diz] in liaison (e.g. *dix ans* 'ten years'), and [si] and [di] before a consonant (see note c), (e.g. *six francs* 'six francs', *dix jours* 'ten days').

(c) 'Before a consonant' in notes a and b relates only to contexts in which the numeral directly governs a following noun (as in *cinq jours*) or adjective (as in *dix beaux livres* 'ten beautiful books'); in contexts such as *dix pour cent* 'ten per cent' this does not apply and the numerals are pronounced [sɛ̃k, sis, dis].

(d) *Neuf* is pronounced [nœf] except in the two phrases *neuf ans* [nœvɑ̃] 'nine years' and *neuf heures* [nœvœːr] 'nine o'clock', so *neuf jours* [nœf ʒuːr] 'nine days', *neuf arbres* [nœf arbr] 'nine trees', etc.

(e) *Vingt* on its own is pronounced [vɛ̃] but it is pronounced [vɛ̃t] not only in liaison (i.e. *vingt et un* [vɛ̃t e œ̃]) but also before a consonant in the numbers '22' to '29' (e.g. *vingt-quatre* [vɛ̃tkatr]); but note that the *-t* of *quatre-vingt(s)* is never pronounced, not even in *quatre-vingt-un*.

(f) In Belgium and Switzerland, '70' and '90' are *septante* (pronounced [sɛptɑ̃ːt] – contrast *sept* [sɛt] and *septième* [sɛtjɛm]) and *nonante* respectively, and hence *septante et un* '71', *nonante-trois* '93', etc. However, '80' is usually *quatre-vingts* though *huitante* does exist in some parts of Switzerland (but not in Belgium).

180 Remarks:

(a) Hyphens should be inserted in compound numbers (but not in fractions) except before or after *et, cent* (or *centième*), *mille* (or *millième*), e.g.:

> *vingt-deux,* twenty-two   *vingt et un*, twenty-one

(b) *Et* is inserted before *un, une* or *onze*, in '21, 31, 41, 51, 61, 71', but not in '81, 91, 101', e.g.:

> *trente et un, soixante et un, soixante et onze,* but *quatre-vingt-un*

(c) *Vingt* and *cent* take an *s* when multiplied by a number unless followed by another number, e.g.:

> *quatre-vingts, quatre-vingt-deux, deux cents, deux cent vingt* (But see **183**.)

(d) In 'one hundred', 'one thousand', the 'one' is not to be translated, e.g.:

> he had only one (or a) thousand men
> *il n'avait que mille hommes*

(e) *Mille* takes no sign of the plural, e.g.:

dix mille hommes   ten thousand men

(f) The normal form for '1100' is *onze cents* 'eleven hundred' (*mille cent* is virtually unused); from '1200' to '1900' (and particularly from '1200' to '1600'), the forms *douze cents* 'twelve hundred', etc., are preferred to *mille deux cents*, etc. The same is true of dates of the Christian era, but note in addition that in this case, if the form in 'one thousand' is used, then the spelling is *mil*, e.g. *en l'an mil huit cent* (no *-s* – see **183**) 'in the year 1800' (but 'the year one thousand' is *l'an mille*).

(g) When 'a thousand and one' means a large indefinite number ('umpteen'), it is *mille et un(e)*, e.g. *J'ai mille et une choses à faire* 'I have a thousand and one things to do'; note too, as an exception, *Les Mille et une nuits* '*The Thousand and One Nights* (i.e. *The Arabian Nights*)'.

(h) For the translation of 'than' before a numeral, see **167**.

(i) Apart from a few fixed expressions, such as (*apprendre quelque chose*) *de seconde main* '(to learn something) at second hand', *en second lieu* 'secondly', *second* and *deuxième* are interchangeable; the 'rule' that *second* is preferred with reference to the second of two (only) and *deuxième* when there are more than two can safely be ignored. Note that *second* is pronounced [səgɔ̃].

181   The numerals given above, both cardinal and ordinal, govern their noun directly, without any preposition. Those given below are nouns and must be followed by *de* if a noun follows:

(a) 'Thousands' is translated by *milliers*, e.g. *des milliers de petits oiseaux* 'thousands of little birds'.

(b) Other similar nouns expressing a round number are:

une huitaine, about eight
une dizaine, about ten
une douzaine, a dozen
une quinzaine, about fifteen
une vingtaine, a score, about twenty
une trentaine, about thirty
une quarantaine, about forty
une cinquantaine, about fifty

une soixantaine, about sixty
une centaine, about a hundred

e.g. *J'ai écrit une vingtaine de lettres*
I've written about twenty letters.

Une huitaine is used particularly in the expression *une huitaine de jours* (i.e. 'a week') and *une quinzaine* whether or not followed by *de jours* frequently means 'a fortnight'. As in English, *une douzaine* 'a dozen' can mean 'precisely twelve' in such expressions as *une douzaine d'œufs* 'a dozen eggs'. The terms *trentaine, quarantaine, cinquantaine* and *soixantaine* can refer to age in such expressions as *atteindre la quarantaine* 'to reach the age of forty', *Elle a dépassé la cinquantaine* 'She is over fifty'.

(c) *un million* 'a million' and multiples thereof and *un milliard* 'a thousand million' (or 'a billion' in American and now increasingly in British usage – the older sense of 'a billion' in British usage is 'a million million', which is also now the official definition of *un billion* in French though it used to be the equivalent of *un milliard*), e.g.:

cinquante millions de Français
fifty million Frenchmen

deux milliards de francs
two thousand million francs

182 Cardinal numerals are invariable, except that *un* has a feminine singular, *une*, and is also used in the plural, to mean 'some', in *les uns* (fem. *unes*) . . . *les autres*. . ., 'some. . . others', e.g.:

Trois fois neuf font vingt-sept
Three times nine make twenty-seven, *or* Three nines are twenty-seven

Un et un font deux
One and one are two

Trois un de suite font cent onze
Three ones in succession make one hundred and eleven (111)

Les uns l'aiment, les autres non
Some like it, others (some) do not

183 Cardinal numbers are used instead of ordinals with dates and names of sovereigns, etc., e.g.:

le trente avril	the thirtieth of April
Henri Quatre	Henry the Fourth
Élisabeth II (= 'deux')	Elizabeth II (= 'the Second')
le pape Jean XXIII (= 'vingt-trois')	Pope John XXIII (= 'the Twenty-third')

But this does not apply to the first of a series, e.g.:

le premier mai	the first of May
François premier	Francis the First

The two following are exceptional:

Charles-Quint	the Emperor Charles the Fifth
Sixte-Quint	Pope Sixtus the Fifth

When a number occurs in other lists or series, such as the number of a house in a street, or a page, etc., in a book, there is very little difference between French and English, e.g.:

chapter ten	have as parallels	*chapitre dix*
the tenth chapter	in French	*le dixième chapitre*
tenth chapter		*chapitre dixième*

In these cases *vingt* and *cent* do not take *-s* and 'number' in this sense must be *numéro*, not *nombre*, e.g.:

Il habite au numéro deux cent
He lives at No. 200

(For 'every second, third', etc., see **317,ii,c**).

184 When a cardinal and *premier* 'first' or *dernier* 'last' are combined, the cardinal comes first in French, e.g.:

Les deux premiers fascicules de ce feuilleton ne me plaisent guère
I do not care for the first two numbers of this serial

les trente dernières années
the last thirty years

185 For 'both', 'all three', etc., see **317,ii,c**.

186 Numeral adverbs are formed with *fois* 'time', e.g., *une fois* 'once', *deux fois* 'twice', *sept fois* 'seven times'. Note also *une fois sur dix* 'once in ten times', *dix fois sur vingt* 'ten times out of twenty', etc.

187 Note the use of the definite article in French but not in English in, e.g., *Il a payé le double de ce que j'ai demandé* 'He paid double what I asked'.

Fractions

188 A 'half' is either (*un*) *demi* or *la moitié*, but the two are by no means interchangeable. We can distinguish three types of function, viz. (i) as nouns, (ii) as adjectives, (iii) as adverbs:

(i) Apart from a few contexts in which it is a nominalized adjective (see ii,c, below), *un demi* exists as a noun only as a mathematical term, e.g. *Deux demis font un entier* 'Two halves make a whole'. Otherwise, *la moitié* must be used (and note that, when it is the subject of the verb, the verb may be either singular or plural, depending on the sense – the same is also true of other fractions), e.g.:

Il n'a écrit que la moitié de son roman
He has only written half his novel

couper une orange en deux moitiés
to cut an orange into two halves

La moitié de la ville a été inondée
Half the town was flooded

La moitié de mes amis habitent à Paris
Half my friends live in Paris

la première (seconde) moitié
the first (second) half

(ii) *Demi* occurs in the following circumstances:

(a) Before a noun in the sense of 'half (a). . .'; it is then invariable and is linked to the noun by a hyphen, e.g. *un demi-pain* 'half a loaf', *un demi-frère* 'a half-brother', *une demi-heure* 'half an hour', *une demi-bouteille* 'half a bottle', *des demi-mesures* 'half-measures'.

(b) After the noun and preceded by *et*, meaning '. . . and a half'; it is then written as a separate word and takes an *-e* if the noun is feminine, e.g. *un kilo et demi* 'a kilo and a half, one and a half kilos', *une heure et demie* 'an hour and a half, one and a half hours, half past one', *trois heures et demie* 'three and a half hours, half past three'.

(c) with an implied noun (as in a above), in contrast to a noun expressing a whole object, e.g. *Vous voulez un pain? Non, un demi* 'Do you want a loaf? No, a half (half a loaf)'; note (in contrast to *une demi-bouteille*, etc., see a above) that *demi* takes *-e* in agreement with a feminine noun when the noun itself is omitted, e.g. *Nous allons commander une bouteille de vin? – Une demie suffira* 'Shall we order a bottle of wine?' 'A half (bottle) will be enough'. Note too the following instances in which the noun has been completely dropped and the adjective has therefore become fully nominalized (see **176**):

> *un demi* 'glass of beer' (originally *un demi-litre*, but now contains less)
>
> *un demi* 'half-back' (in football – for *un demi-arrière*)

(iii) As adverbs, *à demi* and *à moitié* are in most cases interchangeable (but see below), in particular:

(a) before an adjective or participle, e.g.:

> *à demi plein/vide, à moitié plein/vide*
> half full/empty
>
> *à demi ouvert/pourri, à moitié ouvert/pourri*
> half open/rotten

(b) after a verb, e.g.:

> *ouvrir la porte à demi/à moitié*
> to half-open the door
>
> *Vous avez fait le travail à demi/à moitié*
> You have (only) half done the work
>
> *remplir un verre à demi/à moitié*
> to half-fill a glass

Note, however, the use of *à moitié* (but not of *à demi*) in a small number of expressions with nouns, in particular *à moitié prix* '(at) half-price' and *à moitié chemin* 'half-way' (but *à mi-chemin*, see below, is more usual). *Moitié* (without *à*) also occurs in various other expressions such as *moitié moitié* 'half-and-half, fifty-fifty', (*diviser quelque chose*) *par moitié* '(to divide something) in half, in two', *être pour moitié dans quelque chose* 'to be half responsible for something' (for other such expressions, consult a good dictionary).

Finally, the old noun *mi* 'a half' is still to be found used adverbially in such constructions as *mi pleurant et mi souriant* 'half weeping and half smiling', *mi-fil et mi-coton* 'half linen and half cotton', in the expression *mi-clos* 'half-shut', and in a number of expressions with *à mi* including the following (for others, consult a dictionary):

> *à mi-chemin*, half way
> *à mi-hauteur*, half-way up
> *à mi-mât*, at half-mast
> *à mi-pente*, half-way up or down the slope
> (*travailler*) *à mi-temps*, (to work) half-time
> *à mi-voix*, in an undertone

189 'A third' and 'a quarter' are *un tiers* and *un quart* respectively, e.g.:

> *Il ne m'a donné que le tiers de ce que je désirais*
> He only gave me a third of what I wanted

> *La bouteille est aux trois quarts vide*
> The bottle is three-quarters empty

190 Other fractions have (as in English) the same form as the ordinals, e.g. *un cinquième* 'a fifth', *sept huitièmes* 'seven eighths', *un centième* 'a hundredth', etc.

191 When a fraction refers to part of a specific whole (i.e. to one introduced by the definite article or by a demonstrative or possessive determiner), French uses the definite article where English uses either the indefinite article or (especially in the plural) no article, e.g.:

> *Il·a perdu le quart de ses biens*
> He lost a quarter of his possessions

la moitié de la classe
half (of) the class

les sept huitièmes de la population
seven eighths of the population

192 The decimal system as used in France is based not on the point but on the comma, and the figures coming after the comma are often expressed as if they were whole numbers, e.g. 2.35 'two point three five' becomes 2,35 *deux virgule trente-cinq.*

Pronouns and pronominal determiners

Personal pronouns

Introduction

193 These are of two kinds – conjunctive and disjunctive. Conjunctive pronouns stand as the subject or as the direct or indirect object of verbs, without any intervening preposition or other word of any kind. No word can stand between a conjunctive personal pronoun and its verb except another conjunctive personal pronoun and the negative particle *ne* – the latter only when the pronoun is the subject. Conjunctive pronouns cannot take any emphasis (see 216,i).

Disjunctive pronouns are required when the pronoun is separated in some other way from its verb. For these and their uses see 215–220.

194 *Je* 'I' and *nous* 'we' are known as the first person singular and the first person plural respectively; *tu* 'you' and *vous* 'you' (see 196) are the second person singular and the second person plural respectively; *il* 'he, it' and *elle* 'she, it' are the third persons singular, masculine and feminine, and *ils* and *elles* 'they' are the third persons plural, masculine and feminine.

195 *Je* can be either masculine or feminine, depending on the sex of the speaker, e.g. *Je suis heureux* (masc.), *Je suis heureuse* (fem.) 'I am happy'. Likewise, *nous* can be either masculine or feminine, e.g. *Nous sommes heureux/heureuses* 'We are happy' (when *nous* includes persons of both sexes, the masculine agreement is used).

196 *Tu* refers to one person only and is normally used only when addressing a friend, a relative, a child, God, or an animal; used in other contexts it can be (and can be intended to be) offensive. Note that, whereas the corresponding English form *thou* has long since gone out of use (except in some dialects and sometimes in poetic or religious style), the use of *tu* is, if anything, on the increase, particularly among young people.

Those to whom one does not say *tu* are addressed as *vous*, which is therefore both singular and plural depending on whether one is addressing one person or more than one; whether it is singular or plural makes no difference to the verb, but adjectives and participles vary both for gender and for number, e.g. *Vous êtes fou* (masculine singular)/*folle* (feminine singular)/*fous* (masculine plural)/*folles* (feminine plural) 'You're crazy'. (As with *nous*, when *vous* includes persons of both sexes, the masculine agreement is used.)

197 Masculine nouns, whether relating to humans, animals, abstractions or inanimate objects, are referred to as *il* and feminine nouns as *elle; il* and *elle* therefore both mean 'it' as well as 'he' and 'she' respectively, e.g. *Où est ma cuiller? Elle est sur la table* 'Where is my spoon? It's on the table'. When 'they' refers to persons of both sexes or to nouns of both genders, *ils* is used.

Conjunctive personal pronouns

198 The forms of the conjunctive personal pronouns are as follows:

subject	direct object	indirect object	
je, I	*me*, me	*me*, to me	
tu, you	*te*, you	*te*, to you	
il, he, it	*le*, him, it	*lui*, to him ⎤	sometimes
elle, she, it	*la*, her, it	*lui*, to her ⎦	'to it', see **200**
nous, we	*nous*, us	*nous*, to us	
vous, you	*vous*, you	*vous*, to you	
ils, they (masc.)	*les*, them	*leur*, to them	
elles, they (fem.)	*les*, them	*leur*, to them	

(For the terms 'direct object' and 'indirect object', see **17, 18** and **21**.)

With reference to things, the indirect object is often expressed by *y* rather than by *lui* or *leur* – see **200**.

Je, me, te, le and *la* become *j'*, *m'*, *t'* and *l'* before a verb beginning with a vowel or mute *h* and before *y* or *en*, e.g. *J'arrive* 'I arrive', *M'aimes-tu?* 'Do you love me?', *Il l'achète* 'He buys it'.

199 With reflexive verbs, *se* (which becomes *s'* before a vowel) takes the place of *le, la, les, lui* and *leur*; *me, te, nous, vous* also serve as reflexive pronouns, e.g.:

je me lave
I wash myself

vous vous fatiguez
you are tiring yourself

il s'est blessé
he has injured himself

elle s'est blessée
she has injured herself

ils se sont blessés
they have injured themselves

elles se sont blessées
they have injured themselves

il s'est fait mal
he has done harm to (i.e. hurt) himself

elle s'est fait mal
she has done harm to (i.e. hurt) herself

ils se sont fait mal
they have done harm to (i.e. hurt) themselves

elles se sont fait mal
they have done harm to (i.e. hurt) themselves

For the use of *soi* see **219**.
For the reciprocal use of reflexive pronouns see **292**.

200 *Y* is commonly used as an adverb of place meaning 'there'.
As a pronoun it may be used, of things only, instead of *lui* and *leur*. But even of things it should not always be thus used. *Lui* and *leur* are to be preferred when the thing or things in question can be regarded as having a kind of personal existence.

Examples:

> *Venez me chercher au bureau; j'y vais tout à l'heure, et j'y serai jusqu'à midi*
> Come and pick me up at the office; I am going there shortly, and I shall be there till 12

> *Il m'a raconté une longue histoire, mais je n'y ai pas fait attention*
> He told me a long story, but I paid no attention to it

> *Il éprouvait pour* $\left\{ \begin{array}{l} \textit{sa machine} \\ \textit{ses machines} \end{array} \right\}$ *un véritable amour, et*
>
> $\left. \begin{array}{l} \textit{lui} \\ \textit{leur} \end{array} \right\}$ *attribuait beaucoup de son succès*
> He was literally in love with his machine(s) and attributed to it/them much of his success

It is not always easy to decide when 'to it' or 'to them' with reference to things should be *y* and when *lui* or *leur*, but the following indications will cover the great majority of cases:

(i) *y* is used:

(a) with reflexive verbs, e.g. *Il s'y accrochait* 'He was clinging to it'

(b) with the following verbs:

accoutumer, accustom	*prétendre*, lay claim to
appeler, summon	*réfléchir*, to think, reflect
aspirer, aspire	*renoncer*, renounce
habituer, accustom	*songer*, reflect
penser, think	*viser*, aim

e.g.:

> *Ils n'aiment pas la mer; il faudra les y habituer*
> They dislike the sea; we must get them used to it

> *J'y pensais*   I was thinking about it

Note that, with reference to people, these verbs take the preposition *à* and the disjunctive pronouns *lui, elle, eux, elles*, not the conjunctive indirect object pronouns *lui* and *leur*, e.g. *je pensais à lui, . . . à eux* 'I was thinking about him, . . . about them'.

(c) when the English 'it' refers, not to a particular noun, but to the general idea expressed in a previous sentence, e.g.:

Ne partez pas. Rien ne vous y oblige.
Don't leave. Nothing obliges you to (do so).

(d) when 'it' refers to a particular noun, provided that this noun is not personified (see below), e.g.:

Ce bruit ne me dérange pas – je n'y fais pas attention.
That noise doesn't disturb me – I pay no attention to it (I don't notice it).

(ii) *Lui* or *leur* are used when the English 'it' or 'them' refers to a particular noun, if this noun can be regarded as being, in the faintest degree, a living agent, or as having some sort of personality of its own, e.g.:

Je suis heureux de $\left\{ \begin{array}{l} \textit{ma maladie} \\ \textit{mes malheurs} \end{array} \right\}$, *puisque je* $\left\{ \begin{array}{l} \textit{lui} \\ \textit{leur} \end{array} \right\}$

dois votre amitié

I am glad of $\left\{ \begin{array}{l} \text{my illness} \\ \text{my misfortunes} \end{array} \right\}$ since I owe to $\left\{ \begin{array}{l} \text{it} \\ \text{them} \end{array} \right\}$

your friendship

On the whole, this use of *y* is less common than it was. In this connection a passage quoted from Mme de Sévigné in the *Grammaire Larousse du XXᵉ Siècle* is interesting. She wrote, in the 17th century:

Mes pauvres lettres n'ont de prix que celui que vous y donnez
The value which you set on them is the only value my poor letters have

and the authors of the grammar point out that in modern French *y* would here be replaced by *leur*, the letters being, as it were, personified.

201 There is one other conjunctive pronoun, namely *en* (not to be confused with the preposition *en* (see **654–658**), which is a totally different word), meaning 'of it, of them' or 'from there'. *En* is used mainly of animals and things, only rarely of people. When not referring to people:

(i) It takes the place of a personal pronoun of the third person (whatever the gender or number) governed by *de* 'of, about', etc., e.g.:

> *Avez-vous vu sa nouvelle maison? Oui, nous en parlions tout à l'heure*
> Have you seen his new house? Yes, we were talking of it just now
>
> *Avez-vous vu les éléphants? Oui, nous en parlions tout à l'heure*
> Have you seen the elephants? Yes, we were talking of them just now

but with reference to people:

> *Connaissez-vous Henri? Nous parlions de lui tout à l'heure*
> Do you know Henry? We were talking of him just now
>
> *Connaissez-vous Madeleine? Nous parlions d'elle tout à l'heure*
> Do you know Madeleine? We were talking about her just now

(ii) In partitive constructions, it serves as a pronominal equivalent of *de* + a noun, with the value of 'some of it (*or* of them)', or 'any of it (*or* of them)'; and note that, though 'of it, of them' is frequently omitted in English, *en* must be inserted in French, e.g.:

> *Avez-vous du pain? – Oui, j'en ai acheté*
> Have you any bread? – Yes, I've bought some
>
> *Voulez-vous de la bière? – Oui, s'il y en a*
> Do you want some beer? – Yes, if there is any
>
> *Si vous voulez des billets, je peux vous en donner*
> If you want tickets, I can give you some
>
> *Comment! Ils n'ont pas d'argent! Donnez-leur-en; moi, je n'en ai pas*
> What! They have no money! Give them some; I haven't got any

(iii) Where numerals and expressions of quantity are concerned, *en* is inserted in French, often without any English equivalent, provided that the numeral or expression of quantity is either the object or the complement of a verb.

Note that here too, as in (ii) above, the *en* cannot be omitted, e.g.:

> *Voici des billets de vingt francs; je leur en donnerai dix*
> Here are some twenty-franc notes; I will give them ten (of them)

> *C'est ici le beurre que je désire? Eh bien! J'en prends deux kilos*
> Is this the butter I want? Very well! I will have two kilos (of it)

> *La plupart des gens voudraient avoir plus d'argent qu'ils n'en ont*
> Most people would like more money than they have

Note that this use of *en* also applies to people (contrast i above), e.g.:

> *Combien d'enfants avez-vous? – J'en ai quatre*
> How many children have you? – I have four

(iv) It is used, with nouns that denote neither number nor quantity, as the genitive of the neuter pronoun – 'its, of it, their, of them'; in this case, the noun in French is always preceded by the definite article, e.g.:

> *Regardez donc ce toit en béton; le poids en est immense*
> Look at this concrete roof; its weight (*or* the weight of it) is immense

(v) It sometimes has the value of 'for that reason, for that, for it', e.g. :

> *S'il a fait ça, je l'en déteste d'autant plus*
> If he did that, I hate him all the more (for it)

> *S'il ne revient qu'après dix ans, il n'en sera pas moins le bienvenu*
> If he does not come back for ten years, he will be none the less welcome (for that)

(vi) With verbs such as *(re)venir* 'to come (back)', *rentrer* 'to return', *arriver* 'to arrive', *partir* 'to leave, go away', *sortir* 'to go out', it is used in the sense of 'thence, from there', e.g.:

> *J'ai passé une semaine à Paris; j'en reviens à l'instant*
> I have spent a week in Paris; I am just back from there

The position of conjunctive personal pronouns

Subject

202 The subject pronoun normally comes before the verb; however, it follows the verb

(i) in certain types of questions (see **583–584, 589–592**)

(ii) in certain non-interrogative constructions (see **476–478, 596, 599–600**)

As a rule the subject pronoun is best repeated with each verb; but, provided both verbs are in the same tense, it may be omitted with *et, mais* and *ou* (see examples in **210**), and generally is with *ni* 'nor' (see **571**).

No subject is expressed with verbs in the imperative (see **514**).

Pronouns other than subject pronouns

203 Note the insertion in French of object pronouns and of *y* and *en* where their equivalents are merely implied in English, e.g.:

Qui vous l'a dit?   Who told you (it, *or* so)?

J'aime ceux-là; j'en prendrai une demi-douzaine
I like those; I'll take half a dozen (of them)

Quand allez-vous à Paris? J'y vais demain
When are you going to Paris? I'm going (there) tomorrow

204 Except with the affirmative imperative (see **207**), the pronouns stand immediately before the verb of which they are the object, e.g.:

Je t'aime	I love you
La connaissez-vous?	Do you know her?
Mon frère leur écrit souvent	My brother often writes to them
J'en prends six	I'll take six of them
Nous n'y allons pas	We are not going there
Ne les perdez pas	Don't lose them
Nous voulons les vendre	We want to sell them

(In the last of the above examples, 'them' is the object of 'sell' not of 'wish' and so, in accordance with the rule, comes immediately before the infinitive *vendre* 'to sell'.)

In the case of compound tenses (see **448–456**) the pronouns come before the auxiliary and are *never* placed immediately before the past participle, e.g.:

Je vous ai écrit	I have written to you
Ne les avez-vous pas trouvés?	Haven't you found them?
Mon père y est allé	My father has gone there

Exceptions will be found with *faire, laisser* and verbs of the senses – see **209** – and with *envoyer* followed by *chercher* or *dire*, e.g. *Je le lui enverrai dire* 'I will send him word of it', *Je l'enverrai chercher* 'I will send (to look) for him'.

205 In a negative sentence, the *ne* stands immediately before the object pronouns, e.g. *Je ne les aime pas* 'I don't like them'.

206 When there is more than one object pronoun, they stand in the following order:

1 *me, te, se, nous, vous*
2 *le, la, les*
3 *lui, leur*
4 *y*
5 *en*

Examples:

Je vous le donnerai	I will give it to you
Je le lui ai donné	I have given it to her
Me le donnez-vous?	Are you giving it to me?
Les lui a-t-il donnés?	Has he given them to him?
Ne nous les donnez pas	Do not give them to us

Note:

(a) that it is not possible for more than one member of any of groups 1 to 3 above to occur with the same verb (see **208**)

(b) that, though it is possible for up to three of the above pronouns to occur together provided they are from different groups (e.g. *Je m'y en achète* 'I buy some for myself there'), in practice this very rarely happens.

207 With the affirmative imperative (see **514**):

(a) all pronouns follow the verb

(b) *moi* and *toi* are used instead of *me* and *te* except with *en* and *y* (see below)

(c) direct object precedes indirect object

(d) *y* and *en* come last

(e) except for elided forms (*m'*, *t'*, *l'*), pronouns are linked to the verb and to one another by hyphens.

Examples:

Croyez-moi	Believe me
Prends-en	Take some (of it, of them)
Donnez-le-moi	Give it to me
Envoyez-nous-y	Send us there
Prêtez-leur-en	Lend them some
Donnez-m'en	Give me some
Menez-l'y	Take him (*or* her) there
Va-t'en!	Go away!

208 It is not possible to combine:

(i) any two of *me, te, se, nous, vous* (see **206**, note a), or

(ii) any of *me, te, se, nous, vous* as direct object with *lui* or *leur* as indirect object.

In circumstances that might seem to require one of these impossible constructions, the direct object pronoun follows the ordinary rule but the indirect object is expressed by *à* 'to' and a disjunctive pronoun (see **215–220**), e.g.:

Il vous présentera à moi
He will introduce you to me

Voulez-vous me présenter à elles?
Will you introduce me to them?

Présentez-moi à eux si vous les voyez
Introduce me to them if you see them

Nous ne voulons pas nous rendre à lui
We will not surrender to him

Ils se sont rendus à nous
They surrendered to us

209 Conjunctive pronouns governed by an infinitive stand immediately before the infinitive, not before the verb on which it depends; e.g.:

Il n'osera jamais vous le dire
He will never dare say it to you

But *faire, laisser* and verbs of the senses (see **430–438**) are exceptions to this rule, e.g.:

J'aime cette chanson; je la lui ferai chanter
I like this song; I will get him to sing it

210 Conjunctive pronouns governed by more than one verb must be repeated with each verb; e.g.:

Je les crains et je les tiens pour malhonnêtes
I fear them and consider them dishonest

except

(a) when the two verbs convey much the same idea, e.g.:

Je les crains et je les déteste, or *et les déteste,* or *et déteste*
I fear and loathe them

(b) in compound tenses, when the auxiliary is regularly understood with the second participle, e.g.:

Je les ai toujours craints et tenus pour malhonnêtes
I have always feared them and considered them dishonest

Le, or la, les or invariable le?

211 *Le, la, les* (variable) or *le* (invariable) are used in French to refer to something just mentioned, where English often has no corresponding pronoun or other word (though 'so' may sometimes be inserted).

212 *Le, la, les* (variable) always refer to some noun already mentioned. This must be a noun used in a definite sense, i.e. a proper name or a noun preceded by the definite article or by a demonstrative, interrogative or possessive determiner. The pronoun (*le, la, les*) agrees with this noun in gender and number, e.g.:

Elle n'est pas sa femme et elle ne la sera jamais
She is not his wife and she never will be

Êtes-vous les marins qui ont été naufragés? – Nous les sommes
Are you the sailors who have been shipwrecked? – We are

But this is an exclusively literary construction; i.e. it is not used in speech which, instead, in contexts like these would be likely either to repeat the noun (. . . *elle ne sera jamais sa femme*) or to use the invariable *le* (. . . *elle ne le sera jamais* – see **213**) or to use some other expression (e.g. *Oui, c'est nous*).

Le, la, les must also be inserted when the object is put before the verb for the sake of emphasis, e.g.:

$\left.\begin{array}{l} Ces \\ Les \\ Mes \end{array}\right\}$ *bijoux que vous convoitez tant, vous ne les aurez jamais*

$\left.\begin{array}{l} These \\ The \\ My \end{array}\right\}$ jewels which you covet so much you will never get

Ta sœur je la connais!
Your sister I know! (or 'I know your sister' with some emphasis on 'sister')

213   *Le* (invariable) refers to

(i) a noun used in a general sense, i.e. qualified by an indefinite article if singular, a partitive article if plural, e.g.:

Les Cinq-Ports étaient autrefois des places fortes; ils ne le sont plus
The Cinque Ports were formerly fortresses; they are so no longer

(ii) a noun denoting nationality, profession, rank or title – **35,i,b** – except when qualified by a definite article, e.g.:

Est-elle étudiante? Elle le sera l'année prochaine
Is she a student? She will be next year

(iii) an adjective or participle, e.g.:

Sont-elles fâchées? Elles le sont
Are they angry? They are

(iv) the general idea expressed in the previous sentence, e.g.:

Qui sait où il est? Moi, je le sais
Who knows where he is? I do

Notre malade va mieux aujourd'hui? Je l'espère
Is our patient better today? I hope so

This invariable *le* is also inserted:

(v) in short parenthetic sentences, such as 'I admit', 'I know', 'I see', e.g.:

Son explication n'est pas très lucide, je l'avoue
His explanation is not very clear, I admit

(vi) in the second half of a comparison, e.g.:

Vous êtes plus intelligent que je ne le pensais (for the *ne* see 563)
You are cleverer than I thought

(vii) with adverbial clauses (i.e. clauses introduced by a conjunction) when in English 'it', 'so', or some such word might be inserted, or the verb might be repeated in the infinitive without making nonsense, e.g.:

Je viendrai dès qu'on me le permettra
I will come as soon as I am allowed (to come)

Je le ferai si vous le désirez
I will do it if you wish (it, or me to do it)

So too with *comme*, e.g.:

Je suis essoufflé, comme vous le voyez (or *comme vous voyez*)
I am out of breath, as you see

214 Conversely, after certain verbs of thinking (*croire, juger, trouver*) the 'it' of the English is not expressed in French when the complement of the verb of thinking is an adjective followed by a clause introduced by *que*, or by an infinitive governed by a preposition, e.g.:

Je trouve bon que vous partiez après-demain
I think it well that you should leave the day after to-morrow

J'aurais cru impossible de faire gravir une telle pente à une auto
I should have thought it impossible to get a car up such a gradient

Disjunctive personal pronouns

215 The disjunctive pronouns are:

moi, I, me

nous, we, us

toi, you

vous, you

lui, he, him

eux, they, them (masc.)

elle, she, her

elles, they, them (fem.)

They can be combined with *-même(s)* as follows:

moi-même, myself

nous-mêmes, ourselves

toi-même, yourself

vous-même, yourself

vous-mêmes, yourselves

lui-même, himself

eux-mêmes, themselves (masc.)

elle-même, herself

elles-mêmes, themselves (fem.)

They can function, in the circumstances discussed below, as subject of a verb, as direct object, or as the complement of a preposition; when preceded by the preposition *à*, they can function as an indirect object.

216 The disjunctive pronouns are used:

(i) to add emphasis to a conjunctive pronoun (as conjunctive pronouns cannot themselves bear any emphasis); this is done by adding a disjunctive pronoun at the beginning or end of the phrase, in apposition to the conjunctive pronoun to be emphasized. If the latter stands for the indirect object, then the disjunctive pronoun is preceded by *à*, e.g.:

Toi, tu feras ce que tu voudras: lui, il reste ici
You can do what you like: *he*'s staying here

Moi, je le préfère lui
I prefer *him*

Je ne le lui dirai pas à lui (à elle)
I won't tell *him* (*her*)

This disjunctive pronoun is also inserted where the only emphasis in English is that the actions, words, etc., of two people, or sets of people, are contrasted with one another, e.g.:

Moi, je vais en Écosse demain; mon frère ne me rejoindra que plus tard
I am going to Scotland tomorrow; my brother will not join me till later

Note too the use of disjunctive *nous, vous* + *autres* as emphatic forms, particularly when there is an expressed implied distinction between 'us' or 'you' on the one hand and some other group (or other people in general) on the other, e.g.:

Nous autres Français, nous mangeons beaucoup de pain
We French eat a lot of bread

Vous n'êtes jamais contents, vous autres fermiers
You farmers are never content

Nous n'aimons pas ça, nous autres
We do not like that

(ii) when the subject of a verb consists of two pronouns, or of a noun and a pronoun. (See Composite Subject, **392.**)

(iii) as complement of *être* when the subject is *ce*. (See **255** and **258.**)

(iv) when a personal pronoun is governed by any preposition, e.g.:

Nous y sommes allés avec eux
We went there with them

Il était assis entre elle et moi
He was sitting between her and me

(v) when the direct or indirect object pronoun is governed by *ne . . . que . . .* 'only', e.g.:

Je ne connais que lui
I only know him (i.e. him only)

Je n'obéirai qu'à eux
I will only obey them (i.e. them only)

(vi) when the French pronoun is the subject or object of a verb not expressed, but understood from what precedes. In English some verb is usually expressed, e.g.:

Qui a cassé la fenêtre? A vrai dire, moi
Who broke the window? To tell the truth, I (did)

Mon frère est plus intelligent que moi
My brother is cleverer than I (am)

Vous pouvez le comprendre, peut-être; moi non
You can understand it, perhaps; but not I (I cannot)

Qui a-t-on puni pour ça? Moi
Whom did they punish for that? Me

(vii) with an infinitive in exclamations, e.g.:

Lui, nous trahir!   *He* betray us! (see **429**)

217 The third person disjunctive pronouns are sometimes used as the direct subjects of a verb (i.e. in the absence of the corresponding conjunctive pronoun), e.g.:

Les autres l'ignoraient, mais lui le savait
The others were unaware of it, but *he* knew

Nous, nous étions trop loin, mais eux l'ont vu
We were too far away, but *they* saw it

This is not possible in the case of the other disjunctive pronouns, with which the corresponding conjunctive pronoun must be inserted as grammatical subject (see examples in **216**,i, above); this is true even for *nous* and *vous* whose conjunctive and disjunctive forms are the same (see the example with *nous* quoted above).

218 It may be difficult to decide whether to use *de* + the disjunctive pronoun or the possessive determiner. English usage and French usage do not always coincide, e.g.:

à sa vue   at the sight of him
à cause de moi   for my sake

When met with, such differences of idiom should be noted, though, in reality, they are usually only the result of a confusion between a paraphrase and a translation, e.g.:

à sa vue may be rendered 'on his appearance'
à cause de moi may be rendered 'because of me'

219 The reflexive disjunctive pronoun *soi* and its compound *soi-même* are normally used only when they refer to some indefinite subject, such as *chacun, nul, personne, on*, or when the sense of a noun or adjective on which *soi* depends is applied to people in general, e.g.:

On ne devrait pas penser toujours à soi
One ought not to be always thinking of oneself

Il n'est pas naturel de se faire du mal à soi
It is not natural to do harm to oneself

C'est une vertu que d'être mécontent de soi
Self-discontent is a virtue

Il ne faut pas être trop fier de soi (or *soi-même*)
We must not be too proud of ourselves

Chacun pour soi
Everyone for himself

l'approbation de soi
self-approval

Otherwise, the pronouns *lui, elle, eux, elles*, or their compounds *lui-même*, etc. (see **215**), should be used, e.g.:

Il est très fier de lui(-même)
He is very proud of himself

Elle ne pense qu'à elle(-même)
She only thinks of herself

Ceux qui sont mécontents d'eux-mêmes peuvent faire des progrès
Those who are dissatisfied with themselves may improve

(Some modern authors affect the archaic use of *soi* with reference to a definite subject, e.g. *Elle pensait à soi* 'She was thinking of herself', but this usage should not be imitated.)

220   Note also the use of the disjunctive pronoun after *à*:

(i) with verbs of motion such as *aller* 'to go', *courir* 'to run', *accourir* 'to run up, rush', *marcher* 'to walk', *venir* 'to come', when no idea is suggested but that of physical motion towards (but this does not apply to *envoyer* 'to send' except in the kind of circumstances dealt with in **208**), e.g.:

Il vient à moi   He comes to me
Ils ont accouru à nous   They ran up to us

and likewise *appeler* 'to summon' (i.e. make someone come), e.g.:

Elle appela les enfants à elle	She called the children to her

but:

Il me les a envoyés	He sent them to me

(This rule does not apply when no physical motion is implied, e.g. *l'idée m'est venue que* . . . 'the idea came to me that . . .'.)

(ii) with a few other verbs such as *en appeler à* 'to appeal to' (in the sense of 'make an appeal to'), *penser à, songer à* 'to think of', *recourir à* 'to resort to, turn to, appeal to', *renoncer à* 'to renounce, give up', and *être à* 'to belong to', e.g.:

J'en appelle à vous	I appeal to you
Elle pense à moi	She is thinking of me
Elle renonça à lui	She gave him up
Ce livre est à elle	This book belongs to her (is hers)

(iii) with *avoir affaire à* 'to have to do with, to deal with', *avoir recours à* 'to have recourse to', *faire attention à* 'to pay attention to', and a few other such phrases, e.g.:

J'ai toujours recours à lui
I always turn to him

Il ne fait jamais attention à moi
He never pays attention to me

Adverb replacing preposition + pronoun

221 Where English has a preposition governing 'it' or 'them' referring to things, French often puts an adverb, if a suitable one exists; e.g.:

J'arriverai à temps; vous pouvez compter là-dessus (alternative to *y compter*)
I shall arrive in time, you may depend on it

Il y avait un grand feu avec un garde-feu devant (instead of *devant lui*)
There was a big fire with a fire-guard in front of it

Possessive determiners and pronouns

Introduction

222 French, like English, has two sets of possessives, each having different functions, viz.:

(i) possessive determiners (see 23) (more frequently but less satisfactorily known as 'possessive adjectives'), corresponding to English *my, your*, etc. (see 223–226)

(ii) possessive pronouns, corresponding to English *mine, yours*, etc. (see 231–233)

Possessive determiners

223 The possessive determiners in French are:

masc. sing.	fem. sing.	masc. and fem. plur.	
mon	*ma*	*mes*	my
ton	*ta*	*tes*	your
son	*sa*	*ses*	his, her, its
notre	*notre*	*nos*	our
votre	*votre*	*vos*	your
leur	*leur*	*leurs*	their

These always stand before the noun, or the adjective and noun, that they qualify.

They agree with that noun – the thing possessed, not the possessor – in gender and number.

Before a noun or adjective beginning with a vowel or mute *h*, *mon, ton, son*, are used in the feminine instead of *ma, ta, sa*, e.g. *mon idée* 'my idea', *son habileté* 'his skill'.

The distinction between *ton*, etc., and *votre*, etc., corresponds to that between *tu* and *vous* (see 196).

Examples:

> *mon frère* 'my brother', *ta sœur* or *votre sœur* 'your sister', *ses amis* 'his, or her, friends', *nos enfants* 'our children', *leur mère* 'their mother', *leurs vastes terres* 'their vast domains'

(observe that *leur* does not add *e* for the feminine). *Chaque race a ses particularités* 'Every race has its peculiarities'.

In cases such as *son chien, sa maison, ses amis*, where the context does not make it clear whether *son, sa, ses*, mean 'his' or 'her', the disjunctive pronoun with *à* may be inserted after the noun, e.g.:

sa mère à lui, non pas à elle	his, not her, mother
Il a adopté ses enfants à elle	He adopted her children

224 The possessive determiners are used much as in English, except that in most cases they must be repeated with each noun, e.g.:

mon père et ma mère
my father and mother

ma plume et mon crayon
my pen and pencil

mon chapeau et mon pardessus
my hat and coat

But this repetition is unnecessary

(i) if the two nouns mean practically the same thing and are connected by *ou* 'or', e.g.:

Ils passent leurs vacances dans leur appartement ou studio à Paris
They spend their holidays in their flat or flatlet in Paris

(ii) with a few pairs of nouns, alike in sense and together expressing a single idea, e.g.:

ses allées et venues
his comings and goings

en mon âme et conscience
from the bottom of my heart

ses faits et gestes
his exploits and achievements
vos nom et prénoms
your full name

à vos risques et périls
at your own risk

225 The possessive must also usually be repeated with each adjective when a noun is qualified by two adjectives the sense of which is contradictory; but when the second adjective only denotes a further quality of the same person or thing, the possessive is not repeated, e.g.:

Ma meilleure et ma pire performance diffèrent de dix secondes
My best and worst performance differ by ten seconds (obviously two different performances)

Sa pâle et blême figure m'a accablé d'horreur
Her pale, wan face filled me with dismay (only one face)

226 The first person singular possessives *mon*, etc., are used in certain circumstances when addressing someone; in particular:

(i) as a sign of familiarity or affection; e.g. a parent speaking to his or her son or daughter may well use the forms *mon fils* and *ma fille* (where English would probably just use their names), or, speaking to one's children in general, *mes enfants* (which could also be used by a teacher addressing a class); likewise *mon vieux!* 'old chap!', *mon ange!* '(my) angel!'

(ii) as a sign of respect or deference, e.g. *mon père* 'father' (i.e. when one of his children is speaking), or 'Father' (i.e. with reference to a Catholic priest), *mon oncle* 'uncle', *ma tante* 'aunt', etc., and, in the army, when addressing those of higher rank (i.e. where 'Sir!' would be used in English), e.g. a captain and a colonel would be addressed as *mon capitaine* and *mon colonel* respectively by their inferiors, but as *capitaine* and *colonel* by their superiors and by civilians. This practice is at the origin of the forms *monsieur* (originally = 'my lord'), *madame, mademoiselle* (whose plurals are still formed in *mes*, viz. *messieurs, mesdames, mesdemoiselles*) and the ecclesiastical title *monseigneur,* plur. *messeigneurs.*

227 When the English words 'its' or (unless referring to people) 'their' qualify a noun which is the direct object of a verb or the complement of *être, devenir, paraître* or *sembler*, both words are generally translated by *en* (pronoun) rather than by a possessive adjective. In such cases the noun requires the definite article, e.g.:

Je suis entré dans la bibliothèque afin d'en consulter le catalogue
I went into the library in order to use its catalogue

Le proviseur du lycée en connaît tous les élèves
The headmaster of the school knows all its pupils

Cette robe est très jolie mais les manches en sont trop courtes
That dress is very pretty but its sleeves are too short

*Il achetait des livres afin d'en dévorer le contenu plutôt que
d'en admirer la reliure*
He bought books in order to master their contents rather
than to admire their bindings

228   With reference to parts of the body, French commonly uses
the definite article where English uses the possessive determiner.
Two different constructions have to be noted:

(i) When the reference is to something the subject does *with* a part
of his body, the definite article alone is used, e.g.:

J'ai ouvert les yeux
I opened my eyes

Elle hausse les épaules
She shrugs her shoulders

Ils étendirent les bras
They stretched out their arms

and likewise with *fermer la bouche* (*les yeux*) 'to close one's mouth
(eyes)', *grincer des dents* 'to grind one's teeth', *lever la main* 'to put
one's hand up', *secouer la tête* 'to shake one's head', etc. Cf. too
expressions such as *avoir mal aux dents, . . . à la gorge, . . . à la
tête, . . . aux reins* 'to have toothache, a sore throat, a headache,
backache', etc. However, when the part of the body is in any way
qualified, the possessive is used, e.g. *Elle ouvrit ses grands yeux
bleus* 'She opened her big blue eyes'.

(ii) When the reference is to something one does *to* a part of one's
body, the reflexive pronoun (functioning as an indirect object) is
used, as in *Elle se lave les cheveux* 'She washes her hair (*lit*. She
washes the hair to herself)'; cf.:

Vous vous êtes cassé le bras	You have broken your arm
Je me suis coupé le doigt	I have cut my.finger
Elle s'est tordu le bras	She wrenched her arm

A similar construction, using the indirect object pronoun referring to the person affected, occurs when the action is something
one does to a part of someone else's body, e.g.:

Il m'a tordu le bras   He twisted my arm
Elle lui lave les cheveux   She washes his hair
Il lui a craché à la figure   He spat in his face

229   With some verbs two different constructions are possible, e.g.:

Elle s'est $\left\{ \begin{array}{l} \textit{blessée} \\ \textit{brûlée} \end{array} \right\}$ *au genou*

She has $\left\{ \begin{array}{l} \text{hurt} \\ \text{burnt} \end{array} \right\}$ her knee

(*lit.* 'she has hurt/burnt herself in the knee' – *se* is a direct object and so the past participle agrees with it, see **461**), or alternatively:

Elle s'est $\left\{ \begin{array}{l} \textit{blessé} \\ \textit{brûlé} \end{array} \right\}$ *le genou*

(*lit.* 'She has hurt/burnt the knee to herself' – *se* is an indirect object and so the past participle does not agree.)

230   Similarly in describing the circumstances attendant on some action the French definite article may replace an English possessive determiner, e.g.:

Il est entré dans le salon le chapeau sur la tête, la pipe aux dents et les mains dans les poches
He entered the drawing-room with his hat on his head, his pipe in his mouth and his hands in his pockets

Possessive pronouns

231   The French possessive pronouns are

masc. sing.	fem. sing.	masc. plur.	fem. plur.	
le mien	*la mienne*	*les miens*	*les miennes*	mine
le tien	*la tienne*	*les tiens*	*les tiennes*	yours
le sien	*la sienne*	*les siens*	*les siennes*	his, hers
le nôtre	*la nôtre*	*les nôtres*	*les nôtres*	ours
le vôtre	*la vôtre*	*les vôtres*	*les vôtres*	yours
le leur	*la leur*	*les leurs*	*les leurs*	theirs

232   (i) They agree in gender and number with the noun they replace, e.g.:

Ma maison est mieux construite que la leur
My house is better built than theirs

(ii) They may be used as nouns in certain expressions such as:

in the singular: *il y met du sien*, which may mean, according to the context, 'he puts his best into it', or 'he embellishes' (a story);

in the plural:

Les nôtres ont bien joué	Our side played well
Il est des nôtres	He is one of us

(iii) After any part of *être*, 'mine, yours', etc., are usually rendered by *à moi, à vous*, etc. (i.e. 'it belongs to me' rather than 'it is mine'), e.g.:

Ces livres-ci sont à moi
These books are mine

Laquelle de ces clefs est à vous?
Which of these keys is yours?

However, when a contrast is being drawn not so much between two possessors (as in, for example, *Ces livres-ci sont à lui, les autres sont à nous* 'These books are his, the others are ours') as between two sets of things possessed, *le mien*, etc., are used, e.g.:

Ces livres-ci sont les vôtres; les miens sont en bas
These books are yours; mine are downstairs

233 The forms listed in 231 also occur very occasionally without the definite article as adjectives, in particular:

(i) in such expressions as *faire sien* 'to adopt as one's own', *regarder comme sien* 'to consider as one's own', e.g. *Je fais mienne votre réponse* 'I adopt your answer as my own', *Il regardait comme siens tous les revenus de sa femme* 'He considered all his wife's income as his own';

(ii) in the archaic construction, that one still sometimes comes across, *un* or *ce* + demonstrative + noun, e.g. *un mien ami* 'a friend of mine', *ce mien ami* 'this friend of mine'; the normal equivalents of these are *un ami à moi* (or, with a slightly different meaning, *un de mes amis* 'one of my friends') and *cet ami à moi*.

Demonstrative determiners and pronouns

Introduction

234 Unlike English, which uses *this* and *that*, *these* and *those*, both as déterminers (see **23**) and as pronouns, French (as in the case of the possessives, see **222, 223, 231**) has two sets of demonstratives, each having different functions, viz.:

(i) demonstrative determiners (more usually but less satisfactorily known as demonstrative adjectives) (see **235–237**)

(ii) demonstrative pronouns (see **238**)

Demonstrative determiners

235 The demonstrative determiners in French, meaning both 'this/these' and 'that/those' (see **237**) are:

masc. sing.	fem. sing.	plur.
ce, cet	*cette*	*ces*

In the masculine singular, *ce* is used except before a vowel or mute *h* when *cet* is used, e.g. *ce livre* 'this/that book', *cet arbre* 'this/that tree', *ce soldat* 'this soldier', *cet ancien soldat* 'this former soldier', *cet homme* 'this man'.

Note that, as in the case of the other principal determiners, viz. the articles *les* and *des* (**24**) and the possessives, *mes, nos*, etc. (**223**), there is no distinction of gender in the plural.

236 The determiners are used as in English, except that in English the demonstrative may qualify more than one noun at a time, whereas in French it is repeated with each noun in turn, e.g.:

ce monsieur	this (that) gentleman
cet homme	this (that) man
cette femme	this (that) woman
cette idée	this (that) idea
ces arbres	these (those) trees (masc.)
ces maisons	these (those) houses (fem.)

Ces fleurs et ces arbres sont très jolis
These flowers and trees are very pretty

237 The French determiners mean both 'this/these' and 'that/those'. It is possible to make a distinction comparable to the English one by adding after the noun either *-ci* (an archaic form of *ici* 'here') for 'this/these' or *-là* (= 'there') for 'that/those', e.g. *ces jours-ci* 'these days', *ce jour-là* 'that day', but this is usually not necessary. Indeed, it is frequently not only unnecessary but incorrect to add *-ci* or *-là* to the noun. They should be used *only* in the following circumstances:

(i) to express emphasis

(ii) to mark a contrast between 'this' and 'that', or 'these' and 'those'

(iii) when an object is, literally, pointed out.

Examples:

> *Ces gens-ci sont bien ennuyeux*
> These people are very tiresome

> *En laissant ces maisons-ci à droite et ces arbres-là à gauche vous y êtes*
> Leave these houses on your right and those trees on your left, and you are there

> *Qui est ce monsieur-là?*
> Who is that gentleman (there)?

Note that, in familiar speech, the forms in *-là* are frequently used instead of the forms in *-ci* when the context makes it clear what particular item is being referred to, e.g.:

> *Ce train-là va à Paris?*   Does this train go to Paris?

Demonstrative pronouns

238 Whereas, in the case of the demonstrative determiners, French often does not distinguish between 'this/these' and 'that/those' (see 237), in the case of the demonstrative pronouns strictly so called (see 245–246 for other pronouns that are sometimes also considered to be demonstratives) the distinction is compulsory and is expressed, as in the case of the determiners (see 237), by adding *-ci* or *-là* to the pronoun itself. The forms of the demonstrative pronouns are:

	masc. sing.	fem. sing.	masc. plur.	fem. plur.
this, these	*celui-ci*	*celle-ci*	*ceux-ci*	*celles-ci*
that, those	*celui-là*	*celle-là*	*ceux-là*	*celles-là*

Note that, in the singular, English frequently uses 'this one, that one' instead of 'this, that'; in French, *celui-ci, celle-là,* etc., are all that is required – do not attempt to translate the English 'one'. The gender of the pronoun is determined by that of the noun it refers to – 'this one' with reference to a book (*le livre*), for example, is *celui-ci* but with reference to a bottle (*la bouteille*) the feminine, *celle-ci,* is required. *Celui-ci,* etc., also mean 'the latter' (i.e. the one just mentioned, so, in that sense, the nearer, 'this one'), while *celui-là,* etc., mean 'the former'. Examples:

> *A qui sont ces esquisses? Celles-ci sont à moi et celles-là sont à ma cousine*
> Whose are these sketches? These are mine and those are my cousin's

> *Pourquoi ai-je deux billets? Celui-ci est à vous et celui-là est à moi*
> Why have I got two tickets? This (one) is yours, that (one) is mine

> *Laquelle de ces chemises préférez-vous? Je préfère de beaucoup celle-ci*
> Which of these shirts do you prefer? I much prefer this one

> *Marlborough et Eugène étaient presque comme deux frères; celui-ci avait plus d'audace, celui-là l'esprit plus froid et calculateur*
> Marlborough and Eugene were almost like two brothers; the latter was more impetuous, the former more coldly calculating

Celui-là, etc., are frequently used in familiar speech instead of *celui-ci,* etc., when the meaning is clear from the context (cf. 237), e.g.:

> *Quelle robe as-tu choisie? – Je prends celle-là*
> Which dress have you chosen? – I'll take this one

The neuter demonstrative pronouns

239 French has three so-called 'neuter' demonstrative pronouns, viz. *ce, ceci* and *cela* (note that the *-a* of *cela* does not have an accent).

240 *Ce.* Although *ce* is very widely used (i) when followed by a relative clause and meaning 'what, that which' (see 274), and (ii)

as the subject of *être* and meaning 'it' (see **248–261**), it has almost
entirely gone out of use as a real demonstrative. It survives as such
only in a few phrases (all of them characteristic of literary rather
than of spoken usage) such as:

sur ce
thereupon, whereupon

pour ce, pour ce faire
to this end, for this purpose

ce disant
saying this, so saying, with these words

ce faisant
doing this, doing which

and *et ce* 'and that' (in the sense of 'for the reason that', or 'and
that is true', 'I did so', etc.) as in, for example, *J'ai promis de
l'aider, et ce pour le convaincre de mon amitié* 'I promised to help
him, and that in order to convince him of my friendship').

241   *Ceci* 'this' and *cela* 'that' differ from *celui-ci, celui-là*, etc., in
that the latter refer to specific nouns that have already been
mentioned or implied and can often be rendered in English as 'this
one, that one' rather than just 'this, that' (see **238**) whereas *ceci*
and *cela* have a less specific sense. In particular, they refer:

(i) to the general content of a statement, in which case *ceci*
generally refers forward to something that still has to be stated,
whereas *cela* refers back to something already stated, e.g.:

Écoutez ceci
Listen to this (i.e. to what I have to say)

Cela n'est pas vrai
That is not true

Si vous croyez cela, vous êtes fou
If you believe that, you're crazy

*On dit qu'il va donner sa démission; mais cela me paraît peu
probable*
They say he is going to resign; but that seems to me
improbable

Note however that *ceci* refers back in the expression *ceci dit* 'that
said', as in *Ceci dit, parlons d'autre chose* 'That said, let us talk
about something else'.

Note too the construction *ceci/cela* + *de* + adjective + a noun clause, e.g.:

Le problème a ceci (cela) d'intéressant que personne ne sait ce qu'elle fera demain
The problem is interesting in this respect that (*or* what is interesting about the problem is that) no-one knows what she will do tomorrow

(ii) to some unspecified object, i.e. meaning 'this, that' not 'this one, that one' (which must be *celui-ci*, etc.), e.g.:

Je prends ceci	I'll take this
Ceci est son chef d'œuvre	This is his masterpiece
Jetez cela!	Throw that away!

242 Note:

(i) that frequently in speech and sometimes, in an informal style, in writing, *cela* is reduced to *ça*, e.g. *Ça suffit!* 'That's enough!'

(ii) that *ceci* is characteristic particularly of literary usage and is not very much used in conversational French in which it tends to be replaced by *cela*.

243 *Cela* (*ça*) is widely used as a strengthening particle in what would otherwise be one-word questions, e.g.:

Je l'ai vu ce matin. – Où cela?
I saw him this morning. – Where?

Quelqu'un me l'a dit. – Qui ça?
Someone told me. – Who (did)?

and likewise *Comment ça?* 'How?', *Pourquoi ça?* 'Why (so)?', *Quand ça?* 'When?' (but it is **not** used with *quoi?* 'what?').

244 With the verb *être* and a following noun phrase, the two parts of which *cela* originally consisted are still frequently separated, with *ce* serving as the subject of the verb and *là* coming between the verb and the noun phrase (without a hyphen); the meaning however is still 'that' (with sometimes a slight degree of emphasis), e.g.:

C'est là le problème
That's (just) the problem

C'était là ce qu'il voulait dire
That was what he meant

Est-ce là la maison dont vous parlez?
Is that the house you are talking about?

Note that this construction can also occur with a plural verb (cf. 255), e.g.:

Ce sont là les messieurs qui sont arrivés hier
Those are the gentlemen who arrived yesterday

(but the form *sont-ce* should be avoided.)

The simple demonstrative pronouns

245   The simple demonstrative pronouns, i.e. *celui, celle, ceux, celles* without *-ci* or *-là*, can no longer be used as demonstratives in the strict sense of the word, i.e. meaning 'this one, that one, these', etc. They are used as the equivalent of English 'the one(s)' (or, in the literary language, 'that, those') when standing for some previously expressed noun and followed by a defining clause or phrase. The pronoun agrees in gender and number with the noun it stands for, e.g. 'these letters and the ones I wrote yesterday' is *ces lettres et celles que j'ai écrites hier* (*celles* because it stands for *lettres* which is feminine plural).

The defining element may be:

(i) a prepositional phrase introduced by *de*, corresponding to an English phrase of the type 'that of my brother' (or, more frequently, 'my brother's' with no expressed pronoun), e.g.:

sa décision et celle du président
his decision and that of the President

Son jardin est plus grand que celui de Jean
Her garden is bigger than John's

J'aime mieux les romans de Balzac que ceux de Zola
I prefer the novels of Balzac to those of Zola

Nous mangeons ces pommes-ci ou celles de mon frère?
Shall we eat these apples or my brother's?

(ii) a relative clause (see also **246**), e.g.:

Votre maison est plus grande que celle que je viens d'acheter
Your house is bigger than the one I have just bought

ces messieurs et ceux qui arrivent demain
these gentlemen and those (the ones) who are arriving tomorrow

Ce parc n'est pas celui dont je vous ai parlé
This park isn't the one I told you about

Quelle dame cherchez-vous? Celle à qui j'ai parlé hier
Which lady are you looking for? The one I spoke to yesterday

(iii) a noun, adjective, participle, or a prepositional phrase introduced by a preposition other than *de*; however, such constructions are often considered stylistically bad, if not incorrect, and so are best avoided. So, instead of, for example:

tous ceux fonctionnaires d'état
all those who are civil servants

Le niveau qu'il a atteint est inférieur à celui nécessaire à l'obtention du diplôme
The level he reached is lower than that necessary to get the diploma

Je joins à ma lettre celle écrite par le prince (Racine)
I enclose with my letter that (the one) written by the prince

vos esquisses et celles sur la table
your sketches and those on the table

it would generally be considered preferable to write . . . *ceux qui sont fonctionnaires d'état,* . . . *celui qui est nécessaire* . . ., . . . *celle qui a été écrite par le prince* (or . . . *celle que le prince a écrite*) and . . . *celles qui sont sur la table.*

246 *Celui qui* (*que*, etc) and *ceux qui* (*que*, etc.) can also be used in a general sense, i.e. 'he who(m) . . .', 'those who(m)', e.g.:

Heureux celui qui craint le Seigneur!
Blessed is he who fears the Lord!

Ceux qui voyagent beaucoup ont de la chance
Those who travel a lot are lucky

ceux que les dieux aiment
those whom the gods love

247 In a similar construction to the use of *celui qui*, etc., in a general sense (**245**), the 'neuter' pronoun *ce*, which now rarely serves as a strict demonstrative (see **240**), frequently occurs as the antecedent of a relative clause with the meaning 'what, that which', e.g. *ce que je veux* 'what I want' (for fuller details see **274**).

c'est and il est

248 It is a curious fact that such a basic problem as how to translate the expression 'it is' into French is the source of considerable uncertainty and difficulty. No French grammar deals with it entirely adequately. Fortunately, for at least part of the problem, namely the use of *c'est* or *il est* + adjective, we now have an illuminating study in Professor Samuel N. Rosenberg's book, *Modern French Ce* (Paris and The Hague: Mouton, 1970) to which section **250** below in particular owes a lot.

The basic problem, i.e. that of distinguishing between *c'est* and *il est* as equivalents of 'it is', is complicated by two others. One is the fact that *il (est)* in French may be the equivalent either of the English impersonal 'it is', as in 'It is easy to understand him', or of 'he is' or of 'it is' with reference to a specific object, as in 'If you want my dictionary, it is on the desk'. The other is the fact that in some contexts French uses *c'est* where English uses 'he is' or 'she is' (see **251**).

We cannot hope in a few pages to deal with all facets of the problem but what follows will cover the majority of cases in which it arises.

In what follows, 'complement' refers to what comes after the verb 'to be' and 'referent' to whatever the pronoun (*ce, il, elle,* etc.) stands for; for example, in *Jean ne vient pas, il est malade* 'John isn't coming, he's ill' and *C'est beau, la neige* 'Snow is beautiful', *malade* and *beau* respectively are the complements and *Jean* and *la neige* the referents.

Finally, note that (as in, for example, *C'est beau, la neige,* above), an adjectival complement after *c'est* always agrees with *ce,* i.e. it is masculine, even if the referent is a feminine noun or a plural noun (e.g. *C'est important, les traditions* 'Traditions are important').

249 As the subject is a complicated one and a number of different rules and sub-rules are involved, it may help to simplify matters if we give a summary of the contents of sections **250-261**:

I. *C'est* or personal *il est, elle est,* etc.?

250 (i) The complement is an adjective:

(a) The referent is a person

(b) The referent is a thing

(c) The referent is an unspecified object, a neuter pronoun, an adverbial expression of place, or a phrase including a numeral

251 (ii) The complement is a noun or pronoun:

(a) *C'est*

(b) *Il est, elle est*, etc.

(c) The difference between a and b

(d) Some exceptions

252 (iii) The complement is neither an adjective nor a noun or pronoun:

(a) The referent is a person or thing

(b) The referent is *ceci* or *cela*, a noun phrase introduced by *ce qui*, etc., or the name of a place

II. *C'est* or impersonal *il est*?

253 (i) The complement is an adjective

254 (ii) With reference to the time of day

255 (iii) The complement is a noun or pronoun

256 (iv) The complement is an indirect object, adverb, adverbial phrase, or verb phrase

257 *Ce doit être, ce peut être*, etc.

III. *C'est* or *est*?

258 *C'est* is compulsory

259 *C'est* is preferred to *est*

260 Free choice between *c'est* and *est*

261 *C'est* + *que de* + infinitive

I. C'est *or personal* il est, elle est, *etc.?*

250 (i) **The complement is an adjective**

(a) The referent is a person:

Use *il est, elle est*, etc., e.g.:

> 1 *Je connais sa fille. Elle est très jolie*
>   I know his daughter. She is very pretty.

> 2 *Si mon frère arrive, il sera content de vous voir*
>   If my brother arrives, he will be pleased to see you

> 3 *Jean ne vient pas. Il est malade*
>   John isn't coming. He's ill

(b) The referent is a thing – either *c'est* or *il est, elle est*, etc., is possible, but with a difference in meaning. Generally speaking, if *il est, elle est*, etc., are used, then the adjective relates strictly to the referent, whereas, if *c'est* is used, the adjective has a somewhat wider application, referring for example, as the following examples will show, to the context of the referent as well as to the referent itself, or to the referent in a general rather than in a specific sense, or to what is implied by the referent:

> 4 *Est-ce que cette robe vous plaît? – Oui, elle est très jolie*

> 5 *Est-ce que cette robe vous plaît? – Oui, c'est très joli*

Both of these could be translated 'Do you like this dress? – Yes, it is very pretty', but whereas, in 4, *Elle est très jolie* refers only to the dress itself, there is an implication in 5, *C'est très joli*, that the general effect is pretty (the meaning borders on something like 'It looks very pretty on you').

> 6 *Regardez cette table! Elle est affreuse!*

> 7 *Regardez cette table! C'est affreux!*

Both 6 and 7 mean 'Look at that table! It's awful!', but 6 refers rather to the table itself as a piece of furniture and 7 to the table and whatever is on it, the way it is laid or decorated, etc.

> 8 *Voulez-vous du cognac? Il est très bon*
>   Would you like some cognac? It's very good

> 9 *Voulez-vous du cognac? C'est très bon pour la digestion*
>   Would you like some cognac? It's very good for the digestion

In 8, the reference is to the quality of the particular cognac that is being offered; in 9, to a quality attributed to cognac in general.

10 *Elle est belle, la neige!*
The snow is beautiful!

11 *C'est beau, la neige!*
Snow is beautiful!

In 10, the speaker is commenting on the snow that is on the ground, or falling, as he speaks and that he can see; in 11, to snow in general (and note the use of the English definite article 'the' in 10 but not in 11).

12 *Je comprends votre idée. Elle est très simple*
I understand your idea. It is very simple

13 *J'ai une idée. C'est très simple.*
I have an idea. It is very simple.

12 means specifically that the idea itself is simple; 13 has rather the meaning of 'what I have in mind is simple'.

14 *J'aime ce livre. Il est très beau*
I like this book. It's very handsome

15 *Je n'aime pas ce livre. C'est trop triste*
I don't like this book. It's too sad

Whereas 14 refers to the physical appearance of the book, 15 refers to its contents.

16 *C'est important, les traditions*
Traditions are important

refers by implication to all that traditions represent.

(c) The referent is an unspecified object (as in sentence 17 below), or a 'neuter' pronoun such as *cela (ça), ce (qui, que, dont)*, or *le*, or a clause introduced by *comme*, or an adverbial expression of place or the name of a locality (in which case the explanation of the use of *ce* is similar to that given for sentence 15 above), or a phrase including a numeral (including *un*) (and this list is not necessarily complete), e.g.:

17 *Attention! C'est lourd!*   Careful! It's heavy!

In 17, the speaker and his hearer(s) know of course what it is that is heavy (e.g. a rock, a box, a piece of furniture) but the speaker has not specifically mentioned it, hence the use of *ce*.

18 *Ne buvez pas ça! C'est trop fort*
   Don't drink that! It's too strong

19 *C'est vrai, ça!*
   That's true

20 *C'est inquiétant ce que vous dites*
   What you say is worrying

21 *Elle le croit mais ce n'est pas vrai*
   She believes it but it isn't true

22 *C'est incroyable comme on oublie*
   It's unbelievable how one forgets

23 *C'est charmant ici*
   It's delightful here

24 *C'est beau, la Provence*
   Provence is beautiful

In 24, the reference is to all that is conjured up by the name of Provence.

25 *C'est long, une heure!*
   It's a long time, an hour!

26 *Vingt francs, c'est très cher*
   Twenty francs is very expensive

In 26, note that English uses a singular not a plural verb after 'twenty francs' – a further indication that the adjective refers not so much to the nominal referent as to what is implied by it.

251 (ii) The complement is a noun or pronoun

(a) The general rule is that one uses *c'est* when the complement is introduced by a determiner (article, possessive or demonstrative) or when it is a pronoun such as *un, celui, quelqu'un*, e.g.:

C'est un médecin
He is a doctor

C'est l'ami dont je vous parlais
He is the friend I was telling you about

Méfiez-vous de cette femme-là; c'est votre ennemie mortelle
Beware of that woman; she is your deadly enemy

Qui est ce monsieur-là? C'est celui à qui je vous ai presenté hier

Who is that gentleman? He is the man I introduced you to
yesterday

C'était quelqu'un d'important
He was someone important

(b) With nouns indicating a long-term state in life, such as
nationality, profession or family status, it is possible to use *il est,
elle est*, etc., with no article before the complement, e.g.:

Il est médecin	He is a doctor
Elle est étudiante	She is a student
Elle est Américaine	She is an American
Il est grand-père	He is a grand-father

(c) The distinction between types a and b above is basically that in
type b (*Il est médecin*) the noun has a primarily adjectival function,
it serves only to characterize the person, e.g.:

Puis-je présenter mon mari? Il est médecin
May I introduce my husband? He is a doctor

whereas, once any other idea is introduced, type a (*C'est un
médecin*) is likely to be used, e.g.:

Mon mari n'aime pas qu'on fume. C'est un médecin
My husband doesn't like people to smoke. He's a doctor

*Elle fait beaucoup de gestes lorsqu'elle parle. Après tout, c'est
une Italienne*
She makes a lot of gestures when she speaks. After all, she's
an Italian

Consequently, type a must be used whenever the noun is qualified,
e.g.:

C'est un excellent médecin
He is an excellent doctor

C'est un étudiant qui travaille bien
He is a student who works well

(d) In spite of a and b above, the construction *il est, elle est* +
complement introduced by a determiner sometimes occurs, e.g.
when the subject pronoun is strengthened by a disjunctive pronou,
e.g.:

Elle, elle était une petite veuve de trente-trois ans (Courteline)
She was a little thirty-three-year-old widow

or when the uniqueness of the complement is stressed, e.g.:

Elle est la reine	She *is* the Queen
Après tout, il est mon père	After all, he is my father

But such nuances are delicate and difficult to define and, in general, it is advisable to follow the rules set out in a and b above.

252 (iii) **The complement is neither an adjective nor a noun or pronoun**
(a) The referent is a person or a thing expressed by a noun or pronoun – use *il est, elle est*, etc., e.g.:

Où est votre frère? – Il est en France
Where is your brother? – He is in France

Où est mon dictionnaire? – Il est sur la table
Where is my dictionary? – It is on the table

A qui est cette voiture? – Elle est à moi
Whose is this car? – It's mine

Si vous cherchez le chat, il est dans le jardin
If you are looking for the cat, he (it) is in the garden

Je ne comprends pas cette lettre. Elle est en allemand
I don't understand this letter. It's in German

(b) The referent is *ceci* or *cela* (*ça*), or a noun phrase introduced by *ce qui*, etc., or the name of a place, or the idea contained in a preceding clause – use *c'est*, e.g.:

Ça, c'est à voir
That remains to be seen

Je ne comprends pas ce qu'il a écrit. C'est en allemand
I don't understand what he has written. It's in German

Où est Neuchâtel? C'est en Suisse
Where is Neuchâtel? It is in Switzerland

J'aime jouer aux échecs. C'est très intéressant
I like playing chess. It's very interesting

II. C'est *or impersonal* il est?

253 (i) **The complement is an adjective** (see also end of this section)

When the referent has already been expressed, i.e. when the adjective refers *back* to it, *c'est* must be used, but when the referent follows, i.e. when the adjective refers *forward* to it, *il est* is used (but see below), e.g.:

1 *Pourquoi est-il parti? – Je ne sais pas; c'est difficile à comprendre*
   Why has he left? – I don't know; it's difficult to understand

2 *Il est difficile de comprendre pourquoi il est parti*
   It is difficult to understand why he has left

3 *C'est lui qui l'a cassé – Oui, c'est évident*
   It is he who broke it. – Yes, it's obvious

4 *Il est évident que c'est lui qui l'a cassé*
   It is obvious that it was he who broke it

In 1 and 3, the adjectives *difficile* and *évident* refer *back* to what is difficult to understand (viz. his departure) or obvious (the fact that he broke the window) and so *c'est* is used, but in 2 and 4 the adjectives refer *forward* to the same events and so *il est* is used.

However, in speech *c'est* is widely used instead of *il est* with reference forward (e.g. *C'est difficile de comprendre pourquoi il est parti*) and this is usual even in literary usage when the adjective carries any kind of emphasis, e.g. *C'est curieux qu'il ne soit pas venu* 'It is strange that he has not come'.

Other adjectives with which both constructions occur include *agréable* 'pleasant', *certain, essentiel* 'essential', *étonnant* 'surprising', *facile* 'easy', *impossible, juste* 'fair', *nécessaire* 'necessary', *possible, probable, rare, regrettable, surprenant* 'surprising', *triste* 'sad', *vrai* 'true', etc.

Though these constructions occur mainly with adjectival complements, they also apply when the complement is an adverb such as *bien* 'well' used more or less as the equivalent of an adjective (for other adverbs, see **256**), or an infinitive governed by the preposition *à*, e.g.:

Il est bien qu'il soit arrivé à Rome avant Pâques
It is well (a good thing) that he has reached Rome before Easter

Est-il sain et sauf? C'est à espérer
Is he safe and sound? It is to be hoped so

Il est à espérer qu'il est sain et sauf
It is to be hoped that he is safe and sound

254   (ii) **With reference to the time of day,** *il est* is used, e.g.:

Quelle heure est-il?	What time is it?
Il est trois heures et demie	It is half past three

255   (iii) **The complement is a noun or pronoun**, which may or may not be qualified by a relative clause – *c'est* must be used, e.g.:

1 *Qui est-ce? – C'est moi*
  Who is it? – It's me

2 *C'est lui qui l'a fait*
  (It's) he (who) did it

3 *C'est vous que je cherche*
  It's you I'm looking for

4 *C'est Jean qui travaille le mieux*
  (It's) John (who) works best

5 *Avez-vous trouvé votre livre? – Oui, c'est celui-ci*
  Have you found your book? – Yes, it's this one

If the complement is a plural noun or pronoun, then, in the literary language, *ce sont* is used, e.g.:

6 *Ce sont mes frères qui le feront*
  (It is) my brothers (who) will do it

7 *Ce sont eux qui le feront*
  (It is) they (who) will do it

In speech, however, *c'est* is normally used, e.g. *C'est mes frères qui le feront*, and, even in the literary language, *c'est* is always used with *nous* and *vous* even with reference to more than one person, e.g. (*C'est*) *nous* (*qui*) *le ferons* '(It is) we (who) will do it'. (Note that the verb of the relative clause agrees in person with the complement of the preceding clause, as in the example just given or as in, for example, *C'est moi qui l'ai dit* 'It is I who said so'.)

  This construction must be used when, in English, the subject is emphasized with the value 'it is . . . who', as in '*John* is coming' (= 'It is John who is coming') and sentences 2, 4, 6 and 7 above. Likewise with the direct object, except that in English the word-order is different and the form of the personal pronoun may change, e.g.:

8 *C'est Paul qu'elle aime*
  It is Paul she loves, *or* She loves *Paul*

9 *C'est lui que je cherchais*
It is he I was looking for, *or* I was looking for *him*

Note that *c'est* generally remains in the present tense even though the tense of the relative clause may be different, as in sentences 2, 6 and 9 above. The present tense would still be used in French even if one were translating 'It was he who did it', 'It will be my brothers who will do it', and 'It was he I was looking for'. However, sentences like *C'était lui qui chantait* 'It was he who was singing', *Ce sera Jean qui le fera* 'It will be John who will do it', are not impossible.

256 (iv) **The complement is an indirect object, an adverb or adverbial phrase** (but see **253**, end), **a prepositional phrase, or a verb phrase** (either a subordinate clause or a phrase based on an infinitive other than one governed by *à* – see **253**, end – or on a present participle) – *c'est . . . que . . .* must be used, e.g.:

1 *C'est à Pierre que je l'ai donné*
It was Peter I gave it to, *or* I gave it to *Peter*

2. *C'est là qu'il habite*
It's there (that) he lives, *or* He lives *there*

3 *C'est à Paris que nous l'avons rencontré*
It was in Paris (that) we met him, *or* We met him in *Paris*

4 *C'est aujourd'hui qu'il va venir*
It is to-day that he is coming, *or* He is coming *today*

5 *N'est-ce pas assez d'être prisonnier sans être exposé à ces insultes?*
Is it not enough to be a prisoner without being subjected to these insults?

6 *C'est par l'étude des sauvages que ce savant nous donne des connaissances nouvelles sur la primitive humanité* (A. France)
It is by studying savage races that this scholar adds to our knowledge of primitive man

7 *C'est parce qu'il est bête qu'il a fait ça*
It is because he is a fool that he did that

8 *C'est pour vous protéger que je l'ai dit*
It was to protect you that I said it, *or* I said it to protect you

9 *C'est après vous avoir vu que votre frère est parti*
It was after seeing you that your brother left

10 *C'est en travaillant dur que vous y arriverez*
It's by working hard that you'll get there

As in the construction discussed in **255**, *c'est . . . que . . .* serves to emphasize the complement (see all the above examples) and the tense of *c'est* generally remains unchanged (see sentences 1, 3, 7, 8, 9 and 10).

The following idioms are exceptions to what has been said above:

Il en est ainsi
It is so, that is how things are

il en est de même pour . . .
the same is true of . . .

257   (i) In all the examples given in **248–256**, the verb is *être*. Note however that *ce* can still be used when the modal verbs *devoir* and *pouvoir* (and occasionally *aller* and, in the conditional tense only, *savoir*) are followed by *être*, e.g.:

Ce doit être un gros problème
It must be a big problem

Ce ne peut être que lui
It can only be he

Ce pourrait être vrai
It could be true

Ç'allait être difficile
It was going to be difficult

Ce ne saurait être que lui
It could only be he

(Note the cedilla on *ç'* before the *a-* of *allait*; the same is true before the *a-* of *avoir* in compound tenses of *être*, e.g. *ç'avait été* 'it had been'.)

(ii) Note that *c'est* can be combined with other tenses in a following clause introduced by *qui* or *que*, e.g.:

Si vous faites ça, tout ce qui arrivera $\left\{ \begin{array}{l} \textit{c'est} \\ \textit{or} \\ \textit{ce sera} \end{array} \right\}$ *que vous offenserez tout le monde*

If you do that, all that will happen $\left\{ \begin{array}{l} \text{is } or \\ \text{will be} \end{array} \right\}$ that you will

offend everybody

C'est moi (or *C'était moi*) *qu'elle attendait*
It is me (*or* It was me) she was waiting for

C'est (or *Ce fut*) *Zola qui prit la défense de Dreyfus*
It was Zola who defended Dreyfus

But, if *c'est* is not used, then the tense of the two verbs must be the same; in particular, avoid the trap that foreigners often fall into of beginning with *C'était* . . . and then continuing with a preterite or a perfect in the following clause.

III. C'est or est?

258 Note that *c'est* rather than *est* alone must be used

(i) when the complement is a personal pronoun, e.g.:

Mon meilleur ami c'est vous My best friend is you

(ii) when the referent is singular and the complement plural (in which case *ce sont* would be preferred in literary usage, see **255**), e.g.:

Ce que je crains, c'est (or *ce sont*) *mes prétendus amis*
What I fear is (the reaction of) my so-called friends

(iii) when both referent and complement are positive infinitives, e.g.:

Voir c'est croire Seeing is believing
Le voir c'est le détester To see him is to loathe him

(but, if the second infinitive is negative, either *c'est* or *est* may be used, e.g. *Consentir (ce) n'est pas approuver* 'To consent is not to approve').

259 *C'est*, though not absolutely compulsory, is generally used:

(i) when the referent is a clause introduced by *celui*, etc., or *ce* and a relative pronoun, or by a nominalized adjective conveying the same sense as a clause with *ce qui* (e.g. *l'essentiel = ce qui est essentiel*); this is particularly true whenever a superlative is involved, in which case *c'est* rather than *est* should always be used, e.g.:

> *Celui qui travaille le mieux, c'est Paul*
> The one who works best is Paul (it's Paul who works best)

> *Ce qui m'agace* ⎫
> *Ce que je déteste* ⎬ *le plus, c'est la paresse*
> What infuriates me ⎫
> What I hate ⎬ most is idleness

> *Ce dont je me souviens le mieux, c'est ce qui m'est arrivé dans l'enfance*
> What I remember best is what happened to me in childhood

> *Ce à quoi il pense pour la plupart, c'est sa santé*
> What he thinks of mostly is his health

> *Le plus difficile c'est de le faire comprendre*
> The most difficult thing is to make him understand

and, without a superlative:

> *Celui qui travaille bien c'est Paul*
> The one who works well is Paul

> *Ce qui m'agace, c'est* (or *est*) *sa paresse*
> What infuriates me is his idleness

> *L'ennuyeux de* (for *ce qui m'ennuie dans*) *cette affaire, c'est* (or *est*) *qu'il ne veut pas répondre à mes lettres*
> The annoying part of the business is that he will not answer my letters

Note however that, even after a superlative, *est* not *c'est* is used when the complement is an adjective or adjectival participle, or a noun with a value equivalent to that of an adjective, e.g.:

> *Ce que vous trouvez le plus impossible dans cette affaire est néanmoins vrai* (or *la vérité*)
> What you consider most impossible in this business is nevertheless true (or the truth)

(ii) when the complement is an infinitive or a clause introduced by *que*, e.g.:

> *Le problème (c') est de le persuader que tout ira bien*
> The problem is to persuade him that all will be well

La difficulté (c') est qu'il ne comprend rien
The difficulty is that he understands nothing

260 In various other circumstances, there is virtually a free choice between *c'est* and *est*, e.g.:

Se moquer de lui (c') est très facile
To make fun of him is very easy

This is particularly so when the two halves of the sentence are virtually interchangeable, e.g.:

Son grand défaut (c') est la paresse
His great defect is laziness

La paresse (c') est son grand défaut
Laziness is his great defect

In such cases, the insertion of *ce* gives slightly more emphasis.
But when such a sentence is negative, it is more usual not to insert *ce* e.g.:

Son grand défaut n'est pas la paresse, mais l'obstination
His great defect is not laziness, but obstinacy

261 If in a French sentence beginning with *c'est* the second half of the complement is an infinitive and the two halves are interchangeable, this infinitive is often preceded by *que de*, e.g.:

C'est mourir que de vivre ainsi
It is death to live like this

C'est agaçant (que) d'être mécompris
It is annoying to be misunderstood

Ce serait un désastre (que) de perdre cette occasion
It would be a disaster to lose this opportunity

Relative pronouns

262 English has, on the one hand, the invariable relative pronoun 'that', and, on the other, the following which vary according to their function in the sentence *and* according to whether they refer on the one hand to people or, on the other, to things (including animals):

	referring to people	referring to things
Subject	*who*	*which*
Direct object	*whom*	*which*
Genitive (see 19)	*whose, of whom*	*of which, whose*
After prepositions	*whom*	*which*

In French, the distinction between people and things is found only after prepositions and, sometimes, in the genitive; after prepositions there is yet another form used with reference to various 'neuter' pronouns. The distinctions between the various forms are discussed in some detail below (265–273), but in summary form they are:

	referring to people	referring to things	referring to neuter pronouns
Subject	*qui*	*qui*	*qui*
Direct object	*que*	*que*	*que*
Genitive	*dont*	*dont*	*dont*
	duquel, etc. *de qui*	*duquel*, etc.	
After prepositions	*qui* *lequel*, etc.	*lequel*, etc.	*quoi*

Note in particular

(i) that *que* can never be used after a preposition (see 263, 270, 271)

(ii) that *dont* always comes first in its clause (see 268, 272)

263 After prepositions, except *parmi* 'among' and *entre* 'between' (for which see 270), the forms are:

referring to people

after *de*	(see 268–269)
after *à*	*à qui*
after all other prepositions	*avec qui*, *par qui*, etc.

referring to things

	masc. sing.	fem sing.	masc. plur.	fem. plur.
after *de*	*duquel*	*de laquelle*	*desquels*	*desquelles*
after *à*	*auquel*	*à laquelle*	*auxquels*	*auxquelles*
after all other prepositions	*lequel*	*laquelle*	*lesquels*	*lesquelles*

Note that *lequel*, etc., may also be used as alternatives to *qui* with reference to people (e.g. *auxquels* = *à qui*, masc. plur., *sans laquelle = sans qui,* fem. sing.) but *qui* is the more usual (except after *parmi* and *entre*).

264   With three important exceptions, the use of the relatives in French is much the same as in English. The exceptions are:

(i) the direct object pronoun, which is often omitted in English, must always be inserted in French (265)

(ii) clauses of the type 'the man I gave it to, the table you left it on' always take in French the form 'the man to whom I gave it, the table on which you left it' (266)

(iii) there is no French form corresponding exactly in function to the English 'whose'; forms meaning 'of whom' or 'of which' must be used (267–268).

265   In English, the direct object relative pronoun is very frequently omitted; this is not possible in French – the pronoun *que* must *never* be omitted, e.g.:

> *Connaissez-vous la jeune fille que Paul a épousée?*
> Do you know the girl (that) Paul married?

> *Voici les livres que j'ai achetés*
> Here are the books I bought

266   In English one can omit not only the direct object relative pronoun (see 265) but also a relative pronoun serving as the complement of a preposition, in which case the preposition is moved to the end of the clause, e.g. 'the children for whom he bought these presents' becomes 'the children he bought these presents for'. In French, the full form 'for whom he bought . . .', must be used, e.g.:

> *Où est l'homme à qui j'ai donné les billets?*
> Where is the man I gave the tickets to?

> *Je connais les enfants pour qui il achète ces cadeaux*
> I know the children he is buying those presents for

> *Quelle est la table sur laquelle vous avez laissé mes livres?*
> Which is the table you left my books on?

267   As French has no word whose functions correspond closely to those of English 'whose', the choice of the correct equivalent

can present some problems. We shall divide the relevant sentences into two types (**268** and **269**).

268 Clauses introduced by 'whose' + noun (subject or direct object)

In these clauses, *dont* is the relative to use and the word order is always **subject + verb + direct object**, i.e. the normal French word-order, however far from the relative the object may consequently have to stand. The English practice of placing the direct object immediately after the relative 'whose' as in the second of the following examples must **not** be followed in French.

Examples:

> *Voilà le monsieur dont le cheval vient de gagner*
> ('horse' is the subject so the order is as in English)
> There is the gentleman whose horse has just won

> *L'élève dont vous m'avez prêté le livre est malade*
> ('book' is the object, so *livre* follows the verb)
> The boy whose book you lent me is ill

More complicated (but perfectly regular) examples are:

> *La famille dont on dit qu'on a cambriolé hier soir la maison est en vacances*
> The family whose house is said to have been burgled last night is away on holiday

> *Je vais vous présenter demain à la dame dont vous dites désirer depuis longtemps faire la connaissance*
> I will introduce you to-morrow to the lady whose acquaintance you say you have long been anxious to make

269 The construction preposition + 'whose' + noun

When 'whose' stands between a preposition and the word governed by that preposition, 'of whom' should be substituted for 'whose'. The French order will then be exactly the same as the English order, e.g.:

> *Le négociant à la bonne foi duquel* (or *de qui*) *je me fiais a fait faillite*

The merchant on $\left\{ \begin{array}{l} \text{whose good faith} \\ \text{the good faith of whom} \end{array} \right\}$ I was relying

has failed (gone bankrupt)

Note that, in this type of sentence, *dont* can never be used.

270 *Lequel*

As already stated (263) *lequel* must be used with any preposition when the antecedent is a thing (or animal).

It should also be used with *parmi* 'among', and *entre* 'between', even when the antecedent is a person, the relative *qui* being very uncommon with these two prepositions.

Either *lequel* or *qui* may be used of persons after other prepositions but *qui* is commoner (except perhaps after *avec* 'with').

Lequel is generally used as a pronoun, but it may be a determiner as in the third example below.

Further, *lequel* is sometimes required when the use of *qui* or *dont* would involve ambiguity. If this still leaves the antecedent doubtful, some change must be made in the wording of the sentence, as in the last example below.

Examples:

Les singes auxquels nous montrions le miroir faisaient des grimaces
The monkeys to which we showed the mirror were making faces

Les jeunes gens parmi lesquels nous nous trouvions étaient très bruyants
The young people among whom we found ourselves were very noisy

Voici cent francs, laquelle somme vous est due demain
Here are a hundred francs, which sum is due to you to-morrow

Le fils de cette dame, lequel vient d'arriver, devrait être félicité
This lady's son, who has just arrived, ought to be congratulated

> (*le fils de cette dame qui vient d'arriver* would mean that it was the lady who had just arrived, not the son)

Vous rappelez-vous la jeune fille que nous avons rencontrée chez ma sœur et dont vous avez guéri la toux?
Do you remember the girl whom we met at my sister's (and) whose cough you cured?

(the omission of *et* before *dont* would make *sœur* look like the antecedent, and *de laquelle* would be even more ambiguous, as *sœur* is also feminine)

271   The ordinary rule that a relative agrees with its antecedent in gender, number and person has in practice no effect on a French sentence except

(i)   when *lequel* is used, e.g.:

le chemin par lequel		the road by which	we
la route par laquelle	*nous*	the road by which	were
les chemins par lesquels	*allions*	the roads by which	going
les routes par lesquelles			

(ii)   when the relative affects the number or person, or the past participle (see **460**) of the verb in the relative clause, e.g.:

C'est moi qui l'ai dit	It was I who said it
C'est lui qui l'a fait	It was he who did it
C'est nous qui l'avons vu	It was we who saw it
l'homme que j'ai vu	the man I saw
la dame que j'ai vue	the lady I saw
les hommes que j'ai vus	the men I saw
les dames que j'ai vues	the ladies I saw

It is most important to remember that, though English may omit the relative, as in the last four examples above, French can never do so.

272   Except for what has been said in **269** the relative must stand first in its clause, and the antecedent is put, if possible, immediately before it. The English habit of putting 'of which' after the subject or object noun on which it depends must not be imitated in French, e.g.:

Cette histoire, dont l'origine est inconnue, a eu de graves conséquences
This story, the origin of which is unknown, had serious consequences

Cette lettre, dont je peux deviner l'auteur, est tout à fait inepte
This letter, the writer of which I can guess, is thoroughly silly

273   *Quoi* is used as a relative pronoun after a preposition

(i)   when the antecedent is one or other of the 'neuter' pronouns *ce* (see **274**) or *rien* 'nothing', e.g.:

Ce avec quoi j'écris, c'est une plume d'oie
What I am writing with is a goose quill

Il n'a rien de quoi se plaindre
He has nothing to complain of

(ii) when the antecedent is a sentence, e.g.:

Le président pria l'assistance de s'asseoir, après quoi il commença son discours
The chairman asked the audience to sit down, after which he began his speech

(iii) when there is no antecedent expressed, e.g.:

Voilà en quoi je suis sûr d'avoir raison
That is a matter in which I know I am right

and particularly with *avoir* and a few other verbs + *de quoi* + infinitive, meaning 'to have (etc.) the means, the wherewithal, enough, etc., to do something', e.g.:

Il a de quoi vivre
He has enough to live on

Pourriez-vous me donner de quoi écrire?
Could you give me something to write with?

Il n'y a pas de quoi être fier
There is nothing to be proud of

Note that some writers sometimes use *quoi* instead of *lequel* when the antecedent is a noun (singular or plural) referring to a thing, e.g.:

Cette case, vers quoi convergeaient les regards de presque tous les joueurs . . . (Malraux)
This square (i.e. in a board-game) on which the gaze of nearly all the players converged . . .

Les manuscrits anciens par quoi nous connaissons la Grèce . . . (Gide)
The ancient manuscripts from which we know Greece

This usage should not be imitated.

274 When English 'what' is the equivalent of 'that which, that of which', etc., that is how it must be expressed in French. The forms are:

Subject	*ce qui*
Direct object	*ce que*
'that of which'	*ce dont*
With other prepositions	*ce à quoi, ce avec quoi*, etc.

Examples:

Ce qui m'intéresse, c'est la peinture moderne
What interests me is modern painting

Ce que vous craignez est absurde
What you fear is absurd

Ce dont ils parlent ⎱
Ce à quoi ils pensent ⎰ *ne m'intéresse pas*

What they are talking about ⎱
What they are thinking of ⎰ does not interest me

Je leur parlais de ce dont vous m'avez parlé hier
I was talking to them about what you spoke to me about
yesterday

Where this 'what' is used as an adjective in English to qualify a
noun, it is a pronoun in French and is therefore followed by *de*,
e.g.:

Avec ce que j'ai d'argent j'irai assez loin
With what money (*or* such money as) I have I shall get along
all right

Il ramassa ce qu'il lui restait de forces
He gathered up what strength he had left (*or* such strength as
he had left)

275 Note the following archaic constructions that survive *only* in
the circumstances stated and must not be used otherwise:

(i) *Qui* with the value of *celui qui* in a general sense, 'he who',
remains in a number of proverbs and sayings, e.g.:

Qui dort dîne
A sleep is as good as a meal (*lit.* Who sleeps dines)

Qui vivra verra
Time will tell (*lit.* Who lives will see)

Qui va lentement va sûrement
Slowly but surely

Qui s'excuse, s'accuse
To excuse oneself is to accuse oneself

(ii) *Qui* as the equivalent of *ce qui* 'what, that which' (see **274**) survives only in the three expressions:

qui mieux est	what is better
qui pis est	what is worse
qui plus est	what is more

and after *voici* and *voilà*, e.g.:

Voilà qui est intéressant
That is (something) interesting

Voici qui distingue profondément le pessimisme de Tour-gueniev et celui de Flaubert (P. Bourget)
This is what profoundly distinguishes Turgenev's pessimism and that of Flaubert

(iii) An even more archaic construction than those discussed in (i) and (ii) above is the use of *que* with the value of *ce qui* or *ce que* in the following fixed expressions:

Faites ce que bon vous semblera
Do as you think fit (*lit.* what seems good to you)

Advienne que pourra
Come what may

Coûte que coûte
At all costs (*lit.* Let it cost what it may cost)

Vaille que vaille
For what it is worth

276 *Où* 'where' is frequently used as a relative, instead of preposition + *lequel*, not only when the antecedent denotes place but also (see **277**) when it denotes time, e.g.:

le village où nous vivons
the village in which (*or* where) we live

l'époque où nous vivons
the age in which we live

This *où* may be preceded by *de, par* or *jusque*, e.g.:

La maison d'où sortaient les flammes était la mienne
The house from which the flames were issuing was mine

Les villes par où l'armée était passée étaient toutes en ruines
The towns through which the army had passed were all in ruins

Voici jusqu'où nous allons ensemble
This is as far as we go together

277   With reference to time, *où* or *que*, not *quand* (see below), must be used in relative clauses (e.g. in phrases of the type 'the day when . . .', 'one day when . . .', 'at the time when . . .'). No absolute distinction can be made between *où* and *que* but the following comments will cover most cases:

(i) if the noun is preceded by an indefinite article, use *que*, e.g.:

un jour qu'il pleuvait
one day when it was raining

(ii) when nouns like *jour* 'day', *moment, instant, temps* 'time', *époque* 'time', are preceded by a definite article, *où* is preferred, particularly with *le jour où* 'the day when' and *au moment où* 'at the time when'; with other nouns, it is usually possible to use either *où* or *que*, but note that *où* is by far the more usual in speech. Examples:

le jour où vous êtes arrivé
the day (when) you arrived

au moment où je partais
at the moment I was leaving

les jours où il (or *qu'il*) *pleuvait*
the days (when) it rained

du (or *au*) *temps où* (or *que*) *nous étions étudiants*
at the time (when) we were students

dès le moment où (or *que*) *je l'ai vu*
from the moment I saw him

(Note that *du moment que* means 'since' in the sense of 'seeing that', e.g.:

Du moment que vous n'y allez pas, moi je n'y vais pas non plus
Since you are not going, I am not going either.)

When the clause introduced by 'when' is not a relative (and the conjunction therefore cannot be omitted in English as in the examples above), the appropriate French conjunction is *quand* or *lorsque*, e.g.:

> *A cette époque-là, quand elle était étudiante, elle était souvent malade*
> At that time, when she was a student, she was often ill

Interrogative determiners and pronouns

Introduction

278 The interrogative determiners (often termed interrogative adjectives) in English are 'what?' and 'which?' used before a noun, e.g. 'what day?, which book?'.

The interrogative pronouns are 'who(m)?, what? which?'.

The situation in French, as we shall see, is considerably more complicated.

Interrogative determiners

279 French has no distinction comparable to the English distinction between 'which?' and 'what?' as determiners. The forms are:

	sing.	plur.
masc.	*quel*	*quels*
fem.	*quelle*	*quelles*

Examples:

> *Quel livre avez-vous pris?*
> What book have you taken? Which book have you taken?

> *Quelles lettres avez-vous reçues?*
> What letters have you had?

> *Quel est le chemin le plus court?*
> Which is the shortest way?

> *Quelle peut être son idée?*
> What can his idea be?

As shown in the last two examples, *quel* may be separated from its noun by parts of *être*, and also by *être* in combination with modal verbs such as *pouvoir* and *devoir*. Note that in such sentences (i.e.

the construction 'what?' + 'to be' + noun), 'what?' cannot be translated by any of the pronominal forms for 'what?' such as *que, quoi, qu'est-ce que*, etc. (see **283–287**).

Quel may also stand (i) without a verb in exclamations, in the sense of 'What (a) . . .!', (ii) in indirect questions, as in English, e.g.:

Quelle réponse!	What an answer!
Quelle merveilleuse idée!	What a marvellous idea!
Quel temps superbe!	What superb weather
Quelles jolies fleurs!	What pretty flowers!
Je ne sais pas quel livre il a choisi	I don't know what book he has chosen

Interrogative pronouns

280 'Who?' and 'whom?' (both as direct object and as the complement of a preposition) are both rendered by *qui*, while 'whose?' is *de qui*? except in the construction 'Whose is X?', meaning 'To whom does X belong?', which is *A qui est X*?

Examples:

Direct questions

Subject	*Qui a cassé la fenêtre?* Who has broken the window?
Direct object	*Qui avez-vous vu?* Whom did you see?
'whose?' (with *de*)	*De qui a-t-il épousé la fille?* Whose daughter did he marry?
'of whom?'	*De qui parlez-vous?* Of whom you talking (*or, colloquially*, Who are you talking about)?
'to whom?'	*A qui a-t-il fait allusion?* To whom did he allude?
'whose?' (with *à*)	*A qui (est) cette valise?* Whose is this suitcase?

So with all prepositions, e.g.:

> *Avec qui y êtes-vous allé?*
> With whom did you go there? Who did you go with?

Indirect questions

Subject	*Je ne sais pas qui a cassé la fenêtre* I do not know who has broken the window
Direct object	*Dites-moi qui vous avez vu* Tell me whom you saw
'of whom'	*Je ne comprends pas de qui vous parlez* I do not understand whom you are talking about
'to whom'	*Je ne comprends pas à qui il a fait allusion* I do not understand to whom he alluded
Other prepositions	*Je voudrais savoir avec qui vous y êtes allé* I should like to know with whom you went there

281 Besides the form *qui* a longer form with *est-ce* is in common use in direct questions, viz.:

Subject	*qui est-ce qui*
Direct object	*qui est-ce que*
'of whom?'	*de qui est-ce que*
'to whom?'	*à qui est-ce que*

Some of the examples given above would therefore run as follows:

> *Qui est-ce qui a cassé la fenêtre?*
> *Qui est-ce que vous avez vu?*
> *De qui est-ce que vous parlez?*
> *A qui est-ce qu'il a fait allusion?*

282 Note the use of *qui de . . .?* 'which of . . .?' with

(i)   two nouns or personal pronouns joined by *ou* 'or';

(ii) a cardinal number;

(iii) a single pronoun, with which, however, *qui d'entre* is far commoner.

Examples:

(i)   *De votre père ou de votre mère qui serait le plus compréhensif?*
Which would be the more sympathetic – your father or your mother?

Qui de vous ou de moi risquera l'ascension?
Which of us will risk the ascent – you or I?

(ii) *Qui des deux?*
Which of the two?

(iii) *Attendons ici pour voir qui d'entre elles arrivera la première*
Let us wait here to see which of them will arrive first

283   In a direct question the pronoun 'what' is translated in French as follows:

Subject	*qu'est-ce qui*
Direct object	*que* or *qu'est-ce que*
After any preposition	*quoi*

Examples:

Subject	*Qu'est-ce qui fait ce bruit?*
	What is making that noise?
Direct object	*Qu'est-ce que vous faites?*
	Que faites-vous?
	What are you doing?
After prepositions	*De quoi parlez-vous?*
	What are you talking about?
	A quoi pensez-vous?
	What are you thinking about?
	En quoi puis-je vous servir?
	In what way can I help you?
	Avec quoi écrit-il?
	What is he writing with?

Note that English sentences (like the four just quoted) that begin with 'What . . .?' and end with a preposition cannot be translated literally into French, which requires the form 'With what . . .? Of what . . .?', etc.

Que and *qu'est-ce que* also serve as the complement of *être* and *devenir* (see also **285**), e.g.:

Que sera-t-il?
What will he be?

Qu'est-ce que c'était?
What was it?

Qu'est-ce qu'il est devenu ensuite?
What did he become next?

284 In certain circumstances, *quoi* can be used as the subject or direct object of a verb expressed or understood, in particular:

(i) with *de* and an adjective, e.g.:

Quoi de neuf? Quoi de nouveau?
What news?

Quoi de plus simple?
What could be easier?

(ii) as the object of certain common verbs such as *dire, faire, répondre*, particularly to express hesitation or uncertainty, e.g.:

Quoi dire?   What can one say?

(Note that 'what?' as the object of an infinitive is usually *que*, e.g. *Que dire?*)

(iii) in the expression *pour quoi faire* 'for what purpose, etc.', e.g.:

Je vais à Londres demain. Pour quoi faire?
I'm going to London tomorrow. What for?

(iv) for emphasis, when asking for confirmation of what has been said, e.g.:

J'ai perdu le magnétoscope. – Tu as perdu quoi?
I've lost the video-recorder. – You've lost what?

Il va devenir prêtre. – Il va devenir quoi?
He's going to become a priest. – He's going to become what?

(In conversational usage, this has become a normal, unemphatic, way of asking a question, so *Tu as perdu quoi?* = *Qu'as-tu perdu?* or *Qu'est-ce que tu as perdu?* 'What have you lost?')

(v) On its own or with an adverb, particularly as an exclamation or other expression of surprise, e.g.:

> *Quoi! Il est déjà parti?!*
> What! He's gone already?!

> *J'ai fait quelque chose de stupide. – Quoi donc?*
> I've done something stupid. – What?

> *Quoi encore!*
> What next!

> *Il est fou ou quoi?*
> Is he crazy or what?

> *Quoi?* (but *Comment?* is a more polite form)
> What (did you say)?

285   Note the use of *devenir* in the sense of 'become of':

> *Que deviendrai-je?*
> What will become of me? (*lit.* What shall I become?)

> *Qu'est-il devenu?*
> What has become of him? (*lit.* What has he become?)

Two different constructions are possible with the verbs *arriver* and *se passer* 'to happen', viz:

(i) 'What?' may be treated as the subject, so:

> *Qu'est-ce qui arrive?*
> *Qu'est-ce qui se passe?* } What is happening?

(ii) the verbs may be treated as impersonal, with impersonal *il* as subject (as in *Il est arrivé un accident* 'There has been an accident'), in which case 'What?' is treated as the complement, viz:

> *Qu'arrive-t-il?*
> *Que se passe-t-il?* } What is happening?

286   In connection with the English interrogative 'what', the following idioms should be remembered:

> *Qu'y a-t-il?* or *Qu'est-ce qu'il y a?*
> What's the matter?

> *Qu'a-t-elle?* or *Qu'est-ce qu'elle a?*
> What's the matter with her?

Elle est bien laide, mais qu'est-ce que ça fait?
She is very ugly, but what does that matter?

Qu'est-ce? or *Qu'est-ce que c'est?*
What is it?

Qu'est-ce qu'il fait? { (a) What is he? (by trade or profession)
{ (b) What's he doing?

Comment dit-on ... en français?
What is the French for . . .?

Et les billets?
What about the tickets?

Et moi?
What about me?

A quoi ça sert?
What's that for? What's the use of that?

A quoi bon?
What's the point?

Note that *Qu'est-ce que . . .?* can be used without a verb to ask the question 'What is . . .?'. In the longer form, *Qu'est-ce que c'est que . . .?*, the question often expresses surprise, e.g.:

Qu'est-ce que cette fleur-là?
What is that flower?

Qu'est-ce que c'est que cette fleur-là?
What ever is that flower?

287   At this point it may help if we summarize the forms **most generally used** for 'who(m)?' and 'what?', i.e. excluding forms for 'whose?' (see **280**) and various restricted uses of *quoi* (see **284**); we use *avec* to represent any preposition:

(i) 'Who? Whom?'

	short forms	long forms
Subject	*qui*	*qui est-ce qui*
Direct object	*qui*	*qui est-ce que*
After prepositions	*avec qui*	*avec qui est-ce que*

(ii) 'What?'

	short forms	long forms
Subject	—	*qu'est-ce qui*
Direct object	*que*	*qu'est-ce que*
After prepositions	*avec quoi*	*avec quoi est-ce que*

Note:

(a) that there is no short form for 'what?' as subject

(b) that the long forms for 'who(m)' all begin with *qui* and those for 'what?' with *que*

(c) that the long forms for the subject end in the subject relative pronoun *qui* and that those for the direct object end in the direct object relative pronoun *que*.

288 The forms for 'what' in indirect questions are:

Subject	*ce qui*
Direct object	*ce que*
After prepositions	*quoi* (*à quoi, de quoi, avec quoi,* etc.)

Examples:

Subject	*Dites-moi ce qui vous inquiète* Tell me what is worrying you
Direct object	*Je me demande ce qu'il va faire* I wonder what he is going to do
	Je me demande ce que veut dire mon père (see **598**) I wonder what my father means
After prepositions	*Dites-moi de quoi vous parliez* Tell me what you were talking about
	On ne sait jamais à quoi il pense One never knows what he is thinking about
	Savez-vous avec quoi il a ouvert la boîte? Do you know what he opened the box with?

Ce que is also the complement of the verbs *être* and *devenir* (cf. the use of *que* with these verbs in direct questions, 283 and 285), e.g.:

Je me demande ce qu'elle est maintenant
I wonder what she is now

Savez-vous ce qu'il est devenu?
Do you know what he became (*or* what became of him)?

289 As the object of an infinitive in indirect questions, 'what' is not *ce que* but *que* or sometimes (especially in speech) *quoi* (cf. the use of *quoi* in direct questions, 284,ii), e.g.:

Si j'avais su que (or *quoi*) *répondre*
If I had known what to reply

Il ne sait plus que (or *quoi*) *dire*
He no longer knows what to say

Note that *je ne sais,* etc. (i.e. without *pas* - see **561**,b), being characteristic of literary usage, takes *que*, whereas the more colloquial form *je ne sais pas* tends to take *quoi*, e.g.:

Je ne sais que faire/dire $\Big\}$ I don't know what to do/to say
Je ne sais pas quoi faire/dire

Note finally the expression *je ne sais quoi* (literally 'I do not know what') meaning 'an indefinable something', particularly when followed by *de* and an adjective (cf. **667**,i,ii), e.g.:

Elle a je ne sais quoi de distingué
There is something distinguished about her

290 The forms for 'which?' as a pronoun (and note that, as pronouns, there *is* a distinction between 'what?' and 'which?' – contrast **279**), both in direct and in indirect questions, are:

	masc. sing.	fem. sing.	masc. plur.	fem. plur.
Subject Direct object $\Big\}$	*lequel*	*laquelle*	*lesquels*	*lesquelles*
With *de*	*duquel*	*de laquelle*	*desquels*	*desquelles*
With *à*	*auquel*	*à laquelle*	*auxquels*	*auxquelles*

Note that, though these forms are made up of the definite article and *quel*, etc., the two parts cannot be separated, even when combined with *à* or *de* (as in *auxquels, duquel*, etc.)

Examples:

> *Laquelle de ces deux maisons préférez-vous?*
> Which of these two houses do you prefer?
>
> *Duquel de ses frères parlez-vous?*
> Of which of his brothers are you speaking?
>
> *Je ne sais plus dans laquelle de ces boîtes j'ai caché vos documents*
> I don't remember in which of these boxes I hid your documents
>
> *Je vais lui demander lesquelles de ces photos il a prises lui-même*
> I am going to ask him which of these photos he took himself
>
> *Lesquels de ces livres avez-vous lus?*
> Which of these books have you read?

The gender of *lequel* depends on the gender of the noun it refers to; its number is determined by whether the answer expected is in the singular or the plural. In the last example above, the use of *lesquels* indicates that the questioner assumes that more than one book had been read – if the question (which in English would be the same) implied that only one book had been read, it would have been in French *Lequel de ces livres avez-vous lu?* Likewise, if the example immediately before had related to only one photograph, the wording would have been . . . *laquelle de ces photos* . . .

Note finally that *lequel* can stand alone, e.g.:

> *Je viens d'acheter une maison dans votre village. Tiens! Laquelle?*
> I have just bought a house in your village. Fancy that! Which one?

Indefinite adjectives, adverbs, determiners and pronouns

291 The various so-called 'indefinites' are grouped together here primarily for convenience. As will be seen below, they function in many different ways. Consequently, many of them could have been and in some cases are discussed under other headings (see cross-references). In particular, quantifiers and negatives are discussed separately (see **320–337** and **542–558** respectively).

292 *Autre(s)*

(i) *Autre* 'other' may be a pronoun or an adjective and as a rule it is used in the same way as English 'other', e.g.:

Avez-vous un autre livre?
Have you got another book?

Oui, j'en ai beaucoup d'autres
Yes, I have plenty of others (*or* many others)

In the plural *d'autres* is used by itself meaning 'others', e.g.:

Un beau jour d'autres nous remplaceront
Some day others will take our place

So too even after *bien* in spite of what is said in **325**, e.g.:

Bien d'autres sont de mon avis
Many others are of my opinion

(This is in accordance with the rule that *des* is replaced by *de* before an adjective in the plural, *d'autres* here being the equivalent of *d'autres personnes*, i.e. it is in fact an adjective; see **44**.)

(ii) *L'un l'autre, l'une l'autre* (sing.), *les uns les autres, les unes les autres* (plur.), 'each other, one another'.

In this expression *l'autre* or *les autres* may be governed by any preposition, or may be the object of a transitive verb; *l'un* and *les uns* can stand in apposition to either the subject of any verb or the object of a transitive verb, but can never have a preposition before them. The English idiom by which a preposition is put before the whole expression – e.g. 'with each other', 'to one another', etc. – is unknown in French, which must say 'one with the other' *l'un avec l'autre*, 'the ones to the others' *les uns aux autres*, etc., e.g.:

Ils disaient toujours du mal l'un de l'autre (if only two in all are concerned)

Ils disaient toujours du mal les uns des autres (if more than two)
They were always speaking ill of one another

This reciprocal *l'un l'autre*, etc., is often combined with or replaced by (a) a reflexive pronoun, or (b) the preposition *entre* with a disjunctive pronoun (see also **673**) provided that the words 'one another' are the direct or indirect object, e.g.:

Ils se racontaient des histoires les uns aux autres
Ils se racontaient des histoires entre eux

or simply

Ils se racontaient des histoires
They were telling one another stories

(iii) *L'un l'autre*, etc., meaning 'one another', must not be confused with

| *l'un. . ., l'autre. . .*
one. . ., the other. . . | becoming
in the
plural | *les uns. . ., les autres. . .*
some. . ., others. . . |

e.g.

Asseyez-vous, messieurs, s'il vous plaît, les uns à droite, les autres à gauche
Sit down, please, gentlemen, some on the right, the others on the left

For the plural, *qui. . ., qui. . .* is occasionally substituted (see 314).

The difference between *les autres* and *d'autres* (see i above), both meaning 'others', is that *les autres* means '(all) (the) others' while *d'autres* means '(some) others'.

(iv) After *l'un et l'autre* 'both', *ni l'un ni l'autre* 'neither', the verb may be singular or plural according to taste, e.g.:

L'un et l'autre sont morts or *est mort*
Both are dead

Ni l'un ni l'autre ne viendront or *ne viendra*
Neither of them will come

But

(a) When these expressions stand after the verb in apposition to a plural subject, the verb is of course plural, e.g.:

Vos amis ne sont pas arrivés ni l'un ni l'autre
Neither of your friends has arrived

(b) *Ni l'un ni l'autre* takes a verb in the singular when the fact stated can only apply to one of the two, e.g.:

Ni l'un ni l'autre n'obtiendra le premier prix
Neither of them will get the first prize (i.e. only one could)

For the same reason, *l'un ou l'autre* 'one or the other' requires a singular verb, e.g.:

L'un ou l'autre a raison⁻
One or other is right (not both)

(v) For *nous autres, vous autres*, see **216**,i.

293 *Autrui* 'others, other people'

Although *autrui* can be used as the subject or the direct object of a verb, this is uncommon and it is most frequently found as the complement of a preposition, e.g.:

Faites à autrui ce que vous voudriez qu'on vous fît
Do unto others as you would they should do unto you

chercher le bien d'autrui
to seek the happiness of others

Autrui is found in literary usage only – elsewhere, use *les autres*. 'Someone else' can occasionally be translated by *autrui* when it is used in a general sense, e.g. *agir au nom d'autrui* 'to act on someone else's behalf', but note that, whenever the reference is to a specific person, *autrui* cannot be used – use *quelqu'un d'autre*, e.g.:

Je le fais pour quelqu'un d'autre
I'm doing it for somebody else

N.B. *autre chose* 'something else'.

294 *Certains* 'some (people)'

Certains as a pronoun exists in the plural only, with a meaning not far removed from that of *quelques-uns* 'some' but rather more definite. It may be used on its own or followed by *de* and a noun, e.g.:

Certains disent que . . .
Some (people) say that . . .

En entendant ceci certains des élèves se mirent à rire
On hearing this some of the pupils began to laugh

Certains d'entre vous vont pouvoir partir demain
Some of you are going to be able to leave tomorrow

As an adjective preceding the noun (see **146**), *un certain, une certaine,* plural *certains, certaines* (with no article), mean 'a certain (one), certain (ones)', or, in the plural, 'some', e.g.:

> *Un certain écrivain français a dit que . . .*
> A certain French writer has said that . . .

> *Certains jours, je ne me sens vraiment pas bien*
> Some days I don't feel at all well

295 *Chaque, chacun* 'each'

Chaque is a determiner, e.g. *chaque jour* 'each day', *chaque enfant* 'each child'.

Chacun, feminine *chacune,* is a pronoun, e.g.:

> *Chacun fera ce qu'il veut*
> Each (one) will do as he pleases

> *J'ai acheté un cadeau pour chacune de mes sœurs*
> I have bought a present for each of my sisters

There are difficulties in deciding which possessive determiner to use with reference to *chaque* or *chacun*. Note the following rules:

If *chacun* has *de* depending on it ('each of us, of them, etc.'), use *son, sa, ses,* to translate the possessive determiner.

If there is no dependent *de*

> in the 1st and 2nd pers. use *notre, nos; votre, vos;*
> in the 3rd pers. either *son, sa, ses* or *leur, leurs* may be used, unless *chacun* means people in general, in which case the former is required.

Examples:

> *Avant de partir nous avons donné chacun nos conseils* (or *chacun de nous a donné ses conseils*)
> Before going away we each of us gave our advice (*or*, each of us gave his advice)

> *Ils pensaient chacun à son propre intérêt* (or *chacun à leur propre intérêt*)
> Each of them was thinking of his own interest (*or* they were each thinking of their own interest)

> *Chacun à son goût*
> Everyone to his (their) taste

For *chacun* with a reflexive pronoun, see **219**.
See also *tout*, **317**.

296 *De quoi* 'the wherewithal, etc.'

For the use of *de quoi* with an infinitive, meaning 'the wherewithal, the means, etc.' to do something, see **273**,iii.

297 *Différents, divers* 'various'

In the plural only, and when placed before the noun (see **146**) and with no article, the adjectives *différents* and *divers* (which in this construction are more or less interchangeable), mean 'various', etc., e.g.:

> *en différents endroits*
> in various places

> *pour différentes raisons*
> for a variety of reasons

> *divers amis*
> various friends

> *en diverses occasions*
> on several occasions

> *différentes* (or *diverses*) *personnes m'en ont parlé*
> a number of people have spoken to me about it

298 *D'aucuns* 'some (people)'

D'aucuns, which now occurs mainly in the literary language, is an invariable pronoun (and only a pronoun) serving as an equivalent of *certains* (see **294**) or *quelques-uns* (see **306**), e.g.:

> *D'aucuns estiment que cela est faux*
> Some consider that that is untrue

299 *Je ne sais qui, quel, quand*, etc.

There is a whole series of indefinites formed with *je ne sais* and a determiner (*quel*), pronoun (*qui, quoi*), or adverb (*combien, comment, où, pourquoi, quand*) and all expressing uncertainty as to the person, object, time, place, etc., involved, e.g.:

Ils distribuaient je ne sais quel tract politique
They were distributing some political tract or other

Il a demandé à je ne sais qui ce qu'il fallait faire
He asked somebody or other what had to be done

Mon départ a été remis à je ne sais quand
My departure has been postponed till Heaven knows when

Il y a eu je ne sais combien de tués
There were I don't know how many people killed

Also *je ne sais quoi* (see **289**), *je ne sais comment, je ne sais où, je ne sais pourquoi.* Parallel constructions with *on* or another personal pronoun instead of *je* and with *Dieu sait* also occur, but much less frequently than those formed with *je ne sais*, e.g.:

Il a réussi on ne sait comment à s'évader
Somehow he managed to escape

Il est allé s'enterrer Dieu sait où
He has gone and hidden himself away somewhere

300   *Même*

Même has four different senses:

(i) 'same', and usually, as in English, accompanied by the definite article (but see below) (note that 'as' here is translated by *que*), e.g.:

C'est toujours la même chose
It is always the same thing

Ils n'ont pas les mêmes idées que nous
They have not got the same ideas as we (have)

Même 'same' can be preceded by other determiners than the definite article, e.g.:

Ce même individu est revenu un quart d'heure plus tard
That same individual came back a quarter of an hour later

Un même mot peut avoir plusieurs sens différents
One and the same word can have several different meanings

Note the expression *en même temps* 'at the same time' (e.g. *ils sont arrivés en même temps* 'they arrived at the same time', *en même temps que moi* 'at the same time as me'), and the possibility of omitting the definite article with a small number of nouns after *de*, e.g. *de même couleur* 'of the same colour', *de même espèce* 'of the same kind', *de même nationalité* 'of the same nationality', *de même origine* 'of the same origin', *de même taille* 'of the same size', *de même type* 'of the same type', but also *de la même couleur*, etc., and always *du même âge* 'of the same age'.

(ii) 'self', mostly with disjunctive personal pronouns (to which it is joined by a hyphen), e.g. *moi-même* 'myself', *vous-mêmes* 'yourselves', (see 215); also, with nouns denoting inanimate objects, 'itself', e.g.:

Il l'aime plus que lui-même
He loves her more than himself

Nous le ferons nous-mêmes
We shall do it ourselves

Elle est la bonté même
She is kindness itself

(iii) 'very', in which sense *même* follows the noun, e.g.:

le jour même du mariage
the very day of the marriage

Les animaux mêmes frissonnaient d'épouvante
The very animals were shivering with terror

(iv) 'even', an adverb (and therefore never takes an *s*), e.g.:

même maintenant
even now

même à Londres
even in London

Même moi je ne le sais pas
Even I don't know

Même mes cousins sont venus
Even my cousins came

The distinction in sense between ii, iii and iv is very slight; e.g. 'the very animals', 'the animals themselves', and 'even the animals' are almost interchangeable expressions.

Note that, with comparatives, 'even' must be translated by *encore* and not by *même*, e.g.:

Elle est encore plus intelligente que son père
She is even more intelligent than her father

(v) A few idioms should be noted:

(a) *à même*

As a preposition, has the sense of 'on a level with, right up against', etc., e.g.:

> *des bicoques construites à même la falaise*
> shanties built right up against the cliff
>
> *coucher à même le sol*
> to lie on the bare ground
>
> *boire à même la bouteille*
> to drink straight out of the bottle

Followed by *de* and an infinitive, has the sense of 'in a position to, able to, equal to', e.g.:

> *Il est à même de vous servir*
> He is in a position to be of use to you

(b) *au même*

> *Cela revient au même*
> That comes to the same thing

(c) *de même*

'in the same way, alike'; with *que* 'in the same way as, like', e.g.:

> *Quand un Français et un Anglais pensent de même, il faut bien qu'ils aient raison*
> When a Frenchman and an Englishman think alike, they must be right
>
> *Il en est de même des autres*
> It is just the same with the others
>
> *De même que vous, j'ai été voir*
> Like you, I have been to see
>
> *tout de même*
> all the same, notwithstanding

(d) *quand même*

In combination with *quand, même* has two uses:

1. as a conjunction, 'even if, even though', nearly always with the conditional (see **422**), e.g.:

> *Il faut l'essayer, quand même ça ne servirait à rien*
> We must try it even though it may be useless

2. as an adverb, 'notwithstanding, all the same', e.g.:

Ça ne servira à rien, mais il faut l'essayer quand même
It will be quite useless, but we must try it all the same

301   *N'importe qui*, etc.

Another set of indefinites (cf. **299**) is introduced by *n'importe* which means 'it doesn't matter (which, etc.)' and so gives the members of this set the value of 'any (one, etc.) at all', as in *n'importe qui* 'anyone (at all) (*lit.* it doesn't matter who)', *n'importe quand* 'at any time (at all) (*lit.* it doesn't matter when)', e.g.:

N'importe qui vous dira où il habite
Anyone will tell you where he lives

Vous pouvez lui donner n'importe quoi
You can give him anything (you like)

n'importe lequel d'entre vous
any one of you

à n'importe quelle heure de la soirée
(at) any time in the evening

Vous pouvez les laisser n'importe où
You can leave them anywhere

Also *n'importe combien* 'any number', *n'importe comment* 'in any way at all'.

Do not expand the above by means of a relative clause, i.e. do not use them as equivalents for *qui que ce soit qui* 'whoever', *quoi que* 'whatever', *où que* 'wherever, no matter where', etc. (see **315**).

302   *On* 'one'

On can be used only as the subject of the verb. Otherwise, its use is very similar to that of English 'one' or 'you' referring to a person or persons unspecified, e.g.:

On peut s'amuser même quand on est seul
One can enjoy oneself even when one is alone
You can enjoy yourself even when you are alone

(*Vous* should not be used in this general sense – but see the end of this section for its use as the object of the verb.) *On* is however used much more extensively than English 'one' and, in particular, is frequently found where English has a passive, e.g.:

Ici on parle français
French (is) spoken here

Qu'est-ce qu'on dit à Paris?
What is being said in Paris?

On m'en a parlé hier
I was told about it yesterday

On is also often used when some definite person or persons are intended, i.e. as the equivalent of any personal pronoun (particularly of *nous* 'we'); in such cases, though the verb remains in the third person singular, adjectives and participles agree in gender and number with the person or persons concerned, e.g.:

On est fatiguée = Tu es fatiguée?
Are you (fem.) tired?

Avez-vous trouvé ma mère? Qu'a-t-on dit? On a été bien fâchée?
Did you find mother? What did she say? Was she very angry?

On a été contents de vous voir
We (masc.) were pleased to see you

On était heureuses à cette époque
We (fem.) were happy then

In the literary language *l'on* is frequently used for *on* after a word ending in a vowel, especially monosyllables such as *et, ou, où, qui, que, si*, and occasionally at the beginning of a sentence, e.g.:

et l'on y avait construit un monument
and a monument had been built there

C'est un endroit où l'on s'ennuie
It is a place where one gets bored

ceux à qui l'on doit tant
those to whom one owes so much

Si l'on avait su!
If we had known!

L'on is not used however after *dont* or before a word beginning with *l-* (to avoid the alliteration *l- . . . l-*), so could not be substituted for *on* in such contexts as the following:

un roman dont on parle   a novel that is talked about

si on lit son roman   if one reads his novel
quand on l'avait vu   when we had seen him

As has been said, *on* can be used only as the subject of a verb. As reflexive pronouns relating to *on, se* and *soi* are used, e.g.:

On se couche tard   One goes to bed late
On le ferait pour soi(-même)   One would do it for oneself

but this is not possible when 'one' is the object pronoun in English. In such cases, the object pronoun corresponding to 'one' is *nous* or, more frequently, *vous*, e.g.:

La musique vous calme quand on est agité
Music calms one when one is upset

Il est bon de parler de ce qui vous (or *nous*) *inquiète*
It is good to talk about what worries one

But sometimes there is nothing corresponding to English 'one', e.g.:

Cela donne à penser   That makes one think

303   *Pareil* and *tel* 'such'

(i) Both *pareil* and *tel* mean 'such', but *pareil* is never used with *que* for 'such as'. This is always *tel que*.

Both words are commonly used with the indefinite article, but, as in the case of other adjectives, this precedes them, and there is nothing in French to correspond to the English order 'such a. . .'.

'Such a book as that' must be either *un tel livre* or *un livre comme* (or *tel que*) *celui-là*.

Pareil may stand before or after its noun, *tel* (unless followed by *que*) only before, e.g.:

Comment a-t-on pu faire { *une telle chose?*
                           { *une pareille chose?*
                           { *une chose pareille?*
How could they do such a thing?

The article is sometimes omitted before *pareil*, especially:

(a) after a verb in the negative, e.g.:

Je n'ai jamais vu pareille chose
I have never seen such a thing

Je n'ai jamais entendu pareil discours
I have never heard such a speech

(b) in certain prepositional phrases, e.g.:

en pareille occasion on such an occasion
hier à pareille heure yesterday at this time

(ii) Neither word can be used as an adjective with a definite article, any more than the English 'such'. But *pareil* is often treated as a noun meaning 'the like, a match', etc., and agreeing in gender with the thing named, e.g.:

Je n'ai jamais rien entendu raconter de pareil
I have never heard anything like it

Il a un bel alezan pour son carrosse, mais il ne peut pas en trouver le pareil
He has got one fine chestnut for his coach, but he cannot find a match for it

C'est une dame qui pour la vraie bonté a peu de pareilles (or *n'a pas sa pareille*)
She is a lady who for real kindness has few equals (*or* has no equal)

Tel cannot be used as a noun or pronoun except in the idioms *Monsieur un tel* 'Mr So-and-so', *Madame une telle* 'Mrs So-and-so', *les Untel* 'the So-and-sos', and in a few phrases with no article (see below).

Except for the position of the indefinite article mentioned above, it is used just like the English 'such'. With *que* it may mean either 'such as' or 'such that'; e.g.:

La chaleur était telle ⎫
        or   ⎬ *que plusieurs élèves se sont évanouis*
Telle était la chaleur ⎭

The heat was such ⎫
        or   ⎬ that several pupils fainted
Such was the heat ⎭

On devrait se débarrasser de gens tels que ceux-là
We ought to get rid of such people as those

(iii) *Tel* has the further senses of 'a certain', 'such and such a . . .', 'one . . . another', 'like', 'some or other', 'a kind of'; e.g.:

Je connais tel pays où l'on peut herboriser à sa guise
I know a certain country where a man can botanize to his
heart's content

En tel pré on trouve des fritillaires, en tel autre des orchidées
In one (*or* in such and such a) meadow fritillaries are to be
found, in another orchids

*Il fut convenu que je prendrai le train tel jour, à telle heure,
pour telle gare* (O. Mirbeau)
It was agreed that I shall catch such-and-such a train, at
such-and-such a time, for such-and-such a station

Tel père, tel fils
Like father, like son

Il se tenait debout, tel (or *telle*) *une statue de bronze*
He stood like a bronze statue

Note that in sentences on the pattern of this last example, *tel* may
agree with either term of the comparison (i.e., in this example
either with *il*, masculine, or with *statue*, feminine).

(iv) *Tel* is used as a pronoun meaning 'one. . ., another. . .; one
(some) who. . .', e.g.:

Tel l'aime, tel le déteste
One man likes him, another loathes him

Tel l'aimera demain qui le déteste aujourd'hui
Some who loathe him to-day will like him to-morrow

(v) Note the expression *tel quel. . .* 'as it is (was), as they are
(were), etc.', in which both *tel* and *quel* agree with the noun or
pronoun they refer to, e.g.:

Il a acheté la maison telle quelle
He bought the house as it was

Je vais le prendre tel quel
I shall take it as it is

Il faut laisser les choses telles quelles
Things must be left as they are

(vi) When 'such (a)' means no more than 'of this kind', it is often
best translated by *de ce genre, de cette sorte*, e.g.:

J'ai chez moi un instrument de cette sorte
I have such an instrument at home

> *Il a écrit beaucoup de livres de ce genre*
> He has written many such books

(vii) 'Such (a)' with reference to adjectives is *si* or (particularly in speech) *tellement*, e.g.:

> *une si belle vue*
> such a beautiful view
>
> *une ville tellement historique*
> such an historic town
>
> *des problèmes si (tellement) difficiles*
> such difficult problems

(viii) When 'such' refers to quantity (= 'so much'), it is often best translated by *tant de* or *tellement de*, e.g.:

> *Nous avons eu tant* (or *tellement*) *de difficulté*
> We have had such difficulty
>
> *Il faisait tant de bruit*
> He was making such a noise

(but the difference in meaning between these sentences and . . . *une telle difficulté*, . . . *un tel bruit*, which characterize the difficulty and the noise in terms of quality – i.e. their intensity – rather than in terms of quantity, is only slight).

304   *Quelconque* 'some or other, any (one) at all'

Quelconque normally follows a noun introduced by an indefinite article, e.g.:

> *sous un prétexte quelconque*
> on some pretext or other
>
> *Soient deux droites quelconques*
> Let there be any two straight lines
>
> *Avez-vous des livres quelconques?*
> Have you any books of any kind?

(Note that *quelconque* has acquired the meaning of 'mediocre, poor' in such contexts as *C'est un vin quelconque* 'It's a pretty ordinary sort of wine', *Ce film est tout à fait quelconque* 'This film isn't up to much'.)

305 The following indefinites (which will be discussed in the order given here) must be clearly distinguished as they are not in any way interchangeable:

(i) *quelque, quelques* (determiner) 'some' (see **306**)

(ii) *quelque* (invariable adverb) + numeral 'some, approximately' (see **307**)

(iii) *quel que* (variable) + *être* + noun or pronoun 'whatever (= of whatever kind)' (see **308**)

(iv) *quelque(s)* + noun + relative clause 'whatever (+ noun)' (see **309**)

(v) *quelque* (invariable adverb) + adjective + *que* 'however (+ adjective)' (see **310**).

306 *Quelque, quelques* 'some, a few'

Quelque(s) is an indefinite determiner whose meaning in the plural does not differ much from that of the indefinite or partitive article *des*, e.g.:

Nous avons eu quelque difficulté
We had some difficulty

Quelque imbécile m'a cassé les lunettes
Some idiot has broken my glasses for me

Je lui ai acheté quelques fleurs
I bought her some (a few) flowers

In questions or after *si* 'if', *quelque(s)* is sometimes translatable by 'any', e.g. *Avez-vous eu quelque difficulté?* 'Did you have any difficulty?', *Si vous avez quelque difficulté* . . . 'If you have any difficulty . . .'

Note *quelques-uns* (fem. *unes*) as a plural pronoun 'some, a few', e.g.:

Quelques-uns de mes amis sont venus
Some of my friends came

Vous avez perdu toutes vos photos? – Non, mais j'en ai perdu quelques-unes
Have you lost all your photos? – No, but I've lost some (a few) of them

See also *quelque chose* 'something' (311) and *quelqu'un* 'someone' (312).

307 *Quelque* (adverb) 'some, approximately, about'

Note that *quelque* before a numeral and meaning 'some, approximately, about, roughly' is an adverb and therefore invariable (i.e. it does *not* take a plural -*s*), e.g.:

> *J'ai acheté quelque deux cent cinquante timbres*
> I bought about 250 stamps

> *Il est mort il y a quelque cinquante ans*
> He died some fifty years ago

> *Cela m'a valu quelque cent mille francs*
> That brought me in about a hundred thousand francs

308 *Quel que* (variable) 'whatever (= of whatever kind)'

The equivalent of English 'whatever' + 'to be' + a noun or pronoun is *not* the pronoun *quoi que* (see 315,ii) but *quel que* (in which *quel* agrees in gender and number with the noun or pronoun); the reason for the use of *quel que* rather than *quoi que* is that, in an expression such as 'whatever the difficulty may be', we are not really dealing with 'what' it is (a difficulty is a difficulty) but with 'what kind of' difficulty it is. Note too that the verb 'to be', which is regularly omitted in this construction in English ('whatever the difficulty' means the same thing as 'whatever the difficulty may be'), *must* be inserted (in the subjunctive) in French, e.g.:

> *quelle que soit la difficulté*
> whatever the difficulty

> *quelles que soient vos inquiétudes*
> whatever your worries (may be)

> *tous vos problèmes, quels qu'ils soient*
> all your problems, whatever they may be

Être in this construction may be preceded by *devoir* or *pouvoir*, e.g.:

> *quel que doive être le prix de cette noble liberté* (Montesquieu)
> whatever the cost of this noble freedom may be

> *quel qu'il puisse être*
> whatever he may be

309 *Quelque(s)* (determiner) + noun + relative clause 'whatever'

'Whatever' (in the sense of 'whichever') before a noun qualified by a relative clause is *quelque* (sing.), *quelques* (plur.) (note that *quel-* does not vary for gender or number); the relative clause is almost always introduced by *que*, but a *qui*-clause is not impossible, e.g.:

> *quelques fautes que vous ayez commises*
> whatever mistakes you may have made

> *de quelque manière que l'on aborde ce problème*
> in whatever (whichever) way one approaches this problem

> *quelque lien qui pût nous unir* (Musset)
> whatever bond united us

310 *Quelque* (adverb) + adjective 'however'

(i) *Quelque* 'however', modifying an adjective + *que* and the subjunctive, is an adverb and is therefore invariable, e.g.:

> *quelque riche qu'il soit*
> however rich he is

> *quelque grands que soient vos défauts*
> however great your faults (may be)

Note:

(a) that if the subject is a noun it follows the verb, as in the example just quoted

(b) that, though the verb is sometimes omitted in English when the subject is a noun (see the translation of the last example above), this is not possible in French (cf. **308**)

(c) that the verb is in most cases *être* but that the construction is also possible with such verbs as *sembler* 'to seem' and *paraître* 'to appear', and that any of these verbs may be preceded by a modal verb such as *devoir* or *pouvoir*, e.g.:

> *quelque difficile que cela puisse paraître*
> however difficult that may appear

(ii) A similar but much less frequent construction is that in which *quelque* modifies another adverb, e.g.:

> *quelque audacieusement qu'il mente*
> however impudently he lies

(iii) **A number of alternatives to this construction exist. Note the following:**

quelque riche que soit mon père	
si riche que soit mon père	however rich my father
tout riche que soit mon père	may be
pour riche que soit mon père	
aussi riche que soit mon père	

(The construction with *aussi* is sometimes frowned on, but it has been used by good modern writers.)

Tout may also be followed by the indicative, but with a slight difference in meaning in that the construction in question presents the situation as a fact, e.g. *tout riche qu'est mon père* 'rich though my father is' (see also **317,v,b**).

When the subject is a personal pronoun, an even greater range of constructions is available since, with *si* and *aussi*, the *que* may be omitted, in which case the pronoun subject follows the verb; we therefore have, for 'however rich he is' (and not including *tout riche qu'il est* 'rich though he is'), at least seven possibilities, viz.:

quelque riche qu'il soit	
si riche qu'il soit	*si riche soit-il*
tout riche qu'il soit	
pour riche qu'il soit	
aussi riche qu'il soit	*aussi riche soit-il*

(What is more, the constructions *quelque riche soit-il, tout riche soit-il* and *pour riche soit-il* do occur, but only infrequently and should therefore be avoided.)

311   *Quelque chose* 'something'

Note that, though *la chose* 'thing' is feminine, *quelque chose* is masculine.

Note too that, with adjectives, we have the construction *quelque chose d'intéressant* 'something interesting' (see **667,i**) (but *autre chose* 'something else').

In questions or after *si* 'if', *quelque chose* may correspond to English 'anything' (see also **319**), e.g.:

Avez-vous quelque chose à déclarer?
Have you anything to declare?

s'il arrive quelque chose
if anything happens

312   *Quelqu'un* 'someone, somebody'

Quelqu'un is used in much the same way as its English counter-
parts 'someone, somebody', e.g.:

Quelqu'un vous demande
Someone is asking for you

Je connais quelqu'un qui peut le faire
I know someone who can do it

Note with adjectives the construction with *de* (see **667**,i), e.g.
quelqu'un d'important 'someone important', *quelqu'un d'autre*
'someone else'.

In questions or after *si* 'if', *quelqu'un* may correspond to English
'anyone' (see also **319**), e.g.:

Avez-vous vu quelqu'un?	Did you see anybody?
Il y a quelqu'un?	Anybody there?
si quelqu'un vient	if anyone comes

Like English 'somebody', *quelqu'un* can mean 'somebody of
importance', as in *Il se croit quelqu'un* 'He thinks himself somebody'.

313   *Quiconque* 'whoever, anyone (who)'

Quiconque may be used as an indefinite relative pronoun meaning
'whoever, anyone who', in which case it can function at the same
time as the direct or indirect object of one verb and the subject of
another (see the second and third examples below), e.g.:

Quiconque a dit cela doit être fou
Whoever said that must be mad

La loi punit quiconque est coupable
The law punishes anyone who is guilty

Ils vont vendre leurs services à quiconque veut les employer
(Voltaire)
They will go and sell their services to anyone who will
employ them

It may also be used without any relative value in the sense of 'anyone' (in which case it differs little in meaning from *n'importe lequel, n'importe qui,* see **301**), e.g.:

> *Je le sais mieux que quiconque*
> I know it better than anyone

> *Demandez à quiconque des assistants*
> Ask anyone present

314 *Qui . . . qui . . .* 'some . . . some . . .'

Qui, repeated and with no verb, has a distributive value meaning 'some (did this), some (did that)' e.g.:

> *Les clients de l'hotel prenaient, qui du thé, qui du porto, qui un cocktail, qui un whisky au soda* (P. Bourget)
> Some of the hotel's guests took tea, some took port, some a cocktail, some a whisky and soda

Note that, though we have translated *qui . . . qui . . .* as 'some . . . some . . .', in fact, since *qui* does not vary for number, this construction does not specify whether each *qui* refers to only one or to more than one individual.

315 *Qui que (ce soit)* 'whoever', *quoi que (ce soit)* 'whatever', *où que* 'wherever', etc.

(i) 'Whoever'

(a) The form *qui que* remains only as the complement of *être*, e.g.:

> *qui que vous soyez*   whoever you are
> *qui que ce soit*   whoever it is

(b) As subject of the verb, the form *qui que ce soit qui* must be used, e.g. *qui que ce soit qui ait dit cela* 'whoever said that' (see also d below)

(c) As direct object, though the form *qui que* is still given in some grammars (e.g. *qui que vous cherchiez* 'whoever you are looking for'), in practice only *qui que ce soit que* is now in current use, e.g. *qui que ce soit que vous cherchiez* (see also d below)

(d) The constructions given in b and c above, i.e. *qui que ce soit* + a relative clause introduced by *qui* or *que*, themselves function as the subject or object of another verb, e.g.:

Qui que ce soit qui vienne sera obligé de repartir tout de suite
Whoever comes will have to leave again at once

Qui que ce soit que vous rencontriez pourra vous diriger
Anyone whom (whoever) you meet will be able to direct you

*Si par hasard vous rencontriez qui que ce soit qui m'ait envoyé
ce livre, vous pourriez peut-être le remercier de ma part*
If you happened to meet whoever it was that sent me this
book, you might perhaps thank him for me

(e) After prepositions, only *qui que ce soit que* is found, e.g.:

à qui que ce soit que vous ayez écrit
whoever (it is) you wrote to

avec qui que ce soit qu'il voyage
whoever he is travelling with

(f) When not followed by a subordinate clause, *qui que ce soit*
means 'anyone at all', e.g.:

si vous voyez qui que ce soit
if you see anyone at all

Ne le dites pas à qui que ce soit
Don't tell anyone

*Pour le reste du chemin vous n'avez qu'à demander à qui que
ce soit*
For the rest of the way you have only to ask anyone you meet

(ii) 'Whatever'

(a) *Quoi que* serves as the complement of *être*, e.g.:

quoi que ce soit   whatever it is

(Note the difference between *quoi que ce soit* and *quoi qu'il en soit*
'however that may be, be that as it may, at all events'.)

(b) As subject of the verb, only *quoi que ce soit qui* is in current
use (*quoi qui* occurs, but only very rarely and should not be
copied), e.g.:

quoi que ce soit qui vous inquiète
whatever is worrying you

(c) As direct object, the most common form is *quoi que*, e.g. *quoi
que vous fassiez* 'whatever you do', but *quoi que ce soit que* may
also be used, e.g.:

quoi que ce soit que vous fassiez
whatever you do

Quoi que ce soit qu'on lui ait dit l'a bien fâché
Whatever (it was that) was said to him has greatly annoyed
him

(d) After prepositions, *quoi que ce soit que* must be used, e.g.:

sur quoi que ce soit que vous l'écriviez
whatever you write it on

(e) When not followed by a subordinate clause, *quoi que ce soit*
means 'anything at all', e.g.:

Vous pouvez dire quoi que ce soit
You can say anything (at all)

si vous le soupçonnez de quoi que ce soit
if you suspect him of anything at all

(iii) 'Wherever'

(a) 'Wherever' in its strictly indefinite sense is *où que*, e.g.:

Où qu'il aille, il n'est jamais content
Wherever he goes, he is never satisfied

(b) Note however that, in English, 'wherever' followed by a
relative clause is the equivalent of 'anywhere' or 'everywhere', and
this must be expressed in French by *partout où* (literally 'everywhere where'), e.g.:

Partout où vous allez, moi je peux y aller aussi
Wherever (anywhere) you go I can go too

Vous pouvez me conduire partout où vous voudrez
You may take me wherever (anywhere) you like

(c) Note that 'somewhere' and, in questions or 'if' clauses,
'anywhere', are *quelque part*, e.g.:

Je l'ai vu quelque part
I saw him somewhere

L'avez-vous vu quelque part?
Have you seen him anywhere?

si vous le voyez quelque part
if you see him anywhere (somewhere)

Note too *n'importe où* 'anywhere at all' (see **301**).

(iv) 'Whenever'

(a) Note that there is no form based on *quand* corresponding to *où que* 'wherever'. When 'whenever' has a strictly indefinite value, i.e. that of 'at whatever time', it can be expressed by some such turn of phrase as *à quelque moment (qu'il arrive)* 'whenever (= at whatever time) (he arrives)', but in practice *quand* 'when' alone is usually adequate, e.g.:

> *Quand il arrivera, dites-lui de me téléphoner*
> Whenever he arrives, tell him to ring me

(b) Frequently, however, 'whenever' means 'each time that', in which case the French equivalent is *chaque fois que* or *toutes les fois que*, e.g.:

> *Chaque fois qu'elle va à Paris, elle achète beaucoup de vêtements*
> Whenever she goes to Paris, she buys a lot of clothes

(v) 'However'

(a) 'However' in the sense of 'in whatever way' is *de quelque façon que* or *de quelque manière que*, e.g.:

> *De quelque façon que vous vous y preniez, vous n'allez pas réussir*
> However you go about it, you won't succeed

(b) For 'however' with an adjective or an adverb (e.g. 'however difficult'), see **310**.

('However' meaning 'nevertheless' is *cependant, pourtant* or *toutefois*.)

316 *Tel* 'such'

See **303**, *'Pareil* and *tel'*.

317 *Tout* 'all, every, etc.'

(i) *Tout* may be a determiner (as in *tout enfant* 'every child') or a predeterminer (i.e. an element that comes before the determiner, as in *tous les enfants* 'all the children') (see ii below), a pronoun (see iii), a noun (see iv), or an adverb (see v).

As a determiner, predeterminer or pronoun, it has these forms:

	singular	plural
masc.	*tout*	*tous*
fem.	*toute*	*toutes*

Note that the masculine plural form, *tous*, is pronounced:

as a determiner or predeterminer	[tu]
as a pronoun	[tus]

(ii) As a determiner or predeterminer

(a) In the sense of 'any, every' it is used in the singular without the article.

In the sense of 'all' (meaning 'any, every') it is used in the plural, generally with the article. But, as in English, these two uses constantly overlap, and the insertion or omission of the article in the plural is often a matter of taste, e.g.:

Toute ville a son histoire
Every town has its history

Toutes les villes ont leur histoire
All towns have their history

Tout homme est mortel
Every man is mortal

Tous les hommes sont mortels
All men are mortal

Des gens arrivaient { *à tout moment*
                        à tous moments

People were arriving all the time

So 'on all sides' may be *de toute part*, or *de toutes parts*; or, plural only, *de tous côtés*. In such cases *chaque, chacun*, can be substituted for *tout* whenever 'each' or 'each one' is possible in English.

(b) In the sense of 'all', meaning the whole, it is used in the singular with the definite article.

With the indefinite article *entier* usually takes the place of *tout* in the singular, and must always do so with the partitive article in the plural, e.g.:

Toute la ville fut incendiée
All the (*or* the whole) town was burnt

Une ville entière (or, less often, *toute une ville*) *fut incendiée*
A whole town was burnt

Des villes entières furent incendiées
Whole towns were burnt

(c) It is used with a numeral in the sense of

(1) 'every second, third', etc.

(2) 'both', 'all three', etc., e.g.:

tous les deux jours
every other day, *or* both days

tous les trois jours
every third day, *or* all three days

In both senses the article may always be inserted, and must be if the numeral qualifies a noun. It can be omitted only in *tous deux*, 'both', *tous trois* 'all three', *tous quatre* 'all four', and their feminines, when these stand without any noun, e.g.:

Allez vous coucher, tous trois, or *tous les trois*
Go to bed, all three of you

Elles sont parties toutes (les) quatre
They (fem.) have all four left

but

Tous les trois enfants (never *tous trois*) *sont allés se coucher*
All three children have gone to bed

Tous trois etc. are characteristic of literary rather than of spoken usage which prefers *tous les trois* etc.; with numbers above four, the form with the article, *tous les dix* 'all ten', etc., must be used even in literary style.

Tout before the name of a town is invariable when the expression denotes the inhabitants, e.g.:

Tout Rome était dans les rues
All Rome was in the streets

(d) When, in English, the pronouns 'all', 'everyone', 'everybody', 'anyone', are used as antecedents to a relative, the demonstrative pronoun (*celui, celle, ceux, celles*) must, in French, be inserted next after *tout, toute, tous, toutes*, e.g.:

'All who were there' becomes 'all those who were there'

Tous ceux qui y étaient

(e) *Tout* with 'neuter' *ce* and a relative (see **274**) is used to form a kind of superlative in the common expression *tout ce qu'il y a (avait, aura,* etc.) *de,* e.g.:

> *Il était tout ce qu'il y a de charmant*
> He was most charming, as charming as could be

(iii) As a pronoun

(a) *tout* means 'all, everything'; *tous, toutes* mean 'all', e.g.:

> *Tout va bien*
> All is well
>
> *Il a tout perdu, tout*
> He has lost everything, absolutely everything
>
> *Ils sont tous partis*
> They have all left
>
> *Je les connais toutes*
> I know them (*fem.*) all

(b) It is used in apposition to a personal pronoun, when English has 'all of us, you or them'. In this case it always follows the personal pronoun, e.g. *nous tous* 'all of us'.

(iv) As a noun, *le tout* means 'the whole', e.g.:

> *Le tout est plus grand que la somme de ses parties*
> The whole is greater than the sum of its parts
>
> *Trois tiers font un tout*
> Three thirds make one whole

Note the idiomatic use of *le tout* in such expressions as *Le tout est de réussir* 'The thing that matters is to succeed (success is everything)'.

'The whole (of)' + determiner + noun is translated either by the predeterminer *tout* or by the adjective *entier* (see ii, b above), e.g. *Il passe tout son temps à lire* 'he spends the whole of his time (= all his time) reading'.

(v) As an adverb

(a) *tout* means 'quite, wholly, entirely, all', and qualifies adverbs, adjectives or participles. In this case *tout* remains unchanged, except that before feminine adjectives or participles beginning with a consonant or aspirate *h* it becomes in the singular *toute*, in the plural *toutes*, e.g.:

> *Elle était tout facilement la première*
> She was quite easily top
>
> *Elle était tout enchantée, tout heureuse*
> She was quite happy and delighted
>
> *Elle arriva toute fatiguée, toute haletante*
> She arrived quite (wholly) exhausted and out of breath
>
> *Il avait les mains tout écorchées, toutes lacérées*
> His hands were all raw and torn

(b) It is used in the sense of 'however' before an adjective or participle followed by *que* (see also **310**,iii). In this sense also the spelling varies according to the rule given above, e.g.:

> *tout puissants qu'ils soient*
> *toutes puissantes qu'elles soient* } however powerful they are

but

> *tout insensées qu'elles soient*   however crazy they are

How important it is to distinguish between the adverb *tout* and the adjective *tout, toute*, is well illustrated by the following example taken from the *Grammaire Larousse du XXe Siècle*, p. 250:

> *Donnez-moi toute autre occupation que celle-là*
> Give me any other employment than that
>
> *Donnez-moi une tout autre occupation que celle-là*
> Give me some employment completely different from that

(vi) Note *tout le monde* 'everybody', e.g. *Tout le monde le connaît* 'Everybody knows him'. ('All the world, the whole world' is *le monde entier*.)

318 *Un, une* 'one'; *l'un, l'une, les uns, les unes* 'the one, the ones'
   Generally speaking *un, une*, can be used to translate the English 'one' unless

(i) 'one' is indefinite (see *on*, **302**) or

(ii) 'one' is followed by a relative, expressed or understood (see **245**).

Examples:

> *Vous n'avez pas de parapluie? Si, j'en ai un dans la voiture*
> Haven't you got an umbrella? Yes, I've got one in the car

but

> *Quelle belle robe! Je la préfère à celle que vous portiez hier*
> What a pretty dress! I like it better than the one you had on
> yesterday (because the relative 'which' is understood after
> 'one')

(See for *l'un . . . l'autre, les uns . . . les autres,* 292, iii; for
chacun, 295; for *quelqu'un,* 312.)

319   The translation of 'anyone', 'anything'

'Anyone', 'anything', must be variously translated according to the
context:

(i) With 'if', e.g.:

> If anybody comes, say I am out
> *Si quelqu'un vient*   } *dites que je suis sorti*
> *Si l'on vient*

> Wake me if anything happens
> *Éveillez-moi s'il arrive* { *quelque chose*
>   *quoi que ce soit* }

(ii) In comparative sentences, e.g.:

> The richer anyone is, the more taxes he pays
> *Plus on est riche, plus on paie d'impôts*
> *Plus quelqu'un est riche, plus il paie d'impôts*

(iii) Followed by a relative, e.g.:

> Anyone who means to make speeches must get himself
> taught
> *Qui*
> *Celui qui* } *veut faire des discours doit se faire instruire*
> *Quiconque*
> *Si l'on*   } *veut faire des discours,* { *on* } *doit se faire*
> *Si quelqu'un*   { *il* } *instruire*

> *Tous ceux qui veulent faire des discours doivent se faire instruire*

Anything which annoys him is bad for his health
Ce qui ⎫
Tout ce qui ⎭ *l'ennuie nuit à sa santé*

(iv) Meaning 'everyone', 'everything', e.g.:

Anyone can do that ⎰ *Tout le monde peut faire ça* ⎱
⎱ *Il n'y a personne qui ne puisse faire ça* ⎰

Anything is better than disgrace
Tout est préférable au déshonneur

You can say anything
Vous pouvez tout dire
Vous pouvez dire n'importe quoi

(v) Meaning 'someone', 'something', e.g.:

Anyone who is worth anything knows that
Tous ceux qui valent quelque chose savent ça

(vi) In a question, direct or indirect, e.g.:

Is anyone at home?
Y a-t-il quelqu'un à la maison?

Have you anything to declare?
Avez-vous quelque chose à déclarer?

Do you think anything (something) is keeping him?
Croyez-vous que quelque chose le retienne?

(vii) With negatives, see **551**.

(See also *je ne sais qui, quoi,* **299**; *n'importe qui, quoi,* **301**; *quelconque,* **304**; *quiconque,* **313**; *qui que ce soit, quoi que ce soit,* **315**, i,f and ii,e.)

Quantifiers

320 Quantifiers, as the name suggests, define various elements in the sentence in terms of quantity (e.g. how little or how much thereof, how few or how many thereof). Some items that could have been included here (such as 'some' and 'all') have already been dealt with under 'Indefinites', and others could equally well have been included under that heading.

For reasons of convenience, we shall consider together both pronominal and adverbial quantifiers.

321   (i) Note that in English such quantifiers as 'enough, (as, so, too, how) much, (as, so, too, how) many, more, less, few, fewer' can, and usually do, qualify directly the noun that they govern, e.g. 'enough bread, many books, less time'. In French, *de* must be used in comparable contexts, e.g.:

assez de pain	enough bread
trop de voitures	too many cars
autant de difficulté	as much difficulty
tant de problèmes	so many problems
beaucoup de livres	many books
combien d'enfants?	how many children?
plus de temps	more time
moins de danger	less danger
peu d'amis	few friends

(ii) In comparable expressions with a personal pronoun, English either uses 'of' or omits the pronoun altogether, leaving it to be implied from the context; in French, the pronoun *en* 'of it, of them' (see **201**), must not be omitted, e.g.:

Il en vend autant que vous
He sells as many (of them) as you

Et le pain? – Nous en avons déjà assez
What about the bread? – We have enough already

Combien en avez-vous acheté?
How much (how many) did you buy?

When 'of it, of them' are not implied, then there is no *en* in French, e.g.:

Beaucoup ont disparu	Many have disappeared
Combien a-t-il perdu?	How much did he lose?

(iii) Note that when the quantifiers are followed by a definite article in English, the same is true of French; so, we have, without an article, *beaucoup d'étudiants* 'many students', *trop de bière* 'too much beer', *combien de papier?* 'how much paper?', but:

Beaucoup des étudiants de cette université sont Africains
Many of the students at this university are Africans

Il a bu trop de la bière que vous avez achetée
He has drunk too much of the beer that you bought

Combien du papier a été brûlé?
How much of the paper was burnt?

322 *Assez* 'enough' and *trop* 'too (much, many)'

(i) Modifying a noun or pronoun, e.g.:

Ils achètent assez de bonbons pour tous les enfants
They are buying enough sweets for all the children

A-t-il assez d'argent?
Has he enough money?

Nous n'en vendons pas assez
We don't sell enough (of it, of them)

Notre pays importe trop de voitures
Our country imports too many cars

Vous en prenez trop
You are taking too much (too many)

Note that, after a phrase introduced by *assez* or *trop*, a following infinitive is preceded by *pour*, e.g.:

Nous avons assez de temps pour le faire
We have enough time to do it

Il a perdu trop d'argent pour être content
He has lost too much money to be satisfied

(ii) When *assez* and *trop* are the complement of *être*, *en* is not required, e.g. *C'est assez* 'It's enough', *Ça c'est trop* 'that's too much'; but note the idioms *C'en est assez!* 'Enough is enough!' and *C'en est trop!* 'That's going too far!'

(iii) *Assez* and *trop* modifying an adjective or an adverb mean 'enough, quite, rather' and 'too' respectively; as with *assez (trop) de* (see i above), a following infinitive is preceded by *pour*, e.g.:

C'est assez difficile
It's rather difficult

Il est assez intelligent pour comprendre
He is intelligent enough to understand

Ils ont une maison à peine assez grande pour leur nombreuse famille
They have a house hardly big enough for their large family

Nous sommes arrivés à une heure assez avancée de la nuit
We arrived rather late at night

Il marche assez lentement
He walks rather slowly

Il vient assez souvent nous voir
He comes to see us quite often

Il est trop malade pour pouvoir sortir
He is too ill to be able to go out

Nous sommes restés trop longtemps
We stayed too long

(iv) Note that, whereas in English 'enough' follows adjectives ('easy enough') and occasionally follows nouns ('time enough' for 'enough time'), *assez* always precedes both adjectives and nouns (*assez facile, assez de temps*).

(v) When modifying verbs, *assez* means 'enough' and *trop* means 'too much', and are often enough in themselves where English uses some expanded phrase such as 'long enough' or 'too hard', e.g.:

Nous avons assez travaillé pour une journée
We have worked enough for one day

Ils se disputent trop
They argue too much

Avez-vous assez dormi?
Have you slept long enough?

Il travaille trop
He works too hard

As in i and iii above, a following infinitive is preceded by *pour*, e.g.:

Il parle trop pour être pris au sérieux
He talks too much to be taken seriously

323 *Autant* 'as much, as many' and *tant* 'so (as) much, so (as) many'

(i) *Autant* expresses a comparison of equality between nouns or pronouns or between verbs, as *aussi* does between adjectives or between adverbs (see 157), e.g.:

Il mange autant de pain (autant de pommes) que vous
He eats as much bread (as many apples) as you (do)

Mon frère en vend autant que mon père
My brother sells as much (as many) as my father (does)

Je lis autant que mon frère
I read as much as my brother (does)

L'avez-vous assez considéré? – Je l'ai considéré autant que je veux
Have you considered it sufficiently? – I have considered it as much as I want to

As a rule, *autant* follows the word it qualifies, e.g.:

J'y suis intéressé autant que lui
I am as much concerned in it as he (is)

Note that in sentences of the type *Je ne trouve pas ça ton affaire autant que la mienne* (or *Je ne trouve pas ça autant ton affaire que la mienne*) 'I do not consider that (to be) as much your business as mine', *autant* qualifies the verb *être* that is understood, i.e. it does not qualify the noun and hence there is no *de*.

Occasionally, as an alternative to the usual construction *Il est aussi agréable qu'intelligent* 'He is as pleasant as (he is) intelligent' (see 157), one finds the construction *Il est agréable autant qu'intelligent*, in which again *autant* qualifies the verb *être* that is understood (= *Il est agréable autant qu'il est intelligent*).

(ii) In negative and interrogative clauses, both *autant* and *tant* are possible, e.g.:

Il n'a pas autant (or *tant*) *de patience que vous*
He hasn't as much patience as you (have)

Je ne mange pas autant (or *tant*) *(de viande) que vous*
I do not eat as much (meat) as you (do)

Vous y tenez autant (or *tant*) *que ça?*
Are you that keen on it?

(iii) On the optional insertion in English of a verb such as 'to be, to have, to do' after a comparative, where French normally has no such verb, see 157 and 173, and various examples in i and ii above.

(iv) Although *tant* is not usually used to express the comparative of equality in affirmative clauses, it is sometimes so used with the verbs *pouvoir* and *vouloir*, e.g.:

Il pleut tant qu'il peut
It is raining as hard as it can

Je vous en donnerai tant que vous voudrez
I will give you as much as you want

(v) *Tant que* (but not *autant que*) is also used:

(a) of time, meaning 'as long as', e.g.:

Tant que je vivrai, je ne vous oublierai jamais
As long as I live, I shall never forget you

(b) of extent, meaning 'as far as', e.g.:

Tant que la vue s'étend, il n'y a rien qu'une vaste plaine
As far as the eye can see, there is nothing but one vast plain

(vi) *Tant (que)* also means 'so much, so many (that)', another
sense in which *autant* cannot be used, e.g.:

J'ai tant mangé que je ne peux plus me lever
I have eaten so much that I can't get up any more

J'ai tant à faire (or *tant de choses à faire*) *que je ne sais où
commencer*
I have so much (*or* so many things) to do that I don't know
where to begin

Je le plains tant que je me rends aussitôt à Paris pour l'aider
I am so sorry for him that I am going at once to Paris to help
him

In this type of sentence, in which *tant* means 'so much, so many'
and *que* means 'that' not 'as', *tant* can be replaced by *tellement*
(e.g. *j'ai tellement de choses à faire que . . ., je le plains tellement
que . . .*).

Note the following use of *tant* where English puts 'so' + an
adjective or adverb at the beginning of the clause for emphasis:

*Tant ils se sont montrés cruels qu'on finit par se soulever
contre eux*
So cruel did they show themselves that in the end there was a
general rising against them

324 *Beaucoup*, etc. 'much, many'

(i) *Beaucoup* is by far the most widespread French equivalent for
'much, many, a lot of', e.g.:

Il n'a pas beaucoup de patience
He hasn't much (a lot of) patience

Ils vendent beaucoup de fleurs
They sell a lot of flowers

Avez-vous beaucoup d'amis?
Have you many friends?

Je n'en veux pas beaucoup
I don't want much (*or* many)

Il a beaucoup voyagé
He has travelled a great deal

(ii) (a) Before a comparative, when 'much' could be replaced by 'far' in English, *de beaucoup* may be used as an alternative to *beaucoup*, e.g.:

Il est beaucoup plus fort que son ami
Il est de beaucoup plus fort que son ami
He is much (*or* far) stronger than his friend

(b) *De beaucoup*, not *beaucoup* alone, *must* be used as the equivalent of 'much' or 'by far' when placed after a comparative, e.g.:

Il est plus fort de beaucoup que son ami

or when the comparative is not expressed in the same sentence but implied, e.g.:

Est-il plus fort que son ami? – Mais oui, de beaucoup
Is he stronger than his friend? – Yes, much

or with a superlative, expressed or implied, e.g.:

Il est de beaucoup le plus fort de tous
He is by far the strongest of all

Est-il le plus fort de tous? – Mais oui, de beaucoup
Is he the strongest of all? – Yes, by far

(iii) *Beaucoup* can never be qualified by *très* (or any other word for 'very'), *trop* 'too', *aussi* 'as' or *si* 'so'. 'Very much, very many' are usually just *beaucoup*, though *beaucoup, beaucoup* can be used for emphasis, 'too much, too many' are translated by *trop* alone (see **322**), 'as much, as many' by *autant* or (in some circumstances) *tant* (see **323**), and 'so much, so many' by *tant* (see **323**).

Examples:

> *Je l'aime beaucoup*   I like him very much
>
> *Je me suis beaucoup, beaucoup amusé*
> I enjoyed myself *very* much

On the other hand *beaucoup* can qualify *trop, plus,* or *moins*, e.g.:

> *Il a beaucoup trop d'argent*
> He has much too much money
>
> *Il a beaucoup plus (moins) d'argent qu'il ne lui en faut*
> He has much more (less) money than he needs

(iv) For (*le*) *plus* as the comparative and superlative of *beaucoup*, see **165–168**.

(v) A frequent form in conversational French is *pas mal de* 'quite a lot of', e.g.:

> *J'ai eu pas mal de difficulté*
> I had quite a lot of difficulty
>
> *Il en vend pas mal*
> He sells quite a lot of them

Note that the verb is not preceded by *ne* (contrast *pas grand-chose*, vii below).

(vi) Note that *force* 'many' (and occasionally 'much'), which sometimes occurs in the literary language, is not followed by *de* (see also **395**,vi), e.g. *avec force compliments* 'with many compliments'.

(vii) Note the form *grand-chose* which occurs widely in speech but only in the expression *pas grand-chose* 'not much' and which cannot be followed by a noun as a complement; the verb, if there is one, is preceded by *ne* (contrast *pas mal*, v above); e.g.:

> *Il n'a pas dit grand-chose*
> He didn't say much
>
> *Qu'est-ce que vous avez acheté? – Pas grand-chose*
> What have you bought? – Not much

(viii) In the literary language, *maint*, which has the following forms:

	sing.	plur.
masc.	*maint*	*maints*
fem.	*mainte*	*maintes*

when used in either the singular or the plural expresses a plural number, 'many a, many', e.g. *maint Anglais* 'many an Englishman', *maints Anglais* 'many Englishmen'. It is used especially in the expressions *maintes fois* 'many a time', *à mainte(s) reprise(s)* 'on numerous occasions'.

(ix) *Nombre de, quantité de* (with no article before them) can be used with plural nouns in the sense of 'a lot of, a number of', e.g.:

Nombre de députés ont voté contre
A number of MPs voted against

Quantité d'indications laissent supposer qu'il est mort
A number of indications lead one to think he is dead

325 *Bien du, bien de la, bien des* 'much, many'

These expressions for 'much, many' are somewhat less objective than *beaucoup* and convey the idea of a measure of surprise, satisfaction, disapproval, or some other subjective reaction, e.g.:

Il a bien de l'argent
He has plenty of money

Elle vous donne bien de l'inquiétude
She causes you a lot of worry

Bien des gens me l'ont dit
Many people have told me so

Bien de (instead of *du, de la, de l', des*) is used only when an adjective precedes the noun (see **44**) and with *autres* used as a pronoun (see **292,i**), e.g.:

J'ai bien de jolies esquisses à vous montrer
I have many pretty sketches to show you

Bien d'autres sont de mon avis
Many others are of my opinion

326 *Combien?* 'how much? how many?'

(i) Direct questions, e.g.:

Combien de pain?
How much bread?

Combien d'Américains sont venus?
How many Americans came?

Combien en avez-vous?
How much (*or* how many) have you?

Combien sont partis?
How many have left?

Combien est-ce que vous pesez?
How much do you weigh?

(ii) Indirect questions, e.g.:

Je ne sais pas combien il en a acheté
I don't know how much he bought

(iii) Note the following construction in which *combien* corresponds to English 'how' (see also **154**):

Je ne m'étais pas rendu compte combien vous étiez inquiet
I had not realised how worried you were

327   *Davantage* 'more' and *moins* 'less' – see **330**.

328   *Peu* 'little, few', *un peu* 'a little'

(i) When 'little' means 'not much', it must be translated by *peu de* and not by *petit*, e.g.:

Nous avons eu peu de difficulté
We had little difficulty

Note the difference between this, which stresses the negative aspect ('not much'), and *un peu de* 'a little' (and again *petit* cannot be used) which stresses the positive aspect ('there is some'), e.g.:

Nous avons eu un peu de difficulté
We had some (*or* a little) difficulty

Note the expression *peu de chose* 'little, not much', as in *Cela compte pour peu de chose* 'That doesn't count for much'.

(ii) In the plural, *peu* means 'few', e.g. *Il a peu d'amis* 'He has few friends'. There is no plural equivalent of *un peu* (for 'a few' use *quelques,* e.g. *Il a quelques amis* 'He has a few friends', see **306**).

(iii) For *le peu* 'the little, the few', see **395**,ii.

(iv) For *(le) moins* as the comparative and superlative of *peu*, see **165–168**.

329   *La plupart* 'most, the greater part'

La plupart can be either singular, e.g.:

> *la plupart du temps*
> most of the time

> *La plupart de ce qu'il dit est faux*
> Most of what he says is untrue

or plural, e.g.:

> *La plupart sont déjà partis*
> Most have already left

> *La plupart de mes amis sont étudiants*
> Most of my friends are students

330   *Plus* 'more', *moins* 'less', etc.

(i) For the use of *plus* and *moins* to express the comparative and superlative of adjectives and adverbs, see **160–164** and **169–172**

(ii) For (*le*) *plus* as the comparative and superlative of *beaucoup* and (*le*) *moins* as the comparative and superlative of *peu*, see **164–168**.

(iii) For (*ne . . .*) *plus* in negative clauses, see **552**.

(iv) *Davantage* 'more'

(a) *Davantage* generally qualifies only verbs, e.g.:

> *Vous devriez manger davantage*
> You ought to eat more

> *Rien ne pourrait lui plaire davantage*
> Nothing could please him more

Note its use with reference to the pronoun *le* standing for an adjective (though even here it really qualifies the verb *être*), e.g.:

> *Il est vrai que ma sœur est inquiète, mais mon frère l'est davantage*
> It is true that my sister is worried, but my brother is more so

(b) *Davantage que* and *davantage de* are often considered to be incorrect (even though both constructions occurred in Classical French and may still be found in good authors), and are best avoided. However, there is no objection to using *davantage* with the pronoun *en* 'of it, of them', e.g.:

Voulez-vous encore du thé? – Merci, je n'en veux pas davantage
Do you want any more tea? – No, thank you, I don't want any more

Nous n'en dirons pas davantage
We shall say no more about it

(c) In practice, *davantage* usually comes at the end of its clause, though not invariably (e.g. *J'aimerais pouvoir faire davantage pour vous* 'I should like to be able to do more for you').

(d) Note that *davantage* can never be used with numbers, in which case 'more than' is always *plus de* (see **167**).

(v) For the use of *encore* meaning 'more', see **616**,iv.

331 *Plusieurs* 'several'

The use of *plusieurs* is much like that of English 'several'; note that it has the same form for both genders, e.g. *plusieurs Anglais* 'several Englishmen', *plusieurs femmes* 'several women', *plusieurs de mes amis* 'several of my friends', *j'en ai vu plusieurs* 'I have seen several' (with reference to either masculine or feminine nouns).

332 *Presque* 'almost, nearly'

(i) *Presque* can modify adjectives, adverbs, certain indefinite pronouns, and verbs, e.g.:

Il est presque aveugle	He is almost blind
presque tous	almost all (of them)
presque personne (or *rien*)	almost nobody (*or* nothing)
presque immédiatement	almost immediately
Il pleurait presque	He was almost crying

In the above uses, the *-e* of *presque* is never elided before a vowel.

Note the use of *ou presque* 'or almost', expressing a kind of afterthought, e.g.:

C'est impossible, ou presque	It's impossible, or almost
Il pleurait, ou presque	He was crying, or nearly

(ii) Certain nouns may also be modified by *presque*; with the exception of the one word *une presqu'île* 'peninsula', the *-e* is not elided, nor is a hyphen used, e.g.:

J'en ai la presque certitude
I am practically certain of it

la presque totalité des habitants
almost all the inhabitants

être élu à la presque unanimité
to be elected almost unanimously

333 *Que de . . .!* 'what a lot of!'

Que de . . . meaning 'what a lot of' or sometimes 'how much, how many', is often used as a quantifier in exclamations, e.g.:

Que de peine pour rien!
What a lot of trouble for nothing!

Que de fois faut-il que je vous le dise!
How many times must I tell you!

Que nous avons dû visiter de cathédrales!
What a lot of cathedrals we had to go and see!

334 *Si* 'so', *tant* 'so much, so many', *tellement* 'so, so much, so many'

(i) 'So' with an adjective or adverb is *si* or, especially in familiar style, *tellement*; 'so . . . that' is *si* (or *tellement*) . . . *que . . .*; e.g.:

Ce problème est si difficile
This problem is so difficult

Elle est tellement jolie
She is so pretty

J'y suis allé si souvent
I have been there so often

Je me suis levé si tard que j'ai manqué le train
I got up so late that I missed the train

Il est si distingué que je ne le vois plus
He is so grand that I never see him now

This construction must not be confused with *si . . . que* 'as . . . as' after a negative (see 157).

(ii) 'So much, so many' must be rendered by *tant* or *tellement* (see 323,vi) and not by *si*. Note that *si* qualifies only adjectives and adverbs – it never qualifies a verb.

(iii) For the construction *si riche qu'il soit* 'however rich he is', see **310**, iii.

335 *Très*, etc. 'very'

(i) *Très* can be used in almost exactly the same way as its English equivalent 'very', but there are a few limitations to this statement. The most important of these is that *très* cannot qualify *beaucoup* – see **324**, iii.

Très can also be used with past participles more freely than 'very'; while, unlike 'very', it directly qualifies adjectival and adverbial expressions, e.g.:

> *C'est un homme très estimé et très au courant des affaires*
> He is a man highly esteemed and very much in the know

Lastly, though *très* can be used elliptically like 'very', this is much less common in French than in English, e.g.:

> *Êtes-vous très inquiet? Oui, très!*
> Are you very worried? Yes, very!

is possible in French, common in English; but in French, *Oui, très inquiet* would be much more usual.

(For 'very' as an adjective, translated by *même*, see **300**,iii.)

(ii) *Bien* and *fort* can be used for 'very' in much the same way as *très*, except that they cannot be used alone; i.e. they could replace *très* in any of the examples in (i) above except *Oui, très!* However, it is better to avoid using *fort* before another word beginning with *f-*, so *très loin, bien loin, fort loin* 'very far', but preferably only *très facile* or *bien facile* for 'very easy'.

336 *Trop* 'too (much, many)' – see **322**.

337 Note that when the subject of the verb is a quantifier (or an expression introduced by a quantifier, such as *beaucoup de gens*) that can be either singular or plural, the number of the verb and the number and gender of any adjectives or participles depend on the sense of the quantifier and its complement if any, e.g.:

> *Beaucoup de ce qu'il dit est faux*
> Much of what he says is untrue

> *Beaucoup estiment que c'est trop tard*
> Many think it is too late

Combien de temps s'est écoulé?
How much time has elapsed?

Combien de personnes ont été tuées?
How many people were killed?

Tant de convives étaient arrivés que . . .
So many guests had arrived that . . .

Trop de difficultés étaient survenues
Too many difficulties had arisen

Verbs

Introduction

338 Verbs will be discussed according to the following plan:

A The conjugations (definition) (339)
B Moods and tenses (names thereof) (340–341)
C The persons of the verb (definition) (342–343)
D Defective verbs (definition) (344)
E The morphology (forms) of the verb (345–378)
F Reflexive verbs (379–381)
G The passive (382–385)
H Negative and interrogative conjugations (386–389)
I Person and number (390–396)
J Tenses (397–424)
K The infinitive (425–438)
L The present participle (439–447)
M The past participle (448–471)
N The moods (definition) (472)
O The subjunctive (473–506)
P 'May, might, must, ought, should, would' (507–513)
Q The imperative (514–517)
R The complement of verbs (518–538)
S Idioms with *avoir, être* and *faire* (539–541)

A The conjugations

339 The ending of the present infinitive decides the conjugation to which any French verb is said to belong.

There are only four endings for the present infinitive: *-er*, *-ir* (not preceded by *o*), *-re*, *-oir*.

Verbs in *-er* belong to the First Conjugation.
Verbs in *-ir* (not *-oir*) belong to the Second Conjugation
Verbs in *-re* belong to the Third Conjugation.

These are called the 'regular' conjugations. It must not be supposed, however, that all verbs whose infinitive ends in *-er*, *-ir* or *-re* are regular.

The First Conjugation contains several thousand verbs, nearly all of them regular (for exceptions, see **352–357**).

The Second Conjugation contains something approaching 350 verbs of which over 300 are regular.

The Third Conjugation contains about 100 verbs, the great majority of which are irregular.

Verbs with a present infinitive in *-oir* used to be counted as another conjugation; but they are better classified as irregular verbs, as there are only about 30 of them, of which not more than seven belong to any one group.

The first and second conjugations are called the 'living conjugations'; the third conjugation is said to be 'dead'. All this means that is that any new verb coming into the language must be conjugated on the model of either *donner* or *finir* (see **351** and **359**), i.e. it is not possible to create new verbs ending in *-re* (or, of course, *-oir*).

B Names of moods and tenses

340 English usage differs as regards the names of French tenses. The first column below shows the names used in this book; the second, the most usual French names; the third, some alternative

English names used in some grammars (but note that some grammars adopt their own non-standard names for various tenses – none of these are listed here):

Indicative	*Indicatif*	
present	*présent*	
perfect	*passé composé*	
imperfect	*imparfait*	
pluperfect	*plus-que-parfait*	
preterite	*passé simple*	past historic
past anterior	*passé antérieur*	
double-compound past	*passé surcomposé*	
future	*futur*	
future perfect	*futur antérieur*	
Conditional	*Conditionnel*	
present	*présent* (or *futur dans le passé*)	
past	*passé* (or *futur antérieur du passé*)	
Subjunctive	*Subjonctif*	
present	*présent*	
perfect	*passé*	
imperfect	*imparfait*	past
pluperfect	*plus-que-parfait*	
Imperative	*Impératif*	

The tenses of the conditional are sometimes considered as tenses of the indicative, and there is a case for this. However, for the sake of convenience, the conditional is here (as in many other grammars) classified as a separate mood.

The tenses formed on the basis of a part of the verb *avoir* or *être* and the past participle (e.g. *j'ai parlé, il était venu*) are known as **compound tenses** (for a full list with examples, see **449**). For **double-compound tenses**, see **412**. All other tenses are known as **simple tenses**.

341 A form of the verb that shows tense and mood (i.e., as far as French is concerned, a form that has an ending corresponding to one of the six persons of the verb – see **342**) is known as a 'finite verb'. The non-finite forms of the verb are the infinitive (see

425–438), the present participle (see 439–447), and the past participle (see 448–471).

C   The persons of the verb

342   The persons of the verb are associated with the following subject pronouns:

	sing.	plur.
first	*je* 'I'	*nous* 'we'
second	*tu* 'you'	*vous* 'you'
third (masc.)	*il* 'he, it'	*ils* 'they'
(fem.)	*elle* 'she, it'	*elles* 'they'

For further discussion, see 194–197.

Impersonal verbs

343   (i)   An impersonal verb, properly so called, is a verb which

(a) exists in the infinitive, participles and third person singular only;

(b) has no subject except the neuter impersonal pronoun *il* 'it, there';

(c) is never used personally in any sense.

Of these there are in French only two – *il faut* 'it is necessary' and *il neige* 'it snows'.

Both these verbs and other verbs used impersonally (see ii to iv below) have as their subject the pronoun *il* which therefore corresponds both to English 'it' (as in *il neige* 'it is snowing') and to 'there' (as in *il est arrivé une catastrophe* 'there occurred a catastrophe').

(ii) Besides these wholly impersonal verbs, there are others (particularly verbs having to do with the weather) that are either used quite currently both impersonally and personally, e.g.:

Il gèle	It is freezing
Il dégèle	It is thawing

Je gèle   I am freezing
Le lac dégèle   The lake is thawing

or else are usually impersonal but not when used metaphorically,
e.g.:

Il pleut   It is raining
Il tonne   It is thundering

but

Des coups pleuvaient sur lui
Blows were raining upon him

Cent pièces de canon tonnèrent à son arrivée
On his arrival a hundred guns thundered (a welcome)

The verb *grêler* is impersonal when intransitive (*il grêle* 'it is
hailing') but personal when used transitively (e.g. *L'orage a grêlé
les vignes* 'The hail-storm damaged the vines').

(iii) Some verbs are used impersonally only in certain constructions, e.g.:

agir   *il s'agit de*
              it is a question of, a matter of, etc.

aller   *il y va de (sa vie,* etc.)
              (his life) is at stake

avoir   *il y a*
              there is, there are

convenir   *il convient de*
              it is as well (*or* advisable) to

faire   *il fait beau, chaud, froid*, etc.
              it is fine, hot, cold, etc.

              il fait du soleil, du vent, etc.
              it is sunny, windy, etc.

(iv) Some verbs are used impersonally or personally without
change of sense, e.g.:

Alors il est arrivé un événement extraordinaire
Then there occurred an extraordinary event

Alors un événement extraordinaire est arrivé
Then an extraordinary event occurred

Il se trouve là de belles choses
There are some beautiful things to be found there

Là se trouvent de belles choses
Some beautiful things are to be found there

D   Defective verbs

344   Defective verbs are verbs that exist only in certain tenses or even only in parts of tenses. In general, French defective verbs are not in widespread use and there is even uncertainty in some cases as to which forms actually occur other than as exceptionally rare forms that one author or another happens at some time to have used (and may in fact have invented). Defective verbs are all indicated as such in our tables (**377**) in which the forms given are those that are generally recognized as existing.

Defective verbs must not be confused with impersonal verbs (see **343**) which, by virtue of their meaning, exist only in the third person singular, having as their subject the impersonal pronoun *il*.

E   The morphology (forms) of the verb

345   The endings

(i) The endings of the imperfect and future indicative, the conditional and the imperfect subjunctive never vary. They are, for all verbs:

Imperf. Indic.	*-ais*	*-ais*	*-ait*	*-ions*	*-iez*	*-aient*
Fut. Indic.	*-ai*	*-as*	*-a*	*-ons*	*-ez*	*-ont*
Condit.	*-ais*	*-ais*	*-ait*	*-ions*	*-iez*	*-aient*
Imperf. Subjunct.	*-sse*	*-sses*	*-ˆt*	*-ssions*	*-ssiez*	*-ssent*

(In the third person singular of the imperfect subjunctive, note the forms *tînt* and *vînt* for the verbs *tenir* and *venir*, and similar forms for compounds of these two verbs.)

The endings of the present subjunctive vary in *être* and *avoir* only. For all other verbs they are:

.-e	*-es*	*-e*	*-ions*	*-iez*	*-ent*

(ii) The stem and endings of the imperative are the same as those of the present indicative except:

(a) in the second person singular of *-er* verbs and verbs such as *cueillir, couvrir* that are conjugated like *-er* verbs in that tense (see **365**); these lose their *-s* except before *y* and *en*, e.g.:

	2nd sing. pres. indic.	2nd sing. imper.
penser	*tu penses*	*Pense à moi* Think of me
		Penses-y Think about it
donner	*tu donnes*	*Donne-le-moi* Give it to me
		Donnes-en à Jean Give John some

Cf. too for the verb *aller*, second person singular indicative *tu vas*, imperative *va*, but *vas-y*;

(b) in the verbs *avoir, être, savoir* and *vouloir*; see the notes to these verbs in the tables.

Note that *pouvoir*, impersonal verbs and certain defective verbs have no imperative; this fact is referred to in the notes to the verbs in question in the tables.

(iii) If the past participle ends in *-i, -is* or *-it*, the first person singular preterite indicative ends in *-is*; except that *luire* 'shine' (see further **374**,ii), *traire* 'milk' have no preterite or imperfect subjunctive.

If the past participle ends in *-u*, the first person singular preterite indicative ends in *-us*, except for *battre* 'beat', *coudre* 'sew', *tenir* 'hold', *venir* 'come', *vêtir* 'clothe', *voir* 'see', and the verbs ending in *-andre, -endre, -ondre, -rdre*. Of these *tenir* and *venir* have *je tins, je vins*, for the first person singular preterite, and *prendre* has past participle and preterite *pris*. The rest have *-u* in the past participle, *-is* in the first person singular preterite.

346   The stems

(i) Except for *aller, avoir, être, faire, pouvoir, savoir, valoir* and *vouloir*, and any impersonal or defective verbs that do not have a form for the third person plural present indicative, the third person plural present indicative provides the key to the stem of the present subjunctive, e.g.:

	3rd plur. pres. indic.	1st sing. pres. subjunct.
dire	*ils disent*	*que je dise*
prendre	*ils prennent*	*que je prenne*
recevoir	*ils reçoivent*	*que je reçoive*

Note that *aller, valoir* and *vouloir*, like many other irregular verbs, have one stem in the first and second persons plural of the present subjunctive and a different one in the other persons, e.g. *que j'aille, que nous allions*. Note too that, apart from *avoir, être, faire, pouvoir* and *savoir*, the first and second persons plural of the present subjunctive are the same as those of the imperfect indicative, e.g. from *devoir, (que) nous devions, (que) vous deviez*.

(ii) On the stem of the imperative, see **345**,ii.

(iii) The stem of the future and conditional in regular *-er* and *-ir* verbs is the same as the infinitive (e.g. *finir, je finirai*); in all regular and irregular *-re* verbs except *être* and *faire*, it is the same as the infinitive without the final *-e* (e.g. *prendre, je prendrai*); in all verbs, however irregular the stem of the future may be in other respects, it always ends in *-r* (e.g. *être, je serai; voir, je verrai*).

(iv) The stem of the imperfect subjunctive is the same as that of the preterite; the vowel of the ending (*-a-, -i-* or *-u-*) is also the same as that of the preterite; so, in regular first conjugation verbs we have, for example, preterite *je chantai, tu chantas*, etc., imperfect subjunctive *que je chantasse*, etc.; for other verbs, the first person singular imperfect subjunctive may be formed from the first person singular preterite by replacing the *-s* of the preterite by *-sse* (e.g. for the verbs *être, prendre, vivre* and *voir* we have preterite *je fus, je pris, je vécus, je vis*, etc., imperfect subjunctive *que je fusse, prisse, vécusse, visse*, etc.). As this is true for all verbs without exception, the imperfect subjunctive is not listed in the tables that follow.

347 The verbs *avoir* and *être*

The two very common verbs *avoir* and *être* are highly irregular. They each have two distinct uses:

(i) as full verbs with the meanings 'to have' and 'to be' respectively

(ii) as auxiliary verbs; in particular:

(a) *avoir* serves to form the compound tenses of the active voice of most verbs (e.g. *j'ai fini* 'I have finished')

(b) *être* serves to form the compound tenses of the active voice of reflexive verbs and a few others (e.g. *je me suis levé* 'I have got up', *je suis arrivé* 'I have arrived') (see **451–456**) and to form the passive (e.g. *il est soupçonné* 'he is suspected') (see **382–385**).

Note that the active compound tenses both of *avoir* itself and of *être* are formed with *avoir*, e.g. *j'ai eu* 'I have had', *j'ai été* 'I have been'.

As these two verbs are so important, we list their forms in full (**349–350**) before those of the regular verbs.

348 In the tables that follow, the forms of the subjunctive are given with *que* before them, as is usual in French grammars (e.g. first person singular present subjunctive of *être* is given as *que je sois*). It must not however be assumed either that *que* always requires the subjunctive (in fact, *que* is more often followed by the indicative) or that the subjunctive cannot occur without *que* (for the subjunctive without *que*, see **476–478**).

349 *Avoir* 'to have'

		Infinitive		
pres.	*avoir*		past	*avoir eu*
		Participles		
pres.	*ayant*		past	*eu*
		Indicative		
pres.	*j'ai*		perf.	*j'ai eu*
	tu as			*tu as eu*
	il a			*il a eu*
	nous avons			*nous avons eu*
	vous avez			*vous avez eu*
	ils ont			*ils ont eu*
imperf.	*j'avais*		pluperf.	*j'avais eu*
	tu avais			*tu avais eu*
	il avait			*il avait eu*
	nous avions			*nous avions eu*
	vous aviez			*vous aviez eu*
	ils avaient			*ils avaient eu*

pret.	*j'eus*	past ant.	*j'eus eu*
	tu eus		*tu eus eu*
	il eut		*il eut eu*
	nous eûmes		*nous eûmes eu*
	vous eûtes		*vous eûtes eu*
	ils eurent		*ils eurent eu*
fut.	*j'aurai*	fut. perf.	*j'aurai eu*
	tu auras		*tu auras eu*
	il aura		*il aura eu*
	nous aurons		*nous aurons eu*
	vous aurez		*vous aurez eu*
	ils auront		*ils auront eu*

Conditional

pres.	*j'aurais*	past	*j'aurais eu*
	tu aurais		*tu aurais eu*
	il aurait		*il aurait eu*
	nous aurions		*nous aurions eu*
	vous auriez		*vous auriez eu*
	ils auraient		*ils auraient eu*

Subjunctive

pres.	*que j'aie*	perf.	*que j'aie eu*
	que tu aies		*que tu aies eu*
	qu'il ait		*qu'il ait eu*
	que nous ayons		*que nous ayons eu*
	que vous ayez		*que vous ayez eu*
	qu'ils aient		*qu'ils aient eu*
imperf.	*que j'eusse*	pluperf.	*que j'eusse eu*
	que tu eusses		*que tu eusses eu*
	qu'il eût		*qu'il eût eu*
	que nous eussions		*que nous eussions eu*
	que vous eussiez		*que vous eussiez eu*
	qu'ils eussent		*qu'ils eussent eu*

Imperative

aie   ayons   ayez

Notes on *avoir*:

1 The compound *ravoir* 'to get back, recover' is used only in the infinitive.

2 Note that the forms of the imperative are the same as those of the present subjunctive except that the second person singular is *aie* instead of *aies*.

3 Some idioms with *avoir* will be found in **539**.

350 *Être* 'to be'

Infinitive

pres.	*être*	past	*avoir été*

Participles

pres.	*étant*	past	*été*

Indicative

pres.	*je suis*	perf.	*j'ai été*
	tu es		*tu as été*
	il est		*il a été*
	nous sommes		*nous avons été*
	vous êtes		*nous avez été*
	ils sont		*ils ont été*
imperf.	*j'étais*	pluperf.	*j'avais été*
	tu étais		*tu avais été*
	il était		*il avait été*
	nous étions		*nous avions été*
	vous étiez		*vous aviez été*
	ils étaient		*ils avaient été*
pret.	*je fus*	past ant.	*j'eus été*
	tu fus		*tu eus été*
	il fut		*il eut été*
	nous fûmes		*nous eûmes été*
	vous fûtes		*vous eûtes été*
	ils furent		*ils eurent été*
fut.	*je serai*	fut. perf.	*j'aurai été*
	tu seras		*tu auras été*
	il sera		*il aura été*
	nous serons		*nous aurons été*
	vous serez		*vous aurez été*
	ils seront		*ils auront été*

Conditional

pres.	*je serais*	past	*j'aurais été*
	tu serais		*tu aurais été*
	il serait		*il aurait été*
	nous serions		*nous aurions été*
	vous seriez		*vous auriez été*
	ils seraient		*ils auraient été*

Subjunctive

pres.	*que je sois*	perf.	*que j'aie été*
	que tu sois		*que tu aies été*
	qu'il soit		*qu'il ait été*
	que nous soyons		*que nous ayons été*
	que vous soyez		*que vous ayez été*
	qu'ils soient		*qu'ils aient été*

imperf.	que je fusse	pluperf.	que j'eusse été
	que tu fusses		que tu eusses été
	qu'il fût		qu'il eût été
	que nous fussions		que nous eussions été
	que vous fussiez		que vous eussiez été
	qu'ils fussent		qu'ils eussent été

Imperative

sois soyons soyez

Notes on *être*:

1 Observe that the past participle *été* can never take an agreement in gender or number and that its spelling therefore never changes.

2 Note that the forms of the imperative are the same as those of the present subjunctive.

3 Some idioms with *être* will be found in **540**.

First conjugation: verbs in -er

351 *Donner* 'to give'

Infinitive

pres.	donner	past	avoir donné

Participles

pres.	donnànt	past	donné

Indicative

pres.	je donne	perf.	j'ai donné
	tu donnes		tu as donné
	il donne		il a donné
	nous donnons		nous avons donné
	vous donnez		vous avez donné
	ils donnent		ils ont donné
imperf.	je donnais	pluperf.	j'avais donné
	tu donnais		tu avais donné
	il donnait		il avait donné
	nous donnions		nous avions donné
	vous donniez		vous aviez donné
	ils donnaient		ils avaient donné
pret.	je donnai	past ant.	j'eus donné
	tu donnas		tu eus donné
	il donna		il eut donné
	nous donnâmes		nous eûmes donné
	vous donnâtes		vous eûtes donné
	ils donnèrent		ils eurent donné

fut.	je donnerai	fut. perf.	j'aurai donné
	tu donneras		tu auras donné
	il donnera		il aura donné
	nous donnerons		nous aurons donné
	vous donnerez		vous aurez donné
	ils donneront		ils auront donné

Conditional

pres.	je donnerais	past	j'aurais donné
	tu donnerais		tu aurais donné
	il donnerait		il aurait donné
	nous donnerions		nous aurions donné
	vous donneriez		vous auriez donné
	ils donneraient		ils auraient donné

Subjunctive

pres.	que je donne	perf.	que j'aie donné
	que tu donnes		que tu aies donné
	qu'il donne		qu'il ait donné
	que nous donnions		que nous ayons donné
	que vous donniez		que vous ayez donné
	qu'ils donnent		qu'ils aient donné

imperf.	que je donnasse	pluperf.	que j'eusse donné
	que tu donnasses		que tu eusses donné
	qu'il donnât		qu'il eût donné
	que nous donnassions		que nous eussions donné
	que vous donnassiez		que vous eussiez donné
	qu'ils donnassent		qu'ils eussent donné

Imperative

donne   donnons   donnez

Note on *donner*:

The second person singular imperative takes an *-s* before *en* or *y* (see 345,ii), e.g. *Donnes-en à Jean* 'Give John some', *Parles-en à ta mère* 'Speak to your mother about it', *Penses-y* 'Think about it'.

Peculiarities of verbs in -er

Verbs in -cer, -ger

352   Verbs ending in the infinitive in *-cer* require a cedilla under the *c*, and verbs ending in *-ger* require an *e* after the *g*, when (but only when) the ending begins with *a* or *o*, e.g. (from the verbs *avancer, manger*): *nous avançons, il avança, nous mangeons, je mangeais*

Verbs with é or e [ə] in the penultimate syllable

353 Verbs with *é* in the last syllable but one of the infinitive change this *é* into *è* in the whole of the singular and the third person plural of the present indicative and subjunctive and the second person singular of the imperative, i.e. when followed by a final syllable having as its vowel a mute *e*. In the first and second persons plural and throughout all other tenses and in the participles, the *é* is kept, e.g. (from the verb *céder* 'to yield'):

pres. indic.	pres. subjunct.	imper.
je cède	que je cède	
tu cèdes	que tu cèdes	cède
il cède	qu'il cède	
nous cédons	que nous cédions	cédons
vous cédez	que vous cédiez	cédez
ils cèdent	qu'ils cèdent	

But *cédant, cédé,* future *je céderai,,* etc., conditional *je céderais,* etc., imperfect indicative *je cédais,* etc., preterite *je, cédai,* etc., imperfect subjunctive *qu'il cédât,* etc.

Like *céder* are *altérer* 'to impair' (*j'altère,* etc.), *compléter* 'to complete', *espérer* 'to hope', *léguer* 'to bequeath', *protéger* 'to protect', *régner* 'to reign', *refléter* 'to reflect'. Note that, in the case of verbs having *é* in two successive syllables, it is only the second that is affected, e.g. *répéter* 'to repeat' (*je répète,* etc.), *pénétrer* 'to penetrate', *persévérer* 'to persevere', *préférer* 'to prefer', *révéler* 'to reveal'. Note too that verbs such as *agréer* 'to accept' and *créer* 'to create', in which there is no consonant between the *é* and the ending, are not affected by this rule, e.g. *j'agrée, ils créent* (see 358).

354 Some verbs in *-eler* or *-eter* and all other *-er* verbs having *e* [ə] in the last syllable but one of the infinitive (e.g. *mener* 'to lead', *semer* 'to sow', *lever* 'to raise', *peser* 'to weigh', and compounds thereof such as *amener* 'to bring', *emmener* 'to take away', *enlever* 'to remove', *soupeser* 'to feel the weight of') change the *e* into *è* in the whole of the singular and the third person plural of the present indicative and subjunctive and the second person singular of the imperative, *and also throughout the future and conditional tenses,* i.e. when followed by *any* syllable, final or not, having as its vowel a mute *e*. Elsewhere, the *e* is kept, e.g. (from *geler* 'to freeze', *acheter* 'to buy'):

pres. indic.	pres. subjunct.	imper.
je gèle	*que je gèle*	
tu gèles	*que tu gèles*	*gèle*
il gèle	*qu'il gèle*	
nous gelons	*que nous gelions*	*gelons*
vous gelez	*que vous geliez*	*gelez*
ils gèlent	*qu'ils gèlent*	
j'achète	*que j'achète*	
tu achètes	*que tu achètes*	*achète*
il achète	*qu'il achète*	
nous achetons	*que nous achetions*	*achetons*
vous achetez	*que vous achetiez*	*achetez*
ils achètent	*qu'ils achètent*	

Future *je gèlerai, tu gèleras, il gèlera, nous gèlerons, vous gèlerez, ils gèleront, j'achèterai*, etc.; conditional *je gèlerais, j'achèterais*, etc.; but imperfect indicative *je gelais, j'achetais*, etc.; preterite *je gelai, j'achetai*, etc.; imperfect subjunctive *qu'il gelât, qu'il achetât*, etc.; present participle, *gelant, achetant*; past participle *gelé, acheté*.

Similarly *je mène, nous menons, je mènerai*, etc.; *je sème, nous semons, je sèmerai*, etc.; *je lève, nous levons, je lèverai*, etc.; *je pèse, nous pesons, je pèserai*, etc.

Like *geler* are *celer* 'to conceal', *ciseler* 'to chisel', *congeler* 'to (deep-)freeze', *déceler* 'to detect, reveal', *écarteler* 'to tear apart', *modeler* 'to model', *peler* 'to peel'. Like *acheter* are *crocheter* 'to pick (a lock, etc.)', *haleter* 'to pant', *racheter* 'to buy back, redeem'. For other verbs in *-eler, -eter*, see 355 and 356 below.

355 Most other verbs in *-eler, -eter*, double the *l* or the *t* in those forms where *geler, acheter*, etc., take a grave accent, e.g. (from *appeler* 'to call', *jeter* 'to throw'):

pres. indic.

j'appelle	*je jette*
tu appelles	*tu jettes*
il appelle	*il jette*

nous appelons   *nous jetons*
vous appelez   *vous jetez*
ils appellent   *ils jettent*

and similarly in the present subjunctive and the imperative. Future *j'appellerai, je jetterai*, etc.; conditional *j'appellerais, je jetterais*, etc.; but imperfect indicative *j'appelais, je jetais*, etc.; preterite *j'appelai, je jetai*, etc.; imperfect subjunctive *qu'il appelât, qu'il jetât*, etc.; present participle *appelant, jetant*; past participle *appelé, jeté*.

The following verbs (and various other highly uncommon ones) are like *appeler* and *jeter*:

amonceler, to heap up
atteler, to harness
chanceler, to totter
ensorceler, to bewitch
épeler, to spell
étinceler, to sparkle
ficeler, to tie up
grommeler, to mutter
niveler, to level
rappeler, to recall
renouveler, to renew
ruisseler, to stream
cacheter, to seal
caqueter, to cackle, gossip
colleter, to seize by the collar
décacheter, to unseal
épousseter, to dust
étiqueter, to label
feuilleter, to leaf through (a book, etc.)
moucheter, to speckle, fleck
projeter, to project, plan
rejeter, to reject

356 The verb *harceler* 'to harass' can be either like *geler* (e.g. *je harcèle*) or like *appeler* (e.g. *je harcelle*). A few (relatively uncommon) verbs in *-eter* can be treated either like *acheter* or like *jeter*; they include *becqueter* 'to peck' (e.g. *il becquète* or *becquette*), *breveter* 'to patent', and *fureter* 'to ferret about, pry, rummage'.

Verbs in -*yer*

357 Verbs ending in the infinitive in -*oyer*, -*uyer* change *y* into *i* before mute *e*, e.g. *employer* 'to use', *j'emploie*; *nettoyer* 'to clean', future *je nettoierai; ennuyer* 'to bore', *ils ennuient*.

Verbs ending in -*ayer* may either do the same or retain the *y*, e.g. *payer* 'to pay', *je paie* or *paye, je paierai* or *payerai*.

The verb *grasseyer* 'to pronounce the letter *r* gutturally' always retains the *y*, *je grasseye*.

Note that *envoyer* 'to send' is conjugated like *employer*, except that it makes its future and conditional irregularly: *j'enverrai, j'enverrais*, etc. *Renvoyer* 'to send back, dismiss' does the same.

Other verbs in -*voyer*, such as *convoyer* 'to escort', *fourvoyer* 'to lead astray', follow the same pattern as *employer* throughout.

Verbs in -*éer*, -*ier*

358 Difficulty is sometimes caused by the verbs ending in -*éer* or -*ier*. These are quite regular, but to beginners -*ée* or -*ii*- or -*éi*- may seem strange; still more so a feminine past participle with -*éée*.

Examples:

	créer, create	*crier*, shout
past part.	*créé, créée, créés, créées*	*crié, criée, criés, criées*
pres. indic.	*je crée*	*je crie*
	nous créons	*nous crions*
imp. indic.	*je créais*	*je criais*
	nous créions	*nous criions*
fut. indic.	*je créerai*	*je crierai*
	nous créerons	*nous crierons*

Second conjugation: verbs in -ir

359 *Finir* 'to finish'

		Infinitive		
pres.	*finir*	past	*avoir fini*	
		Participles		
pres.	*finissant*	past	*fini*	
		Indicative		
pres.	*je finis*	perf.	*j'ai fini*	
	tu finis		*tu as fini*	
	il finit		*il a fini*	

	nous finissons		*nous avons fini*
	vous finissez		*vous avez fini*
	ils finissent		*ils ont fini*
imperf.	*je finissais*	pluperf.	*j'avais fini*
	tu finissais		*tu avais fini*
	il finissait		*il avait fini*
	nous finissions		*nous avions fini*
	vous finissiez		*vous aviez fini*
	ils finissaient		*ils avaient fini*
pret.	*je finis*	past ant.	*j'eus fini*
	tu finis		*tu eus fini*
	il finit		*il eut fini*
	nous finîmes		*nous eûmes fini*
	vous finîtes		*vous eûtes fini*
	ils finirent		*ils eurent fini*
fut.	*je finirai*	fut. perf.	*j'aurai fini*
	tu finiras		*tu auras fini*
	il finira		*il aura fini*
	nous finirons		*nous aurons fini*
	vous finirez		*vous aurez fini*
	ils finiront		*ils auront fini*

Conditional

pres.	*je finirais*	past	*j'aurais fini*
	tu finirais		*tu aurais fini*
	il finirait		*il aurait fini*
	nous finirions		*nous aurions fini*
	vous finiriez		*vous auriez fini*
	ils finiraient		*ils auraient fini*

Subjunctive

pres.	*que je finisse*	perf.	*que j'aie fini*
	que tu finisses		*que tu aies fini*
	qu'il finisse		*qu'il ait fini*
	que nous finissions		*que nous ayons fini*
	que vous finissiez		*que vous ayez fini*
	qu'ils finissent		*qu'ils aient fini*
imperf.	*que je finisse*	pluperf.	*que j'eusse fini*
	que tu finisses		*que tu eusses fini*
	qu'il finît		*qu'il eût fini*
	que nous finissions		*que nous eussions fini*
	que vous finissiez		*que vous eussiez fini*
	qu'ils finissent		*qu'ils eussent fini*

Imperative

finis   finissons   finissez

Peculiarities of verbs in *-ir*

360   *Haïr* 'to hate' (note the *tréma* – *ï* not *i*) is irregular in the singular of the present indicative, *je hais, tu hais, il hait,* and the second singular of the imperative, *hais* – these forms have no *tréma* and are pronounced [ɛ]. In all other forms, the verb is regular except for the *tréma*, which indicates that the group *-ai-* is pronounced as two syllables, [ai], not as [ɛ], e.g. *nous haïssons, je haïssais, il haïra, j'ai haï,* etc., and, in the preterite and imperfect subjunctive where the *tréma* takes the place of the usual circumflex accent (but in fact these tenses of *haïr* are almost never used even in the literary language), *nous haïmes, vous haïtes, qu'il haït.*

361   *Bénir* 'to bless' is now completely regular. Note however the old past participle *bénit* that is now used only as an adjective meaning 'holy, consecrated' e.g. *du pain bénit* 'consecrated bread', *de l'eau bénite* 'holy water' (but *il a béni ses enfants* 'he blessed his children', etc.).

362   *Fleurir* 'to blossom' is completely regular, but when it has the sense of 'to be prosperous, to flourish', the present participle and imperfect indicative are borrowed from an old verb *florir* (otherwise disused), viz. *florissant, je florissais,* etc. (but *fleurissant* 'blossoming', *les arbres fleurissaient* 'the trees were coming into flower', etc.).

363   Two important sub-classes of *-ir* verbs, viz. *dormir,* etc. (see **364**) and *cueillir, couvrir,* etc. (see **365**), are regular in certain tenses but irregular in others. The two subclasses have in common the fact that they have no *-iss-* (except of course in the imperfect subjunctive, *que je dormisse, que je couvrisse,* etc.).

364   The following verbs and most of their compounds (for exceptions see the end of this section) not only have no *-iss-* but are also irregular in the singular of the present indicative and imperative (they drop the last letter, *-m-, -v-,* or *-t-,* of the stem before the endings *-s, -s, -t*):

dormir, to sleep	*se repentir,* to repent
servir, to serve	*sentir,* to feel
mentir, to lie, tell lies	*sortir,* to come out, go out
partir, to leave, go away	

Examples:

pres. part.	pres. indic.	imperf. indic.	pres. subjunct.	imper.
dormant	*je dors*	*je dormais*	*que je dorme*	
	tu dors			*dors*
	il dort			
	nous dormons			*dormons*
	vous dormez			*dormez*
	ils dorment			
servant	*je sers*	*je servais*	*que je serve*	
	tu sers			*sers*
	il sert			
	nous servons			*servons*
	vous servez			*servez*
	ils servent			
mentant	*je mens*	*je mentais*	*que je mente*	
	tu mens			*mens*
	il ment			
	nous mentons			*mentons*
	vous mentez			*mentez*
	ils mentent			

Compounds conjugated in the same way include *s'endormir* 'to go to sleep', *desservir* '(of buses, trains, etc.) to serve (a certain place)', *démentir* 'to deny', *repartir* 'to go away again', *ressentir* 'to feel', *ressortir* 'to go out again'. Note however that the following are conjugated like *finir*: *asservir* 'to subjugate', *impartir* 'to assign', *répartir* 'to share out', *assortir* 'to match', *ressortir à* 'to come under the jurisdiction of', e.g. *Vous assortissez toujours la couleur de votre robe à celle de vos yeux* 'You always match the colour of your dress to that of your eyes', *L'affaire ressortit (ressortissait) à la Cour suprême* 'The affair comes (came) under the jurisdiction of the High Court'.

365 The following verbs not only have no *-iss-* but are irregular in the present indicative and subjunctive and the imperative, where they are conjugated like *-er* verbs, and, in some cases (see below), in the future and conditional or in the past participle:

cueillir, to gather	*découvrir*, to discover
accueillir, to welcome	*recouvrir*, to recover
recueillir, to gather	*offrir*, to offer
assaillir, to assail	*ouvrir*, to open
tressaillir, to shudder	*rouvrir*, to re-open
couvrir, to cover	*souffrir*, to suffer

Examples:

Pres. part.   *cueillant, assaillant, couvrant*, etc.

Pres. indic.:

je cueille	*j'assaille*	*je couvre*
tu cueilles	*tu assailles*	*tu couvres*
il cueille	*il assaille*	*il couvre*
nous cueillons	*nous assaillons*	*nous couvrons*
vous cueillez	*vous assaillez*	*vous couvrez*
ils cueillent	*ils assaillent*	*ils couvrent*

Imper: *cueille, cueillons, cueillez; ouvre, ouvrons, ouvrez*, etc.

Pres. subjunct.: *que je cueille, que tu assailles, que nous couvrions*, etc.

Imperf. indic.: *je recueillais, tu tressaillais, il offrait*, etc.

Pret.: *je cueillis*, etc.

Imperf. subjunct.: *que j'offrisse*, etc.

Additional irregularities

(a) *cueillir* and its compounds change *-ir-* to *-er-* in the future and conditional: *je cueillerai, il accueillera, nous recueillerions*, etc. (but all the others are regular, e.g. *je tressaillirai, il ouvrira*).

(b) *couvrir* and its compounds, and *offrir, (r)ouvrir* and *souffrir* form their past participles in *-ert: couvert, découvert, recouvert, offert, ouvert, rouvert, souffert.*

The verb *défaillir* 'to faint, weaken, etc.', is defective (see **344**). It is conjugated like *assaillir* but, in practice, occurs only in the plural of the present indicative (*nous défaillons, vous défaillez, ils défaillent*), the imperfect indicative (*je défaillais*, etc.), the preterite (*je défaillis*, etc.), the infinitive, and the participles (*défaillant, défailli*). (Other parts of the verb occur very rarely, and there is much uncertainty as to the correct forms.) *Faillir* is both irregular and defective (see **376** below).

The verb *saillir* is also defective, occurring in practice only in the third persons singular and plural of various tenses, the infinitive, and the participles. When meaning 'to jut out, protrude' (i.e. when indicating state, not movement), it is conjugated like *assaillir* (*il saille, ils saillent, il saillait*, etc., *saillant, sailli*). With the meaning 'to gush out, spurt', it is conjugated like *finir*, but it is now rarely used in this sense.

366 All other verbs in *-ir* are irregular in various respects and are listed among the irregular verbs in **377** below.

Third conjugation: verbs in -re

367 *Vendre* 'to sell'

		Infinitive	
pres.	*vendre*	past	*avoir vendu*
		Participles	
pres.	*vendant*	past	*vendu*
		Indicative	
pres.	*je vends*	perf.	*j'ai vendu*
	tu vends		*tu as vendu*
	il vend		*il a vendu*
	nous vendons		*nous avons vendu*
	vous vendez		*vous avez vendu*
	ils vendent		*ils ont vendu*
imperf.	*je vendais*	pluperf.	*j'avais vendu*
	tu vendais		etc.
	il vendait		
	nous vendions		
	vous vendiez		
	ils vendaient		
pret.	*je vendis*	past ant.	*j'eus vendu*
	tu vendis		etc.
	il vendit		
	nous vendîmes		
	vous vendîtes		
	ils vendirent		
fut.	*je vendrai*	fut. perf.	*j'aurai vendu*
	tu vendras		etc.
	il vendra		
	nous vendrons		
	vous vendrez		
	ils vendront		
		Conditional	
pres.	*je vendrais*	past	*j'aurais vendu*
	tu vendrais		etc.
	il vendrait		
	nous vendrions		
	vous vendriez		
	ils vendraient		

Subjunctive

pres.	*que je vende*	perf.	*que j'aie vendu*
	que tu vendes		etc.
	qu'il vende		
	que nous vendions		
	que vous vendiez		
	qu'ils vendent		
imperf.	*que je vendisse*	pluperf.	*que j'eusse vendu*
	que tu vendisses		etc.
	qu'il vendît		
	que nous vendissions		
	que vous vendissiez		
	qu'ils vendissent		

Imperative

vends   *vendons*   *vendez*

368 Regular verbs in *-re* are mainly those ending in *-andre, -endre, -ondre,* or *-rdre,* of which the following are the most common:

épandre, scatter	*attendre*, wait (for)	*confondre*, confuse	*mordre*, bite
répandre, shed, spread	*défendre*, defend, forbid	*fondre*, melt	*perdre*, lose
	descendre, descend	*pondre*, lay (eggs)	*tordre*, twist
	détendre, relax	*répondre*, reply	
	entendre, hear	*tondre*, shear	
	étendre, spread		
	fendre, split		
	prétendre, claim		
	rendre, give back		
	tendre, stretch		
	vendre, sell		

(Note that *prendre* 'to take' and its compounds *apprendre* 'to learn', *comprendre* 'to understand', etc., are irregular – see **377**.)

369 *Rompre* 'to break' and its compounds *corrompre* 'to corrupt' and *interrompre* 'to interrupt' are similar but have a *-t* in the third person singular of the present indicative.

Battre 'to beat, hit' and its compounds *abattre* 'to fell', *combattre* 'to fight, oppose', *débattre* 'to debate', *rabattre* 'to pull down (e.g. a lid)', etc., and *rebattre* 'to shuffle (cards)' are regular apart from the fact that there is only one *-t-* in the singular of the present indicative and imperative. The present indicative of *rompre* and *battre* runs as follows:

je romps	*je bats*
tu romps	*tu bats*
il rompt	*il bat*
nous rompons	*nous battons*
vous rompez	*vous battez*
ils rompent	*ils battent*

370 *Vaincre* 'to win, conquer', and its compound *convaincre* 'to convince', are regular apart from one purely orthographical feature, namely the fact that *-c-* is replaced by *-qu-* in the plural of the present indicative and imperative and throughout the present subjunctive, imperfect indicative, preterite, imperfect subjunctive, and in the present participle:

Pres. part.: *vainquant*

Past part.: *vaincu*

Pres. indic.: *je vaincs, tu vaincs, il vainc, nous vainquons, vous vainquez, ils vainquent*

Imper.: *vaincs, vainquons, vainquez*

Pres. subjunct.: *que je vainque*, etc.

Imperf. indic.: *je vainquais*, etc.

Pret.: *je vainquis*, etc.

Imperf. subjunct.: *que je vainquisse*, etc.

Fut.: *je vaincrai*, etc.

Condit.: *je vaincrais*, etc.

Note the *-t-* in the interrogative of the third person singular of the present indicative, *vainc-t-il?* etc. (see **388,iii**).

371 All other verbs in *-re* are irregular. Most of these are listed in **377**, but three groups each contain enough verbs to justify separate treatment here (**372–374**).

372 Verbs ending in *-aindre, -eindre, -oindre*
The main verbs in this group are:

contraindre, compel	*enfreindre*, infringe
craindre, fear	*éteindre*, extinguish
plaindre, pity	*étreindre*, hug

astreindre, compel
atteindre, reach, attain
ceindre, gird
dépeindre, depict
déteindre, fade
enceindre, encircle

feindre, pretend
geindre, moan
peindre, paint
restreindre, restrain
teindre, dye

and the verb *joindre* 'to join' and its compounds (*adjoindre, conjoindre, disjoindre, enjoindre, rejoindre*).

The special features of these verbs are (a) that the past participle ends in *-t*, and (b) that *-nd-* changes to *-gn-* when a vowel follows.

Examples:

Pres. part.: *craignant, atteignant, joignant*, etc.

Past part.: *craint, atteint, joint*, etc.

Pres. indic.:

je crains	*j'atteins*	*je joins*
tu crains	*tu atteins*	*tu joins*
il craint	*il atteint*	*il joint*
nous craignons	*nous atteignons*	*nous joignons*
vous craignez	*vous atteignez*	*vous joignez*
ils craignent	*ils atteignent*	*ils joignent*

Imper.: *crains, craignons, craignez*, etc.

Pres. subjunct.: *que je craigne, qu'il atteigne, que nous joignions*, etc.

Imperf. indic.: *je craignais, il atteignait, nous joignions*, etc.

Pret.: *je craignis, il atteignit, nous joignîmes*, etc.

Imperf. subjunct.: *que je craignisse, qu'il atteignît*, etc.

Fut.: *je craindrai, tu atteindras*, etc.

Condit.: *je craindrais*, etc.

The little-used verbs *oindre* 'to anoint' and *poindre* 'to dawn' technically form part of this group, but both are defective (see **344**). *Oindre* now occurs in practice only in the infinitive and the past participle (*oint*) and *poindre* only in the infinitive and the third person singular of the present indicative (*il point*) and of the future (*il poindra*) (its present participle also remains, but only as an adjective, *poignant* 'poignant').

373 Verbs ending in *-aître, -oître*

(i) The main verbs in this group are:

apparaître, appear

connaître, know

disparaître, disappear

méconnaître, misjudge

paraître, appear

reconnaître, recognize

repaître (rare), feed

accroître, increase

décroître, decrease

(For *croître*, see (ii) below.)

Note that the stem of these verbs has -*î*- (with a circumflex accent) before -*t*, but -*i*- (without an accent) elsewhere (e.g. *connaît* but *connais*).

Examples:

Pres. part.: *connaissant, paraissant, accroissant*, etc.

Past part.: *connu, paru, accru, décru*, etc.

Pres. indic.:

je connais	*je parais*	*j'accrois*
tu connais	*tu parais*	*tu accrois*
il connaît	*il paraît*	*il accroît*
nous connaissons	*nous paraissons*	*nous accroissons*
vous connaissez	*vous paraissez*	*vous accroissez*
ils connaissent	*ils paraissent*	*ils accroissent*

Imper.: *connais, connaissons, connaissez*, etc.

Pres. subjunct.: *que je connaisse, qu'il paraisse, que nous accroissions*, etc.

Imperf. indic.: *je connaissais, il paraissait, nous accroissions*, etc.

Pret.: *je connus, il parut, nous accrûmes*, etc.

Imperf. subjunct.: *que je connusse, qu'il parût*, etc.

Fut.: *je connaîtrai, il accroîtra*, etc.

Condit.: *je paraîtrais*, etc.

The verb *paître* 'to graze' falls within this group but is defective (see **344**); it has no preterite or imperfect subjunctive, and its past participle, *pu*, is not in normal use so, in effect, it has no compound tenses either.

(ii) The verb *croître* 'to grow' is conjugated like *accroître* and *décroître* except that it has a circumflex accent in all three forms of the singular of the present indicative, in all forms of the preterite, and, in the masculine singular only, in the past participle. The circumflex is all that distinguishes these forms from the corresponding forms of the verb *croire* 'to believe'. For purposes of comparison, the forms of both verbs are given below:

		Croître	*Croire*
Pres. part.		*croissant*	*croyant*
Past part.		*crû, crue, crus, crues*	*cru, crue, crus, crues*

Indicative

pres.	*je croîs*	*je crois*
	tu croîs	*tu crois*
	il croît	*il croit*
	nous croissons	*nous croyons*
	vous croissez	*vous croyez*
	ils croissent	*ils croient*
imperf.	*je croissais*	*je croyais*
	tu croissais	*tu croyais*
	il croissait	*il croyait*
	nous croissions	*nous croyions*
	vous croissiez	*vous croyiez*
	ils croissaient	*ils croyaient*
pret.	*je crûs*	*je crus*
	tu crûs	*tu crus*
	il crût	*il crut*
	nous crûmes	*nous crûmes*
	vous crûtes	*vous crûtes*
	ils crûrent	*ils crurent*
fut.	*je croîtrai*, etc.	*je croirai*, etc.
condit.	*je croîtrais*, etc.	*je croirais*, etc.

Subjunctive

pres.	*que je croisse*	*que je croie*
	que tu croisses	*que tu croies*
	qu'il croisse	*qu'il croie*
	que nous croissions	*que nous croyions*
	que vous croissiez	*que vous croyiez*
	qu'ils croissent	*qu'ils croient*
imperf.	*que je crusse*, etc.	*que je crusse*, etc.

Imperative

croîs	*croissons croissez*	*crois croyons croyez*

374   Verbs ending in -*uire*

(i) The main verbs in this group are:

cuire, to cook (intransitive)
construire, construct, build
détruire, destroy
instruire, instruct

and a number of compounds of the obsolete verb *duire* 'to lead', including:

conduire, conduct, lead   *produire*, produce
déduire, deduce   *réduire*, reduce
enduire, coat   *séduire*, seduce
introduire, introduce   *traduire*, translate

Examples:

Pres. part.: *cuisant, construisant, traduisant*, etc.

Past part.: *cuit, construit, traduit*, etc.

Pres. indic.:

je construis   *je traduis*
tu construis   *tu traduis*
il construit   *il traduit*
nous construisons   *nous traduisons*
vous construisez   *vous traduisez*
ils construisent   *ils traduisent*

Imper.: *traduis, traduisons, traduisez*, etc.

Pres. subjunct.: *que je construise, que nous traduisions*, etc.

Imperf. indic.: *je construisais, il traduisait*, etc.

Pret.: *je construisis, nous traduisîmes*, etc.

Imperf. subjunct.: *que je conduisisse, qu'il traduisît*, etc.

Fut.: *je construirai, il traduira*, etc.

Condit.: *je construirais*, etc.

(ii) The verbs *luire* 'to shine', *reluire* 'to gleam', *nuire* 'to harm', are similarly conjugated except that (a) their past participles are *lui, relui, nui*, and (b) the preterite and the imperfect subjunctive of *luire* and *reluire* do not normally occur (and, in practice, these two verbs are more or less restricted to the third persons singular and plural even in other tenses).

Verbs in -oir

375 As already stated (see **339**), all verbs in *-oir* are irregular. However, the fact that one sub-group, namely that of verbs ending in *-evoir*, contains as many as seven verbs is grounds enough for giving it separate treatment. The verbs in question are *devoir* 'to owe, to have to' and its compound *redevoir* 'to owe a balance' (when part of a debt has been paid) and five verbs in -*cevoir*, viz. *apercevoir* 'to notice', *concevoir* 'to conceive', *décevoir* 'to disappoint', *percevoir* 'to perceive, collect (taxes, etc.)', *recevoir* 'to receive'. (Note (a) that the past participles of *devoir* and *redevoir* take a circumflex accent in the masculine singular *only*, and (b) that, quite regularly, the -*c*- of verbs in -*cevoir* takes a cedilla when it is immediately followed by *o* or *u*.)

Examples:

Pres. part.: *devant, recevant*

Past part.: *dû, due, dus, dues, reçu*

Pres. indic.:

je dois	*je reçois*
tu dois	*tu reçois*
il doit	*il reçoit*
nous devons	*nous recevons*
vous devez	*vous recevez*
ils doivent	*ils reçoivent*

Imper.: *dois, devons, devez, reçois, recevons, recevez*, etc.

Pres. subjunct.:

que je doive	*que je reçoive*
que tu doives	*que tu reçoives*
qu'il doive	*qu'il reçoive*
que nous devions	*que nous recevions*
que vous deviez	*que vous receviez*
qu'ils doivent	*qu'ils reçoivent*

Imper. indic.: *je devais, il recevait, nous apercevions*, etc.

Pret.: *je dus, il reçut, nous aperçûmes*, etc.

Imperf. subjunct.: *que je dusse, qu'il reçût*, etc.

Fut.: *je devrai, il recevra, nous apercevrons*, etc.

Condit.: *je devrais, il recevrait, nous apercevrions*, etc.

Irregular verbs

376 The following points should be noted:

(1) The forms given below for the simple verb are also correct,

unless otherwise stated, for all verbs formed from it. Note in particular the following:

(i) like *acquérir* are *conquérir* 'to conquer', *s'enquérir* 'to enquire', *requérir* 'to require'; the simple verb *quérir* 'to look for' now occurs (and then only rarely) in the infinitive, in the expressions *aller quérir* 'to go and fetch', *envoyer quérir* 'to send for', *venir quérir* 'to come for'

(ii) like *courir* are *accourir* 'to rush up', *concourir* 'to compete', *discourir* 'to hold forth', *encourir* 'to incur', *parcourir* 'to travel through', *recourir* 'to have recourse (to)'

(iii) like *écrire* are *décrire* 'to describe', and verbs in *-scrire*, such as *inscrire* 'to inscribe', *prescrire* 'to prescribe', *proscrire* 'to ban, proscribe', *souscrire* 'to subscribe', *transcrire* 'to transcribe', etc.

(iv) like *faire* are its compounds *défaire* 'to undo', *contrefaire* 'to imitate', *satisfaire* 'to satisfy', etc.; *parfaire* 'to perfect' is defective, having a past participle (*parfait*) and compound tenses, but no simple tenses

(v) like *mettre* are *admettre* 'to admit', *commettre* 'to commit', *compromettre* 'to compromise', *émettre* 'to emit, transmit, etc.', *omettre* 'to omit', *permettre* 'to permit', *promettre* 'to promise', *soumettre* 'to submit, subject', *transmettre* 'to pass on', etc.

(vi) like *prendre* are *apprendre* 'to learn', *comprendre* 'to understand', *entreprendre* 'to undertake', *surprendre* 'to surprise', etc.

(vii) like *tenir* are *s'abstenir* 'to abstain', *appartenir* 'to belong', *contenir* 'to contain', *maintenir* 'to maintain', *obtenir* 'to obtain', *retenir* 'to hold back, retain', *soutenir* 'to support', etc.

(viii) like *traire* are *abstraire* 'to abstract', *distraire* 'to entertain, distract', *extraire* 'to extract', etc.

(ix) like *venir* are *convenir* 'to agree, suit', *devenir* 'to become', *intervenir* 'to intervene', *parvenir* 'to manage', *se souvenir (de)* 'to remember', etc.

(2) Not listed here are verbs of the following types that are discussed fully above:

(i) *-er* and *-ir* verbs having minor irregularities (see 352–358 and 360–362)

(ii) *dormir, servir, sortir*, etc., and their compounds (see 364)

(iii) *cueillir, assaillir, couvrir*, and other verbs similarly conjugated (see 365)

(iv) verbs in *-aindre, -eindre, -oindre, -aître, -oître, -uire* (see 372–374)

(v) *recevoir* and other verbs in *-cevoir* (see **375**).

(3) In all verbs, the conditional has the same stem as the future, and the imperfect subjunctive has the same stem as the preterite (e.g. from *savoir* and *voir*, future *je saurai, je verrai*, so conditional *je saurais, je verrais*; preterite *je sus, je vis*, so imperfect subjunctive *que je susse, que je visse*); the conditional and the imperfect subjunctive are therefore not listed below.

(4) Unless otherwise stated in a note, the imperative is the same as the second person singular and the first and second persons plural of the present indicative (e.g. from *dire*, present indicative *tu dis, nous disons, vous dites*, imperative *dis, disons, dites*). If these forms do not exist, then neither does the imperative.

(5) Compound tenses are formed in the same way as in regular verbs.

(6) Defective verbs (see **344**) are indicated by †. A dash (—) indicates that the forms in question do not exist (or, in some cases, that they are so exceptionally rare as to be virtually non-existent in present-day French).

Irregular verbs:
principal forms

377   Irregular verbs: principal forms
A number after the infinitive or other part of a verb refers to the notes in 378 below.

infinitive	participles	present indicative	
(1) †*absoudre*[1]	*absolvant*	*j'absous*	*nous absolvons*
'absolve'	*absous*	*tu absous*	*vous absolvez*
	(fem.*absoute*)	*il absout*	*ils absolvent*
(2) *acquérir*	*acquérant*	*j'acquiers*	*nous acquérons*
acquire'	*acquis*	*tu acquiers*	*vous acquérez*
		il acquiert	*ils acquièrent*
(3) *aller*	*allant*	*je vais*	*nous allons*
'go'	*allé*	*tu vas*[2]	*vous allez*
		il va	*ils vont*
(4) *s'asseoir*[3]	*s'asseyant*	*je m'assieds*	*nous nous asseyons*
'sit down'	*assis*	*tu t'assieds*	*vous vous asseyez*
		il s'assied	*ils s'asseyent*
(5) *avoir* 'have' – see **349**			
(6) *boire*	*buvant*	*je bois*	*nous buvons*
'drink'	*bu*	*tu bois*	*vous buvez*
		il boit	*ils boivent*
(7) *bouillir*[4]	*bouillant*	*je bous*	*nous bouillons*
'boil'	*bouilli*	*tu bous*	*vous bouillez*
		il bout	*ils bouillent*
(8) †*braire*[5]	*brayant*	*il brait*	*ils braient*
'bray'	——		
(9) †*bruire*	——	*il bruit*	*ils bruissent*
'rustle', etc.	——		
(10) †*choir*[6]	——	*je chois*	——
'fall'	*chu*	*tu chois*	——
		il choit	*ils choient*
(11) †*clore*[7]	——	*je clos*	——
'close'	*clos*	*tu clos*	——
		il clôt	*ils closent*
(12) *conclure*[8]	*concluant*	*je conclus*	*nous concluons*
'conclude'	*conclu*	*tu conclus*	*vous concluez*
		il conclut	*ils concluent*
(13) *confire*	*confisant*	*je confis*	*nous confisons*
'preserve	*confit*	*tu confis*	*vous confisez*
(fruit, etc.)'		*il confit*	*ils confisent*

pret.	fut. and imperf. indic.	present subjunct.	
——	*j'absoudrai* *j'absolvais*	*que j'absolve* *que tu absolves* *qu'il absolve*	*que nous absolvions* *que vous absolviez* *qu'ils absolvent*
J'acquis	*j'acquerrai* *j'acquérais*	*que j'acquière* *que tu acquières* *qu'il acquière*	*que nous acquérions* *que vous acquériez* *qu'ils acquièrent*
j'allai	*j'irai* *j'allais*	*que j'aille* *que tu ailles* *qu'il aille*	*que nous allions* *que vous alliez* *qu'ils aillent*
je m'assis	*je m'assiérai* *je m'asseyais*	*que je m'asseye* *que tu t'asseyes* *qu'il s'asseye*	*que nous nous asseyions* *que vous vous asseyiez* *qu'ils s'asseyent*
je bus	*je boirai* *je buvais*	*que je boive* *que tu boives* *qu'il boive*	*que nous buvions* *que vous buviez* *qu'ils boivent*
je bouillis	*je bouillirai* *je bouillais*	*que je bouille* *que tu bouilles* *qu'il bouille*	*que nous bouillions* *que vous bouilliez* *qu'ils bouillent*
——	*il braira* *il brayait*	——	——
——	*il bruira* *il bruissait*	——	
il chut	——	——	——
——	*je clorai* ——	*que je close* *que tu closes* *qu'il close*	*que nous closions* *que vous closiez* *qu'ils closent*
je conclus	*je conclurai* *je concluais*	*que je conclue* *que tu conclues* *qu'il conclue*	*que nous concluions* *que vous concluiez* *qu'ils concluent*
je confis	*je confirai* *je confisais*	*que je confise* *que tu confises* *qu'il confise*	*que nous confisions* *que vous confisiez* *qu'ils confisent*

infinitive	participles	present indicative	
(14) *contredire* 'contradict' – see note 11 (on *dire*)			
(15) *coudre*	*cousant*	je couds	nous cousons
'sew'	*cousu*	tu couds	vous cousez
		il coud	ils cousent
(16) *courir*[9]	*courant*	je cours	nous courons
'run'	*couru*	tu cours	vous courez
		il court	ils courent
(17) *croire* 'believe, think' – see 373,ii			
(18) *déchoir*[10]	———	je déchois	nous déchoyons
'decline'	*déchu*	tu déchois	vous déchoyez
		il déchoit	ils déchoient
(19) *devoir* 'owe, have to' – see 375			
(20) *dire*[11]	*disant*	je dis	nous disons
'say'	*dit*	tu dis	vous dites
		il dit	ils disent
(21) †*dissoudre* 'dissolve' – like *absoudre*			
(22) †*échoir*[12] 'fall due, expire'			
(23) †*éclore*	———	il éclot	ils éclosent
'to hatch, open out'	*éclos*		
(24) *écrire*	*écrivant*	j'écris	nous écrivons
'write'	*écrit*	tu écris	vous écrivez
		il écrit	ils écrivent
(25) *élire* 'elect' – like *lire*			
(26) *émouvoir* 'move, upset' – like *mouvoir* (but see note 13)			
(27) †*s'ensuivre*[14] 'ensue'			
(28) *entrevoir* 'glimpse' – like *voir*			
(29) *envoyer* 'send' – see 357			
(30) *être* 'be' – see 350			
(31) *exclure* 'exclude' – like *conclure*			
(32) *faillir*[15]	———	———	———
'almost (do)'	*failli*		
(33) *faire*	*faisant*	je fais	nous faisons
'do, make'	*fait*	tu fais	vous faites
		il fait	ils font
(34) *falloir*[16]	———	il faut	
'be necessary'	*fallu*		
(35) *frire*[17]	———	je fris	———
'fry'	*frit*	tu fris	———
		il frit	———
(36) *fuir*	*fuyant*	je fuis	nous fuyons
'flee'	*fui*	tu fuis	vous fuyez
		il fuit	ils fuient

pret.	fut. and imperf. indic.	present subjunct.	
je cousis	*je coudrai* *je cousais*	*que je couse* *que tu couses* *qu'il couse*	*que nous cousions* *que vous cousiez* *qu'ils cousent*
je courus	*je courrai* *je courais*	*que je coure* *que tu coures* *qu'il coure*	*que nous courions* *que vous couriez* *qu'ils courent*
je déchus	*je déchoirai* ───	*que je déchoie* ─── *qu'il déchoie*	*que nous déchoyions* *qu'ils déchoient*
je dis	*je dirai* *je disais*	*que je dise* *que tu dises* *qu'il dise*	*que nous disions* *que vous disiez* *qu'ils disent*
───	*il éclora* ───	*qu'il éclose*	*qu'ils éclosent*
j'écrivis	*j'écrirai* *j'écrivais*	*que j'écrive* *que tu écrives* *qu'il écrive*	*que nous écrivions* *que vous écriviez* *qu'ils écrivent*
je faillis	*je faillirai* ───	───	───
je fis	*je ferai* *je faisais*	*que je fasse* *que tu fasses* *qu'il fasse*	*que nous fassions* *que vous fassiez* *qu'ils fassent*
il fallut	*il faudra* *il fallait*	*qu'il faille*	
───	*je frirai* ───	───	───
je fuis	*je fuirai* *je fuyais*	*que je fuie* *que tu fuies* *qu'il fuie*	*que nous fuyions* *que vous fuyiez* *qu'ils fuient*

infinitive	participles	present indicative	

(37) *gésir*[18]   *gisant*   *je gis*   *nous gisons*
    'lie'   ——   *tu gis*   *vous gisez*
        il gît   *ils gisent*

(38) *inclure* 'include' – see note 8 (to *conclure*).

(39) *interdire* 'forbid' – see note 11 (on *dire*)

(40) *lire*   *lisant*   *je lis*   *nous lisons*
    'read'   *lu*   *tu lis*   *vous lisez*
        il lit   *ils lisent*

(41) *maudire*   *maudissant*   *je maudis*   *nous maudissons*
    'curse'   *maudit*   *tu maudis*   *vous maudissez*
        il maudit   *ils maudissent*

(42) *médire* 'speak ill of' – see note 11 (on *dire*)

(43) *mettre*   *mettant*   *je mets*   *nous mettons*
    'put'   *mis*   *tu mets*   *vous mettez*
        il met   *ils mettent*

(44) *moudre*   *moulant*   *je mouds*   *nous moulons*
    'grind'   *moulu*   *tu mouds*   *vous moulez*
        il moud   *ils moulent*

(45) *mourir*   *mourant*   *je meurs*   *nous mourons*
    'die'   *mort*   *tu meurs*   *vous mourez*
        il meurt   *ils meurent*

(46) *mouvoir*   *mouvant*   *je meus*   *nous mouvons*
    'move'   *mû*[19]   *tu meus*   *vous mouvez*
        il meut   *ils meuvent*

(47) *naître*   *naissant*   *je nais*   *nous naissons*
    'be born'   *né*   *tu nais*   *vous naissez*
        il naît   *ils naissent*

(48) †*ouïr*   ——   ——   ——
    'hear'   *ouï*

(49) *plaire*   *plaisant*   *je plais*   *nous plaisons*
    'please'   *plu*   *tu plais*   *vous plaisez*
        il plaît   *ils plaisent*

(50) *pleuvoir*[20]   *pleuvant*   *il pleut*
    'rain'   *plu*

(51) *poursuivre* 'pursue' – like *suivre*

(52) *pourvoir* 'provide' – see note 28 (on *voir*)

(53) *pouvoir*[21]   *pouvant*   *je peux, je puis*[22]   *nous pouvons*
    'can, be able'   *pu*   *tu peux*   *vous pouvez*
        il peut   *ils peuvent*

pret.	fut. and imperf. indic.	present subjunct.	
	je gisais		
je lus	je lirai	que je lise	que nous lisions
	je lisais	que tu lises	que vous lisiez
		qu'il lise	qu'ils lisent
je maudis	je maudirai	que je maudisse	que nous maudis-
	je maudissais	que tu maudisses	sions
		qu'il maudisse	que vous maudissiez
			qu'ils maudissent
je mis	je mettrai	que je mette	que nous mettions
	je mettais	que tu mettes	que vous mettiez
		qu'il mette	qu'ils mettent
je moulus	je moudrai	que je moule	que nous moulions
	je moulais	que tu moules	que vous mouliez
		qu'il moule	qu'ils moulent
je mourus	je mourrai	que je meure	que nous mourions
	je mourais	que tu meures	que vous mouriez
		qu'il meure	qu'ils meurent
je mus	je mouvrai	que je meuve	que nous mouvions
	je mouvais	que tu meuves	que vous mouviez
		qu'il meuve	qu'ils meuvent
je naquis	je naîtrai	que je naisse	que nous naissions
	je naissais	que tu naisses	que vous naissiez
		qu'il naisse	qu'ils naissent
je plus	je plairai	que je plaise	que nous plaisions
	je plaisais	que tu plaises	que vous plaisiez
		qu'il plaise	qu'ils plaisent
il plut	il pleuvra	qu'il pleuve	
	il pleuvait		
je pus	je pourrai	que je puisse	que nous puissions
	je pouvais	que tu puisses	que vous puissiez
		qu'il puisse	qu'ils puissent

infinitive	participles	present indicative	

(54) *prédire* 'foretell' – see note 11 (on *dire*)

(55) *prendre*	*prenant*	*je prends*	*nous prenons*
'take'	*pris*	*tu prends*	*vous prenez*
		il prend	*ils prennent*

(56) *prévaloir* 'prevail' – see note 26 (on *valoir*)

(57) *prévoir* 'foresee' – see note 28 (on *voir*)

| (58) †*promouvoir* | *promouvant* | —— | —— |
| 'promote' | *promu* | | |

(59) †*résoudre* 'resolve' – see note 1 (on *absoudre*)

(60) *rire*	*riant*	*je ris*	*nous rions*
'laugh'	*ri*	*tu ris*	*vous riez*
		il rit	*ils rient*

(61) *savoir*[23]	*sachant*	*je sais*	*nous savons*
'know'	*su*	*tu sais*	*vous savez*
		il sait	*ils savent*

(62) *seoir* 'be situated, suit' – see note 3 (on *s'asseoir*)

(63) *sourire* 'smile' – like *rire*

(64) *suffire*	*suffisant*	*je suffis*	*nous suffisons*
'suffice'	*suffi*	*tu suffis*	*vous suffisez*
		il suffit	*ils suffisent*

(65) *suivre*	*suivant*	*je suis*	*nous suivons*
'follow'	*suivi*	*tu suis*	*vous suivez*
		il suit	*ils suivent*

(66) *surseoir*	*sursoyant*	*je sursois*	*nous sursoyons*
'postpone'	*sursis*	*tu sursois*	*vous sursoyez*
		il sursoit	*ils sursoient*

(67) *survivre* 'survive' – like *vivre*

(68) *taire*[24]	*taisant*	*je tais*	*nous taisons*
'hush up'	*tu*	*tu tais*	*vous taisez*
		il tait	*ils taisent*

(69) *tenir*[25]	*tenant*	*je tiens*	*nous tenons*
'hold'	*tenu*	*tu tiens*	*vous tenez*
		il tient	*ils tiennent*

(70) †*traire*	*trayant*	*je trais*	*nous trayons*
'milk'	*trait*	*tu trais*	*vous trayez*
		il trait	*ils traient*

(71) *vaincre* 'conquer' – see 370

(72) *valoir*[26]	*valant*	*je vaux*	*nous valons*
'be worth'	*valu*	*tu vaux*	*vous valez*
		il vaut	*ils valent*

pret.	fut. and imperf. indic.	present subjunct.	
je pris	*je prendrai* *je prenais*	*que je prenne* *que tu prennes* *qu'il prenne*	*que nous prenions* *que vous preniez* *qu'ils prennent*
je ris	*je rirai* *je riais*	*que je rie* *que tu ries* *qu'il rie*	*que nous riions* *que vous riiez* *qu'ils rient*
je sus	*je saurai* *je savais*	*que je sache* *que tu saches* *qu'il sache*	*que nous sachions* *que vous sachiez* *qu'ils sachent*
je suffis	*je suffirai* *je suffisais*	*que je suffise* *que tu suffises* *qu'il suffise*	*que nous suffisions* *que vous suffisiez* *qu'ils suffisent*
je suivis	*je suivrai* *je suivais*	*que je suive* *que tu suives* *qu'il suive*	*que nous suivions* *que vous suiviez* *qu'ils suivent*
je sursis	*je surseoirai* *je sursoyais*	*que je sursoie* *que tu sursoies* *qu'il sursoie*	*que nous sursoyions* *que vous sursoyiez* *qu'ils sursoient*
je tus	*je tairai* *je taisais*	*que je taise* *que tu taises* *qu'il taise*	*que nous taisions* *que vous taisiez* *qu'ils taisent*
je tins	*je tiendrai* *je tenais*	*que je tienne* *que tu tiennes* *qu'il tienne*	*que nous tenions* *que vous teniez* *qu'ils tiennent*
――	*je trairai* *je trayais*	*que je traie* *que tu traies* *qu'il traie*	*que nous trayions* *que vous trayiez* *qu'ils traient*
je valus	*je vaudrai* *je valais*	*que je vaille* *que tu vailles* *qu'il vaille*	*que nous valions* *que vous valiez* *qu'ils vaillent*

infinitive	participles	present indicative	
(73) *venir*	*venant*	*je viens*	*nous venons*
'come'	*venu*	*tu viens*	*vous venez*
		il vient	*ils viennent*
(74) *vêtir*	*vêtant*	*je vêts*	*nous vêtons*
'clothe'	*vêtu*	*tu vêts*	*vous vêtez*
		il vêt	*ils vêtent*
(75) *vivre*	*vivant*	*je vis*	*nous vivons*
'live'	*vécu*	*tu vis*	*vous vivez*
		il vit	*ils vivent*
(76) *voir*[28]	*voyant*	*je vois*	*nous voyons*
'see'	*vu*	*tu vois*	*vous voyez*
		il voit	*ils voient*
(77) *vouloir*[29]	*voulant*	*je veux*	*nous voulons*
'wish'	*voulu*	*tu veux*	*vous voulez*
		il veut	*ils veulent*

pret.	fut. and imperf. indic.	present subjunct.	
je vins[27]	je viendrai je venais	que je vienne que tu viennes qu'il vienne	que nous venions que vous veniez qu'ils viennent
je vêtis	je vêtirai je vêtais	que je vête que tu vêtes qu'il vête	que nous vêtions que vous vêtiez qu'ils vêtent
je vécus	je vivrai je vivais	que je vive que tu vives qu'il vive	que nous vivions que vous viviez qu'ils vivent
je vis	je verrai je voyais	que je voie que tu voies qu'il voie	que nous voyions que vous voyiez qu'ils voient
je voulus	je voudrai je voulais	que je veuille que tu veuilles qu'il veuille	que nous voulions que vous vouliez qu'ils veuillent

378 Notes on irregular verbs

(1) *Absoudre* and *dissoudre* are not usually classified as defective, but strictly speaking they are since they lack the preterite and the imperfect subjunctive. *Résoudre* 'to solve, resolve' is like *absoudre* but usually has the past participle *résolu*.

(2) The second person singular imperative is *va* (but note the special case *vas-y*).

(3) *S'asseoir* may also be conjugated throughout like *surseoir* (i.e. present participle *s'assoyant*, present indicative *je m'assois, nous nous assoyons*, etc., imperfect indicative *je m'assoyais*, etc., imperative *assois-toi, assoyons-nous, assoyez-vous*), but with a difference of spelling in the future and conditional (*je m'assoirai*, etc., but *je surseoirai*, etc.) and the present subjunctive (*que je m'assoie*, etc., but *que je surseoie*, etc.). However, the forms listed above (i.e. *je m'assieds*, etc.) are more usual. *Asseoir* is occasionally used non-reflexively meaning 'to put someone (child, invalid, etc.) in a chair'. More often it has a technical sense, e.g. 'to impose (a tax), lay (a foundation), base (an opinion), etc.' However, it is most frequently used reflexively. It must be remembered that *s'asseoir* means literally 'to seat oneself', and so 'to sit down'. The past participle *assis* 'seated' is therefore equivalent to the English present participle, 'sitting'. *S'asseyant* means 'taking one's seat'. 'I was sitting in the garden all the morning', is *j'étais assis toute la matinée au jardin*, not *je m'asseyais*, which could only mean 'I spent the whole morning taking my seat'. *M'étant assis* means 'having taken my seat, having sat down'.

The simple verb *seoir* in its original sense of 'to sit' remains in legal language in the participles *séant* (e.g. *un tribunal séant à Rouen* 'a tribunal sitting at Rouen') and *sis* 'situated' (e.g. *une maison sise à Versailles* 'a house situated at Versailles'). In the sense of 'suit, be becoming' it has present participle *seyant*, third person singular and third person plural of present indicative, *il sied, ils siéent*, present subjunctive (rare) *qu'il siée, qu'ils siéent*, imperfect indicative *il seyait, ils seyaient*, future *il siéra, ils siéront*, conditional *il siérait, ils siéraient*, but the verb in general is somewhat archaic and none of these forms is widely used.

(4) *Bouillir* is intransitive, e.g. *l'eau bout* 'the water is boiling'; for the transitive, *faire bouillir* must be used, e.g. *Je ferai bouillir de l'eau* 'I will boil some water'.

(5) Although other forms are very occasionally found, in general *braire* occurs only in the third persons singular and plural of the tenses indicated (and some of these are rare). No imperative.

(6) Little used, even in literary style, other than in the infinitive (such expressions as *faire choir* 'to knock over', *laisser choir* 'to drop'). No imperfect subjunctive or imperative.

(7) Little used, even in literary style, other than in the infinitive and past participle.

(8) *Exclure* 'to exclude' is like *conclure*. *Inclure* 'to include' is hardly ever used except in the past participle, *inclus(e)* (contrast *conclu*), and then usually in the form *ci-inclus*, e.g. *la lettre ci-incluse* 'the enclosed letter'.

(9) An old form *courre* survives in a few phrases, e.g. *courre le cerf* 'to hunt stag', *laisser courre les chiens* 'to lay the hounds on', *la chasse à courre* 'hunting' when it is wanted to distinguish hunting from *la chasse au fusil* 'shooting'.

(10) No imperative.

(11) In the compounds of *dire* the second person plural present indicative and second person plural imperative vary:

> *redire* 'to repeat' has *redites*; *contredire* 'to contradict', *interdire* 'to forbid', *prédire* 'to predict', *médire* 'to slander' have *contredisez, interdisez, prédisez, médisez*.

Otherwise, these verbs are conjugated exactly like *dire*. Note, however, that *maudire* 'to curse' is conjugated differently (like *finir*, in fact) and so is listed separately.

(12) Used only in the infinitive, the participles, and in the third persons singular and (even less frequently) plural of the tenses indicated and of the conditional (not imperfect subjunctive).

(13) But the past participle, *ému*, has no accent on the *-u*.

(14) Like *suivre* but used only in the infinitive and the third persons singular and plural (of simple and compound tenses).

(15) No imperfect subjunctive. *Faillir* is constructed with an infinitive, e.g. *J'ai failli tomber* 'I nearly fell'. In the earlier meaning of 'to fail', which is still occasionally found but only as an archaism, some forms occur in addition to those we list, e.g. *Le cœur me faut* 'My heart fails me'.

(16) An impersonal verb and so used with impersonal *il* as its subject; no present participle or imperative, but not usually considered defective.

(17) Imperative has second person singular, *fris*, only; future is little used. The missing tenses are supplied by the locution *faire frire*, e.g. *il faisait frire des pommes de terre* 'he was frying potatoes'. *Faire frire* is also widely used in those simple and compound tenses for which forms of *frire* do exist, e.g. *J'ai frit* or *j'ai fait frire des pommes de terre* 'I have fried some potatoes'. But *faire frire* has no passive — use *être* and the past part. *frit*, e.g. *Le poisson avait été frit* 'The fish had been fried'.

(18) Rarely used other than in the expressions (on tombstones) *ci-gît* 'here lies', *ci-gisent* 'here lie'.

(19) The past participle has no accent in the feminine singular (*mue*) and in the plural (*mus, mues*).

(20) Usually impersonal and so used in third person singular only. However, other persons occasionally occur in metaphorical uses, e.g. *Eau, quand donc pleuvras-tu?* (Baudelaire) 'Water, when will you rain?', *Des coups pleuvent (pleuvaient) sur son dos* 'Blows rain (rained) on his back'.

(21) No imperative.

(22) *Puis* is now rarely used except in inversion (questions, etc.), when it *must* be used (i.e. *peux* cannot be used), e.g. *Que puis-je dire?* 'What can I say?', *Peut-être puis-je vous aider* 'Perhaps I can help you'.

(23) Imperative: *sache, sachons, sachez*.

(24) Most frequently used reflexively, *se taire* 'to be silent'.

(25) Note that *tenir* 'to hold' and *venir* 'to come' are conjugated in exactly the same way in all simple tenses. The forms of the preterite and the imperfect subjunctive of these two verbs are so unusual that these tenses are given in full below:

pret.		imperf. subjunct.	
je tins	je vins	que je tinsse	que je vinsse
tu tins	tu vins	que tu tinsses	que tu vinsses
il tint	il vint	qu'il tînt	qu'il vînt
nous tînmes	nous vînmes	que nous tinssions	que nous vinssions
vous tîntes	vous vîntes	que vous tinssiez	que vous vinssiez
ils tinrent	ils vinrent	qu'ils tinssent	qu'ils vinssent

(26) *Prévaloir* 'to prevail' is conjugated like *valoir* except in the present subjunctive, which keeps *-val-* throughout:

que je prévale	*que nous prévalions*
que tu prévales	*que vous prévaliez*
qu'il prévale	*qu'ils prévalent*

(27) For the full preterite and imperfect subjunctive of *venir*, see note 25, on *tenir*.

(28) *Entrevoir* 'to glimpse', and *revoir* 'to see again, revise', are conjugated like *voir* throughout. *Pourvoir* 'to provide' and *prévoir* 'to foresee' are conjugated like *voir* except that (a) both verbs have their future and conditional in *-voir-*, viz. *je pourvoirai, je pourvoirais, je prévoirai, je prévoirais*, etc., and (b) *pourvoir* has the preterite *je pourvus* and the imperfect subjunctive *que je pourvusse*, etc. (but *je prévis, que je prévisse*, etc.).

(29) The usual forms of the imperative are *veuille, veuillons, veuillez*, but with the expression *en vouloir à quelqu'un* 'to have (hold) something against someone' the more usual forms of the imperative (and, in practice, this is always in the negative) are *veux, voulons, voulez*, e.g. *Ne m'en veux pas, ne m'en voulez pas* 'Don't hold it against me', *Ne lui en voulons pas* 'Let's not hold it against him' (though *Ne m'en veuillez pas*, etc., also occur).

F Reflexive verbs

379 Reflexive verbs in French are verbs whose direct or indirect object, expressed by one or other of the conjunctive pronouns *me, te, se, nous* or *vous* (see **198–199**), refers to the subject of the same verb, e.g. *Jacques se lave* 'James is washing (himself)' means that James is washing James. They include *reciprocal* verbs, e.g. *nous nous aimons* 'we love one another', *ils s'écrivent souvent* 'they often write to one another', and a number of verbs that are used only reflexively (see **534**), in many of which the reflexive pronoun is untranslatable.

380 All verbs when used reflexively are conjugated with *être*. In the compound tenses of such verbs the past participle agrees with the reflexive pronoun if this serves as the direct object, but not if it serves as the indirect object. Take, for example, the verbs *se blesser* 'to injure oneself' in which *se* is the direct object, and *se nuire* 'to do harm to oneself' in which *se* is the indirect object: in the perfect tense we have *elle s'est blessée* (*blessée* is feminine to agree with *se* 'herself') but *elle s'est nui* (*nui* does not agree because *se* is the indirect object). See further on this, 461.

381 Example of the conjugation of a reflexive verb:

se laver 'to wash (oneself)'

Infinitive

pres.	*se laver*	past	*s'être lavé/lavée/*
			lavés/lavées

Participles

pres.	*se lavant*	past	*lavé*

Indicative

pres.	*je me lave*	perf.	*je me suis lavé(e)*
	tu te laves		*tu t'es lavé(e)*
	il se lave		*il s'est lavé*
	elle se lave		*elle s'est lavée*
	nous nous lavons		*nous nous sommes lavé(e)s*
	vous vous lavez		*vous vous êtes lavé(e)(s)*
	ils se lavent		*ils se sont lavés*
	elles se lavent		*elles se sont lavées*
imperf.	*je me lavais*, etc.	pluperf.	*je m'étais lavé*, etc.
pret.	*je me lavai*, etc.	past ant.	*je me fus lavé*, etc.
fut.	*je me laverai*, etc.	fut. perf.	*je me serai lavé*, etc.

Conditional

pres.	*je me laverais*, etc.	past	*je me serais lavé*, etc.

Subjunctive

pres.	*que je me lave*, etc.	perf.	*que je me sois lavé*, etc.
imperf.	*que je me lavasse*, etc.	pluperf.	*que je me fusse lavé*, etc.

Imperative

lave-toi   *lavons-nous*   *lavez-vous*

G The passive

382 The French passive is formed in exactly the same way as the English passive, i.e. with the verb *être* 'to be' and the past participle, e.g. *Il sera tué* 'He will be killed', The past participle varies, agreeing in gender and number with the subject, e.g. *Elle sera tuée* 'She will be killed' (but note that, in the compound tenses, *été* does not change, e.g. *Elle a été tuée* 'She has been killed'), *Elles ont peur d'être blessées* 'They are afraid of being hurt'.

383 Example of the passive conjugation: *être blessé* 'to be hurt or wounded' (passive of *blesser* 'to hurt, to wound'):

Infinitive

pres.	*être blessé* (or *-és, -ée, -ées*) to be hurt	past	*avoir été blessé*, etc., to have been hurt

Participles

pres.	*étant blessé*, etc., being hurt	past	*blessé*, etc., hurt, or having been hurt

Indicative

pres.	*je suis blessé* (or *-ée*), I am hurt	perf.	*j'ai été blessé*, etc., I have been hurt
	tu es blessé (or *-ée*)		*tu as été blessé*, etc.
	il est blessé		*il a été blessé*
	elle est blessée		*elle a été blessée*
	nous sommes blessés (or *-ées*)		*nous avons été blessés*, etc.
	vous êtes blessé (or *-ée, -és, -ées*)		*vous avez été blessé*, etc.
	ils sont blessés		*ils ont été blessés*
	elles ont blessées		*elles ont été blessées*

·Only the masculine past participle is shown in the rest of the conjugation below:

imperf.	*j'étais blessé* I was hurt	pluperf.	*j'avais été blessé* I had been hurt

| pret. | *je fus blessé*
I was hurt | past ant. | *j'eus été blessé*
I had been hurt |
| fut. | *je serai blessé*
I shall be hurt | fut. perf. | *j'aurai été blessé*
I shall have been hurt |

Conditional

| pres. | *je serais blessé*
I should be hurt | past. | *j'aurais été blessé*
I should have been hurt |

Subjunctive

| pres. | *que je sois blessé*
that I am (may be) hurt | perf. | *que j'aie été blessé*
that I (may) have been hurt |
| imperf. | *que je fusse blessé*
that I was (might be) hurt | pluperf. | *que j'eusse été blessé*
that I had (might have) been hurt |

Imperative

| *sois blessé*
be hurt | *soyons blessés*
let us be hurt | *soyez blessé*
be hurt |

384 The passive voice is much less commonly used in French than in English. For this there are three main reasons:

(1) The fact that *on* (see **302**) is much more extensively used than its English equivalent, 'one', e.g. *On dit que* . . ., literally 'One says that . . .', where English would normally say 'It is said that', *On lui a rendu son argent* 'His money was given back to him'

(2) The widespread use of the reflexive as an equivalent of the English passive, e.g. *Cela se comprend* 'That is understood'

(3) The fact that constructions equivalent to the English passive with a direct object, e.g. 'He was given a book', are much less common in French than in English – but the view one sometimes sees expressed, that French has no equivalent construction, is mistaken (see **385**).

385 An English sentence such as 'The teacher gave the boy a book' can be turned into a passive by taking as the subject either the original direct object, 'A book was given to the boy (by the teacher)', or the original indirect object, 'The boy was given a book (by the teacher)'. French has a word-for-word equivalent of the first of these, viz. *Un livre fut donné au garçon (par le professeur)*, but not of the second. However, although many grammars fail to mention the fact, a construction in which the original indirect object is the subject, i.e. a passive in which the original direct object remains the direct object, is possible in

French and, though less common than its English equivalent, is in widespread use, particularly but by no means exclusively in journalistic usage. It involves the verb *voir* 'to see', as in:

> *Les mineurs se voient déjà offrir plus de 16% (Le Monde)*
> The miners are already being offered more than 16%

> *Je me suis vu refuser un visa par le consulat américain*
> I have been refused a visa by the American consulate

The construction can occur even when the subject is inanimate and so cannot 'see' the action that is performed, e.g.:

> *'Le Voyage au bout de la nuit' se vit décerner le prix Théophraste Renaudot par 6 voix sur 10* (J. A. Ducourneau)
> (The novel) *Le Voyage au bout de la nuit* was awarded the Théophraste Renaudot prize by 6 votes out of 10

On the other hand, when the main verb is a verb of saying, the passive auxiliary is usually *entendre* 'to hear' rather than *voir*, e.g.:

> *C'est plutôt rare qu'une femme de ménage s'entende dire ça* (Simenon)
> It's not often a cleaning lady is told that

H Negative and interrogative conjugations

386 Negation and interrogation (questions) are dealt with more fully below in **542–580** and **581–593** respectively. Here, we are concerned only with the basic forms involved.

387 (i) The following table illustrates, from one simple tense (the present) and one compound tense (the perfect), the difference between verbs conjugated affirmatively and those conjugated negatively, or interrogatively, or both:

affirmative ('I speak', etc.)	interrogative ('Do I speak?', etc.)
je parle	(See **389**)
tu parles	*parles-tu?*
il parle	*parle-t-il?*

elle parle	*parle-t-elle?*
nous parlons	*parlons-nous?*
vous parlez	*parlez-vous?*
ils parlent	*parlent-ils?*
elles parlent	*parlent-elles?*
j'ai parlé	*ai-je parlé?*
tu as parlé	*as-tu parlé?*
il a parlé	*a-t-il parlé?*
elle a parlé	*a-t-elle parlé?*
nous avons parlé	*avons-nous parlé?*
vous avez parlé	*avez-vous parlé?*
ils ont parlé	*ont-ils parlé?*
elles ont parlé	*ont-elles parlé?*
negative	negative-interrogative
('I do not speak', etc.)	('Do I not speak?', etc.)
je ne parle pas	(See **389**)
tu ne parles pas	*ne parles-tu pas?*
il ne parle pas	*ne parle-t-il pas?*
elle ne parle pas	*ne parle-t-elle pas?*
nous ne parlons pas	*ne parlons-nous pas?*
vous ne parlez pas	*ne parlez-vous pas?*
ils ne parlent pas	*ne parlent-ils pas?*
elles ne parlent pas	*ne parlent-elles pas?*
je n'ai pas parlé	*n'ai-je pas parlé?*
tu n'as pas parlé	*n'as-tu pas parlé?*
il n'a pas parlé	*n'a-t-il pas parlé?*
elle n'a pas parlé	*n'a-t-elle pas parlé?*
nous n'avons pas parlé	*n'avons-nous pas parlé?*
vous n'avez pas parlé	*n'avez-vous pas parlé?*
ils n'ont pas parlé	*n'ont-ils pas parlé?*
elles n'ont pas parlé	*n'ont-elles pas parlé?*

(ii) Note:

(a) that in the interrogative form, the subject pronoun stands after the verb, and in a compound tense stands after the auxiliary, to which it is linked by a hyphen; for important exceptions, see **388** and **389**

(b) that in the negative form, *ne* and *pas* respectively precede and follow the verb or the auxiliary

(c) that in the negative-interrogative form, *ne* precedes the verb and *pas* follows the pronoun

(d) that the only elements that can come between *ne* and the verb are the conjunctive pronouns (including *y* and *en*) (see **198–201**), e.g. *il ne me les donne pas* 'he does not give them to me', *nous n'en parlons pas* 'we do not talk about it', *ne lui avez-vous pas parlé?* 'haven't you spoken to him?'

(iii) Other verbs and tenses are treated in the same way, e.g.:

vous finissez 'you finish', *finissez-vous? vous ne finissez pas, ne finissez-vous pas?*

tu vends 'you sell', *vends-tu? tu ne vends pas, ne vends-tu pas?*

il viendra 'he will come', *viendra-t-il? il ne viendra pas, ne viendra-t-il pas?*

ils sont partis 'they have left', *sont-ils partis? ils ne sont pas partis, ne sont-ils pas partis?*

nous avions vu 'we had seen', *avions-nous vu? nous n'avions pas vu, n'avions-nous pas vu?*

388 (i) Note that, if the verb ends in a vowel, *-t-* is inserted before *il* or *elle* in the interrogative and negative-interrogative forms, e.g. *parle-t-il? n'a-t-elle pas parlé? viendra-t-il? viendra-t-elle?*

(ii) There is no *-t-* when the verb ends in a consonant, e.g. *est-il?* 'is he?', *voit-elle?* 'does she see?', *vend-il?* 'does he sell?', *avait-il fini?* 'had he finished?'. In such circumstances, the final *-t* and the final *-d* are both pronounced as a [t], e.g. *Que répond-il?* [kə repɔ̃til] 'What does he reply?'.

(iii) The only exception to (ii) above is the present tense of *vaincre* and *convaincre* (see **370**), e.g. *vainc-t-il? convainc-t-elle?*

(iv) Note that this *-t-* also occurs with the pronoun *on* 'one', e.g. *Où va-t-on?* 'Where are we going?' (*lit.* Where is one going?'), *Que cherche-t-on?* 'What are they looking for? (*lit.* What is one looking for?)'.

389 (i) In the present indicative, it is normally only with a few common monosyllabic verbs that *je* is inverted (placed after the verb), in particular *ai-je? dis-je? dois-je? puis-je?* (as the interrogative of *je peux*), *sais-je? suis-je?* and, with a following infinitive, *vais-je?*, e.g.:

> *Ai-je bien compris?*
> Have I understood aright?

> *Que dois-je répondre?*
> What am I to reply?

> *Puis-je vous aider?*
> May I help you?

> *Où vais-je le cacher?*
> Where am I going to hide it?

Je fais and *je vois* may also be inverted, but even less commonly so than the above, which are themselves characteristic of a slightly formal style rather than of everyday spoken usage.

(ii) In the present indicative of first conjugation verbs, many grammars list forms like *parlé-je?* (note the acute accent – but the pronunciation is [parlɛːʒ]), etc. These certainly do exist, but nowadays only rarely occur even in the written language. They should never be used in speech and are best avoided even in writing. (Note that, in any case, this form does not occur with verbs whose stem ends in [ʒ], like *je mange* and *je voyage*.)

(iii) *Je* is **never** inverted in the present indicative of other verbs (e.g. *je finis, je vends, je dors, j'écris*).

(iv) Normally, the interrogative of the *je* form of the present indicative (and frequently of other tenses too) is expressed either by intonation (see **586**) or by *est-ce que?* (see **585**), *qu'est-ce que?* 'what?' (see **283**), etc.; so, an alternative form for the sentences quoted in (i) above would be *Est-ce que j'ai bien compris? Qu'est-ce que je dois répondre? Est-ce que je peux vous aider? Où est-ce que je vais le cacher?*

I Person and number

Introduction

390 The verb agrees with its subject in person and number, but with a composite or collective subject the following additional rules must be observed:

A Composite subject

391   When the subject consists of two or more nouns joined by *et* (either expressed or understood) the verb is put in the third person plural, e.g.:

Le printemps et l'été ont été très secs
The spring and summer have been very dry

392   When the subject consists of two or more pronouns, or of a combination of nouns and pronouns, the verb is plural, and agrees with the first person rather than with the second or third, with the second rather than with the third. These pronouns are disjunctive.

(i)   In affirmative and negative sentences, if the verb is in the first or second person, an additional conjunctive *nous* or *vous* (according to the sense) is generally inserted in the usual position before the verb; if the verb is in the third person, *ils* is not inserted, unless the rest of the subject is put after the verb, as it often is whatever the person and number, e.g.:

     Vous et moi, nous irons ensemble à la gare
or *Nous irons ensemble à la gare, vous et moi*
     You and I will go to the station together

     On m'a dit que vous et votre sœur vous ne voulez pas jouer
or *On m'a dit que vous ne voulez pas jouer, vous et votre sœur*
     They tell me that you and your sister do not want to play

     Jacques et lui sont allés au théâtre
or *Ils sont allés au théâtre, Jacques et lui*
     James and he have gone to the theatre

(ii)   In interrogative sentences, and other forms of sentence in which the subject is a conjunctive pronoun following the verb, this *nous, vous, ils* or *elles* (whichever the sense requires) cannot be omitted, whether the composite subject stands before or after the verb, e.g.:

Votre femme et vous, comptez-vous passer la fin de semaine à Paris?
Do you and your wife mean to spend the week-end in Paris?

A peine étaient-ils partis, mon frère et son ami, que j'ai reçu ce télégramme

Scarcely had my brother and his friend started, when I
received this telegram

(iii) For the number of the verb with *l'un et l'autre*, *l'un ou l'autre*,
ni l'un ni l'autre, see **292**, iv.

B *Collective subject*

393 Collective nouns denote a collection of people or things
considered not as so many individuals but as making up one body
(i.e. a collectivity), e.g. *un bataillon* 'battalion', *le comité* 'committee', *la compagnie* 'company', *la foule* 'crowd', *le gouvernement*
'government', *la maison* 'firm', *une multitude* 'multitude', *le parti*
'(political) party', *le peuple* 'people' (as in, e.g., *le peuple français*
'the French people'), *un tas* 'heap', *une troupe* 'troop'.

394 In English, there is a good deal of freedom in the use of a
singular or a plural verb with collective nouns (e.g. 'The government has decided . . .' or 'The government have decided . . .'). In
French, there is considerably less freedom of choice. The number
of the verb is determined by the following rules:

(i) The verb of which such words are the subject is generally put in
the singular, unless followed by a genitive plural, e.g.:

> *La foule prit d'assaut les barricades*
> The crowd rushed the barricades

> *Le comité entier est d'avis qu'il n'y a rien de plus à y faire*
> The committee all agree that there is nothing more to be
> done about it

> *Le gouvernement italien a démissionné*
> The Italian government has (*or* have) resigned

(ii) Even when a singular collective noun is followed by a genitive
plural, the verb is often put in the singular, e.g.:

> *Un bataillon de soldats marchait par les rues*
> A battalion of soldiers was marching through the streets (a
> single unit, without reference to the individuals who com-
> pose it)

(iii) But when the genitive plural is emphasized by the addition of
plural adjectives or participles, the number of the main verb

becomes a matter of taste, as may be seen in the following examples:

(a) *Un bataillon de soldats affamés, en haillons, couverts de boue et de sang, marchaient* (or *marchait*) *par les rues*
A battalion of soldiers, starving, ragged, covered with mud and blood, was marching through the streets

(They still form a battalion, a single unit, so the verb may be singular; but, as attention is called to the condition of the individual soldiers, the plural is equally possible.)

(b) *Un bataillon de soldats, dispersés par les rues, enfonçaient toutes les portes*
A battalion of soldiers, roaming through the streets, were breaking down all the doors

(The soldiers have ceased to be a single unit, and are acting as separate individuals, so the plural is almost inevitable.)

The rules given above state what appears to be the normal usage, but they are not universally observed.

395 There are, however, a few special cases where the rules are more definite:

(i) When followed by *de* with a plural noun, *un assez grand nombre* 'a fairly large number', *la plupart* and *le plus grand nombre* 'the majority', *une infinité* 'no end of', *nombre* and *quantité* (both without article) 'lots of', require their verb in the plural. *La plupart, le plus grand nombre* and *une infinité* can also be used without any complement introduced by *de* and then too they require a plural verb. Any one of the above six expressions, however, when followed by *de* with a singular noun requires a verb in the singular. (See also **329**, *La plupart*.) Examples:

Le sénat différait d'opinion; la plupart désiraient la guerre
The senate was divided; the majority (*or* most of them) wanted war

La plupart du sénat désirait la guerre
La plupart des sénateurs désiraient la guerre
The majority of the senate (senators) wanted war

(ii) When *le peu (de)* means 'the little (of)' (i.e. 'the small amount (of)'), it takes a singular verb whether it stands alone or is followed by *de* and a singular noun, e.g.:

Le peu d'argent qui me reste me suffira
The little money I have left will be enough for me

When *le peu de* is followed by a plural noun, i.e. when it means 'the few', the verb is singular, i.e. it agrees with *le peu*, if the emphasis is on the smallness of the quantity, e.g.:

Le peu de gens qui nous suit n'y suffira pas
The smallness of our following will not admit of it

but the verb is plural, i.e. it agrees with the plural noun following *de*, if the emphasis is on the number (small though it may be) of individual persons or things denoted by that noun, e.g.:

Le peu de troupes qu'il avait rassemblées ont tenu ferme
The handful of troops (the few troops) he had got together stood firm

For *peu (de)* and *un peu (de)*, see **328**.

(iii) *Tout le monde* 'everybody' and *plus d'un* 'more than one' always take the singular, but *moins de deux*, etc. 'less (fewer) than two', etc., *plus de trois*, etc. 'more than three', etc., always take the plural, e.g.:

Tout le monde est de votre avis; plus d'un voudrait même aller plus loin
Everybody agrees with you; more than one would even like to go further

Moins de deux mois se sont écoulés
Less than two months have elapsed

(iv) *La moitié* 'half', *le tiers* 'a third', *le quart* 'a quarter', *une douzaine* 'a dozen', and other similar collective numerals can be followed by a verb in either the singular or the plural according to the emphasis, e.g.:

La moitié des députés a voté pour et l'autre moitié contre le projet de loi
Half the members voted for and half against the bill

Une bonne moitié des grévistes sont restés dans l'usine
A good half of the strikers stayed in the factory

(v) With *toute sorte de, toute espèce de* 'every kind of, all kinds of', followed by a plural noun, the verb is normally in the plural, e.g.:

Toute sorte de cigarettes sont mauvaises pour la santé
All kinds of cigarettes are bad for one's health

(vi) *Force* 'many, a lot of' (see **324**, vi), which is never followed by *de*, takes a plural verb, e.g.:

Force gens croient être plaisants, qui ne sont que ridicules
Many people think themselves humorous when they are only ridiculous

(vii) Note that 'the rest' with reference to people is never *le reste* (which refers to things, 'the remainder', and takes a singular verb) but *les autres*, which of course takes a plural verb.

396   Phrases connected by 'as', 'as much as', 'as well as', 'and not', 'but not', 'more than', 'less than', etc. are, of course, neither composite nor collective subjects, as these expressions are compound conjunctions introducing a separate clause with the verb understood (see also **129**), e.g.:

Le vaisseau amiral, mais très peu des autres vaisseaux de l'escorte, rentra sans dégâts
The flagship, but very few of the other vessels in the escort, returned undamaged

i.e. the flagship returned undamaged, but very few of the other vessels in the escort did so.

J Tenses

397   There are many similarities but also some fundamental differences between the tense systems of English and French. Among the main differences are the following:

398   (i) The English distinction between simple forms and continuous forms (constructed with the verb 'to be' and the present participle) is not paralleled in French. When it is desired to stress the fact that the action was in progress, French can certainly do so, by using the expression *être en train de* 'to be in the process of' + the infinitive, e.g.:

Il ne faut pas le déranger, il est en train de réfléchir
We mustn't disturb him, he's thinking

Il était en train de téléphoner à sa femme quand je suis arrivé
He was telephoning his wife when I arrived

but this construction should be used only sparingly and not be regarded as an all-purpose equivalent of the English continuous forms. The following will illustrate some of the forms that correspond in the two languages:

I write	I am writing	*j'écris*
I lived	I was living	*j'habitais*
I have worked	I have been working	*j'ai travaillé*

Nor does French have a special form corresponding to the English 'habitual past' expressed by 'used to' – e.g. 'I used to work' is just *je travaillais*.

399   (ii) The English preterite or simple past (e.g. 'I wrote, he came') has a number of different values which in French are expressed by different tenses (see **405–410**).

400   (iii) On the other hand, the French perfect (e.g. *j'ai chanté*) may correspond either to the English perfect ('I have sung') or, very frequently, to the English preterite ('I sang') (see **410**).

401   Note too (though this is not a matter of tense) that French does not use *faire* as English uses 'to do' as a mere auxiliary verb in the negative and interrogative conjugations (e.g. 'I do not sing', 'Do you sing?'), or for the purpose of emphasizing the verb (e.g. 'I do find my work hard') (in such contexts, French uses some such expression as *en fait* 'indeed' or *il est vrai que* 'it is true that').

402   Taken together, the factors referred to in **398–401** lead to such similarities and differences as the following between the two languages:

Present
affirmative

I find (*or* am finding) my work rather hard
Je trouve mon travail assez difficile

I **do** find my work rather hard
Je trouve mon travail assez difficile en fait

negative

I do not find (*or* am not finding) my work hard
Je ne trouve pas mon travail difficile

interrogative

Do you find (*or* are you finding) your work hard?
Trouvez-vous votre travail difficile?

Imperfect (including English preterite forms)
affirmative

At that time I found (*or* was finding, *or* used to find) my work
rather hard
A cette époque je trouvais mon travail assez difficile

At that time I **did** find my work rather hard
*Il est vrai qu'à cette époque je trouvais mon travail assez
difficile*

negative

At that time he did not find (*or* was not finding, *or* used not
to find) his work hard
A cette époque il ne trouvait pas son travail difficile

interrogative

Did he find (*or* was he finding, *or* used he to find) his work
hard?
Trouvait-il son travail difficile?

Perfect (including English preterite forms)
affirmative

Lately I have found (*or* have been finding) my work rather
hard
Dernièrement j'ai trouvé mon travail assez difficile

Yesterday I found my work rather hard
Hier j'ai trouvé mon travail assez difficile

negative

> Lately you have not found (*or* have not been finding) your
> work hard
> *Dernièrement vous n'avez pas trouvé votre travail difficile*

> Yesterday you did not find your work hard
> *Hier vous n'avez pas trouvé votre travail difficile*

interrogative

> Have you found (*or* have you been finding) your work hard
> lately?
> *Avez-vous trouvé votre travail difficile dernièrement?*

> Did you find your work hard yesterday?
> *Avez-vous trouvé votre travail difficile hier?*

Pluperfect

> I had worked (*or* had been working) in Paris
> *J'avais travaillé à Paris*

> I had not worked (*or* had not been working) in Paris
> *Je n'avais pas travaillé à Paris*

> Had he worked (*or* had he been working) in Paris?
> *Est-ce qu'il avait travaillé à Paris?*

Future

> I shall leave (*or* shall be leaving) tomorrow
> *Je partirai demain*

> I shall not leave (*or* shall not be leaving) tomorrow
> *Je ne partirai pas demain*

> Will you leave (*or* will you be leaving) tomorrow?
> *Est-ce que vous partirez demain?*

(For the use of the present instead of the future, and of *aller faire*
'to be going to do', see 414).

403   In sections 404–424 we consider some problems relating to
the use of particular tenses of the indicative. For tenses of the
subjunctive, see 496–506.

The 'historic present'

404 The 'historic present', i.e. the present tense as a narrative and descriptive tense with reference to the past, is very much more widely used in French than in English, e.g.:

> *Le lendemain matin, un homme muni d'un appareil photo pénètre dans la salle à manger de mon hôtel. Il se plante à quelques mètres de moi et, calmement, déclenche son flash* (Sylviane Stein in *L'Express*)
> The next morning a man with a camera made his way into the dining-room of my hotel. He planted himself a few yards from me and, calmly, took a flash photo.

The imperfect, the preterite, and the perfect

405 The preterite is no longer in normal use in spoken French though it survives in the written language (except in an informal style influenced by the spoken language). In discussing the use of these three past tenses, we must therefore distinguish between (i) the written language (see **406–408**) and (ii) the spoken language (see **409–410**).

(i) The written language

406 The imperfect is used:

(a) to refer to a past event regarded as continuous or as being in progress, i.e. it corresponds to the English 'was (were) + . . . ing' which can always be translated by the French imperfect; note however that English sometimes uses the preterite in such contexts, e.g.:

> *Il pleuvait lorsque Jean partit*
> It was raining when John left

> *Pendant que mon père travaillait, mon frère dormait*
> While my father was working, my brother was sleeping
> While my father worked, my brother slept

(b) for descriptions in the past (including descriptions of states of mind, etc.), e.g.:

Sous l'Empire les Romains étaient très civilisés
Under the Empire the Romans were very civilized

Elle ne voulait pas sortir
She did not wish to go out

Le sentier descendait vers un pont qui traversait un petit ruisseau
The path sloped down towards a bridge that crossed a little stream

(c) with reference to habitual actions in the past, i.e. it corresponds to English 'used to do' which can always be translated by the French imperfect; note however that English very often uses the preterite in such contexts whereas French does not; e.g.:

Lorsqu'il voyageait beaucoup, il m'écrivait chaque semaine
When he used to travel a lot, he used to write to me every week
When he travelled a lot, he wrote to me every week

Quand nous étions à Paris, nous allions tous les jours au Bois de Boulogne
When we were in Paris we went (*or* we used to go) to the Bois de Boulogne every day

Note that the important thing is that the action is regarded as **habitual, not merely as frequent or repeated** (in which case the preterite or the perfect is used — see also **407, a**), e.g.:

Pendant les vacances, il lui téléphonait régulièrement
During the holidays, he rang her regularly

Pendant les vacances, il lui téléphona plusieurs fois
During the holidays, he rang her several times

Il lui a déjà téléphoné dix fois
He has already rung her ten times

(d) The imperfect can also be used for various stylistic effects; this is particularly true of what has been termed the 'picturesque imperfect', i.e. the use of the imperfect where the preterite or the perfect would normally be expected (see **407** and **410**) with reference to a completed action in the past, and often with a precise indication of time or date, e.g.:

Louis XIV se remariait deux ans après (É. Faguet)
Louis XIV remarried two years afterwards

Il y a six ans, l'armée française débarquait sur les côtes de Provence (France-Illustration)
Six years ago the French army landed on the coast of Provence

Since one role of the imperfect is to present the action as in progress (see a above), the effect of using it instead of the preterite or perfect is to present the action as unfolding before our eyes, so to speak, and hence to heighten the effect. But this construction should only be used sparingly and with care and is best avoided by learners.

407 The preterite refers to events regarded as completed (i.e. not as continuous or habitual – see **406**) in the past, e.g.:

L'accord fut signé mardi
The agreement was signed on Tuesday

Les alliés débarquèrent en Normandie en 1944
The allies landed in Normandy in 1944

It is frequently used as a narrative tense, expressing successive events in the story, e.g.:

Giuseppa embrassa son fils et rentra en pleurant dans sa cabane. Elle se jeta à genoux devant une image de la Vierge, et pria avec ferveur. Cependant Falcone marcha quelque deux cents pas dans le sentier et ne s'arrêta que dans un petit ravin où il descendit. L'endroit lui parut convenable pour son dessein. (Mérimée)
Giuseppa kissed her son and went back into the hut in tears. She fell upon her knees before an image of the Virgin, and prayed fervently. Meanwhile Falcone walked some two hundred paces along the path, and did not stop till he came to a little gully into which he descended. The place seemed to him suitable for the execution of his plan.

Note:

(a) that while habitual actions are expressed by the imperfect, actions that are merely presented as repeated can be in the preterite (see also **406**, c), e.g.:

Il visita Paris quatre fois pendant les années 50
He visited Paris four times during the 50s

(b) that the length of time taken by the action is irrelevant – an event that lasted years, or centuries, or millions of years, is expressed by the preterite if it is regarded as a completed event in the past, e.g.:

Voltaire vécut 84 ans
Voltaire lived for 84 years

L'ère tertiaire dura cinquante millions d'années
The tertiary era lasted fifty million years

408 The use of the perfect corresponds closely to that of the English perfect; it implies some kind of link between the past event and present time, e.g. that the action has taken place in a period of time (the same day, the same century, someone's lifetime, etc.) that still continues, or that the consequences of the action continue into the present, e.g.:

Je n'ai jamais visité Versailles
I have never visited Versailles (i.e. in the course of my life, which continues)

as contrasted with:

Je passai trois ans à Paris mais je ne visitai jamais Versailles
I spent three years in Paris but I never visited Versailles (i.e. during the three years in question, which are now over)

The difference between the preterite and the perfect is well illustrated by the following example in which they both occur:

Nous nous adressâmes la parole quelques jours plus tard, un dimanche matin, en des circonstances dont j'ai bien gardé la mémoire (Lacretelle)
We spoke to one another a few days later, one Sunday morning, in circumstances that have remained clearly in my memory

(ii) The spoken language

409 The use of the imperfect in speech is the same as in the written language (see **406**).

410 The preterite is no longer in normal use in speech, in which its functions as a narrative past tense have been taken over entirely by the perfect, e.g.:

J'ai visité Paris pour la première fois en 1948
I visited Paris for the first time in 1948

La guerre a éclaté en 1939
War broke out in 1939

Nos cousins sont arrivés ce matin; nous les avons rencontrés dans la Rue de Rivoli
Our cousins arrived this morning; we met them in the Rue de Rivoli

This use of the perfect, as a substitute for the preterite, is increasingly found not only in speech but in writing, especially in journalism and in a narrative style that is modelled on spoken usage, e.g.:

Jeter l'Angleterre à genoux en l'atteignant par les Indes, jamais Napoléon n'a perdu de vue cet objectif. Il l'a poursuivi par toutes les voies
To beat England to her knees by striking at her through India – this was the objective of which Napoleon never lost sight. He tried every road that might lead to its attainment

Note examples such as the following in which the French corresponds once to the English preterite and once to the English perfect:

Je l'ai vu il y a dix ans et je ne l'ai jamais revu
I saw him ten years ago and I have never seen him since

The pluperfect and the past anterior

411 (i) The pluperfect is used as in English, e.g.:

Je croyais qu'il avait terminé son travail
I thought he had finished his work

Note however that, in sentences such as the following in which English can use a preterite instead of the pluperfect that, strictly speaking, the sense requires, the pluperfect **must** be used in French:

Il prétendait que son frère lui avait écrit la semaine précédente
He claimed that his brother wrote (*or* had written) to him the
week before

(ii) The past anterior, like the preterite, is practically unknown in
conversation. It is a literary form used principally:

(a) with temporal conjunctions, such as *quand, lorsque* 'when',
après que 'after', *dès que, aussitôt que* 'as soon as', when the main
verb is preterite, and similarly after *à peine* 'scarcely' followed by a
que-clause, to indicate that one thing happened immediately after
something else had happened, e.g.:

Dès qu'ils eurent mis le nez dehors, l'orage éclata
The storm burst the instant they put their noses outside

A peine eurent-ils mis le nez dehors que l'orage éclata
Hardly had they put their noses outside when the storm burst

(b) occasionally, in a main clause, with an expression of time such
as *bientôt* 'soon', *vite* 'quickly', *en un instant* 'in a moment', to
express the speed with which something happened, e.g.:

Cependant il eut bien vite deviné que . . . (Hugo)
However, he had very quickly guessed that . . .

Ils eurent rejoint la chasse en un instant (Mérimée)
In a moment they had caught up with the hunt

412 The 'double-compound' tenses

(i) The past anterior is, of course, based on the preterite, e.g. *(il)
eut (fini), (il) fut (parti)*. As we have seen (410), the preterite is
replaced in speech, and often in writing, by the perfect. If we now
substitute the perfect of *avoir* or *être* for the preterite in *il eut fini*,
etc., we get the so-called 'double-compound' tense known in
French as the *passé surcomposé*, viz. *il a eu fini, il a été parti*.
Although not all grammars refer to them, such forms as these have
been in use for many centuries and they are well established as
substitutes for the past anterior in those spoken and written styles
that avoid the preterite, e.g.:

Dès que je l'ai eu vu, il s'est mis à courir
The moment I saw him, he started to run

Je l'ai démêlé après que Monsieur a été parti (Marivaux)
I sorted it out after you had left, sir

(ii) Other 'double-compound' tenses formed on the basis of compound tenses of the auxiliaries (e.g. *j'aurai eu fait, j'aurais eu fait, j'avais eu fait*) also exist but in practice rarely occur with the exception (itself by no means common) of the type *j'avais eu fait*, e.g.:

Ils avaient eu vite tourné le câble autour des bittes (R. Vercel)
They had quickly got the cable wound round the bollards

A peine les avais-je eu quittés qu'ils s'étaient reformés (Proust)
Scarcely had I left them than they had formed up again

Tenses with depuis (que), il y a (voici, voilà) . . . que

413   (i) The use of tenses with *depuis que* and *il y a (voici, voilà) . . . que* often causes difficulty.

(ii) *Depuis que* has two meanings:

(a) It refers to a specific event, i.e. to a specific point in time, in which case it is translated as 'since' or sometimes 'after' and takes the same tense as in English (allowing that the French perfect is often the equivalent of the English preterite – see **410**), e.g.:

Je ne le vois plus depuis qu'il s'est marié
I no longer see him since he got married

Depuis qu'il s'est établi à la campagne je le vois presque tous les jours
I see him nearly every day since he settled in the country

Je le voyais souvent depuis qu'il s'était établi à Paris
I used to see him often after he had settled in Paris

– but note that, in examples such as this last one in which English has the option of using the preterite as an alternative to the pluperfect ('. . . after he settled in Paris'), French insists on the pluperfect.

(b) It introduces a verb that relates not to a past event but to a continuing state of affairs, i.e. it expresses duration; in this case, the two languages use different constructions (see iv below).

(iii) (a) When used with expressions of time, *il y a, voici* and *voilà* serve to express the meaning 'ago', e.g. *Je l'ai vu il y a (voici, voilà) dix minutes* 'I saw him ten minutes ago'. When followed by a *que*-clause, they express the meaning of 'since', e.g. *Voilà dix ans qu'il est parti* 'It is ten years since he left'. In such sentences as these, then, French uses the same tense as English (cf. ii,a above).

(b) However, when *il y a* etc. . . . *que* are followed by a verb expressing the duration of a continuing state of affairs, the two languages use different tenses (see iv below).

(iv) When *depuis que, il y a (voici, voilà)* . . . *que* are followed by a verb that refers not to a past event, i.e. not to a point in time, but to a continuing state of affairs, i.e. to duration, French uses

(a) the present tense where English uses the perfect

(b) the imperfect tense where English uses the pluperfect.

Examples:

> *Tiens! Vous voilà à Paris? Combien de chapeaux avez-vous achetés depuis que vous êtes ici?*
> Hullo! You're in Paris, then? How many hats have you bought since you have been here?

$$\left\{ \begin{array}{l} \textit{Il y a} \\ \textit{Voici} \\ \textit{Voilà} \end{array} \right\} \textit{dix ans que je le connais}$$

I have known him for ten years (and still know him)

$$\left\{ \begin{array}{l} \textit{Il y avait} \\ \textit{Voici} \\ \textit{Voilà} \end{array} \right\} \textit{dix ans que je le connaissais}$$

I had known him for ten years (and still knew him)

Similarly, French uses the present or the imperfect (corresponding to the perfect or the pluperfect in English) to express duration in a main clause that includes the preposition *depuis*, or is preceded or followed by a clause introduced by *depuis que*, and in questions introduced by *depuis quand?* or *depuis combien de temps?* 'since when? (for) how long?', e.g.:

> *Je le connais depuis dix ans*
> I have known him for ten years

> *Je le connaissais depuis dix ans*
> I had known him for ten years

> *Je le connais depuis 1970*
> I have known him since 1970

> *Je le connais depuis qu'il est arrivé à Paris*
> I have known him since he arrived in Paris

Je le connaissais depuis qu'il avait écrit son premier roman
I had known him since he had written (*or* wrote – cf. 411,i)
his first novel

Depuis quand êtes-vous à Paris?
How long (*or* since when) have you been in Paris?

Depuis combien de temps étiez-vous à Paris lorsque votre père est mort?
How long had you been in Paris when your father died?

(v) For *depuis (que)* and *il y a, voici, voilà* in negative constructions, see 567.

The future, aller faire, etc.

414 (i) In the case of the future, French and English use much the same forms of expression. The use of the present tense to express future time is very frequent in French (but see ii below), and must be used (as in English) instead of the future after *si* 'if'. Similarly the present indicative of *aller* can be used with the infinitive just like English 'to be going to'.

Examples:

Je pars (or *je vais partir,* or *je partirai*) *demain*
I leave (*or* am leaving, *or* am going to leave, *or* shall leave)
tomorrow

Je ne pars pas (ne vais pas partir, ne partirai pas) avant lundi
I am not leaving (am not going to leave, shall not leave)
before Monday

Quel jour partez-vous (allez-vous partir, partirez-vous)?
What day do you leave (are you leaving, are you going to leave, will you leave)?

But:

Je le verrai s'il vient (**not** *viendra*)
I shall see him if he comes

Je ne viendrai pas si je ne reçois (**not** *recevrai*) *pas une lettre de votre part*
I shall not come if I do not hear from you

Viendra-t-il si je ne lui écris (**not** *écrirai*) *pas?*
Will he come if I do not write to him?

Note the use of the present tense in French in contexts such as *Je vous aide?* 'Shall I help you?'

(ii) Except for *avant que* which requires the subjunctive (see **488**), temporal conjunctions, such as *quand, lorsque* 'when', *dès que, aussitôt que* 'as soon as', *après que* 'after', take the indicative or conditional. With these the English present, when it refers to future time, must **always** be translated by the future or future perfect in French, e.g.:

> I will see him when he comes
> *Je le verrai quand il viendra*

> As soon as we arrive we will order dinner
> *Dès que nous serons arrivés nous commanderons le dîner*

(iii) The future of *avoir* and *être*, and the future perfect (formed on the basis of the future of *avoir* and *être* and the past participle) can express something that is assumed to be true or that is highly likely to be true, e.g.:

> *Il est dix heures. Jean sera déjà à Paris*
> It is ten o'clock. John will be in Paris by now

> *Qui est à la porte? – Ce sera un des enfants*
> Who is at the door? It will be one of the children

> *Il n'est pas encore arrivé? Il aura manqué son train*
> Hasn't he come yet? He must have missed the train

(iv) Contrary to what some grammars state, the construction *aller faire* does not (or not necessarily) express a *futur proche*. It indicates that the future event (which may be a long way in the future) is in some way linked to the present, e.g. as inevitable or as arising out of the present situation or as depending on some decision or intention already known, e.g.:

> *Tôt ou tard, nous allons tous mourir*
> Sooner or later, we are all going to die

> *Dans dix ans, je vais prendre ma retraite*
> In ten years time I am going to retire

(v) For the use of the future as an imperative, see **517**.

The conditional

415 As in English, the so-called 'conditional' tense in French has two quite distinct values:

(i) It expresses a future-in-the-past, e.g.:

> *Il a dit qu'il viendrait*
> He said he would come

– at the time of speaking (*il a dit*), the action of coming was in the future (he presumably said something like *Je viendrai* 'I shall come'), hence the term 'future-in-the-past'; with reference to this use, the term 'conditional' is not really appropriate

(ii) It is used in conditional sentences proper, i.e. in sentences containing (or at least implying) a subordinate clause introduced by *si* and expressing a condition (but note that the conditional is **not** used in the *si*-clause itself), e.g.:

> *Il viendrait s'il savait que vous étiez ici*
> He would come if he knew you were here

> *Dans ce cas-là, je vous écrirais*
> In that case (i.e. if that were so), I should write to you

For fuller discussion of the use of tenses after *si*, see **418–422**.

416 French has the conditional, but English has no 'would' or 'should'

(i) with relatives – when equivalent to 'anyone who', 'anything which'; with expressions of time; and with *comme*; e.g.:

> *On se moquerait de celui qui ferait cela*
> Anyone who did that would be laughed at

> *On le surveillerait à partir du moment où il débarquerait*
> He would be watched from the moment when he landed

> *Vous feriez comme vous voudriez*
> You would do as you liked

(ii) in a sort of implied reported speech, e.g.:

> *A en croire le 'Figaro' la guerre serait inévitable*
> According to the *Figaro* war is inevitable

(By using the conditional the writer implies that the statement is not his own, but the *Figaro*'s.)

(iii) in certain common idioms with *pouvoir*, *savoir* and *vouloir*, e.g.:

Il se pourrait bien qu'il n'arrive jamais
It is quite likely (possible) that he may never get there

Vous ne sauriez le convaincre
You wouldn't be able to convince him

Je voudrais bien être sain et sauf de l'autre côté de la Manche
I wish I were safe and sound on the other side of the Channel

417 Note on the other hand that when, as is occasionally the case, English 'would' is the equivalent of 'used to', the imperfect and not the conditional must be used in French, e.g.:

When we were children, we would spend our holidays every year at the sea-side
Quand nous étions enfants, nous passions nos vacances tous les ans au bord de la mer

Tenses in conditional sentences with si 'if'

418 One of the main uses of the French conditional is in conditional sentences proper, i.e. in sentences containing a subordinate clause introduced by *si* 'if'. (These do not include indirect questions introduced by *si* 'if, whether' – see **423–424**.)
In such sentences:

(i) when English has 'would' or 'should' in the main clause, the French main clause is also conditional
when English has no 'would' or 'should' in the main clause, the French main clause is indicative

(ii) in the main clause the tenses are always the same in both languages

(iii) when the tense used in the main clause in French is present conditional (English 'would' or 'should'), the imperfect indicative is used in French in the *si* clause to represent the English preterite, or the forms 'did', 'should' or 'were to', e.g.:

$$\text{If I} \begin{cases} \text{needed} \\ \text{were to need} \\ \text{should need} \\ \text{did need} \end{cases} \text{anything, I would write to you}$$

Si j'avais besoin de quelque chose, je vous écrirais

If he did not need something, he would not write
S'il n'avait pas besoin de quelque chose, il n'écrirait pas

Note:

(a) that it is important to be sure of this use of the imperfect, since experience shows that students have a tendency to use the conditional instead (even though the conditional is not used in English either); the conditional is never used after *si* in this type of sentence (the conditional after *si* meaning 'whether' is a different matter – see **423–424**)

(b) that the preterite is never used in this type of sentence; the only time the preterite can be used after *si* in conditional sentences (and even then only rarely) is when the *si*-clause in reality expresses a fact, e.g. *S'il quitta la ville en toute hâte, on ne peut pas l'en blâmer* 'If he left the town in a hurry, one cannot blame him for it' (the implication is that he did leave the town in a hurry).

419 Except for this use of the imperfect indicative, the tenses of the 'if' – clause are the same in both languages, including the use of the present indicative with 'if' to represent future time, e.g.:

Si j'ai fait ça, je dois souffrir

$$\text{If I} \begin{cases} \text{did} \\ \text{have done} \end{cases} \text{that, I must suffer for it}$$

S'il arrive demain, vous le verrez
If he arrives tomorrow, you will see him

Before or after an imperative main clause, a *si*-clause is in the present indicative, e.g.:

Si tu m'aimes, écris-mois souvent
If you love me, write to me often

Montrez-les-moi, si vous en recevez
Show them to me if you get any

420 As the result of these rules, observe that after *si* meaning 'if' French ordinarily uses only four tenses, viz.:

present indicative, perfect indicative, imperfect indicative and pluperfect indicative

Examples:

Je vous les montre toujours, si j'en reçois
I always show them to you, if I get any

Je vous les montrerai, si j'en reçois
I will show them to you, if I get any

Je vous les ai toujours montrés, si j'en ai reçu
I have always shown them to you, if I have received any

Je vous les montrais, si j'en recevais
I used to show them to you, if I got any

Je vous les avais montrés, si j'en avais reçu
I had shown them to you, if I had received any

Je vous les montrerais, si j'en recevais
I should show them to you, if I got any

Je vous les aurais montrés, si j'en avais reçu
I should have shown them to you, if I had received any

The pluperfect subjunctive is sometimes used instead of the pluperfect indicative (see also **478,c**), e.g. *Je vous les aurais montrés, si j'en eusse reçu*; this is a literary archaism that should be avoided by learners.

Lastly, when the English 'if' is followed by two clauses, joined by 'and' or 'or', *que* replaces *si* in the second clause, and the verb after *que* is put in the subjunctive, e.g.:

S'il m'écrit, ou qu'il vienne me voir, je vous le dirai
If he writes to me, or comes to see me, I will tell you

(See also **703**.)

421 *Si* with little or no conjunctive force

Si can also be used with little or no conjunctive force:

(i) like English 'supposing', e.g.:

Si nous partions
Let us start, supposing we start, what about starting?

(ii) in wishes (not referring to the future) with imperfect or pluperfect indicative, e.g.:

Si j'étais (j'avais été) plus jeune
Would that (if only) I were (had been) younger

422   The sense of a conditional sentence can also be expressed without the use of *si*:

(i) with *quand* (*quand même* – 300,v,d) or *que*, both verbs being in the conditional, e.g.:

Quand (quand même) il me le jurerait, je ne le croirais pas
or *Il me le jurerait que je ne le croirais pas*
Even if he swore it, I should not believe it

(For this use of *que* see also **701**.)

(ii) by inverting verb and subject, as in questions. This is commonest with the imperfect or pluperfect subjunctive, though the conditional also occurs; these are all characteristic only of the literary language, e.g.:

Dussé-je en mourir, je n'y consentirais jamais
(*devrais-je* is also possible)
Even if I had to die for it, I would never consent

Il se serait retiré, n'eût-il pas pensé qu'il se ferait remarquer
He would have withdrawn, had he not thought he would attract attention

In such sentences *pas* may be omitted.

Tenses in indirect questions after si 'if, whether'

423   *Si* 'if' is also regularly used in indirect questions as the equivalent of 'whether'. In this case it takes any tense of the indicative or conditional that the sense requires, e.g.:

Je me demande s'il viendra

I wonder $\left\{ \begin{array}{l} \text{if} \\ \text{whether} \end{array} \right\}$ he will come

Je me demandais s'il viendrait

I was wondering $\left\{ \begin{array}{l} \text{if} \\ \text{whether} \end{array} \right\}$ he would come

Je ne sais pas s'il a lu ce roman
I don't know if he has read this novel

Je ne savais pas s'il prenait le train ou l'avion
I didn't know whether he was coming by train or by plane

424 Note the emphatic use of what is, in reality, this type of *si*-clause with ellipsis of its main clause, where English would use either an echo-question or an exclamatory expression, e.g.:

Voulez-vous y aller? – Si je le veux!
Do you want to go? – Do I want to?! (I should think I do!)

(this assumes a non-expressed main clause such as *Vous me demandez si* . . . 'You are asking me whether . . .').

K The infinitive

425 The infinitive is frequently used as a verbal noun, and often corresponds to the English verbal noun in *-ing*. It is a verbal noun in the fullest sense of the term, i.e. it functions to some extent as a verb and to some extent as a noun, when it is used without an article:

(i) as the subject of a verb or as the complement of the verb *être*, e.g.:

Penser à vous sera ma seule consolation
Thinking (to think) of you will be my only consolation

Voir, c'est croire
Seeing is believing

Consentir n'est pas approuver
To consent is not to approve

Mieux vaut les garder
Better keep them (i.e. to keep them would be better)

For the use of *c'est* when both subject and complement are positive infinitives, see **258**,iii.

In Classical French and occasionally still in literary usage, the infinitive subject may be preceded by *de*, e.g. *De penser à toi me soutiendra* (Gide) 'Thinking of you will sustain me'; this *de* is required when the infinitive follows the verb, e.g.:

Ma seule consolation sera de penser à vous
My only consolation will be to think of you

Ça m'agace de l'écouter
It irritates me to listen to him

In such cases, the infinitive may also be introduced by *que de*, e.g.:

C'est une honte que de dire cela
It is shameful to say that

(ii) after prepositions, e.g.:

Il a fini par franchir le mur
He ended by getting over the wall

Je l'ai fait pour vous aider
I did it to help you

For the use of the infinitive with prepositions, see further **649**.

426   The infinitive becomes fully a noun when it is used with an article. In some cases, it retains something of its verbal value and is used in the singular only, e.g.:

le boire et le manger	food and drink
au coucher (au lever) du soleil	at sunset (sunrise)
l'heure du coucher	bedtime
le savoir-faire	savoir-faire

but in other cases it is used in every way as an ordinary noun, e.g.:

le baiser	kiss
le devoir	duty
le dîner	dinner
un être (humain)	a (human) being
le sourire	smile
le souvenir	memory

– all of these can be used in the plural, e.g. *des êtres humains* 'human beings', *mes souvenirs* 'my memories'.

427   The infinitive is used in French:

(i) after verbs of the senses (saying, hearing, etc. – see **430**) with a noun that serves both as the direct object of the main verb and as the subject of the infinitive, where English uses either the infinitive without 'to' or the present participle, e.g.:

Avez-vous entendu crier la foule?
Did you hear the crowd shouting (*or* shout)?

On a entendu le roi vanter sa hardiesse
People have heard the king boasting (*or* boast) of his bravery

Vous avez vu des fleurs étiolées s'épanouir parce qu'on leur donnait de l'air
You have seen drooping flowers revive on being given air

(ii) after verbs of saying and thinking, when the subject of both verbs is the same, as an alternative to a *que*-clause, e.g.:

J'ai cru rêver (or *J'ai cru que je rêvais*)
I thought I was dreaming

Il reconnaissait avoir écrit (or *qu'il avait écrit) la lettre*
He admitted writing (having written, that he had written) the letter

It is not possible to tie this down to strict rules – for example, while *Il disait avoir faim* seems entirely acceptable as an equivalent of *Il disait qu'il avait faim* 'He said he was hungry', the infinitive construction would be somewhat unlikely as an alternative to the corresponding statement in the present tense, *Il dit qu'il a faim* 'He says he is hungry'. In case of doubt, it is safer to use a *que*-clause.

(iii) after verbs of saying and thinking introduced by a relative pronoun that is the object of the verb of saying or thinking and whose antecedent is the subject of the infinitive, e.g.:

La reine qu'on croyait ne rien savoir
The queen who they thought knew nothing

Le danger qu'on affirmait être imaginaire
The danger which was declared to be imaginary

An alternative construction would be:

La reine dont on croyait qu'elle ne savait rien
Le danger dont on affirmait qu'il était imaginaire

428 The infinitive is used with the preposition *à* to express what is required by, or possible in, the circumstances. This infinitive occurs most commonly with *être, y avoir, rester* and similar verbs, but it is by no means confined to them, e.g.:

Combien de fenêtres y a-t-il à réparer?
How many windows are there to be mended?

Qu'y a-t-il à faire ici?
What is there to do (*or* to be done) here?

Reste à savoir ce qui va arriver
It remains to be seen what is going to happen

Je ne trouve rien à y redire
I find nothing to object to (*or* to be objected to) in it

appartement à louer
flat to let (to be let)

terrain à vendre
plot to be sold, land for sale

This infinitive is always active in French, but the corresponding English infinitive may usually be either active or passive.

429 In some cases the infinitive stands alone owing to the omission of the words or phrases on which it originally depended. It may then have

(i) an exclamatory force, e.g.:

Que dire? Que faire?
What is – or was – to be said (done)? What can (could) one say (do)?

Où aller?
Where am I (is he, was he, etc.) to go?

S'attaquer à un si brave homme!
(How could one) attack such a worthy man!

(ii) an imperative force, especially in general instructions, etc., e.g.:

Tenir au frais	Keep in a cool place
Tenir la main courante	Hold on to the handrail
Ne pas se pencher en dehors	Do not lean out
Voir chapitre dix	See Chapter 10

The infinitive with *faire, laisser,* and verbs of the senses

430 With *faire* 'to make', *laisser* 'to let', and verbs of the senses such as *écouter* 'to listen to', *entendre* 'to hear', *regarder* 'to look at', *sentir* 'to feel' and *voir* 'to see', the French active infinitive may be used to represent in English an active or passive participle or infinitive, e.g.:

Il y a longtemps que nous regardons bâtir la maison en face
We have been watching the house opposite being built for a long while

Je le ferai chercher
I will have him sent for

Nous ne laisserons pas faire du mal à nos amis
We will not allow harm to be done to our friends (i.e. We will not let our friends be injured [allow our friends to be injured]).

This construction is really the same as that explained in **463–466**, except that the accusative after *faire, laisser*, etc., being indefinite, is understood. Thus in the instances just given the literal sense is:

We have been watching (men) building the house opposite
I will make (someone) fetch him
We will not allow (anyone) to injure . . .

With regard to this use of *faire, laisser*, etc., whether the English is active or passive, the following points must be noted:

431 (i) When there is only one object, whether it is according to the sense the object of *faire*, etc., or that of the infinitive, it is treated grammatically as a direct object, e.g.:

(a) *Faites-le descendre*
Make him come down

(b) *On l'a fait chasser de la ville*
They had him driven from town

In (a) *le* is the object of *faire*, in (b) it is the object of *chasser*. For the position of noun and pronoun direct objects, see **434** and **435**.

(ii) *Faire, laisser*, etc., also take an accusative if the dependent infinitive has an indirect object, e.g.:

Je le ferai renoncer à cette idée
I will make him give up this idea

432 But if the infinitive after *faire, laisser, voir*, etc., has a direct object then the object of *faire* is treated as an indirect object while that of *laisser, voir*, etc., may be treated as either a direct or an indirect object, e.g.:

Faites descendre les bagages au porteur
Get the porter to bring down the luggage

Je lui ferai abandonner cette idée
I will make him give up that idea

J'ai laissé mon fils choisir le métier qu'il préfère
J'ai laissé choisir le métier qu'il préfère à mon fils
I have let my son choose the occupation he prefers

Je l'ai (or lui ai) entendu dire beaucoup de bêtises
I have heard him say a lot of silly things

Nous les (or leur) regardions brûler des documents importants
We used to watch them burn(ing) important documents

(Even with *faire*, both objects are sometimes treated as direct objects if that of *faire* is a personal pronoun, e.g. *Je le ferai abandonner cette idée*, but this is not the usual construction and so is best avoided.)

433   As an alternative to the construction with an indirect object, a construction with *par* 'by' may be used, e.g.:

Il a fait exécuter ses ordres à ses hommes (or *par ses hommes*)
He made his men carry out his orders (*or* had his orders carried out by his men)

434   (i) A noun serving as the direct object of *faire* and the subject of the infinitive follows the infinitive, e.g. *Il a fait partir mon frère* 'He made my brother leave' (the implied sentence is 'my brother leaves' – 'my brother' is the subject). But with *laisser* and verbs of the senses, such a noun may come either before or after the infinitive; the choice may be determined either by considerations of meaning, e.g.:

(a) *Je laisse Pierre venir* ⎫
(b) *Je laisse venir Pierre* ⎬ I am letting Peter come

– (a) is a neutral statement with no implications, whereas (b) may suggest that there are others that I am not letting come (in this case, 'Peter' would be slightly stressed in English), or by stylistic factors; for example, in the case of a lengthy direct object, e.g.:

Je regardais jouer tous les petits enfants du village
I was watching all the little children in the village playing

the alternative construction, i.e. placing the lengthy object first and the much shorter infinitive second, would not be acceptable. But in many cases the two constructions are interchangeable.

(ii) When the construction with *à* or *par* + a noun is used, the infinitive follows *faire*, etc., immediately and the direct object follows the infinitive, e.g.:

> *Il fait construire sa maison à* (or *par*) *un architecte remar-quable*
> He is having his house built by a remarkable architect

(for another example, see **433**).

(iii) A noun that is the direct object of the infinitive always follows the infinitive, e.g.:

> *Je regardais abattre les arbres*
> I was watching the trees being cut down

(i.e. I was watching [someone] cutting down the trees).

435 The following remarks on the position of object pronouns do not apply to reflexive verbs (see **436**).

(i) When there is only one direct object conjunctive pronoun, whether it is, according to the sense, the object of *faire, laisser*, or of the infinitive, it is treated grammatically as the object of *faire*, etc., e.g.:

> *Je l'ai vu courir*
> I saw him run (object of *voir*)

> *Je l'ai vu tuer*
> I saw him killed (= I saw [someone] kill him) (object of *tuer*)

> *Faites-les descendre*
> Have them brought down

(ii) Where both *faire*, etc., and the infinitive have, according to the sense, a direct object pronoun, there are two possibilities:

(a) The object of *faire*, etc., is treated grammatically as an indirect object and both pronouns come before *faire*, etc., e.g.:

> *Je les lui regardais brûler*
> I was watching her burn(ing) them

> *Laissez-les-moi lire!*
> Let me read them!

This is primarily a literary construction.

(b) Each functions grammatically as the object of its own verb, e.g.:

Je la regardais les brûler
I was watching her burn them

Laissez-moi les lire!
Let me read them

This construction is the usual one in speech

(iii) Note the special case of *envoyer* + an infinitive, e.g. *envoyer chercher* 'to send for'; two constructions are possible, e.g.:

Nous l'enverrons chercher ⎱ We shall send for him
Nous enverrons le chercher ⎰

436 When *faire* or, though less frequently, *laisser, envoyer, mener* or *emmener*, is followed by the infinitive of a reflexive verb, the reflexive pronoun may be omitted, e.g.:

Nous les ferons taire or *Nous les ferons se taire*
We shall make them be quiet

Ils vous en feront repentir or *Ils vous en feront vous repentir*
They will make you regret it

This does not apply to the reflexive infinitive after verbs of the senses, after which the reflexive pronoun must be used, e.g.:

Je les entendais se plaindre
I could hear them complaining

The reflexive pronoun must however be inserted after *faire*, etc., when its omission would cause ambiguity; when inserted, it stands before the infinitive, unless the reflexive pronoun and the subject of *faire*, etc., denote the same person, e.g.:

Nous les ferons se tuer
We will make them kill themselves

Se is inserted because *Nous les ferons tuer* means 'We will have them killed'; it does not stand before *ferons* because different persons are concerned.

But in *Il se fera tuer* 'He will get himself killed', *se* precedes *fera*, because only one person is concerned.

Note that in such cases, whether the reflexive pronoun is inserted or not, *faire* takes an accusative, not a dative, e.g., *Nous les ferons se tuer* (see above).

Similarly in *Je le fis s'arrêter* 'I made him stop', the insertion of *se* is needed, because *Je le fis arrêter* means 'I had him arrested'.

437   This use of the infinitive with *faire, laisser*, etc., may easily give rise to ambiguities, e.g.:

Faites-le comprendre

may mean

Make him understand *or*
Make it understood

Nous lui avons vu jouer beaucoup de mauvais tours

may mean

We have seen him play many shabby tricks *or*
We have seen many shabby tricks played on him

If the former sense is intended, it is better to write

Nous avons vu jouer beaucoup de mauvais tours par celui-là
We have seen many shabby tricks played by him

L'homme que j'ai vu peindre may mean 'the man I saw painting' or 'the man whom I saw being painted', i.e., 'whose portrait I saw being painted'.

Such ambiguous expressions should be avoided.

438   In sentences of this class it must not be forgotten that the object of a verb may be a clause introduced by *que* (indirect statement) or by an interrogative (indirect question). Such object clauses are reckoned as accusatives, so that where they occur the second object is in the dative, e.g.:

J'ai fait entendre à Pierre { *qu'il ne devait pas agir de la sorte*
{ *en quoi il avait eu tort*

I made Peter understand { that he must not behave like that
{ in what respect he had been wrong

J'ai entendu dire à quelqu'un que le danger était passé
I heard someone say that the danger was over

But as the second of these examples is ambiguous, and might mean 'I heard it said to someone', i.e. 'I heard someone told', it would be better to write *par* rather than *à*, or, better still, to use the construction *J'ai entendu quelqu'un dire que* . . .

L The present participle

439 The French present participle is used

(i) as an ordinary adjective

(ii) as a participle which governs any case or takes any construction admissible with any other part of the verb to which it belongs

(iii) after *en* (in which case it is often known as the gerund)

The distinction between adjective and participle is this:

the adjective expresses a state or quality descriptive of the noun it qualifies;

the participle expresses action.

The endings of the adjective vary with the number and gender of its noun, viz.:

| masc. sing. | *-ant* | masc. plur. | *-ants* |
| fem. sing. | *-ante* | fem. plur. | *-antes* |

The participle ends invariably in *-ant*.
The outcome of these principles in practice is as follows:

440 The form in *-ant*, etc., is an adjective and therefore variable:

(i) when it stands immediately before or immediately after a noun which it qualifies. In this case nothing but an adverb (qualifying the adjective) can come between it and its noun; and then the only order possible is 1. noun, 2. adverb, 3. adjective, e.g.:

Il y a { *de charmantes gravures* / *des gravures charmantes* } *dans ce livre*

(or, with an adverb, *des gravures absolument charmantes*)

There are some delightful engravings in this book (*or, with an adverb*, some absolutely delightful engravings)

(ii) when it is the complement of *être* or any other link verb (but see **445**,ii), e.g.:

Sa figure était à ce moment rayonnante de joie
Her face was at this moment beaming with joy

441   It is a participle, and therefore invariable:

(i)   when it governs an object (direct or indirect) or describes some action connected with the noun or pronoun to which the sense attaches it, e.g.:

Hier, dans la forêt, j'ai vu des chiens courant un cerf
I saw some dogs chasing a stag in the forest yesterday

Pensant à ces avanies elle grinça des dents
Thinking of these outrages she ground her teeth

Elle accourut, criant et gesticulant
She ran up, screaming and waving her arms

La duchesse restait assise, ne disant rien
The duchess remained seated, saying nothing

(ii)   when it is followed by an adverb or adverbial phrase describing the circumstances in which the action of the verb takes place, e.g.:

Voilà la cavalerie avançant rapidement
Here comes the cavalry advancing rapidly

J'ai vu des chiens courant dans la forêt
I saw some dogs running about in the forest

(iii)   when the participle is an alternative to the infinitive, e.g.:

Nous les avons vus riant et gesticulant
We saw them laughing and gesticulating

But here *Nous les avons vus rire et gesticuler* would be preferable (see **427**,i).

   It follows from (i) above, that the present participle of all reflexive verbs (including *soi-disant* 'so-called') must always be invariable, as the reflexive pronoun must be the direct or the indirect object.

   Ayant and *étant* must likewise always be invariable; their sense prevents their use as adjectives qualifying nouns, e.g.:

La soi-disant comtesse, étant sans vergogne, se mit à rire
The so-called countess, being quite shameless, began to laugh

Ayant dit ça, la grande dame sortit, furieuse
Having said this the great lady went out in a temper

442   After *en* the present participle is a gerund, and its use corresponds to that of the English verbal noun in *-ing* with 'by', 'in', 'on' or 'while', e.g.:

Il s'est endormi (tout) en écrivant son devoir
He fell asleep while writing his exercise

Here the insertion of *tout* is optional. It makes the sentence a little more vivid. Cf. 'while' with 'in the act of'.

On ne convainc pas les gens en les assommant
You do not convince people by hitting them over the head

In this use *en* is occasionally omitted, especially with *aller,* e.g.:

Sa maladie va empirant
His illness keeps getting worse

Compare

généralement parlant   generally speaking

443   When the English present participle follows its noun, it can be translated by a relative clause in French. This is especially common after verbs of the senses. Thus in **441,i, ii** and **iii**:

courant un cerf	could be	*qui couraient un cerf*
avançant rapidement	could be	*qui avançait rapidement*
courant dans la forêt	could be	*qui couraient dans la forêt*
riant et gesticulant	could be	*qui riaient et gesticulaient*

So too in other constructions, e.g.:

Ces marchands de journaux, qui crient par les rues, m'agacent
These newsvendors shouting in the streets infuriate me (i.e. because they shout)

N.B. This use is mainly confined to the present and imperfect.

444   The present participle can also be used absolutely (cf. the absolute use of the past participle, **457**), e.g.:

Les choses ne s'arrangeant pas à son gré, il fut forcé de quitter la France
Things not going as he wanted, he had to leave France

Son chapeau étant perdu, il s'en alla nu-tête
His hat being lost, he went away bareheaded

Present participle in English but not in French

445   In spite of what is said above (**440–442**), the English present participle cannot be translated by a French present participle, either adjectival or gerundial, in the following cases:

(i) The English present participle and a finite verb are used to denote two actions that occur in rapid succession. In such sentences French requires either two finite verbs joined by *et* or, instead of the English present participle, the combination present participle of *avoir* or *être* + a past participle (e.g. *ayant répondu* 'having replied', *étant descendu* 'having come down'), followed by a finite verb, e.g.:

Jumping on his horse he galloped away
Il sauta sur son cheval et s'en alla au galop

Hurriedly paying his bill, he rushed out of the shop
Ayant réglé son compte à la hâte, il quitta précipitamment le magasin

(ii) In English the present participle is used with the verb 'to be' in compound forms of various tenses. This is not possible in French (see **398**) e.g.:

Tomorrow he is coming to spend a week with us
Il vient demain passer huit jours chez nous

You have been dreaming
Vous avez rêvé

In the example given at the end of **440**, *rayonnante* is purely adjectival; it might equally well be replaced by *pleine de joie* or, simply, *joyeuse*, and is equivalent to the English 'radiant'. No action is described.

(iii) When English has the preposition 'by' and a present participle after verbs of beginning or finishing, French requires the infinitive, e.g.:

They ended by agreeing with one another
Ils ont fini par se mettre d'accord

(See also **649**.)

This use must not be confused with such expressions as 'to begin, finish doing something' without any preposition, e.g.:

He began writing (to write) a letter
Il commença à écrire (or *d'écrire*) *une lettre*

(iv) Note that, except for *en* used to form the gerund (see **442**), **no** preposition may be used with the present participle in French (which often uses the infinitive instead, see **649**).

(v) So with various idiomatic phrases, e.g.:

I found him in his room, burning some papers
Je l'ai trouvé dans sa chambre, en train de brûler des papiers

I was just going to ring them up
J'étais sur le point de leur donner un coup de téléphone

(vi) Participles denoting position, such as standing, kneeling, lying, crouching, are deceptive, e.g.:

He was standing (kneeling, lying, crouching) in front of the fire
Il était debout (*agenouillé, couché, accroupi*) *devant le feu*
(For 'sitting' see **378**,n.3.)

446 Verbal adjectives differing from participles

The following verbal adjectives differ in form from the present participles of the corresponding verbs:

pres. part.	adj. in -*ant*	pres. part.	adj. in -*ent*
convainquant	*convaincant*	*adhérant*	*adhérent*
convincing	convincing	adhering	sticky, adhesive
extravaguant	*extravagant*	*différant*	*différent*
raving	extravagant	postponing,	different
fatiguant	*fatigant*	differing	
fatiguing	fatiguing	*divergeant*	*divergent*
intriguant	*intrigant*	diverging	divergent
puzzling,	scheming	*excellant*	*excellent*
scheming		excelling	excellent
suffoquant	*suffocant*	*négligeant*	*négligent*
suffocating	suffocating	neglecting	negligent
vaquant (à)	*vacant*		
attending (to)	vacant	*précédant*	*précédent*
		going ahead of	previous
		violant	*violent*
		violating	violent

447   Nouns differing from participles

Note too the following differences between participles and nouns in -*ant* or -*ent*:

pres. part.	noun
fabriquant, manufacturing	*fabricant*, manufacturer
affluant, flowing	*affluent*, tributary
présidant, presiding	*président*, president
résidant, residing	*résident*, resident

Adhérent and *précédent* (see **446**) are also nouns meaning 'adherent, member' and 'precedent'.

M The past participle

Introduction

448   The French past participle, like the English, is used in three ways: (i) as an ordinary adjective; (ii) as a participle; (iii) absolutely.

As an adjective it presents no difficulty; like all adjectives it agrees in gender and number with its noun, e.g.:

une feuille morte, échappée aux bouleaux
a dead leaf, fallen from the birches

449   As a participle it is used with *avoir* and *être* to form the compound tenses, i.e. the perfect (e.g. *j'ai fini, je suis parti*), the pluperfect (*j'avais fini, j'étais parti*), the past anterior (*j'eus fini, je fus parti*), the future perfect (*j'aurai fini, je serai parti*), the past conditional (*j'aurais fini, je serais parti*), the perfect subjunctive (*que j'aie fini, que je sois parti*), the imperfect subjunctive (*que j'eusse fini, que je fusse parti*), and the double-compound tenses (see **412**). (On the use of *être* to form all tenses of the passive, see **382–385**.)

Compound tenses with avoir

450   With *avoir*, the past participle forms the compound tenses of the active voice of all transitive verbs except reflexive verbs (see

379–381), and of all intransitive verbs (including *être*) except those listed in 451–456, e.g.:

> *J'ai écrit quelques lettres; le reste de la matinée j'ai couru par monts et par vaux*
> I wrote some letters; the rest of the morning I ran about all over the place

Compound tenses with être

451   With *être*, the past participle forms

(a) all tenses of the passive of all verbs (see 382–385)

(b) all compound tenses of the active of all reflexive verbs (see 379–381)

(c) all compound tenses of the active of the following intransitive verbs:

> *aller*, go
> *arriver*, arrive, happen
> *décéder*, die
> *descendre*, come or go down
> *devenir*, become
> *entrer*, enter, go in
> *monter*, come or go up
> *mourir*, die
> *naître*, be born
> *partir*, go away, leave
> *rentrer*, come back, come home
> *rester*, remain, stay
> *retourner*, go back, return
> *tomber*, fall
> *sortir*, come or go out
> *venir*, come

and intransitive compounds of *partir, sortir* and *venir*, except *convenir à* 'to suit' which takes *avoir*. (*Prévenir* 'to warn' is transitive and therefore takes *avoir*.)

For verbs that are sometimes compounded with *avoir* and sometimes with *être*, see 453–456.

Examples:

(a) *Elle est accablée de douleur*
   She is overwhelmed with grief

(b) *Nous nous sommes levés un peu tard ce matin*
We got up rather late this morning

Je me suis coupé le doigt
I have cut my finger

(c) *Mme Duval est montée?*
Has Madame Duval gone upstairs?

Cette année beaucoup de gens sont morts de la grippe
A lot of people have died of flu this year

Il est parti (sorti) de bonne heure et il n'est pas encore rentré (revenu)
He started (went out) early, and he has not come back yet

452   Of the verbs listed in **451** and their compounds, some may also be used transitively, in which case they are compounded with *avoir*; the only ones that are widely so used are:

descendre	(1) descend (ladder, hill, etc.)
	(2) take (bring) down
monter	(1) climb, ascend
	(2) take up
remonter	wind up
rentrer	bring in
retourner	to turn (something) over (etc.)
sortir	take out

Examples:

Elle a descendu l'escalier
She came down the stairs

J'ai monté les bagages
I have brought the luggage up

J'ai remonté ma montre
I have wound up my watch

Il a sorti de sa poche deux bouchons et un canif, et puis il l'a retournée
He took two corks and a knife out of his pocket, and then turned it inside out

Entrer and *tomber* are occasionally transitive in such expressions as *entrer un meuble dans une pièce* 'to get a piece of furniture into a room', *tomber sa veste* 'to take off one's jacket', *tomber quelqu'un*

'to throw someone' (in wrestling), and then they too are compounded with *avoir*.

Verbs compounded with avoir or être

453 Besides the verbs already mentioned the following must be
noted:

    (i) *accourir*, run up to   *apparaître*, appear

are used with *avoir* or *être* indifferently.

454 (ii) *changer*, change   *expirer*, expire
           déménager, move house   *grandir*, grow bigger
           disparaître, disappear   *vieillir*, grow old(er)
           échouer, run aground

are compounded with *avoir*, unless the idea of state or condition
resulting from the action predominates to such an extent that the
participle becomes purely adjectival in sense.

    All of these except *disparaître* and *échouer* can also be transi-
tive, with different meanings, in which case they are of course
compounded with *avoir*.

Examples:

    J'ai changé un billet de banque
    I have changed a bank-note

    Elle a beaucoup changé l'année dernière
    She altered a lot last year

    Elle est bien changée depuis l'année dernière
    She is much altered since last year

    Ce navire a échoué hier soir
    This ship ran aground last night

    Il y a là-bas un navire qui est échoué
    There is a ship aground over there

    Mon bail a expiré hier
    My lease expired yesterday

    Mon bail est expiré et je ne vais pas le renouveler
    My lease is at an end and I am not going to renew it

455   (iii) *demeurer* takes *avoir* when it means 'to dwell, live (at)', but *être* when it is the equivalent of *rester* 'to remain', e.g.:

Avant mon mariage, j'ai demeuré à Paris
Before my marriage I lived in Paris

La police est demeurée sur les lieux
The police remained on the spot

Il est toujours demeuré fidèle
He has always remained faithful

456   (iv) *passer* takes *être* in the sense of 'to call on, visit'; in other intransitive senses it may be conjugated with either *avoir* or *être*, e.g.:

M. le préfet est passé chez moi hier soir
The Prefect called on me yesterday evening

J'ai été malade, mais ça a passé
I have been ill, but it is all over

Après une courte discussion nous avons passé à autre chose
After a short discussion we changed the subject

The absolute use of the past participle

457   The past participle is said to be used absolutely when it is used in combination with a noun or pronoun which is not the subject of any finite verb to explain some circumstance connected with its clause (cf. the absolute use of the present participle, 444), e.g.:

Ses dettes payées, il quitta la ville
His debts paid, he left town

Cela dit, je promets de me taire
That said, I promise to be silent

458   With certain past participles, such as *excepté, vu, y compris, étant donné* and others, this absolute use has developed so far that, when they precede their noun, they are nearly always invariable, and in some cases are hardly distinguishable from prepositions. For further discussion of this, see 134.

The agreement of the past participle

459 (i) When forming part of a compound tense, the past participle can vary for gender and number, e.g.:

arrivé	*arrivée*	*arrivés*	*arrivées*
écrit	*écrite*	*écrits*	*écrites*

according to the following rules (which apply to **all** compound tenses):

(a) The participle compounded with *avoir* agrees with a preceding direct object (see **460**); otherwise it is invariable

(b) the participle of a reflexive verb, even though compounded with *être*, also agrees with a preceding direct object (see **461**)

(c) the participle of other verbs compounded with *être* (see **451**,c, and **453–456**) agrees with the subject (see **462**).

(ii) In the passive, the participle always agrees with the subject, e.g.:

Ma sœur a été retenue par un petit accident
My sister has been delayed by a slight accident

Les livres avaient été vendus
The books had been sold

Elles seront punies
They (*fem.*) will be punished

(Note that *été* never agrees.)

460 The past participle compounded with *avoir* agrees only with a preceding direct object, i.e. with a direct object coming before the verb; this does not mean that the object must necessarily come immediately before the verb – the two are often separated by a number of other elements.

The only words that can come before the verb as its direct object and so cause agreement of the participle are:

(a) the interrogatives *quel, lequel* and *combien de* (see also the notes below)

(b) the exclamatory *que de* 'what a lot of' (see **333**)

(c) the relative pronouns *que* and *lequel*

(d) the conjunctive pronouns *me, te, nous, vous, le, la, les* (for *se* see **461**)

Examples:

Quelle maison a-t-il achetée? (agreement with *quelle maison*)
Which house has he bought?

Je ne sais pas laquelle il a achetée (agreement with *laquelle*)
I don't know which one he has bought

Combien de lettres avez-vous écrites? (agreement with *combien de lettres*)
How many letters have you written?

Que de problèmes il a rencontrés! (agreement with *que de problèmes*)
What a lot of problems he encountered!

Voilà la maison que j'ai achetée (agreement with *que = la maison*)
There is the house I have bought

– Il ne m'a pas vue, dit-elle (agreement with *me*, feminine)
"He didn't see me," she said

Elle ne les avait pas vendus (agreement with *les*)
She had not sold them

(iii) Note the following points:

(a) *combien de* and *que de* take their gender and number from the noun they govern (e.g. *combien de glace?* is feminine singular, *que de difficultés* is feminine plural)

(b) grammarians differ as to whether, and if so when, the participle should agree with *combien* accompanied by the pronoun *en* 'of it, of them', e.g.:

Combien en a-t-il vendu (or *vendus*)?
How many of them has he sold?

It is safest never to make the participle agree in this case. The same applies to the infrequent instances where other quantifiers such as *plus* or *moins* + *en* precede the verb, e.g. *Plus il a acheté de livres, plus il en a vendu(s)* 'The more books he bought, the more he sold'.

(c) *que* takes its gender and number from its antecedent

(d) *qui?* 'whom?' is always treated as masculine singular, even in contexts in which it might be supposed to relate to a female or to more than one person, so, when functioning as the preceding direct object of a verb in a compound tense, it never leads to any agreement other than the masculine singular, e.g. *Qui avez-vous vu?* 'Whom did you see?'

(e) *me, te, nous* and *les* can be masculine or feminine, while *vous* can be masculine or feminine, singular or plural.

(iv) For some less straightforward cases, see **463–470**.

461 The participle of a reflexive verb also agrees with the preceding direct object. If this is the reflexive pronoun itself, it takes its gender and number from the subject (which it refers back to), e.g.:

Elle s'est blessée
She has hurt herself

Ils se sont blessés
They have hurt themselves

Je me suis blessé (the speaker is male)
Je me suis blessée (the speaker is female)
I have hurt myself

Vous vous êtes blessé (one male addressee)
You have hurt yourself

Vous vous êtes blessées (more than one female addressee)
You have hurt yourselves

Note:

(a) that when the reflexive pronoun represents an indirect object, it does not of course bring about agreement, e.g.:

Elle s'est nui (*nuire à quelqu'un*)
She has harmed herself (i.e. her interests)

Elle s'est blessé le doigt
She has hurt her finger (*lit.* She has hurt the finger to herself)

Ils se sont écrit
They have written to one another

(b) that some other element than the reflexive pronoun may be the direct object, e.g.:

J'ai lu les lettres qu'ils se sont écrites
I have read the letters they wrote to one another

in which *écrites* agrees with the preceding direct object *que* whose antecedent is *les lettres* and which is therefore feminine plural.

462   The participle of other verbs compounded with *être* agrees with the subject, e.g.:

> *Votre sœur est-elle arrivée?*
> Has your sister arrived?

> *Jean et Pierre sont déjà partis*
> John and Peter have already left

The past participle with an infinitive

463   When a compound tense of *faire, laisser*, or a verb of the senses such as *voir, entendre*, etc. is followed by an infinitive (see 430), the following rules apply:

464   *faire*

The past participle of *faire* remains invariable, e.g.:

> *Quels livres avez-vous fait venir?*
> What books have you had sent?

> *Voilà la maison que nous avons fait construire*
> There is the house that we have had built

465   *laisser*

The past participle of *laisser*, like that of *faire*, may be treated as invariable, but, more usually, it agrees with a preceding direct object whether that object is, according to the sense, the object of *laisser* (as in *Il la laisse entrer* 'He lets her come in') or the object of the infinitive (as in *Ils se laissent prendre* 'They let themselves be caught', *lit.* 'They let [someone] catch them'), e.g.:

> *Il l'a laissée* (or *laissé*) *entrer*
> He has let her come in

> *Ils se sont laissés* (or *laissé*) *prendre*
> They have let themselves be caught

466   Verbs of the senses

In the case of a verb of the senses such as *entendre* 'to hear', *voir* 'to see', etc. (see 430), the participle agrées with a preceding direct object (see **460**), provided that, according to the meaning, it is the object of the verb of the senses and not the object of the infinitive (in which case there is no agreement). A little thought will usually clear up any difficulty there may be in deciding. For example, in *les acteurs que nous voyons jouer* 'the actors we see act(ing)', *les acteurs* is the object of *voir* and the subject of *jouer* ('we see the actors; the actors act'), whereas in *les pièces que nous voyons jouer* 'the plays that we see acted' (*lit.* 'the plays that we see [someone] act'), *les pièces* is the object of *jouer* ('one acts plays').

There is in fact a simple test that can be applied, viz.:

When the French infinitive can be translated by a present participle in English, the French past participle agrees with any direct object that stands before it; when the present participle is impossible in English, the French past participle remains unchanged, e.g.:

Les acteurs que nous avons vus jouer
The actors whom we have seen act – *or* acting

Les pièces que nous avons vu jouer
The plays which we have seen acted ('acting' makes nonsense)

Les chanteurs que nous avons entendus chanter
The singers whom we have heard sing – *or* singing

Les chansons que nous avons entendu chanter
The songs which we have heard sung ('singing' makes nonsense)

467 With verbs followed by an infinitive governed by *à* or *de*, the same difficulty exists. Here too one has to decide whether the direct object is the object of the main verb or of the infinitive, according to the meaning, e.g.:

Les rapports que je leur ai donnés à écrire sont assez longs
The reports that I gave them to write out are rather long

(*donnés*, because 'I gave them the reports' so, according to the sense, *les rapports* is the object of *donner*)

Les raisons que j'ai essayé de leur expliquer
The reasons that I tried to explain to them

(*essayé* – no agreement – because 'I tried to explain the reasons' so, according to the sense, *les raisons* is the object of *expliquer* not of *essayer*).

468 Similar problems to those presented by *faire, laisser* and verbs of the senses might seem to be presented by modal verbs (e.g. *devoir, pouvoir*) and certain other verbs that are followed by an infinitive without *à* or *de*. In fact, there is no real problem. The participle of such verbs is invariable whether the infinitive is expressed or merely understood since, if there is a direct object, it is in all cases the object of the infinitive not of the other verb.

Such verbs are:

adorer, adore. . .-ing
aimer autant, be just as willing to
aimer mieux, prefer
compter, expect
daigner, deign
désirer, wish
devoir, have to (etc.)
espérer, hope
faillir, be near. . .-ing
oser, dare
paraître, appear
pouvoir, be able
préférer, prefer
savoir, know how to, be able
sembler, seem
souhaiter, wish
vouloir, wish

and the impersonals

falloir	*valoir autant*	*valoir mieux*
be necessary	be just as well to	be better to

Examples:

Il y avait tant de choses que nous avions espéré voir
There were so many things which we had hoped to see

Nous avons fait tous les préparatifs que nous avons pu (faire is understood)
We have made all the preparations we could

Je vais vous montrer la maison qu'il avait désiré acheter
I'll show you the house that he had wanted to buy

Many of these verbs may also be used without an infinitive and then follow the usual rule of agreement of the participle. Contrast these two examples:

La femme qu'il avait tant adoré voir à la maison était morte
The wife he had so much adored seeing about the house was
dead

La femme qu'il avait tant adorée était morte
The wife he had so much adored was dead

– in 'he had adored his wife' the word 'wife' is the direct object of
the verb 'to adore' whereas in 'he had adored seeing his wife about
the house' the word 'wife' is the object of 'to see'.

Problematic cases not connected with the infinitive

469 *courir, coûter, marcher, peser, valoir*

The participles of these verbs are invariable when they are
followed by an expression of amount, time, or distance. The
reason is that, in sentences such as *Ce paquet pèse trois kilos* 'This
parcel weighs three kilos', *J'ai couru huit kilomètres* 'I ran eight
kilometres', *J'ai marché deux heures* 'I walked (for) two hours',
the expressions *trois kilos, huit kilomètres, deux heures* are not
really direct objects but adverbial expressions of amount, distance
or time, and so the relative pronoun *que* standing for them is not a
direct object either and so, in a compound tense, does not cause
agreement. Note however that *courir, coûter, peser* and *valoir* do
take a direct object (and so the participle takes agreement) when
they are used metaphorically, and that *peser* in the sense of 'to
weigh (an object)' also has a normal direct object.

Examples:

Malgré les huit kilomètres qu'il avait couru, il n'était guère
essoufflé
In spite of the five miles he had run, he was hardly out of
breath

Malgré les dangers qu'il avait courus, il n'était guère ému
In spite of the dangers he had run, he was almost unmoved

Les trente mille livres que vous a coûté votre maison ne vous
reviendront jamais
You will never get back the £30,000 your house has cost you

La peine que lui avait coûtée cette affaire lui revint à l'esprit
He recalled the trouble this business had cost him

Il aurait voulu peser les cinquante kilos qu'il avait pesé
autrefois

He wished he could have weighed the fifty kilos he used to weigh

Les raisons que vous m'avez données, et que j'ai pesées avec soin, ne sont pas suffisantes
The reasons which you have given me, and which I have carefully weighed, are inadequate

Voici les pommes que j'ai pesées
Here are the apples I have weighed

Cette propriété combien de francs a-t-elle valu avant la guerre?
How much was this property worth before the war?

Combien de jours de détention vous a valus cette escapade?
How many days' detention did this escapade cost you?

470 *attendre, demeurer, dormir, durer, vivre*

With these and other similar intransitive verbs, expressions denoting duration of time are treated as adverbial, not as being in any way the object of the verb. The past participles of such verbs are therefore invariable.

Examples:

J'ai complètement perdu les deux heures que j'ai attendu
I have completely wasted the two hours I have been waiting

Combien d'heures avez-vous dormi sans bouger?
How many hours did you sleep without stirring?

Les vingt-quatre heures que la grève a duré m'ont paru très longues
The twenty-four hours that the strike lasted seemed very long to me

Note however that *passer* 'to spend (time)' does take a direct object, e.g.:

Les dix heures que nous avons passées sur le bateau ont été assommantes
The ten hours we spent on the boat were shattering

Past participles used as nouns

471 A number of past participles are used as nouns, e.g.:

masc.	fem.
le dû, dues	*l'allée*, path, avenue
l'écrit, written exam, etc.	*les allées et venues*, comings and goings
le fait, fact	*l'arrivée*, arrival
le reçu, receipt	*l'étendue*, extent
le réfugié, refugee (male)	*l'entrée*, entry, entrance
	la réfugiée, refugee (female)
	la revue, review, magazine
	la sortie, way out, exit
	la vue, view, eyesight

N   The moods

472   There is so little agreement among grammars of French as to just how many 'moods' French has and what they are that we shall not attempt to define the term 'mood' but shall concentrate on discussing the ways in which each so-called mood is used.

The moods recognized by some though, as we have said, not all grammars are the following (of which the first three are agreed by everyone to be moods):

(i) The indicative – for a brief general discussion of the difference between the indicative and the subjunctive, see **473**; the tenses of the indicative are discussed above, under 'J: The tenses'

(ii) The subjunctive – discussed at length below, **474–506**

(iii) The imperative – see **514–517**

(iv) The conditional – discussed above under 'Tenses', see **415–423**.

(v) The infinitive – see **425–438**

(vi) The participles – see **439–471**

(vii) The gerund – here included under the present participle (see **439**,ii, and **442**)

O The subjunctive

Introduction

473 If one thing is certain about the use of the subjunctive in Modern French, it is that it cannot be reduced to a few easy rules. It is true that, in many cases, one can give precise guidance, i.e. one can say that in certain circumstances one **must** use the subjunctive (and, in others, that one **must** use the indicative). But there are other circumstances that allow the use of either the indicative or the subjunctive. Often the choice is a meaningful one, each mood having a real and distinctive, if not always easily definable, expressive value. But sometimes the distinction is merely stylistic – the literary language, for example, may still prefer the subjunctive where in speech, and even in educated speech, the indicative is well established.

With these reservations, it is not too much of a simplification to say that, in general, the indicative presents an event as a fact, whereas the subjunctive expresses it as, for example, a possibility or an aim, or calls it into doubt or denies its reality, or expresses a judgement on it.

474 Many errors made by students in the use of the subjunctive can be avoided if one remembers that, with the exception of a few fixed expressions and certain constructions in which its use is little more than a relic of an earlier stage of the language (see **476–478**), the subjunctive occurs **only**:

(i) in clauses introduced by *que* or conjunctions ending in *que* (e.g. *quoique* 'although') (see **486–491**) – but *most* clauses introduced by *que* have the indicative, and

(ii) in certain types of relative clauses (see **492–495**) – but, again, *most* relative clauses have the indicative.

475 We shall discuss first the exceptional cases referred to above. These are of three types:

(i) fixed expressions, i.e. expressions that cannot be varied in any way (**476**)

(ii) constructions allowing a slight amount of variation, but only within very strict limits (**477**)

(iii) constructions allowing a greater degree of variation than those referred to under (ii) (**478**).

476 (i) Fixed expressions

The subjunctive without *que* occurs in a small number of fixed expressions (many of them having religious associations), e.g.:

advienne que pourra	come what may
grand bien vous fasse	much good may it do you
ainsi soit-il (after a prayer)	amen (*lit.* so be it)
soit dit entre nous	between you and me
coûte que coûte	at all costs (*lit.* let it cost what it costs)
n'en déplaise à . . . (*ne vous en déplaise*, etc.)	with all due respect to . . ., if you have no objection
fasse le ciel que . . .	Heaven (God) grant that . . .
Dieu vous bénisse!	(when someone sneezes) God bless you!
Dieu soit loué!	God be praised!
A Dieu ne plaise!	God forbid!

Note that the English equivalents are in some cases also fixed expressions involving the subjunctive, *Come what may, God be praised, God forbid,* etc.

477 (ii) Constructions allowing a minimum of variation

The subjunctive without *que* occurs in the following constructions, all of them other than (a) and (b) being characteristic of literary rather than of spoken usage:

(a) with *vivre* 'to live': *Vive la France!* 'Long live France!', *Vivent les Belges!* 'Long live the Belgians!' – occurs only when the subject is a noun (which may however be any noun that makes sense in the context)

(b) with *venir* 'to come': *vienne la fin du mois* 'come the end of the month', *viennent les beaux jours* 'when the fine weather comes' – the subject is usually a noun referring to a point in time

(c) with *pouvoir* 'may': *Puisse-t-il arriver à temps!* 'May he arrive (= if only he can arrive) in time!', *Puissiez-vous réussir* 'May you succeed', *Puissent vos beaux yeux ne jamais pleurer* (Vigny) 'May your lovely eyes never weep' – can occur with all persons of the verb (note the form *puissé-je*)

(d) with *être* 'to be': *Soit un triangle ABC* 'Let there be a triangle ABC', and similar expressions used in geometry

(e) with *savoir* 'to know': *je ne sache pas que. . .* "I am not aware that . . .' (with a subjunctive in the following clause) – normally found only with *je* or *on* (e.g. *On ne sache pas qu'il ait jamais fait de grands efforts* 'It is not known that he has ever made any great effort'); similarly *Je ne sache rien de plus agréable* 'I know of nothing more pleasant', and comparable expressions with *ne . . . personne* 'no-one', *ne . . . guère* 'scarcely', etc.

478 ' (iii) **Constructions allowing a greater degree of variation**

(a) *The imperfect subjunctive in conditional clauses*, e.g. *fût-il du sang des dieux aussi bien que des rois* (Corneille) 'were he of the blood of gods as well as of kings', *dût-il* (*dussiez-vous*, etc.) *en mourir* 'had he, were he (you, etc.) to die because of it (i.e. even if . . .)', *dussent mille dangers me menacer* 'were a thousand dangers to threaten me', *voulût-il le faire* 'even if he wanted to do so' – the subject may be a personal pronoun (note the forms *fussé-je, dussé-je*), or *ce*, or *on*, or a noun, but note that, if it is a noun, complex inversion (see **596**) is obligatory in the case of *être* and *vouloir*, e.g. *la situation fût-elle encore plus grave* 'were the situation even more serious', but not in the case of *devoir*

(b) *The pluperfect subjunctive with inversion of the subject in 'if' clauses*, e.g. *Pierre Louis m'eût-il encouragé* (Gide) 'had Pierre Louis encouraged me'; this highly literary construction is the equivalent of the usual *si Pierre Louis m'avait encouragé*

(c) *The pluperfect subjunctive in both parts of conditional sentences*. In constructions of the type *S'il avait parlé, j'aurais répondu* 'If he had spoken, I should have replied', the pluperfect indicative in the *si* clause and the past conditional in the main clause (or, sometimes, one of the two but not both) may be replaced by the pluperfect subjunctive, *S'il eût parlé, j'eusse répondu*; similarly, with verbs taking *être*, one may find *si elle fût partie*, etc., for *si elle était partie* 'if she had left', etc.

Note (1) that this construction occurs *only* as the equivalent of the pluperfect and the past conditional and that no parallel construction exists as the equivalent of the construction *S'il parlait, je répondrais* 'If he spoke, I should reply', and (2) that it is in any case a highly literary and even somewhat archaic construction and should not be imitated.

(d) As an alternative to the construction *si* (*quelque . . ., aussi . . ., tout . . ., pour. . .*) *riche qu'il soit* 'however rich he may be' (see **310**) one sometimes finds the construction *si riche soit-il* 'however rich he is (may be)', but only when the subject is *il, elle, ils* or *elles.*

The subjunctive introduced by que

479 We shall divide the clauses introduced by *que* and taking the subjunctive into three categories, viz:

(i) those in which the *que* clause is not dependent on some preceding verb, adjective, noun, or adverb (**480**)

(ii) those in which the *que* clause *is* dependent on a preceding verb, adjective, noun, etc. (**481–485**)

(iii) those in which *que* is part of a conjunction (the majority of which are in fact what in French are known as *locutions conjonctives*, i.e. compound conjunctions such as *à moins que* 'unless', *en sorte que* 'so that', *pourvu que* 'provided that') (**486–491**)

(The distinction between (ii) and (iii) is sometimes uncertain – for example, *de crainte que* 'for fear that, lest', could well fit into either category.)

The subjunctive in independent clauses

480 The subjunctive occurs in the following types of clauses in which *que* is not dependent upon a preceding element (verb, noun, etc.):

(i) In clauses expressing an order (a kind of third person imperative) or an exhortation; these can often be rendered in English by 'Let X do so-and-so', though in practice some other equivalent usually occurs, e.g. *Qu'il vienne me voir demain* 'Let him come and see me (he can come and see me, tell him to come and see me) tomorrow', *Qu'elles rentrent avant minuit* 'Let them be back (they'd better be back) by midnight', *Qu'ils fassent bien attention* 'Let them (they'd better) take care', *Que tout le monde sorte* '(Let) everybody leave'

(ii) the subjunctive is usual when *que* introduces a noun-clause (i.e. a clause functioning as a noun in relation to some other clause), placed at the beginning of the sentence; the noun-clause may function as the subject of another clause, e.g. *Qu'il soit mécontent est certain* 'That he is displeased is certain' (*qu'il soit mécontent* is the subject of *est*), or stand in some other relation to the other clause, e.g. *Qu'il puisse partir demain, tout le monde le sait* 'That he may leave tomorrow everybody knows', *Que vous ayez raison, j'en suis certain* 'That you are right I am sure of'. (The indicative can occur when the factual nature of the statement is stressed, e.g. *Que Louis XVIII ne l'aimait pas (. . .), cela, il le savait* (Aragon) 'That Louis XVIII did not like him, that he knew').

(iii) In certain types of hypothetical (conditional) clause, in particular:

(a) in a *que*-clause as the equivalent of a *si*-clause at the beginning of the sentence, e.g. *Qu'il fasse beau demain (= s'il fait beau demain), (et) j'irai à la pêche* 'If (provided) it's fine tomorrow, I shall go fishing' (note that the following clause is often introduced by *et*); *Que l'ennemi vienne, le lâche s'enfuit* 'Should the enemy come, the coward runs away'.

(b) as the equivalent of *si* introducing a second hypothetical clause, e.g. *s'il fait beau et qu'il ne fasse pas trop chaud . . . (= s'il ne fait pas trop chaud)* 'if it's fine and if it's not too hot. . .'

(c) after *soit que . . . soit que* or *soit que . . . ou que* 'whether . . . or (whether)', e.g. *Soit qu'il ne comprenne pas, soit qu'il (or ou qu'il) ne veuille pas comprendre, il est de toute façon très entêté* 'Whether he does not understand, or whether he does not wish to understand, he is at all events very stubborn'.

(d) in the construction *que . . . ou que* (or *ou non*) 'whether . . . or whether (or not)', e.g. *Qu'il fasse beau ou qu'il pleuve (qu'il fasse beau ou non), j'irai à la pêche* 'Whether it's fine or whether it rains (whether it's fine or not), I shall go fishing'.

The subjunctive in dependent que-clauses

481 Broadly speaking, *que*- clauses involving the subjunctive fall into four categories, each expressing – if sometimes rather vaguely – a particular value which is something other than a mere factual statement. The following indications (and in many cases they *are* indications rather than rules) are not exhaustive, and there are frequent exceptions, i.e. instances where the indicative occurs when the subjunctive might be expected, and *vice versa*. The four categories in question are the following (in each case, we use the term 'event' to indicate the action or idea expressed by the verb):

(i) Clauses in which the event is presented as something to be accomplished (**482**)

(ii) Clauses in which the event is presented as merely possible, or is called into doubt (**483**)

(iii) Clauses in which the reality of the event is denied (**484**)

(iv) Clauses expressing a judgement on or reaction to the event (**485**).

The *que*-clause may be dependent on a verb or an adjective or, occasionally, on a noun or an adverb.

482   (i) **The event is presented as something to be accomplished**

(a) after verbs expressing a wish, a request, an order, an expectation, permission, etc.; these include:

vouloir que	to wish, want	*insister pour que*	to insist
souhaiter que	to wish	*tenir à ce que*	to insist, be keen
désirer que	to wish, desire	*veiller à ce que*	to take care, see to it
demander que	to ask	*attendre que*	to wait (until)
exiger que	to demand, require	*s'attendre à ce que*	to expect
ordonner que	to order	*permettre que*	to allow
recommander que	to recommend	*consentir à ce que*	to agree, consent

e.g. *Je veux qu'il parte* 'I want him to leave', *Il a demandé que toutes les lettres soient brûlées* 'He asked that all the letters be burnt', *Nous insistons pour que vous veniez nous voir* 'We insist that you come and see us', *Mon frère veillera à ce que ce soit fait* 'My brother will see that it is done', *Attendons que le courrier arrive* 'Let's wait until the mail arrives (for the mail to arrive)'.

Note that other verbs, such as *dire* 'to say', *crier* 'to shout', may sometimes express an order and so take a subjunctive, e.g. *Dites-lui qu'il parte tout de suite* 'Tell him to leave at once', *Ils crient qu'on les serve* "They are shouting to be served'.

With most of the above verbs, the infinitive **must** be used instead of a *que*-clause when the subject of both verbs is the same, e.g. *Je veux le faire* 'I want to do it', *Il a demandé à descendre* 'He asked to get down', *Mon frère insiste pour vous voir* 'My brother insists on seeing you', *Nous nous attendons à partir demain* 'We expect to leave tomorrow'. On these and other infinitive constructions (e.g. *Dites-lui, permettez-lui de partir* 'Tell him, allow him, to leave') see 527–533 and 535–536.

(b) after the following impersonal verbs:

> *il convient que*, it is advisable
> *il faut que*, it is necessary
> *il importe que*, it is important
> *il suffit que*, it is enough
> *il vaut mieux que*, it is better

e.g. *Il faut que vous partiez maintenant* 'It is necessary that you leave (you must leave) now', *Il suffit que je le dise* 'It is enough that I say so (for me to say so)', *Il vaut mieux qu'il le sache* 'It is better that he should know (for him to know)'.

(c) after such adjectives as:

> *essentiel*, essential   *nécessaire*, necessary
> *important*   *préférable*
> *indispensable*   *utile*, useful

e.g. *Il est nécessaire que vous achetiez ce livre* 'It is necessary for you to buy this book'.

(d) after nouns such as *besoin* 'need', e.g. *Nous avons besoin que vous nous aidiez* 'We need you to help us', *avoir soin que* 'to take care that'.

(e) in the construction *assez X pour que*, where 'X' is an adjective or an adverb, e.g. *Ce livre est assez simple pour qu'un enfant le comprenne* 'This book is easy enough for a child to understand', *Il parle assez lentement pour que tout le monde comprenne* 'He is speaking slowly enough for everyone to understand'.

483   (ii) The event is presented as doubtful or as merely possible

(a) After *douter que* 'to doubt that (whether)', and *il se peut que* 'it is possible that', e.g. *Je doute que ce soit vrai* 'I doubt whether it is true'. But the indicative (or the conditional) may be used instead of the subjunctive after *douter* in the interrogative or negative, when the reality of the event is stressed, e.g.:

$$\textit{Il ne faut pas douter qu'il } \begin{Bmatrix} \textit{fera} \\ \textit{ferait} \end{Bmatrix} \textit{ ce qu'il } \begin{Bmatrix} \textit{pourra} \\ \textit{pourrait} \end{Bmatrix}$$

It cannot be doubted that he $\left\{ \begin{array}{l} \text{will} \\ \text{would} \end{array} \right\}$ do all he $\left\{ \begin{array}{l} \text{can} \\ \text{could} \end{array} \right\}$

(b) After verbs of thinking and saying *in the negative or interrogative*, in particular:

croire que, to think, believe
penser que, to think
trouver que, to be of the opinion that
espérer que, to hope that
affirmer que, to assert
déclarer que, to declare
dire que, to say

e.g. *Je ne crois pas qu'il l'ait fait* 'I don't think he did it', *Trouvez-vous qu'elle soit jolie?* 'Do you think she's pretty?', *Est-ce qu'il espère que j'y aille?* 'Does he hope that I shall go there?', *Je ne dis pas qu'il m'écrive souvent* 'I don't say he writes to me often'. Likewise with other verbs when they express a similar idea, e.g. *Je ne vois pas qu'il puisse arriver à temps* 'I don't see that (how) he can arrive in time'.

The indicative is used after such verbs when they are neither negative nor interrogative, e.g. *Je crois qu'il viendra* 'I think he will come', *Nous espérons qu'il recevra demain notre lettre* 'We hope he will receive our letter tomorrow'. The indicative may also occur even after a negative or interrogative if one is stressing the reality or virtual certainty of the event, e.g. *Je ne crois pas qu'il pleuvra* 'I don't think it will rain' (i.e., in effect, 'I think, I feel sure, it won't rain').

(c) Verbs like *sembler, paraître*, are followed by the indicative ɔ the subjunctive depending on the degree of certainty or doubt it s intended to convey, e.g. *Il semble qu'ils sont malades* 'It seems they are ill' (i.e. the speaker accepts that they are ill), *Il semble qu'ils soient malades* 'It seems they are ill' (the speaker is not vouching for the fact). In practice, the indicative is usually found when it is stated that 'it seems *to someone* that . . .', e.g. *Il me semble (il me paraît) que vous avez raison* 'It seems (appears) to me that you're right'. When the verbs in question are in the negative or the interrogative, the subjunctive is usual, e.g. *Il ne (me) semble pas qu'on puisse partir aujourd'hui* 'It doesn't seem (to me) that we can leave today'.

(d) After adjectives such as *douteux* 'doubtful', *possible, rare*, e.g. *Il est possible que mon père aille à Paris* 'It is possible that my father may go to Paris', *Il est rare qu'un Français comprenne le gallois* 'It is rare for a Frenchman to understand Welsh'.

Also after *peu probable* 'improbable, unlikely', and (usually though not invariably) after the adjectives *certain, sûr* 'sure', *vrai* 'true', in negative and interrogative constructions, *Il est peu probable que, il n'est pas certain (sûr, vrai) que mon père ait reçu la lettre* 'It is unlikely, not certain (true) that my father has received the letter', *Est-il vrai que vous soyez malade?* 'Is it true that you are ill?' – but *Il est probable, certain, vrai, que mon père a reçu la lettre* 'It is probable, certain, true, that my father has received the letter'.

(e) The subjunctive is frequently (but not invariably) used in miscellaneous constructions (here admittedly grouped somewhat uneasily together) in which the event seems to be envisaged as a possibility rather than as a fact, e.g.:

(1) After

il arrive que	it happens that
ignorer que	to be unaware that
l'idée que	the idea that

e.g. *Il arrive que nous nous trompions* 'It (sometimes) happens that we are wrong', *L'idée qu'il revienne m'effraie* 'The idea that he is coming (might come) back frightens me', *J'ignorais qu'il fût arrivé* 'I did not know that he had come'.

(2) After verbs such as *admettre* 'to admit', *comprendre, s'expliquer* 'to understand', *supposer* 'to suppose', which take the indicative when the event is presented as a fact (or, at least, as a supposed fact), e.g. *J'admets que vous avez raison* 'I admit that you are right', *Je comprends que cela vous est difficile* 'I understand that that is difficult for you', *Je suppose que vous avez été à Paris* 'I assume you have been to Paris', but the subjunctive when the event is merely envisaged as a possibility, e.g. *Admettons (supposons) que vous ayez raison* 'Let us admit, suppose (i.e. for the sake of argument) that you are right', *Je comprends que vous en soyez mécontent* 'I understand (how it is) that you are displeased about it', *Je m'explique mal qu'il soit déjà parti* 'I find it difficult to understand that he has already left'. Similarly after some other verbs such as *se souvenir* 'to remember' in the negative or interrogative, e.g. *Vous souvenez-vous qu'il a écrit* (indicative) *à son frère?* 'Do you remember [the fact] that he has written to his

brother?', but *Vous souvenez-vous qu'il ait écrit* (subjunctive) *à son frère?* 'Do you recall whether he has written to his brother?'.

(3) After *si (tellement, tant) . . . que* in interrogative or imperative clauses, or clauses containing a suggestion of obligation or duty, e.g. *Est-ce que vous habitez si (tellement) loin qu'on soit obligé de prendre un taxi?* 'Do you live so far out that one has to take a taxi?', *A-t-il tant de travail qu'il soit toujours fatigué?* 'Has he so much work to do that he is always tired?', *Parlez* (or *il faut parler*) *si éloquemment qu'on ne puisse rien vous refuser* 'Speak (*or* you must speak) so eloquently that no-one can refuse you anything', *Faites-vous tant aimer qu'on ne puisse . . .* (etc.) 'Make yourself so much loved that no one can . . . (etc.)'.

For the subjunctive after these adverbs in negative clauses, see **484**,d.

484   (iii) **The reality of the event is denied**

(a) After such verbs as:

> *nier que*, to deny
> *défendre que*, to forbid
> *interdire que*, to forbid
> *éviter que*, to avoid
> *empêcher que*, to prevent
> *s'opposer à ce que*, to oppose, object

e.g. *Je nie que ce soit vrai* 'I deny that it is true', *Évitez (empêchez) qu'il ne vienne* (note the *ne*) 'Avoid having him come, prevent him from coming', *Il s'oppose à ce que vous y alliez* 'He is opposed to (is against) your going there'.

Nier in the negative is followed either by the subjunctive (*Je ne nie pas que vous ayez raison* 'I don't deny that you are right') or, if the reality of the event is being stressed, by the indicative (*Je ne nie pas qu'il m'a écrit* 'I don't deny that he wrote to me').

(b) After expressions such as *ce n'est pas que . . .*, e.g. *Ce n'est pas que je me sente malade* 'It is not that I feel ill', *il s'en faut de beaucoup que . . .*, e.g. *Il s'en faut de beaucoup qu'elle soit belle* 'She's far from being beautiful'.

(c) After adjectival expressions like *il est impossible que . . .*, *il n'est pas possible (vrai) que . . .* 'it is impossible, not possible, not true, that . . .'.

(d) After *trop X pour que* . . . (where X is an adjective or an adverb), e.g. *Il est trop jeune pour que vous lui donniez du vin* 'He's too young for you to give him wine', *Il est trop tard pour qu'elle arrive ce soir* 'It's too late for her to arrive this evening', and after *si (tellement)* . . . *que, tant* . . . *que*, in a negative or interrogative clause, e.g. *Il n'est pas si riche* (or *tellement riche*) *qu'il puisse s'offrir une Rolls-Royce* 'He's not so rich that he can afford a Rolls-Royce' (for the subjunctive after these adverbs in interrogative clauses, see 483,e,3). Cf. also the subjunctive after *bien loin que*, e.g. *Bien loin qu'il vous pardonne, il est toujours fâché* 'Far from forgiving you, he's still cross'.

(e) After a variety of negative constructions in which *que* depends on a noun, e.g. *ce n'est pas la peine que* 'it is not worth', *il n'y a aucune chance que* 'there is no chance that', *il n'y a pas de danger que* 'there is no fear (risk, danger) that', e.g. *Ce n'est pas la peine que tu lui écrives* 'It's not worth (while) your writing to him'.

(f) In surprised or indignant exclamations, where the *que*-clause may appear to be an independent clause but is not really so, as the main clause is understood, e.g.:

> *Moi, que je trahisse mon pays!*
> I betray my country!

where some such idea as 'Do you think that I would . . .?' is understood.

485 (iv) **The clause expresses a judgement on or reaction to the event**

(a) Expressions of acceptance, approval or pleasure, including verbs like

> *accepter que*, to accept
> *approuver que*, to approve
> *aimer mieux que*, to prefer
> *préférer que*, to prefer
> *se réjouir que*, to be delighted

adjectives like *content* 'pleased', *heureux* 'happy', *fier* 'proud', *ravi* 'delighted', *satisfait* 'satisfied'; impersonal expressions of the type *il est bon* 'it is good', *inévitable, juste* 'fair, right', *logique* 'logical', *naturel* 'natural', *normal* 'normal, natural', *préférable* 'preferable', e.g. *Je préfère que vous restiez* 'I prefer you to stay', *Elle est fière que son fils ait appris à nager* 'She is proud that her son has learned how to swim', *Il est juste qu'il soit puni* 'It is right that he (should) be punished'.

(b) Expressions of curiosity or surprise, including *s'étonner que* 'to be amazed that', *être étonné, surpris que* 'to be amazed, surprised that', *il est bizarre, curieux, extraordinaire que* 'it is odd, curious, extraordinary that'.

(c) Expressions of indifference, annoyance, anger, or sorrow, e.g. verbs like

ennuyer que, to bother	*se plaindre que*, to complain
se fâcher que, to be annoyed	*regretter que*, to regret

the impersonal verb *peu (m') importe que* 'it matters little (I don't mind, etc.)', adjectives like *désolé* 'upset', *fâché* 'annoyed', *furieux* 'angry', *triste* 'sad'. e.g. *Cela m'ennuie que tu sois triste* 'It bothers, upsets, me that you are sad', *Peu m'importe qu'il soit déjà parti* 'I don't care if he has gone already'.

(d) Expressions of fear, including *avoir peur* 'to be afraid', *craindre* 'to fear', *de crainte que, de peur que* 'for fear, lest'; in the literary language, these are usually followed by a redundant *ne* (see 564), e.g. *Je crains que ce ne soit trop tard* 'I fear it is too late', *de peur qu'il ne nous voie* 'for fear, lest, he (should) see us'.

The subjunctive after conjunctions formed on the basis of *que*

486 As in the case of dependent *que*-clauses in the subjunctive (481–485), these clauses usually express something other than a mere factual statement of the event. The commonest conjunctions taking the subjunctive are discussed in sections 487–491 – others are listed in 697.

487 Conjunctions meaning 'although', of which the commonest are *quoique* (note that this is written as one word) and *bien que*, e.g.:

Il le fera bien que ce soit défendu
He will do it although it is forbidden

Quoique mon frère ait reçu ma lettre, il ne vient pas
Although my brother has received my letter, he is not
coming

(The reality of the event may well be accepted, but it is discounted
– e.g., in the second of these examples it is accepted that the letter
has been received, but, *in spite of that fact*, the brother is not
coming.)

Bien que and *quoique* occasionally take the indicative or conditional when 'though' is almost the same as 'but', e.g.:

Il nous faut le faire, bien que nous n'y gagnerons rien

We must do it, $\left\{ \begin{array}{l} \text{though} \\ \text{but} \end{array} \right\}$ we shall gain nothing by it

But, generally speaking, the subjunctive should be used.

Other conjunctions meaning 'although' and taking the subjunctive are *encore que* (exclusively literary) and *malgré que* (familiar,
and frowned on by some grammarians – see **698**).

Note that *alors que* and *tandis que*, both meaning 'whereas',
always take the indicative.

488 The conjunctions *avant que* 'before' and *jusqu'à ce que* and
en attendant que 'until', e.g.:

Nous le verrons avant qu'il parte
We shall see him before he leaves

Restons ici jusqu'à ce qu'il vienne, . . . en attendant qu'il
vienne
Let's wait here until he comes

Note that, when 'not . . . until' is the equivalent of 'not . . .
before', *avant que* must be used, e.g.:

Je ne partirai pas avant qu'il vienne
I shall not leave until he comes (= before he comes)

but

Je n'attendrai pas jusqu'à ce qu'il vienne (or *qu'il vienne*
without *jusqu'à ce*)
I shall not wait till he comes ('before he comes' does not
make sense)

Note too that comparable expressions based not on *que* but on *où* 'when', in particular *avant le moment où* 'before (the time when)', *jusqu'au moment où, en attendant le moment où* 'until (the time when)', always take the indicative. (Even *jusqu'à ce que* occasionally takes the indicative, but it is safer to stick to the subjunctive which is always correct.)

Other conjunctions relating to time, e.g. *aussitôt que* 'as soon as', *pendant que* 'while' (for a full list, see **693–695**), take the indicative. But note that, whereas according to strict grammar *après que* 'after' takes the indicative, there is an increasing tendency to use the subjunctive (presumably by analogy with *avant que*); those whose French is not at a really advanced level are advised to stick to the indicative.

489 Conjunctions meaning 'in order that, so that' (i.e., conjunctions expressing purpose, introducing what are often known as 'final' clauses – Latin *finis* and French *la fin* mean 'purpose' as well as 'end'); these include *afin que* and *pour que*, e.g.:

J'ai brulé la lettre afin que personne ne la lise
I burnt the letter so that no-one should read it

Je vous le dis pour que vous le sachiez
I am telling you so that (in order that) you may know

Like English 'so that', the following are both final (i.e. expressing purpose) and consecutive (i.e. expressing consequence, result):

de (telle) façon que
de (telle) manière que } so that, in such a way that
de (telle) sorte que
en sorte que

They take the subjunctive when any idea of purpose is implied, e.g.:

Le professeur expérimenté s'exprime de (telle) sorte que sa classe puisse le comprendre
An experienced teacher expresses himself in such a way that his class can understand him

Il parle toujours de (telle) façon que tout le monde l'entende
He always speaks so that (in such a way that) everyone may hear him

or when they express a result that is to be avoided (this too implies purpose), e.g.:

> *Je ne veux pas agir de (telle) sorte (façon, manière) qu'on me déteste*
> I do not want to act in such a way as to get myself disliked

But when they express a result that is merely stated as a fact, they take the indicative, e.g.:

> *Il parle toujours de (telle) façon que tout le monde l'entend*
> He always speaks in such a way that everybody hears him

> *Il a agi de telle sorte qu'il s'est fait détester*
> He acted in such a way that he got himself disliked

Note that *de façon à ce que* and *de manière à ce que* 'so that' have only a final value and so always take the subjunctive.

This use of the subjunctive is extended to *si . . . que* and *tant que* when the main clause

(i) is imperative, or suggests a duty or obligation, as with *il faut, devoir*, e.g.:

> *Agissez* ⎱
> *Il faut agir* ⎰ *si vite qu'on ne sache pas ce que vous faites*
> You must act so quickly that no one can know what you are doing

(ii) contains a negative, or an interrogative suggesting a negative sense, e.g.:

> *Vous n'êtes pas si essoufflé que vous ne puissiez dire quelques mots*
> You are not so much out of breath that you cannot say a few words

> *Es-tu si stupide que tu veuilles partir tout de suite?*
> Are you so stupid that you want to leave straight away?

490   Certain conjunctions expressing conditions, hypotheses or suppositions, including:

au cas que, en cas que   in case (note that *au cas où, dans le cas où*, take the indicative or the conditional)

à moins que (usually with *ne*, see **566**)	unless
pour peu que	if only, if ever, etc.
pourvu que	provided that
à supposer que, supposé que	supposing
si tant est que	so long as, provided that

Examples:

A moins que tu ne partes tout de suite
Unless you leave at once

Pour peu que vous répondiez à sa lettre, il consentira à rester
You've only got to answer his letter and he'll agree to stay

A supposer qu'il ne vienne pas, qu'allez-vous faire?
Supposing he doesn't come, what are you going to do?

Note that *à (la) condition que, sous (la) condition que* 'on condition that' may take either (a) the subjunctive or (b) the future indicative or the conditional (but **not** other indicative tenses), e.g. *Vous pouvez rester à (la) condition que vous vous taisiez* (or *tairez*) 'You can stay on condition that you keep quiet'.

Autant que and *pour autant que* 'as far as' can take either the indicative or the subjunctive depending on the degree of certainty or uncertainty the clause is intended to express, e.g.:

(pour) autant que je peux (or *puisse*) *en juger*
as far as I can judge

491 Conjunctions that deny the reality of the event, e.g.:

non que, non pas que	not that
loin que	far from (. . .ing)
sans que	without (. . .ing)

Examples:

non (pas) qu'il ait peur
not that he's afraid

Loin qu'il puisse m'aider, il ne comprend même pas le problème
Far from being able to help me, he doesn't even understand the problem

Il est parti sans que nous le sachions
He left without our knowing

de peur que, de crainte que (usually with *ne*, see **564**) 'lest, for fear', e.g.:

> *Partons tout de suite de peur qu'il (ne) nous voie*
> Let's leave at once for fear (in case) he sees us

The subjunctive in relative clauses

492   The subjunctive can occur in three types of relative clause

(i) when the relative clause relates not to an actual individual or individuals but to a possible member or members of a class (**493**)

(ii) when the antecedent is qualified by a superlative or equivalent expression (**494**)

(iii) after the so-called 'indefinite relatives' (the equivalent of English 'whoever', 'whatever', 'wherever', etc.) (**495**).

493   The subjunctive in relative clauses relating to a possible member or members of a class. (This is sometimes known as the 'generic subjunctive' – *generic*: 'relating to a class or group'.)

An example will help to make this clear. If I ask someone: 'Could you show me the road that leads to the station?', the relative clause 'that leads . . . etc.' describes a particular road that I know (or, at any rate, that I assume) actually exists – the French equivalent has the indicative, *Pourriez-vous m'indiquer le chemin qui conduit à la gare?* Likewise, if I say: 'I am looking for a road [i.e. a road that I know exists and that I am describing] that leads to the station', the French equivalent is: *Je cherche un chemin qui conduit à la gare*. But if I ask: 'Could you show me a road that leads to the station?' (i.e. I am in fact enquiring whether any such road exists), or if I say: 'I am looking for a road that [if such a road exists] leads to the station', the relative clause rather than describing a particular road indicates the *type* of road that I want, i.e. it relates to any members of the class (which may or may not exist) of 'roads leading to the station'. In such cases, French has the subjunctive, viz. *Pourriez-vous m'indiquer un chemin qui conduise à la gare?*, of *Je cherche un chemin qui conduise à la gare*. Likewise, the subjunctive is of course used when the existence of the class in question is represented as hypothetical, as in 'If you know a road that leads to the station', *Si vous connaissez un chemin qui conduise à la gare*, or is denied (cf. **484**), as in 'There is no road that leads to the station', *Il n'y a pas de chemin qui conduise à la gare*. For similar reasons, a relative clause depending on *peu* 'little, few, not many' (see **328**) requires the subjunctive. Examples:

> *Pouvez-vous me montrer une dame qui soit mieux habillée que moi?*
> Can you show me a lady who is better dressed than I am?
>
> *Il lui faut un ami qui lui écrive régulièrement*
> He needs a friend who will write to him regularly
>
> *J'attends* ⎱ *une explication qui soit du moins raisonnable*
> *Je désire* ⎰
> I am waiting for ⎱ an explanation which is at least
> I want ⎰ reasonable
>
> *Il n'y a personne qui veuille m'aider*
> There is no-one who is willing to help me
>
> *Il n'y a rien que vous puissiez lui dire*
> There is nothing you can say to him
>
> *Je voudrais une chambre où l'on n'entende pas ce bruit*
> I should like a room where you can't hear that noise
>
> *Donnez-moi une plume avec laquelle je puisse écrire*
> Give me a pen I can write with
>
> *Il y a ici peu de gens que je connaisse*
> There are not many people I know here

Contrast these with the following, in which the relative clause relates to an actual and not a possible or hypothetical member of a class and so takes the indicative:

> *Pouvez-vous me montrer la dame qui est mieux habillée que moi?*
> Can you show me the lady who is better dressed than I am?
>
> *Il a un ami qui lui écrit régulièrement*
> He has a friend who writes to him regularly
>
> *J'ai une chambre où l'on n'entend pas ce bruit*
> I have a room where you can't hear that noise
>
> *Voilà une plume avec laquelle je peux écrire*
> Here is a pen I can write with

494   The subjunctive in relative clauses after a superlative

When the antecedent of the relative pronoun *qui* or *que* is qualified by a superlative adjective (*le plus beau*, etc.), or by one of the adjectives *premier* 'first', *dernier* 'last', *seul* 'only', or *unique* 'only', which are in some respects the equivalent of a superlative, the relative clause usually takes the subjunctive, e.g.:

> *Elle est la seule personne qui puisse m'aider*
> She is the only person who can help me
>
> *C'est l'histoire la plus fascinante qu'on puisse imaginer*
> It is the most fascinating story one can imagine
>
> *Pierre est le meilleur ami que nous ayons*
> Peter is the best friend we have

The indicative sometimes occurs, however, when the strictly factual nature of the superlative is being emphasized, e.g. *C'est le dernier livre que j'écrirai* 'It's the last book I shall write'. In general, the indicative is more likely to occur in familiar style (e.g. conversational speech or informal letters) than in literary usage.

Note that after expressions such as *la première (dernière) fois que* the indicative **must** be used, e.g. *C'est la première (dernière) fois que ça m'est arrivé* 'It's the first (last) time that that has happened to me'. (Beware of sentences in which the superlative is followed by a genitive plural, e.g. 'It is the best of the books I have read', which do *not* come under the above rule since the meaning is either 'The book I have read is the best one, i.e. *C'est le meilleur des livres que j'ai lu'*, or 'Of those books that I have read it is the best', i.e. *C'est le meilleur des livres que j'ai lus*.)

495   The subjunctive after indefinite relatives

The subjunctive **must** be used after

(i) *qui que ce soit qui* 'whoever' (subject), *quoi que ce soit qui* 'whatever' (subject), e.g. *qui que ce soit qui le dise* 'whoever says so'

(ii) *qui que ce soit que* 'whoever' (object), *quoi que, quoi que ce soit que* 'whatever' (object), e.g. *qui que ce soit que vous voyiez* 'whoever you see', *quoi (que ce soit) qu'il fasse,* . . . *qu'il ait fait* 'whatever he does, . . . he has done'.

(iii) *où que* 'wherever', e.g. *où que j'aille* 'wherever I go'.

(iv) *quelque(s)* + noun, 'whatever', e.g. *Quelques fautes que vous ayez commises, vous faites tout de même des progrès* 'Whatever mistakes you (may) have made, you are making progress all the same'.

(v) Note that with the verb *être* (used alone or preceded by *pouvoir* or *devoir*), the construction *quel* (variable) + *que* + verb in the subjunctive + noun is used (see **308**), e.g. *quels que soient les problèmes* 'whatever the problems', *quelle qu'ait pu être sa conduite* 'whatever his behaviour may have been'. A variant on this is the construction *Les difficultés, quelles qu'elles soient, ne sont pas insurmontables* 'The difficulties, whatever they are, are not insurmountable'.

(vi) Note the use of *quelque* or *si* + adjective or adverb, meaning 'however' (see **310**), e.g. *quelque intelligents qu'ils soient, si intelligents qu'ils soient* 'however intelligent they are' (note that *quelque* here is an adverb and does not vary for gender or number), *quelque heureuse, si heureuse qu'elle puisse paraître* 'however happy she may appear', *Quelque* (or *si*) *lentement que nous parlions, il ne comprend pas* 'However slowly we speak, he doesn't understand'.

Aussi, tout or *pour* can occur in place of *quelque* or *si*, e.g. *aussi riche, tout riche, pour riche qu'il soit* 'however rich he is'; *tout* may also take the indicative when the factual nature of the statement is stressed, e.g. *tout riche qu'il est* 'rich though he is'; for the agreement of *tout* see **317,v**. On the alternative construction *si riche soit-il*, etc., see **310,iii**.

The tenses of the subjunctive

496 The French subjunctive has only four tenses, viz. two simple tenses:

    the present   the imperfect

and two compound tenses:

    the perfect   the pluperfect

The imperfect and pluperfect subjunctive are virtually never used now in speech and there is an increasing tendency to avoid them even in writing. The rules that we give in **497–499** should therefore be regarded as characteristic only of a very conservative literary style. In practice, the principles set out in sections 500–506 should be followed.

497   The subjunctive in independent clauses (see **476, 477** and **480**) is normally in the present or the perfect tense, as the meaning requires; for constructions taking the imperfect or the pluperfect subjunctive, see **478**.

498   (i) In a conservative literary style (see **496**), the choice of tense of the subjunctive is determined in most cases (for exceptions see **499**) by a 'rule for the sequence of tenses' that can be simply stated. (Note that, in what follows, the verb of the clause on which the subjunctive clause depends is referred to as the 'main verb' – e.g. in *Je ne crois pas qu'il soit malade* 'I don't think he is ill', *crois* is the main verb; strictly, this 'main verb' is sometimes itself a subordinate verb, as in *Elle dit qu'elle ne croit pas qu'il soit malade* 'She says that she doesn't think that he is ill', but this is of little practical consequence for our present purpose and, having now drawn attention to the matter, we shall not refer to it any more.)

(ii) The 'rule for the sequence of tenses' runs as follows:

If the main verb is:	the subjunctive is:
present future perfect imperative	present or perfect

If the main verb is:	the subjunctive is:
preterite imperfect pluperfect conditional past conditional	imperfect or pluperfect

(iii) The present or imperfect is used when the event expressed by the verb in the subjunctive is considered to take place at the same time as or later than that of the main verb – note therefore that there is normally no distinction between present and future (but see **506**). The perfect or pluperfect is used when the event expressed by the verb in the subjunctive is considered to have taken place before that of the main verb.

The application of the rule can be illustrated thus:

Je ne crois pas	
Je ne croirai pas	(a) *qu'il vienne*
Je n'ai jamais cru	(b) *qu'il soit venu*
Ne croyez pas	

I do not believe	
I shall not believe	(a) that he is coming, that he will come
I have never believed	(b) that he has come
Do not believe	

Je ne crus pas	
Je ne croyais pas	
Je n'avais pas cru	(a) *qu'il vînt*
Je ne croirais pas	(b) *qu'il fût venu*
Je n'aurais pas cru	

I did not believe	
I did not believe	(a) that he was coming, that he would come
I had not believed	
I should not believe	(b) that he had come
I should not have believed	

499 The sequence of tenses given in **498** should not be applied too mechanically. Sometimes the sense requires us to depart from it, as when, for example, a main verb in the present is followed by a verb that, in the indicative, would be in the imperfect, e.g. corresponding to *il était heureux* 'he was happy':

> *On ne peut pas croire qu'il fût heureux*
> One cannot believe that he was happy

or when a main verb in the past is followed by a verb referring to an event that is present or future at the time of speaking, e.g.:

> *Il n'avait pas voulu croire que mon frère vienne demain*
> He had not wanted to believe that my brother is coming tomorrow

500 Even in literary French, the sequence of tenses is frequently not followed when the main verb is in the conditional, which is treated as a member of the first rather than of the second group of tenses given in **498**,ii, e.g. *Je ne croirais pas qu'il vienne* rather than *Je ne croirais pas qu'il vînt* 'I should not believe that he would come'.

501 As is mentioned in section **496** above, the imperfect and pluperfect subjunctive are no longer used in ordinary speech and are indeed increasingly avoided in writing. The following principles should therefore be followed as far as possible:

502 In writing, in a formal style, the imperfect subjunctive may still be used:

(i) with the verbs *avoir* and *être*

(ii) in the third person singular of other verbs (e.g. *qu'il chantât*).
   Otherwise it should be avoided so, for example, such forms as *que je vinsse, que nous chantassions, qu'ils écrivissent* should **never** be used.

Two possible ways of avoiding the imperfect subjunctive, both of them widely used, not only when that tense really must be avoided but when its use is still tolerated in a literary style, i.e. in the circumstances stated in (i) and (ii) above, are:

(a) to recast the sentence in such a way as to avoid the subjunctive altogether; for example, instead of:

Les propriétaires n'avaient jamais permis que nous y entrassions
The owners had never allowed us to go in

Il ordonna qu'on déposât les armes
He ordered them to lay down their arms

one could write:

Les propriétaires ne nous avaient jamais permis d'y entrer
L'ordre fut donné de déposer les armes

(b) to use the present subjunctive instead of the imperfect, as in the following examples from literary texts:

Il fallait que Lucienne réponde (A. Orain)
It was essential that Lucienne should answer

Il n'aurait jamais dû permettre que sa femme s'en aille seule (Maurois)
He ought never to have allowed his wife to go away alone

Il suffisait que je regarde le banc, la lampe, le tas de poussier, pour que je sente que j'allais mourir (Sartre)

I only had to look at the seat, the lamp, the heap of coal-dust, to feel that I was going to die

Nous avions passé une semaine angoissée côte à côte avant que je ne reparte pour l'été chez mes parents (Sagan)
We had spent an agonized week side by side before I left for my parents' place for the summer

503 The pluperfect subjunctive, based as it is on the imperfect subjunctive of *avoir* or *être* (see **502**,ii), e.g. *qu'il eût fini, qu'ils fussent partis*, is still in use in a literary style, but, on the other hand, is frequently replaced by the perfect subjunctive.

504 In speech, the imperfect and pluperfect subjunctive should **always** be either (i) avoided (cf. **502**,a), or (ii) replaced by the present or the perfect subjunctive respectively, e.g.:

Ma femme voulait que j'aille voir (Simenon)
My wife wanted me to go and see

Je craignais qu'il soit déjà parti
I was afraid he had already left

505 Where the use of the present subjunctive in place of the imperfect could cause ambiguity, the perfect may be used instead; for example, corresponding to the indicative *Il travaillait jeudi* 'He was working on Thursday', we could have *Je ne crois pas qu'il ait travaillé jeudi* 'I don't think he worked on Thursday', since *Je ne crois pas qu'il travaille jeudi* would mean 'I don't think he is working (*or* will be working) on Thursday'.

506 Where the use of the present subjunctive as the equivalent of a future indicative could cause ambiguity, the subjunctive of *devoir* and the infinitive may be used to form a kind of future subjunctive, e.g. *Je ne crois pas qu'il doive le faire* 'I don't think he will do so' in contexts in which *Je ne crois pas qu'il le fasse* would be likely to be interpreted as 'I don't think he is doing so'.

P 'May, might, must, ought, should, would'

507 It is important to be aware that, though English 'may, might, should, would' often correspond to a subjunctive in French, very often they do not. These particular modal verbs in English correspond in reality to a number of different constructions in French and great care must be taken in translating these forms, and the closely related modals 'must' and 'ought'. Note in particular the constructions dealt with below.

508 May

'May'

(i) corresponds to the French subjunctive expressing purpose, after *pour que* or *afin que* or sometimes *que* alone, e.g.:

> *Pour que vous compreniez, je vais vous expliquer ce que cela veut dire*
> So that you may understand, I am going to explain what that means

(ii) corresponds to the French subjunctive, expressing a wish, e.g.:

> *(Que) Dieu vous bénisse!*   May God bless you!

(iii) corresponds to the French subjunctive in a variety of other contexts, e.g.:

> *J'y vais de peur qu'il ne soit inquiet*
> I'm going for fear he may be worried

> *quelque riche qu'il soit*
> however rich he may be

(iv) expresses possibility, in which case French uses either the verb *pouvoir*, e.g.:

> *Cela peut être vrai*   That may be true
> *Il a pu le faire*   He may have done it

(in this last example, note that French uses the perfect of *pouvoir* and the present infinitive where English uses the present of 'may' and the past infinitive – cf. 510, ii), or *il est possible que* or *il se peut que* 'it is possible that' followed by a subjunctive clause, e.g.:

> *Il est possible que* ⎫
> *Il se peut que*   ⎬ *ce soit vrai* It may be true

or *peut-être* 'perhaps', e.g.:

Il viendra peut-être demain   He may come tomorrow

(v) expresses permission, in which case French uses *pouvoir* and not the subjunctive, e.g.:

Vous pouvez vous asseoir si vous voulez
You may sit down if you wish

Peut-on entrer?
May we come in?

509   Might
'Might'

(i) is used (somewhat loosely) in English as an alternative to 'may' in contexts such as those dealt with in **508, i, iii** and **iv**

(ii) in its strict usage is the past tense of 'may' and so corresponds to the French imperfect subjunctive in such contexts as the following (corresponding to the use of the present subjunctive as in **508,i, iii** and **v**):

Je lui écrivis afin qu'il ne fût plus inquiet
I wrote to him so that he might no longer be worried

J'y allai de peur qu'il ne fût inquiet
I went for fear he might be worried

Il était possible que ce fût vrai
It was possible that it might be true

(For restrictions on the use of the imperfect subjunctive in French, see **500–504**.)

(iii) is used much like 'may' in **508,ii**, but suggests less hope of fulfilment, e.g.:

Oh, que ce fût vrai!
Oh, that it might be true!

(iv) expresses a possibility (often a slight possibility) (cf. **508, iv**):

Ça pourrait être vrai, mais j'en doute
That might be true, but I doubt it

(v) is used to request permission (cf. **508,v**), e.g.:

Pourrais-je vous suggérer que c'est idiot?
Might I suggest that this is idiotic?

510 Must

'Must'

(i) expresses a moral certainty, something that is regarded as being inevitably so, e.g.:

> *Cela doit être vrai*
> That must be true

> *Vous devez croire que je suis bête*
> You must think that I am stupid

(ii) expresses obligation – note that in this case *devoir* is not strong enough and that some such expression as *il faut que* or *il est nécessaire que* 'it is necessary that' has to be used, e.g.:

> *Il faut que nous partions tout de suite*
> We must leave at once

Note that, where English uses 'must' and the past infinitive, French usually has a compound tense of *devoir* and the present infinitive (cf. 508, iv), e.g.:

> *Il a dû partir*
> He must have left

> *Je supposais qu'il avait dû partir la veille*
> I assumed he must have left the day before

511 Ought

'Ought' is translated by the conditional of *devoir*, e.g.:

> *Je devrais y aller*   I ought to go

or, when English has 'ought to have' and the past participle, by the past conditional of *devoir* and the infinitive, e.g.:

> *J'aurais dû y aller*   I ought to have gone

512 Should

'Should'

(i) is often the expression of the conditional (see 415–423) in the first persons singular and plural, e.g.:

> *Je ne vous le dirais pas, même si je le savais*
> I should not tell you, even if I knew

(ii) is sometimes the equivalent of 'were to' in *if*-clauses; in such cases, it must **not** be translated by the French conditional but by the imperfect of *devoir* and the infinitive, e.g.:

S'il devait arriver ce soir, donnez-moi un coup de fil
If he should arrive (were to arrive) this evening, give me a ring

(iii) is sometimes the equivalent of 'ought to', in which case it must be translated as in **511**, e.g.:

Vous devriez y aller
You should go (= You ought to go)

(iv) is sometimes used with verbs of believing or doubting as a less categorical assertion than would be the case if the present tense were used, e.g. 'I should think he will come', 'I should doubt whether he will come'; in such contexts, French would usually use the present indicative, i.e. *Je crois qu'il viendra, Je doute qu'il vienne*, or some kind of circumlocution, e.g. *Je suis porté à croire qu'il viendra* 'I am inclined to think he will come'.

513 Would

'Would'

(i) is very frequently the sign of the conditional (see **415–423**), e.g.:

Ils ne vous le diraient pas, même s'ils le savaient
They would not tell you even if they knew

(ii) expresses determination, in which case it is usually stressed in English and should be rendered in French by *vouloir* 'to wish' or *tenir à* 'to insist on (doing)', which are often strengthened by an adverb, e.g.:

Il voulait (absolument) y aller ⎱ He *would* go
Il tenait (absolument) à y aller ⎰

(iii) in 'would that', expresses a wish and is rendered in French by a *si*-clause, e.g.:

Si j'étais (j'avais été) plus jeune
Would that I were (had been) younger

(iv) occasionally expresses an habitual action or state in the past, in which case French uses the imperfect indicative (see **417**), e.g.:

Un jour il était insensé de fureur; le lendemain il oubliait ses griefs et devenait l'ami de tout le monde
One day he would be beside himself with rage; the next he would forget his grievances and make friends with everybody

Q   The imperative

514   Generally speaking, the imperative is used to express commands in French in much the same way as in English. Note however:

(i) that, whereas it is possible in English to use the subject pronoun 'you' with the imperative for purposes of emphasis, this is not possible in French which instead uses, depending on the precise type of emphasis required, either the appropriate form for 'yourself' or 'yourselves', e.g.:

Fais-le toi-même!
Faites-le vous-même!   } *You* do it!
Faites-le vous-mêmes!

or some such circumlocution as *Il faut que toi tu le fasses* '*You* must do it (= *You* do it'), or *Vous pourriez peut-être le lui dire* 'You might perhaps tell him (= *You* tell him, please)'

(ii) that French has a first person plural imperative corresponding to 'Let us (do something)' and that neither the verb *laisser* nor *que* and the subjunctive (as in **515**) must be used, e.g.:

Partons tout de suite   Let's leave at once

515   A kind of third person imperative can be expressed by means of *que* and the subjunctive, e.g. *Qu'il attende* 'Let him wait' (see also **480**,i).

516   For the use of the infinitive as the equivalent of an imperative in general instructions, etc., see **429**,ii.

517   The future tense may be used as a polite imperative, i.e. to express a request rather than a command, e.g.:

Quand il arrivera, vous me le direz, s'il vous plaît
When he comes, please let me know

R   The complement of verbs

518   Linking verbs

A certain number of verbs, in particular *être* 'to be' but also *devenir* 'to become', *sembler* 'to seem', *paraître* 'to appear', *rester* 'to remain' and a few others, can function as 'linking verbs'. This means that they take as their complement (i.e. complete their sense with) not a direct or indirect object but a noun (or noun phrase) or adjective (or adjectival phrase) relating to the subject, e.g. 'Peter is a doctor', 'She is becoming a very attractive girl', 'These books seem too difficult'.

The main differences between English and French in their treatment of the complement of linking verbs are the following:

(i) in French, the adjective has to agree with the subject (see 127–130), e.g.:

Il est petit
He is small

Elle en est devenue furieuse
She became angry at it

Vos sœurs paraissent intelligentes
Your sisters seem intelligent

Ils sont restés calmes
They remained calm

(ii) in English, one might hesitate in the case of personal pronouns between the more formal 'It is I', 'It was he', etc., and the more informal 'It's me', 'It was him', etc.; in French there is no problem since the disjunctive pronoun must always be used, e.g. *C'est moi*, *C'était lui*.

519   Verbs other than linking verbs

In French, any verb other than *être* or another verb used as a linking verb (see 518) can, if necessary, take as its complement (i.e. complete its sense with) one of the following:

(i) a direct object (otherwise referred to as an object in the *accusative* – see 17), e.g. *Il a acheté ce livre* 'He bought this book', *Je les connais* 'I know them' (for direct object personal pronouns, see 198–199)

(ii) an indirect object (otherwise referred to as an object in the *dative* – see 18) introduced by the preposition *à*, or one or other of the dative conjunctive pronouns *me, te, nous, vous, se, lui, leur* or *y* (see 198–200)

(iii) a *genitive* phrase introduced by the preposition *de* (see 19), or the genitive conjunctive pronoun *en* 'of it, of them, etc.' (see 201)

(iv) a noun or pronoun preceded by some other preposition – e.g. *avec, dans, en, sur*

(v) an infinitive alone without a preposition

(vi) an infinitive introduced by *de*

(vii) an infinitive introduced by *à*

(viii) an infinitive introduced by some other preposition – e.g. *après, par, pour, sans*

(ix) a present participle introduced by the preposition *en*

(x) a clause introduced by a conjunction or by some interrogative word.

520 The lists below are an attempt to classify the verbs which present difficulties because of a difference in construction between French and English.

For the terms *accusative, dative* and *genitive*, see 17–19 and 519, i–iii.

521 List 1

Verbs with no preposition in English, but used in French either with the genitive pronoun *en*, or with a noun or pronoun governed by *de*:

> *abuser de*, misuse
> *démordre de*, let go
> *douter de*, doubt
> *hériter de*, inherit[1]
> *jouer de*, play (an instrument)[2]
> *jouir de*, enjoy

médire de, backbite, disparage
redoubler de, redouble[3]
user de, use (with accus., use up, wear out)

Examples:

J'en doute
I doubt it

Pouvez-vous jouer du piano?
Can you play the piano?

Ne médisez pas des absents
Do not disparage the absent

Notes

1   *hériter* is used in three ways, viz. *hériter d'une fortune* 'to inherit a fortune', *hériter une fortune de quelqu'un* 'to inherit a fortune from someone', *heriter de quelqu'un* 'to be someone's heir'

2   *jouer d'un instrument* but *jouer à* with reference to games, e.g. *jouer au football* 'to play football'

3   *redoubler de* = 'to redouble' in the expression *redoubler d'efforts* 'to redouble one's efforts'; otherwise *redoubler de patience, de violence*, etc. 'to be even more patient, violent, etc.'. For other meanings of *redoubler* (e.g. *redoubler une classe* 'to repeat a year (in school or college)'), consult a good dictionary.

522   List 2

Verbs with no preposition in English, but used in French either with a dative pronoun or with a noun governed by *à*

(a) The following verbs take only one object, viz. a direct object in English and an indirect object in French:

aller à, suit
attenter à, attack
contrevenir à, infringe
convenir à, suit
déplaire à, displease
désobéir à, disobey
entrer à, enter[1]
grimper à, climb[2]

>   *jouer à*, play (a game)
>   *nuire à*, harm
>   *obéir à*, obey
>   *obvier à*, obviate
>   *parvenir à*, reach, attain
>   *plaire à*, please
>   *remédier à*, cure, remedy, make good
>   *renoncer à*, renounce, abandon, give up
>   *répondre à*, answer (answer for, *de*)
>   *résister à*, resist
>   *ressembler à*, resemble, be like, look like
>   *subvenir à*, to meet (a need, expense, etc.)
>   *succéder à*, follow, succeed
>   *surseoir à*, postpone (mostly legal)
>   *survivre à*, survive

Examples:

>   *Ce costume lui va très bien*
>   This costume suits her very well
>
>   *Il faut obéir aux ordres du roi*
>   The king's orders must be obeyed
>
>   *J'y ai renoncé*
>   I've given it up
>
>   *Le martinet ressemble fort à l'hirondelle*
>   A martin is very like a swallow

Notes

1   *Entrer* takes *à* only in the sense of 'become a member of', e.g. *entrer au parti* 'to join the party'. When 'enter' denotes literal movement into some place, it must in French be followed by *dans*, e.g. *Il est entré dans la tente* 'He entered the tent'.

2   *Grimper* can also take *dans* or *sur* when the sense allows, e.g. *grimper à l'échelle, aux arbres* 'to climb the ladder, to climb trees', *grimper dans un arbre* 'to climb up into a tree', *grimper sur le toit* 'to climb on to the roof'.

(b) The following verbs always take a direct object in English but in French take either a direct object or an indirect object depending on the meaning:

>   *insulter* 'to insult' takes a direct object with reference to a person (*insulter quelqu'un* 'to insult someone'), but other-

wise an indirect object (e.g. *insulter à l'intelligence de quel-qu'un* 'to insult someone's intelligence'); *toucher* takes a direct object when it merely means 'to touch' physically (e.g. *toucher le mur* 'to touch the wall', *toucher quelqu'un à l'épaule* 'to touch someone on the shoulder'), but an indirect object when it conveys the idea of 'meddling with' (e.g. *Ne touchez pas à mes papiers* 'Don't touch my papers') and in certain other cases (e.g. *Il n'a pas touché à son petit déjeuner* 'He hasn't touched his breakfast (i.e. he hasn't eaten any of it)', *toucher à une question* 'to touch on a question') – consult a good dictionary.

(c) Note that in English 'one asks or forgives someone for something' whereas in French *on demande ou on pardonne quelque chose à quelqu'un*, e.g.:

J'ai demandé cent francs à mon frère
I asked my brother for a hundred francs

Je lui pardonnerai son absence
I shall forgive him for his absence

(d) Verbs such as *défendre* 'to forbid', *dire* 'to tell', *offrir* 'to offer', *ordonner* 'to order', *permettre* 'to allow, permit', *promettre* 'to promise', *raconter* 'to tell', *refuser* 'to refuse' and others of similar meaning that can have both a direct and an indirect object have the same construction in both languages, but whereas in English the indirect object is often identical in form with the direct object, i.e. it is not accompanied by the preposition 'to' (e.g. 'to promise **somebody** something' = 'to promise something **to some-body**'), in French the indirect object must always be expressed by a dative pronoun or by *à* + a noun phrase, e.g.:

Il faudra le dire à Pierre
We shall have to tell Peter

Voulez-vous permettre aux enfants de sortir?
Will you allow the children to go out?

Je lui ai promis cent francs
I promised him a hundred francs

Le consulat leur refuse un visa
The consulate refuses them a visa

523   List 3

Verbs taking a preposition in English but a direct object in French.

admettre, admit of
approuver, approve of
attendre, wait for
chercher, look for
coucher en joue, aim at
demander, ask for
écouter, listen to
envoyer chercher, send for
escalader, climb over
espérer, hope for
fournir, supply with (see also **524**)
habiter, live in[1]
payer, pay for
regarder, look at[2]
rencontrer, meet with
reprocher, reproach for[3]
viser, aim at

Examples:

Attendons le bus
Let's wait for the bus

Je n'ai pas écouté un mot de son discours
I did not listen to a word of his speech

Le détenu s'est échappé en escaladant la muraille
The prisoner escaped by climbing over the wall

Il lui fournit une grande somme d'argent
He supplied him with a large sum of money

J'ai payé le dîner à mes amis
I paid for my friends' dinner

Il rencontra un obstacle imprévu
He met with an unforeseen obstacle

Notes

1   *Habiter* with an accusative is used of the house, room, town, etc., in which one lives, e.g.:

Il habite la maison en face .
He lives in the house opposite

It can also be used absolutely, e.g.:

Il habite depuis quelques mois en Italie
He has been living for a few months in Italy

Il habite près de Paris
He lives near Paris

2 *Regarder à* means 'pay attention to', 'be particular about', e.g.:

Je ne regarde pas à des bagatelles
I am not particular about trifles

3 *Reprocher*: in English one reproaches someone for something, in French *on reproche quelque chose à quelqu'un*, e.g.:

Il reprocha au garçon ses fautes
He reproached the boy for his mistakes

524 List 4

After the verbs in list (a), *de* corresponds to English 'with'; after those in list (b), *à* corresponds to English 'from'.

(a)
accabler de, overwhelm with
armer de, arm with
broder de, embroider with
brûler de, burn with (metaph.)
charger de, load with, entrust with
combler de, overwhelm with
couronner de, crown with
couvrir de, cover with
cribler de, riddle with
douer de, endow with
écraser de, overwhelm with
entourer de, surround with (passive also 'by')
entremêler de, intermingle with
environner de, surround with (passive also 'by')
faire de, do with
fourmiller de, swarm with
fournir de, supply with[1] (see also **523**)
gémir de, groan with
grever de, burden, encumber with
grouiller de, crawl, swarm with

menacer de, threaten with
munir de, provide with
orner de, adorn with
parer de, deck; adorn with
planter de, plant with
pourvoir de, provide with
regorger de, overflow with
remplir de, fill with
semer de, sow with
souiller de, soil with
tacher de, stain with
tapisser de, carpet with; hang, cover (walls) with
trembler de, tremble with[2]
vêtir de, clothe with

So, too, especially in the passive, *coiffer* 'to put on one's head'.

Examples:

Ces nouvelles l'accableraient de honte
This news would overwhelm him with shame

Le gazon fourmille d'insectes
The turf is swarming with insects

L'enfant tremblait d'effroi
The child was trembling with fright

un homme coiffé d'un béret
a man wearing a beret

Qu'avez-vous fait de votre livre?
What have you done with your book?

J'ai les mains souillées de goudron
My hands are soiled with tar

Notes

1   *Fournir* takes either *de* or, more usually nowadays, *en*, e.g.
fournir quelqu'un de viande or *en viande* 'to supply someone
with meat'.

2   *Trembler de* can also mean 'to tremble in', e.g. *Il tremble de
tous ses membres* 'He is trembling in every limb'.

(b)

acheter à, buy from
arracher à, snatch away from

cacher à } hide from
celer à }
dérober à, steal from, hide from
échapper à, escape (from)[1]
emprunter à, borrow from
enlever à } take away from
ôter à }
louer à, rent, hire from
prendre à, take from (also *dans* , 659, iii, *sur*, **685**)
retirer à, remove from
soustraire à, abstract from (maths, subtract, *de*)
se soustraire à, withdraw from (intrans.)
voler à, steal from[2]

Examples:

Il cacha son dessein à ses amis
He hid his plan from his friends

Je vais emprunter mille francs à mon frère
I am going to borrow a thousand francs from my brother

On lui a volé sa montre
Someone has stolen his watch from him

Notes

1   *Échapper à* implies 'not being caught' and so is usually to be translated 'to escape' (with a direct object) rather than 'to escape from', e.g. *Il a échappé à la police* 'He escaped the police' (i.e. 'He avoided being caught'), *échapper au gibet* 'to escape the gallows'; 'to escape from' in the sense of 'to get out of' is *s'échapper de* (as in *Il y a de l'eau qui s'échappe de ce tuyau* 'There is water escaping from this pipe') or, particularly in the sense of escaping from prison, etc., *s'évader de*.

2   *Voler* meaning 'to rob (a person)', when the thing stolen is not mentioned, takes a direct object, e.g. *voler ses clients* 'to rob one's clients', *On l'a volé* 'They have robbed him' or 'He has been robbed'.

525   List 5

After the following verbs various English prepositions have to be translated by *de* (list a) or by *à* (list b):

(a) *de*

abreuver de, steep in, overwhelm with
abriter de, shelter from (also *contre*)
accompagner de, accompany with, by
affranchir de, free from
s'alarmer de, become alarmed by, at
bénir de, bless with
complimenter de, compliment on
débarrasser de, free from, rid of
déjeuner de, lunch on (i.e. have something for lunch)
délivrer de, deliver from
dépendre de, depend on
dîner de, dine on
éloigner de, separate from
embarrasser de, encumber with
encombrer de, encumber with
envelopper de, wrap up in, envelop in
hérisser de, bristle with
se moquer de, laugh at, make fun of
se nourrir de, feed on
se passer de, dispense with, do without
se repaître de, feed on (figurative), revel in
répondre de, answer for, guarantee
rire de, laugh at
rougir de, blush for, with
tenir de, take after
triompher de, triumph over
vivre de, live on

Examples:

Vous vous moquez de moi
You are laughing at me

Elle rougit de chagrin, de plaisir
She blushed for vexation, with pleasure

Le paquet était enveloppé de papier gris
The parcel was wrapped up in brown paper

(b) *à*

assister à, attend, be present at[1]
compatir à, sympathize with (someone's sorrow, etc.)

connaître à, know by[2]
reconnaître à, recognize by[2]
croire à or *en*, believe in[3]
employer à, employ in, for
mêler à, mix up in
pendre à, hang on (trans. or intrans.)
penser à, think of[4]
pourvoir à, provide for
présider à, preside over (also with direct object)
réfléchir à, reflect upon (also *sur*)
réserver à, reserve for
songer à, think of
suspendre à, hang on (trans.)
veiller à, attend to, see to (things)[5]

Examples:

Il a pourvu à tous nos besoins
He has provided for all our needs

Je veux bien songer à votre projet
I am quite ready to think over your plan

Notes

1   *Assister* meaning 'to help' takes a direct object.
2   *Connaître* and *reconnaître* take *à* to denote some distinctive peculiarity, *par* or *de* in the sense of 'known by (or to), recognized by people (or animals)', e.g. *Il fut reconnu à sa cicatrice par un vieil ami* 'He was recognized by his scar by an old friend'. *De* is used in such expressions as *connaître de vue, de nom* 'to know by sight, by name'.
3   *Croire* sometimes takes a direct object, sometimes not:

   croire quelque chose
   to believe a thing is true

   croire quelqu'un
   to believe someone, to believe what he says

   croire à quelque chose, à quelqu'un
   to believe in something or someone, i.e. to believe in its or his existence

   croire en quelqu'un
   to have confidence in someone

e.g. *Croyez-vous cette histoire?* 'Do you believe that story?', *Je vous crois* 'I believe you', *Je ne crois pas aux miracles* 'I do not believe in miracles', *croire au Saint-Esprit, au diable, aux fées* 'to believe in the Holy Spirit, in the devil, in fairies' (but *croire en* with names, e.g. *croire en Dieu, en Jésus-Christ* 'to believe in God, in Jesus Christ'), *Je crois en mes amis* 'I believe in (i.e. I have confidence in) my friends'. For other uses of *croire* with *à* or *en*, consult a good dictionary.

4   *Penser à* 'think of' in the sense of 'have in mind, keep in mind, remember, reflect on', e.g.:

> *A quoi pensez-vous?*
> What are you thinking about?

penser de 'think of' in the sense of 'have an opinion about, form a judgement on', e.g.:

> *Que pensez-vous de ces gens?*
> What do you think of these people?

5   *Veiller à*, as in *veiller à l'ordre public* 'to see to it that public order is maintained'. *Veiller sur* is 'to watch over, keep an eye on (people)', e.g. *Il me faut veiller sur ces enfants* 'I have to keep an eye on these children'. *Veiller* in the sense of 'to sit up with (a sick person or a dead body)' takes a direct object.

526   Lists 1 to 5 do not apply to cases in which the complement contains an infinitive. These are dealt with below.

Observe that (with the exceptions noted in List 6c) an infinitive after a verb used impersonally always requires *de*, e.g.:

> *Il lui arriva d'être emporté par des brigands*
> It happened that he was carried off by brigands (*lit*. It happened to him to be carried off by brigands)

As such infinitives stand in apposition to the subject, and are in no sense the object of the impersonal verb, they do not appear in the following lists.

527   List 6. Verbs requiring no preposition with the infinitive are:

(a) most verbs of 'saying' and 'thinking', provided that both verbs refer to the same person, e.g.:

> *Je crois m'être égaré*
> I think I have lost my way

In all such sentences, however, the ordinary construction with *que* can be used and is generally safer for beginners, e.g.:

Je crois que je me suis égaré

If the subject of both verbs is not the same, *que* must be used, e.g.:

Je crois qu'il s'est égaré   I think he has lost his way

Among such verbs are:

affirmer, assert	*jurer*, swear
assurer, maintain	*nier*, deny
avouer, admit	*penser*, think
confesser, confess	*prétendre*, assert
croire, think	*protester*, declare
déclarer, declare	*reconnaître*, acknowledge
déposer, testify	*soutenir*, maintain
dire, say	*témoigner*, testify
juger, consider	

(b) several verbs of motion, when the infinitive expresses purpose. Among such verbs are:

accourir, run up, rush
aller, go
courir, run
descendre, come (or go) down
envoyer, send
mener, lead (and compounds)
monter, come (or go) up
retourner, return
revenir, come back
venir, come

Note the idioms *envoyer chercher quelqu'un* 'to send for someone', *envoyer dire à quelqu'un* 'to send word to someone'.

Examples:

On accourut lui annoncer l'heureuse nouvelle
People came running up (in order) to announce the good tidings to him

Il m'a emmené voir ses roses
He took me to see his roses

Je suis venu vous féliciter de votre succès
I have come to congratulate you on your success

(c) the following verbs, many of which have appeared in the list of
modal and similar verbs (468):

adorer, adore
aimer autant, be just as willing[2]
aimer mieux, prefer[2]
compter, intend, expect[4]
daigner, deign
désirer, wish[4]
détester, detest (also *de*)
devoir, ought, have to
écouter, listen[3]
entendre, hear[3]
espérer, hope
faillir, be near . . .-ing
faire, make, get[1]
falloir, be necessary[1]
se figurer, fancy
s'imaginer, imagine
laisser, let, allow[3]
oser, dare
ouïr, hear (only with *dire*)
paraître, appear[1]
pouvoir, be able[1]
préférer, prefer[4]
regarder, look at[3]
savoir, know how to, be able
sembler, seem[1]
sentir, feel[3]
souhaiter, wish (also *de*)
valoir autant, be just as well[1,2]
valoir mieux, be better[1,2]
voir, see[3]
vouloir, wish[5]

Examples:

J'adore monter à cheval
I adore riding

Elle a failli s'évanouir
She nearly fainted

Regardons jouer les enfants
Let us watch the children playing

Notes

1 *Faire, falloir, paraître, pouvoir, sembler, valoir (autant, mieux)* are used impersonally without *de* (see **526**), e.g. *Il fait bon prendre un bain de soleil sur la plage* 'It is nice sun-bathing on the beach', *Il vaudrait mieux partir maintenant* 'It would be better to leave now'.

2 In a comparison after *aimer autant, aimer mieux, valoir autant* and *valoir mieux*, and generally after the adverb *plutôt* 'rather', *de* is used before the second infinitive, e.g.:

Plutôt
J'aime mieux
Il vaut mieux } *partir aussitôt que d'attendre le train du soir*
Autant vaut

I would rather start at once than }
We had better start at once than } wait for the evening train
As well start at once as }

3 *Faire, laisser* and verbs of the senses, of which only the commonest are listed here (viz. *écouter, entendre, regarder, sentir, voir*), take an infinitive only when the infinitive has a subject expressed (e.g. *Je vois arriver mon frère* 'I see my brother arriving' – i.e. my brother is arriving) or understood (e.g. *Je fais construire une maison* 'I am having a house built' = 'I am causing [someone] to build a house' – i.e. someone [unspecified] is building a house).

4 The use of *compter, désirer, préférer* with *de* (e.g. *Il désire de partir* for *Il désire partir* 'He wishes to leave') is an archaism that should not be imitated.

5 Note that *vouloir* only takes the infinitive when the subject of both verbs is the same, e.g. *Je veux le faire* 'I want to do it'; otherwise *que* and the subjunctive must be used, e.g. *Je veux que vous le fassiez* 'I want you to do it'.

528 List 7 (a).

The following verbs can take *de* with the infinitive when they have no other complement:

avoir accoutumé de, be in the habit of[1] (compound tenses only)

achever de, finish . . .-ing

affecter de, pretend to

ambitionner de, aspire to

appréhender de, dread to

brûler de, long to

cesser de, cease to

choisir de, choose to

commencer de, begin to (also *à*)

continuer de, continue to (also *à*)

craindre de, fear to

décider de, decide to

dédaigner de, disdain to

désespérer de, despair of . . .-ing

détester de, detest . . .-ing (see also **527**,c)

différer de, postpone . . . .-ing (also *à*)

discontinuer de, leave off . . .-ing

enrager de, be infuriated by, loathe . . .-ing

entreprendre de, undertake to

essayer de, try to

éviter de, avoid . . .-ing

feindre de, pretend to

finir de, finish . . .-ing

frémir de, tremble to

gémir de, bemoan . . .-ing

haïr de, hate to[1]

hasarder de, risk . . .-ing

jurer de, swear to

ne pas laisser de, not to fail to[1,2] (etc.)

ne pas manquer de, not to fail to[2] (etc.)

mériter de, deserve to

mourir de, die of . . .-ing

négliger de, neglect to

obtenir de, get leave to

offrir de, offer to

omettre de, omit to

oublier de, forget to
parler de, speak of . . .-ing
projeter de, plan to
promettre de, promise to
recommencer de, begin again to (also *à*)
refuser de, refuse to
regretter de, regret to
risquer de, risk . . .-ing
rougir de, blush, be ashamed to
souffrir de, be grieved to
souhaiter de, wish to (see also **527**,c)
soutenir de, endure to
tâcher de, try to
tenter de, try to
trembler de, fear to[3]

Examples:

Il a choisi d'y demeurer
He has chosen to live there

Il commençait $\left\{ \begin{array}{c} de \\ à \end{array} \right\}$ *désespérer de se faire entendre*
He was beginning to despair of making himself heard

Son attitude ne laisse pas de me surprendre
His attitude surprises me nevertheless

Je ne manquerai pas d'y aller
I shall not fail to go there

Si tu ne rougis pas de pécher, rougis au moins de ne pas rougir en péchant
If you are not ashamed to sin, at least be ashamed of sinning unashamedly

Mes lettres n'avaient pas accoutumé de se suivre de si près
My letters were not in the habit of following one another so closely

Notes

1   *Avoir accoutumé de, haïr de* · and *ne pas laisser de* are now characteristic only of literary usage.

2   *Ne pas laisser de* and *ne pas manquer de* are used only in the negative.

3   *Trembler* may be used in a different sense with *à*. *Je tremble de le voir* means 'I am afraid to see him' but *Je tremble à le voir* means 'I tremble when I see him'.

529   List 7(b)

The following verbs can take *à* with the infinitive when they have no other complement:

aboutir à, end in
aimer à, like to[1]
apprendre à, learn to
aspirer à, aspire to
avoir à, have to
balancer à, hesitate to
chercher à, try to
commencer à, begin to (also *de*)
concourir à, combine to
condescendre à, condescend to
consentir à, consent to
consister à, consist in . . .-ing
conspirer à, conspire to
continuer à, continue to (also *de*)
contribuer à, contribute to
demander à, ask to[2]
descendre à, descend to . . .-ing
exceller à, excel in . . .-ing
gagner à, gain by . . .-ing
hésiter à, hesitate to
parvenir à, succeed in . . .-ing, manage to
passer à, go on to
pencher à, be inclined to
persévérer à, persevere in . . .-ing
persister à, persist in . . .-ing
prétendre à, aspire to
recommencer à, begin again to (also *de*)
renoncer à, give up . . .-ing
répugner à, detest, loathe . . .-ing[3]
réussir à, succeed in . . .-ing
songer à, think of . . .-ing

suffire à, be enough to (also *pour*)[4]
tendre à, tend to
tenir à, be anxious to
travailler à, work at . . .-ing
trouver à, manage to
viser à, aim at . . .-ing

Examples:

J'ai dû renoncer à y aller
I have had to give up going there

Nous n'avons pas encore réussi à les trouver
We have not succeeded in finding them yet

Notes
1 *Aimer* is also used without a preposition, e.g. *J'aime voyager* 'I like travelling'; this is the most usual construction in speech and it must always be used with *aimer autant*, e.g. *J'aimerais autant partir tout de suite* 'I would just as soon leave right away', and *aimer mieux* 'to prefer'. *Aimer de* is archaic and should not be used.
2 For *demander à* or *demander de* + infinitive, see **532**, note 2.
3 Though *répugner* when used personally takes *à*, e.g. *Je répugne à suivre ses conseils* 'I am reluctant to take his advice', it is more often used impersonally, in which case it takes *de*, e.g. *Il me répugne de le faire* 'I hate doing it, it is repugnant to me to do it'.
4 *Suffire*, whether used personally or impersonally, takes *à* or *pour* when the infinitive expresses what something or other is sufficient for, e.g. *Cette somme suffira à* (or *pour*) *payer ses dettes* 'That sum will be enough to pay his debts', or, impersonally, *Il a suffi de trois jours pour achever le travail* 'Three days were enough to complete the work'. But when the impersonal *il suffit* introduces an infinitive expressing what it is that is sufficient, the infinitive is preceded by *de*, e.g. *Il suffira de lui écrire* 'It will be enough to write to him' (i.e. 'Writing to him is all that will be necessary').

530 List 8(a)
Verbs that take a direct object followed, when necessary, by *de* with an infinitive.[3]

accuser de, accuse of
applaudir de, applaud for
avertir de, warn to
blâmer de, blame for
charger de, desire, commission to, burden with
conjurer de, conjure, beg to
contraindre de, compel to[1]
dégoûter de, disgust with, deter from
détourner de, divert from
dispenser de, exempt from, let off . . .-ing
dissuader de, dissuade from
empêcher de, hinder from
excuser de, excuse for . . .-ing
féliciter de, congratulate on
forcer de, force, compel to[1]
gronder de, scold for
louer de, praise for
obliger de, compel, oblige to[1]
persuader de, persuade to[2]
plaindre de, pity for
presser de, press to, with, urge to
prier de, beg to
punir de, punish for
remercier de, thank for
reprendre de, reprove for
sommer de, summon to
soupçonner de, suspect of
supplier de, entreat, beg to

Examples:

Il m'applaudit d'avoir parlé si franchement
He applauded me for having spoken so frankly

Il les blâme tous deux d'avoir tiré l'épée
He blames them both for having drawn the sword

Le médecin va vous gronder de vous être levé
The doctor will scold you for getting up

Je vous supplie de m'aider
I beg you to help me

Notes
1   *Contraindre, forcer* and *obliger* usually take *à* in the active,
    e.g. *Je vais les obliger à partir* 'I am going to compel them to

leave' (see list 8,b); in the passive, *à* is used when the verbal value is strongly present, especially when an agent is expressed, e.g. *J'ai été obligé par mon père à partir* 'I was compelled to leave by my father', but *de* is used when the verbal value is weak, i.e. when *Je suis contraint, forcé, obligé de*, etc., mean merely 'I have to . . .', e.g. *Je suis obligé de partir tout de suite* 'I have to leave at once'.

2   *Persuader* takes either a direct or an indirect object, i.e. either *persuader quelqu'un de faire quelque chose* or, more usually nowadays, *persuader à quelqu'un de faire quelque chose* 'to persuade someone to do something'.

3   Note that *de* is also used with a few verbs that are normally followed by an infinitive only when in the passive, such as *être charmé de, être enchanté de* 'to be delighted to', *être vexé de* 'to be upset or annoyed to'.

531 List 8(b)

Verbs that take a direct object followed, when necessary, by *à* with an infinitive.

accoutumer à, accustom
admettre à, admit, permit
aider à, help
amener à, induce, persuade
animer à, rouse, incite
appeler à, summon
astreindre à, compel
autoriser à, authorize
condamner à, condemn
conduire à, lead, induce
contraindre à, compel[1]
convier à, invite
dépenser à, spend in, on
destiner à, destine[2]
déterminer à, decide (someone) to
disposer à, induce
dresser à, train
employer à, employ
encourager à, encourage
engager à, urge
exciter à, incite
exercer à, train

exhorter à, exhort
exposer à, expose
forcer à, force[1]
habituer à, accustom
inciter à, incite
incliner à, incline
induire à, induce
inviter à, invite
mettre à, set someone to work at
obliger à, oblige[1]
passer à, spend (time) in
porter à, induce, cause
pousser à, urge
préparer à, prepare
provoquer à, provoke
réduire à, reduce[2]

Examples:

Vous ne l'amènerez jamais à avouer sa faute
You will never induce him to admit his mistake

Je les ai encouragés à persévérer
I encouraged them to persevere

Je vais le pousser à se raviser
I shall urge him to reconsider his decision

Notes
1   For *contraindre, forcer* and *obliger* + *à* or *de,* see **530,** note 1.
2   *Destiner* and *réduire* + *à* + infinitive are found particularly in
     the passive, *être destiné (réduit) à,* e.g. *destiné à disparaître*
     'doomed to disappear', *J'en ai été réduit à boire de l'eau* 'I was
     reduced to drinking water'.

532   List 9

Verbs that take an indirect object followed, when necessary, by *de*
with an infinitive.

accorder de, grant, allow
commander de, command
conseiller de, advise
crier de, shout to
défendre de, forbid

demander de, ask[1]
déplaire de, displease[4]
dire de, tell
écrire de, write to
enjoindre de, enjoin upon
importer de, be important
jurer de, swear to
offrir de, offer
ordonner de, order
pardonner de, pardon for . . .-ing
parler de, speak of . . .-ing
permettre de, allow
persuader de, persuade[2]
plaire de, please[4]
prescrire de, prescribe, ordain
promettre de, promise
proposer de, propose
recommander de, urge
reprocher de, reproach for . . .-ing
répugner de, be repugnant, disgust[4]
suggérer de, suggest

Examples:

Il lui a conseillé de ne pas le faire
He advised him not to do it

Il leur demanda (permit) de s'en aller
He asked (allowed) them to go away

Je lui ai dit de rester
I told him to stay

Il répugne à une mère de voir sa fille mal habillée
A mother hates (*lit.* it disgusts a mother) to see her daughter
badly dressed

Notes
1   'To ask someone (else) to do something' is *demander à
    quelqu'un de faire quelque chose*, but 'to ask to (be allowed to)
    do something (oneself)' is *demander à faire quelque chose*, e.g.
    Il a demandé à partir 'He asked to (be allowed to) leave'.
2   For *persuader* + direct or indirect object + infinitive, see **530**,
    note 2.

3   *Déplaire, plaire* and *répugner* (see **529**, note 2) are followed by
    de and an infinitive only when used impersonally, e.g. *Il me*
    plaît de vous écouter 'I like listening to you'.

533   List 10

Verbs with indirect object of the person which can have for their
direct object sometimes a noun in the accusative, sometimes an
infinitive governed by *à*.

apprendre ⎫
enseigner ⎬ teach
montrer   ⎭
donner, give
laisser, leave it to someone to
offrir, offer

Note that *apprendre* without an indirect object means 'to learn'.

Examples:

Il apprend à jouer du piano
He is learning to play the piano

Il apprend le latin
He is learning Latin

but

Je lui apprends à jouer du piano
I am teaching him to play the piano

Je lui apprends le latin
I am teaching him Latin

Sa mère lui apprit à écrire
His mother taught him to write

Il montre aux plus hardis à braver le danger
He teaches the boldest to face danger

Cela lui donna à penser
That gave him something to think about

Laissons aux astronomes à mesurer la grandeur des astres
Let us leave it to astronomers to measure the size of the stars

Il leur offrit de l'argent
He offered them money

Il leur offrit à boire
He offered them something to drink

When no mention is made of the thing taught, use *enseigner* (not *apprendre*) with a direct object of the person, e.g. *enseigner des enfants* 'to teach children'.

Reflexive verbs

534 List 11

Some verbs in French are only used in the reflexive form. The chief of these are:

s'abstenir, abstain
s'accouder, lean on one's elbows[2]
s'accroupir, crouch[2]
s'adonner (à), devote oneself to, etc.[2]
s'arroger, lay claim to
se blottir, huddle (up)[2]
se démener, fling oneself (about)
se désister, stand down
s'écrier, cry out
s'écrouler, collapse[2]
s'efforcer, struggle
s'emparer (de), seize
s'empresser, hasten, bustle[2]
s'en aller, go away
s'enquérir, inquire
s'éprendre (de), fall in love with[2]
s'évader, escape[2]
s'évanouir, faint[2]
s'évertuer, strive
s'extasier, go into ecstasies
s'ingénier, contrive
se méfier (de), mistrust
se méprendre, be mistaken
se moquer (de), make fun of[1]
s'opiniâtrer, persist
se raviser, change one's mind
se rebeller, rebel
se récrier, cry out
se réfugier, take refuge[2]
se rengorger, puff oneself up
se repentir, repent[2]
se souvenir (de), remember

Notes

1 Although *se moquer de* is included in this list, the non-reflexive form *moquer* 'to mock' still sometimes occurs in a somewhat archaic literary usage and more generally in the passive, *être moqué* 'to be mocked'.

2 Note the following past participles:

(a) *adonné à* 'addicted to', *blotti* 'huddled (up)', *écroulé* 'collapsed, tumbledown', *épris de* 'enamoured of, in love with', *évanoui* 'unconscious, in a faint'

(b) corresponding to English present participles: *accoudé* 'leaning (on one's elbows)', *accroupi* 'crouching'

(c) used in an active sense: *empressé* 'attentive, assiduous', *repenti* 'penitent, repentant'

(d) used as nouns: *un(e) évadé(e)* 'escapee', *un(e) réfugié(e)* 'refugee'.

535 List 12(a)

The following verbs require *de* with a following infinitive. Most of them can also be used with *de* and a following noun or pronoun (or else the pronoun *en* – see **201**). Some of them also have the same construction when not reflexive.

> *s'affliger de*, grieve to
> *il s'agit de*, it is a question of
> *s'arrêter de*, stop . . .-ing
> *s'attrister de*, regret to
> *s'aviser de*, take it into one's head to
> *se charger de*, undertake to
> *se contenter de*, be content with, put up with
> *se dépêcher de*, hasten to
> *se désaccoutumer de* ⎫
> *se déshabituer de* ⎭ get out of the habit of
> *s'efforcer de*, struggle to[1]
> *s'empresser de*, be anxious to
> *s'ennuyer de*, be bored with
> *s'enorgueillir de*, pride oneself on
> *s'étonner de*, be surprised to
> *s'excuser de*, apologize for
> *se fâcher de*, be vexed at, to
> *se flatter de*, flatter oneself on

se garder de, take care not to
se glorifier de, be proud of
se hâter de, make haste to
s'impatienter de, long to, be dying to
s'indigner de, be indignant at, chafe at
s'inquiéter de, be anxious about, care for
s'irriter de, be angry at[2]
se lamenter de, lament
se lasser de, to weary of[3]
se mêler de, take it upon oneself to
s'occuper de, deal with[4]
s'offenser de, be offended at
se passer de, do without
se piquer de, pride oneself on
se plaindre de, complain of
se presser de, hurry to
se réjouir de, rejoice at, be glad to
se rengorger de, preen oneself on
se repentir de, regret, be sorry for
se soucier de, care for, or about
se souvenir de, remember
se vanter de, boast of

Examples:

Il s'est arrêté de travailler
He has stopped working

Il s'excuse d'être en retard
He apologizes for being late

Vous souvenez-vous de l'avoir vu?
Do you remember having seen him?

Note that a number of verbs that take *de* with a noun or pronoun (or else the pronoun *en* – see above) are not used with a following infinitive; they include:

s'apercevoir de, notice
se douter de, suspect
s'emparer de, seize
s'éprendre de, fall in love with
se jouer de, dupe
se méfier de, mistrust
se moquer de, make fun of

se munir de, provide oneself with
s'offenser de, be offended at
se tromper de, make a mistake about

Notes

1   *S'efforcer à faire quelque chose* also exists but is archaic.
2   With a following noun or pronoun, *s'irriter* takes *de* with reference to things but *contre* with reference to people.
3   *Se lasser à faire quelque chose* means 'to tire oneself out by doing something'.
4   *S'occuper à faire quelque chose* means 'to busy oneself, be engaged in doing something'.

536   List 12(b)

The following verbs require *à* with a following infinitive. Many of them can also be used with *à* and a following noun or pronoun (or else the pronoun *y* – see 200).

s'abaisser à, condescend to
s'accorder à, agree to [1]
s'accoutumer à, be accustomed to
s'acharner à, persist in, be bent on[2]
s'amuser à, enjoy . . .-ing
s'appliquer à, apply oneself to
s'apprêter à, get ready to, or for
s'astreindre à, bind oneself to
s'attacher à, be intent on
s'attendre à, expect to
se borner à, confine oneself to
se complaire à, take pleasure in
se dévouer à, devote oneself to[1]
se disposer à, arrange to, prepare to
s'égayer à, be highly amused at . . .-ing
s'employer à, apply oneself to
s'engager à, undertake to
s'entendre à, know how to, be expert in
s'entêter à, persist in
s'essayer à, try one's hand at
s'évertuer à, strive to
se fatiguer à, wear oneself out with[3]
s'habituer à, get used to
se hasarder à, risk
s'intéresser à, be interested in

se lasser à, tire oneself out by[4]
se mettre à, begin to
s'obliger à, bind oneself to
s'obstiner à, persist in
s'occuper à, busy oneself with[5]
s'offrir à, offer to
se plaire à, delight in
se prendre à, begin to
se refuser à, refuse to
se résigner à, resign oneself to
se résoudre à, resolve to

Examples:

Je m'attends à recevoir bientôt de vos nouvelles
I expect to hear from you soon

Je m'habitue à me coucher de bonne heure
I am getting used to going to bed early

Il s'est mis à pleurer
He began to cry

A few verbs that take *à* with a noun or pronoun (or else the pronoun *y* – see above) are not used with a following infinitive; they include:

s'adresser à, apply to, be directed at
se fier à, trust
s'opposer à, oppose
s'en prendre à, blame

Notes:
1 *S'accorder* and *se dévouer* can also take *pour*, e.g. *Ils se sont accordés pour voyager ensemble* 'They agreed to travel together'.
2 *S'acharner* in the sense of 'pursue a person relentlessly' takes *après*, *contre* or *sur*.
3 Note that the past participle *fatigué* 'tired (of)' takes *de*.
4 For *se lasser* with *de* or *à*, see 535, note 3.
5 For *s'occuper* with *de* or *à*, see 535, note 4.

537 List 13. **Unclassified**
The following verbs do not lend themselves to classification. They mostly have more than one sense and more than one construction, and the construction usually alters with the sense.

approcher

1 Transitive: 'bring near (or nearer)' ('to' *de*), e.g.:

> *Approchez la table du feu*
> Bring the table near (*or* nearer to) the fire

2 Intransitive: may be used (a) literally, (b) metaphorically:

(a) 'come, get near (or nearer) ('to' *de*), e.g.:

> *Nous approchons de Paris*
> We are getting near (*or* nearer to) Paris

(b) 'come near' (to, *de*), e.g.:

> *L'éléphant est l'animal qui approche le plus de l'homme par l'intelligence*
> The elephant is the animal which comes nearest to man in intelligence

> *Il approchait de dix ans*
> He was nearly ten years old

3 *s'approcher de* (reflexive), only used literally, 'come, draw near'; whereas *approcher de* refers only to the fact of drawing near(er), *s'approcher* usually implies an intention to do so, e.g.:

> *Il s'approcha de la porte*
> He walked towards the door

> *Elle s'approcha de moi*
> She came up to me

changer has many meanings, including the following (for others, consult a good dictionary):

1 Transitive:

(a) 'change, alter', e.g.:

> *Il a changé ses habitudes*
> He has changed his habits

> *Je veux changer un billet de banque*
> I want to change a bank-note

(b) '(ex)change one thing for another (*contre* or *pour*)', e.g.:

> *Je vais changer ma voiture contre* (or *pour*) *une nouvelle*
> I am going to change my car for a new one

(c) *changer en* 'to change one thing into another, transform', e.g.:

> *Circé changea en bêtes les compagnons d'Ulysse*
> Circe changed the companions of Ulysses into animals

2 Intransitive:

(a) 'change (i.e. become different)', e.g.:

> *Le temps va changer*
> The weather is going to change
>
> *Vous n'avez pas changé du tout*
> You haven't changed at all

(b) 'change (trains, etc.)', e.g.:

> *Il faut changer à Dijon*
> You have to change at Dijon

(c) *changer de* 'change, alter' – in the sense of transference from one place, position, idea, etc., to another – is used in a large number of idioms, e.g.:

changer d'avis	to change one's mind
changer de train	to change (trains)
changer de route	to take another road
changer de place	to change one's seat
changer de coiffure	to change one's hair-style

3 Reflexive:

(a) 'to change, turn into', e.g.:

> *Les souris de Cendrillon se sont changées en chevaux*
> Cinderella's mice turned into horses

(In this sense, *se transformer* is very often used.)

(b) 'to change (one's clothes)', e.g.:

> *Il faut que je me change avant de sortir*
> I must change before I go out

convenir

1 Personal, with an indirect object, 'suit, be fitting, agree with', e.g.:

> *Ses vêtements conviennent à sa position*
> His clothes suit (are in keeping with) his position

Ce climat ne leur convient pas
This climate does not suit them (agree with them)

2 Impersonal followed by *de* and an infinitive, 'to be fitting, appropriate, advisable', e.g.:

Il convient de ne pas trop en parler
It is advisable not to say too much about it

3 *Convenir de* 'to agree'

(a) with an infinitive, e.g.:

Nous avons convenu d'y être à midi
We have agreed to be there at noon

(b) with a noun or pronoun (including *en* 'of it, of them' – see 201), e.g.:

Nous allons convenir du prix
We are going to agree on the price

(c) note *être convenu de* with either an infinitive or a noun or pronoun, 'to be in agreement', e.g.:

Nous sommes convenus de nous taire
We are in agreement to say nothing

Nous sommes convenus du prix
We are agreed on the price

4 *Convenir de* with a noun or pronoun (including *en* – see 201), 'to acknowledge, recognize, admit', e.g.:

Il a convenu de son erreur
He has acknowledged his mistake

J'ai eu tort – j'en conviens
I was wrong – I admit it

coûter 'to cost'

1 Indirect object of the person, direct object of the price, e.g.:

Cela lui coûtera mille francs
That will cost him a thousand francs

La guerre a coûté la vie à des milliers d'hommes
The war cost thousands of men their lives

2 With *à* and an infinitive to express the nature of the expense, e.g.:

Combien un cheval coûte-t-il à nourrir?
How much does a horse cost to feed?

3 Impersonal with *de* and an infinitive, e.g.:

Il ne coûte rien d'être poli
It costs nothing to be polite

4 *En coûter (à quelqu'un)* 'to be painful, difficult', with *de* and an infinitive, e.g.:

Il lui en coûtera de les quitter
It will be a wrench for him to leave them

décider ⎫
déterminer ⎬ 'decide, settle, induce, be determined'

1 When transitive, reflexive or passive, take *à* with the infinitive; when intransitive, take *de* with the infinitive, e.g.:

On n'a pu décider (déterminer) que trois cents soldats à monter à l'assaut
Only three hundred soldiers could be induced to go into the attack

Il s'est décidé (déterminé) à partir
He has decided to start

Nous sommes décidés (déterminés) à y aller
We are determined to go

Il a décidé (déterminé) de renvoyer son domestique
He has decided to dismiss his servant

2 'Decide, settle upon', with a direct object, e.g.:

déterminer un rendez-vous
to settle on a meeting-place

décider une querelle
to settle a quarrel

3 *Décider* (but not *déterminer*) can be used with *de* before a noun or pronoun (or else the pronoun *en* – see **201**) in the sense of 'deciding (on or about), coming to a decision about', e.g.:

des événements qui décident de la fortune des empires
events which decide the fate of empires

Le gouvernement a décidé de l'avenir du projet
The government has decided on the future of the project

Le comité en décidera
The committee will decide about it

défier

1 'Challenge (to any form of competition)', direct object followed by *à* with noun or infinitive, e.g.:

défier quelqu'un $\left\{ \begin{array}{l} \textit{aux échecs} \\ \textit{à se battre en duel} \end{array} \right\}$

to challenge someone $\left\{ \begin{array}{l} \text{to a game of chess} \\ \text{to fight a duel} \end{array} \right\}$

2 'Defy someone to (suggesting that he cannot do something)', direct object followed by *de* with infinitive, e.g.:

Je vous défie de deviner cette énigme
I defy you to guess this riddle

3 'Defy' (with direct object), e.g.:

instruit à défier le péril et la mort
taught to defy danger and death

4 Reflexive, *se défier de* 'distrust', e.g.:

Nous nous défions de nous-mêmes
We distrust ourselves

In this sense *se méfier* is commoner.

devoir

1 'Owe', e.g.:

Je lui dois mille francs
I owe him a thousand francs

2 In simple tenses (other than the conditional – see 3 below), when followed by an infinitive, 'be to' or 'have to' or, sometimes, 'must' (but see also 510), e.g.:

Je dois y aller demain
I am to (have to) go there tomorrow

Cela doit être vrai
That must be true

Il devait partir le lendemain
He was to leave the next day

Je devrai lui écrire
I shall have to write to him

Je dus y aller
I had to go there

3 In the conditional when followed by an infinitive, 'ought' or 'should' (expressing obligation) – see 511 and 512,iii

4 In compound tenses when followed by an infinitive, two quite distinct meanings (see also 510,ii):

Il a dû écrire à son frère
(a) He had to write to his brother
(b) He must have written to his brother

Je supposais qu'il avait dû le faire
(a) I supposed that he had had to do it
(b) I supposed that he must have done it

5 For *devoir* and an infinitive as the equivalent of a future subjunctive, see 506

6 The past participle, used adjectivally, means 'due' or 'owing', e.g.:

Il a payé la somme due à ses créanciers
He has paid the sum due to his creditors

falloir (impersonal only)

1 'Be necessary, be required, must'

(a) with *que* and the subjunctive, e.g.:

Il faut qu'il parte   He must go

(b) dative of personal pronoun and infinitive without a preposition, e.g.:

Il leur faut le voir
It is necessary for them to (they must) see him

(c) dative of object (noun or pronoun) with a noun in apparent apposition to *il*, e.g.:

... un cahier
... needs a notebook

(d) dative of object (noun or pronoun) with a noun in apparent apposition to *il* followed by an infinitive with *pour*, e.g.:

> *Il faudra des heures à nos amis pour y arriver*
> Our friends will require hours to get there

In connection with all these uses notice the common use of *le* to avoid repetition, e.g.:

> *Il viendra s'il le faut* (i.e. *s'il lui faut venir*)
> He will come if necessary

2 *S'en falloir* 'be lacking'

(a) with an expression of amount introduced by *de*, e.g.:

> *Le compte n'y est pas; il s'en faut de cinq francs*
> The account is wrong; it is five francs short

> So *Il s'en faut de beaucoup* 'Far from it'.

(b) The same expressions followed by *que* and the subjunctive mean 'it is far from being the case that. . .', e.g.:

> *Il s'en faut de beaucoup que je le comprenne*
> I am far from understanding it

(c) So also with *peu*, e.g.:

> *Peu s'en* $\left\{ \begin{array}{l} \textit{fallut} \\ \textit{faut} \end{array} \right\}$) *qu'il ne* $\left\{ \begin{array}{l} \textit{fût} \\ \textit{soit} \end{array} \right\}$ *tombé*

> He very nearly fell

(d) Similar constructions without *de*, e.g. *Il s'en faut beaucoup* (or *peu*), *Il s'en faut cinq francs* still exist in the literary language but are not in general use and should not be imitated.

manquer

Manquer is used in a variety of constructions and with a number of different meanings of which the following are the most important (for the whole range of meanings, consult a good dictionary):

1 Transitive, 'miss, fail in, etc.', e.g.:

manquer un train	to miss a train
manquer une classe	to miss a class

> *Je les ai manqués à la gare*   I missed them at the station
> *Il a manqué son coup*   He failed in his attempt

.2 Intransitive:

(a) 'fail' (*échouer* is more usual in this sense), e.g.:

> *L'expérience a manqué*   The experiment failed

(b) 'be lacking, missing', with, when necessary, *à* = 'from' and/or *de* and an infinitive, e.g.:

> *La première page manque à ce livre*
> The first page is missing from this book
>
> *Rien ne manque*
> Nothing is missing
>
> *Les occasions ne m'ont pas manqué de visiter Paris*
> I haven't lacked opportunities to visit Paris

(c) *manquer à* 'fail (someone), fail in (something)', etc, e.g.:

> *Les mots me manquent*   Words fail me
> *manquer à son devoir*   to fail in one's duty
> *manquer à sa promesse*   to break one's promise

Note the idiom *A manque à B* = 'B misses A' (i.e. 'regrets his absence'), e.g.:

> *Elle me manque beaucoup*
> I miss her a lot

(d) *manquer de* 'lack (= not have any of, or enough of)', e.g.:

> *Il manque de patience*
> He lacks patience
>
> *Je manque de temps pour le faire*
> I haven't (enough) time to do it

3 *Manquer* followed by an infinitive

(a) *manquer de faire* or *manquer faire* translated by 'nearly', e.g.:

> *J'ai manqué (de) tomber*
> I nearly fell

(*Faillir* is more usual in this sense, e.g. *J'ai failli tomber.*)

(b) *ne pas manquer de faire* 'not to fail to do', e.g.:

Ne manquez pas de nous écrire
Don't fail to write to us (*or* Mind you write to us)

Je ne manquerai pas de vous le dire
I shan't fail to tell you

In the negative (as in the above examples), this construction is still in current use. In the affirmative, however, *manquer de faire* and its alternative *manquer à faire* are now characteristic only of a somewhat archaic literary usage; *négliger de* 'to neglect to' or *omettre de* 'to omit to' should be used instead for 'to fail to do something' in the sense of 'not to do', e.g.:

Il a négligé de répondre à ma lettre
He failed to answer my letter

4 Impersonal 'be missing, lacking', with, when necessary, *à* = 'from', e.g.:

Il ne manque pas de candidats
There is no shortage of candidates

Il manque vingt pages à ce livre
There are twenty pages missing from this book

Il nous manque cent francs
We are a hundred francs short

5 Impersonal and reflexive, *s'en manquer*

Il s'en manque is a less widely used equivalent of *il s'en faut* (see above under *falloir*), e.g.:

Il s'en manque de beaucoup   Far from it

rester

1 'Remain, stay', e.g.:

J'y suis, j'y reste
Here I am and here I stay

Elle y est restée dix jours
She stayed there for ten days

2 'Remain, be left (over)' e.g.:

tout ce qui reste
all that remains

les quelques amis qui lui restaient
the few friends who remained to him (that he had left)

With reference to precise amounts remaining, the impersonal construction (see 3 below) is more usual.

Note the construction in which the verb comes first and is translated into English as 'there remain(s), there remained', etc., e.g.:

Restait le problème des pays en voie de développement
There remained the problem of the developing countries

Restent deux solutions
There remain two solutions

3 Impersonal, 'to be left', with an indirect object of the person, e.g.:

Il ne leur restait que cent francs
They had only a hundred francs left (*lit.* there remained to them only a hundred francs)

4 Impersonal with *à* and the infinitive, 'it remains to', e.g.:

Il ne me reste qu'à vous remercier de votre bonté
It only remains for me to thank you for your kindness

Reste à voir
It remains to be seen

5 *En rester à* 'stop, stop at', e.g.:

Où en sommes-nous restés? Nous en sommes restés à la page deux cent
Where did we stop? We stopped at page two hundred

servir

1 Transitive, 'serve' in a wide range of contexts, including the following:

(a) 'be of service to (a person, a cause)', e.g.:

servir le roi	to serve the king
servir un client	to serve a customer
servir la cause de la paix	to serve the cause of peace

(b) with a thing as direct object, e.g.:

> *servir la balle* to serve the ball (at tennis)
> *servir un repas* to serve a meal

2 Intransitive, in various senses, e.g.:

> *J'ai servi pendant la guerre*
> I served in the war
>
> *Il sert dans un café*
> He serves (i.e. he is a waiter) in a café
>
> *C'est à vous de servir*
> It is you to serve (*or* your service) (at tennis)

3 *Servir à* 'be of use to or for, be for', with a noun or pronoun or with an infinitive (N.B. an infinitive representing the subject is introduced by *de*), e.g.:

> *Cela ne sert à rien*
> That is (of) no use
>
> *Mes paroles ne servaient qu'à l'irriter*
> My words only served to annoy him
>
> *Une pelle sert à creuser des trous*
> A spade is for digging holes
>
> *A quoi sert de pleurer?*
> What is the use of crying? (i.e. What purpose does crying serve?)

4 *Servir de* 'serve as, act as', e.g.:

> *Mon nom sert de rempart à toute la Castille*
> My name serves as a bulwark to all Castile
>
> *Je lui ai servi d'interprète*
> I acted as interpreter for him
>
> *Cette pièce sert de salle à manger*
> This room serves as a dining-room

5 *Se servir*

(a) 'help oneself (to food)', e.g.:

> *Servez-vous (de légumes)*
> Help yourself (to some vegetables)

Je me suis servi de poisson
I've taken some fish

(b) *se servir de* 'use, make use of' e.g.:

Il vaut mieux vous servir d'un dictionnaire
You had better use a dictionary

tarder

1 'Delay, linger, be a long time (doing)', with *à* and an infinitive where necessary, e.g.:

Vous avez tardé à venir
You have been a long time coming

Il ne va pas tarder
He won't be long

Je suis venu sans tarder
I came without delay

2 Impersonal, 'long to, be impatient to', with dative of the person and *de* with the infinitive, e.g.:

Il lui tarde de partir
He is longing to start

traiter

1 'To treat (a person)' – 'as' is either *comme (un)* or *en*, e.g.:

Il me traitait durement
He used to treat me harshly

traiter un malade
to treat a patient

Traitez-moi comme (un) ami
Treat me as a friend

traiter quelqu'un en enfant
to treat someone as a child

2 *Traiter quelqu'un de* 'call someone something', e.g.:

Il nous a traités d'imbéciles
He called us fools

3 *Traiter un sujet* and *traiter d'un sujet*, 'deal with'

Traiter un sujet implies a systematic treatment of a subject, whereas *traiter d'un sujet* implies no more than that the subject is dealt with in the book, article, etc., in question, perhaps even only incidentally, e.g.:

> *Ce rapport traite le problème de l'énergie nucléaire*
> This report deals with the problem of nuclear energy
>
> *Tous ses romans traitent du problème des relations entre parents et enfants*
> All his novels deal with the problem of relations between parents and children

venir

1 'Come (and)' – *venir* and infinitive, i.e. no word for 'and' and no preposition, e.g.:

Venez me voir demain	Come and see me tomorrow
Il est venu me remercier	He came to thank me

2 *Venir de* 'to have just', e.g.:

Je viens de lui écrire	I have just written to him
Il venait de les voir	He had just seen them

This construction does not occur with tenses other than the present (for 'have just, has just') and the imperfect (for 'had just').

3 *Venir à* with an infinitive, 'happen to', e.g.:

> *Un de mes amis vint à passer*
> · One of my friends happened to pass
>
> *Si vous veniez à le voir*
> · If you happened to see him

4 *En venir à* with a noun or an infinitive, 'come to, turn to, be reduced to, etc.', e.g.:

> *J'en viens maintenant au problème principal*
> I now come (*or* turn) to the main problem
>
> *Il en était venu à mendier*
> He had been reduced to begging

5 For the difference between *Il vient à moi* 'He comes to me', etc., and *L'idée me vient que . . .* 'The idea comes to me that . . .', etc., see 220,i.

538   Alphabetical list of the verbs in 521–537

(Verbs that can occur either reflexively or non-reflexively, e.g. *arrêter, s'arrêter,* are indexed only under the non-reflexive form.)

abaisser	12 b	*apprendre*	7 b, 10
aboutir	7 b	*apprêter*	12 b
abreuver	5 a	*approcher*	13
abriter	5 a	*approuver*	3
s'abstenir	11	*armer*	4 a
abuser	1	*arracher*	4 b
accabler	4 a	*arrêter*	12 a
accompagner	5 a	*s'arroger*	11
accorder	9, 12 b	*aspirer*	7 b
s'accouder	11	*assister*	5 b
accourir	6 b	*assurer*	6 a
accoutumer	7 a, 8 b, 12 b	*astreindre*	8 b, 12 b
s'accroupir	11	*attacher*	12 b
accuser	8 a	*attendre*	3, 12 b
acharner	12 b	*attenter*	2
acheter	4 b	*attrister*	12 a
achever	7 a	*autoriser*	8 b
admettre	3, 8 b	*avertir*	8 a
s'adonner	11	*aviser*	12 a
adorer	6 c	*avoir*	7 b
adresser	12 b	*avouer*	6 a
affecter	7 a	*balancer*	7 b
affirmer	6 a	*bénir*	5 a
affliger	12 a	*blâmer*	8 a
affranchir	5 a	*se blottir*	11
s'agit, il	12 a	*borner*	12 b
aider	8 b	*broder*	4 a
aimer	7 b	*brûler*	4 a, 7 a
aimer autant	6 c	*cacher*	4 b
aimer mieux	6 c	*celer*	4 b
s'alarmer	5 a	*cesser*	7 a
aller	2, 6 b	*chagriner*	12 a
s'en aller	11	*changer*	13
ambitionner	7 a	*charger*	4 a, 8 a, 12 a
amener	8 b	*chercher*	3, 7 b
amuser	12 b	*choisir*	7 a
animer	8 b	*coiffer*	4 a
apercevoir	12 a	*combler*	4 a
appeler	8 b	*commander*	9
applaudir	8 a	*commencer*	7 a, 7 b
appliquer	12 b	*compatir*	5 b
appréhender	7 a	*complaire*	12 b

complimenter	5 a	*dépendre*	5 a
compter	6 c	*dépenser*	8 b
concourir	7 b	*déplaire*	2, 9
condamner	8 b	*déposer*	6 a
condescendre	7 b	*dérober*	4 b
conduire	8 b	*désaccoutumer*	12 a
confesser	6 a	*descendre*	6 b, 7 b
conjurer	8 a	*désespérer*	7 a
connaître	5 b	*déshabituer*	12 a
conseiller	9	*désirer*	6 c
consentir	7 b	*se désister*	11
consister	7 b	*désobéir*	2
conspirer	7 b	*destiner*	8 b
contenter	12 a	*déterminer*	8 b, 13
continuer	7a, 7 b	*détester*	6 c, 7 a
contraindre	8 a, 8 b	*détourner*	8 a
contrevenir	2	*devoir*	6 c, 13
contribuer	7 b	*dévouer*	12 b
convenir	2, 13	*différer*	7 a
convier	8 b	*dîner*	5 a
coucher en joue	3	*dire*	2, 6 a, 9
courir	6 b	*discontinuer*	7 a
couronner	4 a	*dispenser*	8 a
coûter	13	*disposer*	8 b, 12 b
couvrir	4 a	*dissuader*	8 a
craindre	7 a	*donner*	10
cribler	4 a	*douer*	4 a
crier	9	*douter*	1, 12 a
croire	5 b, 6 a	*dresser*	8 b
daigner	6 c	*échapper*	4 b
débarrasser	5 a	*écouter*	3, 6 c
décider	7 a, 13	*écraser*	4 a
déclarer	6 a	*s'écrier*	11
dédaigner	7 a	*écrire*	9
défendre	2, 9	*s'écrouler*	11
défier	13	*s'efforcer*	11, 12 a
dégoûter	8 a	*égayer*	12 b
déjeuner	5 a	*éloigner*	5 a
délivrer	5 a	*embarrasser*	5 a
demander	2, 3, 9	*s'emparer*	11, 12 a
se démener	11	*empêcher*	8 a
démettre	12 a	*employer*	5 b, 8 b, 12 b
démordre	1	*s'empresser*	11, 12 a
dépêcher	12 a	*emprunter*	4 b

encombrer	5 a	*finir*	7 a
encourager	8 b	*flatter*	12 a
engager	8 b, 12 b	*forcer*	8 a, 8 b
enjoindre	9	*fourmiller*	4 a
enlever	4 b	*fournir*	3, 4 a
ennuyer	12 a	*frémir*	7 a
enorgueillir	12 a	*gagner*	7 b
s'enquérir	11	*garder*	12 a
enrager	7 a	*gémir*	4 a, 7 a
enseigner	10	*glorifier*	12 a
entendre	6 c, 12 b	*grever*	4 a
entêter	12 b	*grimper*	2
entourer	4 a	*gronder*	8 a
entremêler	4 a	*grouiller*	4 a
entreprendre	7 a	*habiter*	3
entrer	2	*habituer*	8 b, 12 b
envelopper	5 a	*haïr*	7 a
environner	4 a	*hasarder*	7 a, 12 b
envoyer	6 b	*hâter*	12 a
envoyer chercher	3	*hérisser*	5 a
s'éprendre	11, 12 a	*hériter*	1
escalader	3	*hésiter*	7 b
espérer	3, 6 c	*imaginer*	6 c
essayer	7 a, 12 b	*impatienter*	12 a
étonner	12 a	*importer*	9
s'évader	11	*inciter*	8 b
s'évanouir	11	*incliner*	8 b
s'évertuer	11, 12 b	*indigner*	12 a
éviter	7 a	*induire*	8 b
exceller	7 b	*s'ingénier*	11
exciter	8 b	*inquiéter*	12 a
excuser	8 a, 12 a	*insulter*	2
exercer	8 b	*intéresser*	12 b
exhorter	8 b	*inviter*	8 b
exposer	8 b	*irriter*	12 a
s'extasier	11	*jouer*	1, 2, 12 a
fâcher	12 a	*jouir*	1
faillir	6 c	*juger*	6 a
faire	4 a, 6 c	*jurer*	6 a, 7 a, 9
falloir	6 c, 13	*laisser*	6 c, 7 a, 10
fatiguer	12 b	*lamenter*	12 a
feindre	7 a	*lasser*	12 a, 12 b
féliciter	8 a	*louer* (hire)	4 b
figurer	6 c	*louer* (praise)	8 a

manquer	7 a, 13	*penser*	5 b, 6 a
médire	1	*permettre*	2, 9
méditer	7 a	*persévérer*	7 b
se méfier	11, 12 a	*persister*	7 b
mêler	5 b, 12 a	*persuader*	8 a, 9
menacer	4 a, 7 a	*piquer*	12 a
mener	6 b	*plaindre*	8 a, 12 a
se méprendre	11	*plaire*	2, 9, 12 b
mériter	7 a	*planter*	4 a
mettre	8 b, 12 b	*porter*	8 b
monter	6 b	*pourvoir*	4 a, 5 b
montrer	10	*pousser*	8 b
se moquer	5 a, 11, 12 a	*pouvoir*	6 c
mourir	7 a	*préférer*	6 c
munir	4 a, 12 a	*prendre*	4 b, 12 b
négliger	7 a	*préparer*	8 b
nier	6 a	*prescrire*	9
nourrir	5 a	*présider*	5 b
nuire	2	*presser*	8 a, 12 a
obéir	2	*prétendre*	6 a, 7 b
obliger	8 a, 8 b, 12 b	*prier*	8 a
s'obstiner	12 b	*projeter*	7 a
obtenir	7 a	*promettre*	2, 7 a, 9
obvier	2	*proposer*	9
occuper	12 a, 12 b	*protester*	6 a
offenser	12 a	*provoquer*	8 b
offrir	7 a, 9, 10, 12 b	*punir*	8 a
omettre	7 a	*se raviser*	11
s'opiniâtrer	11	*se rebeller*	11
opposer	12 b	*recommander*	9
ordonner	9	*recommencer*	7 a, 7 b
orner	4 a	*reconnaître*	5 b, 6 a
oser	6 c	*se récrier*	11
ôter	4 b	*redoubler*	1
oublier	7 a	*réduire*	8 b
ouïr	6 c	*réfléchir*	5 b
paraître	6 c	*se réfugier*	11
pardonner	2, 9	*refuser*	2, 7 a, 12 b
parer	4 a	*regarder*	3, 6 c
parler	7 a, 9	*regorger*	4 a
parvenir	2, 7 b	*regretter*	7 a
passer	5 a, 7 b, 8 b, 12 a	*réjouir*	12 a
payer	3	*remédier*	2
pencher	7 b	*remercier*	8 a
pendre	5 b	*remplir*	4 a

rencontrer	3	suspendre	5 b
se rengorger	11, 12 a	tacher	4 a
renoncer	2, 7 b	tâcher	7 a
repaître	5 a	tapisser	4 a
se repentir	11, 12 a	tarder	13
répondre	2, 5 a	témoigner	6 a
reprendre	8 a	tendre	7 b
reprocher	3, 9	tenir	5 a, 7 b
répugner	7 b, 9	tenter	7 a
réserver	5 b	toucher	2
résigner	12 b	traiter	13
résister	2	travailler	7 b
résoudre	8 b	trembler	4 a, 7 a
ressembler	2	triompher	5 a
rester	13	tromper	12 a
retirer	4 b	trouver	7 b
retourner	6 b	user	1
réussir	7 b	valoir autant	6 c
revenir	6 b	valoir mieux	6 c
rire	5 a, 7 a	vanter	12 a
risquer	7 a	veiller	5 b
rougir	5 a, 7 a	venir	6 b, 13
savoir	6 c	vêtir	4 a
sembler	6 c	viser	3, 7 b
semer	4 a	vivre	5 a
sentir	6 c	voir	6 c
servir	13	voler	4 b
sommer	8 a	vouloir	6 c
songer	5 b, 7 b		a
se soucier	12 a		
souffrir	7 a	*List*	*Paragraph(s)*
souhaiter	6 c, 7 a	1 =	521
souiller	4 a	2 .=	522
soupçonner	8 a	3 =	523
soustraire	4 b	4 =	524
soutenir	6 a, 7 a	5 =	525
se souvenir	11, 12 a	6 =	527
subvenir	2	7 =	528–529
succéder	2	8 =	530–531
suffire	7 b	9 =	532
suggérer	9	10 =	533
supplier	8 a	11 =	534
surseoir	2	12 =	535–536
survivre	2	13 =	537

S Idioms with *avoir, être, faire*

539 Idioms with *avoir*

(a) where *avoir* with a noun is represented in English by 'to be' with an adjective, the noun in French having no article:

avoir faim, to be hungry
avoir soif, to be thirsty
avoir froid, to be cold
avoir chaud, to be hot
avoir dix ans, to be ten years old
avoir raison, to be right
avoir tort, to be wrong
avoir honte, to be ashamed
avoir peur, to be frightened
avoir sommeil, to be sleepy

(b) where *avoir* with a noun is followed by *de* or *à* and a noun, pronoun or infinitive:

avoir affaire à, to have to deal with
avoir besoin de, to need, have need of
avoir envie de, to want, feel inclined to
avoir pitié de, to have pity on
avoir soin de, to take care of

(c) where *avoir* with a noun is translated by various English verbs, e.g.:

Il eut une exclamation d'étonnement
He uttered an exclamation of surprise

Il eut un sourire amical
He gave a friendly smile

Il eut un mouvement de colère
He made an angry gesture

(d) where *avoir* is preceded by *en*, e.g.:

J'en ai assez
I have had enough, I am sick of it

J'en ai pour des années

I have enough $\left\{ \begin{array}{l} \text{to keep me busy} \\ \text{to last me} \end{array} \right\}$ for years

C'est à vous qu'il en a
It is you that he is cross with

(e) Notice also

avoir la vue longue
to have long sight, to be long-sighted

avoir la vue $\left\{ \begin{array}{l} \textit{courte} \\ \textit{basse} \end{array} \right.$

to have short sight, to be short-sighted

Qu'avez-vous?
What is the matter with you?

avoir $\left\{ \begin{array}{l} \textit{bonne} \\ \textit{mauvaise} \end{array} \right\}$ *mine*

to look $\left\{ \begin{array}{l} \text{well} \\ \text{ill} \end{array} \right.$

avoir l'air
to look, seem

e.g.:

Elle a l'air distrait (or *distraite*)
She looks preoccupied (as if she were thinking of something else) (the adjective may agree either with the subject or with *air*)

Elle a l'air de nous avoir oubliés
She seems to have forgotten us

540 Idioms with *être*

être bien (or *mal*) *avec quelqu'un*
to be on good (or bad) terms with someone

y être	to see the point
cela étant	this being so
ainsi soit-il	1, so be it; 2, amen

en être

en être à	to have come to, to have got to
en être pour	to be let in for, spend in vain;
C'en est trop!	That's a bit too much!
C'en est assez!	Enough of that! That will do!
en être de (impers.)	to be with

Examples:

Ah! j'y suis; d'abord je ne vous avais pas bien compris
Oh! I see; I did not understand you at first

J'en suis au dernier chapitre
I have got to the last chapter

Ils en étaient à mourir de faim
They had reached starvation point

Vous en serez pour dix mille francs
You will be out of pocket to the tune of ten thousand francs

Il en est de lui comme de ses camarades
It is with him as with his companions

s'en fut

Être with *s'en* is also used, in the preterite only (mostly in the 3rd sing.), in the sense of *aller* or *s'en aller*. When so used, it is followed, if the sense requires, by an infinitive without a preposition; e.g.:

Ce disant il s'en fut
So saying he made off (departed)

La voyant dans l'allée il s'en fut démarrer le moteur
Seeing her on the drive he went off to start the engine

541 Idioms with *faire*

faire accueil (or *bon accueil*) *à*	1. to welcome; 2. to give favourable consideration to
faire mauvais accueil à	to give a cold reception to
faire face à	face (literally and metaphorically)
faire honte à	shame, put to shame
faire horreur à	horrify, be repugnant to
faire mal à	hurt
faire du mal (du bien) à	do harm (good) to

faire tort à, faire du tort à	do damage to, wrong
faire plaisir à	give pleasure to
faire signe à	beckon, signal to
faire part à quelqu'un de quelque chose	inform someone of something
faire cas de	value
faire attention (à)	pay attention (to)
faire naufrage	be shipwrecked
faire peur à	frighten
faire pitié	arouse pity
faire semblant de	pretend to
c'en est fait de	it is all up with

Faire alone, like the English 'does', 'have', etc., is used as a substitute for a verb which would otherwise have to be repeated, e.g.:

Il mange des escargots comme le font les Français
He eats snails as the French do

Il est merveilleux qu'ils aient tenu bon comme ils l'ont fait
It is wonderful that they have held out as they have

This is not possible when the subsitute verb is stressed in English, in which case various corresponding expressions are found in French, e.g.:

She sings well. – Yes, she does
Elle chante bien. – Oui, en effet (or *c'est vrai*)

He doesn't like cheese. – Yes he does!
Il n'aime pas le fromage. – Mais si!

'Make' must be translated by *rendre*, not by *faire*, when the sense is 'to cause someone or something to become what they were not previously', and the new condition is described by an adjective, e.g.:

La guerre l'a rendu très pauvre
The war made him very poor

But this rule does not apply to the reflexive *se faire* 'become, get', e.g.:

Il se fait tard
It is getting late

Le bruit se faisait insupportable
The noise was becoming intolerable

The Structure of the Sentence

Negation

Introduction

542 We shall discuss negation under the following headings:
- A: Negation with a verb
- B: The negative conjunction *ni* 'neither, nor'
- C: Negation of an element other than a verb

A *Negation with a verb*

Introduction

543 Negation with a verb is expressed by the use of *ne* (or *n'* before a vowel or mute *h*) before the verb and, in most cases, of another element which may be a determiner (*aucun, nul* 'no, not any'), a pronoun (*personne* 'nobody', *rien* 'nothing', *aucun, nul*), an adverb (*aucunement, nullement* 'in no way, not at all', *guère* 'hardly, scarcely', *jamais* 'never', *plus* '(no) longer', *que* 'only', and what are often termed the negative particles *pas* and *point* 'not'). Some of these elements always follow the verb, others may either precede or follow depending on meaning or on the degree of emphasis they carry. All are discussed at greater length below.

Note that *faire* must not be used as the equivalent of 'do' in negative constructions, e.g.:

Ils ne parlent pas français
They do not speak French

For the use of *ne* alone, see **559–567**.

Ne and another element

ne . . . pas, ne . . . point *'not'*

544 (i) The normal way of making a verb negative is to use *ne*
. . . *pas*. *Pas* comes immediately after the verb or, in compound
tenses, after the auxiliary (but see also ii below), e.g.:

Je ne viens pas
I am not coming

Il n'est pas venu
He has not come

Mon frère ne la connaissait pas
My brother did not know her

However, *ne pas* come together before an infinitive, e.g.:

Je préfère ne pas le voir
I prefer not to see him

Je suis content de ne pas le lui avoir dit
I am glad not to have told him

(The construction *ne* + infinitive + *pas* exists but is archaic and
should not be imitated.)

(ii) Nothing can come between the verb (or auxiliary) and *pas*
except the subject pronoun in a negative-interrogative clause or
certain adverbs, mainly adverbs of affirmation or doubt (see
627–628), such as *certainement* 'certainly', *même* 'even', *peut-être*
'perhaps', *probablement* 'probably', *sûrement* 'certainly' and the
adverbial phrase *sans doute* 'doubtless', e.g.:

Ne vient-il pas?
Isn't he coming?

Ne vous l'avions-nous pas dit?
Had we not told you?

Il ne viendra certainement pas
He certainly won't come

Il ne m'a même pas regardé
He did not even look at me

Vous ne l'avez peut-être pas vu
Perhaps you did not see him

Il ne la connaissait probablement pas
He probably didn't know her

The only items that can come between *ne* and the verb are the conjunctive personal pronouns, *me, le, vous*, etc. – see 387,ii,d, and some of the examples quoted above.

(iii) The only case in which *pas* can precede the verb is when it forms part of the expression *pas un (seul)* 'not (a single) one' as subject of the verb, e.g.:

De tous mes amis, pas un (seul) n'a voulu m'aider
Of all my friends, not one was willing to help me

Pas un oiseau ne chantait dans la forêt
Not a single bird was singing in the forest

545 Some grammars state that *point* expresses a 'stronger' negation than *pas* (some, indeed, go so far as to translate it as 'not at all'). **This is not so.** For 'not at all', some such expression as *pas du tout* or *absolument pas* must be used. *Point* nowadays is used mainly by writers who wish to give a slightly archaic or a provincial flavour to their French. Many modern writers never use it and foreigners are well advised to avoid it altogether.

Note that, although (subject to the above remarks) *point* could replace *pas* in any of the examples given in **544** (i) and (ii), it cannot be substituted for *pas* in *pas un* – see **544** (iii).

546   *aucun* 'no, not any, etc.'

Aucun is used:

(i) In the singular only, as a pronoun, e.g.:

Aucun de mes amis n'est venu
Not one of my friends came

Aucune de ces raisons n'est valable
None of these reasons is valid

De tous mes amis, aucun ne m'a aidé
Of all my friends, not one helped me

In compound tenses it follows the past participle, e.g.:

Je n'en ai acheté aucun
I did not buy one (any) of them

(ii) As a determiner, e.g.:

Aucun exemple ne me vient à l'esprit
No example comes to my mind

Je n'ai aucune intention d'y aller
I have no intention of going there

As a determiner, *aucun* is not used in the plural except sometimes with nouns that have no singular (e.g. *aucuns frais* 'no expenditure') or are used in the plural with a meaning they do not have in the singular (e.g. *aucuns gages* 'no wages').

547 *nul* 'no, not any, etc.'

(i) *Nul* is characteristic of the literary rather than of the spoken language.

(ii) As a pronoun it is used, usually only in the singular and only as the subject of the verb:

(a) with reference to some person or thing already mentioned (in which case the spoken equivalent is *aucun*), e.g.:

De toutes les maisons que je connais, nulle n'est plus agréable que la vôtre
Of all the houses I know, none is more pleasant than yours

(b) meaning 'nobody' (in this sense *personne*, not *aucun*, is used in speech), e.g.:

Nul ne sait ce qu'il est devenu
Nobody knows what has happened to him

(iii) As a determiner, *nul* is used in the literary language, mainly in the singular but occasionally (though this should not be imitated) in the plural, as the equivalent of *aucun*, e.g.:

Je n'ai nulle envie de le faire
I have no desire to do so

548   *aucunement, nullement* 'not at all'

Aucunement and, especially in the literary language, *nullement* serve to negate the verb more emphatically than *pas*; they follow the verb (or the auxiliary, or the infinitive if the sense requires it), e.g.:

> *Je n'en suis aucunement* (or *nullement*) *froissé*
> I am in no way (*or* not at all) put out about it

> *Je ne crains nullement* (or *aucunement*) *la mort*
> I am not in the least afraid of death

> *Il semble ne vouloir aucunement y aller*
> He seems to be by no means anxious to go there

549   *ne . . . guère* 'hardly, scarcely'

Ne . . . guère is used both as an adverb, e.g.:

> *Cela n'est guère probable*
> That is hardly likely

> *Je ne comprends guère ce qu'il dit*
> I scarcely understand what he says

and as a quantifier, e.g.:

> *Je n'ai guère d'argent*   I have hardly any money

In compound tenses it precedes the past participle, e.g.:

> *Je ne l'aurais guère cru*
> I should hardly have believed it

550   *ne . . . jamais* 'never'

Jamais usually follows the verb or the auxiliary, e.g.:

> *Je ne bois jamais de vin*   I never drink wine
> *Il n'a jamais dit ça*   He never said that

but it comes before the infinitive, e.g.:

> *Il décida de ne jamais revenir*
> He decided never to come back

For emphasis, it may be placed first, e.g.:

> *Jamais je ne dirais ça!*   I would *never* say that!

551 *ne . . . personne* 'nobody', *ne . . . rien* 'nothing'

Personne and *rien* can serve either as the subject or as the object of a verb or as the complement of a preposition, e.g.:

Personne n'arrivera ce soir
Nobody will arrive this evening

Rien ne le satisfait
Nothing satisfies him

Je ne vois personne
I can't see anyone

Je ne dirai rien
I shall say nothing

Je ne travaillais avec personne
I wasn't working with anybody

Je ne pensais à rien
I wasn't thinking of anything

Note that, in compound tenses, *rien* follows the auxiliary but *personne* follows the past participle, e.g.:

Je n'ai rien vu
I saw nothing (I haven't seen anything)

Je n'ai vu personne
I saw no-one (I haven't seen anyone)

Nous n'avions rien fait d'intéressant
We hadn't done anything interesting

(*Rien* may however sometimes follow the participle if it is qualified, e.g. *Je n'ai trouvé rien qui vaille la peine* 'I found nothing worth while'.)

Likewise, *rien* goes before and *personne* after the infinitive, e.g.:

Il a décidé de ne rien faire
He decided to do nothing

Il a décidé de n'accepter personne
He decided to accept nobody

552 *ne . . . plus* 'no longer, not any more'

Ne . . . plus means 'no more' **only** in the sense of 'no longer, not any more', e.g.:

Je n'y travaille plus
I don't work there any more, I no longer work there

Nous n'avons plus de pain
We have no more bread (i.e. no bread left)

('No more' in a strictly comparative or quantitative sense is *ne . . . pas plus*, e.g. *Ce livre n'est pas plus intelligible que l'autre* 'This book is no more intelligible than the other one', *Je n'ai pas plus de temps que vous* 'I have no more time than you'.)

Plus follows the verb or auxiliary, but precedes the infinitive, e.g.:

Je n'y suis plus allé
I never went there any more

J'ai décidé de ne plus y aller
I have decided not to go there any more

553   *ne . . . que . . .* 'only'

(i) Whereas in unaffected English (as distinct from pedantic English) 'only' can go before the verb even when it relates to something else, provided the meaning is clear from the context (e.g. 'He only works on Saturdays' = 'He works only on Saturdays'), the *que* of *ne . . . que . . .* always goes immediately before the element it relates to, e.g.:

Je n'en ai que trois
I only have three

Il ne travaille que le samedi
He only works (= works only) on Saturdays

Je ne l'ai dit qu'à mon frère
I only told (told only) my brother

(ii) As *que* must also follow the verb, there might seem to be a problem when 'only' relates to the verb itself, as in 'She only laughed' or 'On Saturdays he only works' (i.e., 'All he does on Saturdays is work'); what happens in French is that the verb *faire* 'to do' is used to express the relevant person, tense and mood, which *que* can then follow while at the same time preceding the infinitive of the verb it relates to, e.g.:

Je ne faisais que plaisanter
I was only joking

Elle n'a fait que rire
She only laughed

Le samedi il ne fait que travailler
All he does on Saturdays is work

Il ne fera que te gronder
He'll only scold you

(iii) Though the use of *ne pas . . . que . . .* to mean 'not only' is frowned on by some purists, it is well established in literary as well as spoken usage and there is no good reason to avoid it, e.g.:

Ne pensez pas qu'à vous (A. France)
Don't only think of yourself

Il ne négligea pas que l'église (Mauriac)
It was not only the church he neglected

Il n'y a pas que l'argent qui compte
It is not only money that counts (i.e. Money isn't everything)

554 *ne . . . rien* 'nothing'

See **551**, *ne . . . personne* and *ne . . . rien*.

555 'Fossilized' negative complements

In a few idioms, *goutte* and *mot* replace *rien*. *Goutte* occurs only with *voir* 'to see' *comprendre* 'to understand', and *entendre* in the sense of 'to understand' (not in the sense of 'to hear') and usually with *y* before the verb or, failing that, *à* + a noun, e.g.:

La lune est cachée, on n'y voit goutte (Mauriac)
The moon is hidden, one cannot see a thing

L'électeur moyen n'y comprend goutte (Le Monde)
The average voter understands nothing about it

Ils ne comprennent goutte à ma conduite (Flaubert)
They completely fail to understand my behaviour

Mot still retains its meaning of 'word' and occurs only with *dire* 'to say', *répondre* 'to answer' and in the idioms *ne (pas) sonner mot* and *ne (pas) souffler mot* 'not to utter a word', e.g.:

Le curé souriait (. . .) mais ne disait mot (Mauriac)
The priest smiled but said nothing

Il n'en souffle mot à personne (P.-J. Hélias)
He says nothing about it to anyone

556   Multiple negative complements

Pas and *point* cannot be combined with any of the other negative complements discussed in **546–555** (except in the expression *ne . . . pas que*, see **553**,iii). Various combinations of other complements are however possible, e.g.:

Personne n'a rien dit
Nobody said anything

Personne ne peut plus le supporter
Nobody can stand him any more

Il n'a jamais blessé personne
He has never hurt anyone

Nous n'avons jamais eu aucun problème
We never had any problem

Cela ne me regarde plus guère
That hardly concerns me any more

Il se décida à ne jamais plus rien supporter de la sorte
He decided never to put up with anything of the kind again

Negation without *ne*

557   *pas* without *ne*

When the verb of a negative clause is dropped, the *ne* of course drops with it and *pas* alone expresses the negation; for example, in answer to the question *Est-il arrivé?* 'Has he arrived?', instead of the complete sentence *Il n'est pas encore arrivé* 'He has not yet arrived', one is likely to find simply the expression *Pas encore* 'Not yet'. This is a construction one constantly comes across. Further examples:

Est-ce que vous l'admirez? – Pas du tout (or even *Du tout*)
Do you admire him? – Not at all

Tu viens? – Pas tout de suite
Are you coming? – Not immediately.

Qu'est-ce que je dois prendre? – Pas ça!
What am I to take? – Not that!

Qui l'a dit? – Pas moi, de toute façon
Who said so? – Not me, at any rate

Likewise *certainement pas* 'certainly not', *pourquoi pas?* 'why not?', *pas là!* 'not there!', etc.

For other negative complements without *ne*, see **558**,iii.

558

aucun,	*jamais,*	*personne,*	*plus,*	*rien*	without *ne*
any	ever	anybody	more	anything	

(i) As *sans* 'without' implies a negative, these five words may be used after *sans* or *sans que* 'without', e.g.:

sans aucune raison, sans raison aucune
without any reason

sans jamais le dire
without ever saying so

sans voir personne
without seeing anyone

sans plus tarder
without delaying any more, without further delay

sans rien dire
without saying anything, saying nothing

Il est parti sans rien
He left without anything

Elle est partie sans que personne le sache
She left without anyone knowing

sans que rien soit fait
without anything being done

(ii) The five words in question originally had a positive value and this survives in questions and comparisons and after *si* 'if', e.g.:

Y a-t-il aucune raison pour ça?
Is there any reason for that?

Je le respecte plus qu'aucun autre homme
I respect him more than any other man

Vous le savez mieux que personne
You know better than anyone

Avez-vous jamais rien entendu de si absurde?
Have you every heard anything so absurd?

Si jamais vous le voyez, dites-le-moi
If ever you see him, tell me

On *jamais*, see also **618**.

Plus retains a positive value generally, not just in the circumstances mentioned above – see **164–168**.

(iii) As is explained in **557**, *pas* retains a negative value when the verb (and hence the *ne*) of a negative clause is dropped. The same is true of *aucun, jamais, personne, plus* and *rien*. Each of these originally had a positive value but, through their constant association with negative constructions, they have themselves acquired a negative value in the circumstances in question, e.g.:

Y a-t-il aucune raison pour ça? – Aucune
Is there any reason for that? – None

Le lui avez-vous jamais montré? – Jamais
Have you ever shown it to him? – Never

Qui vous l'a dit? – Personne
Who told you so? – Nobody

Plus de discussions!
No more arguing!

Qu'est-ce qu'il t'a dit? – Rien de très intéressant
What did he tell you? – Nothing very interesting

Ne *alone*

559   In medieval French, *ne* was frequently used on its own (i.e. without *pas* or any other complement, though these were in fact already in use) to negate a verb, e.g. *Ne m'oci!* 'Don't kill me!' There are relics of this in modern French, falling into three categories, viz.:

(i) Fixed expressions and proverbs (**560**)

(ii) Constructions in which *ne* is a literary alternative to *ne . . . pas* (**561**)

(iii) Constructions in which *ne* is superfluous (and where English has no negative at all) (**562–567**)

(i) Ne *on its own in fixed expressions and proverbs*

560   *Ne* is used on its own:

(a) In a number of fixed expressions, including:

A Dieu ne plaise!
God forbid!

N'ayez crainte!
Fear not! Never fear!

N'importe or *Il n'importe*
It doesn't matter

Qu'à cela ne tienne!
Never mind that! No problem!

(b) A few constructions that can vary slightly in respect of their subject and/or tense and/or complement, and mainly involving one or other of the verbs *avoir* and *être*, e.g.:

n'avoir cure de
not to be concerned about

n'avoir (pas) de cesse que. . .
not to rest until. . .

n'avoir garde de (faire)
to take good care not to

n'avoir que faire de (+ noun)
to have no need of, no use for, to manage very well without

n'était
but for, were it not for

n'eût été
but for, had it not been for

si ce n'est (+ noun or pronoun)
if not . . . , apart from

Examples:

Il n'avait garde de contredire sa fille (Mérimée)
He took care not to contradict his daughter

Je n'ai que faire de ses conseils
I can manage very well without his advice

N'était son arrogance, il serait sûr de réussir
Were it not for his arrogance, he would certainly succeed

On ne voyait rien si ce n'est le ciel (Barbier d'Aurevilly)
Nothing was to be seen apart from the sky

Three such expressions involving other verbs are *n'en déplaise à* 'with all due respect to', *n'empêche que* 'the fact remains that', and *savoir* in the conditional meaning 'to be able' (of the constructions listed here, these last two are the only ones that are current in conversational usage), e.g.:

> *N'empêche qu'il a tout à fait tort*
> The fact remains that he is quite wrong

> *Je ne saurais répondre à votre question*
> I can't answer your question

(c) A few proverbs beginning with *il n'est*. . . 'there is not' e.g.:

> *Il n'est pire eau que l'eau qui dort*
> Still waters run deep (*lit.* There is no worse water than sleeping water)

> *Il n'est pire sourd que celui qui ne veut pas entendre*
> There is none so deaf as he who will not hear

(ii) Ne *as a literary alternative to* ne . . . pas

561 In a variety of constructions, the use of *ne* alone is still possible, particularly in the literary language. The principal constructions in question are:

(a) With the verb *cesser* 'to cease', but only when followed by *de* and an infinitive, *daigner* 'to deign', *oser* 'to dare', *pouvoir* 'to be able' and occasionally *bouger* 'to move', e.g.:

Il ne cesse de pleurer	He never stops crying
Je n'ose l'avouer	I dare not admit it
Je ne peux vous aider	I cannot help you
Ne bougez d'ici!	Don't move from here!

(b) With *savoir* followed by an indirect question (in which case it is better to use *ne* alone rather than *ne* . . . *pas*), e.g.:

> *Je ne sais pourquoi*
> I don't know why

> *Il ne sait quel parti prendre*
> He does not know what course to take

or in answer to a question:

> *Qu'allez-vous faire? – Je ne sais encore*
> What you going to do? – I don't yet know

(c) In rhetorical or exclamatory questions introduced by *qui?* 'who?', *quel?* + noun 'what?', *que* 'what?' or *que?* 'why', e.g.:

> *Qui ne court après la Fortune?* (La Fontaine)
> Who does not chase after Fortune?

> *Que ne dirait-on pour sauver sa peau?*
> What would a man not say to save his skin?

> *Que ne sommes-nous arrivés plus tôt!*
> Why did we not get here sooner! If only we had got here sooner!

(d) After *si*, especially when the main clause is negative, e.g.:

> *Je ne vous lâcherai pas si vous ne l'avouez*
> I will not let you go unless you confess

> *Si je n'étais Alexandre, je voudrais être Diogène*
> If I were not Alexander, I should like to be Diogenes

> *Le voilà qui arrive, si je ne me trompe*
> Here he comes, if I am not mistaken

(e) After *non que, non pas que, ce n'est pas que* 'not that', e.g.:

> *Non qu'il ne veuille vous aider . . .*
> Not that he does not want to help you

> *Ce n'est pas qu'il ne fasse des efforts, mais qu'il oublie tout*
> It is not that he doesn't try, but that he forgets everything

(f) In relative clauses taking the subjunctive after a negative (expressed, or implied in a question) in the preceding clause, e.g.:

> *Il ne devrait être personne qui ne veuille apprendre le français*
> There ought to be no one who does not want to learn French

> *Y a-t-il personne qui ne veuille apprendre le français?*
> Is there any who . . .? etc. (= Surely there is no one who . . . etc.)

> *Il n'y a si bon cheval qui ne bronche*
> There is no horse so good that it never stumbles

(g) In a *que*-clause expressing consequence after *tellement* or *si* meaning 'so', e.g.:

Il n'est pas tellement (or *si*) *bête qu'il ne comprenne ça*

He is not so stupid $\left\{ \begin{array}{l} \text{as not to} \\ \text{that he does not} \end{array} \right\}$ understand that

(h) In a dependent clause meaning 'without . . .-ing'; *que . . . ne* in this sense is equivalent to *sans que*, e.g.:

Je ne le vois jamais $\left\{ \begin{array}{l} qu'il\ ne\ me\ prie \\ sans\ qu'il\ me\ prie \end{array} \right\}$ *de passer chez lui*

I never see him without his asking me to drop in on him

(i) For *ne* or *ne . . . pas* after *depuis que*, etc., see **567**.

(iii) Ne *inserted where English has no negative*

562 Besides these cases where the negative sense is expressed by *ne* without *pas* there are a number of others where from the English point of view *ne* seems superfluous, or, as it is generally called, redundant. (Other terms used in various grammars are 'pleonastic *ne*' and 'expletive *ne*'.)

The reason for the presence of the *ne* is that, though the utterance is not strictly negative, there is in every case, as we shall see, a negative implication of some kind or other. Notice however that in speech the *ne* is dropped more often than not, and that it is often dropped also in writing in an informal style.

The constructions in question can be classified as follows:

(a) after comparatives (**563**)

(b) after verbs and expressions of fearing (**564**)

(c) after certain other verbs and their equivalents (**565**)

(d) after the conjunctions *avant que* 'before' and *à moins que* 'unless' (**566**)

(e) after the conjunction *depuis que* 'since' and comparable expressions (**567**)

563 (a) *Ne* **after comparatives**

In an affirmative clause after a comparative and *que* 'than', e.g. *Il en sait plus qu'il n'avoue* 'He knows more than he admits'; the use of *ne* can be explained by the fact that the *que*-clause contains a negative implication, viz. 'He does not admit to knowing as much as he does'. Other examples:

Il a agi avec plus d'imprudence que je ne croyais
He has acted more rashly than I thought

Il est moins riche qu'il ne l'était
He is less rich than he was

Also with *autre(ment) que* 'other than, otherwise than', e.g.:

Il agit autrement qu'il ne parle
He acts differently from the way he speaks

Note however that, when the main clause is interrogative or negative, the *ne* is not usually used unless the negative of the first clause also covers the second clause, e.g.:

Avez-vous jamais été plus heureux que vous l'êtes maintenant?
Have you ever been happier than you are now?

Jamais homme n'était plus embarrassé que je le suis en ce moment
Never was a man more embarrassed that I am at this moment

Vous ne réussirez pas mieux que nous n'avons réussi nous-mêmes
You will not succeed any better than we have
(i.e. 'We have not succeeded and you will not succeed')

(*Ne* is sometimes used, after questions, particularly when the question is rhetorical, e.g.:

Peut-on être plus bête qu'il ne l'est?
Can anyone be stupider than he is?)

564 (b) *Ne* **after verbs and expressions of fearing**

The use of *ne* after verbs and expressions of fearing such as *craindre que* 'to fear that', *avoir peur que* 'to be afraid that', *de crainte que, de peur que* 'for fear that', is explained by the fact that a fear that something may happen implies a hope or wish that it may not happen; for example, *J'ai peur que ce ne soit vrai* 'I am afraid it may be true', and *Il est parti de peur qu'elle ne le voie* 'He left for fear she might see him', imply respectively a hope that it might not be true and that she should not see him.

Note that after a verb of fearing that is itself negative there is no *ne* and that the problem does not of course arise when the verb of the *que*-clause is itself negative. We therefore have the following constructions:

Je crains qu'il ne vienne
I am afraid he will come

Je ne crains pas qu'il vienne
I am not afraid he will come

Je crains qu'il ne vienne pas
I am afraid he will not come

Je ne crains pas qu'il ne vienne pas
I am not afraid he will not come

565 (c) *Ne* after other verbs and their equivalents

After *douter* 'to doubt' when negative or interrogative, e.g.:

Je ne doute pas qu'il ne vienne
I have no doubt he will come

Doutez-vous qu'il ne vienne?
Do you doubt whether he will come?

but, after *douter* in the affirmative:

Je doute qu'il vienne　　　I doubt if he will come

Il n'est pas douteux que . . . takes either the subjunctive with or without *ne* or the indicative without *ne*, e.g.:

Il n'est pas douteux qu'il (ne) vienne ⎫ There is no doubt
Il n'est pas douteux qu'il viendra ⎭ that he will come

Other negative expressions of doubt are usually followed by the indicative without *ne* e.g.:

Il n'y a pas de doute qu'il viendra ⎫ There is no doubt
Sans doute qu'il viendra ⎭ that he will come

Nier 'to deny' when affirmative follows the same rule as *douter*; but, when negative, it can have any of the constructions illustrated below:

Je nie qu'il l'ait fait	I deny that he did it
Je ne nie pas qu'il ne l'ait fait	
Je ne nie pas qu'il l'ait fait	I do not deny that he did it
Je ne nie pas qu'il l'a fait	

After *nier* in the interrogative, the verb of the *que*-clause is usually in the subjunctive, with or without *ne*, e.g.:

Niez-vous qu'il (ne) l'ait fait? .
Do you deny that he did it?

Note that, if the person is unchanged, the infinitive can be used, e.g.:

> *Il ne nie pas l'avoir fait*
> He does not deny doing it (that he did it)

Empêcher que 'to prevent' and *éviter que* 'to avoid' are followed by *ne* whether they are used affirmatively or negatively, e.g.:

> *Rien n'empêche qu'on ne fasse la paix*
> Nothing prevents peace from being made

> *J'évite qu'il ne m'en parle*
> I avoid having him speak to me about it

But note that *empêcher* is very frequently followed by an infinitive, e.g. *Il m'empêche de partir* 'He prevents me from leaving'.

Ne is optional after *peu s'en faut que* or *il s'en faut que* (for which no even approximately literal translation is possible), e.g.:

> *Peu s'en fallut qu'il (ne) tombât dans la mer*
> He very nearly fell into the sea

> *Il s'en faut de beaucoup que cette somme soit suffisante*
> This sum is far from being enough

A few moments' thought ought to be enough to identify the negative implication in the above examples – for example, 'to prevent something from happening' is 'to ensure that it does not happen'.

566   (d) *Ne* after *avant que* 'before' and *à moins que* 'unless'

The use of *ne* after *avant que* 'before' and *à moins que* 'unless' is optional, but it is in general preferred in modern literary usage (much more so than in Classical French), e.g.:

> *Je le verrai avant qu'il (ne) parte*
> I shall see him before he leaves

> *Avant qu'ils n'eussent atteint la galerie* . . . (J. Green)
> Before they had reached the gallery . . .

> *Il va y renoncer à moins que vous (ne) l'aidiez*
> He is going to give up unless you help him

The negative implication of such examples as these is clear – 'he has not yet left', 'they had not reached the gallery', 'if you do not help him'.

Note that the use of *ne* after *sans que* 'without' that one sometimes comes across is best avoided, e.g.:

> *Il est parti sans que ses parents le sachent*
> He left without his parents knowing about it

567 (e) *Depuis que* and comparable expressions

The two interlocking problems that arise with the use of *depuis que*, viz. that of the choice of tense and that of the choice between *ne* and *ne . . . pas*, can best be explained if we first take an example. 'Ten years have passed since I saw him' (a sentence in which, in English, there is no negative) may be translated either by:

> *Dix ans se sont écoulés depuis que je ne l'ai vu*
> (i.e. with the perfect tense and *ne*), or by:

> *Dix ans se sont écoulés depuis que je ne le vois pas* (or *plus*)
> (i.e. with the present tense and either *ne . . . pas* or *ne . . . plus*).

The sense of the second of these forms becomes plain if one takes *depuis que* as an equivalent of 'during which', i.e. 'Ten years have passed during which I do not (*or* I no longer) see him'.

Furthermore, the first type has influenced the second and so one often comes across the construction:

> *Dix ans se sont écoulés depuis que je ne l'ai pas vu*

Alternative constructions to *depuis que* are provided by *il y a, voici, voilà* + expression of a period of time (e.g. *dix ans* 'ten years', *longtemps* 'a long time') + *que*, e.g.:

> *Il y a* ⎫
> *Voici* ⎬ *dix ans que je ne le vois pas* (or *plus*)
> *Voilà* ⎭
> It is ten years since I saw him

or, alternatively:

> *Il y a* ⎫
> *Voici* ⎬ *dix ans que je ne l'ai vu*
> *Voilà* ⎭

Another alternative construction is provided by *cela (ça) fait*, e.g. *Ça fait dix ans que je ne l'ai pas vu.* But note that since *cela (ça) fait* is a somewhat informal construction and the use of *ne* alone is a literary construction, the two should not be combined, i.e. with *cela fait* or *ça fait* always use *ne . . . pas*

Similarly with reference to the past:

Dix ans s'étaient écoulés depuis que $\left\{ \begin{array}{l} \textit{je ne l'avais (pas) vu} \\ \textit{je ne le voyais pas (or plus)} \end{array} \right.$

Ten years had elapsed since I saw (*or* had seen) him

$\left. \begin{array}{l} \textit{Il y avait} \\ \textit{Voilà} \end{array} \right\}$ *dix ans que* $\left\{ \begin{array}{l} \textit{je ne l'avais (pas) vu} \\ \textit{je ne le voyais pas (or plus)} \end{array} \right.$

It was ten years since I had seen him

Note that the use of *pas* or *plus* is optional with the compound tenses (i.e. the perfect and the pluperfect) but compulsory with the simple tenses (the present and the imperfect). Generally speaking, *plus* is more widely used than *pas* with the simple tenses.

De, du, *etc.*, un(e) *and the direct object of negative verbs*

568 *De* is normally substituted for the partitive or the indefinite article with the direct object of a verb in the negative (for exceptions, see **569** and **570**), e.g.:

Nous avons une maison
We have a house

Nous n'avons pas de maison
We haven't a house

Ils vendent du fromage
They sell cheese

Ils ne vendent pas de fromage
They don't sell cheese

Nous avons eu de la difficulté
We have had some difficulty

Nous n'avons jamais eu de difficulté
We have never had any difficulty

Note that, in the construction *il y a* 'there is, there are' followed by a noun (e.g. *Il y a des pommes* 'There are (some) apples'), the noun is the direct object of the verb *a* (from *avoir*) and so the rule applies (e.g. *Il n'y a pas de pommes* 'There aren't any apples').

Note too that *ne . . . que* 'only' is not negative in sense and so does not follow the rule, e.g. *Il n'y a que des pommes* 'There are only apples'.

569 The use of the indefinite article, *un, une*, is not impossible after a negative, but there is a difference in meaning between this construction and the usual construction with *pas de* discussed in **568**. Whereas *pas de* expresses the negation in an unemphatic way ('not a'), *pas un* is somewhat emphatic ('not one, not a single'), e.g.:

Il n'y a pas de communiste qui soit capitaliste
There is no communist who is a capitalist

Il n'y a pas un communiste qui soit capitaliste
There is not a single communist who is a capitalist

Je ne vois pas de cheval
I can't see a horse

Je ne vois pas un cheval
I can't see a single horse

(This last sentence might be spoken to express one's disappointment, for example, at not seeing any horses in circumstances where one had been expecting to see some.) Some circumstances virtually exclude the construction with *pas un*: for example, one might very well say of a woman *Elle n'a pas de mari* 'She hasn't got a husband', but it is difficult to imagine any kind of normal context in which one could say *Elle n'a pas un mari*.

Similarly in negative questions. Whereas *N'avez-vous pas de crayon?* merely means 'Haven't you got a pencil?', to ask *N'avez-vous pas un crayon?* has something of the same implication as 'You haven't (by any chance) a pencil, have you?' (i.e., if so, may I borrow it?).

570 The construction discussed in **568** must be clearly distinguished from others that are superficially similar (or even, in English – but not in French – identical), but have a very different meaning.

One of these is the construction in which the negation applies, according to the sense, not to the verb but to the direct object. For example, 'I didn't buy a typewriter' may carry the implication that, or be followed by a specific statement that, 'I bought something else (e.g. a video-recorder)'. So, in French we have *Je n'ai pas acheté une machine à écrire (mais un magnétoscope)*. The meaning in effect is 'I bought not a typewriter but a video-recorder', i.e. the negation, according to the sense, applies not to the verb 'bought' but to the direct object 'typewriter'.

Another similar construction is that in which the negation applies, according to the sense, neither to the verb nor to the direct object but to some other element in the sentence. For example, an utterance such as 'One doesn't keep a dog in order to eat it', has the implication 'If one keeps a dog, it is not in order to eat it'. So, in French one has *On n'a pas un chien pour le manger.*

B   *The negative conjunction* ni *'neither, nor'*

571   (i)   *Ni* is used to join two independent negative statements.

(a) If these statements have only one finite verb expressed, *ni* is repeated in each part and *ne* stands before the finite verb; this also applies when the auxiliary is the only finite verb expressed in two compound tenses, e.g.:

Ni lui ni moi ne serons prêts à temps
Neither he nor I will be ready in time

Je n'ai ni prié ni ordonné qu'on le fasse
I have neither asked nor ordered that it should be done

Il ne comprend ni l'anglais ni le français
He understands neither English nor French

Je ne suis ni riche ni avare
I am neither rich nor miserly

(b) If there are two finite verbs, the first is negatived by *ne* alone, the second by *ni ne*, e.g.:

Je ne peux ni ne veux y consentir
I neither can nor will agree to it

(ii) French uses *ni* where English uses 'and' or 'or' after a negative or after *sans* or *sans que* 'without', e.g.:

sans père ni mère
without father or mother, with neither father nor mother

Il faut le faire sans qu'il voie ni (qu'il) entende rien
It must be done without his seeing or hearing anything

La vieille aristocratie française n'a rien appris ni rien oublié
The old French aristocracy has learnt nothing and forgotten nothing

(iii) Note the use of *ni* to introduce a kind of afterthought after a negative construction with *ne . . . pas*, e.g.:

> *Il ne faut pas s'asseoir ni même se remuer avant que la reine n'ait donné le signe*
> No-one must sit down or even move till the queen gives the signal

> *Il ne comprend pas le français, ni l'anglais d'ailleurs*
> He doesn't understand French, or indeed English

When the newly introduced element is the equivalent of the subject, English has the construction 'neither' + some such verb as 'is, has, does, shall, will, can, must' + the subject; French has the construction *ni* (optional – see below) + subject (disjunctive form if it is a personal pronoun) + *non plus*, e.g.:

> *Il n'y va pas, (ni) son frère non plus*
> He is not going (and) neither is his brother

> *Je ne regarde jamais la télé, (ni) ma femme non plus*
> I never watch TV, (and) neither does my wife

> *(Ni) moi non plus*
> Neither am I (have I, can I, do I, etc.)

> *Elle ne travaillait jamais. – (Ni) lui non plus*
> She never worked. – Neither did he

In speech, the form without *ni* is the more usual, the form with *ni* being rather more emphatic.

C   Negation of an element other than a verb

572   'No' or 'not' as the equivalent of a negative sentence.
The English 'no' in answer to a question, or by way of being a comment, an objection, a warning, etc., is translated by *non* or, more emphatically, by *mais non!*, e.g.:

> *Vous partez demain? – Non, monsieur*
> Are you leaving tomorrow? – No, sir

> *Non! non! non! Ce n'est pas comme ça qu'il faut le faire!*
> No! no! That's not the way to do it!

> *Vous partez demain, n'est-ce pas? – Mais non! Je reste encore trois jours*

You're leaving tomorrow, aren't you? – No! I'm staying another three days

573 As an exclamatory negative (usually with a sense of protest against the suggestion made), *que non* is sometimes used, e.g.:

A votre avis, votre mari est-il coupable? Oui, ou non? – Que non! Oh, que non!
In your opinion, is your husband guilty? Yes, or no? – No! Oh, no!

574 After verbs of saying or thinking and a few others such as *espérer* 'to hope', and after certain adverbs of affirmation or doubt (see **627–628**) such as *heureusement* 'fortunately' and *peut-être* 'perhaps', 'not' or 'no' can take the place of an object clause; e.g. 'I hope not' as an answer to 'Is he coming?' is the equivalent of 'I hope he is not coming' (it is not therefore the equivalent of 'I do not hope'). The French equivalent of this, and also of 'not . . . so' in such sentences as 'I don't think so', is *que non*, e.g.:

Il part déjà? – J'espère que non/Je crois que non
Is he leaving already? – I hope not/I don't think so

Tu viens à la piscine? – J'ai déjà dit que non
Are you coming to the swimming pool? – I've already said no
(*or* . . . said I'm not)

Vous feriez mieux de ne pas lui écrire. – Peut-être que non.
You had better not write to him. – Perhaps not.

(For a similar use of *que oui* and *que si*, see **628**,ii.)

Non, non pas, pas 'not'

575 When 'not' negates some element other than the verb, there are three possible forms, viz. *non, non pas,* or *pas*. These are interchangeable in some circumstances but not, unfortunately, in all circumstances. We have to distinguish between a number of different constructions. The following summary is based on the admirably clear explanation given by R.-L. Wagner and J. Pinchon in their *Grammaire du français classique et moderne*, Paris, Hachette, 1962, pp. 401–2.

All depends on whether (i) two items are presented as being in opposition to one another, or (ii) two elements are presented as being alternatives, or (iii) only one item is expressed (and, of course, in the negative). Further distinctions are necessary in (i) according to whether it is the first or the second element that is negatived, and in (ii) according to whether or not the second element is or is not expressed. These distinctions should become clear from the examples that follow.

576 (i) Two elements are presented as being in opposition (i.e. we have one or other of the constructions 'not X but Y' or 'X not Y'):

(a) The first element is negatived – 'not' is *non* or *non pas*, e.g.:

> *Il a l'air non fatigué mais malade*
> *Il a l'air non pas fatigué mais malade*
> He looks not tired but ill

> *Elle arrive non mardi mais jeudi*
> *Elle arrive non pas mardi mais jeudi*
> She is arriving not on Tuesday but on Thursday

> *Henri sera mon cavalier, non (pas) qu'il soit beau, mais parce qu'il danse à ravir*
> Henry shall be my partner, not that he is handsome, but because he dances divinely

(b) The second element is negatived – 'not' is *non, non pas*, or *pas*,

> *Il a l'air fatigué, non malade*
> *Il a l'air fatigué, non pas malade*
> *Il a l'air fatigué, pas malade*
> He looks tired, not ill

> *Elle arrive mardi, non jeudi*
> *Elle arrive mardi, non pas jeudi*
> *Elle arrive mardi, pas jeudi*
> She is arriving on Tuesday, not on Thursday

> *Il l'a fait par mégarde, non (non pas, pas) avec intention*
> He did it by mistake, not on purpose

577 (ii) Two elements are presented as being alternatives (i.e. we have one or other of the constructions 'X or not X' or 'X or not'):

(a) The second element is expressed – 'not' is usually *pas*, e.g.:

> *Fatigué ou pas fatigué, il part demain*
> Tired or not tired, he is leaving tomorrow

> *Qu'il parle bien ou pas bien, peu importe*
> Whether he speaks well or not well, it doesn't much matter

(b) The second element is not expressed – 'not' is *non* or *pas*, e.g.:

> *Fatigué ou non, il part demain*
> *Fatigué ou pas, il part demain*
> Tired or not, he is leaving tomorrow

> *Qu'il parle bien ou non, peu importe*
> *Qu'il parle bien ou pas, peu importe*
> Whether he speaks well or not, it doesn't much matter

> *Les uns l'aiment, les autres non*
> *Les uns l'aiment, les autres pas*
> Some like it, others not

578 (iii) Only one (negative) item is expressed – not is *non* or *pas*, e.g.:

> *Il habite non loin de Paris*
> *Il habite pas loin de Paris*
> He lives not far from Paris

> *Il était furieux et non content de ce qu'il avait vu*
> *Il était furieux et pas content de ce qu'il avait vu*
> He was angry and not pleased with what he had seen

579 We therefore have the following pattern:

(i)	a	non	non pas	–
	b	non	non pas	pas
(ii)	a	–	–	pas
	b	non	–	pas
(iii)		non	–	pas

Note in particular:

(a) that *non pas* is used **only** to express opposition;

(b) that *pas* may be used in all constructions **except** to negative the first of two elements in opposition.

Note also that, where there is a choice between *non* and *pas*, the former is characteristic of a more formal, the latter of a more familiar style.

580   *Non* is used before a past participle not compounded with *être* or *avoir*, e.g.:

une leçon non sue	a lesson not known
vin non compris	wine not included
les pays non-alignés	the non-aligned countries

before a present participle used purely as a noun or qualifying adjective, e.g.:

un non-combattant	a non-combatant

and to form compounds (many of them technical) with various nouns and adjectives, e.g.:

non-conducteur
non-conductor

le point de non-retour
the point of no return

non-réussite
failure

non valable
invalid (excuse, etc.), not valid (ticket, etc.)

une manifestation non-violente
a non-violent demonstration

Interrogative sentences (questions)

Introduction

581   Questions are either:

(i) Direct – e.g. 'Are you coming?', 'What is he doing?', 'Why did the cat eat the goldfish?'

or (ii) Indirect – e.g. '(He asked) if I was coming', '(I wonder) what he is doing', '(Nobody knows) why the cat ate the goldfish'.

Direct questions fall into one or other of two categories:

(i) Total interrogation – i.e. 'yes–no' questions, e.g. 'Is she happy?', 'Have you any change?', 'Did the cat eat the goldfish?';

(ii) Partial interrogation – i.e. questions introduced by an interrogative expression, e.g. 'Who?', 'What?', 'When?', 'Where?', 'How?', 'Why?', 'How many?', 'Which book?', 'For what reason?'

We shall discuss interrogative sentences under the following headings:

A: Direct questions: total interrogation

B: Direct questions: partial interrogation

C: Indirect questions

582 In direct questions, in either total or partial interrogation, English makes much use of the verb 'do', which has no function other than to turn a statement into a question, e.g.:

I saw him	Did I see him?
My brother smokes too much	Does my brother smoke too much?
She bought a book	What did she buy?
They eat too much	Why do they eat too much?

Note that, in French, the verb *faire* 'to do' is never used in this way.

A Direct questions – total interrogation

583 The basic interrogative form of a 'yes–no' question when the subject is a personal pronoun or one or other of the pronouns *on* and (with *être* only) *ce* is obtained by inverting the subject, i.e. placing it after the verb, e.g.:

je suis	*suis-je?*	*vous venez*	*venez-vous?*
elle chante	*chante-t-elle?*	*ils peuvent*	*peuvent-ils?*
on dit	*dit-on?*	*c'est vrai*	*est-ce vrai?*

For the interrogative conjugation of a typical verb, see **387**.

For the use of -*t*- when a verb form ending in a vowel is followed by *il, elle* or *on*, see **388**.

Note that, in the present tense, the inversion of *je* is not possible with most verbs (see **389**).

Further examples:

> *Puis-je vous aider?*
> May I help you?

> *A-t-il terminé son travail?*
> Has he finished his work?

> *Viendra-t-elle nous voir?*
> Will she come and see us?

> *Aviez-vous beaucoup de voisins?*
> Did you have many neighbours?

584 A noun subject cannot be inverted in total interrogation. The equivalent construction is obtained by leaving the noun subject at the beginning and inverting the appropriate personal pronoun, e.g.:

> *Le chat a-t-il mangé le poisson rouge?*
> Has the cat eaten the goldfish?

> *Marie habitait-elle à Paris?*
> Did Mary live in Paris?

> *Les Français boivent-ils trop de vin?*
> Do the French drink too much wine?

> *Vos sœurs seront-elles contentes?*
> Will your sisters be pleased?

585 An alternative and widely used way of asking questions is to preface the affirmative form with *Est-ce que . . .?* (literally 'Is it that . . .?' – but it must not be translated thus), e.g.:

> *Est-ce qu'elle viendra nous voir?*
> Will she come and see us?

> *Est-ce que Marie habitait à Paris?*
> Did Mary live in Paris?

This is an effective way of coping with those contexts in which *je* cannot be inverted, e.g.:

> *Est-ce que je parle trop?*
> Do I talk too much?

> *Est-ce que je pars tout de suite?*
> Do I leave immediately?

Note that *est-ce que* is often used for the sake of emphasis, expressing indignation, surprise or doubt, e.g.:

> *Est-ce que je vais me confier à de telles gens?*
> Do you think I am going to entrust myself to such people?

586 The excessive use of *est-ce que* should be avoided. In writing, this can be done by using inversion (see **583–586**). In speech, questions are very frequently formed by means of intonation alone, keeping the same word-order as in statements, e.g.:

> *Je parle trop?*   Am I talking too much?
> *Tu pars déjà?*   Are you leaving already?
> *Mon père est sorti?*   Has my father gone out?

587 The only French equivalent for English tag-questions, i.e. brief questions such as 'Don't I?', 'Isn't she?', 'Haven't you?', 'Won't they?', tacked on to an affirmative sentence, is *n'est-ce pas?*, e.g.:

> *Elle est très heureuse, n'est-ce pas?*
> She's very happy, isn't she?
>
> *Vous êtes allé à Paris, n'est-ce pas?*
> You've been to Paris, haven't you?
>
> *Ils voyageaient beaucoup, n'est-ce pas?*
> They used to travel a lot, didn't they?
>
> *Vous me prêterez votre voiture, n'est-ce pas?*
> You'll lend me your car, won't you?

N'est-ce pas? can also be used after a negative, as the equivalent of 'Is she?', 'Did they?', etc., e.g.:

> *Tu ne pars pas maintenant, n'est-ce pas?*
> You're not leaving now, are you?
>
> *Il n'a jamais dit ça, n'est-ce pas?*
> He never said that, did he?

B Direct questions – partial interrogation

588 For questions involving the interrogative pronouns *qui?* 'who?', *qu'est-ce qui?*, *qu'est-ce que?*, *que?*, *quoi?* 'what', *lequel?* 'which?', see **280–290**.

For questions introduced by *combien?* 'how much?', 'how many?', see **326**.

589   In questions introduced by one of the interrogative adverbs *où?* 'where?', *quand,* 'when?', *comment?* 'how?', *pourquoi?* 'why?', or an interrogative phrase including *quel?* 'which?', the subject, if a personal pronoun, *on* or (with the verb *être* only) *ce*, is inverted, as in total interrogation, e.g.:

> *Où avez-vous garé la voiture?*
> Where have you parked the car?
>
> *Quand viendra-t-elle nous voir?*
> When will she come to see us?
>
> *Pourquoi dit-on cela?*
> Why do they say that?
>
> *Comment le savaient-ils?*
> How did they know?
>
> *Pour quelle compagnie travaille-t-il?*
> Which company does he work for?

As in total interrogation, *est-ce que?* may be used, in which case the order Subject – Verb remains, e.g. (as alternatives to the above):

> *Où est-ce que vous avez garé la voiture?*
> *Quand est-ce qu'elle viendra nous voir?*
> *Pour quelle compagnie est-ce qu'il travaille?* etc.

590   When the subject of a question introduced by *où? quand? comment? pourquoi?* or an expression including *quel?* is a noun (or a pronoun other than a personal pronoun, *on* or *ce*), it may (contrary to what is the case in total interrogation, see **584**) be inverted, subject however to certain restrictions (see **591–592**), e.g.:

> *Où travaillait votre père?*
> Where did your father work?
>
> *Quand arrivent les enfants?*
> When are the children coming?
>
> *D'où est venue cette idée?*
> Where has that idea come from?

A quelle heure est la conférence?
What time is the lecture?

An alternative is to invert the appropriate subject pronoun, in which case the noun subject may go either before or after the interrogative word, e.g.:

Votre père où travaillait-il?
Où votre père travaillait-il?

Again, in speech in particular, *est-ce que?* provides a further alternative, e.g.:

Où est-ce que votre père travaillait?
Quand est-ce que les enfants arrivent?

591 The inversion of the noun subject is not possible with *pourquoi* and tends to be avoided with other interrogative words and phrases of more than one syllable. In such cases, one or other of the constructions referred to in **590** should be used, e.g.:

Pourquoi les enfants pleuraient-ils?
Why were the children crying?

Comment est-ce que votre frère le sait?
How does your brother know?

Combien votre sœur a-t-elle perdu?
How much has your sister lost?

592 The noun subject cannot be inverted when the verb has a direct object (other than a conjunctive pronoun) or some other complement to which it is closely linked and from which it should not be separated, e.g.:

Où est-ce que votre frère gare sa voiture?
Where does your brother park his car?

Quand les étudiants passent-ils leurs examens?
When do the students sit their exams?

Quand les enfants partaient-ils en vacances?
When were the children leaving on holiday?

593 A non-literary construction that is very current in speech is to put the interrogative word not first but after the verb (and, in most cases, at the end), e.g.:

Vous allez où?
Where are you going?

Henri est arrivé quand?
When did Henry arrive?

Vous en voulez combien?
How many do you want?

Ton frère part quel jour?
What day is your brother leaving?

Il fait ça pourquoi?
Why is he doing that?

Elle écrit à qui?
Who is she writing to?

C Indirect questions

594 Indirect questions corresponding to total interrogation are introduced by *si* 'if, whether', e.g.:

Il m'a demandé si je pouvais l'aider
He asked me if I could help him

Nous ne savions pas si le train arriverait à temps
We didn't know whether the train would arrive in time

595 Indirect questions introduced by one of the interrogative expressions discussed in **588–589** have the same word order as in affirmative clauses, e.g.:

Nous ne savions pas pourquoi il était parti
We didn't know why he had left

Il m'a demandé à quelle heure le train partait
He asked me what time the train left

Je me demande où mon frère va acheter sa nouvelle voiture
I wonder where my brother is going to buy his new car

However, inversion of the noun subject is possible provided the indirect question is not introduced by *pourquoi* and there is no direct object and no other complement closely linked to the verb, e.g.:

Dites-moi où habite votre frère
Tell me where your brother lives

Je ne comprends pas comment vivaient les hommes des cavernes
I don't understand how cavemen lived.

Inversion

596   In certain circumstances, the subject comes after the verb instead of before it. This is called 'Inversion'. It may take three forms:

(i)   the subject pronoun follows the verb, e.g.:

Est-il arrivé? Peut-être viendra-t-il demain
Has he arrived? Perhaps he will come tomorrow

(ii)   the subject noun follows the verb, e.g.:

C'est là qu'habite mon frère
That is where my brother lives

Non, monsieur, répondit le garçon
'No, sir,' the boy replied

(iii)   a noun subject comes first and the corresponding conjunctive pronoun is added after the verb, e.g.:

Peut-être ma mère avait-elle changé d'avis
Perhaps my mother had changed her mind

Vos enfants sont-ils en vacances?
Are your children on holiday?

Types (i) and (ii) are sometimes known as 'simple inversion' and type (iii) as 'complex inversion'.

597   For inversion:

in direct questions, see **583–584** and **589–592**

with the subjunctive, expressing wishes, see **476–477**

in hypothetical constructions, in the sense of '(even) if, supposing, etc.', see **478**.

598   (i) Inversion may occur when the subject is a noun (for exceptions, see ii, below) in indirect questions, relative clauses, and other subordinate clauses, e.g.:

Je ne peux pas deviner ce que veut faire ici cet homme-là (or *ce que cet homme-là veut faire ici*)
I cannot imagine what that fellow wants here

Il ne comprenait pas de quoi se fâchaient les indigènes (or *les indigènes se fâchaient*)
He did not understand what the natives were getting annoyed about

Je ne connais pas les hommes dont parlait mon père (or *dont mon père parlait*)
I do not know the men of whom my father was speaking

Voici le livre qu'a acheté mon frère (or *que mon frère a acheté*)
Here is the book my brother bought

Elle avait été heureuse tant qu'avait vécu son époux (or *tant que son époux avait vécu*)
She had been happy for as long as her husband had lived

(ii) Inversion of the noun subject is not however possible in such clauses if this would have the effect of separating the verb from some element with which it is closely linked, such as a direct object, e.g.:

Voici la librairie où mon frère achète ses livres
Here is the bookshop where my brother buys his books

or the complement of *être* or another linking verb (see **518**), e.g.:

C'est en 1959 que de Gaulle est devenu Président de la République
It was in 1959 that de Gaulle became President of the Republic

or an adverbial complement modifying the verb, e.g.:

. . . *tant que son époux avait travaillé à Paris*
. . . for as long as her husband had worked in Paris

(iii) Inversion is not possible in such clauses when the subject is a conjunctive pronoun, *on* or *ce*, e.g.:

Je ne peux pas deviner ce qu'il veut faire ici
I cannot imagine what he wants here

Je ne connais pas les hommes dont il parlait
I do not know the men of whom he was speaking

> *. . . tant qu'il avait vécu*
> . . . for as long as he had lived

(iv) It goes without saying that inversion is impossible when *qui* or *ce qui* is itself the subject.

599 In short parenthetical expressions reporting someone's words, inversion is essential. This applies not only to verbs explicitly referring to speech, such as *dire* 'to say', *s'écrier* 'to exclaim', *demander* 'to ask', *continuer* 'to continue (speaking)', *répondre* 'to reply', but also to a few verbs such as *penser* 'to think', *se demander* 'to wonder' when they imply that the subject is inwardly addressing himself, e.g.:

> *Je ne sais pas, répondit mon frère*
> 'I don't know,' my brother answered

Hélas!
$$\begin{cases} \textit{dit-il,} \\ \textit{cria-t-il,} \\ \textit{s'écria-t-il,} \\ \textit{pensa-t-il,} \\ \textit{a-t-il dit,} \\ \textit{disait-il,} \end{cases}$$
que vais-je devenir?

> 'Alas!' he said (he shouted, he exclaimed, he thought, he said), 'what will become of me?'

With other verbs that occasionally have a similar value, inversion is optional, e.g.:

Il est bizarre,
$$\begin{cases} \textit{ai-je réfléchi,} \\ \textit{j'ai réfléchi,} \end{cases}$$
en relisant sa lettre, qu'il n'en ait rien dit

> It is odd, I reflected, as I re-read his letter, that he has not mentioned it

600 Certain adverbs and adverbial expressions cause inversion more or less regularly (though not invariably) when they stand first in the clause. In the case of a noun subject, we have complex inversion (see **596**, end).

Of the expressions in question, *à peine* 'scarcely' nearly always causes inversion, and *peut-être* 'perhaps' and *sans doute* 'doubtless' usually do so (except when followed by *que* – see below and **642**), e.g.:

> *A peine se fut-il assis que le train partit*
> Scarcely had he sat down when the train started
>
> *Peut-être arrivera-t-il demain*
> Perhaps he will arrive tomorrow
>
> *Sans doute ma sœur vous a-t-elle écrit*
> Doubtless my sister has written to you

but also, as an alternative, *Peut-être qu'il arrivera demain*, etc.

Toujours is always followed by inversion in the expression *toujours est-il que*. . . 'the fact remains that. . .'

Among other adverbs and adverbial expressions that frequently (and in some cases more often than not) cause inversion are:

ainsi, thus	*encore plus*, even more
aussi, and so	*en vain*, in vain
aussi bien, and yet	*rarement*, rarely
du moins, at least	*tout au plus*, at most
(et) encore, even so	*vainement*, vainly
encore moins, even less	

Inversion also sometimes occurs after various other adverbs. Examples:

> *Ainsi la pauvre dame a fini* (or *a-t-elle fini*) *par s'échapper*
> Thus the poor lady ended by escaping
>
> *En vain luttait-il* (or *il luttait*); *rien ne lui réussit*
> In vain he struggled; nothing went right for him
>
> *Vous avez demandé des nouvelles de son mari! mais on vient de l'arrêter; du moins on le dit* (or *le dit-on*)
> You inquired after her husband! why, he has just been arrested; so they say at any rate
>
> *Tout au moins auriez-vous pu m'en avertir plus tôt*
> At least you might have warned me sooner

Note that 'at least' in its literal sense, i.e. before an expression of quantity, is always *au moins* and that, in this case, there is no inversion, e.g.:

> *Au moins trois cents personnes en moururent*
> At least three hundred people died of it

601   A different type of inversion is that in which the verb (which may or may not be preceded by an adverbial expression) has relatively little significance and serves mainly to introduce the subject which is the really important element. In equivalent sentences in English, the verb is regularly introduced by a meaningless 'there' or 'it', e.g.:

Suivit une âpre discussion en russe (Duhamel)
There followed a sharp discussion in Russian

Restent les bijoux (Chamson)
There remain the jewels

Reste à voir ce qu'il fera
It remains to be seen what he will do

A ce moment surgit un petit homme en casquette (Benoit)
At that point there appeared a little man in a cap

Adverbs, Prepositions and Conjunctions

Adverbs

Introduction

602 Adverbs can be conveniently classified as follows:

A: Adverbs of manner; these generally, but not invariably, end in -*ly* in English and in -*ment* in French (see 603–613)

B: Adverbs of time (see 614–623)

C: Adverbs of place (see 624–625)

D: Adverbs of quantity (see 'Quantifiers', 320–337)

E: Adverbs of affirmation or doubt (see 627–628)

F: Adverbs of negation (see 544–558)

G: Interrogative adverbs (see 630–633)

A   Adverbs of manner

603 Most adverbs of manner and some others are formed from adjectives by the addition of -*ment*. (For convenience, we shall include in the following sections some of the adverbs in -*ment* that are not adverbs of manner.)

604 In practice, the following rules apply:

Rule 1. When the adjective ends in a vowel, the adverb is formed by adding -*ment* without any other change (but see 605), e.g.:

aisé, easy	*aisément*, easily
hardi, bold	*hardiment*, boldly
utile, useful	*utilement*, usefully

Rule 2. When the adjective ends in *-ant* or *-ent*, *-nt* becomes *m* before *-ment* is added (but see **606**), e.g.:

brillant, brilliant	*brillamment*, brilliantly
constant, constant	*constamment*, constantly
fréquent, frequent	*fréquemment*, frequently
violent, violent	*violemment*, violently

Rule 3. When the adjective ends in any consonant other than the group *-nt*, *-ment* is added to the feminine form (but see **607**), e.g.:

clair, clear	*clairement*, clearly
discret, discreet	*discrètement*, discreetly
doux, gentle	*doucement*, gently
public, public	*publiquement*, publicly
soigneux, careful	*soigneusement*, carefully

605 Exceptions to Rule 1

(a) The following adverbs take *-é*, although derived from adjectives ending in *-e* mute:

aveuglément, blindly	from *aveugle*
commodément, conveniently	from *commode*
incommodément, inconveniently	from *incommode*
conformément, according (*à*, to)	from *conforme*
énormément, enormously	from *énorme*
immensément, immensely	from *immense*
intensément, intensely	from *intense*
uniformément, uniformly	from *uniforme*

(b) The following add an acute to the feminine adjective:

communément, commonly	from *commun*
confusément, confusedly	from *confus*
diffusément, diffusedly	from *diffus*
expressément, expressly	from *exprès*
importunément, importunately	from *importun*
opportunément, opportunely	from *opportun*
inopportunément, inopportunely	from *inopportun*
obscurément, obscurely	from *obscur*

précisément, precisely   from *précis*
profondément, profoundly   from *profond*
profusément, profusely   from *profus*

(c) The following derived from adjectives in *-i* are peculiar:

gaiement, or *gaîment*, gaily   from *gai*, gay
impunément, with impunity   from *impuni*, unpunished

(d) Six adjectives ending in *-u* add *-ment* without any other change, according to Rule 1. They are:

absolu, absolute   *absolument*, absolutely
ambigu, ambiguous   *ambigument*, ambiguously
éperdu, distracted   *éperdument*, distractedly
ingénu, ingenuous   *ingénument*, ingenuously
irrésolu, irresolute   *irrésolument*, irresolutely
résolu, resolute   *résolument*, resolutely

Other adverbs formed from adjectives in *-u* have a circumflex, viz.:

assidûment, assiduously   *goulûment*, gluttonously
congrûment, appropriately   *incongrûment*, inappropriately
continûment, incessantly   *indûment*, unduly
crûment, crudely   *nûment*, nakedly, bluntly
dûment, duly

606   Exceptions to Rule 2

Three words keep *-nt* and add *-ment* to the feminine, viz.:

lent, slow   *lentement*, slowly
présent, present   *présentement*, at present
véhément, vehement   *véhémentement*, vehemently

607   Exceptions to Rule 3

(a) The adverbs corresponding to *bon* 'good' and *mauvais* 'bad' are *bien* 'well', *mal* 'badly'.

The 'regular' adverb *bonnement* exists, but only in the expression *tout bonnement* 'just, simply, plainly', e.g. *il a répondu tout bonnement que* . . . 'he merely answered that . . .', *Je lui ai dit tout bonnement la vérité* 'I just told him the truth, I told him the plain truth'.

(b) The adverb corresponding to *bref* 'brief' is *brièvement* (from an old adjective *brief*, feminine *briève*, that no longer exists).

(c) *Gentil* (pronounced [ʒɑ̃ti]) 'nice', has as its adverb *gentiment*.

(d) The adverb corresponding to *traître* (originally a noun) 'treacherous' (feminine *traîtresse*) is *traîtreusement*.

608 The adverbs *journellement* 'every day', *notamment* 'notably, in particular', *nuitamment* 'by night', *précipitamment* 'hurriedly', *sciemment* 'knowingly', have no corresponding adjective. Nor has *grièvement*, which exists only in the expression *grièvement blessé* 'gravely wounded'.

609 As in English, a few adjectives can be used as adverbs qualifying certain verbs, e.g.:

Elle marcha droit devant elle
She walked straight ahead

Il travaille très dur
He works very hard

The following list gives the adjectives most commonly used as adverbs and the verbs with which they are generally used:

bas, with *jeter*, 'down'; with *chanter, parler*, 'low, in a low voice' (often *tout bas*)

bon, with *sentir*, '(smell) good, nice'; with *tenir*, '(hold) fast, (stand) firm'

cher, with *acheter, coûter, vendre*, 'dear'

clair, with *voir*, 'clearly'

court, with *s'arrêter*, '(stop) short'; with *couper*, '(cut) short'; with *demeurer, rester, se trouver*, 'be at a loss for words'

droit, with *aller, marcher*, 'straight'; also *tout droit* 'straight ahead'

dru, with *pleuvoir*, 'hard'; with *semer*, 'thickly'; with *tomber* 'thick and fast'

dur, with *travailler, jouer*, 'hard'

faux, with *chanter, jouer*, 'out of tune'; with *sonner*, 'have a false ring'

ferme, with *discuter*, 'vigorously'; with *tenir*, '(stand) fast, firm'; with *travailler*, 'hard'

fort, with *déplaire, douter*, etc., 'greatly'; with *sentir*, 'have a strong smell'; with *frapper, jouer*, 'hard'; with *crier, parler*, 'loudly'

gros, with *écrire*, 'big'; with *gagner, perdre*, 'heavily, a lot' *haut*, with *lire*, 'aloud'; with *parler*, 'loudly'; with *placer*, 'high'

juste, with *tirer*, '(shoot) straight'; with *deviner, raisonner, voir*, 'correctly, accurately'

long, in *en savoir long sur quelque chose*, 'to know all about something'

lourd, with *peser*, 'heavy, heavily'

mauvais, with *sentir*, '(smell) bad'

net, with *se casser*, 'snap in two'; with *dire, parler*, etc., 'plainly'; with *refuser*, 'point blank'; with *trancher*, '(cut) short (e.g. a discussion)'; with *tuer*, 'outright'; etc.

ras, with *couper, tondre*, 'close'

sec, with *boire*, 'heavily'; with *parler, répondre*, etc., 'curtly'

serré, with *jouer*, 'cautiously'

610 (i) The above follow the verb they qualify and are invariable. But note that *frais* 'freshly' used adverbially before a participle, and *grand* and *large* 'wide' before the one participle *ouvert* 'open', vary like adjectives, e.g.:

des fleurs fraîches cueillies
freshly picked flowers

les yeux $\left\{\begin{array}{c} grands \\ larges \end{array}\right\}$ *ouverts*
with wide open eyes

une fenêtre grande ouverte
a wide open window

(ii) In (*tout*) *battant neuf*, (*tout*) *flambant neuf* 'brand new', *tout* and *neuf* normally agree but *battant* and *flambant* are usually invariable, e.g. *des vêtements (tous) battant neufs* 'brand new clothes', *une voiture (toute) flambant neuve* 'a brand new car' – but occasionally the form in *-ant* agrees (and, just to complicate things, sometimes *neuf* does not, e.g. *des bâtiments flambant neuf* 'brand new buildings').

(iii) For a general statement of the conditions in which *tout* does or does not vary when used adverbially, see 317,v,a.

611 French sometimes uses adverbial phrases of the type *de* or *d'une façon, de* or *d'une manière* + (feminine) adjective, i.e. 'in such-and-such a way', as the equivalent of an adverb of manner modifying a verb, e.g. *agir discrètement* or *d'une manière discrète* 'to act discreetly', *différemment* or *de manière différente* 'differently', *inexplicablement* or *d'une façon inexplicable* 'inexplicably'.

Another possibility is to use *avec* and a noun, e.g. *soigneusement* or *avec soin* 'carefully', *impatiemment* or *avec impatience* 'impatiently'.

In the case of a small number of adjectives that have no corresponding adverb, some such alternative construction **must** be used, e.g. *d'une manière tremblante* 'tremblingly', *Il regardait autour de lui d'un air content* 'He looked contentedly around him', *avec concision* 'concisely'.

Note that these alternative constructions can be used **only** when they modify a verb or the clause in general; so, *agréablement* could not be replaced by *d'une manière agréable* in, for example, *agréablement surpris* in which it modifies a participle.

612 Adverbs of manner that have no corresponding adjective include:

ainsi, thus
debout, standing
exprès, deliberately, on purpose
vite, quickly

and also, taking the term 'adverb of manner' in a very wide sense:

ensemble, 'together'   *plutôt*, rather

For *bien* 'well' and *mal* 'badly', see **161–163**.

613 *Comme* and *comment*

(i) With *être* and sometimes with other linking verbs such as *devenir* 'to become', *paraître* 'to appear', *comme* after an adjective expresses a comparison in a large number of fixed expressions such as:

Il est fort comme un bœuf
He is as strong as an ox

Elle est devenue blanche comme un linge
She turned as white as a sheet

malin comme un singe
as artful as a monkey

noir comme (du) jais
as black as soot (*lit.* jet)

blanc comme neige
as white as snow

Note that this construction is limited to such expressions and is **not** used as a general equivalent of *aussi . . . que . . .* (see 157); it could not, for example, be substituted for *aussi . . . que . . .* in *il est aussi intelligent que son frère* 'he is as intelligent as his brother'.

(ii) As a conjunction expressing a comparison between two verbs, *comme* means 'as', e.g.:

Il écrit comme il parle
He writes (in the same way) as he speaks

Il se conduit comme se conduirait un enfant
He behaves as a child would behave

When, as is frequently the case, the verb of the second clause would merely repeat the first, e.g. 'He behaves as a child behaves', I consider him as I (would) consider a brother', it may be omitted in French as in English, e.g.:

Il se conduit comme un enfant
He behaves like a child

Je le considère comme un frère
I consider him as a brother

and in many expressions of the type:

courir comme un lièvre
to run like a hare

travailler comme un forçat
to work like a galley-slave

For other uses of *comme* as a conjunction, see 154.

(iii) In the sense of 'how', *comme* must not be confused with *comment*.

(a) In direct questions, 'how?' is *comment?* (see 589–590)

(b) With an exclamatory value, 'how' is translated as *comme* or as *que* when qualifying an adjective, e.g.:

Comme il est (or *Qu'il est*) *facile de se tromper!*
How easy it is to be mistaken!

Comme elle est (or *Qu'elle est*) *belle!*
How beautiful she is!

but usually as *comme* (or, in conversational French, *ce que* or even *qu'est-ce que*) when modifying a verb or an adverb, e.g.:

Comme elle a pleuré!
Ce qu'elle a pleuré! } How she wept!
Qu'est-ce qu'elle a pleuré!

Comme elle chante bien!
Ce qu'elle chante bien! } How well she sings!
Qu'est-ce qu'elle chante bien!

(c) In indirect questions either *comme* or *comment* may be used, with however a significant difference in meaning. *Comment* refers strictly and objectively to the way something is done, e.g.:

Observez bien comment il travaille
Notice how he does his work

while *comme* (in line with b above) is somewhat exclamatory and conveys the idea of the extent to which something is done, e.g.:

Observez bien comme il travaille
Notice how hard he works

(d) The English 'What!', half question, half exclamation, is also translated by *Comment!*, e.g.:

Comment! Pas encore parti!
What! Not gone yet!

B   Adverbs of time

614   Adverbs of time include, among a number of others:

actuellement, at present
alors (see **615**), then
après, afterwards
aujourd'hui, today
auparavant, beforehand
autrefois, formerly

avant, before
bientôt (see 622), soon
déjà, already
demain, tomorrow
depuis, since
désormais, henceforward
donc (see 615), then
encore (see 616), again
enfin, at last
ensuite (see 615 and 617), then, next
hier, yesterday
jamais (see 618), ever, never
longtemps, for a long time
parfois, sometimes
maintenant (see 620), now
précédemment, previously
puis (see 615), then (next)
quelquefois, sometimes
souvent, often
tard (see 621), late
tôt (see 622), early
toujours, always, still

615 *Alors, puis, ensuite, donc, lors* 'then'

(i) The above five adverbs can all be translated as 'then', but in fact they mean very different things and, apart from *puis* and *ensuite*, they are not in general interchangeable.

(ii) *Alors* is used when 'then' means (a) 'at that time', e.g.:

J'étais à Paris. L'affaire Dreyfus était alors à son comble
I was in Paris. The Dreyfus affair was then at its height

or (b) 'so (= therefore)', e.g.:

Alors vous viendrez après tout
Then (*or* So) you will come after all

(iii) *Puis* and *ensuite* are used where 'then' means 'afterwards' or 'next', e.g.:

Nous sommes allés d'abord à Bougival et ensuite (or *puis*) *à Versailles*

We went first to Bougival and then to Versailles

On *ensuite*, see also **617**.

(iv) *Donc* means 'therefore, so, then', and, with the meaning of 'therefore' (i.e. expressing the conclusion of a logical argument), it comes first in the clause, e.g.:

Je pense; donc je suis
I think; therefore I exist

When meaning 'therefore' in a rather weaker sense, i.e. 'so, then', it usually follows the verb, e.g.:

On m'a téléphoné; je sais donc ce qui est arrivé
They telephoned to me; so I know what has happened

Il est donc de retour?
So he's back? (He's back then?)

But *donc* is mainly used to emphasize some word or phrase immediately preceding it, with a suggestion of protest or annoyance. In this case it stands early in its clause, but not first, and never precedes the verb except with an interrogative pronoun, adjective or adverb, e.g.:

Voulez-vous donc vous taire!
Can't you be quiet!

Qu'est-ce donc qui vous embête?
What on earth is annoying you?

Combien de fois donc dois-je vous dire ça?
However many times must I tell you that?

(v) For *lors*, see **619**.

616 *Encore* 'again, still, yet'
(i) Strictly as an adverb of time, *encore* has three senses:
(a) 'Again', e.g.:

J'espère que nous nous rencontrerons encore
I hope we shall meet again

It is often difficult to distinguish *encore* meaning 'again' from *de nouveau*. The latter faintly suggests restarting something: the former mere repetition; e.g. *Nous nous rencontrerons de nouveau* would imply 'starting a fresh series of meetings'. Thus one might say of two dogs *Ils se battent de nouveau* 'They are beginning a fresh fight'.

A nouveau means 'afresh'; without any idea of repetition, e.g.:

Il faut commencer à nouveau
We're got to start life all over again (a new kind of life, not the kind we've lived hitherto)

(b) 'Still (i.e., up to the present time)', e.g.:

Il est encore là   He is still there

Je suis encore à chercher une explication
I am still trying to find an explanation

But in this sense *encore* is sometimes ambiguous and so it is often advisable to use *toujours* instead, e.g.:

Il travaille toujours?   Is he still working?

(c) With a negative, 'yet', e.g.:

Personne n'est encore arrivé? Pas encore, heureusement! Rien n'est encore prêt!
Has nobody come yet? No, not yet, luckily! Nothing is ready yet

The position of *encore* in this sense is generally as shown in this example, i.e. after *pas*, or, if there is no *pas*, after the verb, or, in a compound tense, after the auxiliary.

(ii) With expressions denoting past time, *encore* may sometimes be translated as 'only', e.g.:

Hier encore il gelait; aujourd'hui nous voici en plein été
Only yesterday it was freezing; and to-day here we are in the middle of summer

(iii) Note the use of *encore* for the sake of emphasis, meaning 'too, even, actually, into the bargain', e.g.:

Outre l'amende il fut encore condamné à la prison

Besides the fine he was $\left\{ \begin{array}{l} \text{actually sentenced to prison} \\ \text{sentenced to prison into the bargain} \end{array} \right\}$

(iv) When 'another' means 'one more, an additional one' rather than 'a different one', *encore* should be used, not *un autre*, e.g.:

Il a demandé encore une banane
He asked for another (one more) banana

Il a demandé une autre banane
He asked for another (different) banana

Likewise, 'more' meaning 'some more' can be rendered by *encore* and the partitive article (but note that 'no more' is *ne . . . plus*), e.g.:

Désirez-vous encore du vin? Merci, je n'en veux plus
Would you like some more wine? No thank you, I don't want any more

(v) Note that 'even' with a comparative must be translated by *encore* (cf. English 'yet more' = 'even more'), not by *même*, e.g.:

Elle est encore plus intelligente que ses collègues
She is even more intelligent than her colleagues

J'aime encore mieux votre maison que la mienne
I like your house even better than my own

(vi) Finally, a couple of contexts in which *encore* either will not do (as in a below) or is not entirely adequate (as in b):

(a) The English idiom 'as (big) again', meaning 'twice as (big)' must be translated by *deux fois plus grand*, 'twice as (big) again' by *trois fois plus (grand)*, etc., e.g.:

Elle est deux fois plus jolie que sa sœur
She is as pretty again as her sister

Cette maison est trois fois plus grande que la mienne
This house is twice as big again as mine

(b) When 'yet' means 'as yet, up to this time', it should generally be translated by *jusqu'ici*, e.g.:

Je le connais de nom mais jusqu'ici je ne l'ai jamais vu
I know him by name, but I have never yet seen him

617 *Ensuite* and other expressions based on *suite*

Ensuite (see 615) was originally two words, viz. *en suite*, and it is worth noting a number of other adverbial and prepositional expressions formed on the basis of *suite*:

de suite	(1) in succession, one after another;
	(2) immediately
tout de suite	immediately

    par la suite   later on, subsequently
    par suite de   as a result of, in consequence of
e.g.:

    et ainsi de suite
    and so on

    Je viens tout de suite
    I am coming at once

    Nous verrons par la suite
    We will see later on

    Par suite de cet accident il fut fait prisonnier
    As a result of this accident he was made prisoner

618   *Jamais* 'ever'

Jamais is used particularly in direct and indirect questions, after comparisons, and after *si* 'if', e.g.:

    L'avez-vous jamais vu?
    Have you ever seen him

    Je t'aime plus que jamais
    I love you more than ever

    Si jamais je le vois, je le lui dirai
    If ever I see him, I'll tell him

and in a few expressions like *à jamais, à tout jamais* 'for ever'.
For *jamais* in the sense of 'never', see **550** and **558**.

619   *Lors*

Lors is not used on its own but only when preceded or followed by a preposition. The combinations *depuis lors* and *dès lors* mean 'since then, from that time, thenceforth', *pour lors* means 'for the time being, at the moment' (with reference to the past), while the prepositional phrase *lors de* means 'at the time of, in the days of', e.g.:

    Depuis (or *dès*) *lors de longues années se sont écoulées*
    Since that time (since then) long years have elapsed

    Le roi craignait pour ses États d'Hanovre, où il était pour lors
    The king was anxious about his possessions in Hanover where he was at the moment

    Lors de notre enfance nous jouions ensemble
    In the days of our childhood we used to play together

620 *Maintenant, or* 'now'

Maintenant means 'now' only of time. *Or* means 'now' in an introductory sense, and is used for emphasis, never of time. It must stand first in its clause, e.g.:

> *Il est maintenant colonel*
> He is now a colonel

> *Tous s'écrièrent de nouveau, disant, Non pas celui-ci, mais Barabbas. Or Barabbas était un brigand*
> Then cried they all again, saying, Not this man, but Barabbas! Now Barabbas was a robber

In English 'now' is often used in narrative of past time. French in such cases usually has *alors* (though *maintenant* also occurs), e.g.:

> *Alors ils se rendirent enfin compte du danger*
> Now at last they realized the danger

621 *Tard, en retard* 'late'

Tard means 'late' in the sense of 'at an advanced stage in some period of time'; but in the sense of 'too late' (i.e. after an appointed time) *retard* must be used, either with *en* or as an ordinary noun, e.g.:

> *Il se fait tard; il nous faut rentrer*
> It is getting late (i.e. in the day); we must go home

> *Il se développa tard*
> He developed late (i.e. in his life)

but

> *Le train est en retard de dix minutes* (or *Le train a dix minutes de retard*)
> The train is ten minutes late (i.e. after the time fixed for it)

> *Vous voilà, en retard comme d'habitude*
> Here you are, late as usual

622 *Tôt* 'soon, early' and compounds thereof

(i) *Tôt* 'soon, early' rarely stands by itself as *bientôt* is nearly always used for 'soon' and *de bonne heure* is the more usual equivalent of 'early'. Instances of the independent use of *tôt* are:

> *se lever (se coucher) tôt*
> to get up (go to bed) early

tôt ou tard
sooner or later

avoir tôt fait de + infinitive
not to take long about doing

(ii) *Tôt* may be qualified by other adverbs, the two words remaining separate, e.g.:

Vous arrivez très tôt; trop tôt en fait
You are here very early; too early in fact

Le train est parti plus tôt que d'ordinaire
The train started earlier (sooner) than usual

le plus tôt possible
as soon as possible

au plus tôt
(1) as soon as possible; (2) at the earliest

Je n'y serai pas aussi (or *si*) *tôt que vous*
I shall not be there as early as you

(iii) In certain cases, *tôt* is compounded with other adverbs in a single word, viz.:

aussitôt, immediately
bientôt, soon
plutôt, rather
sitôt, as soon
tantôt, this afternoon

tantôt . . . tantôt, sometimes . . . sometimes

e.g.:

J'irai aussitôt, bientôt, etc.   I will go at once, soon, etc.

With *que, aussitôt* and *sitôt* are used in the sense of 'as soon as', *plutôt* in the sense of 'rather than', e.g.:

Je vous écrirai aussitôt que je pourrai
I will write to you as soon as I can

Je mourrai plutôt que de vous trahir
I will die sooner than betray you

Il était tantôt heureux, tantôt triste
He was sometimes happy, sometimes sad

Aussitôt and *sitôt* may be used in the same sense with a past participle, e.g.:

Aussitôt (sitôt) dit, aussitôt (sitôt) fait
No sooner said than done

Aussitôt (sitôt) la lettre reçue, il partit
As soon as the letter was received, he left

In certain phrases *aussitôt* develops from this use into a preposition, e.g.:

Aussitôt son retour nous allons à la campagne
Immediately on his return we are going to the country

623   *Tout à coup* and *tout d'un coup*

Both of these adverbial expressions can be translated 'all at once'. But this phrase may mean either 'suddenly', which is *tout à coup*, or 'at one blow, with one movement', etc., which is *tout d'un coup*, e.g.:

La tempête fit tout à coup éclater la fenêtre
The gale suddenly shattered the window

La rafale emporta tout d'un coup la toiture du pigeonnier
The squall at one fell swoop carried away the roof of the dovecote

As will be seen from these examples, the two senses differ little from one another and are sometimes barely distinguishable.

C   Adverbs of place

624   Adverbs of place include:

ailleurs (see **625**), elsewhere	*devant*, in front
autour, around	*ici*, here
dedans, inside	*là*, there
dehors, outside	*loin*, far
derrière, behind	*partout*, everywhere
dessous, below	*près*, near
dessus, above	*proche*, near

625   *Ailleurs* 'elsewhere' and *d'ailleurs* 'besides, moreover'

D'ailleurs, 'besides', must be distinguished from *ailleurs,* 'elsewhere', e.g.:

> *Je ne peux pas quitter Londres; d'ailleurs je n'aime pas voyager*
> I cannot leave London; besides I don't care for travelling
>
> *J'ai cherché dans ma chambre et partout ailleurs, et je ne le trouve pas*
> I have looked in my room and everywhere else, and I can't find it

But note that *ailleurs* can sometimes be preceded by *de* 'from', in which case *d'ailleurs* of course means 'from somewhere else'.

D   Adverbs of quantity

626   For adverbs of quantity, see 320–327 ('Quantifiers').

E   Adverbs of affirmation or doubt

627   Adverbs of affirmation or doubt include:

apparemment, apparently
assurément, most certainly
certainement, certainly
certes, of course, admittedly
· *peut-être*, perhaps
probablement, probably
oui (see **628**), yes
si (see **628**), yes
sûrement, certainly
volontiers, willingly
vraiment, really
vraisemblablement, in all likelihood

628   (i) French has two words for 'yes', *oui* and *si*. In most contexts *oui* is used, while *si* is used in answer to a question expressed in the form of a negative, e.g.:

Ne m'avez-vous pas entendu?–Mais si, je vous ai entendu
Didn't you hear me?–Oh yes, I heard you

This *si* is further used to contradict a negative statement, e.g.:

Vous n'y réussirez jamais.–Mais si!
You will never succeed.–Oh yes I shall!

Que si and *si fait* are sometimes found as emphatic alternatives for *si*.

(ii) Note the use of *que oui* and *que si* after verbs of saying or thinking, after *espérer* 'to hope', and after *peut-être* 'perhaps', e.g.:

Est-ce qu'il peut partir maintenant? – J'ai déjà dit que oui
May he leave now? – I've already said yes (said so, said he can)

Est-ce qu'il arrive aujourd'hui? – J'espère que oui (Je crois que oui)
Is he arriving today? – I hope so (I think so)

Peut-être que oui
Perhaps so

Il n'acceptera jamais de le faire. – Ah, je crois que si.
He will never agree to do it. – Oh, I think he will

(Cf. the use of *que non*, **574**.)

F   Adverbs of negation

629   For adverbs of negation, see **544–558**.

G   Interrogative adverbs

630   The interrogative adverbs (see also **589–593** and **595**) are:

combien? (see **326**)	how much? how many?
comment?	how?
où?	where?
pourquoi?	why?
quand?	when?
que . . . ne. . .? (see **632**)	why . . . not . . . ?

631   On the basis of *où?* 'where?' is formed *d'où?* 'whence? where from?', e.g.:

> *D'où vient-il?*
> Where does he come from?

632   In the literary language, *que?* can have the meaning of 'why?', expressing at the same time an emotional reaction such as regret or surprise; in practice, this construction now seems to occur only in negative questions (though this restriction did not always apply in Classical French), and note that *que . . . ne . . .?* 'why . . . not?' is not accompanied by *pas*, e.g.:

> *Olivier et Roland, que n'êtes-vous ici?* (Hugo)
> Oliver and Roland, why are you not here?

633   Interrogation is also expressed by a variety of adverbial phrases, e.g. *de quelle manière?* 'how? in what way?', *pour quelle raison?* 'why? for what reason?', *à quel moment?* 'at what time?', *pendant combien de temps?* 'for how long?'

The comparison of adverbs

634   For the comparison of adverbs, see 'The comparison of adjectives and adverbs' (155–174).

The position of adverbs

635   The position of adverbs is to some extent a matter of taste and may vary in the interests of special emphasis or other stylistic effect. The observations that follow should therefore be taken as indications of general practice, which is often deviated from, rather than as hard-and-fast 'rules'.

Adverbs ending in -ment

636   (i) As a general principle adverbs in *-ment* (mostly adverbs of manner) stand before any word or phrase which they modify except a verb, so that in most cases their position is the same as in English, e.g.:

Il nous a donné une explication complètement incompréhensible
He gave us a completely incomprehensible explanation

Comme spectacle, cette pièce est absolument sans pareille
As a spectacle this play is absolutely without equal

Essayez d'écrire lisiblement
Try to write legibly (because *lisiblement* here qualifies a verb)

When, however, a past participle is used adjectivally, a qualifying adverb can be placed either before or after it; e.g.:

Un diner parfaitement cuit (or *cuit parfaitement*)
A perfectly cooked dinner (or a dinner cooked perfectly)

(For a past participle used in the compound tenses of a verb see 637.)

637 (ii) More often than not adverbs in *-ment* qualifying a verb stand after the verb in simple tenses, and between the auxiliary and the past participle in compound tenses.

But they must follow the past participle in a compound tense when the adverb has other words depending on it, and may also do so if the adverb is fairly long, e.g.:

Ils se battent fréquemment
They frequently fight (or fight frequently)

Ils se sont fréquemment battus
They have frequently fought (or fought frequently)

Ils se sont battus indépendamment les uns des autres
They fought independently of one another

Ils se sont battus furieusement (or *furieusement battus*)
They fought furiously

638 (iii) Various adverbs of affirmation or doubt in *-ment*, such as *apparement* 'apparently', *heureusement* 'fortunately', *probablement* 'probably', may stand either in the ordinary position after the verb, or first in the sentence and followed by *que* (see also **642**), e.g.:

Vous le connaissez heureusement
You know him, fortunately

Heureusement que vous le connaissez
Fortunately you know him

Il arrivera probablement mardi
He will probably arrive on Tuesday

Probablement qu'il arrivera mardi
Probably he will arrive on Tuesday

Adverbs not ending in *-ment*

639   (i) **Manner**

Bien, mieux, mal, pis, like adverbs in *-ment*, follow the verb in simple tenses, and more often than not come between the auxiliary and the participle in compound tenses, except that *si bien, si mal*, can be used like the English 'so well', 'so badly', e.g.:

Si bien a-t-il prononcé son morceau qu'on l'a entendu partout
So well did he pronounce his piece that he was heard everywhere

or
$\left\{\begin{array}{l}\textit{Il a si bien prononcé son morceau} \\ \textit{Il a prononcé si bien son morceau} \\ \textit{Il a prononcé son morceau si bien}\end{array}\right\}$ *(que . . .)*

Most other adverbs of manner not ending in *-ment* can likewise stand where emphasis requires. Some of them, if put at the beginning of a sentence, may cause inversion (see **600**).

640   (ii) **Time and place**

Adverbs of time and place usually come after the verb they qualify, but never between the auxiliary and participle. For the sake of emphasis they sometimes stand before both verb and subject, e.g.:

Il n'est pas arrivé aujourd'hui, mais il viendra demain
He has not come to-day, but he will come to-morrow

Nous sommes allés partout, et partout nous avons cherché des curiosités
We have been everywhere, and everywhere we have hunted for curios

Il est fatigué aujourd'hui
He is tired today

Aujourd'hui il est fatigué mais demain il va travailler
Today he is tired but tomorrow he is going to work

Like adverbs in *-ment*, these adverbs of time and place usually have the same position as in English.

641 (iii) **Quantity**

Adverbs of quantity generally stand after the verb in simple tenses and between the auxiliary and the participle in compound tenses and the past infinitive, e.g.:

Il voyage beaucoup
He travels a lot

Il a beaucoup voyagé
He has travelled a lot

Vous avez tant souffert
You have suffered so much

Nous avons assez travaillé
We have worked (long) enough

Il croyait avoir trop bu
He thought he had drunk too much

642 (iv) **Affirmation or doubt**

Peut-être 'perhaps' and the adverbial phrase *sans doute* 'doubtless' can either stand after the verb or else comes first and be followed by *que*, like *heureusement*, etc. (see **638**), or, in addition, they can come first and be followed by inversion of the subject pronoun (see **600**), e.g.:

Mon frère vous écrira sans doute ⎤
Sans doute que mon frère vous écrira ⎬ My brother will doubtless write to
Sans doute mon frère vous écrira-t-il ⎦ you

Il viendra peut-être mardi ⎤
Peut-être qu'il viendra mardi ⎬ Perhaps he will come on Tuesday
Peut-être viendra-t-il mardi ⎦

643 (v) **Interrogatives**

In literary French, interrogative adverbs always precede the verb both in direct and in indirect questions, e.g.:

Pourquoi veut-il y aller?
Why does he want to go there?

Je me demande pourquoi il veut y aller
I wonder why he wants to go there

Quand partez-vous?
When are you leaving?

But note that in spoken French there is a widespread tendency to put the interrogative last in direct questions, e.g.:

Vous partez quand?   When are you leaving?
Vous en voulez combien?   How many do you want?

For more on this, see **593**.

Prepositions

Introduction

644   Prepositions are of two kinds:

(1) **Simple** – those consisting of a single word.

(2) **Compound** – those formed of two or more words and usually ending in *à* or *de* (for exceptions see **648**).

Simple prepositions

645

à, to, at
*après, after
*avant, before (of time)
*avec, with
chez, at the house of
*contre, against
dans, in, into
de, of, from
*depuis, since, from
*derrière, behind
dès, from (of time)
*devant, before (of place)
en, in, into

entre, between
envers, towards
hormis, except
hors, outside, except
malgré, in spite of
*outre, besides
par, by, through
*parmi, among
*pour, for
sans, without
sauf, except, save
*selon, according to
sous, under
sur, on, upon
vers, towards

*The prepositions marked with an asterisk can also be used as adverbs; so also can *par derrière*, *par-dessous*, *par-dessus* (see **669**, **671**, **684**), e.g.:

Allez avant; nous viendrons après et les autres avec
You go ahead; we will come after and the others too (lit. 'with' = 'with us')

646 There are, besides, a few participles (present and past) used as prepositions.

Present participles

concernant, concerning
durant, during
pendant, during

suivant, according to
touchant, touching

To these may be added, as being participial in origin:

moyennant $\begin{cases} \text{in consideration for} \\ \text{on payment of} \end{cases}$

*nonobstant (archaic), notwithstanding

Past participles

attendu, considering
compris, including
excepté, except

passé, beyond, after
supposé, supposing
vu, considering

(See **134**.)

Compound prepositions

647 The English equivalents given here do not always cover the whole range of meanings of the French preposition in question; for fuller information, consult a good dictionary.

à

> *grâce à*, thanks to
> *jusqu'à*, up to, as far as
> *quant à*, as to
> *par rapport à*, with respect to

de

> *en amont de*, above ⎫ of places on
> *en aval de*, below ⎭ a river
> *en arrière de*, behind
> *en avant de*, ahead of
> *auprès de*, near, compared with
> *autour de*, around
> *à cause de*, because of
> *à côté de*, beside
> *du côté de*, to or from the direction of
> *au* ⎫ *dedans de*, inside
> *en* ⎭
> *au* ⎫ *dehors de*, outside
> *en* ⎭
> *au delà de*, beyond
> *au-dessous de*, below
> *au-dessus de*, above
> *(aller) au-devant de*, (to go) to meet
> *à l'exception de*, except
> *en face de*, opposite
> *faute de*, for lack of
> *à fleur de*, on the surface of
> *à force de*, by dint of
> *à l'insu de*, without the knowledge of
> *au lieu de*, instead of
> *au* (or *le*) *long de*, along, throughout
> *lors de*, at the time of

à moins de, without, barring
à partir de, as from
près
proche } *de*, near
à propos de, in connection with, apropos of
à raison de, at the rate of
à
au } *rebours de*, against, counter to
au sujet de, about
à titre de, by way of, as
au travers de, through
en travers de, across, athwart
vis-à-vis de, opposite, in relation to

As in English, a possessive adjective is with *à côté de* sometimes, and with *à l'insu de* always, substituted for a personal pronoun, e.g. *à côté de moi* or *à mes côtés* 'beside me' or 'at my side', *à mon insu* 'without my knowledge'.

648 Compound prepositions not ending in *à* or *de*

A few compound prepositions do not come into either of the categories mentioned in **644**, as they do not consist of a single word, and yet do not end in *à* or *de*. The only ones in regular use are:

d'après, according to, in the style of
à travers, through, across
par derrière, behind, round the back of (see **669**)
par-dessous, 'under', *par-dessus* 'over' (see **671** and **684**)

Government of verbs by prepositions

649 A few prepositions can stand before verbs. Of these, *en* is followed by the present participle, e.g. *en travaillant* 'working, by working'. The rest can only be used with the infinitive. They are:

Simple   *à*
              après (see below)
              de

                    entre (rare)
                    par (after verbs of beginning and ending only)
                    pour
                    sans

Compound   *avant de* (see below)
                    faute de
                    à force de
                    jusqu'à
                    au lieu de
                    à moins de
                    près de
                    proche de
                    quant à

Examples:

Il a commencé par l'éviter
He began by avoiding him

Il a fini par comprendre
He ended up understanding, he finally understood

Il alla jusqu'à la menacer de mort
He went so far as to threaten her with death

A moins de prendre un taxi nous serons en retard
Unless we take a taxi we shall be late

Elle était près de s'evanouir
She was nearly fainting

Note:

(a) that 'before' with an infinitive is *avant de* and never *avant* alone, e.g. *avant de partir* 'before leaving'

(b) that *après* always takes the perfect infinitive, i.e. *avoir* and the past participle or, in the case of those verbs that form their perfect tense with *être* (see **347**), *être* and the past participle (which agrees with the implied subject), e.g. *après avoir chanté* 'after singing, after having sung', *Après être tombée, elle a voulu se reposer* 'After falling, she wanted to rest'.

For the use of prepositions – mainly *à* and *de* – to form
(a) the complement of certain verbs, see **519–538**
(b) the complement of certain adjectives, see **686–690**

Repetition of prepositions

650 (i) **à, de, en**

When *à, de* or *en* govern two or more nouns, pronouns, infinitives or present participles, they should be repeated with each, e.g.:

> *Il doit son succès à son intelligence et à sa bonne volonté*
> His success is due to his intelligence and good will
>
> *Il est né d'une mère anglaise et d'un père français*
> He is the son of an English mother and a French father
>
> *Je vais en France et en Suisse*
> I am going to France and Switzerland
>
> *Il commence à grandir et à se développer*
> He is beginning to grow and develop
>
> *Il répondit en riant et en se moquant de leurs conseils*
> He replied by laughing and making fun of their advice

651 (ii) **other prepositions**

Prepositions other than *à, de* or *en*

(1) must be repeated when the governed nouns express opposite ideas; e.g.:

> *Dans la prospérité et dans l'adversité il montra la grandeur de son âme*
> In prosperity and adversity he showed his greatness of soul

(2) are generally not repeated when the governed nouns have much the same meaning; e.g.:

> *Il est amolli par le luxe et l'oisiveté*
> He is enervated by luxury and idleness

(3) when the ideas expressed by the governed nouns are neither opposite nor similar, the preposition may be repeated or not according to taste. Its omission is rather commoner in English than in French.

The meaning and use of individual prepositions

652 The sense of most prepositions varies widely in different contexts. The main uses are given below; a good many others will be found in various parts of the book, especially in the paragraphs referred to at the end of **649**.

653 *à*, normal meanings 'to, at'

(i) The preposition *à* denotes possession when used with the verb *être*, e.g.:

> *A qui est ce livre? Il est à Charles, mais l'autre est à moi*
> Whose is this book? It is Charles's, but the other one is mine

or with disjunctive personal pronouns, particularly for purposes of emphasis, e.g.:

> *Il a des idées à lui*
> He has ideas of his own
>
> *mes amis à moi et ses amis à elle*
> *my* friends and *her* friends

(ii) *à* and *de* may both be used between two nouns, the second of which qualifies the first. In such cases:

(a) *de* is used when 'of, made of', is expressed or understood

(b) *à* is used when the sense suggests 'with', 'for', 'for the purpose of making, producing, etc.', 'driven, worked, etc., by', e.g.:

de	*à*
une tasse de thé	*une tasse à thé*
a cup of tea	a tea-cup (i.e. a cup for tea)
un marchand de tabac	*un bateau à vapeur*
a tobacconist (i.e. seller of tobacco)	a steamship (i.e. worked by steam)
une robe de soie	*un ver à soie*
a silk dress (i.e. made of silk)	a silk worm (i.e. for producing silk)
	un moulin à café
	a coffee mill (i.e. for the purpose of grinding coffee)

also used in the sense of

(1) by	à force de	by dint of
	peu à peu	little by little
	deux à deux	two by two, i.e. two at a time
	fait à la main	made by hand, handmade
	vendre au poids	to sell by weight
	vendre aux enchères	to sell by auction
	à l'heure	by the hour
	à la lumière d'une bougie	by candle light

(For *à* meaning 'by' see also 433.)

(2) for	à jamais	for ever
	mot à mot	word for word
(3) in	à la campagne	in the country
	au bois	in the wood
	au lit	in bed
	à l'ombre	in the shade
	au milieu de	in the middle of
	à mon avis	in my opinion
	à la hâte	in haste
	à temps	in time
	avec un bâton à la main	with a stick in his hand
	au désespoir	in despair
(4) on	à bord	on board
	à pied	on foot
	à cheval	on horseback
	à droite, à gauche	on the right, left hand side
	à son départ	on his departure
	il se mit à genoux	he knelt down (lit. placed himself on his knees)
	à condition que	on condition that
	au contraire	on the contrary
	à l'heure	on time
(5) with	un garçon aux cheveux longs	a boy with long hair
	le monsieur au parapluie	the man with the umbrella
	une chemise à raies bleues	a shirt with blue stripes
	à grandes enjambées	with long strides
	avoir affaire à quelqu'un	to have to deal with someone
	abattre un arbre à coups de cognée	to fell a tree with (blows of) an axe
	à grand'peine	with great difficulty
	à regret	with regret
(6) within	à portée de fusil, etc.	within range (of rifle, etc.)
	à portée de la main	within reach
	à portée de voix	within hail
	à portée de vue	within sight

Note too:

(7) the use of *à* with an infinitive as the equivalent of an English present participle denote a way of spending time, e.g.:

Il était perché sur le toit à regarder attentivement l'horizon
He was perched on the roof carefully scanning the horizon

Il passe son temps à lire des romans
He spends his time reading novels

(8) the use of *à la* for *à la mode* (with adjectives) or *à la mode de* (with nouns), e.g. *à l'américaine* 'in the American way', *des petits pois à la française* 'peas French-style', *des poésies à la Victor Hugo* 'poems in the style of Victor Hugo'.

For the use of the dative *à* with verbs denoting 'to take something from someone' see **524**, list 4 b.

à, dans, en

654 Great care is needed in translating 'at, to, in, into' when used of place. The three usual equivalents are *à, dans* and *en*, each of which can be used both of motion towards (= 'to, into') or of position at a place (= 'at, in') – but **they are not interchangeable**, e.g.:

Il est à la maison
He is in the house

Il vient à la maison
He is coming to the house

Il se trouvait dans la chambre
He was in the room

Il entra dans la chambre
He went into the room

Il est en prison
He is in prison

On l'a envoyé en prison
He has been sent to prison

For further details, see **655–659**.

For the use of these prepositions with reference to time, see **709** and **713**.

655   'To', 'at' and 'in' with names of towns are all translated by *à*,
e.g.:

Je vais à Paris	I am going to Paris
Je demeure à Paris	I live in Paris
Il est étudiant à Dijon	He is a student at Dijon

If the name of the town includes an article, as in *Le Havre* and *les
Andelys*, the usual contractions apply (see 25), i.e. *au Havre, aux
Andelys*, but, in the feminine singular, *à la Haye* 'at or to The
Hague'. See also **659**,ii, for the use of *dans* with names of towns.

656   The translation of 'to' or 'in' with names of continents,
countries, provinces, etc., depends on their gender (see **52**,b). In
general, 'to' and 'in' are both translated by *en* (without an article)
with feminine names but by *au* (or, in the plural, *aux*) with
masculine names, e.g.:

I go to	France	*Je vais*	*en France*
	China		*en Chine*
I am in	America	*Je suis*	*en Amérique*
I go to	Denmark	*Je vais*	*au Danemark*
	Mexico		*au Mexique*
I am in	the United States	*Je suis*	*aux États-Unis*

The few masculine singular names that begin with a vowel are an
exception and require *en*, e.g. *en Afghanistan* 'in *or* to Afghanistan', *en Équateur* 'in *or* to Ecuador'.

657   Distinction between *dans* and *en*

(i) *En* is not used with the definite article except in certain fixed
expressions such as the following:

en l'absence de
in the absence of

en l'air
in the air (lit. and figurative)

en l'an 1980
in the year 1980

en l'église de
at the church of (used in connection with some ceremony)

en l'espace de
within the space of (a period of time)

en l'honneur de
in honour of

en la matière
on the subject, in the matter (e.g. *je suis ignorant en la matière*)

en la personne de
in the person of

en la présence de
in the presence of

Note that all the above expressions involve the use of *en l'* or *en la*; the use of *en* with *le* or *les* is very rare and should be avoided as it is usually unacceptable.

(ii) *Dans*, on the other hand, must always be followed by an article – definite, indefinite or partitive – or by another determiner (see 23), except with names of towns or people (see 659,ii) or with a numeral, e.g. *dans le tiroir* 'in the drawer', *dans votre sac* 'in your handbag', *Dans quel roman avez-vous trouvé cette citation?* 'In what novel did you find that quotation?', *dans trois villes différentes* 'in three different towns'.

The result of this is that *dans* is in many cases more definite than *en*, e.g.:

Il est en prison
He is in jail (place unspecified)

Il est dans la prison de Poitiers
He is in Poitiers jail (a definite place)

658   Special uses of *en*

Note that in the following cases *en* is used, not *dans*:

(a) in the sense of 'as', e.g.:

Il le traita en enfant	He treated him as a child
déguisé en agent de police	disguised as a policeman

(b) in the sense of 'on', e.g.:

en garde	on guard
en vacances	on holiday
en moyenne	on (an) average

(c) to denote the material of which a thing is made, the colour it is painted, or its shape, e.g.:

une montre en or	a gold watch
une maison bâtie en briques	a house built of brick
un mur peint en blanc	a wall painted white
une fenêtre en ogive	a pointed window

(d) to denote the way in which a person is dressed; e.g.:

en grande tenue	in full dress uniform
en bras de chemise	in shirt sleeves

(e) with verbs of 'changing into' and 'dividing into', e.g.:

Le cinéma va être transformé en supermarché
The cinema is going to be turned into a supermarket

La grenouille s'est changée en prince
The frog changed into a prince

changer des dollars en francs
to change dollars into francs

Il coupa le gâteau en tranches
He cut the cake into slices

(f) with reference to months, seasons, years, e.g.:

en juin (or *au mois de juin*)
in June

en été, en automne, en hiver
in summer, in autumn, in winter

en 1934	in 1934
en quelle année?	in what year?

but *au printemps* 'in spring'.

(g) before *plein* when English has 'in' (or occasionally 'on'), e.g.:

Il le frappa en pleine poitrine	He hit him right in the chest
en plein hiver	in the middle of winter
en plein jour	in broad daylight
en pleine mer	on the high seas

(h) to form adverbial expressions; e.g.:

en bas	below, downstairs
en haut	above, upstairs

en avant	in front, forward
en arrière	behind, back
en face	opposite
en tout cas	anyhow
en plus	in addition, besides

Note in particular the use of *de . . . en . . .* with comparatives of the type 'more and more (or less and less) difficult', e.g.:

de mieux en mieux	better and better
de plus en plus difficile	more and more difficult
de moins en moins souvent	less and less often

For the use of *en* with a present participle, see **442**.

659 Distinction between *à* and *dans*

(i) *Dans* slightly emphasizes the boundaries or limits of the space named, whereas *à* suggests that something is happening in the particular area as opposed to any other area; e.g.:

Monsieur X est-il à la maison?
Is Mr. X in the house? (as opposed to any other place)

Il est quelque part dans la maison
He is somewhere in the house

Non, il est au jardin
No, he is in the garden (as opposed to the house)

Il met des plantes dans les plates-bandes
He is putting some plants in the flower-beds (strictly within the limits of the beds)

Il a été blessé à l'épaule
He has been wounded in the shoulder (as opposed to any other part of his body)

Si j'étais à votre place, je ne le ferais pas
If I were in your place, I should not do it (but your place is distinct from my place)

Je l'ai trouvé dans la poche de son pardessus
I found it in the pocket of his overcoat (obviously confined within the limits of the pocket)

(ii) 'In' or 'at' with the name of a town, regarded as a place where something is situated or where some event takes place, is normally *à*, e.g. *Il travaille à Londres* 'He works in London', *Je l'ai vu à Paris* 'I saw him in Paris'. *Dans* may however be used to express the idea of 'within, (right) inside', e.g. *L'ennemi est déjà dans Paris* 'The enemy is already inside Paris', or to stress the idea of the town as an area (within which one can move about, for example) rather than as a point on a map, e.g. *J'aime me promener dans Paris* 'I like going for walks in Paris, walking about Paris'. *Dans* is also used if the name of a town is qualified by an adjective or adjectival expression, e.g.:

> *A l'exposition on se plonge dans le vieux Paris*
> At the exhibition we plunge into old Paris
>
> *Dans le Paris d'aujourd'hui on ne sait guère s'orienter*
> In present-day Paris one can hardly find one's bearings

With the name of a person, *dans* means 'in the works of', e.g. *Vous le trouverez dans Molière* 'You will find it in Molière'.

(iii) Note the use of *dans* where English uses 'out of' in such contexts as:

> *On a bu dans ce verre*
> Someone has been drinking out of this glass
>
> *un article découpé dans le journal*
> an article cut out of the paper
>
> *Prenez un mouchoir dans le tiroir*
> Take a handkerchief out of the drawer

– i.e. French indicates where the object was before it was moved while English expresses the direction in which it is moved (cf. *sur* 'on' where English uses 'from, off', **685**).

(iv) *dans* is also used in the sense of

with	*dans ce but*	with this object
	dans l'idée d'en finir	with the idea of putting an end to it
within	*L'ennemi est dans les murs*	The enemy is within the walls
	dans les limites de la légalité	within the limits of the law
	Nous y serons dans (les) vingt-quatre heures	We shall be there within twenty-four hours

660 *après*, normal meaning 'after'

Après, when used with a verb, takes the past infinitive (see **649**).

It sometimes has the sense of 'next to', e.g.:

Après le ski, j'aime mieux la natation
Next to skiing, I like swimming best

(For *d'après*, see **648**.)

661 *à travers, au travers de, en travers de*

In spite of what some grammars say, there is little or no distinction
in meaning between *à travers* and *au travers de* meaning 'through';
à travers (which, note, is never followed by *de*) is the more usual,
e.g. *à travers un verre, les nuages, la foule* 'through a glass, the
clouds, the crowd', *Il avait reçu un coup d'épée au travers du bras*
(or *à travers le bras*) 'He had received a sword-thrust through the
arm'. *A travers* occasionally means 'across', e.g. *à travers champs*
'across country', but note carefully the following points in connection with the translation of 'across':

(a) 'across' meaning 'placed across, lying across' is *en travers de*,
e.g. *Il y a un arbre en travers de la route* 'There is a tree (lying)
across the road' (but *un pont sur le ruisseau* 'a bridge across the
stream')

(b) when 'across' means 'on the other side of', none of the forms
based on *travers* will do, e.g. 'I saw him across the square' is best
rendered by *Je l'ai vu de l'autre côté de la place*

(c) where English uses a verb of motion (e.g. 'to swim, to run')
and 'across', French normally uses *traverser* 'to cross' and an
adverbial expression expressing the type of motion involved, e.g.:

> *traverser la Manche à la nage*
> to swim across the Channel

> *Il traversa la place en courant*
> He ran across the square

but 'to walk across' is often just *traverser*, e.g. *traverser le pont* 'to
walk across the bridge'.

662 *auprès de*

Auprès de expresses:

(a) propinquity to, attendance on, or opportunity of communica-
tion with, e.g.:

> *Il était ambassadeur auprès du Saint-Siège*
> He was ambassador to the Holy See

(b) dealings or relations with those with whom one is thus in contact, e.g.:

> *Il était bien auprès du roi*
> He stood well with the king

> *faire des démarches auprès de quelqu'un*
> to take a matter up with someone

(c) comparison, e.g.:

> *Il trouvait cette perte légère auprès des premières*
> He considered this loss trifling compared with his original losses

663   *avant, devant*, normal meaning 'before'

Both denote priority – *avant*, of time, *devant*, of place. When they are used metaphorically *avant* denotes preference, *devant* means 'in view of', 'in the eyes of', e.g.:

> *Il arriva avant l'heure*
> He arrived before the time

> *Il fut amené devant le juge*
> He was brought before the judge

> *Je choisirais ça avant tout*
> I should choose that in preference to anything

> *Tous sont égaux devant la loi*
> All are equal in the eyes of the law

Note also:

(1) *en avant de* 'ahead of, in front of', e.g.:

> *marcher en avant du défilé*
> to walk ahead of the procession

(2) *au-devant de* (with verbs of motion) 'to go, run, etc., to meet', e.g.:

> *Il courut au-devant de son père*
> He ran to meet his father

> *Il va toujours au-devant du danger*
> He always goes to meet danger (courts danger)

664 *avec*, normal meaning 'with'

Used in most of the senses of the English 'with', but see throughout this section the use of other prepositions where English uses 'with'.

665 *chez*, normal meaning 'at the house (or shop) of'

Il est chez lui
He is at his house, at home

Il sort de chez lui
He is coming out of his house

Je l'ai vu chez Jean
I saw him at John's

chez le boulanger
at the baker's

Also used in sense of

with	*C'est une habitude chez moi*	It's a habit with me (or 'of mine')
among	*Ça se fait chez les Anglais*	This is done among the English
in (the works of)	*l'emploi du subjonctif chez Racine*	the use of the subjunctive in Racine

and note too *chez nous* 'in our country', etc.

666 *contre* normal meaning 'against'

Also used in sense of

with	*se fâcher contre quelqu'un*	to get angry with someone
from	*Il s'abrita contre le vent*	He took shelter from the wind
for	*la haine qu'elle éprouvait contre son gendre*	her hatred for her son-in-law
	échanger x contre y	to exchange x for y
to	*six voix contre cinq*	six votes to five

667 *de* (see also 650, 653), normal meanings 'from', 'of', possessive *'s'*

Also used in sense of

(1) for	*le respect de la vérité*	respect for truth
	de longue date	for a long time (past)
(2) with	*de tout mon cœur*	with all my heart
	rouge de colère (see also 524, 688)	purple with rage

(3)	in	*d'un ton sec*	in a dry voice
		(cf. *le ton dont il parlait*, the tone in which he spoke) ·	
		de cette façon	in this way
		augmenter (baisser) de prix (see also 171)	to go up (or down) in price
		jamais de la vie	never in my life

So with words denoting physical or mental qualities or defects, e.g.:

	sain de corps et d'esprit	sound in body and mind
	aveugle de chaque œil et boiteux d'un pied	blind in both eyes and lame in one foot
(4) by	*de naissance*	by birth
	de vue	by sight
	de nature	by nature
	de nom	by name

So of time:

Il est parti de nuit (see also under *par* and 171)	He started by night

(5)	on	*de tous côtés*	on all sides
		de garde	on duty
(6)	than	(see 166–167)	

(i) One important construction involving the use of *de*, and one that must be carefully noted since it does not correspond at all to English usage, is the compulsory insertion of *de* when such indefinite pronouns as *quelqu'un* 'someone', *personne* 'nobody', *quelque chose* 'something', *rien* 'nothing', *aucun, pas un* 'not one', are followed by an adjective or past participle, e.g.:

Quelqu'un d'important demande à vous parler
Somebody important is asking to speak to you

Je ne connais personne de plus charmant
I don't know anyone more charming

Il y a quelque chose de louche dans cette affaire
There's something suspicious about this business

Rien de grave!
Nothing serious!

Je n'ai jamais rien vu de pareil
I've never seen anything like it

Parmi tous ces hommes il n'y en avait aucun (or *pas un*) *de capable*
Among all these men there wasn't one who was efficient

Note in particular *personne d'autre, rien d'autre, quoi d'autre?* 'nobody else, nothing else, what else?'

(ii) The same rule applies after such expressions as *ce qu'il y a* 'what (= that which)', *quoi?* 'what?', *qu'est-ce qu'il y a?* 'what?', *il n'y a . . . que . . .*, e.g.:

Ce qu'il y a d'intéressant c'est que . . .
What's interesting is that . . .

Quoi de neuf?
What news?

Qu'est-ce qu'il y a ⎫
Quoi   ⎬ *de plus beau que . . . ?*
What is more beautiful than . . .?

Il n'y a d'important que la vérité
There is nothing important but truth

Note that in both of these types the adjective remains invariable (contrast iii below).

(iii) The same construction can also occur (a) after a noun introduced by an indefinite article, in which case the preposition serves to detach the adjective from the noun in much the same way as a relative clause, e.g.:

si vous avez une journée libre
if you have a free day

but

si vous avez une journée de libre
if you have a day (which is) free

and (b), with a similar value, after a numeral or some other expression of quantity such as *plusieurs* 'several', *la moitié* 'half', *encore un* 'another one', *beaucoup* 'a lot', *combien?* 'how many?', e.g.:

Sur ces quatre verres, il y en a trois de sales
Of these four glasses, there are three dirty

Il y a déjà la moitié de mes crayons de perdus
There are already half my pencils lost

Encore une journée de perdue!
Another day wasted!

Il y aura beaucoup de soldats de tués
There will be a lot of soldiers killed

Note that in type (iii) the adjective or participle agrees in gender and number with the noun or pronoun to which it refers (contrast i and ii above).

Another idiomatic use of *de* is found in French (where English also often has 'of') between two nouns, the first of which qualifies the second, e.g.:

un vrai fripon d'enfant
a regular rascal of a boy

un pauvre diable de mendiant
a poor devil of a beggar

un imbécile de douanier
a fool of a customs officer

une chienne de vie
a rotten life

un amour de petit chien
a cute little dog

Note:

(a) that, in this construction, *diable* is often treated as feminine with a following feminine noun, e.g. *une diable d'affaire* 'a wretched business', *une diable d'idée* 'a weird idea'

(b) the use of *un* or *une drôle de* meaning 'strange, odd', e.g. *un drôle de type* 'a strange fellow', *une drôle d'idée* 'an odd idea'; note too *la drôle de guerre* 'the phoney war' (i.e. the first few months of World War II when nothing much seemed to be happening).

Notice that all the above constructions express some kind of value judgement (in most – but not all – cases unfavourable).

For the use of *de* instead of an indefinite or a partitive article, see **43–45**.

For the use of *de* to express the possessive relationship, see **22**.

668 *depuis*, normal meanings 'since, for'
Examples:

Il est absent depuis hier
He has been absent since yesterday

Il est absent depuis un an
He has been absent for a year

(For the tense, see **413**,iii. For *depuis lors* see **619**.)

Depuis is also used in the sense of 'from' of time or place, e.g.:

depuis le matin jusqu'au soir
from morning till evening

J'ai été malade depuis Calais jusqu'à Douvres
I was sick from Calais to Dover

La France s'étend depuis les Alpes jusqu'à l'Océan
France stretches from the Alps to the Ocean

669   *derrière, en arrière de, par derrière*, normal meaning 'behind'
Derrière is only used of place in a literal sense. For 'behind, behindhand with' in a metaphorical sense *en arrière de* is used (and may also be used in a literal sense), e.g.:

Il se cacha derrière la porte
He hid behind the door

Il est en arrière des autres élèves
He is behind the other pupils (i.e. in his school work)

Par derrière implies movement, e.g.,:

Il est passé par derrière la maison
He went round the back of the house

670   *dès*, normal meaning 'from the time of, right from'
Examples:

dès sa première enfance   from his earliest infancy
dès le début   right from the beginning

Dès is also used with expressions of place when these denote a point in time, e.g.:

Dès Orange le train augmente de vitesse
From (the moment of leaving) Orange the train's speed increases

(For *dès lors* see **619**.)

671 *dessus, au-dessus de, par-dessus*, normal meanings 'over, above'

Up to the middle of the seventeenth century, *dessus* was regularly used as a preposition, e.g. *Le peuple* . . . *se rua dessus lui* (Regnier) 'The people rushed upon him', but this use now remains only as an archaism that should not be imitated. In practice, *dessus* is now only an adverb. (Cf. *dessous*, **684**.)

Par-dessus nearly always suggests (1) movement over something, or (2) an addition to something ('over and above'), e.g.:

> *Il sauta par-dessus la haie*
> He jumped over the hedge
>
> *par-dessus le marché*
> into the bargain
>
> *Il porte un gros manteau par-dessus son habit*
> He wears a big cloak over his coat

Au-dessus de is used to translate 'over' or 'above' in practically every other case; e.g.:

> *Son portrait pend au-dessus de la cheminée*
> His portrait hangs over the mantelpiece

672 *du côté*

Note the distinction between (i) the prepositional phrase *du côté de*, which is invariable (i.e. *côté* can never be qualified by an adjective), and (ii) the adverbial phrase *du côté* with an adjective and which may or may not be followed by *de*. The principal meanings of these two expressions are:

(i) *du côté de*

(a) 'in the direction of, towards', e.g. *La voiture filait à toute vitesse du côté de Vendôme* 'The car was speeding towards Vendôme'

(b) 'from the direction of, from', e.g. *Le vent vient du côté de la mer* 'The wind is coming from (the direction of) the sea'

(c) 'in the area of', e.g. *Il habite du côté de la place de la République* 'He lives somewhere near the place de la République'

(ii) *du côté* (qualified)

(a) 'to the . . . side', e.g. *Passez de l'autre côté de la rue* 'Cross to the other side of the street'

(b) 'from the . . . side, direction', e.g. *Le vent vient du mauvais côté* 'The wind is coming from the wrong direction (*or* quarter)'

(c) 'on the . . . side', e.g. *L'hôtel de l'Europe se trouve du côté sud de la place* 'The Hôtel de l'Europe is on the south side of the square'

673 *entre, parmi*, normal meanings $\left\{\begin{array}{l} \textit{entre } \text{'between'} \\ \textit{parmi } \text{'among'} \end{array}\right.$

Entre may, however, also mean 'among'. It is used in this sense chiefly with words and expressions which denote 'choosing', 'distinguishing', 'distributing', 'excelling'.

Note that with some of these expressions English, like French, often uses 'between' instead of 'among'.
Examples:

Lequel entre tous ces livres faut-il choisir? (*d'entre* also possible – see below)
Among all these books which am I to choose?

Il ne distinguait pas entre tous ces enfants
He did not distinguish between (*or* among) all these children

Elle était belle entre toutes
She was loveliest of all – literally 'among them all'

Le ciel vous prépare une place entre les immortels
Heaven is preparing a place for you among the gods

L'un l'autre with or without a preposition is sometimes replaced by *entre* and a disjunctive personal pronoun, e.g.:

Ils se ressemblent entre eux (or *l'un à l'autre*)
They are like one another

Parmi, on the other hand, never means 'between' in the sense of 'between two'. Its original meaning is 'in the middle of'. It applies, therefore, firstly to place, and from this is extended to a group or circle; e.g.:

Il se cachait parmi les buissons
He was hiding among the bushes

Il était assis parmi ses brebis
He was sitting among his sheep

674   *d'entre*

After (a) an expression of quantity, (b) a negative pronoun, or (c) an interrogative pronoun, the English word 'of' followed by a disjunctive pronoun should be translated by *d'entre,* 'from among'; e.g.:

> *plusieurs d'entre eux*
> several of them
>
> *la plupart d'entre nous*
> the majority of us
>
> *Personne d'entre vous ne sait rien*
> None of you know(s) anything
>
> *Lequel d'entre eux a dit ça?*
> Which of them said that?

So *deux d'entre vous* 'two of you', when there are more than two people concerned. But for 'there are two of you', meaning that two is the total number, the French is *vous êtes deux.*

This use of *d'entre* may be extended to nouns when 'among' or 'from among' are natural alternatives to 'of' in English.

However, *de* + a disjunctive pronoun is possible as an alternative to *d'entre* after *chacun* 'each', *l'un* 'one', *pas un* 'not one', *aucun* 'not one', *qui?* 'who?', and occasionally *la plupart* 'most', e.g.:

> *chacun d'eux* (or *d'entre eux*)
> each of them
>
> *l'un de nous* (or *d'entre nous*)
> one of us
>
> *qui de vous?* (or *d'entre vous?*)
> who among you?

Note that *de* (not *d'entre*) must be used when the pronoun is qualified, e.g. *Personne de nous trois n'est coupable* 'None of us three is guilty'.

675   *envers* (see **687, 689**), *vers*, normal meanings 'towards, to'

Envers denotes conduct or attitude towards people. *Vers* refers to physical motion towards; with expressions of time it means 'about'.

Examples:

> *sa générosité envers sa famille*
> his generosity to (towards) his family

> *Il courut vers moi*
> He ran towards me

> *Il leva les yeux vers le ciel*
> He raised his eyes to (towards) heaven

> *vers trois heures*
> about three o'clock

676 *hormis, sauf, excepté*, normal meaning 'except'

Hormis is rather rare; *sauf* and *excepté* are used just like the English 'except':

> *Tout le monde est arrivé, sauf ma sœur*
> Everybody has come except my sister

> *Ils sont tous partis, excepté les trois Allemands*
> They have all left, except the three Germans

Note however that *excepté*, which was originally a past participle, occasionally follows the noun to which it refers, and then it agrees with it in gender and number, e.g. *Elles sont toutes mariées, la fille aînée exceptée* 'They are all married, the eldest daughter excepted (apart from the eldest daughter)' (see also **134**).

677 *hors, hors de, en dehors de, fors*, normal meanings 'out of, outside'

In this literal sense *hors* is chiefly confined to certain phrases, e.g.:

> *hors concours*
> outside the competition, i.e. not competing (at a show)

> *hors commerce*
> not on general sale

> *hors jeu*
> offside

> *hors ligne*
> incomparable, outstanding

> *mettre hors la loi*
> to outlaw

It is also, though rarely, used in the sense of 'except'.

Hors de and *en dehors de* are both used literally of place; e.g.:

> *Ils se trouvèrent hors de la ville,* or *en dehors de la ville*
> They found themselves out of the town, or outside the town

Hors de can also be used metaphorically; e.g.:

> *Il est hors de danger*
> He is out of danger

> *hors d'haleine*
> out of breath

> *hors de combat*
> disabled, out of action

Fors is an old form of *hors*, meaning 'except' and has now gone almost totally out of use except in the saying *Tout est perdu fors l'honneur* 'All is lost save honour'.

678 *malgré*, normal meanings 'in spite of, notwithstanding', e.g.:

> *Malgré sa colère il ne dit rien*
> In spite of his fury he said nothing

> *malgré tout*
> in spite of everything

> *malgré moi*
> in spite of myself, against my better judgement

679 *outre, en outre de*, normal meanings: *outre* 'besides, beyond, in addition to'; *en outre de* 'besides'

Outre is used in a few compounds such as:

> *outre-Manche*, across the Channel (i.e. in England)
> *outre-mer*, overseas
> *outre-Atlantique*, across the Atlantic
> *outre-Rhin*, beyond the Rhine
> *outre-tombe*, beyond the grave

Otherwise it is rare except in the phrases:

> *outre mesure*, beyond measure
> *outre cela*, besides that

and adverbially in

> *passer outre,* to press on regardless
> *en outre*, besides

'Besides' can generally be translated by *en outre de*, but French more often uses *en plus de*, or turns the sentence with *sans compter*, or, where English has 'other', by *autre. . .que*; e.g.:

> *En plus du service ordinaire il y a un train spécial à huit heures*
> Besides the ordinary service there is a special train at 8 a.m.

> *J'ai d'autres paquets que le sien à expédier ce soir*
> I have other parcels besides his to send off tonight

680 *par*, normal meanings 'by', 'through'

(a) 'by'

When used to express the agent after a passive verb *par* may often be replaced by *de*, especially with verbs of the senses (*voir, entendre*, etc.) and verbs denoting encirclement (*entourer, environner*, etc.) or mental emotion (*aimer, haïr*, etc.).

(b) 'through'

When used of place 'through' may usually be translated by *par*, although *à travers* (see **661**) or the verb *traverser* are sometimes preferable.

Also used in the sense of

(1) in	*par une pluie battante*	in driving rain
	par un temps neigeux	in snowy weather
	par bouffées	in puffs
	par écrit	in writing
(2) for	*par exemple*	for instance
	par pitié	for pity's sake
	remarquable par sa bonté	remarkable for his kindness
	(so with many adjectives such as *admirable, célèbre*, etc., followed by a noun denoting a quality)	
(3) on	*par terre*	on the ground (but note *tomber, jeter, par terre* 'fall to the ground, throw on the ground')
	par une belle journée d'été	on a fine summer's day
(4) out of	*jeter q.ch. par la fenêtre*	to throw something out of the window

and in various adverbial expressions, e.g.:

par ici	(Come) this way!
par conséquent	consequently
par mégarde	inadvertently
par intervalles	intermittently

(cf. *parfois* 'sometimes', *partout* 'everywhere', which have come to be simple adverbs, written as one word)

681 *pour*, normal meaning 'for'

Pour is used in almost all the senses of the English 'for', except that with expressions of time it can only be used when there is an idea of purpose or intent – see **712**.

Note also its use in percentages, e.g.:

dix pour cent   ten per cent

For its use with adjectives see **687, 689**.
For 'for' with expressions of price, see **717**.

682 *sans*, normal meanings 'without, except for, but for'

Examples:

J'y serai à dix heures sans faute
I will be there at ten o'clock without fail

Sans le capitaine nous aurions été tous noyés
But for the captain we should all have been drowned

683 *selon*, normal meaning 'according to'

Examples:

Selon votre père vous avez eu tort
According to your father you were wrong

selon moi
in my opinion

684 *sous, au-dessous de, par-dessous, dessous*, normal meanings 'under, below, underneath, beneath'.

Though similar in meaning, these prepositions are not however interchangeable. The distinction is basically that:

sous means 'directly below, underneath'

au-dessous de means 'lower down than, beneath (figurative)'

par-dessous suggests motion

Up to the seventeenth century, *dessous* was regularly used as a preposition, but except as an occasional archaism (e.g. *dessous la table* 'under the table') that should not be imitated, this use has died out and *dessous* remains only as an adverb. (Cf. *dessus*, **671**.)

Examples:

Le chien est sous la table
The dog is under the table

Le thermomètre est au-dessous de zéro
The thermometer is below zero

Ce métier est au-dessous de lui
This occupation is beneath him

Il rampa par-dessous la haie
He crawled under the hedge

Sous is also used in the sense of

in	*sous le règne de*	in the reign of
	sous presse	in the press (printing)
	passer sous silence	to pass over in silence
	sous ce rapport	in this respect
	sous forme de cachets	in tablet form
	sous la forme d'une sorcière	in the form (guise) of a witch
on	*sous quelle condition?*	on what condition?
	sous peine de mort	on pain of death
	sous serment	on oath

685   *sur*, normal meanings 'on, upon, on to'

Examples:

Il se mit debout sur la table
He stood up on the table

Il était debout sur la table
He was standing on (*or* upon) the table

Il monta sur la table
He got up on to the table

Also used in the sense of

over	*Il jeta une planche sur le fossé*	He threw a plank over the ditch
	Il s'endormit sur son travail	He went to sleep over his work
	Il n'avait plus d'influence sur sa fille	He had no longer any influence over his daughter
in	*La clef est sur la porte*	The key is in the door
	une fois sur dix	once in ten times
	Il m'en a parlé sur un ton dédaigneux	He spoke of it in a scornful tone
for	*Les autobus sur Toulon sont rares*	There are few buses for Toulon
from, off	*Il prit son chapeau sur la patère*	He took his hat from the peg
	Il prit son livre sur la table	He took his book off the table
out of	*treize sur vingt*	thirteen out of twenty
	deux mariages sur trois	two out of every three marriages
towards	*sur les dix heures*	towards ten o'clock
	Il dirigea ses pas sur cette lumière	He directed his steps towards this light
by	*cinq centimètres sur dix*	five centimetres by ten
	Il régla sa montre sur la mienne	He set his watch by mine
	sur mes conseils	by my advice
about	*Je l'ai questionné sur ses mouvements*	I questioned him about his movements
	Il est très bien renseigné sur cette affaire	He is very well informed about this business
	Avez-vous un canif sur vous?	Have you got a penknife about (on) you?

Prepositions used with adjectives or past participles

686 The following adjectives and participles require in French a preposition which is not the ordinary equivalent of the one used in English. When used with other prepositions, many adjectives have other senses besides those given below.

N.B. No adjective can ever govern an infinitive without a preposition.

687 List 1

A noun or an infinitive depending on one of the following adjectives is usually joined to it by *à*.

adj.	Eng.	remarks
adroit *adroit au tir* a skilful shot	skilful in, at	with *de* *adroit de ses mains*, clever with one's hands
agile *agile à sauter* a good jumper	nimble in	with *de* *agile de ses doigts*, nimble- fingered
âpre *âpre à exiger un droit* relentless in claiming a right *ardent à poursuivre la gloire* ardent in the pursuit of glory	keen on, relentless in	
assidu *assidu au travail* devoted to work	persistent in, devoted to	Notice the use of *auprès de*, e.g. *être assidu auprès de quel-* *qu'un* to be paying marked attention to someone
bon *bon à manger* good to eat *bon à rien* good for nothing	good for, to	When *bon* means 'kind' use *pour*, or *envers*; e.g.: *il a été très bon pour moi* he has been very kind to me
exact *exact au rendez-vous* punctual in keeping an appointment	exact, punctual in, to	With a noun may also take *dans*
habile	clever at, skilled in	With a noun may also take *dans*, *en*
hardi *hardi à agir* bold in taking action	bold in	With a noun may also take *dans*: *hardi dans l'exécution* bold in execution
impropre	unfit for, to	
prêt	ready for, to	
propre *du bois propre à bâtir* wood fit for building	fit for, to; peculiar to	
semblable	similar to, like	

As in the case of *bon*, the English preposition 'to' is not translated by *à* after *doux, dur*, e.g.:

$$\left.\begin{array}{l} doux \\ dur \end{array}\right\} \; envers \text{ (or } p\breve{o}ur) \; tout \; le \; monde$$

gentle (harsh) to everyone

688 List 2

A noun or an infinitive depending on one of the following adjectives or participles is usually joined to it by *de*. Only those specified take an infinitive. For other verbs whose past participles are used in this way see also **525a, 530, 535**

adj.	Eng.	remarks
abasourdi	dazed by, stunned by	also *par*; also with infin.
absent	absent from	
accompagné	accompanied by	
admiré	admired by	
adoré	adored by	

un roi adoré de son peuple
a king adored by his people

affamé	hungry for, thirsting for	also with infin.

un cœur affamé de gloire
a heart thirsting for glory

affranchi	freed from	
alarmé	alarmed by	
alteré	thirsting for	
ambitieux	ambitious for	also with infin.

		ambitieux de vaincre
ambitieux du pouvoir		ambitious to conquer
ambitious for power		

amoureux	in love with, enamoured of	

follement amoureux de la célébrité
madly enamoured of fame

avide	greedy for	
béni	blessed by	
bouillant	boiling with	

bouillant de colère
boiling with rage

certain	certain of, that	also with infin.

		certain de réussir
Il est certain de succès		certain to succeed
He is certain that he will succeed		

charmé	delighted with, to	also with infin.
complice	accessory to, a party to	
confus	embarrassed, dazed by, at	also with infin.

		confus d'être pris sur le fait
Je suis tout confus de votre bonté		embarrassed at being caught red-handed
I am quite embarrassed by your kindness		

connu	known to, by	
consterné	dismayed at, by	

content	contented, pleased with, to	also with infin.
Il était content de son sort		Je suis très content de vous voir
He was contented with his lot		I am very glad to see you
contrarié	vexed with	
curieux	curious to, interested in	also with infin.
Mon ami est curieux de tout		Je serai curieux de savoir la fin de l'affaire
My friend is interested in everything		I shall be curious to know the end of the business
débarrassé	freed from, rid of	
délivré	delivered from	
différent	different from	
éloigné	distant, separated from	also with infin. – but *loin* is commoner
un récit éloigné de la vérité		Il était bien éloigné de jouir de son triomphe
a tale far removed from the truth		He was far from enjoying his triumph
embarrassé	encumbered with, at a loss to	also with infin.
enchanté	delighted with, to	also with infin.
encombré	encumbered with	
ennemi	hostile to, averse from	
exempt	exempt from, quit of	also with infin.
fou	mad with	
Il est fou de colère		
He is mad with rage		
furieux	furious at a thing, at . . .ing a thing – but furious with a person, *contre*	also with infin.
gai	of things – gay, bright with	
une salle gaie de lumière		
a brightly lighted room		
gros	swollen with	
hérissé	bristling with	
heureux	glad of, to, happy to	also with infin.
Je suis très heureux de son succès		Je serai très heureux d'assister à la cérémonie
I am much pleased at his success		I shall be very happy to attend the ceremony
humide	damp with	
inconnu	unknown to	
inconsolable	inconsolable for	

Ils sont inconsolables de leur perte
Nothing will console them for their loss

inquiet	uneasy about, at	also with infin.
inséparable	inseparable from	
ivre	intoxicated with	

un peuple ivre de joie
a nation intoxicated with joy

libre	free from, to	also with infin.

Vous êtes libres d'essayer or *Libre*
    à vous d'essayer
You are free to try

lourd	heavy with	
mécontent	discontented with	
précédé	preceded by	
ravi	delighted with, by	also with infin.

J'ai été ravi de son discours	*Je suis ravi de vous voir*
I was delighted with his speech	I am charmed to see you

reconnaissant	grateful for	also with infin. (for 'grateful to', see **689**)
redevable	indebted for	

C'est à vous seul que nous en sommes redevables
We are indebted for it to you alone

responsable	responsible for	
satisfait	satisfied with	also with infin.
soigneux	careful about	
soucieux	anxious about, to	also with infin.
surpris	surprised at, by, to	also with infin.
trempé	soaked with, in	
tributaire	tributary to, dependent on	
triste	sad about, sorry for	also with infin.
voisin	bordering on, adjacent to	

689   List 3

Envers can be used in the sense of 'to' or 'towards' with the adjectives given below, but the other prepositions noted are often substituted.

adj.	Eng.	remarks
affable	affable	also *à*, *avec*

Il est affable $\left\{ \begin{array}{l} envers \\ à \\ avec \end{array} \right\}$ *tout le monde*

He is affable to everybody

aimable	amiable	also *pour, avec*
bon	kind	also *pour*
charitable	charitable	
civil	civil	also *à*
clément	merciful	also *pour*
cruel	cruel	also *à, pour*
doux	gentle	also *pour*
dur	stern to, hard upon	also *pour*
généreux	generous	
grossier	rude, ill-mannered	
honnête	decent, honourable	also *avec*
impoli	rude	also *avec*
indulgent	indulgent	also *à, pour*
ingrat	ungrateful	also *à*
injuste	unjust	also *avec, pour*
insolent	insolent	also *avec*
juste	just	also *à, pour*
libéral	liberal	also *pour*
malhonnête	rude	
miséricordieux	merciful	
poli	polite	also *avec*
prodigue	lavish	also *à, pour*
reconnaissant	grateful	also *à*
respectueux	respectful	
responsable	responsible	also *à, devant*
rigoureux	harsh	also *pour*
sévère	severe	also *à, pour*

690   List 4

En or *dans* can be used in the sense of 'in' or 'of' with the adjectives given below.

For the difference between *en* and *dans* see **656–657**.

adj.	Eng.	remarks
abondant	abounding in, having plenty of	
expert	expert in	with infin. *à*
	un ennemi expert en tromperies	*expert à faire du ski*
	an enemy expert in deception	expert at skiing
fécond	fruitful in	
fertile	fertile in	
	une langue féconde (fertile) en excuses	
	a tongue prolific in excuses	
fort	good at, sound in (a subject of instruction)	strong (a) in a part of the body, (b) as the result of anything, use *de*
	good at a game is *à*	

Il est très fort en mathématiques He is very good at mathematics		*Il est fort des bras* He is strong in the arms
Il est très fort au tennis He is very good at tennis		*Je suis fort de son assentiment* I am in a strong position because of his agreement
ignorant	ignorant of (a subject of instruction)	generally *de*; also *sur*
riche	rich in (also *de*)	*de* also means 'to the extent of' *riche de deux millions* a millionaire twice over
savant	learned (in a subject), also *sur*	

Conjunctions

Introduction

691   Conjunctions are of two kinds: (i) co-ordinating; (ii) subordinating

(i) Co-ordinating

These join like to like, namely a noun to a noun, an adjective to an adjective, a verb in the indicative to a verb in the indicative, a clause to a clause, and so on.

They are in English: 'and, or' (negative 'nor'), 'but', 'for'; in French: *et, ou* (negative *ni*), *mais, car*; and also 'either . . . or . . .', *soit . . . soit . . .*

Observe that the English habit of joining two co-ordinate clauses, nouns, etc., by 'both . . . and . . .' is much less common in French. Instead of *et . . . et . . .*, either *à la fois . . . et . . .* or a subordinating expression such as *en même temps que, autant* (or *tant*) *que* should generally be used; e.g.:

Il craignait en même temps qu'il désirait de parler
He both feared and wished to speak

C'était un enfant à la fois sage et espiègle
He was a child both sensible and roguish

(ii) Subordinating

There are only three subordinating conjunctions besides *que* and compounds of *que*:

comme	as	(see 613)
si	if	(see 414,i, 415, 418–424)
quand	when	(see 315,iv, 414,ii, 422)

These are constructed with the indicative or conditional, not with the subjunctive. When they govern more than one verb in the same sentence, they are usually not repeated, *que* alone being substituted (see 703).

Conjunctions not requiring the subjunctive

692   *Que* 'that, as' is not only by far the commonest of all French conjunctions but is also really the conjunctive part of all compound conjunctions. (For the sake of convenience, conjunctions written as one word are called 'simple' while those written as two or more words are said to be 'compound'. Of words formed with *que*, only three, *lorsque* 'when', *puisque* 'since' and *quoique* 'although', are written as single words and therefore rank as simple conjunctions.)

693   The following conjunctions take the indicative or the conditional, not the subjunctive. In the case of those listed in **694**, *que* is comparative and means 'as'. In the case of those listed in **695**, *que* is not comparative and so is not translated as 'as' (except in the one case of *dès que* which, though not itself based on comparative *que*, corresponds to an English expression based on comparative 'as', viz. 'as soon as').

For the use of the future tense after temporal conjunctions such as *aussitôt que, tant que, après que, lorsque, pendant que*, etc., see **414**,ii.

694

    ainsi que as, as well as, just as
      à mesure que
      à proportion que } (in proportion) as

aussi. . .que (affirm. or neg.) *si. . .que* (neg. only) as . . . as (see **157**)

aussitôt (or *sitôt*) *que* as soon as
autant que as much as, as far as (but see **490**)
de même que the same as, just as
selon que ⎫
suivant que ⎬ according as
tant que (see **696**) as long as, while

695

alors que, whereas
après que, after
attendu que, seeing that, since
depuis que, since (the time when)
dès que, as soon as
étant donné que, since, given that
excepté que, except that
lorsque, when
outre que, besides the fact that
parce que, because
pendant que, (see **696**), while
puisque, since
sinon que, except that
tandis que, (see **696**), while, whereas
toutes les fois (*chaque fois*) *que*, whenever, as often as
une fois que, once
vu que, seeing that, since

696   *pendant que, tant que, tandis que*

Pendant que 'while' and *tant que* '(for) as long as' are both temporal conjunctions, but whereas *pendant que* merely indicates an action during the course of which something else happens, *tant que* refers to an action throughout the whole time of which something else happens, e.g.:

Pendant que j'étais en Espagne j'ai visité l'Escurial
While I was in Spain I went to see the Escurial

Tant que j'étais chez eux, il a fait affreusement chaud
While (i.e. all the time) I was with them it was terribly hot

Tandis que 'while' originally had the same value as *pendant que* and sometimes still does in literary usage, but its normal value nowadays is that of 'whereas', i.e. it implies a contrast, e.g.:

Son père a peiné jusqu'à la mort, tandis que lui n'a jamais rien fait
His father laboured to the end of his life, while he has never done anything

Conjunctions requiring the subjunctive

697   The following conjunctions take the subjunctive:

although even though though	*bien que* (see 487) *encore que* (see 487) *quoique* (see 487)
before	*avant que* (see 488 and 566)
despite the fact that, although	*malgré que* (see 698)
far from . . .-ing	*loin que* (see 491)
for fear, lest	*de crainte que. . .ne* (see 491, 564) *de peur que. . .ne* (see 491, 564)
if only	*pour peu que* (see 490)
in case	*au cas que* (see 490) *en cas que* (see 490)
in order that	*afin que* (see 489) *pour que* (see 489)
not that	*non que, non pas que* (see 491)
provided that	*pourvu que* (see 490)
so long as, provided that	*si tant est que* (see 490)
supposing that	*à supposer que, supposé que* (see 490)
unless	*à moins que* (see 490)
until	*en attendant que* (see 488) *jusqu'à ce que* (see 488)
whether . . . or	*soit que. . .soit que* (see 480,iii,c)
without . . .-ing	*sans que* (see 491) *que. . .ne* (see 561,h)

698 *malgré que*

Although frowned on by some grammarians, *malgré que* is widely used in speech, and increasingly in literary usage too, with the meaning 'although', e.g. *malgré qu'il ait obtenu tous les prix de sa classe* (Mauriac) 'although he won all the prizes in his class'.

Que *as subordinating conjunction*

699   In subject or object clauses

Except in an indirect question, if one clause is the subject or object of the verb in another clause – or is in apposition to that subject or object – the two clauses will be connected by *que*, e.g.:

Il sortit afin de dire à sa sœur qu'un accident était arrivé
He went out in order to tell his sister (that) there had been an accident

Il craignait qu'on ne mît le feu à la maison
He was afraid (that) the house might be set on fire

Je veux qu'il s'en aille
I want him to go away

On a ordonné que toute lumière soit éteinte à minuit
Orders have been given that all lights should be put out at midnight

Il est évident qu'il a tort
It is obvious that he is wrong

Qu'il soit mécontent est certain
That he is displeased is certain

(See also **480**,ii.)

700   In alternative conditions

In alternative conditional sentences introduced by 'whether . . . or . . .', *que* is used with each dependent verb expressed, e.g.:

Qu'il pleuve ou qu'il fasse beau, je vais sortir
Whether it's raining or whether it's fine, I shall go out

Qu'il soit d'accord ou non, moi je reste ici
Whether he agrees or not, I am staying here

(See also **480**,iii,d.)

701   With one of two verbs in the conditional

When *que* stands with the second of two verbs in the conditional, English has no equivalent for it. The sentence must be translated by placing 'though', 'even if', before the first verb, e.g.:

Il m'offrirait des richesses inouïes que je ne le ferais pas
Though he should offer me untold wealth, I would not do it

(See also 422,i.)

702   *Que* in place of other conjunctions

Que sometimes serves as the equivalent of

afin que, pour que, puisque, sans que (see 561,h)
avant que, jusqu'à ce que, depuis que

and other temporal conjunctions such as *quand* – especially after *à peine*, or, in a negative clause, a comparative. If purpose is suggested, *que* is followed by the subjunctive.

Examples:

Mettez-vous là que je vous voie de face
Stand there that I may see you full face (purpose)

Vous n'êtes donc pas sorti que votre imperméable est toujours sec?
You have not been out then since your raincoat is still dry? (=*puisque*)

(Note that when *que* is used in this sense, the main clause expresses or implies a question.)

Ne venez pas que vous n'ayez de mes nouvelles
Do not come till you hear from me (temporal) *or* without hearing from me (*sans que*)

(Note that *que* in this sense requires *ne* with its verb.)

A peine s'était-il assis qu'on sonna
Scarcely had he sat down when the bell rang (temporal)

Attends que j'aille la chercher
Wait while I go and look for her (temporal)

(For *depuis que* see 413.)

703 To avoid repetition, a conjunction which applies to two or more verbs is replaced by *que* with all but the first verb.

When *que* thus replaces *si* (conditional), though the first verb remains in the indicative, *que* requires the subjunctive (see **420**).

With all other conjunctions the mood after *que* is the same as that taken by the original conjunction.

Examples:

Si quelque chose vous retient et que vous ayez le temps, envoyez-moi un petit mot
If anything detains you and if you have time, drop me a line

Quand il travaillait à Londres et qu'il gagnait beaucoup d'argent, il était toujours très content
When he was working in London and earning a lot of money, he was always very happy

Quoiqu'il le voulût bien et qu'il l'eût promis, il n'y pouvait rien
Although he was willing to and had promised, it was quite beyond his power

704 When *si* is used in an indirect question, i.e. when 'if' is equivalent to 'whether' (see **423**), it cannot be replaced by *que*, e.g.:

Le contrôleur demanda à la dame si elle allait à Londres et si elle avait pris son billet
The ticket-inspector asked the lady if she was going to London and if she had got her ticket

705 For *que* in comparisons, see **166**; after *tout,* **317**,v,b; after *quelque*, etc., **308–310, 315**.

Appendices

I The expression of age, time, price, dimensions, speed

Age

706   Age is reckoned by years, months, etc., as in English, but in French the words *ans* 'years', *mois* 'months', etc., can never be omitted, e.g.:

> *Quel âge avez-vous?*
> How old are you?

> *J'ai quatorze ans et trois mois*
> I am fourteen and a quarter

> *une jeune fille de dix ans* (or *âgée de dix ans*)
> a girl of ten

Note the use of *aîné* 'older, eldest', and *cadet* 'younger, youngest', in comparing the ages of brothers and sisters; they cannot be used with *que* 'than', e.g.:

> *Lequel est l'aîné de ces frères?*
> Which is the older (*or* eldest) of these brothers?

> *Henri est plus âgé de trois ans que Guillaume*
> Henry is three years older than William

> *Madeleine est leur sœur cadette*
> Madeleine is their younger (*or* youngest) sister

Âgé applies to old and young alike, e.g.:

Il n'a que cinq ans; il n'est pas assez âgé pour y aller tout seul
He is only five; he is not old enough to go there alone

Time

707   The names of the days of the week and the months are:

dimanche, Sunday	*janvier*, January
lundi, Monday	*février*, February
mardi, Tuesday	*mars*, March
mercredi, Wednesday	*avril*, April
jeudi, Thursday	*mai*, May
vendredi, Friday	*juin*, June
samedi, Saturday	*juillet*, July
	août, August
	septembre, September
	octobre, October
	novembre, November
	décembre, December

Note that capital initials are not used.

708   Where English uses 'on' with days of the week or month, French has no preposition. Note too the difference between *lundi*, etc. (no article) 'on Monday' (i.e. one particular Monday, last Monday or next Monday) and *le lundi* (singular, definite article) 'on Mondays' (i.e. regularly), but *le* (+ day) + date.

Examples:

J'écrirai lundi
I will write on Monday

J'y vais toujours le samedi
I always go there on Saturdays

Il est parti le quinze août
He left on the fifteenth of August

Il doit arriver le vendredi premier septembre
He is due to arrive on Friday, September 1st

709   Where English uses 'at' of the time of day, the French is *à*.
   The time of day is reckoned much as in English, except that 'o'clock' is translated by *heures* which

(a) is naturally always plural except for *une heure* 'one o'clock'

(b) can never be omitted

(c) is not used of 'twelve o'clock', which is

either   *midi*, 12 (noon)
or   *minuit*, 12 (midnight); e.g.:

Je serai de retour à midi, à une heure, à cinq heures, à minuit
I shall be back at 12 (noon), at one o'clock, at five o'clock,
at 12 (midnight)

710 'Half past' is *et demi* with *midi* and *minuit* but *et demie* when
the word *heure* is involved, e.g.:

Il est midi et demi
It is half past twelve

Il arrive à deux heures et demie
He arrives at half past two

'Quarter past' and 'quarter to' are usually *et quart* and *moins le
quart* (though *un quart* and *moins un quart* also occur), e.g.:

A minuit et quart j'ai été réveillé par l'orage
At a quarter past midnight I was woken up by the thunder-
storm

Attendons jusqu'à trois heures moins le quart
Let's wait until a quarter to three

Otherwise, 'so many minutes past the hour' is expressed by the
appropriate figure, and 'so many minutes to the hour' by *moins*
and the appropriate figure, usually without the word *minutes* in
either case, e.g.:

Il est trois heures dix-sept
It is seventeen minutes past three

Je pars à quatre heures moins vingt
I am leaving at twenty to four

When necessary, 'a.m.' can be rendered by *du matin* and 'p.m.'
by *de l'après-midi* or *du soir*, e.g. *trois heures de l'après-midi* '3
p.m.'.

711   Time is frequently expressed according to the 24-hour clock, not only for administrative purposes (timetables, appointments, radio and TV programmes, etc.), but in ordinary conversational usage too. This is very easy. All hours are expressed, as in the other system (see **709**), by *heures*, including twelve noon (*douze heures*) and twelve midnight (*vingt-quatre heures* or *zéro heure*). Minutes are expressed as minutes past the hour (never as so many minutes 'to' the hour), e.g.:

02h.15 (deux heures quinze)   two fifteen (a.m.)

18h.35 (dix-huit heures trente-cinq)   six thirty-five (p.m.)

712   Duration of time

(i) *Pour* 'for' is usually not the correct equivalent of English 'for' with relation to time. It is however used with reference to a period of time that is later than the time of the action expressed by the verb, in which case it also includes an idea of purpose, e.g.:

Je croyais qu'il n'était venu que pour trois jours
I thought he had only come for three days

Je vais à Paris pour une semaine
I am going to Paris for a week

Note that in such contexts 'for' does not express the time that the action (of coming or going respectively) lasts.

(ii) 'For' meaning 'time during which' is usually to be translated by *pendant* 'during', e.g.:

L'an dernier j'ai été malade pendant trois mois
Last year I was ill for three months

La pièce a duré deux heures; pendant le premier quart d'heure nous nous sommes affreusement ennuyés
The play lasted two hours; for the first quarter of an hour we were terribly bored

(iii) Note the use of *depuis* 'since' instead of *pendant* with reference to a period of time that still continues at the time of the action expressed by the verb, e.g.:

J'insiste là-dessus depuis dix ans
I have been insisting on it for ten years (and still am)

Il est malade depuis trois mois
He has been ill for three months (and still is)

Lorsque je suis arrivé, il était malade depuis trois jours
When I arrived, he had been ill for three days (and still was)

(See also **668**.)

713 *En* and *dans*.

The difference between *en* and *dans* in expressions of time must be noted. The English preposition 'in' is used of time in two senses:

(i) to denote duration; this in French is *en*, e.g.:

Aujourd'hui on peut faire la traversée de la Manche en trente minutes
Nowadays the Channel can be crossed in thirty minutes

(ii) to denote the period of time that will elapse before an action takes place; this in French is *dans*, e.g.:

Nous partons pour Paris dans un quart d'heure
We are starting for Paris in a quarter of an hour

En is also used in dates, e.g. *Il est mort en 1807* 'He died in 1807'.

714 'From' with reference to time

The time from which something starts may be expressed in various ways, including *de* 'from', *dès* 'as from', *depuis* 'since' (see **668**), *à partir de* 'as from, starting from', and *après* 'after', e.g.:

du lever au coucher du soleil
from sunrise to sunset

Dès ce moment essayons d'être sages
From now on, let us try to be good

A partir de dix heures je ne serai plus à la maison
From ten o'clock onwards I shall be out

Téléphonez-moi après dix heures
Ring me after ten

de temps en temps }
de temps à autre } from time to time

715 Miscellaneous observations

(i) *ici* and *là* are used of time in phrases such as the following:

Jusqu'ici il n'y a rien de nouveau
Up to now there is nothing to report

D'ici là tout peut arriver
Between now and then anything may happen

(ii) The use of English adverb 'often' with 'how' in a question has no counterpart in French. 'How often?' must be translated by *combien de fois?* 'how many times?'

But if the question is asked about something which happens at more or less regular intervals, *combien* may be treated as a noun, e.g.:

D'ici à Chartres les trains vont tous les combien?
How often do trains run from here to Chartres?

(iii) Similarly, 'how long?' is expressed by 'how much time?'; 'for how long?' by 'since how much time? since when?', e.g.:

Combien de temps vous faudra-t-il pour faire ça?
How long will it take you to do that?

Depuis combien de temps ⎱ *y travaillez-vous?* (for tense see
Depuis quand   ⎰ **413**)

How long (or since when) have you been working at it?

(iv) When 'whenever' means 'every, each time that', it must be translated by something meaning just that, e.g.:

Toutes les fois ⎱ *qu'il venait, il était le bienvenu*
Chaque fois   ⎰

Whenever he came he was welcome

For 'whenever' meaning 'no matter when', see **315,iv**.

(v) 'B.C.' and 'A.D.' are, respectively, *av. J.-C.* (= *avant Jésus-Christ*) and *ap. J.-C.* (= *après Jésus-Christ*), e.g. *au IVe siècle av. J.-C.* 'in the 4th century B.C.', *en 336 ap. J.-C.* 'in 336 A.D.'

716   Idiomatic expressions of time

What time is it?
Quelle heure est-il?

It is past five
Il est cinq heures passées

It is exactly seven (o'clock)
Il est sept heures précises

about 6 p.m.
vers (les) six heures du soir

Is that eleven o'clock striking?
Est-ce onze heures qui sonnent?

He arrived on the stroke of ten
Il est arrivé sur le coup de dix heures

to arrive in time
arriver à temps

to arrive on time
arriver à l'heure

in the time of our fathers
du temps de nos pères

You will succeed in time
Avec le temps vous réussirez

He gets up early
Il se lève de bonne heure

He goes to bed late
Il se couche tard

He came late (after the time fixed)
Il arriva en retard

The train is ten minutes late
Le train a dix minutes de retard

My watch is ten minutes slow
Ma montre retarde de dix minutes

My watch is ten minutes fast
Ma montre avance de dix minutes

I tried to tell you next morning
J'ai essayé de vous le dire le lendemain matin

I shall see him next Friday
Je le verrai vendredi prochain

I see him on the last Saturday of each month
Je le vois le dernier samedi de chaque mois

I saw him last Saturday
Je l'ai vu samedi dernier (or *passé*)

(Note that *dernier* only follows its noun when there is no article in English. In such cases *passé* is a common alternative.)

last Sunday week
il y a eu dimanche huit jours

next Sunday week
il y aura dimanche huit jours

a fortnight ago
$\left.\begin{array}{l}\textit{voici} \\ \textit{il y a}\end{array}\right\}$ *quinze jours,* or *une quinzaine*

How often do you see him on average each week?
Combien de fois par semaine le voyez-vous en moyenne?

twice a week
deux fois par semaine

today week, a week today
aujourd'hui en huit

tomorrow fortnight
demain en quinze

several days running
plusieurs jours de suite

every year, annually
tous les ans, or *chaque année*

in the previous week
la semaine précédente

in the following week
la semaine suivante

just now, presently
tout à l'heure

sooner or later
tôt ou tard

at once, a moment ago
à l'instant

What day of the month is it to-day? What's the date?
C'est le combien aujourd'hui?

after ten days, ten days later
au bout de dix jours

Price

717   (i) No preposition corresponding to English 'for' is normally used to indicate the price for which something is bought or sold, e.g.:

Il a acheté (vendu) ce tableau 150 000 francs
He bought (sold) this picture for 150,000 francs

(though *pour 150 000 francs* is also possible).

Ces pommes se vendent 8F. le kilo
These apples sell (*or* are sold) at 8 francs a kilo

Note too that *payer* means not just 'to pay' but also 'to pay for', so no preposition is used in such contexts as:

J'ai payé ces billets 200 francs
I paid 200 francs for these tickets

Je les ai déjà payés
I have already paid for them

(ii) In the absence of a verb, the price at which something is sold (i.e. 'at' meaning 'costing') is indicated by *à*, e.g.:

du vin à vingt francs la bouteille
wine at twenty francs a bottle

du tissu à cent francs le mètre
material costing a hundred francs a metre

trois timbres à cinq francs
three five-franc stamps

(iii) With *coûter* 'to cost' and *valoir* 'to be worth, to cost', the construction is the same as in English, e.g.:

Ce tissu coûte (vaut) 50 francs le mètre
This material costs (is worth) 50 francs a metre

(iv) For the use of the definite article where English uses the indefinite article (*dix francs le kilo* = 'ten francs a kilo'), see **36**,a.

Dimensions

718   (i) Expressions of length, height, breadth or depth may be used either (a) with nouns which they qualify, or (b) as complement or object with *être* or *avoir*. The different ways in which such sentences can be translated are given below.

He built a tower fifteen metres high	*Il a bâti une tour*
	haute de quinze mètres,
	de quinze mètres de hauteur,
	d'une hauteur de quinze mètres
The tower will be fifteen metres high	*La tour*
	sera haute de quinze mètres,
	aura quinze mètres de hauteur,
	aura une hauteur de quinze mètres

In the second example of each of the above groups the word *hauteur* (height) can be replaced by *haut*. Similarly *largeur* (breadth or width) can be replaced by *large*, *longueur* (length) by *long*, but *épais* thick and *profond* deep can never be used for *épaisseur* and *profondeur*, e.g.:

La colonne a dix mètres de hauteur (or *de haut*) *et un mètre d'épaisseur* (**not** *d'épais*)
The column is ten metres high and one metre thick

Le terrain de football a cent vingt mètres de long (or *de longueur*) *sur quatre-vingts de large* (or *de largeur*)
The football field is 120 metres long by 80 metres wide

A question with no unit of measurement (feet, metres, etc.) mentioned, is expressed by *combien de* with *hauteur, longueur,* etc., e.g.:

Ce fleuve a combien de largeur?
How wide is this river?

(ii) Square measurements are expressed by the use of *carré* 'square', e.g.:

Cent est le carré de dix
A hundred is the square of ten

Dix est la racine carrée de cent
Ten is the square root of a hundred

dix mètres carrés
ten square metres

For 'X metres (etc.) square', note the expression *X mètres sur X*, e.g.:

un tapis de cinq mètres sur cinq
a carpet five metres square

Speed and fuel consumption

719   The distance travelled in a given time and the fuel consumed in travelling a given distance are both expressed by *à* and the article, e.g.:

Cette voiture fait du 160 (cent soixante) à l'heure
This car does 160 kilometres (= 100 miles) an hour

La consommation d'essence de cette voiture est de onze litres aux cent (kilomètres)
This car does twenty-six miles to the gallon (*lit.* uses eleven litres for a hundred kilometres)

Observe that in the first of these examples the rate of speed is reckoned both in French and English by taking as the unit of measurement a given time (one hour); and that in the second the fuel consumption is reckoned in English by taking as the unit of measurement a given amount consumed (one gallon), in French by taking as the unit of measurement a given distance covered (one hundred kilometres).

II Glossary of words easily confused

720

un air	air (either 'atmosphere' or 'appearance')
une aire	threshing floor
une amande	almond
une amende	fine (penalty)
en avance	early, ahead of one's time
en avant	forward, ahead (of motion)
l'aveuglement	moral or mental blindness; (physical blindness is *la cécité*)
aveuglément	blindly
bai (adj.)	bay (-coloured)
un bai	bay (horse)
une baie	1 bay, gulf; 2 berry
un bal	ball, dance
une balle	1 bullet; 2 ball (cricket, tennis, etc.)
un ballon	1 balloon; 2 football; 3 any large, inflated ball
un brick	brig

une brique	brick
une cane	(female) duck
une canne	cane, stick
le capital	capital (business)
la capitale	capital (town)
la chair	flesh
la chaire	1 pulpit; 2 lecturer's desk; 2 professorship
la chaise	chair
la chasse	hunting, shooting, etc.
la châsse	shrine
le col	1 collar (of shirt, etc.); 2 col, pass (of mountain)
le collier	1 dog-collar, horse-collar, etc.; 2 necklace
la colle	paste, glue
coller	to stick (trans. or intrans.), to glue
un comte	Count (title)
un compte	account, bill
un conte	account, story
un comté	county
un comité	committee
un coq	cock (bird)
une coque	1 hull (of ship); 2 shell (of egg)
la côte	1 hillside, slope; 2 coast; 3 rib
le côté	side (of body)
la cote	rating, quota, etc.
la cotte (*de mailles*)	coat of mail
le cou	neck
le coup	blow
la cour	court, courtyard
le cours	1 course; 2 (university) lecture
la course	race
le court	court (tennis)
court (adj.)	short
le cuir	leather
cuire	to cook
le cuivre	copper
la date	date (time)
la datte	date (fruit)
le dé, pl. *dés*	1 thimble; 2 dice
dès	as from, right from (of time)
des	of the, some (plural) (see 25, 40)
le dessein	design
le dessin	drawing
ébaucher	to sketch out roughly (picture or scheme)
embaucher	to engage (workmen)
le fil [fil], pl. *fils*	thread
le fils [fis], pl. *fils*	son
la file	file (of people or things following each other)
la foi	faith
le foie	liver

une fois	once; *trois fois*, three times; *la première fois*, the first time, etc.
la fosse	pit, grave
le fossé	ditch, moat
le fond	further end, bottom
le fonds	fund, etc.
les fonts baptismaux	font
la fonte	cast-iron
font	3rd plur. pres. ind. of *faire*, to make, do, etc.
la forêt	forest
le foret	drill
le furet	ferret
fumer	1 to smoke; 2 to manure
la fumée	smoke
le fumet	aroma
le fumier	dung
le fumoir	smoking-room
le gaz	gas
la gaze	gauze
la grêle	hail
grêle (adj.)	thin
la guerre	war
guère (adv.)	hardly, scarcely
la gueule	mouth (of animal)
le gueules	gules (heraldic)
la houille	coal
la houle	swell, ground-swell (of sea)
une humeur	humour, good or bad temper
un humour	humour
jeune (adj.)	young
un jeûne	fast, period of abstinence (Note *être à jeun*, to be fasting, to have had nothing to eat)
le lac [lak]	lake
le lacs [la]	snare
le lézard	lizard
la lézarde	crack, crevice
le lieu	place
la lieue	league (distance)
le loup	wolf
la louve	she-wolf
la loupe	1 wen; 2 magnifying-glass
le mâcon	wine from the Mâcon district
le maçon	mason
(le) mat	mate, checkmate (chess)
le mât	mast
mat (adj.)	dull, unpolished
le mépris	scorn
la méprise	mistake (Note *je m'y suis mépris*, etc. I made a mistake)

la mer	sea
la mère	mother
le matin	morning
le mâtin	mastiff
une émeute	riot
une meute	pack of hounds
(le) meurtrier	murderer, murderous
(la) meurtrière	murderess, murderous
la meurtrière	loophole (fortification)
le moral	spirit, state of mind, morale
la morale	morals, moral (of a tale), ethics
(le) mort	dead man, (past participle) dead
la mort	death
la morte	dead woman
le mors	bit (of bridle)
mord	3rd sing. pres. ind. of *mordre,* bite
le mousse	cabin-boy
la mousse	1 moss; 2 froth, mousse
le mur	wall
la mûre	blackberry
mûr, mûre (adj.)	ripe
mure	3rd. sing. pres. ind. of *murer,* wall up, immure
le navet	turnip
la navette	1 shuttle; 2 rape (plant, seed, etc.)
ombragé	shady (of trees, etc.)
ombrageux	taking umbrage easily – i.e. of people, touchy; of horses, nervous
orgue	organ (mus.) (For gender see 71)
un organe	organ (of body), paper (e.g. the organ of a party)
pair (adj.)	even (of numbers)
le pair	1 peer (nobleman); 2 an equal; 3 par (of exchange, etc.)
la paire	a pair
la part	share (suggesting something claimed as a right) used in numerous adverbial phrases, e.g.:

> *nulle part,* nowhere
> *de toutes parts,* on or from all sides
> *de la part de,* on behalf of
> *à part,* aside
> *faire part à,* inform

la partie	1 part, portion (as opposed to whole)
	2 game
	3 party, when the persons who compose it are not specified; if they are, *la bande, le groupe,* etc., should be used, e.g.

> *une partie de chasse,* shooting party
> *une bande* (or *un groupe*) *de chasseurs,* a party of hunters

le parti	1 party (political)
	2 match (matrimonial)
	3 decision (mainly with *prendre*)
	4 advantage (with *tirer*)
la pâte	paste, dough
les pâtes	pasta
le pâté	1 pie, pâté; 2 block of houses; 3 (ink-)blot
la pâtée	mash, swill (as food for animals)
la patte	paw, (animal's) foot
la pêche	peach
le pêcher	peach-tree
la pêche	fishing
pêcher	to fish
le pêcheur	fisherman
le péché	sin
pécher	to sin
le pécheur	sinner
le pèlerin	pilgrim (male); *la pèlerine*, pilgrim (female)
la pèlerine	cape
le pieu	stake; *les pieux*, stakes
pieux (adj.)	pious
le poids	weight
le pois	pea
la poix	pitch
la poignée	1 handful; 2 handle; 3 *donner une poignée de main à*, shake hands with
le poignet	wrist
la poule	hen
le poulet	chicken
la poulie	pulley
le pouls [pu]	pulse
la porte	door
le port	harbour
le port	carriage, deportment
le pore	pore
le porc	pork, pig
le pré	meadow
le prêt	loan
prêt (adj.)	ready
près (adv.)	near
la preuve	proof
une épreuve	trial, test
le prodige	prodigy Note { *l'enfant prodige*, infant prodigy
prodigue (adj.)	prodigal { *l'enfant prodigue*, prodigal son
la rame	oar, scull
ramer	to row
la rame	1 ream of paper; 2 (underground) train
le rameau	bough
la ramée	arbour

le ramage	1 warbling of birds; 2 floral design (on wallpapers, cottons, silks, etc.)
le ramier	wood-pigeon
rassembler	to collect
ressembler	to resemble, be like
recouvrer	to recover, regain
recouvrir	to re-cover (umbrella, etc.), cover (entirely)
le repaire	lair, haunt
le repère	reference (number, etc.); mostly in *un point de repère*, landmark
repartir	1 to start again; 2 to reply
répartir	to distribute
le ris	laugh (poet.)
le ris	reef (in sail)
le ris de veau, d'agneau	sweetbread
le riz	rice
le rose	rose-colour, pink – also an adjective
la rose	rose (flower), rose-window
le roseau	reed
la rosée	dew
la roue	wheel
la rue	1 street; 2 (bot.) rue
le sarment	1 vine-shoot; 2 creeper (with woody stem)
le serment	oath
le saut	leap, jump
le sceau	seal, stamp
le seau	pail, bucket
sensé	sensible, possessing sound judgment
sensible	sensitive, appreciative, perceptible, appreciable
censé	reputed
son (adj.)	his, her, its
le son	sound
le son	bran.
souffler	to blow
le soufflé	soufflé, light omelette
le souffle	breath, puff
le soufflet	1 pair of bellows; 2 blow, slap (in the face)
le souffleur	1 blower (organ, glass, etc.); 2 prompter (stage)
sur (prep.)	on
sur (adj.)	sour
sûr (adj.)	sure
la tache	stain
tacher	to stain
la tâche	task
tâcher	to try
le teint	colour (of dye or complexion)
la teinte	tint, shade (of a colour), tinge (metaph.)
la tempe	temple (of head)
le temple	temple (building), Protestant church

le tourment	torment
la tourmente	storm, gale; – *de neige*, blizzard
la tribu	tribe
le tribut	tribute
la trombe	water-spout
la trompe	1 trumpet, horn; 2 trunk (elephant), proboscis
le vaisseau	vessel (receptacle or ship)
la vaisselle	crockery, dishes
la veille	vigil, i.e. watching and praying on the eve of a festival, and so 1 watching; 2 the day before (cf. Christmas Eve, etc.)
le veilleur	night watchman
la veilleuse	nightlight, sidelight (of car)
veiller	to watch (over)
la vieille	old woman
vieillir	to grow old
la vielle	hurdy-gurdy
le ver	worm
le vers	verse, line of poetry
vers (adv.)	towards
le verre	glass
vert (adj.)	green
la verge	rod
la vergue	yard (of ship)
le verger	orchard
la vierge	virgin
la voie	way
la voix	voice
voir	to see
voire	indeed, nay, in truth
la volée	1 flight (or birds); volley (games or of missiles)
voler	1 to fly; 2 to steal
le volet	shutter

III   Proverbs

721

A beau jeu beau retour	One good turn deserves another
A bon entendeur, salut	A word to the wise is enough; verb. sap.
A bon vin point d'enseigne	Good wine needs no bush
A brebis tondue Dieu mesure le vent	God tempers the wind to the shorn lamb
A l'œuvre on connaît l'artisan	A man is judged by his works
L'appétit vient en mangeant	The more one has the more one wants
Après la pluie le beau temps	After the storm comes the calm; every cloud has a silver lining

A quelque chose malheur est bon	It's an ill wind that blows nobody any good
Au royaume des aveugles les borgnes sont rois	In the kingdom of the blind, the one-eyed man is king
A voleur, voleur et demi	Set a thief to catch a thief
Bon jour bonne œuvre	The better the day the better the deed
Le caque sent toujours le hareng	What's bred in the bone will out in the flesh
C'est en forgeant qu'on devient forgeron	Practice makes perfect
Ce qui nuit à l'un duit à l'autre	One man's meat is another man's poison
Charité bien ordonnée commence par soi-même	Charity begins at home
Chat échaudé craint l'eau froide	Once bitten twice shy
Le chat parti, les souris dansent	When the cat's away the mice will play
Chien qui aboie ne mord pas	His bark is worse than his bite
Chien mort ne mord pas	Dead dogs don't bite
Un chien regarde bien un évêque	A cat may look at a king
Comme on fait son lit, on se couche	As you make your bed, so must you lie
Dans le doute, abstiens-toi	When in doubt, don't
Deux avis valent mieux qu'un	Two heads are better than one
Dis-moi qui tu hantes, je te dirai qui tu es	A man is known by the company he keeps
Faute de grives on mange des merles	Half a loaf is better than no bread
L'habit ne fait pas le moine	Fine feathers don't make fine birds
Une hirondelle ne fait pas le printemps	One swallow doesn't make a summer
Un homme averti en vaut deux	Forewarned is forearmed
Il n'est pire eau que l'eau qui dort	Still waters run deep
Il n'est pire sourd que celui qui ne veut pas entendre	There's none so deaf as he who will not hear
Il n'est sauce que d'appétit	Hunger is the best sauce
Il ne faut pas vendre la peau de l'ours avant de l'avoir tué	Don't count your chickens before they are hatched
Il n'y a pas de fumée sans feu	There is no smoke without fire
Il y a loin de la coupe aux lèvres	There's many a slip 'twixt cup and lip
Loin des yeux, loin du cœur	Out of sight, out of mind
Les loups ne se mangent pas entre eux	Dog doesn't eat dog; there is honour among thieves
Un malheur n'arrive jamais seul	Misfortunes never come singly; it never rains but it pours
Les mauvais ouvriers ont toujours de mauvais outils	A bad workman blames his tools
Mieux vaut tard que jamais	Better late than never
Morte la bête mort le venin	Dead dogs don't bite
Les morts ne parlent pas	Dead men tell no tales
Nécessité fait loi	Any port in a storm
Nécessité n'a pas de loi	Necessity knows no law
Ne réveillez pas le chat qui dort	Let sleeping dogs lie
L'occasion fait le larron	Opportunity makes the thief

On ne fait pas d'omelette sans casser d'œufs	You can't make an omelette without breaking eggs
On ne peut pas être et avoir été	You can't have your cake and eat it
Petit à petit l'oiseau fait son nid	Constant dripping wears away a stone
Petite pluie abat grand vent	Little strokes fell mighty oaks
Pierre qui roule n'amasse pas mousse	A rolling stone gathers no moss
Plus on est de fous, plus on rit	The more the merrier
Un point à temps en épargne cent	A stitch in time saves nine
Point de rose sans épine	There is no rose without a thorn
Prudence est mère de sûreté	Discretion is the better part of valour
Quand on parle du loup on en voit la queue	Talk of the devil and he's sure to appear
Qui aime bien châtie bien	Spare the rod and spoil the child
Qui ne s'occupe à rien s'occupe du mal	Satan finds work for idle hands
Qui sème le vent récolte la tempête	Who sows the wind reaps the whirlwind
Qui se ressemble s'assemble	Birds of a feather flock together
Qui veut noyer son chien l'accuse de la rage	Give a dog a bad name and hang him
Rira bien qui rira le dernier	He who laughs last laughs loudest
Tant va la cruche à l'eau qu'à la fin elle se casse	The pitcher that goes oft to the well is broken at last
Tel père, tel fils	Like father, like son
Un tiens vaut mieux que deux tu l'auras	A bird in the hand is worth two in the bush
Tous les chemins mènent à Rome	All roads lead to Rome
Tout ce qui reluit n'est pas or	All that glistens is not gold
Tout vient à point à qui sait attendre	Everything comes to him who waits
Vouloir c'est pouvoir	Where there's a will there's a way

Index

References are to sections, not to pages.

The following points should be noted:

1 Reflexive verbs are indexed under the form for the verb itself, the *se* being ignored, so, for example, *se lasser* comes between *large* and 'last'.

2 Words included in lists, such as those for gender, masculine and feminine forms of adjectives, plurals, verbs (but see 3 and 4 below), adverbs, prepositions, and conjunctions, are not indexed.

3 Irregular verbs included in **377** *are* indexed.

4 A special index of the verbs listed in various sections under 'The complement of verbs' (**518–538**) is provided in **538**.

For a list of abbreviations used, see p. xiv.

'a, an' (*see* indef. art.)

à
   after adjs 687
   equivalent of 'from' 524
   equivalent of other English
     prepositions 525
   meaning and use 652–656, 659
   repeated 650
   with def. art. 25
   with disjunct. pron. 220
     replacing poss. pron. 232
   with indirect obj. 18, 21, 536
   with infin. 428, 529, 531, 533, 536
   + compl. = Eng. direct obj. 422

à (la) condition que 490
à même 300
à moins que 490, 566

à partir de 714
à peine
   + inversion 600
   + past ant. 411
à supposer que 490
à travers 661
absolument pas 545
absolute constructions
   past part. 457
   pres. part. 444
absolute superlative 174
absoudre 377
abstract nouns, with def. art. 28
accents 9
accepter 485
s'accorder pour 536
accoudé 534

accourir 453
(*avoir*) *accoutumé de* 528
accroître 373
accroupi 534
accueillir 365
accusative case 17
s'acharner après (*contre, sur*) 536
acheter 354
'across' 661
acquérir 372
adjectival clause 13
adjectival phrase 13
  after *celui*, etc. 245
adjectives
  agreement of 127–154, 518
    sing. with plur. nouns 153
    with more than one noun 152
  compound 136
  corresponding to proper names 4
  fem. of
    spoken French 77–81
    written French 82–96
  followed by *à* 687
  followed by *dans* 690
  followed by *de* 45, 688
  followed by *en* 690
  followed by *envers* 689
  followed by subjunct. 482, 483, 485
  introduced by *c'est* or *il est?* 248,
    250, 253
  invariable 95–96, 126
  of nationality 4
  plur. 122–126
  position 139–154
  preceded by *de* 44, 241, 311, 312,
    667
  use of diaeresis in fem. 11
  used as advs 608
  used as nouns 175–177
    gender 74
  used in one gender only 96
  verbal adjs, differing from pres.
    part. 446
admettre 483
adonné 534
adverbial expressions 38, 46
adverbs
  followed by inversion 600
  interrogative advs 630–633
  numerals 186
  of affirmation or doubt 627–628
  of manner 603–613
  of negation 544–558
  of place 624–625

  of quantity 320–337
  of time 614–623
  position 635–643
  preceding *pas* 544
  replacing preposition + pron. 221
  same form as adj. 609
  used as nouns, plur. 117
  with no corresponding adj. 608
afin que 489
'again' 616
age, expression of 706
agenouillé 445
agreement of adjectives 127–138
agreement of past part. 380, 459–470
-*ail*, plural of words in 106
ailleurs 625
aimer 529
aimer autant (*mieux*) 485, 527
-*aindre*, verbs in 372
-*aine*, numerals in 181
  + sing. or plur. verb 395
ainsi 256, 612
ainsi que, agreement with nouns linked
  by 129
-*aître*, verbs in 373
-*al*, plur. of words in 105, 124
aller 377
  imper. 345
  pres. subjunct. 346
  used impersonally 343
aller faire 414
alors 615, 620
alors que 487
alphabet 1
'although' 487
amour 65
'another'
  rendered by *encore* 616
  (see also *autre*)
-*ant*, nouns in, differing from pres.
  part. 447
'any'
  rendered by *n'importe* + pron. or
    adv. 301
  rendered by partitive art. 41
  rendered by *quelque*(s) 306
  rendered by *tout* 317
'anyone' 301, 312, 313, 315, 319, 416
'anything' 301, 311, 315, 319, 416
'anywhere' 301, 315
apparaître 453
appeler 355
apposition, non-use of articles 27, 35
apprendre 532

(*s'*) *approcher*   537
approuver   485
après   660, 714
  with past infin.   649
après que
  + fut.   414
  + indic. or subjunct.   488
  + past ant.   411
arriver   451
  il arrive que   483
articles: *see* definite article, indefinite
  article, partitive article
'as . . . as'   156, 157, 323
  'as long as'   323
  'as much as, as many as'   323
aspirate *h*   3
assaillir   365
s'asseoir   377
assez   45, 154, 322
  assez . . . pour que   482
assister   525
'at'   653, 655, 659
  with ref. to price   717
  with ref. to time of day   709
'at least'   600
atteindre   372
attendre
  agreement of past part.   470
  + subjunct.   482
s'attendre
  à ce que + subjunct.   482
  + *y* where Eng. has no compl.   536
attendu   134
-*au*, plural of words in   103
au cas que (*où*)   490
au même   300
au moins   600
au travers de   661
aucun   298, 546, 556, 557, 667, 674
aucunement   548
aucuns   546
au-dessous de   684
au-dessus de   671
au-devant de   663
auprès de   662
aussi 'as'   157
  aussi . . . que   310, 495
aussi bien que   129
aussitôt   622
aussitôt que
  + fut.   414
  + indic.   488
  + past ant.   411
autant   45, 323

autant que   129, 490
autre(s)   182, 216, 292
autre chose   293
autrui   293
avancer   352
avant (*de*)   649, 663
avant que   488, 566
avec   38, 664
  + noun = adv.   611
avoir
  forms in full   349
  idioms with   539
  pres. subjunct.   346
  as auxiliary and as full verb   347
avoir affaire à   220
avoir l'air   130
avoir peur   485, 564
avoir recours à   220
ayant + past part.   441, 445

battant neuf   610
battre   345, 369
beaucoup   45, 165, 324
'before'   488, 663
bénir   361
(*avoir*) *besoin* + subjunctive   482
'best'   161–163
'better'   161–162
bien   161, 607
  bien d'autres   292
  bien du, des, etc.   325
  used adjectivally   253
  'very'   335
bien loin que   484
bien que   487
bientôt   622
  with past ant.   411
bizarre   485
blotti   534
boire   377
bon   161
bon marché   162
bonnement   607
'both'   317
  'both . . . and' rendered by
    subordinating conjunction   691
bouger, with *ne* alone   561
bouillir   377
braire   377
breadth, expression of   718
bref, brièvement   607
bruire   377
'by'   667, 680

after verbs of beginning or
    ending   445
  'by . . .-ing'   442

ça   9, 242
  after interrogatives   243
çà   9
capitals   4
  accents sometimes omitted on   9
ce (pronoun)
  c'est or est?   258–261
  c'est or impersonal il est?   253–257
  c'est or personal il est, elle est,
    etc.?   250–252
  full demonst.   240
  tout ce + rel. clause   317
  + rel. clause   247, 274
  + rel. clause in indirect
    questions   288
ce n'est pas la peine que   484
ce n'est pas que   484, 561
ce que, exclamatory ('how')   613
c'est . . . qui, que . . ., use of
    tenses   257
ceci   241, 242
céder   353
cedilla   10
  before parts of aller or avoir   257
  on some parts of recevoir, etc.   375
  on some parts of verbs in -cer   352
cela   9, 241
  after interrogatives   243
  separable (ce . . . là)   244
cela fait . . . que   567
celui, etc.   238
  with -ci, -là   238
  without -ci, -là   245–247
  + de   22, 245
  + rel. clause   245, 246
cent(s)   180, 183
certain 'sure'   483
certain(s) 'certain, some'   294
certainement   627
  precedes pas   544
cesser, with ne alone   561
chacun   219, 295, 674
changer   454, 537
chaque   295
chaque fois   315
chez   665
choir   377
chose   66
ci
  with demonst.   8, 237–238
  + adv.   8

ci-inclus, ci-joint   134
clore   377
collective nouns, sing. or plur.
    verb   393–396
colour, adjectives of   95, 126, 147
combien   45, 154, 326
  as preceding direct obj.   460
commander   532
commands, use of definite article
    in   28
comme   154, 613
  agreement with nouns linked
    by   129
comment   589–590, 613
comparatives
  followed by redundant ne   563
  irregular   154
comparison
  of adjs and advs   155–174
  of equality or inequality   157–159,
    172
  of superiority or inferiority   160–173
comparisons   613
  use of le in second part   213
complement
  of a preposition   20
  of être   216, 518
  of linking verbs   518
  of the subject   16
  of verbs   518–538
composite subject, person and number
    of verb   391–392
compound nouns
  use of def. art. with
  gender   57–63
  prepositions with
  plur.   109–116
compound tenses   340, 376
  agreement of past part.   459, 460
  of refl. verbs   380, 451
  position of obj. prons   204
  with avoir   450, 453–456
  with être   451–456
comprendre   483
  with ne . . . goutte   555
compris   134
compter (+ de) + infinitive   527
conclure   377
conditional
  endings   345
  is or is not the equivalent of
    'should'   512
  mood or tense?   340
  stem   346, 376
  values   415–417

conditional sentences   418–422, 701
confire   377
conjugations   339
conjunctions   691–705
  co-ordinating   691
  elision of *-e*   12
  simple and compound   692
  subordinating   691
    repetition avoided by use of
      que   691
  taking indic. or condit.   694–695
  taking subjunct.   486–491, 697
conjunctive pronouns (*see* personal
  pronouns)
connaître   373, 525
conseiller   532
consentir à ce que + subjunctive   482
construire   374
content   485
continuous forms (verbs)
  (English)   398
contraindre   530
contre   665
contredire   377
convenir   343, 451, 537
  il convient que   482
couché   445
coudre   345, 377
countries, names of   30–31
  gender   52
  prepositions with   30, 656
  use of def. art. with   30
courir   377
  agreement of past part.   469
court   141
coûter   537, 717
  agreement of past part.   469
couvrir   345, 365
craindre   372, 485
  followed by redundant *ne*   564
créer   353, 358
crier   358
  + subjunct.   482
croire   373, 525
croître   373
'crouching'   445
cueillir   345, 365
cuire   374
curieux   485

-d pronounced as [t]   388
daigner, with *ne* alone   561
d'ailleurs   625
dans
  after adjs   690

meaning and use   654, 657, 659, 713
dans le cas où   490
dates of the Christian era   180
dates of the month   183
dative case   18
d'aucuns   298
d'autres   292
davantage   330
days of the week   4, 707
  translation of 'on' with   708
de   667
  after adjs   688
  after negatives   35, 43, 568
  after quantifiers   32
  as alternative to *d'entre*   674
  before infin.   261, 425, 528
  elision   12
  equivalent of 'by'   45
  equivalent of 'with'   45, 524
  equivalent of other Eng.
    prepositions   525
  expressing measure of
    difference   171
  expressing possession   19, 22
  impersonal verb + *de* + infin.   526
  linking indef. pron. and adj.   44,
    241, 311, 312, 530, 532, 535
  'than'   167–168
  with def. art.   25
  with disjunct. pron.   218
  with names of countries   30
  + compl. of refl. verbs   535
  + compl. = Eng. direct obj.   653
  = 'made of', etc.   653
de beaucoup   324
de bonne heure   162
de crainte que   485, 491, 561
de façon (à ce) que   489
de manière (à ce) que   489
de même   256, 300
de même que   129
d'entre   674
de peur que (see *de crainte que*)
de quelque façon (manière) que   309,
  315
de quoi   273
de suite   617
de telle façon (manière, sorte) que   489
debout   612
décéder   451
déchoir   377
de-ci de-là   8
décider   537
decimal numerals   192
découvrir   365

défaillir 365
defective verbs 344, 345, 376–378
défendre 'forbid' 484, 522
défier 537
definite article 24–33
  after *de* 32
  corresponding to Eng. indef. art. 36
  elision of *le, la* 12
  omission 27
  replacing poss. 230
  repetition of 28
  used in Fr. but not in Eng. 28
  with days of the week 708
  with *double*, etc. 187
  with fractions 191
  with geographical names 30, 31
  with titles, saints' days, etc. 29
délice 67
demander
  à faire 529, 532
  à q.un de faire 532
  q.ch. à q.un 522
  + subjunct. 482
déménager 454
demeurer 455
  agreement of past part. 470
demi 131, 188
demonstrative determiners 235–237
demonstrative pronouns 238–247
  neuter demonst. prons 239–244
departments (French), names of,
  gender 52
déplaire 532
depth, expression of 718
depuis 668, 712, 714
  tenses with 413
depuis que
  tenses with 413, 567
  with *ne* or *ne . . . pas* (*plus*) 567
dernier 28, 142, 184
  mood after 494
derrière 669
dès 670, 714
  dès lors 619
dès que
  + fut. 414
  + past ant. 411
descendre 451, 452
désirer
  (+ *de*) + infin. 527
  + subjunct. 482
désolé 485
dessous 684
dessus 671
destiner 531
déterminer 537

determiners 23
  arts 24–46
  demonst. 234–237
  indefs and quantifiers 294, 295, 297,
    306, 317, 324, 331
  interrogatives 278–279
  negatives 546–547
  numerals 178
  poss. 222–230
  rels (*lequel*) 270
deuxième and *second* 180
devant 663
devenir
  compl. of 518
  compound tenses 451
devoir 375, 510, 537
  condit. = 'ought' 511
  dût-il, etc. 478
  renders 'should' 512
  + infin., agreement of past
    part. 468
  + infin. as equivalent of fut.
    subjunct. 506
se dévouer pour 536
diable de 667
diaeresis 11
différents 297
dimensions, expression of 718
dire 377
  dire à q.un de + infin. 532
  q.ch. à q.un 522
  with *ne . . . mot* 555
  + subjunct. 482
direct object 17, 198, 216, 519, 533
  Eng. direct obj. rendered by *à* +
    compl. 522
  Eng. direct obj. rendered by *de* +
    compl. 521
  preceding, agreement of past part.
    with 460, 461
  verbs taking direct obj. in Fr. but
    requiring a preposition in
    Eng. 523
  verbs taking direct obj. + *à* +
    infin. 531
  verbs taking direct obj. + *de* +
    infin. 530
  with *faire, laisser*, verbs of senses, +
    infin. 431–435
disjunctive pronouns (see personal
  pronouns)
disparaître 454
dissoudre 377
divers 297
'do'
  used in negative constructions in

Eng. but not in Fr. 401, 543
used in questions in Eng. but not in
    Fr. 401, 582
donc 615
donner 351
dont 262, 268
    replaced by *de qui, duquel*, etc. 270
dormir 364
    agreement of past part. 470
d'où 631
double-compound tenses 412
douter
    followed by redundant *ne* 565
    mood after 483
douteux 483
drôle de 667
du côté de 672
d'une façon (*manière*) + adjective 611
durer, agreement of past
    participle 470

'each' 295
'early' 622
-*eau*, plural of words in 103
(*s*') *échapper* 524
échoir 377
échouer 454
echo-questions 424
éclore 377
écrire 377
écroulé 534
s'efforcer 535
-*eindre*, verbs in 372
'either' 691
élire 377
elision 3, 12
'else' ('someone else, something
    else') 293
emmener + reflexive verb 436
émouvoir 377
empêcher 484
en (preposition)
    after adjs 690
    forming adjectival or adverbial
        expressions 46
    meaning and use 654, 656–658, 713
    repetition of 650
    + pres. part. (= gerund) 439, 442,
        649
en (pronoun) 201, 203, 321
    instead of poss. 227
    en appeler à, with disjunctive
        pronoun 220
    en arrière de 669
    en attendant que 488

en avant de 663
en cas que 490
en dehors de 677
en outre de 679
en retard 621
en sorte que 489
(*être*) *en train de* 398
en travers de 661
en un instant, with past anterior 411
encore 300, 616
encore que 487
endings, verbs
    condit. 345
    fut. 345
    imper. 345
    imperf. indic. 345
    imperf. subjunct. 345
    infin. 339
    past parts in -*i*, -*u* 345
    pres. subjunct. 345
    pret. in -*is*, -*us* 345
English words
    plur. 118
    pronunciation of *w* 1
    plur. words corresponding to a sing.
        in Fr. 121
ennuyer 485
'enough' 45, 154, 322
enseigner 532
ensemble 612
ensuite 615, 617
s'ensuivre 377
-*ent*, nouns in, differing from present
    participle 447
entendre
    s'entendre dire q.ch. 385
    with *ne . . . goutte* 555
entre 673
    + rel. pron. 264
entrer 451, 522
entrevoir 377
envers 675, 689
envoyer 357
    + infin. 435, 436
    + refl. verb 436
épais 718
épris 534
equative degree of comparison 156
-*er* verbs
    forms in full 351
    imper. 345, 350
essentiel 482
est-ce que? 389, 585, 590
et
    in numerals 180
    linking two adjs 150–151

étant 441
 + past part. 445
étant donné 134, 458
été, no agreement 350, 459
étonné 485
s'étonner 485
être
 forms in full 350
 fût-il, etc. 478
 idioms with 540
 pres. subjunct. 346
 serves as auxiliary and as full
  verb 347
 soit 'let there be' 477
 soit que 480
 used to form the passive 382
 with *à* + disjunct. pron. 220, 232
-eu, plural of words in 103
évanoui 534
'even' 300
 encore with a comparative 616
'every' 317
'every second (third, etc.)' 317
'everyone' 317, 319
'everything' 317, 319
éviter 484
 followed by redundant *ne* 565
excepté 134, 458, 676
exclure 377
exiger 482
expectation, verbs expressing, +
 subjunctive 482
expirer 454
s'expliquer 483
exprès 612
extraordinaire 485

fâché 485
se fâcher 485
faillir 365, 377
faire 377
 faire sien, etc. 233
 idioms with 541
 ne faire que + infin. 553
 not an equivalent of 'to do' in
  negative constructions and
  questions 401
 pres. subjunct. 346
 used impersonally 343
 + infin. 430–438, 527
  agreement of past part. 464
  position of obj. prons 209,
   431–435

use of direct or indirect
  obj. 431–435
 + refl. verb 436
faire attention à 220
falloir 343, 377, 537
 il faut que 482, 510
 + infin. 527
'far . . .-er than' 324
'far from . . .-ing' 491
fatigué de 536
(*il*) *faut* (see *falloir*)
faux 144
fearing, verbs and expressions of
 followed by redundant *ne* 564
 + subjunct. 485
feminine of nouns and
 adjectives 75–96
feu 'late' 26, 135
'(a) few' 306, 309
fier 485
finir 359
finite verbs 341
'first' 178, 183–184
first conjugation (see *-er* verbs)
fixed expressions
 use of *ne* alone in negation 560
 with the subjunct. 476
flambant neuf 610
fleurir 362
fois
 la première (*dernière*) *fois que* 494
'for'
 after certain verbs 536
 as expression of indirect obj. 18, 21
 with ref. to price 717
 with ref. to time 712
'for fear' 485, 491
force 324, 395
forcer 530
foreign words
 plur. 118
 pronunciation of *w* 1
 value of *h* 3
'(the) former' 238
fors 677
fort 'very' 335
fournir 524
fractions 188–192
 sing. or plur. verb 395
frais, as adverb, variable 610
frire 377
'from'
 transl. by *à* 524
 with ref. to time 714

'from there' 201
fuel consumption, measurement
    of 719
fuir 377
furieux 485
future 402, 414
    endings 345
    expressing polite imper. 517
    expressing probability 414
    replaced by pres. 414
    stem 346
future-in-the-past 415
future perfect, expressing
    probability 414
future subjunctive
    devoir + infin., equivalent of 506

geler 354
gender 47–74
    adjs used as nouns 74
    anomalies 65–73
    compound nouns 57–63
    gender according to meaning 50–51
    gender and sex 48–49
    letters of the alphabet 1
    place-names 52
    shown by ending 54–56
generic subjunctive 493
genitive case (phrase) 19, 22, 519
gens 68
gentiment 607
geographical names (*see* place-names)
gerund 439, 442
gésir 377
(*ne . . .*) *goutte* 555
grand, as adverb, variable 610
grand-chose 324
grandir 454
grimper 522
(*ne . . .*) *guère* 549, 556

h, two varieties in French 3
habiter 523
habitual past tense (English) 398
haïr 360, 528
'half' (see *demi, mi, moitié*)
'half past' (time) 710
'hardly' 549
haut 718
height, expression of 718
hériter 521
heureusement 638
    h. que non 574

heureux 485
historic present 404
hormis 676
hors (*de*) 677
'how' 154, 326, 613
    'how high (long, wide, etc.)?' 718
    'how long?' (time) 413, 715
    'how much? how many?' 326, 333
'however' 315
    + adj. or adv. 310, 317, 478, 495
huit, huitième, no elision 12
hyphens 6, 8
    in interrogative conjugation 387
    in numerals 180
hypothetical clauses with *que* +
    subjunctive 480

ici, with reference to time 715
(*l'*)*idée que* 483
idioms
    of time 716
    with *avoir* 539
    with *être* 540
    with *faire* 541
'if' (see *si* 'if')
'if only, if ever' 490
ignorer 483
il en est ainsi 256
il en est de même 256
il est or *c'est*?
    impersonal *il* 248, 253–257
    personal *il, elle*, etc. 248–252
il n'y a aucune chance que 484
il n'y a pas de danger que 484
il s'en faut (*de beaucoup*) (*que*) 484, 537, 565
il se peut que 483
il y a 343
    tenses with 413, 567
    with *ne* or *ne . . . pas* (*plus*) 567
imperative 376, 514–517
    endings 345
    expressed by fut. 517
    expressed by infin. 429
    que + subjunct. as 3rd pers. imper. 480, 515
    stem 345
    use of prons with 207
imperfect indicative 402, 406, 409
    endings 345
    renders 'would (do)' 513
    used after *si* 'if' 418
imperfect subjunctive 496–505

avoidance of in speech   496, 501,
  504
avoidance of in writing   496, 501,
  502, 505
endings   345, 346
in condit. sentences   422
stem   346, 376
impersonal verbs   343–345
  + *de* + infin.   526
  + subjunct.   482
important   482
(*il*) *importe que*   482
importer (see (*il*) *importe que*,
  n'importe, peu importe)
impossible   484
'in, into'   653–659, 667, 680, 690, 713
'in case'   490
'in . . .-ing'   442
'in order that'   489
inclure   377
indefinite adjectives, pronouns,
  etc.   291–319
indefinite article   24, 34–39
  in prepositional phrases   38
  plur.   24
  repetition of   39
  replaced by *de* in certain negative
    constructions   568
  used after negative
    constructions   569, 570
  used in Eng. but not in Fr.   26
indicative, after various
  conjunctions   487, 488, 489
indispensable   482
indirect object   18, 21, 200, 208, 215,
  216, 519, 533, 536
  replacing poss.   228
  verbs taking indirect obj. + *à* +
    infin.   533
  verbs taking indirect obj. + *de* +
    infin.   532
  with *faire, laisser*, verbs of senses, +
    infin.   431–435
inévitable   485
infinité + sing. or plur. verb   395
infinitive   425–438
  à + infin. with passive value   428
  after *faire*   430–434
  after *laisser*   430–434
  after prepositions   425, 649
  after verbs of saying and
    thinking   427
  after verbs of the senses   427,
    430–435
  as compl. of verb   258, 259

as equivalent of Eng. pres.
  part.   430
as subject   258
in exclamations   216, 429
instead of subjunct. with identical
  subjects   482
introduced by *de*   261, 425
introduced by *que de*   261, 425
preceded by preposition   649
pure infin. (no preceding
  preposition)   527
used as a noun   426
with imper. value   429
with *ne pas* (*point*)   544
with or without *de*, as subject   425
insister pour que   482
inspirer   532
insulter   522
interdire   377, 484
interrogative
  advs   630–633
  conjugation   387
  determiners   278–279
  prons.   278, 280–290
  sentences (*see* questions)
  words placed last   593, 643
intonation, expressing
  interrogation   389, 586
intransitive verbs
  compound tenses with *avoir*   450
  compound tenses with *être*   451
inversion (of subject)   310, 596–601
  after advs and adverbial
    expressions   600
  in hypothetical constructions   478
  in questions   583, 584, 589, 590
  not after *pourquoi*   591, 595
  when avoided   591–592, 598
  with subjunct. expressing
    wishes   476–477
-*ir* verbs
  forms in full   359
  irregular verbs   377
  peculiarities of some verbs   360–366
irregular verbs
  important introductory note   376
  principal forms   377
  notes   378
islands, names of   31
'it'
  en 'of it'   201
  il, elle   197, 248–252
  not used with verbs of thinking + *que*
    or infin.   214
  replaced by an adv.   221

transl. by *ce*   248–257
y 'to it, etc.'   200
'its'
   son, sa, ses   223
   transl. by *en*   227

jamais 'ever'   618
(*ne . . .*) *jamais* 'never'   35, 550, 556, 557
je
   inverted only with certain verbs   389
   masc. or fem. agreement   195
je ne sais que (*qui, quoi, quand,* etc.)   289, 299
jeter   355
joindre   372
jouer   521
jusqu'à ce que   488
jusque, elision   12
jusque-là   8
jusqu'ici   616
'just' ('to have just done')   537
juste   485

'kneeling'   445

là
   with demonst.   8, 237–238
   with *être*,   244
   with ref. to time   715
   + adverb   8
laisser
   ne pas laisser de   528
   position of obj. prons   209, 431–435
   use and agreement of past part.   465
   use of direct or indirect obj.   431–435
   + infin.   430–438, 527
   + refl. verb   436
languages, names of
   capital initials not used   4
   def. art. with   28
large   718
   as adverb, variable   610
se lasser   535
'last'   28, 142, 184
'late' (see *feu, en retard, tard*)
Latin phrases used as nouns   118
'(the) latter'   238
se laver   381
le (invariable)   211–213
'least'   160, 164
length, expression of   718
lequel, etc.   262–263, 266, 270, 271, 290

as preceding direct obj.   460
duquel, etc.   269
'less'   45, 156, 160, 164, 167, 330
'lest'   485, 491
'let . . .', expressed by *que* + subjunctive   480
letters of the alphabet
   gender   1, 50
   no elision   12
   plur.   117
liaison   3, 7, 99
linking verbs   518, 613
lire   377
'little'   328
   (see also (*un*) *peu, peu de*)
logique   485
loin que   491
long   141, 718
'(no) longer'   552
lors   615, 619
lorsque, tenses after   414
'(a) lot of'   324, 325
luire   345, 374
'lying'   445

maint   324
maintenant   620
mal   161, 607
malgré   678
malgré que   487, 698
manger   352
manquer   537
(*ne pas*) *manquer de*   528
'many, as many, not many, so many, too many'   45, 145, 322–324, 328, 334
marcher, agreement of past part.   469
maudire   377
mauvais   161, 163
'may'   508
meanings
   different in sing. and plur.   120
   different with adjs before and after noun   146
médire   377
meilleur   154, 161–162
même   300, 544
   with disjunct. pron. (*lui-même*, etc.)   8, 215, 300
mener   436
-ment, forming adverbs of manner   603–608
mentir   364
mettre   377
mi   131, 188

mieux   154, 161–162
'might'   509
mil   180
mille   180
milliard, million   181
millier   181
modal verbs   507–513
   + infin.   527
   + infin., agreement of past
      part.   468
moindre   161, 164
moins   45, 160–161, 163, 170, 172, 330
moins de deux, plural verb   395
moitié   188
   sing. or plur. verb   395
monter   451, 452
months   4
moods, classification   472
moquer   534
'more'   45, 156, 160, 165–168, 173, 330
   'no more'   552
'most'   156, 160, 165, 174
   = 'the greater part'   329
(*ne* . . .) *mot*   555
motion, verbs of, + infinitive   527
moudre   377
mourir   377, 451
mouvoir   377
'much, as much, not much, so much,
   too much'   45, 145, 322–325, 334
'must'   510
mute *h*   3, 12, 223, 235

naître   377, 451
naturel   485
ne
   elision   12
   position   387
   used on its own   559–567
      as a literary alternative to *ne* . . .
         pas   561
      in fixed expressions and
         proverbs   560
      where Eng. has no negative
        after *avant que* and *à moins*
           que   566
        after comparatives   563
        after *depuis que*, etc.   567
        after verbs and expressions of
          fearing   564
        after other verbs and their
          equivalents   568
   with a negative particle or other
      compl.   543–555

ne . . . *aucun, aucunement, guère,*
   jamais, nul, nullement, pas,
   personne, plus, point, que, rien (see
   aucun, aucunement, guère, etc.)
nécessaire   482
negation   542–580
   of an element other than a
      verb   572–580
   of the verb   543–570
negative complements
   (particles)   542–558
   multiple negative compls   556
negative conjugation   387
negative-interrogative
   conjugation   387, 388
n'est-ce pas?   587
neuter demonstrative
   pronouns   239–244
'never'   35, 550
'next'   28, 142
ni   571
ni l'un ni l'autre   292
nier   484, 565
n'importe comment, quel, qui,
   etc.   301
'no' (see *aucun, non, non pas, nul, pas*)
'nobody, no-one'
   nul   547
   personne   551
nombre de   35, 324
   sing. or plur. verb   395
nominative case   15
non   572, 575–580
   in compound nouns and adjs   580
   que non   573, 574
   with past or pres. part.   580
non pas   575–579
non pas que   491, 561
non plus   571
non que   491, 561
'none'   544, 546, 542
non-finite forms of the verb   341
normal   485
'not' (*see* negation, *ne, non, non pas,*
   pas)
   'not as (so) . . . as'   157
   'not at all'   545, 557
   'not one' (*see* 'none')
   'not that'   491
'nothing'   551
noun clause
   definition   13
   with subjunct.   480
noun phrase

definition 13
functions 14–22
nouns
    used as adjs 95, 126
    (*see also* gender, plur.)
nous autres 216
nouveau 143
'now' 620
    transl. by *ici* 715
nu 132
nuire 374
nul 219, 547
nullement 548
number of verb
    after quantifiers 337
    with collective subjects 393–396
    with composite subjects 391–392
numerals 178–192
    accompanied by *en* 201
    advs 186
    cardinal 178, 182–184
    followed by *de* 181
    hyphens, use of 8, 180
    ordinal 178
    plur. 117
    pronunciation 179
    used as nouns, plur. 117
    with names of kings, etc. 27, 183

object (*see* direct object, indirect
    object)
obliger 530
s'occuper 535
œuvre 69
'of' (see *de*, possessive relationship)
    construction 'a friend of mine' 233
offrir 365, 522
oindre 372
-oindre, verbs in 372
-oir verbs
    verbs in *-evoir* 375
    other (irregular) verbs 377
-oître, verbs in 373
'on' 653, 658, 667, 672, 680, 685
    'on . . .-ing' 442
    with days of the week 708
on 219, 302
    agreement of adjs with 130
    preceded by *-t-* 388
    used instead of passive 384
'one'
    indef. pron. (see *on*)
    numeral (see *un*)
    'one another' 292

'one . . . another' 303
'one more' 616
'only' 43, 145, 216, 553, 616
    'not only' 553
onze, onzième, no elision before 12
s'opposer 484
'or' 292, 691
or 620
order, verbs expressing an, +
    subjunctive 482
ordonner
    q.ch. à q.un 522
    + subjunct. 482
orge 70
orgue 71
oser, with *ne* alone 561
'other(s)' (see *autre, autrui*)
ou
    agreement with nouns linked
        by 128
    linking two adjs 150
    ou que 480
où 589
    used as rel. pron. 276–277
    with ref. to time 277, 488
-ou, plural of words in 104
où que, 315, 495
'ought' 511
oui 628
    no elision before 12
ouïr 377
'out (of)' 659, 677, 680
outre 679
ouvrir 365

paître 373
Pâque(s) 72
par 680
    faire faire par 433, 434
    to translate Eng. indef. art. 37
    + infin. after verbs of beginning and
        ending 445
par (la) suite 617
paraître 373
    compl. of 518
    mood after 483
    + infin. 527
par-ci par-là 8
par derrière 669
par-dessous 684
par-dessus 671
pardonner 522
pareil 303
parfaire 376

parler
 negative and interrogative
  conjugations 387
 parler (le) français, etc. 28
parmi 673
 + rel. pron. 264
partial interrogation 581–582,
  588–593
partir 364, 451
partitive article 24, 40–46
 after prepositions 46
 omitted 45
 plur. 24
 replaced by *de* in certain negative
  constructions 568
partout 315
(*ne . . .*) *pas* 544, 556
 pas or *non, non pas?* 575–579
 pas de with no art. 35, 43
 position 387, 544
 with infin. 544
 with words meaning 'since' 567
 without *ne* 557
pas du tout 545
pas grand-chose 324
pas mal de 324
pas un (seul) 544, 667, 674
passé 134
passé surcomposé (*see*
  double-compound tenses)
passer 456
 agreement of past part. 470
passive 382–385
 alternatives to 384
 conjugation of 383
 passive value of *à* + infin. 428
past anterior 411
past historic (*see* preterite)
past participle 448–471
 after *celui*, etc. 245
 agreement
  in compound tenses 459, 460, 462
  in passive 459
  when followed by infin. 463–468
  with refl. verbs 380, 459, 461
 endings 345
 for Eng. present part. to denote
  position 445, 534
 used as adj. 147
 used as noun 471, 534
 used as preposition 134, 646
 used in an active sense 534
 used to form compound tenses with
  avoir 450, 453–456

used to form compound tenses with
  être 451–456
payer 717
pendant 712
pendant que 488, 696
penser 525
 with *à* + disjunct. pron. 220
perfect indicative 400, 402
 spoken language 410
 written language 408
perfect subjunctive 496–498
 used instead of imperf.
  subjunct. 508
 used instead of pluperf.
  subjunct. 504
permettre
 q.ch. à q.un 522
 + subjunct. 482
permission, verbs expressing, +
  subjunctive 482
personal names
 hyphenated 8
 plur. 119
 use of diaeresis 11
personal pronouns 193–221
 conjunctive 193, 198–214
  as preceding direct obj. 460
  impossible combinations 208
  order 206–210
  position 204, 387
  repetition 210
 direct obj. forms 17, 198
 disjunctive 193, 200, 208, 215–220,
   223, 518
 elided forms 8, 12
 hyphenated 8
 indirect obj. forms 18, 198
 refl. 199
 subject forms 193–197
  following verb in interrogative
   conjug. 387
  not used with imper. 514
  position 202, 387
  repetition 202
  use of disjunct. prons 216–217
(*ne . . .*) *personne* 551, 556, 558, 667
 gender 73
 indef. pron. 219
persons of the verb 342
 after *c'est (moi*, etc.) *qui . . .* 255
 agreement with 392
persuader 530, 532
petit 161, 164
(*un*) *peu, peu de* 45, 161, 328

sing. or plur. verb   395
peu importe que   485
peu s'en faut   565
peut-être   627
   inversion after   600
   position   642
   precedes *pas*   544
   + *que*   574
phonetic symbols   2
phrases used as nouns, plural   117
pire   161, 163
pis   161, 163
place-names
   gender   52
   hyphenated   8
   use of arts   30–31
se plaindre   485
plaire   377, 532
plein   135
pleuvoir   377
(la) plupart   329, 674
   sing. or plur. verb   395
pluperfect indicative   402, 411
pluperfect subjunctive
   as an archaic alternative to pluperf.
     indic.   420
   avoidance of in speech   496, 501,
     504
   avoidance of in writing   496, 501,
     502
   in condit. sentences   422, 478
plural of adjs   122–126
plural of nouns
   spoken Fr.   97–100
   written Fr.   101–119
     compound nouns   109–116
     foreign words   118
     nouns with two plurs   108
     personal names   119
plural nouns denoting a class, use of
   definite article   28
plus   45, 154, 160, 165, 169–170, 172,
   330
   agreement of past part. with   460
(ne . . .) plus   552, 556, 557
   with words meaning 'since'   567
plus d'un, singular verb   395
plus que, agreement with nouns linked
   by   129
plusieurs   331
plutôt   612, 622
poindre   372
(ne . . .) point   544, 556
   not a 'strong' negation   545

position, verbs denoting
   past part. corresponding to Eng.
     pres. part.   445, 534
possessive determiner   222–229
   alternating with *de* + pron.   218
   repetition   224–225
   replaced by def. art. with parts of
     body   228–230
   replaced by *en*   227
   replaced by indirect obj.   228
   replaced by refl. pron.   228, 229
   use of *à lui*, etc., to clarify meaning of
     son, sa, ses   223
possessive pronouns   222, 231–233
   replaced by *à moi*, etc.   232
   without def. art.   233
possessive relationship   22
possible   133, 483, 484, 508
pour   681
   after *assez, trop*   322
   pour . . . que 'however'   310, 495
   with indirect obj.   18, 21
   with ref. to time   712
pour autant que   490
pour peu que   490
pour que   489
pourquoi   589
   no inversion of noun subject
     after   591, 595
poursuivre   377
pourvoir   377
pourvu que   490
pouvoir   345, 377
   corresponds to 'may'   508
   corresponds to 'might'   509
   pres. subjunct.   346
   puisse-t-il, etc., expressing wish   477
   with *ne* alone   561
   + infin.   527
   + infin., agreement of past
     part.   468
prédire   377
préférable   482, 485
préférer   485, 527
premier   183–184
   mood after   494
prendre   377
prepositional phrases
   after *celui*, etc.   245
   with or without art.   38, 46
prepositions   644–689
   before infin.   425, 649
   compound   644, 647–649
   government of verbs by   649

repetition   650–651
simple   645–646
used as nouns, plur.   117
various Eng. prepositions transl. as *à*
    or *de*   525
verbs requiring a preposition in Eng.
    but direct obj. in Fr.   523
with or without art.   38, 46
with pres. part. (only *en*)   445
present indicative   402
expressing the fut.   414
present participle   439–447
differing from verbal adj.   446
in Eng. but not in Fr.   445
invariable when used as part.   441
rendered by past part. of verbs
    denoting position   445, 534
rendered by rel. clause   443
used as adj.   147, 439–440, 445
used as gerund (*en . . .-ant*)   439,
    442
used as preposition   646
present subjunctive   496–504
endings   345
in independent clauses   497
instead of imperf. subjunct.   502,
    504
stem   346
presque   332
elision   12
preterite
after *si* 'if'   418
endings   345
spoken language   410
written language   407
preterite (English), French equivalents
    of   402
prévaloir   377
prévenir   377
prévoir   377
price, expression of   717
probability expressed by future or
    future perfect   414
probable   483
probablement   627, 638
precedes *pas*   544
prochain   28, 142
profond   718
promettre   522
promouvoir   377
pronouns (*see* demonstrative,
    indefinite, interrogative, personal,
    possessive, reflexive, relative
    pronouns)
proverbs   721

use of *ne* alone in negation   560
'provided that'   490
puis   615
punctuation   5
in decimal numerals   192

quand
interrogative   589
meaning 'even if'   422
meaning 'whenever'   315
tenses and moods after   416
quand même   300
meaning 'even if'   422
quantifiers   320–327
quantité de   324
sing. or plur. verb   395
quantity, expressions of   45
accompanied by *en*   201
que, elision   12
que (conjunction)   699
in clauses dependent on a previous
    verb, adj., etc.   481–485
in hypothetical clauses   480, 700
in independent clauses   480
que . . . ou que . . .   480
replacing *si* 'if'   480, 703
replacing other conjunctions   702,
    703
que (exclamatory)   154, 613
que de   333, 460
Type: *que je trahisse. . .!*   484
que (interrogative)   283, 285, 287, 289
que (relative)   262
equivalent of *ce qui, ce que*   275
gender and number taken from
    antecedent   460
never omitted   264, 265
with ref. to time   277
que 'than'   166, 168
que? 'why?'   561, 632
que de
exclamatory   333, 464
introducing infin.   261, 425
que . . . ne . . . 'without'   561
que non, que oui, que si   573, 574, 628
(*ne . . .*) *que* 'only'   43, 216, 553, 568
quel (interrogative)   35, 279
as preceding direct obj.   460
with *ne* alone   561
quel . . . que   308
quelconque   304
quelque
elision   12
invariable   307, 310
quelque . . . que   310, 495

variable (see *quelque(s)*)
quelque chose 311, 667
quelque part 315
quelque(s) 306, 309
  quelque(s) . . . *que* 495
quelques-uns 306
quelqu'un 312, 667
quérir 376
qu'est-ce qui, que 283, 285–287, 389, 667
  exclamatory *qu'est-ce que* 'how' 613
questions 581–595
  direct questions 280–287, 290, 583–593
  echo-questions 424
  est-ce que . . .? 389
  indirect questions 280, 288–290, 545–595
  introduced by *si* 423
  use of intonation 389
  (*see also* interrogative)
qui (interrogative) 280, 287
  treated as masc. sing. 460
qui (relative)
  after prepositions 263, 266
  equivalent of *celui qui, ce qui* 275
  qui . . . *qui* . . . 'some . . . some' 314
  subject 262
  with *de* or *d'entre* 674
qui est-ce qui/que? 281, 287
qui que (*ce soit*) 315, 495
quiconque 313
quoi? (interrogative) 283, 284, 287, 289, 667
quoi (relative) 262, 273–274
quoi que (*ce soit*) 315, 495
quoique 487

raconter 522
rare 483
ravi 485
ravoir 349
-*re* verbs
  forms in full 367
  irregular verbs 372–374, 377
    verbs with -*aindre*, -*eindre*, -*oindre* 372
    verbs in -*aître*, -*oître* 373
    verbs in -*uire* 374
  principal regular verbs 368
  slightly irregular verbs 369–370
recevoir 375
reciprocal verbs 379
recommander, + subjunctive 482

reconnaître 373, 528
recourir, with *à* + disjunctive pronoun 220
recueillir 365
redoubler 521
réduire 531
reflexive pronouns 199, 219
  possible omission after *faire, laisser*, etc. 436
  replacing poss. 228, 229
reflexive verbs 379–381, 534
  after *faire, laisser*, etc. 436
  agreement of past part. 461
  compound tenses 380
  conjugation of 381
  pres. part. 441
  used instead of passive 384
  + *à* + infin. 536
  + *de* + infin. 535
refuser 522
regarder (*à*) 523
regarder comme sien 233
regretter 485
se réjouir 485
relative clauses 262–267
  subjunct. in 492–495
  with *ne* alone 561
relative pronouns 262–277
remonter 452
renoncer à + disjunctive pronoun 220
rentrer 451, 452
se repentir 364
repetition.
  of def. art. 28
  of demonst. determiner 236
  of indef. art. 39
  of possess. determiner 224, 225
répondre, with *ne* . . . *mot* 555
reprocher 523
répugner 529, 532
request, verbs expressing, + subjunctive 482
résoudre 377
'(the) rest' 395
(*le*) *reste* 395
rester 451, 537
  compl. of 518
retourner 451
(*ne* . . .) *rien* 551, 556, 557, 667
rire 377
rivers, names of, gender 52
rompre 369

s, with apostrophe (in English) 19, 22
saillir 365

saints' days, use of definite article 29
'same' 300
sans 682
  followed by *ni* 571
  implying a negative 558
sans doute
  position 642
  preceding *pas* 544
  + inversion 600
sans que 491
  followed by *ni* 571
  implying a negative 558
  without following *ne* 566
satisfait 485
sauf 676
savoir 377
  je (*ne*) *sache pas que*. . . 477
  pres. subjunct. 346
  with *ne* alone 561
saying, verbs of
  mood after 483
  + infin 427, 527
'scarcely' 549
se 199, 206, 208
seasons, *à* or *en* 658
second conjugation (see *-ir* verbs)
'self'
  non-refl. 8, 300
  refl. 199, 219
selon 683
sembler
  compl. of 518
  mood after 483
  + infin. 527
senses, verbs of
  with following infin. 427, 430–438,
    527
    agreement of past part. 466
    use and position of obj.
      prons 209
    use of direct or indirect
      obj. 432–435
    + refl. verb 436
sentir 364
seoir 377
sequence of tenses
  governing tenses of subjunct. 498
    departures from 499–500
servir 364, 537
seul 145
'several' 331
'should' (*see also* conditional) 512
si 'if, whether'
  elision 12

introducing echo-questions 424
introducing indirect questions 423,
  594
renders 'would that' 513
tenses after 415, 418–422
with *ne* alone 561
with no conjunctive force 421
si 'so, as' 157, 334
  in negative comparisons 157
  si + adj./adv. + *que* +
    subjunct. 483, 484, 489
  Type: *si riche qu'il soit* 310, 495
  Type: *si riche soit-il* 478
  with *ne* alone in *que* clause 561
si 'yes' 628
si fait 628
si tant est que 490
simple tenses 340
'since' 413
'since when?' 413, 715
sitôt 622
'so' 158, 159
  rendered by *le* 213
  'so . . . that' 323
'so long as' 490
'so that' 489
soi 219
soi-disant 136, 147, 441
(*avoir*) *soin*, + subjunctive 482
soit 477
soit que 480
'some'
  certains 294
  d'aucuns 298
  en 201
  partitive art. 41, 42
  quelconque 'some or other' 304
  quelque (= 'approximately') 307
  quelque(*s*) 'some, a few' 306
  quelques-uns/unes 306
  'some . . . some' 314
'someone' 319
  'someone else' 293
'something' 319
  'something else' 293
'somewhere' 315
  'somewhere else' 625
songer, with *à* + disjunctive
  pronoun 220
sonner, with *ne . . . mot* 555
'soon' 622
sortir 364, 451, 452
souffler, with *ne . . . mot* 555
souffrir 365

souhaiter, + subjunctive 482
sourire 377
sous 684
sous (*la*) *condition que* 490
se souvenir 483
sovereigns, names of
  no art. used 27
  with cardinal or ordinal
    numbers 183
speed, measurement of 719
spoken language
  fem. of adjs 77–81
  past tenses 409–410
  plur. 97–100
square measurements 718
stems
  condit. 346
  fut. 346
  imper. 345
  pres. subjunct. 346
'still' 616
subject 15
  agreement of past part. with in
    compound tenses with *être* 462
  agreement of past part. with in
    passive 459
subjunctive 473–506
  after adjs 482, 483
  after conjunctions denying the reality
    of the event 491
  after conjunctions expressing
    conditions, hypotheses or
    suppositions · 490
  after conjunctions formed on the
    basis of *que* 486–491
  after expressions of acceptance,
    approval or pleasure 485
  after expressions of curiosity or
    surprise 485
  after expressions of fear 485
  after expressions of indifference,
    annoyance, anger or sorrow 485
  after impersonal verbs 482
  after nouns 482
  after *que*
    expressing the event as something
      to be accomplished 482
    expressing the event as doubtful or
      merely possible 483
    expressing a judgement or
      reaction 484
    expressing an order or
      exhortation 480
    in hypothetical clauses 480

in noun clauses 480
after verbs expressing a wish,
  request, order, expectation,
  permission 482
forms given with *que* 348
in rel. clauses 492–495
  after a superlative 494
  after indef. art. 495
  generic subjunct. 493
  tenses 496–506
  without *que* 476–478
substances, definite article with names
  of 28
'such' 303
'such and such' 303
suffire 377, 529
  il suffit de 529
  il suffit que 482
suivre 377
superlative
  absolute superlative 176
  of superiority or inferiority 160–173
  subjunct. after 494
supposé que 490
supposer 483
sur 685
sûr 483
sûrement 627
  preceding *pas* 544
surpris 485
surseoir 377
survivre 377
syllables, division into 6

-t- in interrogative conjugation 388
tag-questions 587
taire 377
tandis que 487, 696
tant 45, 154, 323, 334
  tant . . . que + subjunct. 483, 484,
    489
tant que 323, 696
tantôt 622
tard 621
tarder 537
'teach' 532
tel 303
tellement 159, 334
  tellement . . . que + subjunct. 483,
    484
  with *ne* alone 561
tel quel 303
tenir 377
  imperf. subjunct. 345

pret.   345
tenir à + infin.   513
tenir à ce que + subjunct.   482
tenses
    differences between Eng. and
        Fr.   397–402
    names   340
'than'   166–168
'that'
    corresponding *que*, etc., never
        omitted   264, 265
    (*see also* demonstrative determiners
        and pronouns, *que* (relative))
'then'   615
    transl. by *là*   715
thickness, expression of   718
thinking, verbs of
    mood after   483
    no 'it' when followed by *que* or
        infin.   214
    with following infin.   527
third conjugation (see *-re* verbs)
'through'   661, 680
time, expression of   254, 707–716
titles   4, 29
'to'   653–656
tomber   451
'too, too much, too many'   322, 324
tôt   162, 622
total interrogation   581–587
toucher   522
toujours est-il que   600
tout   26, 317
    tout . . . que   310, 495
tout à coup   623
tout de même   300
tout de suite   617
tout d'un coup   623
tout le monde   317
    with sing. verb   395
toute sorte (espèce) de, with plural
        verb   395
tout-puissant   136
towns, names of
    gender   52
    with or without art.   31
traduire   374
traire   345, 377
traiter   537
transitive verbs, compound tenses with
    avoir   450
tréma (diaeresis)   11
trembler   524, 528
très   335
tressaillir   365
triste   485

trop   45, 322
    trop . . . pour que   484
tu and *vous*, when used   196
twenty-four hour clock   711

-uire, verbs in   374
un(s), *une(s)*
    as indef. art.   34
    as numeral   178
    as pron.   318
    l'un et l'autre   182, 292
    l'un l'autre, etc. 'one another'   292
    l'un . . . l'autre, les uns . . . les autres,
        etc.   292
    plur. (*les uns*)   292, 318
    sometimes no elision before   12
'until'   488
'used to do'   398

vaincre   370, 388
valoir   377, 717
    agreement of past part.   469
    + infin.   527
valoir autant (mieux)
    + infin.   527
    + infin., agreement of past
        part.   468
    + subjunct.   482
veiller   525
    veiller à ce que + subjunct.   482
vendre   367
venir   377, 537
    compound tenses   451
    expressions in *vienne(nt)*   477
    imperf. subjunct.   345
    pret.   345
    venir de 'to have just'   537
verbal adjectives, differing from
    present participle   446
verbs (*see* compound tenses,
    conditional, conjugations,
    continuous forms, defective verbs,
    'do', double-compound tenses,
    endings, *-er* verbs, finite verbs,
    future, future-in-the-past, future
    perfect, future subjunctive, generic
    subjunctive, habitual past tense,
    imperative, imperfect indicative,
    imperfect subjunctive, impersonal
    verbs, indicative, infinitive,
    interrogative conjugation,
    intransitive verbs, *-ir* verbs,
    irregular verbs, linking verbs, modal
    verbs, moods, negative conjugation,
    negative-interrogative conjugation,
    non-finite forms, number of verb,

passive, past anterior, past
    participle, perfect indicative,
    perfect subjunctive, present
    indicative, present participle,
    present subjunctive, preterite, *-re*
    verbs, reciprocal verbs, reflexive
    verbs, sequence of tenses, simple
    tenses, stems, subjunctive, tenses,
    transitive verbs, 'used to do', and
    entries for individual verbs)
vers 675
'very' 300, 324, 335
'very many, very much' 324
vêtir 345, 377
vieillir 454
vingt(s) 180, 183
vite 612
    with past ant. 311
vivre 377
    agreement of past part. 470
    vive! etc. 477
voici, voilà . . . que
    tenses with 413, 567
    ne or *ne . . . pas (plus)* 567
voir 345, 377
    construction *se voir offrir q.ch.* 385
voler 524
vouloir 377
    expressing determination 513
    + infin. 527
    + subjunct. 482
vous and *tu*, use of 196
vous autres 216
vrai 483
vu 134, 458

weather, verbs to do with 343
'well' 161
'were to' 512
'what' 258, 259, 273–275
    exclamation 284, 613
    'what a . . .' 35, 279
    'what a lot of . . .' 333
'what?' 279, 283–287
    in indirect questions 288–289
'whatever' 315
    Type: 'whatever the difficulty' 308
    Type: 'whatever mistakes' 309
'when'
    transl. by *où* 277
    transl. by *que* 277
    (see also *quand*)
'whenever' 315, 715
'wherever' 315
'(the) wherewithal' 296

'whether' 423
    rendered by *que . . . ou que* 480
    rendered by *soit que* 480
'which?' 279, 282, 287, 290
'while . . .-ing' 442
'who(m)?' 280–281, 287
'whoever' 313, 315
'(the) whole' 317
'whose' 262, 264, 268–269
width, expression of 718
wish, verbs expressing, +
    subjunctive 482
'with' 664
    transl. as *de* 524, 659, 667
'without' 682
    'without . . .-ing' 491, 561, 566, 571
    (see also *sans, sans que*)
word-order
    advs preceding *pas* 544
    in direct questions 583–593
    in indirect questions 595
    interrogative words placed last 593,
        643
    inversion of subject 310, 583, 584
    position of adjs 139–154
    position of advs 635–643
    position of conjunctive
        prons 204–210
    position of obj. with *faire, laisser*,
        verbs of senses + infin. 434–435
    position of rel. prons 268–269, 272
    with imperf. subjunct. in condit.
        clauses 478
    with negation 544–558
        (see also under specific words,
            aucun, jamais, pas, etc.)
words easily confused, glossary of 720
'worse, worst' 161, 163
'would' 513
    expressed by condit. 415, 418
    expressed by imperf. indic. 417, 513
written language
    fem. of adjs 82–96
    past tenses 406–418
    plur. 101–108

y 200, 203
y compris 134, 458
'yes' 628
'yes–no' questions (*see* total
    interrogation)
'yet' 616
'you'
    distinction between *tu* and *vous* 196
    transl. by *on* 302